Data Structures using Python

Shriram K. Vasudevan
Principal,
K. Ramakrishnan College of Technology,
Samayapuram, Trichy,
Tamil Nadu

Abhishek S. Nagarajan
Data Scientist, [24]7.ai Innovation Labs,
Bangalore

Karthick Nanmaran
Assistant Professor, Department of CSE,
SRM Institute of Science and Technology, Chennai

OXFORD
UNIVERSITY PRESS

Oxford University Press is a department of the University of Oxford. It furthers the University's objective of excellence in research, scholarship, and education by publishing worldwide. Oxford is a registered trade mark of Oxford University Press in the UK and in certain other countries.

Published in India by
Oxford University Press
22 Workspace, 2nd Floor, 1/22 Asaf Ali Road, New Delhi 110002

First Edition published in 2021

ISBN-13 (print edition): 978-0-19-012408-3
ISBN-10 (print edition): 0-19-012408-3

eISBN-13 (eBook): 978-0-19-099236-1
eISBN-10 (eBook): 0-19-099236-0

Typeset in Times New Roman and Helvetica LT Std
by Ideal Publishing Solutions, Delhi
Printed in India by Rakmo Press, New Delhi 110 020

Cover image: © Alok Rawat

For product information and current price, please visit www.india.oup.com

Dedicated to

Baby Hasini, Sai Lakshmi and Master Saihari
Shriram K. Vasudevan

My parents, Usharani and Nagarajan
Abhishek S. Nagarajan

Features of

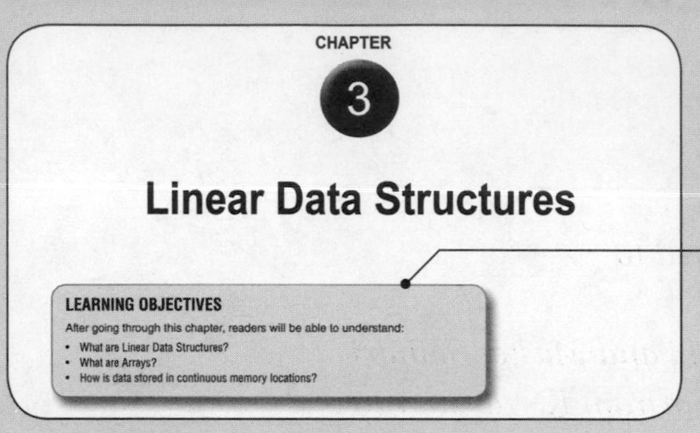

Learning Outcomes
Each chapter begins with learning outcomes listing the topics covered in detail.

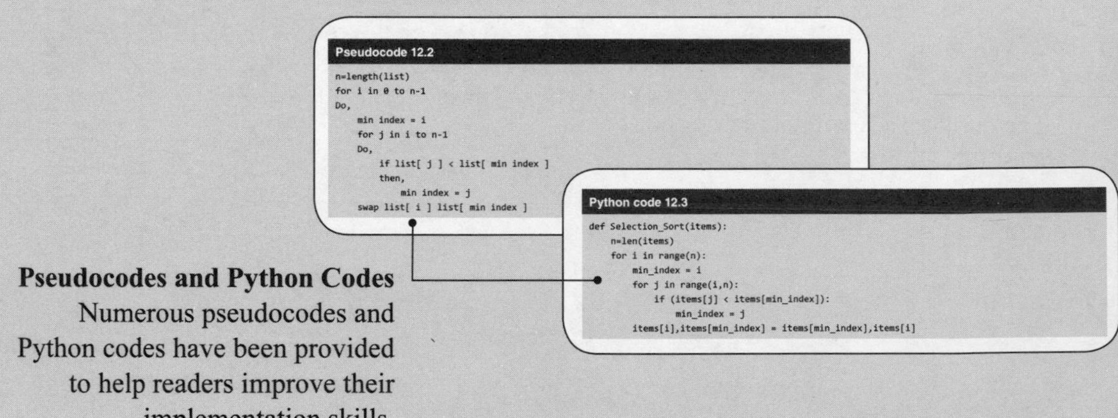

Pseudocodes and Python Codes
Numerous pseudocodes and Python codes have been provided to help readers improve their implementation skills.

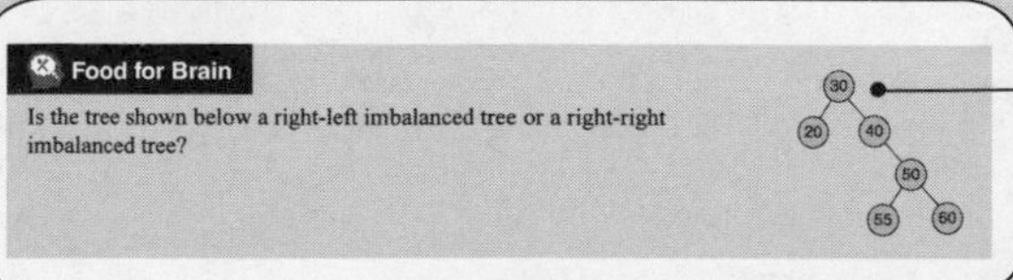

Food for Brain
Mid-chapter 'Food for Brain' questions given in each chapter help readers think out of the box.

the Book

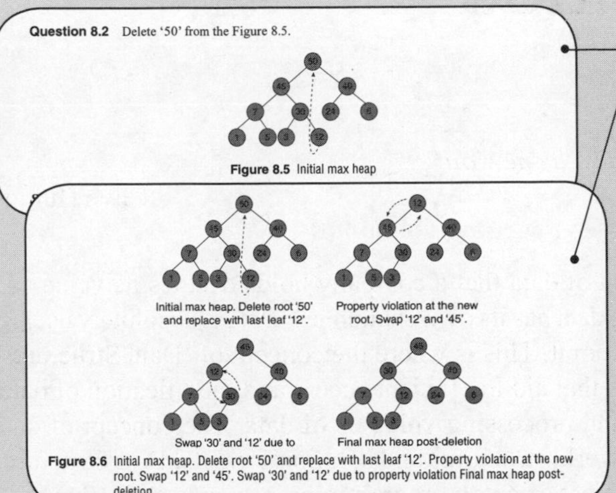
Question 8.2 Delete '50' from the Figure 8.5.

Figure 8.5 Initial max heap

Initial max heap. Delete root '50' and replace with last leaf '12'.

Property violation at the new root. Swap '12' and '45'.

Swap '30' and '12' due to

Final max heap post-deletion

Figure 8.6 Initial max heap. Delete root '50' and replace with last leaf '12'. Property violation at the new root. Swap '12' and '45'. Swap '30' and '12' due to property violation Final max heap post-deletion

Mid-chapter Solved Questions with Pictorial Representation

Each chapter includes solved questions with pictorial representation of data structures' operation to ensure proper understanding of feature and visualization of transformation.

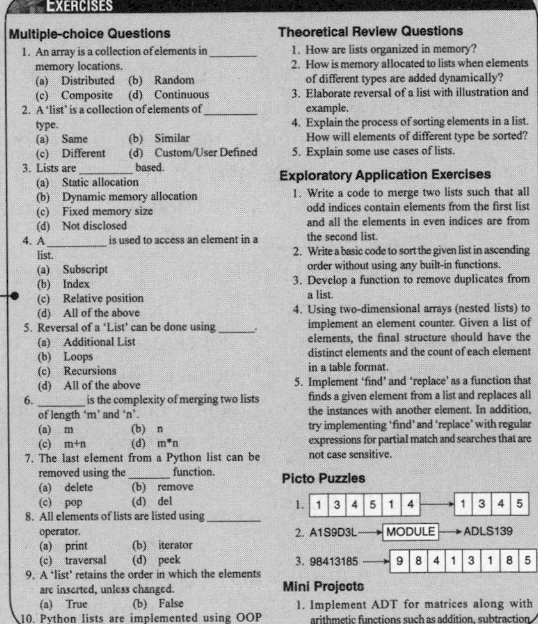
EXERCISES

Multiple-choice Questions

1. An array is a collection of elements in ________ memory locations.
   (a) Distributed (b) Random
   (c) Composite (d) Continuous
2. A 'list' is a collection of elements of ________ type.
   (a) Same (b) Similar
   (c) Different (d) Custom/User Defined
3. Lists are ________ based.
   (a) Static allocation
   (b) Dynamic memory allocation
   (c) Fixed memory size
   (d) Not disclosed
4. A ________ is used to access an element in a list.
   (a) Subscript
   (b) Index
   (c) Relative position
   (d) All of the above
5. Reversal of a 'List' can be done using ______.
   (a) Additional List
   (b) Loops
   (c) Recursions
   (d) All of the above
6. ________ is the complexity of merging two lists of length 'm' and 'n'.
   (a) m (b) n
   (c) m+n (d) m*n
7. The last element from a Python list can be removed using the ______ function.
   (a) delete (b) remove
   (c) pop (d) del
8. All elements of lists are listed using ________ operator.
   (a) print (b) iterator
   (c) traversal (d) peek
9. A 'list' retains the order in which the elements are inserted, unless changed.
   (a) True (b) False
10. Python lists are implemented using OOP

Theoretical Review Questions

1. How are lists organized in memory?
2. How is memory allocated to lists when elements of different types are added dynamically?
3. Elaborate reversal of a list with illustration and example.
4. Explain the process of sorting elements in a list. How will elements of different type be sorted?
5. Explain some use cases of lists.

Exploratory Application Exercises

1. Write a code to merge two lists such that all odd indices contain elements from the first list and all the elements in even indices are from the second list.
2. Write a basic code to sort the given list in ascending order without using any built-in functions.
3. Develop a function to remove duplicates from a list.
4. Using two-dimensional arrays (nested lists) to implement an element counter. Given a list of elements, the final structure should have the distinct elements and the count of each element in a table format.
5. Implement 'find' and 'replace' as a function that finds a given element from a list and replaces all the instances with another element. In addition, try implementing 'find' and 'replace' with regular expressions for partial match and searches that are not case sensitive.

Picto Puzzles

1. 1 3 4 5 1 4 → 1 3 4 5
2. A1S9D3L → MODULE → ADLS139
3. 98413185 → 9 8 4 1 3 1 8 5

Mini Projects

1. Implement ADT for matrices along with arithmetic functions such as addition, subtraction

Chapter-end Exercises

The book comes with numerous objective questions with answers, theoretical review questions, exploratory application exercises, pictorial puzzles, and mini projects for self-check and practice.

KEY POINTS TO REMEMBER

- Linked lists are non–primitive data structures. It is a linear collection of elements or nodes not stored in continuous memory locations.
- A linked list has no particular order of motion. It has no constraint on data insertion and removal.
- The different types of linked lists are as follows:
  - Singly linked list
  - Doubly linked list
  - Circular linked list
  - Circular doubly linked list
- A singly linked list has only one pointer or link to the next node present in the list.
- In a doubly linked list, each node contains two pointers called 'NEXT' and 'PREV' pointing to the next and previous node, respectively.
- In circular linked lists, the last node is connected to the first node, that is, the last node does not contain 'Null' but contains a pointer to the first node of the list.
- In a circular linked list with one element, the node should point to itself.

KEY TERMS

Linked lists A linear data structure designed to store elements in non-continuous memory locations using pointers from one memory location to the next location.

Singly linked lists/SLLs A linked list with pointer to traverse in forward direction. Every node will have a 'Next' pointer to move to the consecutive node, whereas there will not be any way to reach the previous node.

Doubly linked lists/DLL A linked list where every node has both 'Next' and 'Previous' pointers.

Circular linked lists A linked list where the last element points back to the first element to create a circular structure.

Head pointer The dedicated pointer that marks the first node/start point of the list.

Pointer-based linear data structures A data structure that uses pointers to associate a memory location to another memory location.

Summary and Glossary

Quick recap of the concepts learnt and glossary of key terms are provided at the end of each chapter.

Preface

"Data is the new oil"

– Clive Humby

In this data-driven technical era, the amount of data that a company holds decides its value and impact on the society. However, handling the data has its own challenges. Data is absolutely useless if no meaningful information is extracted from it. This is where the concept of 'Data Structures' comes into play. Data structures are formats that aid in efficient access and modification of data. These were designed for efficient storing and processing volumes of data. The concept of data structures is completely inspired from real-world structures and solution formats. Data structures can be implemented in any language, but object oriented programming concepts add value to it.

Data structures play an important role in solving everyday problems. The choice of the apt data structure optimizes the solution of any problem to a great extent. With the power of data structures on its side, Python can claim to be the fastest growing, major programming language. Python is capable of handling data and along with data structures concepts it can perform miracles in the data world.

"Data Structures is a difficult subject" is a myth that needs to be disproven. It is a skill and a way of thinking that can be developed with practice. The book *Data Structures using Python* helps students in doing just that. It helps them to learn the concepts of various data structures, and enables them to start implementing their solutions to strengthen their algorithmic and implementation skills with the help of codes and exploratory questions given at the end of each chapter in this book.

About the book

Data Structures using Python is a textbook cautiously designed for undergraduate and post-engineering students of computer science, information technology, and allied disciplines. The core objective of this book is to introduce different types of data structures and make the readers strong in data structure application for solution implementation. It will also serve as a go-to reference book for professionals to understand important data structures widely used in the industry.

The book starts with highlighting the importance of data structures and slowly moves towards the idea of basic data structures. The evolution of data structures along with the motivation of each structure from real-life objects is analogically explained in the book to aid in faster and clearer understanding for the readers. Data structures are broadly classified as continuous memory-based, pointer-based, hierarchical, non-linear, and non-hierarchical. The chapters are also organized in the same evolutionary order to enhance understanding of concepts.

Each data structure is first explained, followed with a question and its solution. Then, the algorithm/pseudocode is shared and finally the Python implementable code is provided. When there is scope for Python's capabilities to optimize the algorithm further, a concise version of the code is added as well. This particular order of explanation/code is designed in such a way that the readers can clearly comprehend the concepts and implement the same, without which the learning curve of data structures stays incomplete. All these programs have already been implemented and tested using Python 3.6 in Anaconda and Python 3 compilers online. The book also has an Appendix on the useful Python functions and libraries. To further enhance the understanding of the subject, application ability and analytical ability of the students, there are numerous objective, subjective, and programming exercises at the end of each chapter. Above these, each chapter has a set of innovative pictorial puzzles, where the logic behind the questions to be solved and then coded using data structures is given. Finally, each chapter has a set of mini projects, which include some real-world complex problems where data structures have come to the rescue.

Salient Features

The salient features of the book include:

- *Simple and lucid explanations* for complex Data Structures concepts using analogy of real-world objects/systems.
- *Pictorial representation and problem solving* of each data structures operation to ensure proper understanding of feature and visualization of transformation.
- *Base case analysis* with pictorial solving for important corner cases of primary algorithms.
- Plenty of implementable *programs* to help readers improve their implementation skills.
- Mid-chapter exploratory questions in the form of *food for brain* to help think out of the box and explore upcoming concepts on their own.
- Implementation promoting coding style where *pseudocode* is given before *Python codes* using which the readers can try out the code before referring to the given snippet.
- *Case-studies* to show the power of each data structure within each chapter.
- *Evolutionary style explanation* where every data structure talks about the problem in the previous structure and how it is overcome with the abilities of the next structure.
- Abundant and variety of chapter-end exercises including *objective questions* with *answers, theoretical review questions, exploratory application exercises, pictorial puzzles*, and *mini projects* for self-check and practice.
- *Glossary* of key terms and point-wise *summary* at the end of each chapter to help readers quickly revise important concepts learnt.

Organization of the book

The book is divided into 13 chapters and one appendix.

Chapter 1 provides an introduction to Data Structures, why the concept was introduced, and how to read Data Structures.

Chapter 2 discusses the concept of Abstract Data Type and how is it useful in implementing data structures. It introduces the Asymptotic Notations which is the way to measure the cost of an algorithm. The chapter also deals with recursive functions and methods to measure their performance.

Chapter 3 deals with the most primitive and simplest data structure – Array, and operations on arrays. It also describes various built-in functions for Python Lists.

Chapter 4 is dedicated to linear data structures which are traditionally continuous memory- based, and implemented based on Arrays/List – Stack & Queue. It deals with different types of Queue structures along with the behavioural functionalities of all the structures.

Chapter 5 takes up the first non-continuous structure. The different types of Linked Lists, their implementation, and working functions are discussed in this chapter. Since Python does not have the concept of pointers, this chapter shows how nested objects are used to implement non-contiguous structures.

Chapter 6 unleashes the concept of hierarchical data structures. The concept of associating the object to multiple objects makes non-linear data structures possible. 'Tree' is the basic non-linear, hierarchical data structure and this chapter introduces the basic tree concepts and behaviour.

Chapter 7 presents one of the most widely used hierarchical data structures. It deals with different types of Search trees, where there is a constraint with respect to organizing elements in a tree. For all the search trees, the advantages of every structure over the previous are clearly depicted along with the operations aiding the apt use of the structure in data intensive applications.

Chapter 8 shows how a non-linear tree structure can be used for a dynamic linear requirement. This chapter is mainly based on Heaps which a binary tree-like structure using which priority queues are implemented at optimal cost.

Chapter 9 covers other non-linear data structures such as Trie, Sets, Hash Tables, and Dictionaries. Trie is a complex form of tree and hash table is used to aid faster storing and searching of data. Other structures deal with association of various data points, without any particular associativity amongst themselves.

Chapter 10 is dedicated to the B+ Tree structure which is widely used in data storage. It shows various functionalities and explains why it is faster while handling data. Other than B+ Tree, it also throws light on different data structures used in various instances of operating systems.

Chapter 11 handles the non-linear, non-hierarchical data structure, Graphs. First, the various representations of graph along with their implementations are shared followed with various algorithms for problems. Algorithms like connectivity, topological sorting, minimum spanning tree, and shortest distance between any given pair are all explained to aid realistic problem solving.

Chapter 12 explains various sorting techniques. Sorting is the technique of arranging the elements of a list in a specific order. This chapter deals with a wide range of sorting algorithms which vary in performance. Sorting techniques such as bubble sort, selection sort, insertion sort, and distribution sort are discussed. Non-sorting problem solving with techniques like divide and conquer is also explained.

Chapter 13 is dedicated to efficient accessing techniques. Binary search which utilizes the power of a sorted data is shared in this chapter. This chapter also shows how structures like tree and hash table can be used to search data efficiently.

The **Appendix** at the end of the book discusses some of the important utility functions and libraries in Python. This can help in optimizing the implementation codes.

Acknowledgments

The writing of this textbook was a mammoth task for which a lot of help was required from many people. We take this moment to thank all our family and friends who supported us in completing this book.

We would like to sincerely thank and acknowledge [24]7.ai family for their support in writing the book and Abhilaash Nagarajan, Dinesh S, and Apurva Mandalika for extending their help towards organizing the content and testing programs.

Last but not the least, we would like to thank the editorial team at the Oxford University Press, India for their help and support.

Comments and suggestions for the improvement of the book are welcome. Please write to us at shriramkv@gmail.com.

Shriram K. Vasudevan
Abhishek S. Nagarajan
Karthick Nanmaran

Detailed Contents

CHAPTER

1

Data Structures—Introduction

LEARNING OBJECTIVES

After going through this chapter, readers will be able to understand:

- What is a data structure?
- Why are data structures needed?
- How to study and understand data structures?
- How are data structures implemented?
- Why do data structures appear difficult?
- Real-life scenarios for data structures
- DBMS vs Data Structures

1.1 INTRODUCTION

Before taking a deep dive into the programming and algorithmic aspects of data structures, it is inevitable for someone to understand certain fundamental things. What is a data structure? Why do we need a concept called data structure? How to prepare for this subject? Why does it appear to be one of the toughest courses of all times in computer science? How to select your appropriate data structure? All these points shall be clarified in this chapter. It shall serve as a platform for understanding the rest of the chapters.

1.2 WHAT IS A DATA STRUCTURE?

A data structure is a format for storing data in an organized manner. The readers could even be surprised to know that they have already been familiar with data structures. If terms such as array, record, or file are familiar to the reader, then data structure is also familiar.

The next question in the minds of the readers would be, why should the data be organized or why do we need data structure? Assume that you have a rack with a lot of books catering to different subjects such as Computer Science, Biology, and Physics. The books are not organized and randomly piled up. One can refer to Figure 1.1 to understand what is being portrayed.

It is very easy to interpret that picking out one book on a particular topic from the unorganized rack is a tough task and a nightmare if the table is huge with more number of books in place.

Figure 1.1 An unorganized rack of books

Coming to the next scenario, assume a rack which is neatly organized with books properly sectioned as shown in Figure 1.2. The question now is, how much difficult it would be to spot a book from this organized rack? It would not take much time and shall be very easy. This is the difference a reader should understand.

Figure 1.2 An organized rack

Coming back to computer science, data structure is all about organizing, managing, and storing data. This shall enable efficient access with increased ease of access. Let us get the understanding better with more discussion.

1.3 WHY DO WE NEED DATA STRUCTURES?

Most of the interviews, examinations, and discussions will certainly have this question. The understanding of the need for data structures shall inculcate the interest in the reader to learn the subject and concepts deeper. Data structure is a method/technique for storing and organizing the information in a computing machine. Since it is all organized and well maintained, storage is properly taken care of and the data being searched for can be retrieved very easily and fast, hence effectively increasing the productivity. There is no single type of data structure that the reader is going to be introduced with. There are many types of classifications and each of these is unique. Data structures are generally classified as primitive and non-primitive and one can choose the appropriate option based on the requirements and suitability.

Experienced programmers shall agree to this point that the efficiency and speed at which a program runs depends on the choice of data structures and its implementation. Hence, data structures are important to organize data and to make sure the retrieval happens fast during data search.

1.4 HOW TO STUDY/PREPARE DATA STRUCTURES? WHY DOES IT APPEAR DIFFICULT?

First and foremost point to be understood is that 'data structure is not tough'. It is like any other subject which needs attention and a bit of patience to understand the flow. Every concept in a data structure has to be related to a real-time/real-life example. This approach would solve half the problem. Every data structure is inspired by some real-life scenario and this is well articulated in this book. For instance, if you take the data structure 'queue', it is inspired by the queue we stand in everyday for one purpose or other. In case of 'stack', bread slices can be cited as an example. Likewise, there are many real-life examples present in our day-to-day situations and all that is required is to correlate the examples to these data structures.

To make it simple, first identify the example related to a particular data structure, understand it and then navigate to technical learning. Realizing the data structure through implementation is very important. For implementation and to build the code, C, C++, or Python are preferred. Hence, the fundamental knowhow of any of these languages is a must. Here, in this book, we have used Python and it is one of the best options.

Data Structures = Concepts + Programming Skills

1.5 DIFFERENT TYPES OF DATA STRUCTURES

There are three major types of data structures:

1. Linear data structurcs
2. Non-linear, hierarchical data structures
3. Non-linear, non-hierarchical data structures

As the name suggests, in linear data structures, every data point can associate itself to a maximum of two data points only, one before and one after it. Here, the data points can be in continuous memory location. However, it is not mandatory to have the data points in continuous memory location. In non-linear data structures, the data points can never be stored in continuous memory locations as every data point can be associated with more than two data points. In hierarchical data structures, the data points maintain a hierarchical relationship among themselves. The last form of non-hierarchical is the most random form of data structures. Here, any data point can be associated with anything and the complete relationship is to be captured in a single structure.

1.6 HOW TO SELECT A DATA STRUCTURE?

Selection of a data structure for a scenario is completely based on the scenario and answering the following questions in order will help:

1. What is the associativity/relation among the data points?
2. Does the order of element have any significance in the solution?

3. Does the solution involve any order while processing, that is, can any element be modified directly or will there be any constraints on it?
4. What is the most frequently done operation in the solution?
5. Is there any specific behaviour expected from the structure in the solution?

Every time when a data structure is to be selected, do not feel that a particular feature of the data structure is an obstacle in the solution. Instead, pick the closest data structure and modify it as required. Always remember that a data structure is used to find a solution and the problem/solution will usually not be tailor-made for it. You will need to find a closest match.

1.7 HOW ARE DATA STRUCTURES IMPLEMENTED?

Data structures are implemented based on the object oriented programming (OOP) methodology. The features and associativity are defined in the form of classes and applied for the solution. It uses the OOP concept of abstraction and functional programming more. By defining the behaviour as functions inside classes, code reusability is achieved. For a user, it is sufficient if the behaviour of the data structure is known. It is not mandatory for the user to understand how the particular feature is defined. Thus, the functions inside the class abstract the unwanted information from the user. These are achieved by defining data structures as ADTs, called Abstract Data Types, explained in detail in Chapter 2.

1.8 REAL-LIFE SCENARIOS FOR DATA STRUCTURES

Figures 1.3-1.6 show the data structures that you see in the real-life elements every day. This is the approach used in the book throughout. Figure 1.3 is a train which is exactly the concept behind the linked lists. Figure 1.4 has a set of books piled, which is the idea behind the stack data structure. Needless to say, Figure 1.5 shows a tree which was behind the tree concepts in data structure. Followed by these is the Queue in data structure which is inspired through a real-life queue (Figure 1.6).

Figure 1.3 Train as 'Linked Lists'

Figure 1.4 Piled-up books as 'Stack'

Figure 1.5 Tree as 'Tree Data Structure'

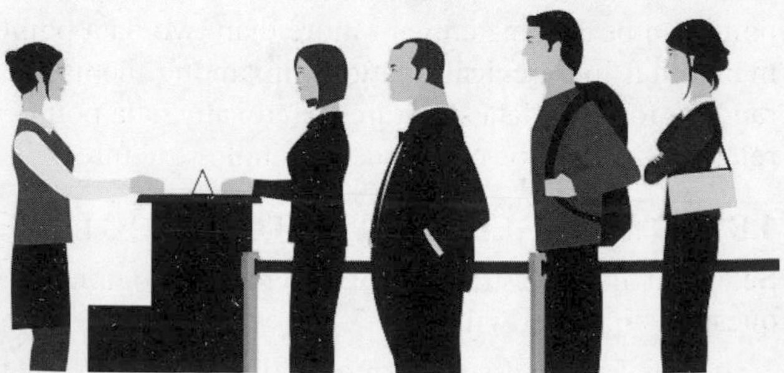

Figure 1.6 Real-life queue—'Queue Data Structure'

Considering the above points, it can be understood that learning data structure with appropriate examples and concepts in place would be easier. The complete book is framed with a lot of examples and real-life references for detailed, fast learning. Examples of objects such as marbles, playing cards, buckets, etc. have been used in this book for easy understanding of concepts.

Food for Brain

Find some more examples of real-time data structures.

Question 1.1 How to represent the relationship of a grand-father to father to son while processing?

Solution: The relationship is shown in Figure 1.7.

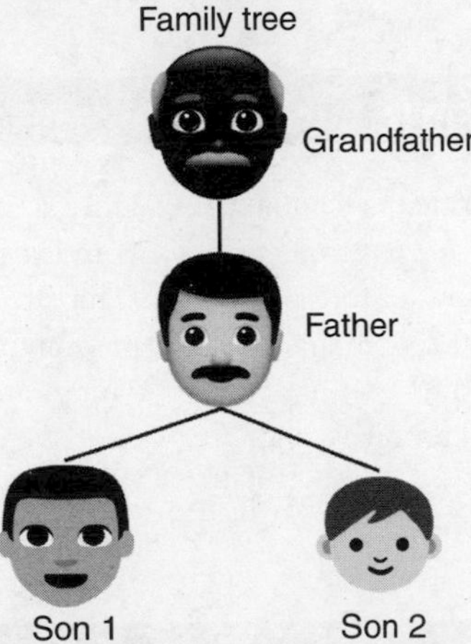

Figure 1.7 Relationship tree

Question 1.2 How to represent few cities and distance between them in order to plan a road trip easily using the information?

Solution: The information for the road trip is shown in Figure 1.8.

Figure 1.8 Road trip linked list charts

1.6 DIFFERENCE BETWEEN DATA STRUCTURES AND DATABASE MANAGEMENT SYSTEMS

All real-time data can be organized as objects, with each object having a lot of features. Multiple objects can have similar features if they ideally belong to the same class. At one time, two different objects may have a relationship. Database is a collection of similar objects. A table is a collection of similar objects, where each row is an object. The relationship among objects is represented as relation between tables. All the fields in the table are the features of that particular object. Database deals with permanent memory and stores data and relationship in real time, whereas data structure functions only at run time. Data Structures are more suitable for organizing data for efficient processing. In memory, all data is nothing but a collection of memory locations and values in them. In RAM, how these memory units are associated for efficient processing is all about data structures. They are not a permanent storage. In database, processing constraints cannot be applied as it only handles organizing and storing data by establishing relationships. All processing constraints are from data structures, with the key intent of improving performance of a solution.

KEY POINTS TO REMEMBER

- A data structure is a format for storing the data in an organized manner.
- Data structure is all about learning how to store and retrieve data in an effective and efficient manner.
- The simplest data structure is an array.
- Data structures can be classified as primitive and non-primitive data structures.
- Only when the real-life examples are connected with learning, it becomes easier.
- Data structure is a combination of concepts and programming approach to implement the concepts.
- Things and components existing in real life can be related easily to data structures. Simple examples start with train, trees, books on the table, etc.

EXERCISES

Multiple-choice Questions

1. Data structures are broadly classified into __________categories.
   (a) 2 (b) 5
   (c) 3 (d) None of the above
2. What is the most important point while selecting the data structure for a problem?
   (a) Associativity among the data points
   (b) Most common operation optimally required in the solution
   (c) Any behaviour required while storing and retrieving the information
   (d) All of the above
3. Linear data structures can be significantly differentiated into how many types?
   (a) 2 (b) 3
   (c) 4 (d) 5
4. A data point can always be associated to a maximum of two data points only?
   (a) True (b) False
5. Data structures' behaviour is implemented in classes to achieve_______.
   (a) Abstraction
   (b) Functional programming
   (c) Polymorphism
   (d) Object oriented programming methodology

Theoretical Review Questions

1. Define data structures.
2. Explain why data has to be structured. What are the implications one would face in case the data is not structured.
3. Express your views about the connection between data structures and speedy execution.

4. Mention the types of data structures you are aware of.
5. Mention some of the real-life elements which can be connected to data structures.

Exploratory Application Exercises

1. Write a function to sort the given numbers.
2. From a file with one million numbers, find all the given numbers.
3. Develop a function for enquiry of subject's registration so that while enquiring for a process the prerequisites can be directly checked and registered if not done.
4. Write a program to check if a given string is a palindrome or not.
5. Represent places and distances in a structure and identify the shortest distance between any two places.

Picto Puzzles

Identify the logic for all the picto puzzles given below.

1. DATA STRUCTIRE ⟶ ERUTCURTS ATAD
2. '3 + (5 * 4)' ⟶ 23
3. '3x + 4y' + '4x – 7y' ⟶ 7x – 3y
4. 1 2 3 4 5 ⟶ 5 4 3 2 1
5. 7 2 9 4 3 ⟶ 2

Mini Projects

1. Develop a system to represent places and the distance among them. The system must also be able to identify if every place is connected to every other place either directly or indirectly.
2. Design a module to handle the tasks in an operating system. It should have the ability to take in new jobs as they are created along with a priority. Based on the priority, the next job is executed. Every job will have the total time for execution as well. When a job is waiting for more than a threshold, its priority will increase further. This module will act as a scheduler and return the order in which the jobs will be executed.
3. Design a structure to represent a family tree. The structure should maintain the hierarchy properly. It should also have a function to print the members in hierarchy.

Answers to Multiple-choice Questions

1. (c) 2. (d) 3. (a) 4. (b) 5. (d)

CHAPTER

2

Abstract Data Type and Analysis

LEARNING OBJECTIVES

After going through this chapter, readers will be able to understand:

- What is an ADT?
- How to measure the performance of any algorithm?
- What is a recursive function?
- How does working of recursive functions differ from normal functions?

2.1 INTRODUCTION— ABSTRACT DATA TYPE

An abstract data type (ADT) is a type or class object which has its own behaviour and properties. Only a very few data structures are pre-defined in any programming language. An ADT is the best solution for data structures that are not defined. It is just a class defined in a standalone manner. The class has definitions of all the properties and functionalities defined in it. Whenever a data structure is required, the ADT file can be imported and objects of that class can be created and used directly. Abstraction means just to show the users what they want and hide the unwanted technical details. This is achieved through classes and objects. In addition, ADT can also be used to strictly stick to a complexity. There can be dedicated functions defined for performance computation and maintenance as well. The level of abstraction is not only for internal values and variables, but also for internal functionalities, such as maintenance, that may be triggered by some functions. The new program, where the ADT is imported and called using a data structure object is referred to as the client code. This client code contains only the data structure object, and the remaining definition is based on the solution designed.

This chapter will explain how to implement data structures and how to design the solution optimally. There can be more than one implementations of any solution. The most optimal implementation can be selected using asymptotic notations, which represent the cost for resources used by the function. This chapter will help the readers understand the computation and representation of this cost along with cost comparison, paving way to efficient selection and usage of data structure in the solution.

2.2 COMPLEXITY

Any algorithm should have a way to measure it. The standardized way of comparing algorithms is complexity. All algorithms will have two complexities—time complexity and space complexity. Time complexity is the measure of running/execution time of an algorithm, whereas space complexity is the measure of total memory used by an algorithm.

2.2.1 Time Complexity

The running time of algorithms may vary from one processor to another, based on their processing speed and memory. Even in the same processor, based on the internal resource availability, the running time of an algorithm may differ across instances. To overcome all these pitfalls, asymptotic notations were introduced. Before discussing notations, it is important to understand the computation of runtime and the reason behind the importance of time complexity in solution design. Time complexity gives the total runtime of an algorithm. Thus, when a solution is designed, every module must be highly optimized for time complexity, in order to prevent wastage of CPU resources during execution.

Every single step of execution in a program will consume one unit time. For universal standards, this unit is not assigned any metric and computation of all the steps is done at this basic time unit level. When an algorithm includes just one step, it is a single time unit, whereas if an algorithm is made up of five steps, then the complexity sums up to five unit time. Be it any constant, if the number of steps in an algorithm is irrespective to the number of inputs, then it is a constant running time algorithm. So, for any large input, the algorithm will complete execution in a fixed time without any scaling. This can be understood by analysing the below code snippets and their complexity explanations.

Python code fragment 2.1

```
def age_diff():
    age1=int(input("age1: "))
    age2=int(input("age2: "))
    print(age2-age1)
```

Python code fragment 2.2

```
def IsEven():
    a=int(input("number: "))
    if(a%2):
        return False
    else:
        return True
```

Python code fragment 2.3

```
def ToEven():
    a=int(input("number: "))
    if(a%2):
        n=int(a/2)*2
        return n
    else:
        return a
```

The function in Python code fragment 2.1 is simple and straight forward. It reads two integers and finds their difference. Irrespective of the input value, the number of steps executed in the function will be '3'. This is the simplest example of constant running algorithm since the number of steps is unaffected by the value inputted.

The function in Python code fragment 2.2 reads a number and identifies if it is even or not. Since there is a conditional block in the code, the steps are calculated individually for all the possible combinations of execution and then the worst case/most number of steps from any block can be taken as the final number of steps for the function. Here, reading input is a step and checking the function is another step. When the condition is true, it has just one step, but when it is false, it again has just one step. Thus, the total number of steps remains '3'.

The function in Python code fragment 2.3 has different steps in '`if`' and '`else`' blocks. When the given input is even, it just has '1' step. However, when the given input is odd, it has '2' steps, which means computing the previous even number and then returning the same. The final steps of the function may be '4' for odd number and '3' for even number. So, the total number of steps from the function should be '4'.

All the above algorithms have fixed number of steps and hence their running time is also a constant number. However, in real time, algorithms do not have fixed steps. Consider a loop that is iterating across an array of elements. If an array is of length '7', then the number of steps will be '7' or a multiple of '7', however, if an array is an input from the user and the number of inputs is not known, then the running steps also become unpredictable. For 'n' inputs, the loop will have 'n' steps or a multiple of 'n' steps. So, the complexity becomes linearly proportional to the inputs. This is explained further with the help of snippets below.

Python code fragment 2.4

```
a = input().split(" ")
for i in a:
    print(i)
```

Python code fragment 2.5

```
def FirstN():
    N=int(input("number: "))
    for i in range(1,N+1):
        print(i)
```

Python code fragment 2.6

```
def Fibo():
    N=int(input("number: "))
    a=0
    b=1
    print(a)
    print(b)
    for i in range(2,N):
        c=a+b
        print(c)
        a=b
        b=c
```

Python code fragment 2.7

```
def Tables():
    N=int(input("number: "))
    for i in range(1,N+1):
        for j in range(1,11):
            print(i," * ",j," = ",i*j)
        print(" ")
```

Python code fragment 2.4 has a simple read and print operation of an array. The snippet gets all the elements of a list in a space separated format. List is a collection of elements in Python. The input is read in one step, but printing it element by element is done using a loop. The interesting part is that the loop runs based on the number of elements given in the input. Thus, to generalize, the number of steps in the loop is referred to as 'n', where 'n' is the number of elements in the input. Thereby, the total number of steps in this snippet is '1+ n'. This mathematical expression that represents the cost is referred to as the cost function.

The function in Python code fragment 2.5 is another version of the same '1+ n' steps. Here, the input is just one element but the loop runs 'n' number of times, where 'n' is the input number, making the final steps to be '1+ n'. In both the snippets, the loop has only one step. When the loop has more steps, the final number of steps also gets impacted.

The function in Python code fragment 2.6 is 'fibo( )', which reads the number 'n' and prints the first 'n' Fibonacci numbers. Each iteration of the loop has '4' steps. The final step should have a component '4n', however, the number of iterations is not 'n' in this function. Instead, the loop runs for 'n-2' iterations, which means the loop runs for '4*(n-2)' number of steps. Therefore, the total number of steps in the function is '5 + 4*(n-2)'. This snippet has multiple steps in the loop. What happens when a loop has another loop within it? Such a function is given in Python code fragment 2.7.

This function in Python code fragment 2.7 reads a number and prints the multiplication tables of all the numbers from '1' to 'n'. For computing the number of steps, we begin with the innermost loop. The innermost loop always runs for '10' iterations as the condition is independent of 'n'. So, it has '10' steps in total, taking all the steps and iterations into consideration. Now, the outer loop is considered. It runs for 'N' iterations. Every outer iteration has the inner loop and one print statement. The number of steps in a single iteration of outer loop becomes '10+1', which is '11'. So, the number of steps executed by the outer loop is '11*n'. The input reading step adds '1' to this component and gives the total steps in the given function as '1 + 11*n'. In this case, the inner loop/nested loop runs for a constant number of times. It can also depend on 'n', such as the cases discussed below.

Consider the case of nested loops. In one level of nesting, both the inner and outer loops run 'n' steps in every iteration. So, the inner algorithm runs 'n' steps for each iteration of the outer loop. It means that there are, in total, 'n*n' steps which correspond to 'n^2' steps. This can be further analysed with Python code fragment 2.8.

Python code fragment 2.8

```
def Series():
    N=int(input("Size: "))
    for i in range(1,N+1):
        k=i
        for j in range(1,N+1):
            k=k*k
        print(k)
```

This snippet is a series generator which takes a number from the user and prints the '8th' power of all the numbers from '1' to 'N'. Here, the inner loop has 'n' number of steps. For every iteration of the outer loop, there is the inner loop and two more steps, which make 'n+2' steps per iteration. Given that outer loop runs 'n' times, the total number of steps is computed as 'n*(n+2)'. Thus, the cost function is 'n^2+2n'. This computation is easy, as it is just multiplication of the outer and inner iterations. However, it is not this easy when the inner iteration is relatively dependant on the outer iteration. Such a function is explained in Python code fragment 2.9.

Python code fragment 2.9

```
def Series():
    N=int(input("Size: "))
    for i in range(1,N+1):
        k=i
        for j in range(i,N+1):
            k=k*k
        print(k)
```

This is where the actual complication of running steps' calculation is seen. The inner loop runs 'n' times for the first iteration of the outer loop. However, as the outer loop's iteration increases, that is, as 'i' increases, the number of iterations of the inner loop decreases since it is running from 'i' to 'N+1' and not from '1' to 'N+1'. When 'i' is '1', the inner loop runs 'n' times. When 'i' is '2', the inner loop runs for 'n-1' times. Similarly, when 'i' is '3', the inner loop runs for 'n-2' iterations. This continues until 'i' becomes 'n' where the inner loop executes just once. So, when the number of steps in the inner loop differs for each iteration of the outer loop, both cannot be multiplied directly to compute the number of steps. Therefore, the total number of steps in the function is computed manually by adding the number of steps in each iteration. This results as [(2+n) + 2+(n-1) + 2+(n-2) + 2+(n-3) + ... + 2+(1) + 2]. When this is reduced, it becomes [(2*n) + ((n)+(n-1) + (n-2)+(n-3) + ... + (1))]. By adding '2' from all the elements separately, we get '2*n' components and the remaining as a series of (n+ n-1 + n-2+ n-2 + ...+1). The series can be seen as sum of numbers from '1' to 'n', which is solved as 'n(n+1))/2'. Thus, the series component can be reduced to [(n^2/2) + (n/2)]. After several reductions, the final cost function for the steps will be [(2*n) + (n^2/2) + (n/2)]. Thus, such nested loops also get the 'n^2' component into the cost function.

As the level of nesting increases, the total number of steps is calculated by multiplying the number of steps in individual loops, when all the loops run for the same number of steps, say 'n'. So, with each level of nesting, the steps increase the degree by '1'. For a one-level nested loop, it is 'n^2', 'n^3' for two-level,

Python code fragment 2.10

```
def Series(N):
    for i in range(1,N+1):
        for j in range(1,N+1):
            for k in range(1,N+1):
                print(i*j*k)
```

'n^4' for three-level nesting, and so on. A simple algorithm with 'n^3' steps is shown in Python code fragment 2.10.

Loops do not always need to have 'n' steps. Some loops may run for lesser or more steps. For example, 'for' loops run for 'n' steps, whereas the number of steps are different for 'while' loops. A case when a 'while' loop has steps lesser than 'n' is shared in Python code fragment 2.11. In languages other than Python, such a case is possible in 'for' loops as well.

Python code fragment 2.11

```
def Series(N):
    i=N
    while(i>0):
        print(i)
        i=int(i/2)
```

In Python code fragment 2.11, the incrementing part is modified as it is divided by '2'. Assume 'n' is '8', so in first iteration, '8' will be divided by '2' to result in '4'. Then, it will be further divided in consecutive iterations into '2' and '1', and finally '0'. Thus, the loop is executed '3' times. This can be computed as '$2^x = n$', where 'x' is the number of iterations. When 'n' is not a perfect exponent of '2', say '$n = 10$', even then the number of iterations is '3', which is equal to the power of '2' for the exponent before it. Thus, the total number steps in the loop, in terms of 'n', is represented as '$\log_2(n)$'. In algorithms, this is generalized as 'log n'. So, when the loop divides 'n' by any constant, the running steps are expressed as 'log n'.

Other than linear programs, loops have more importance in computation of running steps as they are complex for computation.

Question 2.1 Compute the number of running steps in Python code fragment 2.12.

Python code fragment 2.12

```
def Series(N):
    for i in range(0,N):
        j=i*N
        while(j>0):
            print(j)
            j=int(j/2)
```

Solution: The inner loop executes 'log n' steps and the outer loop runs for 'n' iterations. When nested together, this function's steps are represented as 'n*(1 + log n)', which can be reduced to 'n + n*(log n)'.

Food for Brain

What will be the total number of steps in this algorithm?

```
def Series(N):
    for i in range(0,N):
        for j in range(0,N):
            print(i*j)
```

(contd)

(contd)

```
    for i in range(0,N):
        j=i*N
        while(j>0):
            print(j)
            j=int(j/2)
    K=int(N*6/4)
    for i in range(K,7*N):
        print(int(N/7))
```

2.2.2 Space Complexity

While time complexity is based on the number of steps, space complexity is the measure of the total memory spaces required by the code. Just like time complexity, space complexity also has the same metric problem for measuring. In this case, every single memory space is treated as unit space and used to represent the total number of spaces in a code. As in case of time complexity, it is equally important to optimise the code for space complexity. If the code deals with a fairly large data set and memory spaces, then the solution demands huge resources, increasing the cost exponentially. Thus, space complexity is significant while designing solutions. There will not be a wide range of combinations for space complexity.

When the function has only one/constant number of variables to be stored, the number of memory spaces is the sum of the variables (spaces) used in the program. A normal 'for' loop has just one variable and the memory space used is also '1'.

Python code fragment 2.13

```
for i in range(0,5):
    print(i)
```

In Python code fragment 2.13, 'i' is the only variable and the number of spaces used is '1'. Just like time complexity, the goal is to create a mathematical function to represent the total spaces used in the code.

Python code fragment 2.14

```
def age_diff():
    age1=int(input("age1: "))
    age2=int(input("age2: "))
    print(age2-age1)
```

This function in Python code fragment 2.14 has two variables and the number of memory spaces is a constant again, that is, 2. A data structure stores all the elements. So space used by any data structure can never be lesser than 'n', as it is supposed to store all the elements. Consider the list which receives the value from the user, then the spaces used is equal to the number of inputs given, that is, 'n'.

Python code fragment 2.15

```
a = input().split(" ")
```

In this list statement in Python code fragment 2.15, the elements are received from the user and stored as individual elements in list 'a'. So, the memory spaces used can be simply represented as 'n'.

Python code fragment 2.16

```
a=input().split(" ")
j=a[0:2]
print(j)
```

In Python code fragment 2.16, the list 'a' uses 'n' spaces. The list 'j' is a sub-list taking the first two elements from 'a'. The memory spaces used by 'j' can only be a maximum of '2'. Thus, the total spaces used can be represented as '2+ n'. When 'a' gets lesser than '2' elements, the size of 'j' will also be lesser than '2', making the memory space lesser than the represented equation. Considering the worst possibility, the mathematical representation is left unchanged. From this explanation, it is clear that memory spaces can never be 'log n'. Even for a matrix, the space is 'n', as irrespective of the dimensions of the function, the total elements are considered as 'n'.

Food for Brain

When two cost equations have different components with different powers, how can they be compared for choosing the optimal solution?

2.3 ASYMPTOTIC NOTATIONS

The equations, discussed in Sections 2.2.1 and 2.2.2, formed in computing the running steps for time complexity and the memory spaces used in space complexity are treated as a mathematical model. For easy comparison and evaluation of the same, asymptotic notations are used. The need of asymptotic notations can be understood well from the below scenario.

Consider a function with running steps '2n+7'. Now, say the same functionality can be achieved by another function with running steps 'n^2'. So, which implementation should be used in a real-time application? This requires comparison of running time of both the functions. When 'n' is '3', function1 will result in '13' steps and function2 will result in '9' steps. For all 'n' lesser than or equal to '3', function2 will perform better than function1. However, when 'n' crosses 3, function1 starts performing better over function2, which means the number of running steps will be optimally less in case of function1. Thus, in real-time, the comparison becomes difficult while handling those mathematical models due to fluctuating values. Asymptotic notations are used to represent the worst case and best case of the functions and many such metrics aiding in comparison.

The above scenarios have made the necessity of an asymptotic notation clear, however, the question is, 'what does asymptotic mean?'. Asymptotic means approaching a curve or a point as close as possible. Therefore, when representing a function in its asymptotic notation, it is very important to keep in mind that the notating function should be arbitrarily close enough to the original function.

2.3.1 Big–O

Big-O is represented as 'O( )'. This is the widely used asymptotic notation, which signifies the worst case running time of a function. Formally, the Big-O function is defined as a limiting function. It aims at setting an upper limit for a function with another function. A function, '$f(x)$' = 'O($g(x)$) as $x \to \infty$', when the absolute value of '$f(x)$' is lesser than or equal to a multiple of 'C' and '$g(x)$' for all 'x' greater than or equal to a threshold 'x_0' and any constant 'C'. This is mathematically represented as:

$$|f(x)| \leq C * g(x), x \geq x_0 \quad (2.1)$$

For visualizing '$g(x)$' for any '$f(x)$', the graph in Figure 2.1 can be referred.

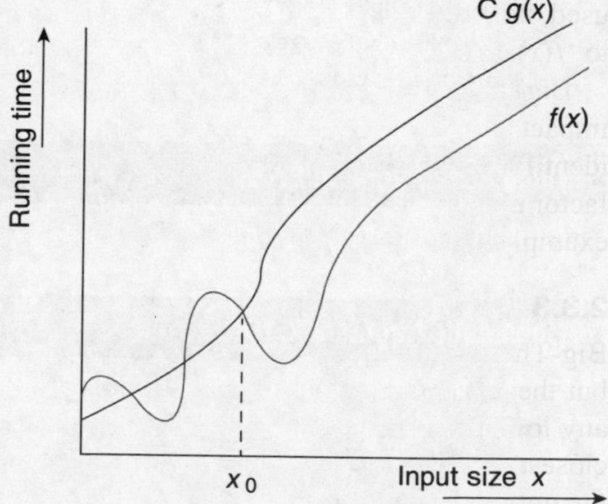

Figure 2.1 Big-O function representation

In the function, it can be clearly seen that '$g(x)$' is always greater than '$f(x)$', after the threshold 'x_0'. For any function, there can be any number of '$g(x)$' forming an upper border but the core task in identifying the apt function is to ensure that '$g(x)$' is as close as possible to the base function '$f(x)$' and to maintain 'x_0' as minimum as possible.

For identifying this easily in asymptotic notations, the first step is to identify the maximum impact creating component in the equation of running steps/memory spaces. Say, in the function, '(2*n) + (n²/2) + (n/2)', the component with the highest impact is '(n²/2)'. This term can further be reduced, that is, when 'n' is high, 'n²' will also be very high. When the constant '2' is compared with a very high 'n²', '2' becomes negligible. Thus, any type of independent constant in the term can be removed. The remaining part in the component is only 'n²'. Thus, the given function is 'O(n²)'. Simply, the Big-O is the largest component in the function with all constants removed.

With this explanation, let us try to identify the Big-O of '3*(logn)+7n'. Mathematically, 'logn' is always lesser than 'n'. So, the function is 'O(n)'. Similarly, it is important to remember the fact that 'nlogn' is lesser than 'n²', only because 'logn' is lesser than 'n'.

2.3.2 Big–Omega

Big-Omega is represented as 'Ω ( )'. While 'O( )' marks the upper bound for a function, 'Ω ( )' marks the lower bound. A function, '$f(x)$' = 'Ω ($g(x)$)' as 'x→∞', when the absolute value of '$f(x)$' is greater than or equal to a multiple of 'C' and '$g(x)$' for all 'x' greater than or equal to a threshold 'x_0' and any constant 'C'. This is mathematically represented as:

$$|f(x)| \geq C * g(x), x \geq x_0 \qquad (2.2)$$

For visualizing '$g(x)$' for any '$f(x)$', the graph in Figure 2.2 can be referred.

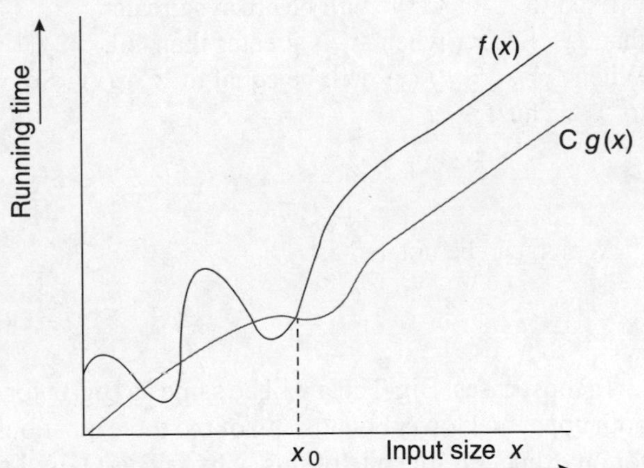

Figure 2.2 Big-Omega function representation

It is clearly seen in the graph that '$g(x)$' is always lesser than '$f(x)$' after a threshold. Say '$f(x)$' is '$x^2 + 5*x$', then '$g(x)$' can be any function which is always lesser than or equal to the '$f(x)$'. Even '$f(x) = \Omega(g(1))$' is right, as '$f(x)$' can never be lesser than '1' at any point. Even though by definition it is right, such a representation will always be misleading and hence this notation is rarely used. Even after these shortcomings, if 'Ω' notation is to be used, it is to be maintained as close as possible to '$f(x)$'.

Big-O identifies the element with the highest impact, however, Big-Omega targets towards identifying the component with the least impact. After identification of the component, any constant factor must be removed. Now, the component can be represented as Big-Omega. For '$f(x)$' in the above example, the ideal 'Ω' should be 'Ω(x)'.

2.3.3 Big–Theta

Big-Theta is the average case. Big-O marked the upper bound and Big-Omega marked the lower bound, but there was a problem in both the notations. Big-O can be any high function and Big-Omega can be any low function, but these are not mandatorily the optimal functions. The optimal Big-O must be the closest upper bounding function and Big-Omega must be the closest lower bounding function. To ensure the optimal function is used, Big-Theta can be considered. In Big-Theta, a function '$g(x)$' is selected to be both the upper bound and lower bound of '$f(x)$'. A function, '$f(x)$' = 'Θ($g(x)$)' as 'x→∞', when the absolute value of '$f(x)$' is within the range of '$C_1 g(x)$' and '$C_2 g(x)$' for all 'x' greater than or equal to threshold 'x_0' and any constants 'C_1, and 'C_2'. This is mathematically represented as,

$$C_1 * g(x) \leq |f(x)| \leq C_2 * g(x),\ x \geq x_0 \tag{2.3}$$

For visualizing '$g(x)$' for any '$f(x)$', the graph in Figure 2.3 can be referred.

In Big-Theta, the same function is multiplied by two different constants, which mark the upper and lower bounds correspondingly based on the value of the constant. This is a notation to optimally represent and mark the upper and lower bounds.

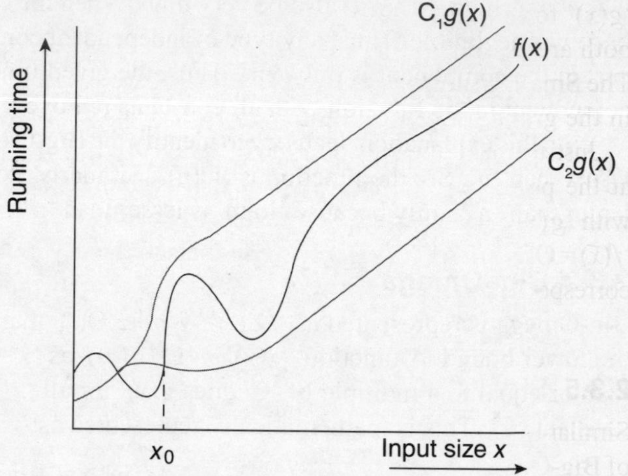

Figure 2.3 Big-Theta function representation

For the same '$f(x)$', '$x^2 + 5*x$', '$g(x)$' for Θ will be 'x^2'. However, how can the lower bound be 'Θ(x^2)'? For any value of 'x', 'x^2' will be lesser than '$x^2 + 5*x$' as '$f(x)$' has a '$5x$' term in addition. Thus 'C_1', the constant for lower bound, is fixed to '1'. For upper bound, 'C_2' is fixed to '2' as '$2*x^2$' will be always greater than '$x^2 + 5*x$', when 'x' is greater than '6'. When 'x' is '5', '$f(x)$' will be equal to '$C_2 g(x)$'. So, with 'C_1' as '1' and 'C_2' as '2', '$g(x)$' can be fixed to 'x^2'. Thus,

$$x^2 \leq x^2 + 5*x \leq 2*x^2,\ \text{for } x \geq 5$$

Which can be notated as,

$$f(x^2 + 5*x) = \Theta(x^2),\ \text{for } x \geq 5$$

In most cases, Big-Theta will be same as Big-O for a function. Given Big-Theta marks the function in both upper and lower bounds, out of the three notations, Θ is the best and most asymptotic representation for any function. In spite of this, why is Big-O used widely? For performance comparison, it is always important to analyse 'How the program will behave in the worst case?' and 'What will be the resources required at worst case?' Thus, Big-O becomes more significant.

2.3.4 Small–O

Small-O is a stricter version of Big-O. Small-O also marks the upper bound of a given function like Big-O, but the definition is stricter. A function '$f(x)$' = 'o(g(x))' as '$x \to \infty$', when the absolute value of '$f(x)$' is lesser than a multiple of 'C' and '$g(x)$' for all 'x' greater than or equal to a threshold 'x_0' and any constant 'C'. This is mathematically represented as,

$$|f(x)| < C * g(x),\ x \geq x_0 \tag{2.4}$$

This difference can be clearly understood by referring to the graph shown in Figure 2.4.

In the above graph, '$f(x) = O(g(x))$'. It can be seen at a point when '$x = k$', '$f(x) = g(x)$'. In spite of the functions meeting at a point, Big-O definition is still fine with '$g(x)$' marking the upper bound for '$f(x)$', whereas Small-O definition does not allow '$g(x)$' to mark the upper bound for '$f(x)$', as they both are equal for a particular 'x' greater than 'x_0'. The Small-O along with Big-O and '$f(x)$' are shared in the graph shown in Figure 2.5.

Just to make the function move away from '$f(x)$' at the point '$x = k$', the constant that is multiplied with '$g(x)$', is increased. So, it is clearly evident that '$f(x) = O(g(x)) = o(g(x))$' for two constants 'C_1' and 'C_2' correspondingly, such that '$C_2 > C_1$'.

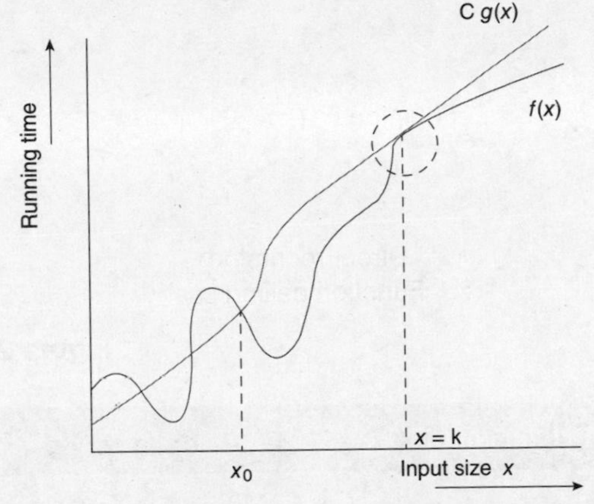

Figure 2.4 Graph to prove non-strictness of Big-O

2.3.5 Small-Omega

Similar to Small-O, Small-Omega is a stricter version of Big-Omega. A function '$f(x) = \omega(g(x))$' as '$x \to \infty$', when the absolute value of '$f(x)$' is greater than a multiple of 'C' and '$g(x)$' for all 'x' greater than or equal to a threshold 'x_0' and any constant 'C'. This is mathematically represented as:

$$|f(x)| > C * g(x), x \geq x_0 \quad (2.5)$$

As there has already been sufficient explanation of Big-Omega and the difference between 'Big-' and 'Small-' notations, it is left for the users to further explore the 'Small-Omega' notation.

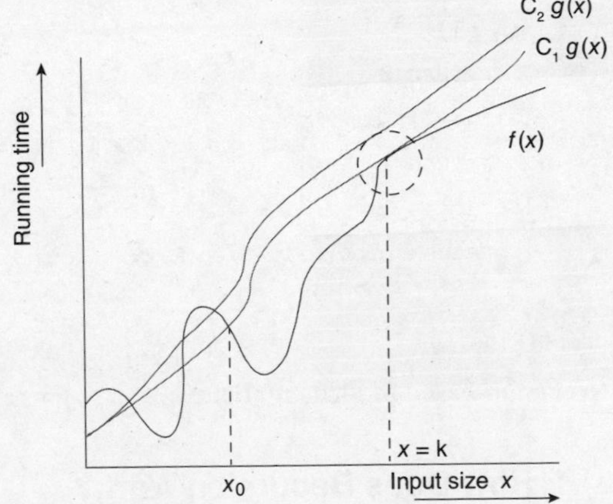

Figure 2.5 Big-O and Small-O for a function

2.4 RECURSION

Recursion is a type of function which calls itself. Recursion can either be direct or indirect. Direct recursion means a function calling itself, whereas in indirect recursion, a function calls another function, and that in turn, calls the prior function. This can be seen as a cycle of function calls. Both these types of recursions can be seen in the graphical cycle representation in Figure 2.6.

Recursion can be seen as a replacement of loops in some regular programs. Ideally, all recursive functions can be re-written to work with iterations, but some might require additional data structure support for passing values from one state to another. A simple recursion to iteration program for Fibonacci series is given in Python code 2.1.

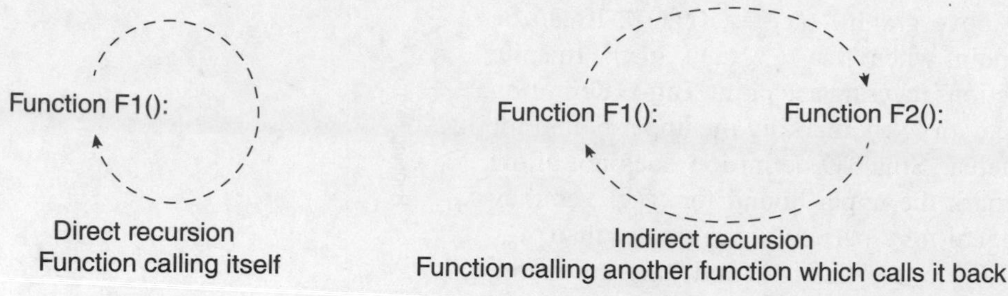

Figure 2.6 Types of recursion

Python code 2.1

```
def Fibo(N):
    if(N==1):
        return 0
    elif(N==2):
        return 1
    else:
        return Fibo(N-1)+Fibo(N-2)

print(Fibo(5))
```

Recursion-based implementation

```
def Fibo(N):
    a=0
    b=1
    fibo=[]
    fibo.append(a)
    fibo.append(b)
    for i in range(2,N):
        c=a+b
        a=b
        b=c
        fibo.append(b)
    return(fibo[N-1])

print(Fibo(5))
```

Iteration-based implementation

2.4.1 How Does Recursion Work?

As already introduced, recursive functions are functions that call themselves either directly or indirectly. Before jumping into recursions, a brief description of how function calls are handled in a Computer System (PC) is given to ensure proper understanding of recursive function calls. In a PC, there is a dedicated memory called 'System Stack'. Stack is a data structure which is explained in detail in Chapter 4. While executing an instruction, there will be many context variables and values. Context variables are defined in the local scope and are available only for those specific set of instructions. If the current instruction is a function call, then the control must move from one function to another. This changes all the context and environment variables as well. So, before moving control to new functions, the current context is saved in a block called as Process Control Block (PCB), which is placed in the system stack. Then, the control moves to the new function and execution of the instruction begins. The PCB also stores the address of the instruction, so that when the function's execution is completed control can go back to the same instruction. This results in a new context with corresponding local variables. However, once the end of the function is reached, the function gets completed and the control is to be transferred back to the instruction that actually called it. The PCB at top of the system stack is taken out and the control is transferred to that instruction. Additionally, the local scope variables are also set back to create the same context again for that program to continue execution. The graphical depiction of this process is shown in Figure 2.7. This function call handling is defined in the operating system of the PC and just a brief up of the process is shared in here, as elaborating the same might deviate from the core aim of the book.

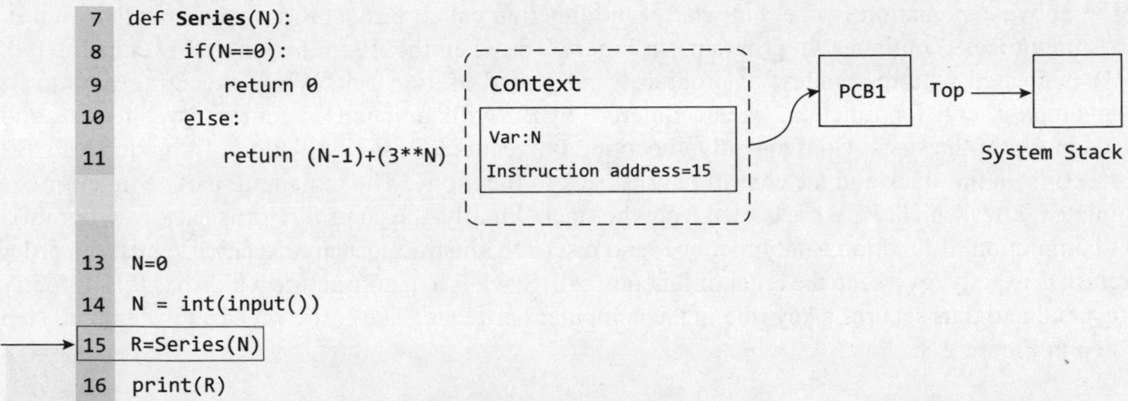

7 def Series(N):
8 if(N==0):
9 return 0
10 else:
11 return (N-1)+(3**N)
13 N=0
14 N = int(input())
15 R=Series(N)
16 print(R)
Context
Var:N
Instruction address=15
PCB1
Top
System Stack

Instructions 13 to 16 are in the main program. While executing instruction at 15, function call is encountered.

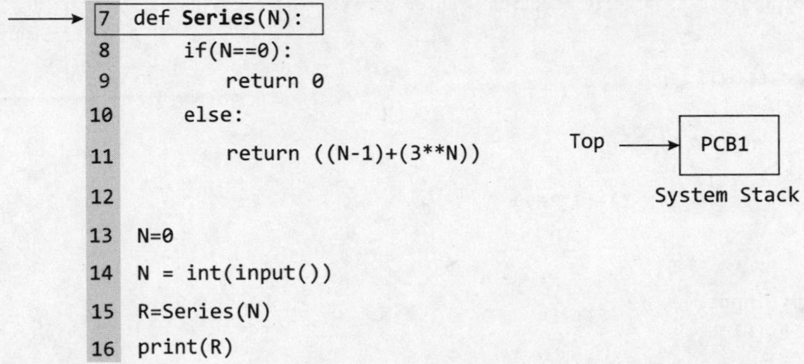

7 def Series(N):
8 if(N==0):
9 return 0
10 else:
11 return ((N-1)+(3**N))
12
13 N=0
14 N = int(input())
15 R=Series(N)
16 print(R)
Top
PCB1
System Stack

When control moves to function, at instruction 7, the context is placed as PCB in system stack.

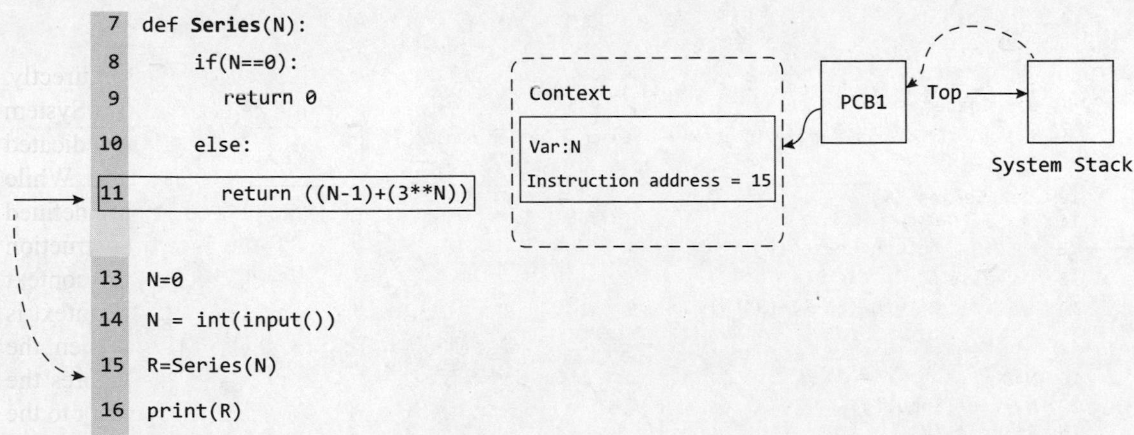

7 def Series(N):
8 if(N==0):
9 return 0
10 else:
11 return ((N-1)+(3**N))
13 N=0
14 N = int(input())
15 R=Series(N)
16 print(R)
Context
Var:N
Instruction address = 15
PCB1
Top
System Stack

While executing instruction 11, the function is completed. So, the previous context is loaded from the stack and control is returned to the location in the PCB. Control moves to instruction 15 and the main program completes execution.

Figure 2.7 Step-by-step illustration of function call and system stack handling it

The above explanation is fine, but what if the function called has another function call within it. The same process continues. In program1 in Figure 2.8, when the first function call is encountered, PCB1 is created with the context of program1 and placed in the stack. While executing function1, when function call for function2 is encountered, PCB2 with function1's context is generated and placed in top of the stack. Consequently, function2 is executed. Post-completion of function2, PCB2 is loaded from the stack and the control returns back to function1. The remaining part of function1 is completed, after which, PCB1 is loaded from the stack. Finally, the control returns back to program1, post-completion of function2 and function1, and rest of the instructions are executed. Thus, the order of return is exactly reverse to the order of function call. Stack is a data structure which has this property of reversal and thus secures a key role in the computer hardware. The entire scenario is depicted step by step in Figure 2.8.

```
def Graze():
        print("This is a graze function...Enter a better number")

def Series(N):
    if(N==0):
        return Graze()
    else:
        return ((N-1)+(3**N))

N=0
N = int(input())
R=Series(N)
print(R)
```

PCB1 Top → System Stack

Program1 is executing and encounters the first function call to function1. PCB1 has context of program1 and is placed in stack.

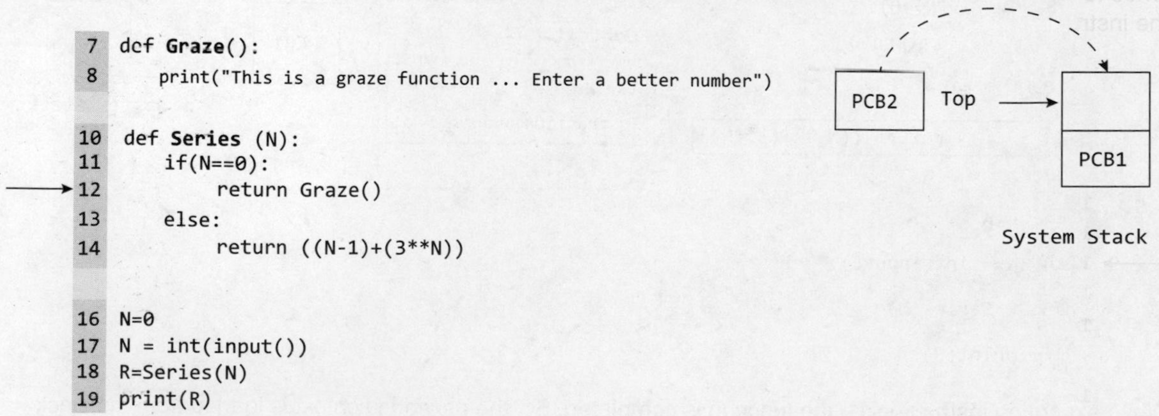

In function1, call to function2 is encountered. Context of function1 is placed in PCB2 and then is placed in stack.

(contd)

(*contd*)

```
def Graze():
    print("This is a graze function...Enter a better number")

def Series(N):
    if(N==0)
        return Graze()
    else:
        return ((N-1)+(3**N))

N=0
N = int(input())
R=Series(N)
print(R)
```

Top → PCB2
PCB1

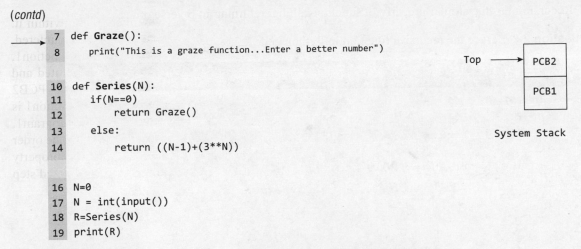

System Stack

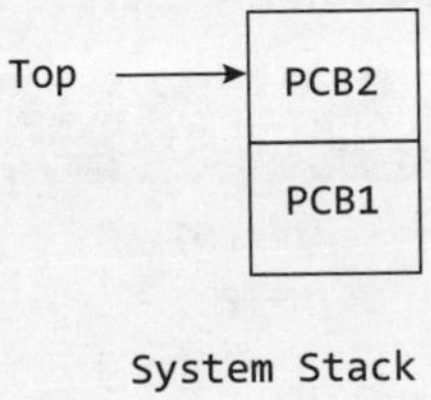

While function2 is executing, the stack will have two elements—PCB2 and PCB1.

```
def Graze():
    print("This is a graze function ... Enter a better number")

def Series (N):
    if(N==0):
        return Graze()
    else:
        return ((N-1)+(3**N))

N=0
N = int(input())
R=Series(N)
print(R)
```

PCB2 Top →
PCB1

System Stack

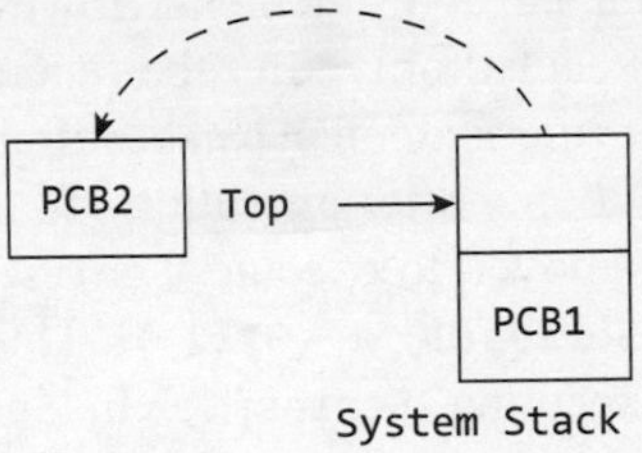

Once function2 completes execution, the top element from the stack is taken out and control is transferred to the instruction address present inside PCB2.

```
def Graze():
    print("This is a graze function ... Enter a better number")

def Series (N):
    if(N==0):
        return Graze()
    else:
        return ((N-1)+(3**N))

N=0
N = int(input())
R=Series(N)
print(R)
```

PCB1 Top →

System Stack

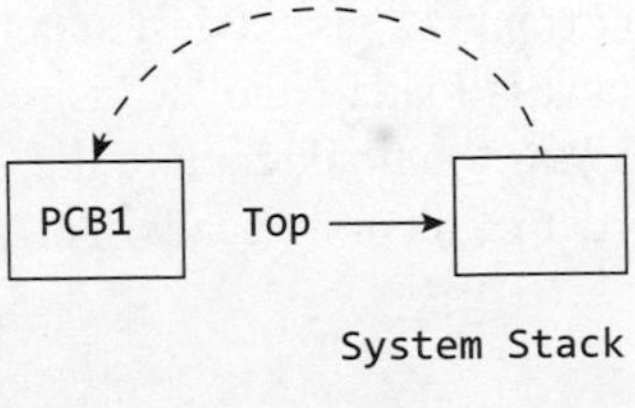

Then, the `return` statement in function1 removes another element from the stack and loads the PCB1. Control is transferred back to that instruction address with return values, if any.

Figure 2.8 Step-by-step illustration of nested function calls

Recursion has the similar property of function calling, returning in reverse order.

Question 2.2 Trace the recursive function in Python code 2.2.

Python code 2.2

```
def Series(N):
    if(N==0):
        return 0
    else:
        return (Series(N-1)+(3**N))

print(Series(3))
```

Solution: The function call '`Series(3)`' assigns '3' to 'N'. This falls under `else` block, which just has one `return` statement. However, the `return` statement has a function call in it. Thus, the return will be executed only after the function call (recursive call) completes execution and returns value. Thus, the `return` statement can be reframed as '`return (Series(2) + (3**3))`', in which '3**3' is reduced to '27' but only after execution of '`Series(2)`'. Thus, the statement placed is the same in PCB and the control is moved to execute '`Series(2)`'. Again, it results in a recursive call at the `return` statement, '`return (Series(1) + (3**2))`'. This statement is again placed in the PCB and the control moves forward for executing '`Series(1)`'. In '`Series(1)`', another recursive call is created at the same instruction, '`return (Series(0) + (3**1))`'. This statement is also placed in the PCB and the control moves forward to execute '`Series(0)`'. The '`Series(0)`' function does not have any recursive calls further and just returns '0'. This is called the base case, where the recursion brakes. If the program is written without this recursion braking condition, then the function will never end and thus result in run-time exception. When '`Series(0)`' returns '0', the control should be transferred to the previous call. Thus, the PCB from the top of stack is loaded and '0' is sent to it. The statement, '`return (Series(0) + (3**1))`', becomes '`return (0+(3**1))`' which on simplification becomes '`return 3`'. From this, it can be clearly understood that '`Series(1)`' returns '3'. This again loads the next PCB from stack and returns value to that stack . The statement, '`return (Series(1) + (3**2))`' becomes '`return (3 + (3**2))`'. Simplifying further gives '`return 12`' as the last statement of the function call, '`Series(2)`'. Eventually, the last PCB from the stack is loaded and '12' is received by the instruction. This forms '`return (12+(3**3))`', which gives '39' as the final result to the user. Thus, the returning order in recursive calls is also exact reverse of the order of recursive calls. This step-by-step explanation is depicted in Figure 2.9.

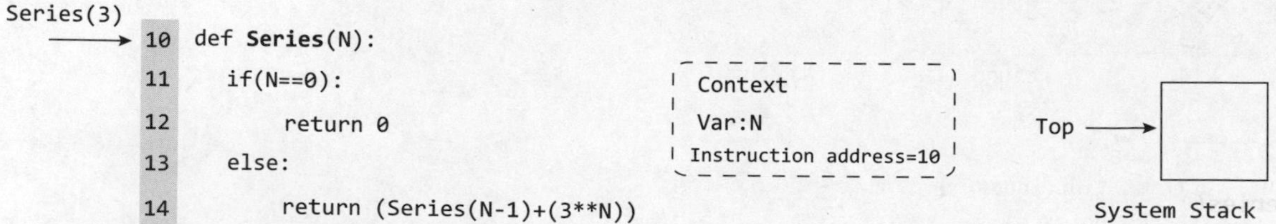
Series(3)
10 def Series(N):
11 if(N==0):
12 return 0
13 else:
14 return (Series(N-1)+(3**N))
Context
Var:N
Instruction address=10
Top
System Stack

Function' 'Series' is called with argument '3'

(contd)

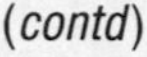

(*contd*)

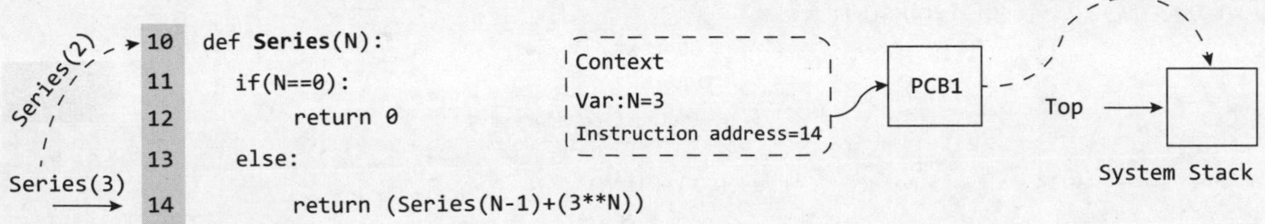

Recursive call '`Series(2)`' is encountered. Context of '`Series(3)`' is placed as PCB1 in system stack.

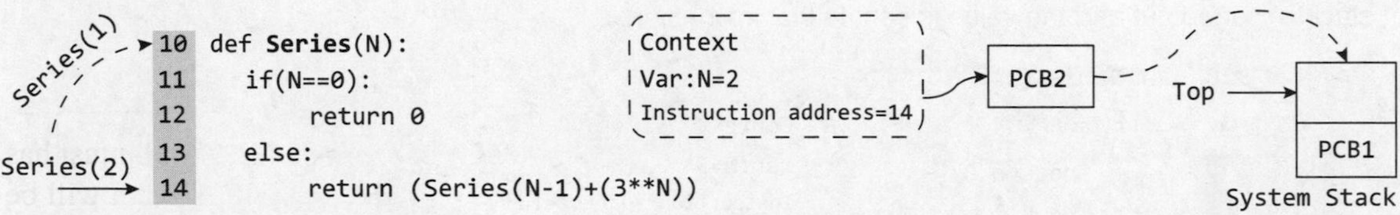

Inside '`Series(2)`', recursive call '`Series(1)`' is encountered. Context of '`Series(2)`' is placed as PCB2 in system stack.

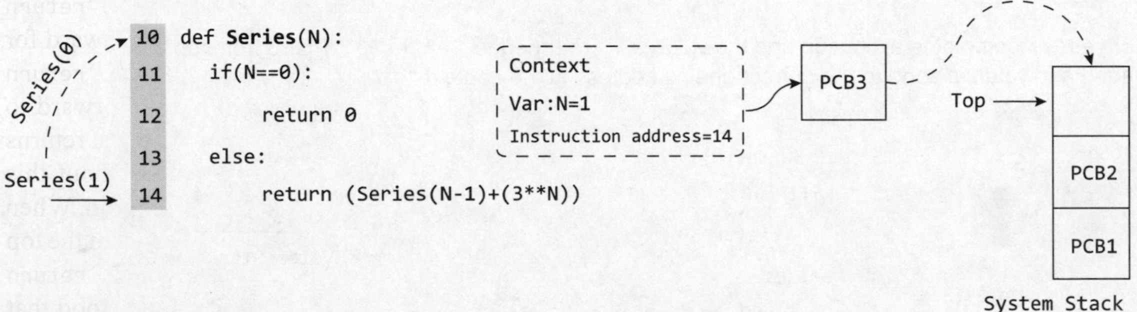

Inside '`Series(1)`', recursive call for '`Series(0)`' is encountered. Context of '`Series(1)`' is placed as PCB3 in system stack.

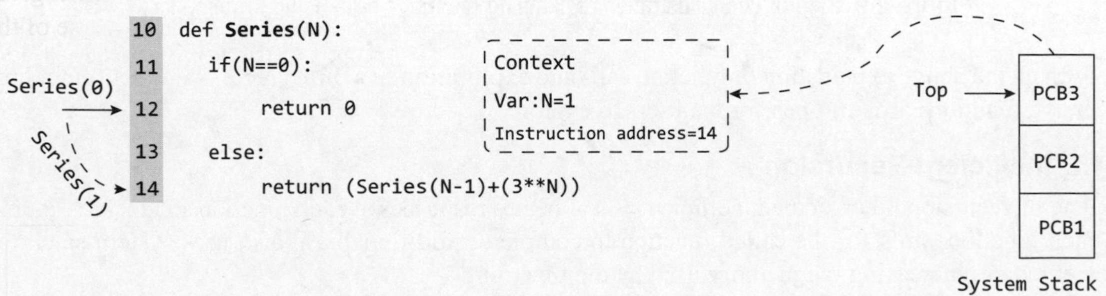

'`Series(0)`' completes execution. '0' is to be returned to '`Series(1)`'. The PCB3, which is at the top of the stack, is loaded into the context. The instruction address is taken from the PCB and the return value is passed here.

(*contd*)

(*contd*)

```
10 def Series(N):
11    if(N==0):
12        return 0
13    else:
14        return (Series(N-1)+(3**N))
```

Series(1)

Series(2)

Context
Var:N=2
Instruction address=14

Top → PCB2
PCB1
System Stack

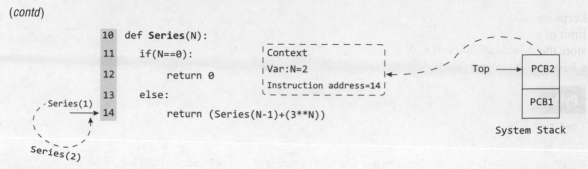

Function 'Series(1)' completes execution. Return value '12' is to be returned to 'Series(2)'. PCB2 from top of stack is loaded out and the value is sent to that instruction.

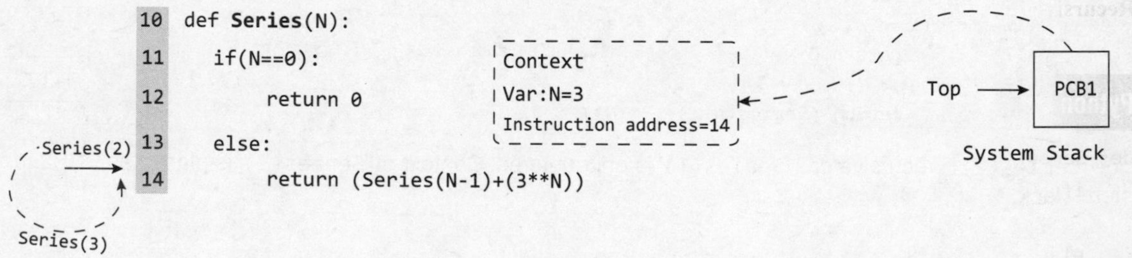

'Series(2)' completes execution and the value 39 is returned to 'Series(3)'. PCB3 from top of stack is loaded and value is send to the corresponding address in the context.

```
10 def Series(N):
11    if(N==0):
12        return 0
13    else:
14        return (Series(N-1)+(3**N))
```

Series(3)

Top →

System Stack

'Series(3)' completes execution and value is returned to the instruction that called it. The stack will be empty to show all the recursive calls have been completed. Thus, the returning order is the exact reverse of the calling order of recursion.

Figure 2.9 Step-by-step illustration of handling recursive calls using system stack

With all the above explanation of function calls and exploration of a direct recursive function, indirect recursive functions are left open for the users to explore.

2.4.2 Inefficient Recursion

In general, recursion is considered inefficient as it allocates resources to each function and locks resources as each function waits for the called function to complete. Additionally, it also uses system stack to a greater extent, increasing the memory used by the function.

Four Rules of Recursion

Any recursion must follow four rules. These rules are discussed below.

Rule 1 Every recursion must have a base case. As explained in Section 2.4.1, base case is the condition when there is no recursive call. The section will be executed based on a condition and will break any further recursive calls. If the recursive function does not have any base case, then the function continuously keeps on calling itself. This consequently increases the elements in the system stack. After a point, the limit of system stack is reached and no further recursive calls are handled since there is no space left to store the contexts. Such a scenario is referred to as *Stack Overflow Exception*. A sample recursion without a base case is shared below (Python code fragment 2.17).

Python code fragment 2.17

```
def Series(N):
    if(N==0):
        return 0
    else:
        return (Series(N-1)+(3**N))
```

Recursive function with base case

```
def Series(N):
    return (Series(N-1)+(3**N))
```

Recursive function without base case

In the above case, the function in the right will be never ending as there is just a statement which is a recursive call. This shows the importance of base case for breaking the recursion. Ideally, a recursion without a base case is of no significance.

Python code fragment 2.18

```
def Series(N):
    if(N==0):
        return 0
    else:
        return (Series(N-1)+(3**N))
```

Rule 2 The recursive call must always be towards the base case. If the increment or decrement of the condition variable is not towards the base case, Stack Overflow Exception occurs.

In the snippet shown in Python code fragment 2.18, in every recursive call, 'N' is decremented by '1' and the base case is 'N= =0'. So, the recursion is perfectly fine as it narrows 'N' towards the base case. Python code fragment 2.19 shows steps when only the recursive call is changed.

Python code fragment 2.19

```
def Series(N):
    if(N==0):
        return 0
    else:
        return (Series(N+1)+(3**N))
```

In this snippet, the recursive call is continuously incrementing 'N'. For any positive 'N', the base case will never be met and the Stack Overflow Exception will be fired again. Thus, it is important for the recursive call to move towards the base case.

Rule 3 The third rule is very straight. All recursive calls in a function should work. There is no point in writing a function with a recursive call that never gets executed. Will this even be possible? Refer to Python code fragment 2.20.

In this snippet, there is a recursive call under else case. This recursive call is towards the base case, but it is a `return` statement. So, when the recursive call returns a value, the function terminates and returns the same value. Ideally, any statement after the `return` statement will not be executed and hence the last recursive call will never be executed. So, what is the problem with such a case? The problem can be understood through Python code fragment 2.21.

Python code fragment 2.20

```
def Series(N):
    if(N==0):
        return 0
    else:
        return (Series(N-1)+(3**N))
    return Series(N-2)
```

In this snippet, there is a base case to break recursion. So, 'Rule 1' is satisfied. There are two recursive calls. The first call does not modify the condition variable, but the second call alters the

Python code fragment 2.21

```
def Series(N):
    if(N==0):
        return 0
    else:
        return (Series(N)+(3**N))
    return Series(N-2)
```

Python code fragment 2.22

```
def Fibo(N):
    if(N==0):
        return 0
    elif(N==1):
        return 1
    else:
        return Fibo(N-1)+Fibo(N-2)
```

Python code fragment 2.23

```
def Fibo(n, a=0, b=1):
    if n==0:
        return a
    if n==1:
        return b
    return Fibo(n-1, b, a+b)
```

condition variable towards the base case. Thus, 'Rule 2' is also satisfied. However, the problem is that the recursive call that satisfied 'Rule 2' will never be executed, as it is after the `return` statement. In spite of passing 'Rule 1' and 'Rule 2', this snippet results in stack overflow again. Thus, 'Rule 3' becomes important. There cannot be any unnecessary recursive calls in the function.

Rule 4 The final rule states that no task should be duplicated in recursion. In recursive calls, a task can be computed from a particular recursive call. It is to be ensured that the same task must not be re-computed using another recursive call. This rule can be better understood using Python code fragment 2.24.

Assume the call '`Fibo(3)`' for the above snippet. This will result in recursive call, '`Fibo(2) + Fibo(1)`'. Now, '`Fibo(2)`' will again have recursive calls, '`Fibo(1) + Fibo(0)`'. Thus, it can be seen that '`Fibo(1)`' is called twice. So, duplication of effort is involved as same value has been computed twice and the old answer has not been used. When the calling argument becomes high, this repetition also increases. To overcome this and satisfy the rule, the result calculated from the previous call should be used for the next call. Python code fragment 2.23 represents the modified code.

In this snippet, there is only one recursive call. The call takes both the left and right elements as arguments and moves forward, thus duplication of effort for the same value is just skipped. Such a call is called a tail call.

Higher Order Recursion Any recursive function which does not satisfy the above four rules is considered inefficient and should be avoided or modified in any application. Other than these rules, there is a classification of recursive functions. When a recursive function has more than one recursive calls, it is referred to as *Higher order recursion*. The problem is the kind of overlapping with 'Rule 4', which states that a value should be computed only once and not multiple times. The best example of higher order recursive functions is the `Fibo( )` function (refer to Python code fragment 2.22).

Python code fragment 2.24

```
def Fibo(N):
    if(N==0):
        return 0
    elif(N==1):
        return 1
    else:
        return Fibo(N-1)+Fibo(N-2)
```

Let us take a structure on the calls with '`Fibo(5)`'. '`Fibo(5)`' will result in '`Fibo(4)`' and '`Fibo(3)`', whereas '`Fibo(4)`' will result in '`Fibo(3)`' and '`Fibo(2)`', thus double computing '`Fibo(3)`'. Similarly, the call grows down and all the numbers from '3' will be computed more than once. The structure of the function calls is represented in Figure 2.10. It shows the number of times each value is computed.

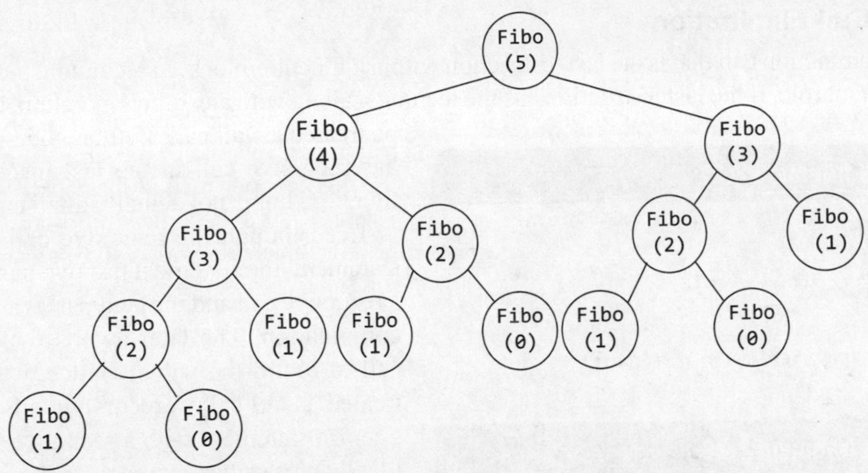

Figure 2.10 Hierarchical structure of recursive calls resulted by '`Fibo(5)`' in higher order recursive definition of Fibonacci series

Thus, higher order functions actually increase the order by exponentially increasing the number of recursive calls. Such recursive functions are ineffective and can be overcome with the same solution of 'Rule 4'.

When recursive functions have these inefficiencies, loops can never be considered as fully efficient. Most of the rules for recursion are applicable for loops as well. Any loop should have a condition to break the iterations, just like 'Rule 1' of recursion. The condition variable should be incremented or decremented towards reaching the break condition and ending the iterations. If the condition variable is not moved towards the breaking condition, the loop will be ever running and will have no significance. This is similar to 'Rule 2' of recursion. 'Rule 3' and 'Rule 4' will not be applicable for loops, as iterations are not controlled by any calls and the process is designed internally.

Python code fragment 2.25

```
def PrintN(N):
    for i in range(N):
        a=2
        b=1
        print(N*(a+b))
```

Python code fragment 2.26

```
def PrintN(N):
    a=2
    b=1
    for i in range(N):
        print(N*(a+b))
```

Another issue in loops is the loop indifferent statements inside a loop. A loop might have some statements which do not affect the loop execution directly, such as some assignment statements. If these statements are moved outside the loop, even then the logic can work and the same result can be received. These statements can be moved out for efficiency of the loop. This can be understood with Python code fragment 2.25.

In this snippet, the loop runs 'N' iterations and prints the first 'N' multiples of '3'. The values of 'a' and 'b' are assigned as '2' and '1', respectively, and in every iteration the assignment also takes place. This assignment operation in every iteration has no significance and in fact is an overhead for the program. This is an inefficient way for writing loops. This can be handled by moving the irrelevant/unchanging instructions out of the loop. The above program can be modified as shown in Python code fragment 2.26 with better efficiency and reduced overhead for the processor.

This topic is not about preventing the use of recursions or iterations in a program. Instead, we intend to efficiently write loops/recursions in applications with optimal overhead to the compiler and processor.

2.4.3 Tail Call Elimination

A *tail call* is a function call that is the last instruction within a function/block. In recursion, the tail call plays a very important role. If the last instruction has the recursion along with any other operation, then it will not be treated as tail call. Python code fragment 2.27 has recursive call in the last instruction of the function, but is not actually a tail call.

Python code fragment 2.27

```
def Series(N):
    if(N==0):
        return 0
    else:
        return (Series(N-1)+(3**N))
```

Python code fragment 2.28

```
def Fibo(n, a=0, b=1):
    if n==0:
        return a
    if n==1:
        return b
    return Fibo(n-1, b, a+b)
```

Even though the recursive call is in the last statement, the statement has two parts. The first is a recursive call and the next part is a mathematical computation. The later awaits for the recursive call to return the value. Hence, it is ideally not treated as tail call. A recursive tail call is simply a return statement with a recursive function call. Ideally, this statement receives the value returned by the function call and returns the same, just like a mediator. This can be seen in Python code fragment 2.28.

In modern compilers, this tail call is handled very efficiently. Modern compilers understand that the tail call has no significance in bringing the return value and the context is just important in identifying the correct instruction address to return the value. So, compilers avoid using the stack for tail call based recursion and instead pass on the return address to the function along with the arguments, thus optimizing recursive functions to a huge extent. This optimization is referred to as *Tail call elimination*. Thus, recursion with a tail call is better than general recursive functions.

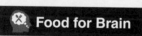

Food for Brain

Can every recursion be converted into a tail call based recursive function?

2.4.4 Analysis of Recursive Functions

Recursion finds a place in this book because the core intent of learning data structures is to design and implement solutions for problems. While designing, it is important to have the optimistic solution in place. This is when asymptotic notations play an important role. However, for recursive solutions, the cost computation is different and it is explained in this section. To identify the complexity of any recursive function, the total running steps have been computed and then represented with asymptotic notations. Just like loops, the total number of steps depends on the number of times a recursive function will be called/executed. Going forward, the number of steps in executing the function once without considering the recursive call is computed first. The base case steps are skipped, as these are executed separately in the end as last iteration. Thus, if the function is executed 'n' times, then the number of steps is multiplied with 'n-1', excluding the breaking case recursion. This is because the last execution of the function is the base case and may have different steps when compared to the block with recursive call. Then, the number of steps in base case execution is added to the product from the previous step. This provides the complete steps of a mathematical equation. Consider the functions shown in Python code fragment 2.29 and their computation.

The regular recursive case in the function shown above has '3' instructions. There is a condition check in the beginning to identify if it is a base case. So, in recursive case, there are '4' steps. These

Python code fragment 2.29

```
def Series(N):
    if(N==0):
        return 0
    else:
        d=(3**N)
        R=Series(N-1)
        return R+d
```

Python code fragment 2.30

```
def Series(N):
    if(N==0):
        return 0
    else:
        return (Series(N-1)+(3**N))
```

three steps will be executed 'N-1' times. The final execution will have just '2' steps, the condition check and single statement in that block. So, total steps from this recursive function are '4(N-1) + 2'. Thus, the worst case complexity is 'O(N)'. In tail calls, the recursive call is inside the return statement, so it is added as a single statement. So, the use of stack can be eliminated, but while computing run-time complexity, it does not make a difference.

Python code fragment 2.30 is another implementation of the same function. Here, there is only one statement in both recursive case and base case. So, the total number of steps equals '2(N-1)+2'. This is again 'O(N)'. The point to be noted in here is, irrespective of the number of terms, the impacting term will be 'N'.

Question 2.3 Compute the running steps for functions (i.e., in Python code fragment 2.31) with more than one recursive call.

Python code fragment 2.31

```
def Fibo(N):
    if(N==0):
        return 0
    elif(N==1):
        return 1
    else:
        return Fibo(N-1)+Fibo(N-2)
```

Solution: In the function shown in Python code fragment 2.31, recursive calls can be arranged as a tree as shown in Figure 2.10. The height of the tree is 'log n', from which the number of recursive calls can be computed as 'O(2n)'. Thus, when a recursive function has more than one recursive calls, its running complexity is linear and represented as 'O(kn)', where 'k' is the number of recursive calls in the definition.

Other than the runtime, while computing, space recursive calls will correspond to 'O(n)' as the system stack is used to store the context for each recursive call. When the number of recursive calls is more than one, space complexity also grows linearly, just like time function.

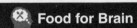

What will be the space complexity when the tail call is eliminated by the compiler?

2.5 APPLICATIONS OF RECURSION

Ideally, all the functionalities demanding loops/iterations can be achieved easily through recursion. Other than this, since recursion is based on function calls, parameters can be passed from first execution to second execution. This is very useful in many critical algorithms such as machine learning. Some critical applications of recursion are:

1. Learning algorithms
2. Traversal of data structures that do not have a size limit, especially non-linear
3. Sorting process
4. Puzzles and Exponential algorithms

POINTS TO REMEMBER

- ADT means Abstract Data Type. It is used for defining new structures' principle and behaviour without essentially disclosing the definition and implementation.
- Complexity is the measure of cost for running/storing a program.
- Asymptotic notations are used to represent the complexity in a generalized and easily comparable way.
- Big-Oh, represented as 'O( )', is used to represent the worst case complexity. It is important for comparison and choosing a program.
- The number of running steps in a loop is product of the number of instructions and the number of iterations.
- Recursive functions are functions that call itself.
- Every recursion should have a base case to terminate the calls and the condition variable should be moved towards the breaking condition.
- Each recursive function must have only one recursive call and should not have any unreachable statements.
- Recursion uses system stack to store the context and return to the calling point after completion of execution.
- When the recursion does not end, it results in stack overflow error.
- The tail call is a recursive function with the recursive call in the last statement.
- In modern compilers, the process of recursion for tail calls is optimized by passing the return location to the function along with the arguments in the recursive call. This avoids the use of stack for storing context.
- The runtime of recursive functions is computed by calculating the product of number of instructions and the number of recursive calls. Thus, runtime is majorly dominated by the number of recursive calls.

KEY TERMS

Abstract data types/ADT User-defined classes that behave like data structures defined as functions and lists internally to store values.

Asymptotic notation Notations for standard representation and comparison of functions from a performance and memory point of view.

Big-O A mathematical function that marks the upper bound of another function.

Big-Theta A mathematical function that marks the average case, both upper bound and lower bound, of another function.

Big-Omega A mathematical function that marks the lower bound of another function.

Recursion A function which calls itself.

EXERCISES

Multiple-choice Questions

1. ADT uses _______ .
   (a) Abstraction
   (b) Inheritance
   (c) Modular programming
   (d) All of the above
2. Running time is measured in _______ .
   (a) Seconds
   (b) Milliseconds
   (c) Unit step running time
   (d) All of the above

3. Can a Small-O also be Big-O of a function?
   (a) Yes (b) No
4. Big-Theta notation can accommodate _______ in the representation.
   (a) Big-O
   (b) Big-Omega
   (c) Both (a) and (b)
   (d) None of the above
5. Recursive function is a function _______.
   (a) That calls itself
   (b) With one line
   (c) With exponential complexity
   (d) Empty function
6. An ideal recursive function should not have _______.
   (a) Multiple recursive calls
   (b) Unreachable statements
   (c) Repetitive computation of the same value
   (d) All of the above
7. Loop computation is worsened by_______ .
   (a) Declaration statements
   (b) Loop indifferent statements
   (c) Assignment statements
   (d) All of the above
8. What is a tail call?
   (a) Recursive call in the last statement of a function
   (b) Multiple recursive calls in the last statement of a function
   (c) Useless recursive call in the last statement of a function
   (d) All of the above
9. System stack is used for _______.
   (a) Storing temporary variables
   (b) Storing variables' address table
   (c) String context of functions to return back post-execution of the called function
   (d) None of the above
10. Higher order recursion has _______.
   (a) No breaking condition/base case
   (b) More than one recursive calls
   (c) No tail call
   (d) All of the above

Theoretical Review Questions

1. What is an ADT and why is it important?
2. What is run time complexity and how is it computed?
3. Explain asymptotic notations. Why are they called so?
4. How are recursive functions handled in a Computer System? Elaborate with an example.
5. How is tail call a threat for recursive functions? How to eliminate the same?

Exploratory Application Exercises

1. Design an algorithm to convert a higher-order recursive function into a single-order recursive function.
2. Is Big-O always tight upper bound? Explain with an example.
3. What is dynamic programming? Can it be a replacement of recursion?
4. Compare and contrast higher-order Fibonacci series program and dynamic programming based Fibonacci series.
5. Does conversion of a recursion to iteration function always result in the same run-time complexity? Elaborate with supportive examples.

Mini Projects

1. Write a Python script to take in a Python code and compute the run-time complexity in terms of Big-O.
2. Implement a stack data structure, which takes in a set of elements and returns them in reverse order.

Answers to Multiple-choice Questions

1. (d) 2. (c) 3. (a) 4. (c) 5. (a) 6. (d) 7. (d) 8. (a) 9. (c)
10. (b)

CHAPTER

3

Linear Data Structures

LEARNING OBJECTIVES

After going through this chapter, readers will be able to understand:

- What are Linear Data Structures?
- What are Arrays?
- How is data stored in continuous memory locations?

3.1 ARRAYS—INTRODUCTION

Figure 3.1 Ice cube tray

An array is a collection of memory locations. It is a pre-defined data structure in all programming languages. Consider an ice tray in the Figure 3.1. It has six empty spaces, so it can hold '6' ice cubes. The spaces can be left unused, but more than '6' ice cubes cannot be held in it. The same is the case with arrays. The memory locations cannot be split from each other, so if there is some empty space, it just goes waste. In addition, arrays cannot be interchanged. For example, an ice tray can hold only ice cubes and an egg tray can have only eggs. An array is a collection of variables of same type. It cannot hold variables of different types. All the blocks in an array are of same size, as it holds only the same type of variables. Visual representation of an array is shown in Figure 3.2. This chapter discusses various operations that can be performed in an array.

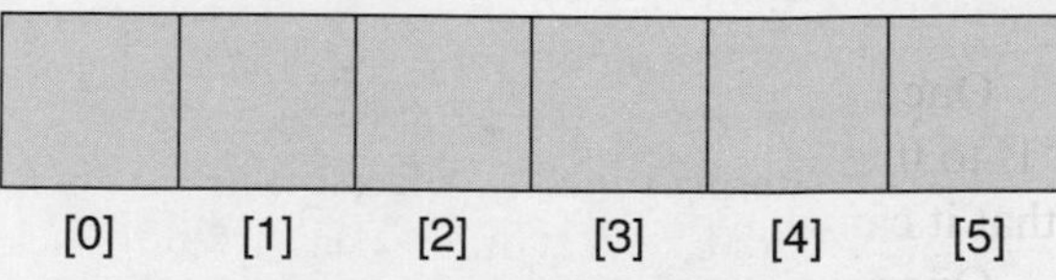

Figure 3.2 Visual representation of an array

3.2 DECLARATION OF ARRAYS

The position of each memory space is indicated by a number. It is called the index or subscript. The memory address of the first location is stored alone in the variable declaration, while others are calculated relatively. Say, 'a' is the name of the array. Then, 'a[3]' = address of 'a[0] + 3'. While declaration, the address of 'a[0]', that is the starting address of the array, will be associated with the variables named 'a' in the internal symbol table. Arrays can also be declared using pointers in C or C++ (not in Python and Java, as these do not have pointers). This is possible only because arrays are always continuous. So, the initial address can be referenced to a pointer and the rest can be used by relative accessing. Another way is to allocate a chunk of memory and assign it to a pointer, which is known as Dynamic Memory Allocation (DMA) in C/C++. By using pointers, the limit on number of elements or size of an array can be eliminated. Arrays are defined in the form of 'Lists'. Even though Python does not have pointers, 'Lists' are by default designed in a dynamic way without any limit.

Some points to be noted about an array are:

- It is a continuous chunk of memory with equally sized blocks
- The subscript always begins with '0' and goes until 'n-1', which is also continuous
- Any memory location can be directly accessed using its subscript
- Static arrays have issues, such as memory wastage and memory leak, and also have constraints over the size. These are overcome by using dynamic arrays or DMA using pointers.
- Since it is a continuous chunk of memory, it has internal issues such as fragmentation and memory leaks.
- This is the basic and naive data structure. Many other data structures are built using arrays.

Python lists have properties similar to an array, but do not require any size for declaration. The list is continuously growing with the elements being added to it, thus designed in a dynamic manner. Hence, lists overcome the problem of memory wastage and memory leak of arrays, as only the required memory blocks are associated with the list variable. Apart from these properties, Python lists have a special property. It can have data of any types within the same lists, which is not possible in generic arrays in other programming languages. Thus, Python lists are better than basic array implementation in programming languages like C/C++.

3.3 IMPLEMENTATION

Python lists can be initialized in one of the following ways. The list can be created empty or with elements.

```
a = []            #empty list
a = [1,2,3,4,5] #list with 5 elements
a = [] * (5)      #Empty list of size 5
```

Once the list is created, elements can be accessed using the subscript. For example, to assign a value '1' to the 4th position of the list created above, 'a[3] = 1' can be used. One additional property of lists is that it can contain data of any type, unlike arrays.

Once the list is declared using either of the above ways, it is ready and settled in the memory. The basic operations on lists are:

1. Insertion
2. Deletion
3. Merging

3.3.1 Insertion

The only way of inserting a new element into a list is to assign it to a specific subscript. For example, if '2' is to be inserted into 'a' at index '3', it is mandatory to initiate 'a[3]' with '2', that is, 'a[3]=2'. Now, '2' is inserted at subscript '3' of list 'a', but this may have multiple cases.

Case 1 Consider 'a[3]' as empty, then inserting '2' will engage the location and '2' will then occupy the memory space 'a[3]' as shown in Figure 3.3.

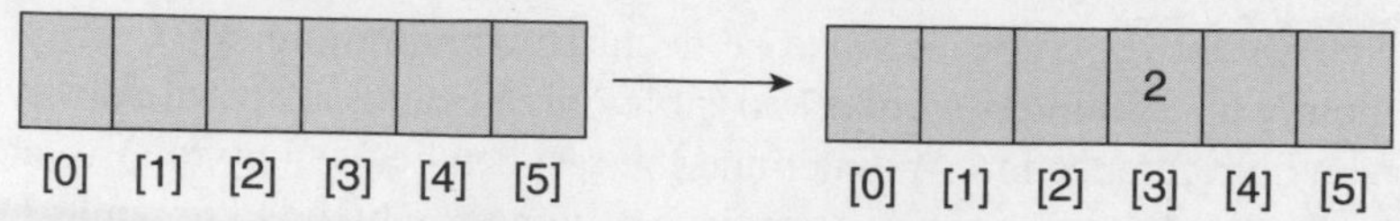

Figure 3.3 Inserting in an empty location

Case 2 Consider 'a[3]' to be already occupied, then inserting '2' will overwrite the content in the location and '2' will occupy the memory space 'a[3]' as shown in Figure 3.4. Now, the old data in the location will be completely lost.

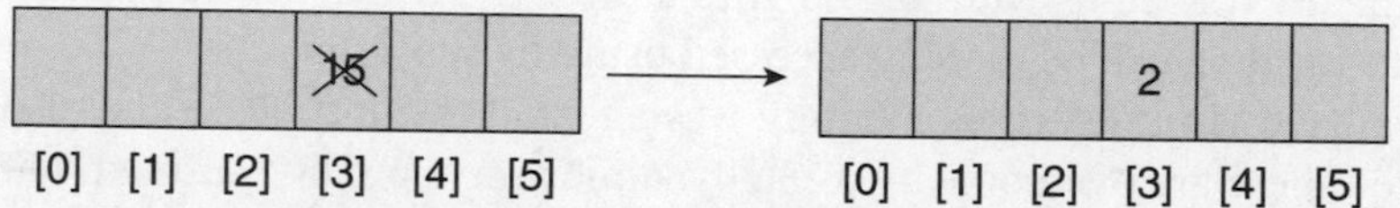

Figure 3.4 Inserting in an occupied location

This is the default way for inserting elements into an array. For inserting without loss of existing data, Algorithm 3.1 is designed and implemented in Python.

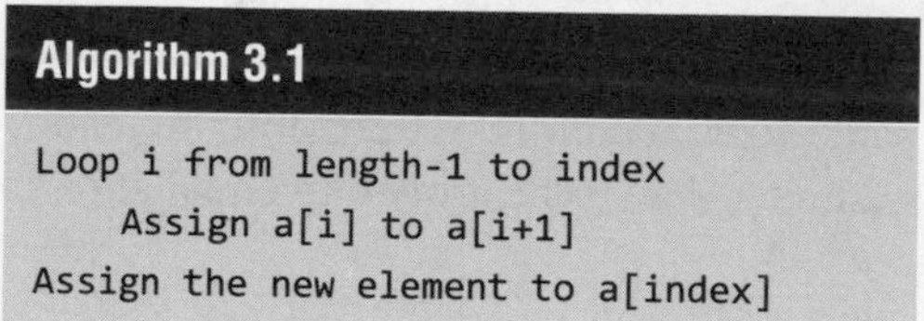

Algorithm 3.1

```
Loop i from length-1 to index
    Assign a[i] to a[i+1]
Assign the new element to a[index]
```

Start from the penultimate element of the array, that is, index 'n-2'. Move every element to the right by '1' position until the index where the new element is to be inserted is reached. Now, assign the location with the new value. All the elements before the particular index remain unchanged.

Question 3.1 Insert '2' at index '1' of a list containing {1, 3, 4}.

Solution: The process is explained in Figure 3.5.

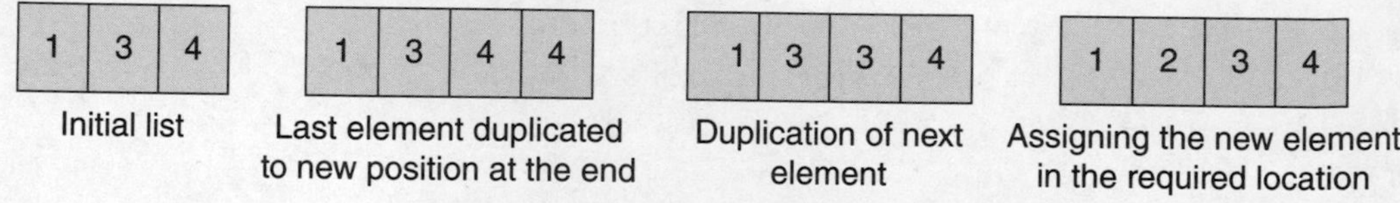

Figure 3.5 Inserting an element inside a list

Note Another advantage of using Python lists is that functions are pre-defined and can be simply called for usage. This function is called as '`list.insert(index, element)`'.

Food for Brain

What will be the time complexity for inserting an element into a list?

3.3.2 Deletion

The only way to delete an element is by using its subscript. So, for deleting an element, its subscript is mandatory. If the subscript of an element is not known, then the element is searched in the list and then deleted. Deleting an element in the middle of the list will move all the following elements to the left, which is depicted in Algorithm 3.2.

Start from the index next to the element to be deleted. Move every element to the left by one position until the end. Finally, free/delete the last element, as it will be duplicated. All the elements before the particular index remain unchanged as shown in Figure 3.6.

Algorithm 3.2

```
def delete(a[ ], element)
    index = 0
    Loop i in a
        if a[i]=element
        then,
            index = i
            break
    Loop i from index+1 to n-1
        Assign a[i] to a[i-1]
    Delete a[i-1]
    Return element
```

Question 3.2 Delete '2' at index '1' from an array of size '4' containing {1, 2, 3, 4}.

Solution: The process is explained in Figure 3.6.

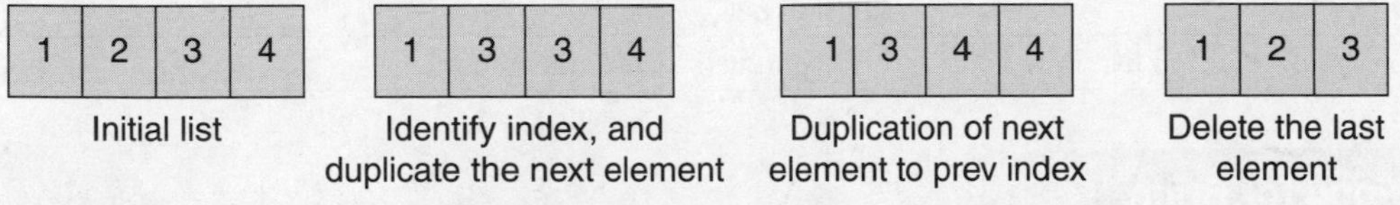
1 2 3 4
Initial list
1 3 3 4
Identify index, and duplicate the next element
1 3 4 4
Duplication of next element to prev index
1 2 3
Delete the last element

Figure 3.6 Deletion illustration in a list

Note Just like insert, this is also pre-defined in Python in the name of remove, called as '`list.remove(element)`'.

3.3.3 Merging

Another notable operation is merging two lists. It is basically concatenating the contents of one list into a new list. In addition, some patterns can be followed while merging the lists like all elements in odd indices of the merged list are from list1 and all elements in even indices are from list2. Such operations are rarely used. A normal merge operation involves creating a new list with list1 elements and appending list2 elements behind it. This utility is as well predefined in Python as 'list1+list2'. This is achieved through operator overloading of '+' operator.

3.3.4 Some More Operations

There are many other utility functions defined for lists. These can be used in basic read, write, or modify functionalities of the list. Table 3.1 has a list of available pre-defined functions, a brief description, and complexity of the same.

Table 3.1 Pre-defined functions for lists

Function	Description
`List.append(element)`	Appends the new element to the end of the list
`List.count(element)`	Returns the number of instances of the given element, if it is present in the list

(contd)

(contd)

Function	Description
List.extend(sequence)	Appends the elements of the sequence into the list
List.index(element)	Searches for the first instance of the element in the list and returns the index
List.pop( )	Removes and returns the last element from the list. This function can also take an optional argument, which is the index of the element to be removed and returned.
List.reverse( )	Reverses the given list
List.sort( )	Sorts the given list in ascending order. A comparison function may be given as an optional argument, based on which it will be sorted.

Other than these built-in functions, there are some operators overloaded for special utilities. All the available operators for a list are shared in Table 3.2.

Table 3.2 Operators available for lists

Operator	Syntax	Description
Length	Len(list)	Returns the length of the list
Concatenation	List1 + list 2	Concatenates list1 and list 2 and returns a new list
Repetition	[element] * number	Creates a list while repeating the element for a specified number of times
Membership	x in ['x', 'y', 'z']	Returns 'True' or 'False' signifying if the given element is present in the given list or not
Iteration	for i in list: print i	Traverses through each element in the list

Given a list object can have elements of any type, how can multi-dimensional lists be implemented using this list object?

3.3.5 Complexity Analysis

The possible operations in an array are insertion and deletion. The basic insertion or deletion processes described earlier with simple assignments are all operations of complexity 'O(1)', since direct access to the location is involved. However, the algorithm for traditional way of inserting or deleting elements into an array has a complexity of 'O(n)'. Consider the case of inserting an element at index '0', then all the other elements must be pushed to the right by '1'. Consider deleting an element at index '0', so all the other elements must be pushed to the left by '1'. Both the above are the worst cases of insertion and deletion and make a cost of 'O(n)'. The complexity of merging two arrays of size 'm' and 'n', respectively, is 'O(m+n)', as all the 'm+n' elements are to be read and stored in the resultant array.

The discussion of other possible operations and processing of lists like search and sort discussed in Chapters 12 and 13, respectively, with the analysis of their complexities. Further data structures will be implemented based on lists in Python.

3.4 APPLICATIONS

The primary application of arrays/lists is storing elements in a linear fashion. Original arrays just store elements of same type, whereas 'Lists' can have elements of any type. If a group of elements is to be stored without any particular constrain/arrangement order, then lists would be the first choice. However, a more important application of lists is in implementation of other data structures. Other linear data structures are built over basic lists with add-on behaviour definition. One real life direct application of lists is string handling. A string is a sequence of characters. So for handling/processing a string, it should be stored in a linear fashion just in the order it was given, which is best done by lists.

3.5 PYTHON SEQUENCES

Ideally, lists are a form of Python sequences. There are some more sequences supported in Python too. Those sequences and their significance is explained in this section. Their behaviour is similar to authentic arrays. The available sequences in Python are:

1. String
2. Lists (discussed above)
3. Tuple
4. Byte Sequences
5. Byte Arrays

Strings

Strings are nothing but a character version of lists. Strings store all the elements only as characters. Even if a string has numbers in it, everything will be saved as characters internally. A string can be initialized by calling the 'str' class. Python code fragment 3.1 shows how to declare a string.

Python code fragment 3.1

```
S = str( ) #Empty String
S = str('Data Structure') #String with 'Data Structure' stored in it
```

All the operations in lists are supported in strings as well.

Tuples

Tuples can be interpreted as immutable lists. It can be recognized using the '( )' around the elements in the declaration unlike '[ ]' around lists (refer to Python code fragment 3.2). Once the elements are placed inside the tuple or are initialized, these cannot be modified. Just as strings, tuples can be initialized using the 'tuple' constructor. However, there cannot be an empty tuple, as these are immutable.

Python code fragment 3.2

```
S = tuple('Data Structure', 'Oxford')
S = tuple(['Data Structure', 'Oxford'])  #tuple using an array of '2' elements
```

Byte Sequences and Byte Arrays

The other two sequences are byte oriented. Byte sequences have all the elements stored in a binary form. A byte sequence can be initialized using a 'bytes' constructor. Byte sequences are also immutable, so should be initialized with the value directly. However, the bigger question in here is, 'how to convert any given value into bytes?'. Standard encoding techniques, such as ASCII, UTF, and some more, can be used to convert a string/number into bytes. Thus, the constructor also has parameters to specify the encoding techniques. The syntax and usage is shared in Python code fragment 3.3. While printing the bytes, 'b' is used as prefix. These are then printed in a hexadecimal format, as byte formats are longer and difficult to interpret by human. The alphabet 'b' signifies that the value following it is binary.

Python code fragment 3.3

```
#Syntax bytes(Src, [encoding, error])
S = bytes([1,2,3])
#b '\0x01\0x02\0x03'
S = bytes('data') #This will throw runtime error, as compiler cannot understand the encoding
directly
S = bytes('data', 'acsii')
# b 'data' #Here, ascii encoding is used to convert the string into bytes
S = bytes('data', 'acsii', 'ignore')
# b 'data' #Here, error works on ignore mode
```

The third argument in the constructor in the above Python code fragment is to let the constructor know how to handle errors that may occur while encoding the string. Errors can be handled in three modes:

- Strict
- Ignore
- Replace

In 'Strict' mode, if any character is not recognized in the selected encoding technique, then immediately an exception is raised. In 'Ignore' mode, a particular character is ignored and all other characters are converted into bytes. In 'Replace' mode, those particular characters are replaced with a specified character.

Byte arrays are just a mutable form of bytes. These can be initialized using 'bytearray' constructor which is also similar to 'bytes' constructor with the same arguments and same behaviour. Python sequence functions, such as 'count' and 'len', for arrays are also supported for these byte sequences. A very popular use of byte sequences is in string handling and comparison. When multiple strings are to be processed, it is always preferred to encode them in the same way and then process the same.

Points to Remember

- Linear data structures are a type of data structure that store a collection of elements one after the other in a linear sequence.
- A 'List' is a primitive heterogeneous data type (i.e., data of different types). The data elements are stored in continuous memory locations.
- Referential accessing is possible in arrays, as memory blocks are in continuous address.
- The first block address is referred to as base address of the array and all other blocks can be relatively accessed using the formula 'basing address + number of blocks'.
- Lists are implemented using classes in Python.
- Lists have many operators overloaded like '+' for concatenation and '*' for repeating an element for 'n' times.
- Strings are lists for characters in Python.
- Byte sequences encode the string and then save those as bytes.
- Tuples are an immutable list.

Key Terms

Arrays The basic linear data structure which stores elements of same type in continuous memory locations.

Python lists A class in Python which is implemented as a data structure to store a collection of elements of various different types in a sequential pattern in continuous memory locations.

Insertion into a list The operation of adding a new element into a list

Deletion from a list The operation of removing an element from a list

List operation Basic operations on elements in a list

Primitive data structure A basic data structure in-built in all the programming languages

EXERCISES

Multiple-choice Questions

1. An array is a collection of elements in ________ memory locations.
   (a) Distributed (b) Random
   (c) Composite (d) Continuous
2. A 'list' is a collection of elements of ________ type.
   (a) Same (b) Similar
   (c) Different (d) Custom/User Defined
3. Lists are ________ based.
   (a) Static allocation
   (b) Dynamic memory allocation
   (c) Fixed memory size
   (d) Not disclosed
4. A ________ is used to access an element in a list.
   (a) Subscript
   (b) Index
   (c) Relative position
   (d) All of the above
5. Reversal of a 'List' can be done using ______.
   (a) Additional List
   (b) Loops
   (c) Recursions
   (d) All of the above
6. ________ is the complexity of merging two lists of length 'm' and 'n'.
   (a) m (b) n
   (c) m+n (d) m*n
7. The last element from a Python list can be removed using the _______ function.
   (a) delete (b) remove
   (c) pop (d) del
8. All elements of lists are listed using ________ operator.
   (a) print (b) iterator
   (c) traversal (d) peek
9. A 'list' retains the order in which the elements are inserted, unless changed.
   (a) True (b) False
10. Python lists are implemented using OOP methodology internally.
    (a) True (b) False

Theoretical Review Questions

1. How are lists organized in memory?
2. How is memory allocated to lists when elements of different types are added dynamically?
3. Elaborate reversal of a list with illustration and example.
4. Explain the process of sorting elements in a list. How will elements of different type be sorted?
5. Explain some use cases of lists.

Exploratory Application Exercises

1. Write a code to merge two lists such that all odd indices contain elements from the first list and all the elements in even indices are from the second list.
2. Write a basic code to sort the given list in ascending order without using any built-in functions.
3. Develop a function to remove duplicates from a list.
4. Using two-dimensional arrays (nested lists) to implement an element counter. Given a list of elements, the final structure should have the distinct elements and the count of each element in a table format.
5. Implement 'find' and 'replace' as a function that finds a given element from a list and replaces all the instances with another element. In addition, try implementing 'find' and 'replace' with regular expressions for partial match and searches that are not case sensitive.

Picto Puzzles

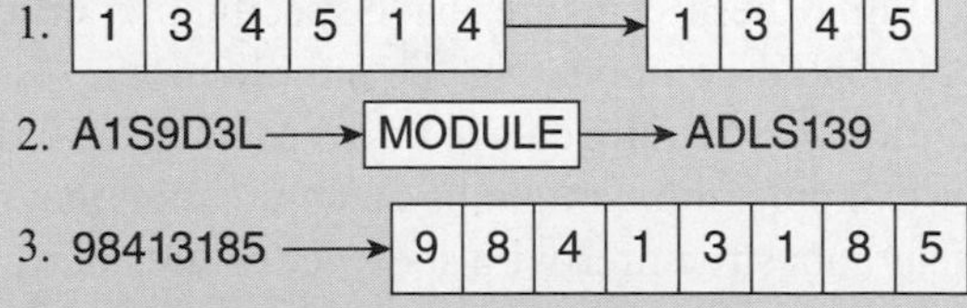

Mini Projects

1. Implement ADT for matrices along with arithmetic functions such as addition, subtraction, and multiplication.

Answers to Multiple-choice Questions

1. (d) 2. (c) 3. (b) 4. (d) 5. (d) 6. (c) 7. (c) 8. (b) 9. (a) 10. (a)

CHAPTER

Continuous Memory-Based Linear Data Structures

LEARNING OBJECTIVES

After going through this chapter, readers will be able to understand:

- Linear data structures other than arrays
- How data stored in continuous memory locations forms new data structures?
- What is a stack and how is it different from an array?
- What are Queues, and when and how to use them?
- Different types of Queues

4.1 INTRODUCTION

Other than 'Lists' and 'Arrays', there are many types of linear data structures that are introduced in this chapter. Continuous memory based linear data structures are designed and implemented in such a way that all the elements in the structure are stored in consecutive memory locations. Other than memory locations, these structures have specific properties in accessing elements and processing them. The core goal behind complicating the simple processes of read/write from arrays is solution optimization. A solution may require data to be saved in linear fashion and specific operations to be performed frequently. For example, there might be an application that requires reversal of elements frequently. Such complex linear data structures with specific features perform complex operations efficiently with minimum cost, which may not be possible in arrays.

4.2 STACK

Stack is a non-primitive data structure. It is a linear data structure designed only with linear access instead of random access with the data stored in continuous memory locations. Consider a pile of books as shown in Figure 4.1 or a stack of files. As the books lay one above the other, the data is visualized as one above the other. To take a book from the bottom, the books on the top must be removed and kept aside, which will prevent the pile from collapsing. Once the required book is taken, the remaining books can be replaced above the pile. However, for ready access, the book on the top of the pile is always available. The same is the case with stack data structure, which means to access an element, one must traverse across the elements above it (in preceding memory locations). In this case too, the contents of the first cell are always readily available. The visual representation of a stack is shown is Figure 4.2.

Figure 4.1 Stack of books

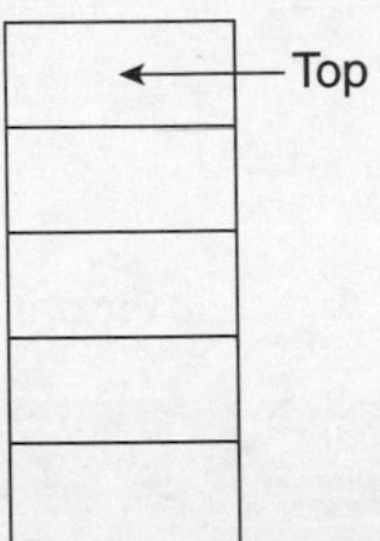

Figure 4.2 Visual representation of a stack

As shown in Figure 4.2, the first element of the stack is pointed by a pointer, 'TOP'. This is the only way of accessing any element in the stack, thus forcing linear access. The movement of data in the stack is commonly referred as 'Last In First Out (LIFO)' process, which means an element that comes first into the stack is placed at the bottom and all the new elements are placed one above the other. So, the element that gets inserted first always exists at the bottom of the stack. While removing the elements, the latest element moves out first as it is present at the top of the stack. All the elements are removed in the order of new to old, and the element at the base of the stack is the last one to be removed. The process is termed LIFO, as the last element comes out first.

Some points to be noted about a stack are:

1. It stores elements in continuous memory locations.
2. Only the top element of the stack can be accessed using the 'TOP' pointer.
3. Accessing any other element is by linear traversal using the 'TOP' pointer.
4. The movement of data is LIFO, so while reading, the data will be in reverse order.

As stacks are stored in continuous memory, it may face problems such as memory constraints and fragmentation issues. So, it is implemented using lists in Python. There are only three notable operations over a stack. They are:

1. Push
2. Pop
3. Top

4.2.1 Working—Push Operation

'Push' is the act of adding an element into the stack. It is named 'Push' as we push data into the top of the stack. Data can be placed only on top of the stack, so if you want the stack to be in a specific order, re-arrange the elements in that order and push it one by one. As said previously, stack does not have any size restriction. So, to push an element, no other parameter is required. It is also important to update and maintain the 'Top' pointer, as losing the 'Top' pointer or misplacing it will cause loss of data (refer to Pseudocode 4.1). Loss of data means that the data is present in the memory, in an unknown location, merely as garbage.

Initially, the size is '0' and 'Top' is pointed to null.

Question 4.1 Push 2,3,1,4 into stack 'a' which is initially empty.

Solution: Figure 4.3 illustrates pushing 2, 3, 1, 4 into the stack 'a'.

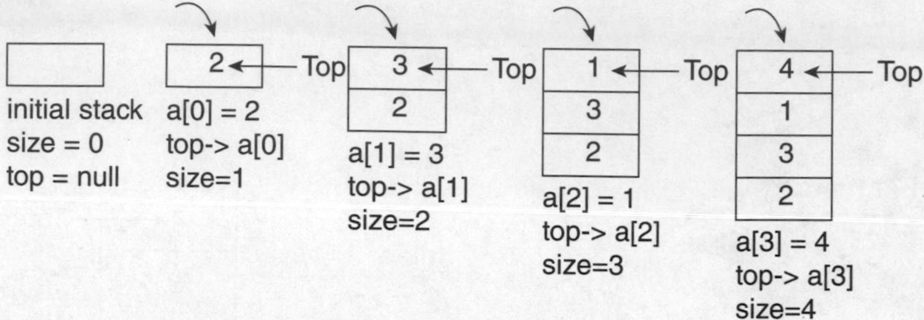

Figure 4.3 Illustration of pushing 2,3,1,4 into stack 'a'

Pseudocode 4.1

```
Assign the new element to a[size]
Update Top pointer to a[size]
size++
```

Food for Brain

How should 'Push' function be modified for a stack with a limit on the number of elements?

4.2.2 Working—Pop Operation

'Pop' is the operation of removing an element from the stack. 'Pop' always removes the data at the top of the stack. 'Top' pointer points to the element at the top of the stack. If the 'Top' pointer is not consistently maintained, then 'Pop' may not work as expected. Similarly, after removing the top element, the 'Top' pointer should be updated to the next element, else the entire stack is lost (refer to Pseudocode 4.2). Using the 'Pop' operation on an empty stack leads to a memory exception problem.

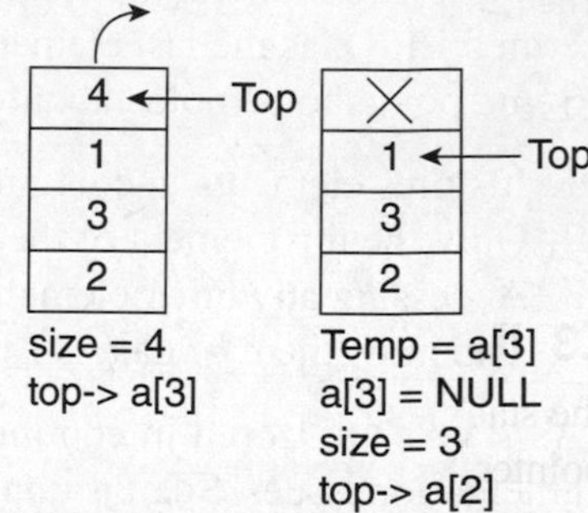

Figure 4.4 'Pop' operation illustration

Question 4.2 Pop '4' from the stack 'a' containing 2,3,1,4.

Solution: Figure 4.4 illustrates the 'Pop' operation.

Pseudocode 4.2

```
If stack is not empty
Then,
        Temp = value at Top
        Stack[size - 1 ] = 0
        size--
        Update Top to stack[size - 1]
        Return Temp
Else,
        Return 0 or any delimiter to show stack is empty
```

4.2.3 Working—Top Operation

'Top' is the simplest operation in a stack. It just returns the element on top of the stack and leaves the stack unchanged. Again, this should not work when the stack is empty, else might throw some memory exceptions. It solely depends on the 'Top' pointer. Had there been any inconsistency in maintaining the 'Top' pointer at the time of 'Push' or 'Pop', this function would not have worked as expected (refer to Pseudocode 4.3). The 'Top' operation is also referred to as 'Peek' operation in some popular implementations.

Question 4.3 Find 'Top' from stack 'a' containing 2,3,1,4.

Solution: Figure 4.5 illustrates the 'Top' operation.

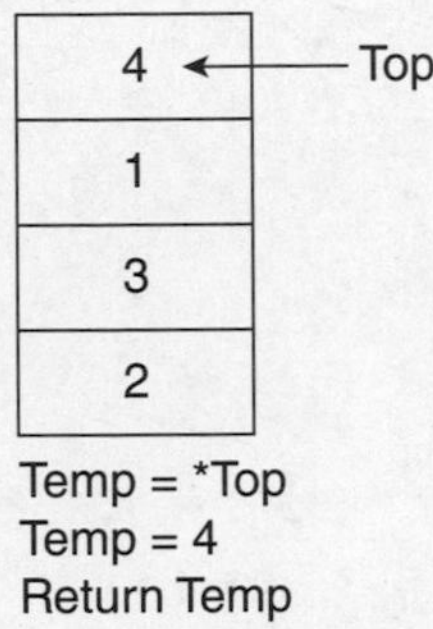

Figure 4.5 'Top' operation and its result from a sample stack

Pseudocode 4.3

```
If stack is not empty
Then,
        Return value at Top
Else,
        Return 0 or any delimiter to show stack is empty
```

4.3 IMPLEMENTATION OF STACK USING POINTERS

The stack data structure is implemented as class for attaining OOP benefits. The members include an array (pointer) or a vector based on implementation. The size is maintained by keeping a count of elements entering the stack. The three basic operations of 'Push', 'Pop', and 'Top' are the member functions. Some additional member functions, such as 'isEmpty', 'Size', and 'Print', ease the process of handling data. The 'Print' function prints the entire content of the stack. Python code 4.1 shows implementation of stacks using pointers.

Python code 4.1

```
class stack:
        def __init__(self):
                self.__s = []
                self.__top = -1
        def push(self,element):
```

(contd)

(*contd*)

```
            self.__top += 1
            self.__s.append(element)
    def print_stack(self):
            if (self.isEmpty()):
                    print("stack empty")
            else:
                    print("top to down order:")
                    print(self.__s[::-1])
    def isEmpty(self):
            if (self.size() == 0):
                    return 1
            return 0
    def size(self):
            return self.__top + 1
    def pop(self):
            if (self.isEmpty() == 0):
                    res = self.__s.pop(self.__top)
                    self.__top -= 1
                    return res
            else:
                    return -1
    def top(self):
            if (self.isEmpty() == 0):
                    return self.__s[self.__top]
            else:
                    return -1
```

Note The LIFO list is also available in Python. The 'queue' class with 'LifoQueue' constructor has all the stack functionalities. The 'Push' function is implemented as 'Put' and 'Pop' function is implemented as 'Get'. The logic remains the same. Just like Python lists, these are additional classes pre-defined for utility.

4.4 COMPLEX OPERATIONS

Standard complex operations for any data structure are searching and sorting as these are used in most of the applications of a data structure.

4.4.1 Searching

As stack allows only linear accessing, the top element must be checked. If it is not the required element, it must be popped out and placed in a new stack or array as only then the next element can be checked. This process is to be continued until the required element is found or the end of the stack is reached. The Pseudocode 4.4 for searching returns '1' if the element is present or else returns '0'. There is no index in stack and cannot return any position. Still, the algorithm can be tweaked to return the position for any lateral use.

Question 4.4 Find '2' in a stack containing 1,2,3,4.

Solution: The process is explained in Figure 4.6.

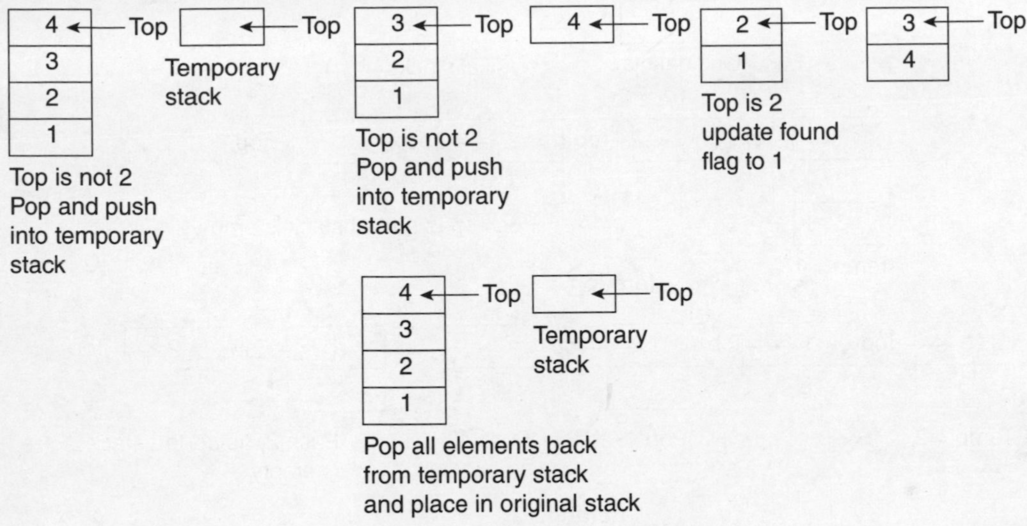

Figure 4.6 Search operation in a stack

Pseudocode 4.4

```
found_flag =0
While found_flag is not 1 or Original_stack is not empty
Do,
        If(Original_stack.top() is equal to required element)
        Then,
                    Found_flag = 1
        Else,
                    Temporary_stack.push(Original_stack.pop())
While Temporary_stack  is not empty
Do,
        Original_stack.push(Temporary_stack.pop())
Return found_flag
```

4.4.2 Sorting

Sorting also requires a new stack, where the elements are placed in sorted order (consider descending order in here). Every element popped from the original stack is compared with the top of the new stack. If it is smaller than the top, then it is placed at the top else in a temporary memory. Then, all the elements from the new stack that are smaller than it are popped. These popped elements are pushed back into the original stack. Once a value greater than the required value is found, the value from the temporary memory is pushed into the new stack. This process is continued until the old stack is empty. The new stack will have the elements in a descending order (refer to Pseudocode 4.5).

Question 4.5 Sort the stack containing 3, 2, 1 in a descending order.

Solution: Figure 4.7 explains sorting 3, 2, 1 in a step-by-step process.

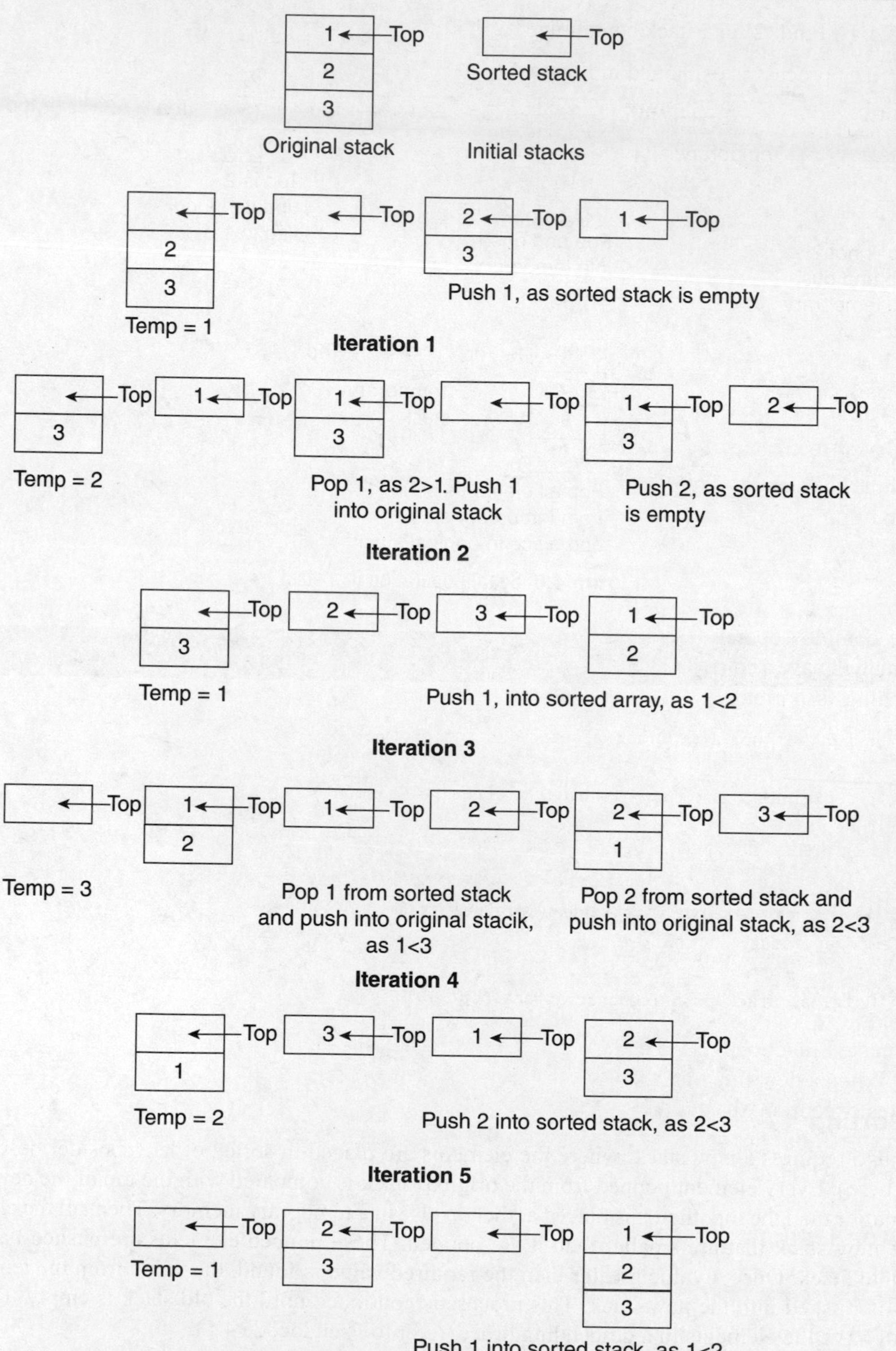

Figure 4.7 Step-by-step illustration of sorting the stack containing 3, 2, 1 in a descending order

Pseudocode 4.5

```
While Original_stack is not empty
Do,
        Temp = Original_stack.pop()
        If (Temp is less than sorted_stack.top())
        Then,
                  Sorted_stack.push(Temp)
        Else,
                  While sorted_stack.top() is less than Temp or Sorted_stack is not empty()
                  Do,       Original_stack.push(sorted_stack.pop())
Sorted_stack.push(Temp)
```

4.4.3 Complexity Analysis

All the three basic operations of the stack are of constant complexity, 'O(1)'. 'Push' is adding the element at the top, 'Pop' is removing the element from the top, and 'Top' is just reading the element at the top. As the 'Top' pointer is maintained well, the operations are straight forward and have constant complexity. Even the additional functions involved inside it such as '`isEmpty( )`' and '`size( )`' are all of complexity 'O(1)', as the count is also maintained.

Some complex operations in the stack like searching, sorting, etc. will have higher complexities. Searching will have a complexity of 'O(n)', as it wants to traverse across all the elements. This complexity of searching is normal, even though the algorithm uses additional stack, at any point the same 'n' elements are distributed across the two stacks summing to 'O(n)'. Thus no additional space is required, which is also in line with arrays. Sorting will have the worst case complexity of '$O(n^2)$' and the space complexity of 'O(n)'. The worst case running of the algorithm occurs when the original stack is already in the required order and we do not know it. So, for every new element to be pushed into the new stack, all the old elements of the stack are to be popped and pushed back again. Thus, summing up to '$O(n^2)$'.

4.5 APPLICATIONS OF STACKS

Stacks play an important role in working of computers and micro controllers. All these devices have basic functionalities defined as modules, which are called during the execution. When a function is called, the current context is stored somewhere and fetched back when the called function completes execution. In case of nested functions, the context is gained back in reverse order. This is where stacks come into the picture. When a new function is called, the current context is pushed into the stack and when a function completes execution, the context at the top of the stack is fetched back.

Other important applications of stack are infix-to-postfix expression conversion and evaluation of a prefix expression.

4.5.1 Application: Infix-to-Postfix Conversion

A normal expression is infix expression. A postfix expression is one in which the operators follow its operands. A prefix expression is the opposite of postfix, as operators are followed by operands. So, a+b becomes ab+ in postfix and +ab in prefix. When operators of different precedence exist in an expression, it becomes a little tricky. In that case, a+b*c becomes abc*+ and +a*bc. The change is just to make sure that multiplication is followed by addition in any expression. More exploration of prefix and postfix expression is suggested before going forward with the below algorithm.

Step-by-step infix-to-postfix conversion algorithm (refer to Python code 4.2):

1. Traverse through the expression
2. If the current character is a variable, append it to output
3. Else if the current character is an operator, check the top of the stack
   3.1. If the top of the stack has an operator of lesser precedence or if the stack is empty, push the operator into the stack.
   3.2. Else if the top of the stack has an operator of higher precedence, then pop all the operators of higher precedence and append it into the output. Then, push in the current operator.
4. Else if the scanned operator is a '(', then push it into the stack
5. Else if the scanned operator is a ')', then pop all the content of the stack and append it into the output until a '(' is encountered
6. Continue the same until the end of the expression is reached
7. If the stack is not empty, pop all the contents and append it to the output.

Python code 4.2

```
def InfixToPostfix(e):
    res = []
    opr_stack = stack()
    for i in exp:
        if isOperand(i):
            res.append(i)
        elif i == '(':
            opr_stack.push(i)
        elif i == ')':
            while((not opr_stack.isEmpty() and opr_stack.top()!='('):
                res.append(opr_stack.pop())
            if(not opr_stack.isEmpty() and opr_stack.top() != '('):
                return -1
            else:
                temp = opr_stack.pop()
        else:
            while(not opr_stack.isEmpty() and ntGrtPrece(i,opr_stack.top())):
                res.append(opr_stack.pop())
            opr_stack.push(i)
        while not opr_stack.isEmpty():
            res.append(opr_stack.pop())
        return "*".join(res)
def isOperand(i):
    return i.isalpha()
def ntGrtPrece(op1,op2):
    precedence = {'+':1, '-':1, '*':2, '/':2, '^':3}
    try:
        o1 = precedence[op1]
        o2 = precedence[op2]
        return True if o1 <= o2 else False
    except  KeyError:
        return False
```

4.5.2 Application: Evaluation of Prefix Expression

Step-by-step evaluation of a prefix expression algorithm (refer to Python code 4.3) is:

1. Traverse across the expression from the right end
2. If the current character is a value, push it into the value stack
3. Else if it is an operator, pop two values for the value stack, perform the operation, and place the result back into the value stack
4. After the expression is complete, the value stack is left with only one value which is the final result

Python code 4.3

```
def prefixEvaluation(exp):
        value_stack = stack()
        e = exp.split(" ")
        l = len(e)
        while (l > 0):
                i = e[l-1]
                if isOperator(i):
                        if (value_stack.size() > 1):
                                tmp = eval(value_stack.pop(), value_stack.pop(),i)
                                value_stack.push(str(tmp)) # before pushing the result
                                                           # back convert it into
                                                           # string
                        else:
                                print("value stack empty, wrong expression")
                                return -1
                elif i != ' ':
                        value_stack.push(i)
                l = l-1
        if(value_stack.size() == 1):
                return int(value_stack.pop())
        else:
                print("wrong expression")
                return -1
def isOperator(o):
        operator = ['+' , '-', '*', '/', '^']
        return True if o in operator else False
def eval(v1,v2,o):
        val1 = int(v1)
        val2 = int(v2)
        return {
        '+':val1+val2,
        '-':val1-val2,
        '*':val1*val2,
        '/':val1/val2,
        '^':val1^val2}[o]
```

Some other common applications of stacks are:

- Handling recursion, where the last called function returns the value first
- Parsing in a compiler, where the data stream is to be maintained for undo, error recovery, and pattern check

- Tower of Hanoi problem
- String reversal
- Palindrome checking

Food for Brain

List some real-time applications of stacks.

4.6 QUEUES

Queue is a non-primitive linear data structure, designed with restricted random access. This also stores data in continuous memory locations. Even though it seems like arrays and stacks, it has its own uniqueness in organizing and accessing data. This is the most common data structure that can be seen in our day-to-day life. In a queue of people shown in Figure 4.8, when a new person enters, he stands at the end of the queue. When the counter is open, the first person moves out and the second person moves in the front, and the process continues. So, if a person standing in the middle of the queue wants to move out, then either all the people before or after him have to come out. Once the person gets out, others can return to their original position. Similarly, in this structure, the first data is always readily accessible. The visual representation of a queue is shown in Figure 4.9.

Figure 4.8 Queue of people in a counter

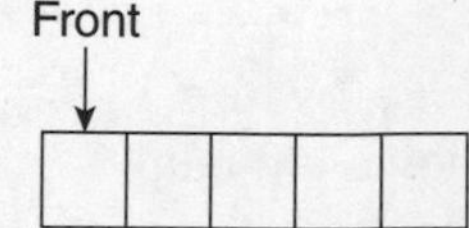

Figure 4.9 Visual representation of a queue

As shown in Figure 4.9, the first element of the queue is pointed by the 'Front' pointer and can be accessed directly, whereas, the rear end of the queue is maintained by the 'Rear' pointer. The movement of data across this structure is in the 'First In First Out (FIFO)' order, which means that an element that enters first will go out first. Any new element that comes into the queue is placed after the 'Rear' pointer and then the pointer is updated. A major difference between the stack and queue is that the elements are removed out in the same order as they enter in case of queues, whereas in stacks, the data is removed in the reverse order.

Some points to be noted about queues are:

- It stores elements in continuous memory locations
- Only the first element of the queue can be accessed using the 'Front' pointer
- The end of the queue is marked by the 'Rear' pointer
- Accessing the elements is possible only through linear traversal using the 'Front' pointer
- Movement of data is FIFO, so it will be read in the same order

There are three types of queues:

1. Single-ended Queue (The normal queue)
2. Double-ended Queue (Deque)
3. Priority queue

4.7 SINGLE-ENDED QUEUES

Single-ended queues are one-way queues. The data can move only in forward direction. The elements enter at the rear and leave from the front. Consider a boarding queue at the airport. The queue shown in Figure 4.10 is one such queue. Here, the passengers can enter into the queue, but not move out from the back. Only once their procedure is over, they get to move to the next counter, lounge, or aircraft. However, they cannot move out of the queue from the rear end. In this data structure, elements can enter at the rear end and can exit only at the front.

Figure 4.10 One-way queue

As shown in Figure 4.11, 'Enqueue' is based on the 'Rear' pointer and 'Dequeue' is based on the 'Front' pointer. The 'Front' pointer is accessible to the user and the 'Rear' pointer is used for internal reference.

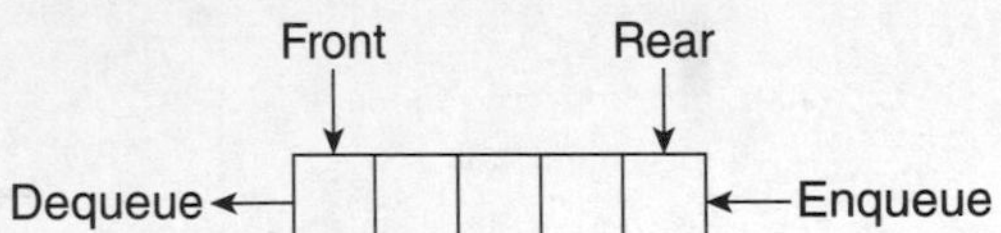

Figure 4.11 Visualization of single-ended queues

Queues also store the data in continuous memory locations. Thus, it is also implemented using lists in Python. There are only three basic operations supported in this data structure:

1. Enqueue
2. Dequeue
3. Front

4.7.1 Working—Enqueue Operation

This is the operation of adding an element into the queue. Data can be added to the end of the queue. So, if you want the queue to have data in some order, arrange the data in the same order and enqueue it one by one into the queue. As the position cannot be determined, no other parameter is required for the function. It is always important to internally update the 'Rear' pointer and maintain it correctly after every 'Enqueue' operation. If the 'Rear' pointer is not consistently maintained, data might be lost as any new data is added only based on this pointer (refer to Pseudocode 4.6). Inconsistency in the 'Rear' pointer may result in two cases- overwriting of data (i.e., losing some old data) or discontinuity within the queue that will collapse the whole structure.

Initially, size will be '0' and Front, Rear will be NULL.

Question 4.6 Enqueue 2,3,1,4 into a queue 'a', which is initially empty.

Solution: The process of enqueueing 2, 3, 1, 4 into an empty queue is shown in Figure 4.12.

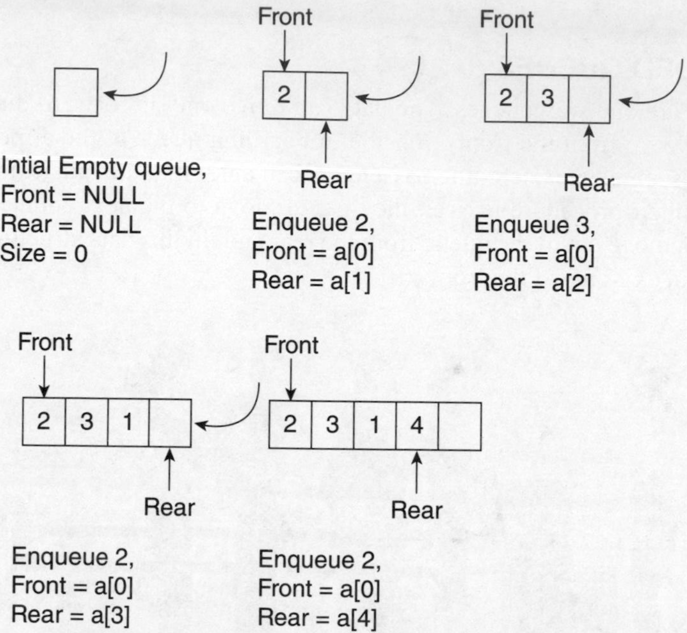

Figure 4.12 Illustration of enqueue in an empty queue

Pseudocode 4.6

```
If Queue is empty
Then,
        Assign data in queue[0]
        front->queue[0]
        Rear->queue[1]
        Increment size
Else,
        Assign data to Rear
        Increment Rear
        Increment size
```

4.7.2 Working—Dequeue Operation

'Dequeue' is the opposite of 'Enqueue' operation. It is the process of removing the element out of the queue. As the queue is one way, the elements can come out only from the front end. As discussed previously, the elements come out in the order they enter. The 'Front' pointer marks the first element and the process of dequeue depends solely on it. So, after removing every element, it is equally important to consistently update the 'Front' pointer. Failing to update the same would cause loss of data. Data in a queue with only 'Rear' pointer is of no use and treated as garbage, as the 'Front' pointer which aids the user access the queue is lost.

Pseudocode 4.7 shows the 'Dequeue' operation. Another important point to notice is that when the queue is empty, access to the pointer results in memory exceptions. Thus, a base case for checking the queue is not empty is added in the algorithm.

Question 4.7 Dequeue '2' times from a queue 'a' containing 2,3,1,4.

Solution: The process of dequeueing is shown in Figure 4.13.

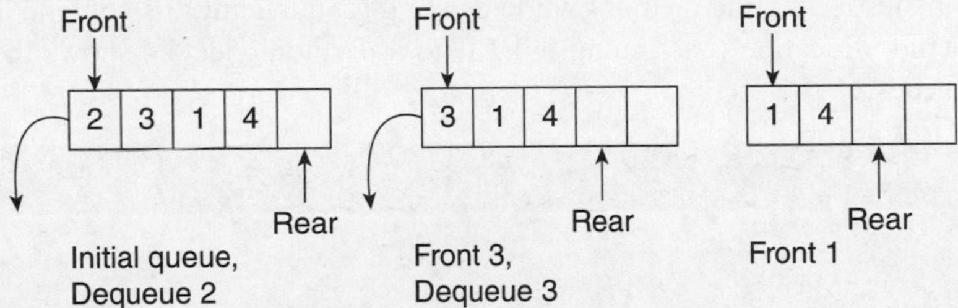

Figure 4.13 Dequeue illustration

Pseudocode 4.7

```
If Queue is not empty
Then,
        Temp = value at front
        Increment Front
        Decrement size
        Return Temp
Else,
        Return 0 or a delimiter to specify queue is empty
```

4.7.3 Working—Front Operation

This is similar to the 'Top' function used in stacks. It is just reading the first element in the data structure. Thus, it is the simplest operation of the data structure. This is fully based on the 'Front' pointer which is to be maintained properly by the 'Dequeue' operation (refer to Pseudocode 4.8). Again, this should not work when the queue is empty, as it might result in memory exceptions.

Question 4.8 Find 'Front' of a queue 'a' containing 3, 1, 4.

Solution: Figure 4.14 shows the 'Front' operation.

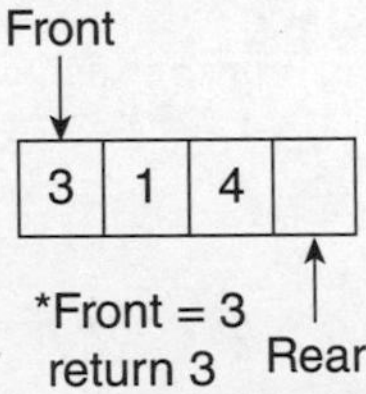

Figure 4.14 'Front' operation and its result in a sample queue

Pseudocode 4.8

```
If Queue is not empty
Then,
        Return value at front
Else,
        Return 0 or a delimiter to specify queue is empty
```

4.7.4 Implementation of Single-Ended Queues using Lists

The members of the class are arrays (Lists) or vectors along with the size, and 'Front' and 'Rear' pointers. The member functions are the basic operations- 'Enqueue', 'Dequeue', 'Top' along with size, 'is Empty', and 'Print' for ease of handling the data. The 'Print' function prints the entire content of the data structure, driven by the 'Front' and 'Rear' pointers. The function, isEmpty(), is for internal usage only. It is called mostly for base cases of operations, such as 'Dequeue' and 'Front', to avoid memory exception. While using arrays, it is better to free the memory while deleting (dequeueing) its content. The simplest way of cleaning the memory location is assigning 'NULL' to it. Python code 4.4 shows the implementation of single-ended queues.

Python code 4.4

```
class queue:
        def __init__(self):
                self.__q = []
                self.__front = -1
                self.__rear = -1
        def enqueue(self,element):
                if (self.isEmpty() == 1):
                        self.__front = 0
                        self.__rear = 0
                        self.__q.append(element)
                        self.__rear += 1
                else:
                        self.__q.append(element)
                        self.__rear += 1
        def dequeue(self):
                if (self.isEmpty() == 0):
                        self.__rear -= 1
                        return self.__q.pop(self.__front)
                else:
                        return -1
        def print_queue(self):
                if (self.isEmpty() == 0):
                        print("front to rear:")
                        print(self.__q[self.__front:])
                else:
                        print("queue empty")
        def front(self):
                if (self.isEmpty() == 0):
                        return(self.__q[self.__front])
                return -1
        def size(self):
                if (self.isEmpty()==0):
                        return(self.__rear - self.__front)
                else:
                        return 0
        def isEmpty(self):
```

(*contd*)

(*contd*)

```
            if(self.__front == self.__rear):
                        return 1
            return 0
```

Here the 'Front' pointer points to the first element, whereas the 'Rear' pointer points to the next empty location. This can be changed based on the design, but all the cases affected by it have to be modified. In this case, only when the queue is empty, 'Front' and 'Rear' pointers will point to the same position. So, 'isEmpty' uses a condition like 'front == rear'. When the size of the queue is '1' and the implementation of 'Rear' is changed, the current condition fails.

Just like stacks, single-ended queues can also be implemented as a class in Python. The same queue class initiated using 'Queue' constructor will initialize a single-ended queue. The 'Enqueue' and 'Dequeue' operations are implemented as 'put' and 'get' functions.

4.7.5 Complex Operations

Keeping aside more complex operations on the data structure, we will go deeper into searching and sorting of queues.

Searching

Queue is a closed linear structure in which only the first element is always accessible. So, to find an element, it must be compared with only the first element. If the required number is in front, then a positive signal is returned. If it is not the required element, the element is dequeued and enqueued back into the queue. The number of elements removed and pushed back must be tracked. Even when the required element is found, the process of enqueueing and dequeueing must continue until all the elements are shifted back. This process is just to make sure that the elements are back in order. When all the elements are shifted back but the required element is still not found, send a negative signal to indicate the absence of that element. The algorithm can also be tweaked to send the number of elements crossed before finding the required element. This number is indirectly the position of the required element and can be useful in various applications. The algorithm is based on the FIFO movement of data. Enqueueing and dequeueing of all elements one by one will retain the original position, as the elements come out in the same order they are entered. Thus, it does not require any additional memory. Pseudocode 4.9 shows the search operation.

Question 4.9 Search '3' in 2, 3, 1.

Solution: The step-by-step process to search '3' in 2, 3, 1 is shown in Figure 4.15.

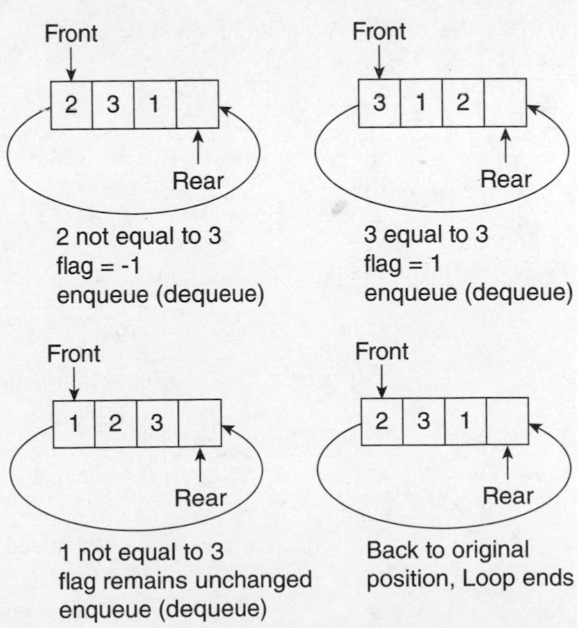

Figure 4.15 Search illustration

Pseudocode 4.9

```
Flag = -1
For i in range of 0 to n
Do,
        check if Front is required element
        Then,
                Flag = 1
        Dequeue(enqueue)
Return Flag
```

Sorting

Unlike searching, sorting requires additional space. In one-way queues, the last element is also not accessible. So, an additional queue along with one extra space is used. The first element is moved from original queue to sorted queue. Then, the next element is picked and placed in a temporary location. For every element in the sorted queue, it is checked if value of the first element is lesser than what is stored in the temporary location. If lesser, one element is removed from the sorted queue and inserted back into the same sorted queue. In case the first number is not less than the value at the temporary location, the value in the temporary location is inserted into the sorted queue and the first element of the sorted queue is then removed. This removed value is now placed into the temporary location. Once this process is over for all the elements of the sorted queue, that is, when the number of iterations is equal to the size of the sorted queue, the final step is performed. The element that is finally present in the temporary location is pushed into the sorted queue and then the next element from the original queue is moved to the temporary location, and so on. This procedure is continued until the original queue is empty. Pseudocode for sorting is a complex algorithm as compared to searching. The sole reason is that the last element of the queue is not accessible. Pseudocode 4.10 shows the sorting operation.

Question 4.10 Sort a queue containing 5, 1, 4, 3 in an ascending order.

Solution: The step-by-step process is explained in Figure 4.16.

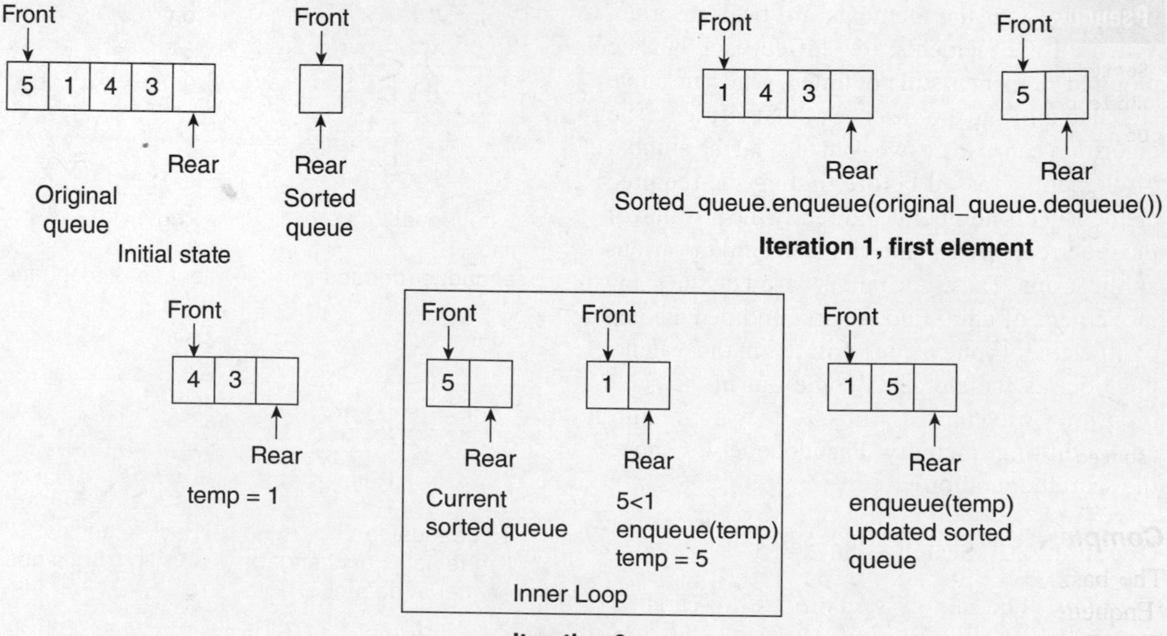

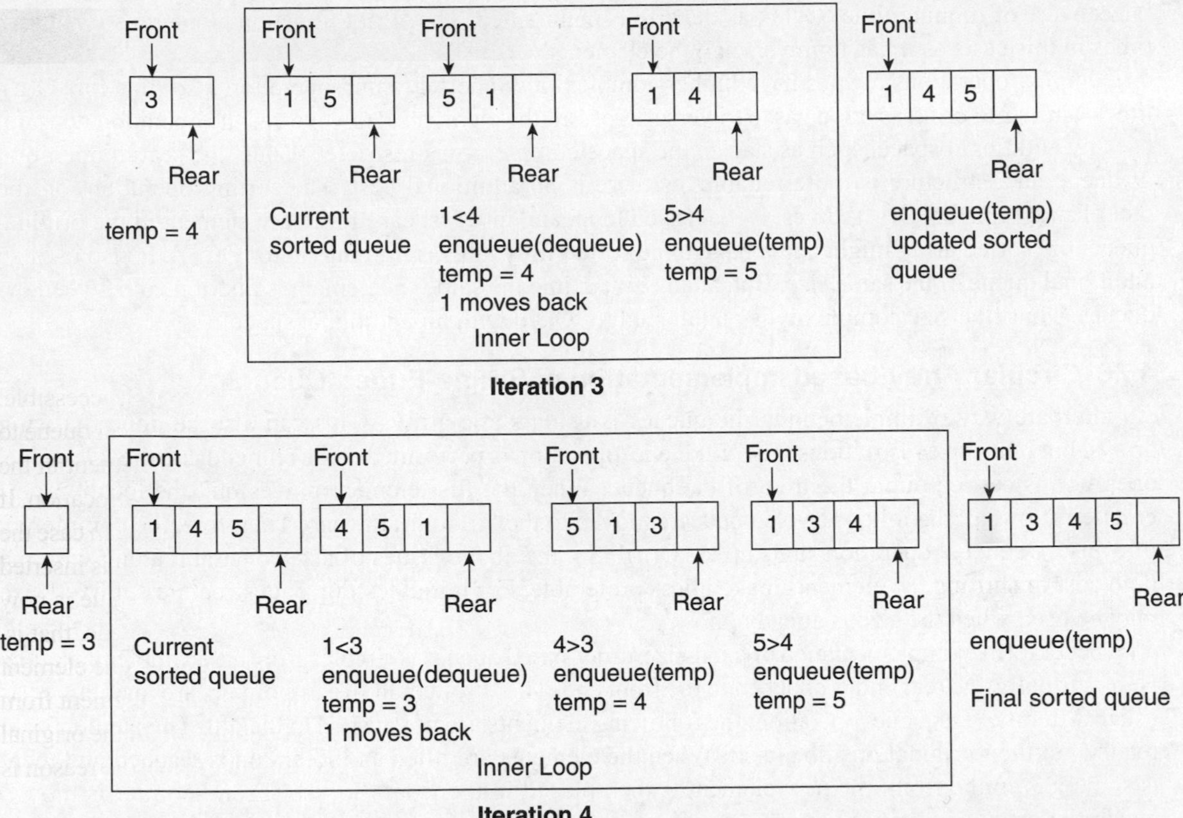

Figure 4.16 Sort illustration

Pseudocode 4.10

```
Sorted_queue.enqueue(Original_queue.dequeue)
While original queue is not empty
Do,
    temp = original_queue.dequeue
    for i in range of 0 to sorted_queue.size
    Do,
        If sorted_queue.front is less than temp
        Then,
            sorted_queue.enqueue (sorted_queue.dequeue)
        Else,
            Sorted_queue.enqueue (temp)
            temp = sorted_queue.dequeue
sorted_queue.enqueue (temp)
```

Complexity Analysis

The basic operations of 'Enqueue', 'Dequeue', and 'Front' are all of constant running time, 'O(1)'. 'Enqueue' is adding a new element at the end, while 'Dequeue' is removing an element from the front. The 'Front' operation is simpler than the other two. Even the additional functions like 'isEmpty( )' and 'size( )' are of running time 'O(1)', as the size is maintained. The 'Print' function alone runs for 'O(n)' times in this case, as it has to traverse all the elements.

Complex operations always have higher complexities. The searching operation also runs for 'O(n)' times, similar to print, as it too has to traverse across all the elements. However, as the operation does not use any additional space, such as stacks, the space complexity is restricted. Thus, the search operation of queue data structure is more reliable, as there is no additional cost. The sorting operation, on the other hand, runs for 'O(n^2)' times. It is a nested loop, and in worst case for every element in the original queue, the sorted array might again have to be sorted fully, thus, summing up to 'O(n^2)'. It also uses an additional queue of the same size. But, at any given time the same 'n' element is distributed between the queues. Thus, the size complexity is maintained to 'O(n)' with no additional space.

4.7.6 Circular Array-based Implementation of Single-Ended Queues

An alternate way of implementing the queues is using static arrays. This can also be done by using arrays, but it has size restrictions. The 'Enqueue' operation is performed at the rear end and the 'Dequeue' operation is carried out at the front of the queue. When the first element moves out, the location gets emptied. Now, all the following elements are moved to the left to fill the gap. Therefore, the complexity of every 'Dequeue' operation sums up to 'O(n)'. So, the above issues of size constraint along with the high cost of shifting the elements make it less preferable. For initial testing, data structures of fixed size may be used when the size is already known.

A better form of implementation of fixed-size, array-based queues is circular array based implementation. Here, virtually, the rear end is attached to the front end. The 'Front' and 'Rear' pointers are maintained as usual. After the 'Dequeue' operation, the following elements are not pushed to the left. The elements are retained at their original position itself. When the elements are filled and Rear end is reached and there is some gap in the front, the new element is then placed in the front. So, the 'Front' pointer is moved inside the array and does not stay at the front permanently. Similarly, the 'Rear' pointer is moved to the front and further moved inside the array. The 'Rear' pointer never crosses the 'Front' pointer in iteration. Unlike the above implementation (Python code 4.4), the 'Rear' pointer here points to the last element and not to the next spot where the element will be filled. It minimises the cost of shifting elements after 'Enqueue', bringing the complexity back to 'O(1)'. Now, the only size constraint is to make it better. Below is the code for implementation (Python code 4.5). Figure 4.17 depicts the visual representation of circular array-based queues.

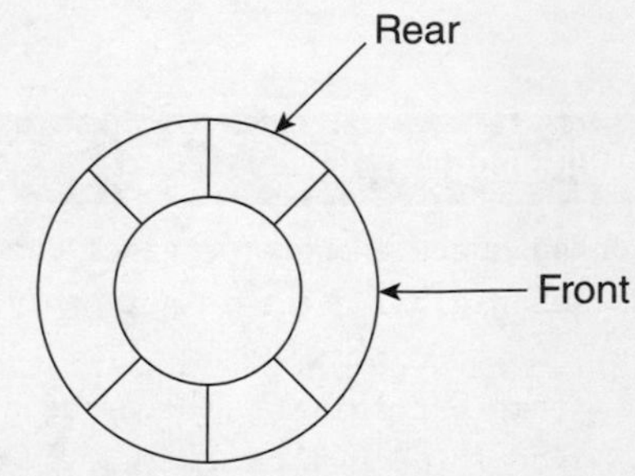

Figure 4.17 Circular array-based queue

Python code 4.5

```
class queue:
        def __init__(self,n):
                self.__max_queue_size = n
                self.__q = [0] * (self.__max_queue_size)
                self.__front = -1
                self.__rear = -1
```

(contd)

(*contd*)

```
    def enqueue(self,element):
        if (self.isEmpty() == 1):
                self.__front = 0
                self.__rear += 1
                self.__rear %= self.__max_queue_size
                self.__q[self.__rear] = element
        elif (self.isFull() == 1):
                print("queue full")
        else:
                self.__rear += 1
                self.__rear %= self.__max_queue_size
                self.__q[self.__rear] = element
    def dequeue(self):
        if (self.isEmpty() == 0):
                temp =  self.__q[self.__front]
                self.__q[self.__front] = 0
                self.__front += 1
                self.__front %= self.__max_queue_size
                return temp
        else:
                return -1
    def print_queue(self):
        if (self.isEmpty()==0):
                print("front to rear:")
                i = self.__front
                print(self.__q[i],",")
                while (i<>self.__rear):
                        i += 1
                        i %= self.__max_queue_size
                        print(self.__q[i],",")
                print(" ")
        else:
                print("queue empty")
    def front(self):
        if(self.isEmpty() == 0):
                return self.__q[self.__front]
        return -1
    def size(self):
        if (self.__front != -1):
                return ((self.__max_queue_size + self.__rear - self.__front) %
                self.__max_queue_size)+1
        else:
                return 0
    def isEmpty(self):
```

(*contd*)

(*contd*)

```
        if(self.__front == -1 or self.size() == 0):
                return 1
        return 0
    def isFull(self):
        if (self.size() == self.__max_queue_size):
                return 1
        return 0
```

Question 4.11 Enqueue 1, 2, 3, 4, 5 into a circular, array-based queue of size '5'.

Solution: Enqueue 1, 2, 3, 4, 5 into a queue of size '5'. Dequeue once after that. Finally, enqueue '6' into the queue. Once the queue is created, it is of size '5'. In addition, the 'Front' and 'Rear' pointers are maintained as indices in here, but are pointed in the same way as done in the previous examples. When an element is put in or out, only the position of these pointers changes and the size of the queue remains the same. Figure 4.18 shows how circular arrays bring 'Rear' to the starting end of the array when there is empty space.

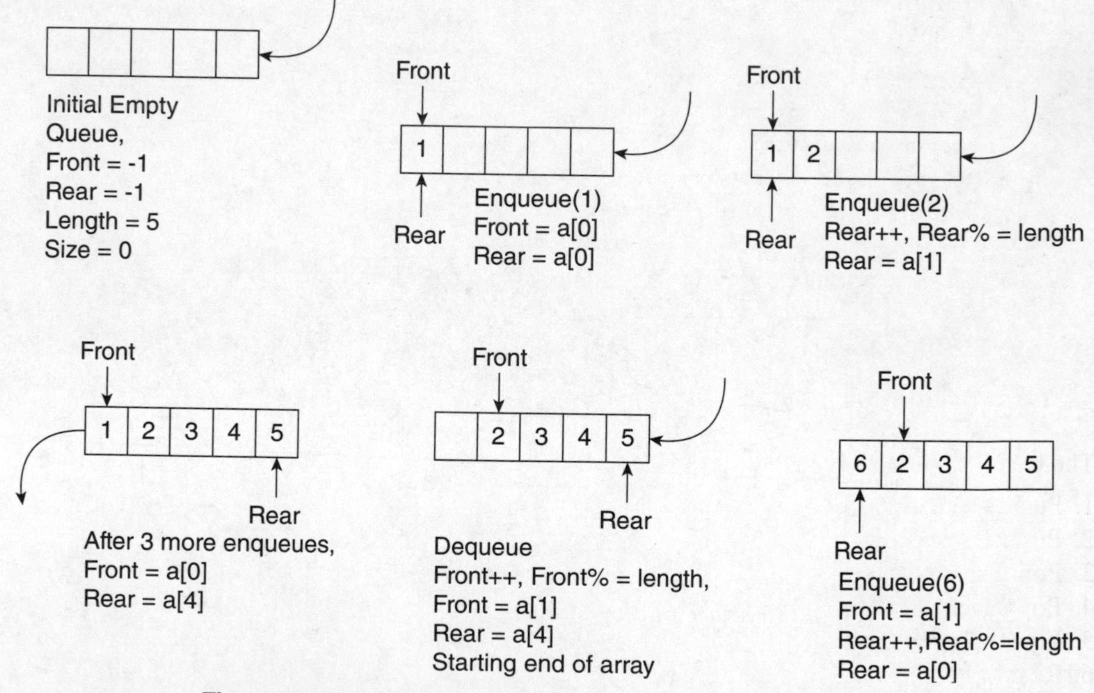

Figure 4.18 Illustration of importance of circular array-based trees

As 'Rear' continuously gets incremented and comes back to the starting end, 'Front' also gets incremented for every 'Dequeue' operation, and on reaching the final point, the other end comes back to initial position, a[0]. Thus, it moves the pointers rather than the elements for each 'Enqueue' or 'Dequeue' operation and limits the complexity. Such an implementation is not required in Python as Python lists, by default, do not have any size limit.

This implementation can also be done for other types of queues as discussed in the following sections.

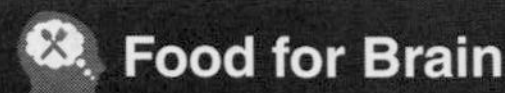

Can a queue be implemented using a Stack ADT?

4.8 DOUBLE-ENDED QUEUES

Consider the scenario of a queue in a theatre. One by one, each person gets the ticket and then the people move forward. When all the tickets are sold and the theatre reaches its maximum capacity, people have to turn back and come out of the queue from the rear end. Alternatively, consider a situation when a premium customer is directly moved to the front of the queue by the manager. Such a queue is depicted in Figure 4.19. This behaviour is replicated exactly by double ended queues, shortly referred to as 'deques'. Deques allow insertion of data at both the ends of the queue, front and rear. The element can leave either the front or the rear end. Both the ends are accessible to the user. Figure 4.20 shows the visual representation of a deque.

Figure 4.19 Double-ended queue

The basic operations of a deque are:

1. Push_Front
2. Push_Back
3. Pop_Front
4. Pop_Back
5. Front
6. Rear

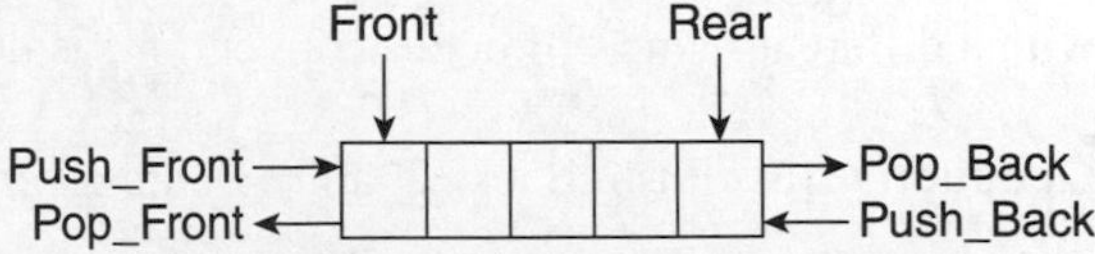

Figure 4.20 Visual representation of a deque

The 'Push_Front' and 'Pop_Front' operations are based on the 'Front' pointer, whereas the 'Push_Back' and 'Pop_Back' operations are based on the 'Rear' pointer.

4.8.1 Working: Push_Front Operation

This is the operation of adding an element at the front of the queue. Only one value can be sent at a time and the new element is placed at the beginning. This entirely thrives based on the 'Front' pointer (refer to Pseudocode 4.11). So, again, maintaining the 'Front' pointer is mandatory and the risk of inconsistent 'Front' pointer prevails here as well.

Question 4.12 Push_Front '4' in a deque containing 2, 3, 1.

Solution: The process is shown in Figure 4.21.

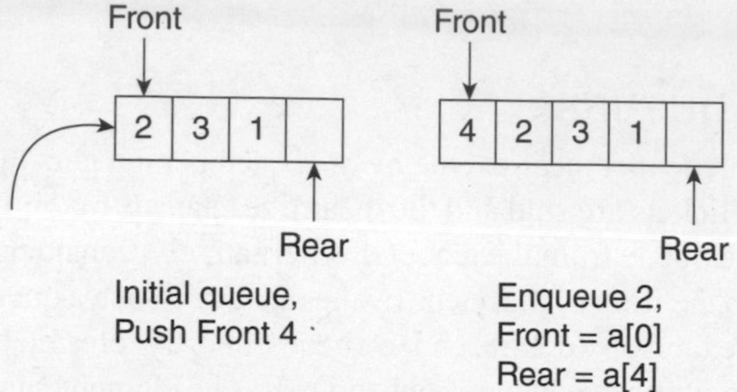

Figure 4.21 Push_Front in a sample deque

Pseudocode 4.11

```
If Queue is empty
Then,
        Assign data in queue[0]
        front -> queue[0]
        rear -> queue[1]
        Increment size
Else,
        Decrement Front
        Assign data to Front
        Increment size
```

4.8.2 Working: Push_Back Operation

This is the normal 'Enqueue' operation of single-ended queues. This depends on the 'Rear' pointer (refer to Pseudocode 4.12). All the conditions and risks remain the same. Basically, it is the same operation with a different name, for better convention, as deques have more features.

Question 4.13 Push_Back '2' and '3' into an empty deque.

Solution: The process is shown in Figure 4.22.

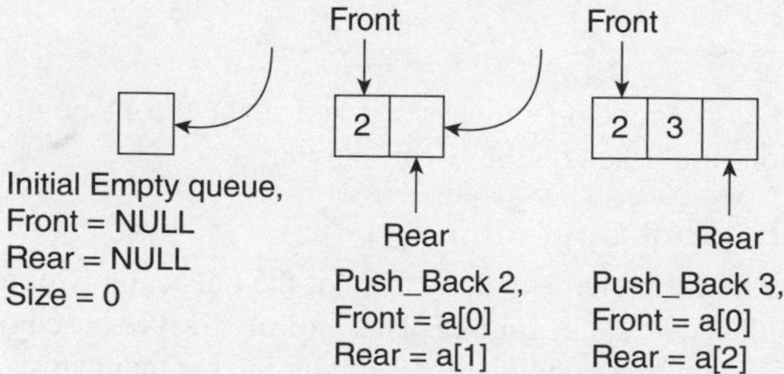

Figure 4.22 Push_Back in a sample deque

Pseudocode 4.12

```
If Queue is empty
Then,
        Assign data in queue[0]
        Front -> queue[0]
        Rear -> queue[1]
        Increment size
Else,
        Assign data to Rear
        Increment Rear
        Increment size
```

4.8.3 Working: Pop_Front Operation

'Pop_Front' is the deque operation of a normal queue. It is similar to the 'Push_Back' operation. The algorithm for the process changes only to meet all the base cases of deques. The working is shown in Pseudocode 4.13.

Question 4.14 Pop_Front a queue containing 2, 3, 1, 4.

Solution: The process is shown in Figure 4.23.

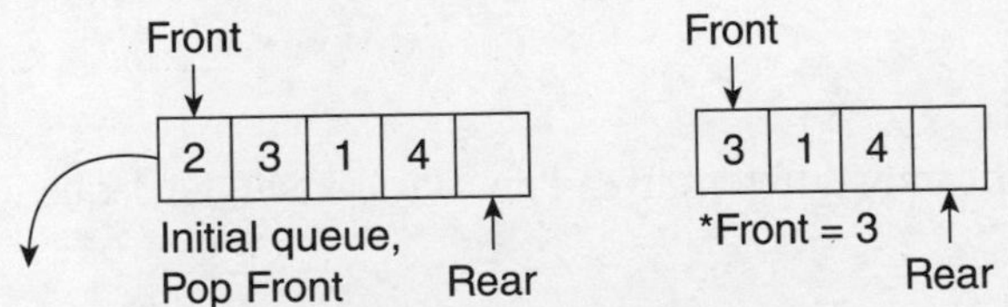

Figure 4.23 Pop_Front in a sample deque

Pseudocode 4.13

```
If Queue is not empty
Then,
        Temp = Value at Front
        Increment Front
        Decrement size
        Clear memory location
        Return Temp
Else,
        Return 0 or delimiter to specify queue is empty
```

4.8.4 Working: Pop_Back Operation

This is the process of removing an element from the rear end of the deque. This also runs based only on the 'Rear' pointer. Basically, it is two operations, that is, updating the 'Front' pointer and updating two other 'Rear' pointers (refer to Pseudocode 4.14).

Question 4.15 Pop_Back from a deque containing 2, 3, 1, 4.

Solution: The process is shown in Figure 4.24.

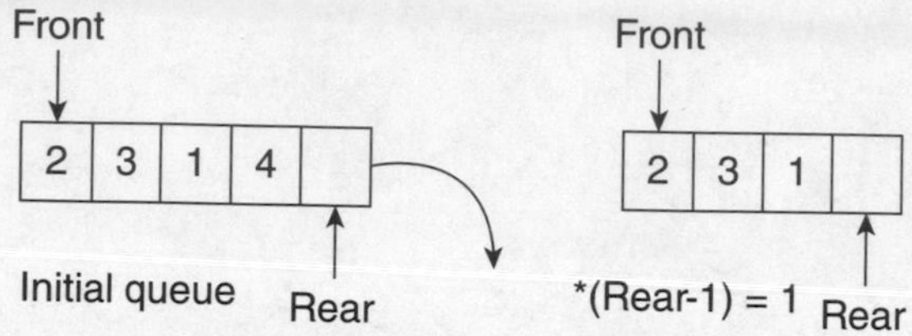

Figure 4.24 Pop_Back in a sample Deque

Pseudocode 4.14

```
If Queue is not empty
Then,
        Temp = value at Rear - 1
        Decrement count
        Decrement Rear
        Clear memory location
        Return Temp
Else,
        Return 0 or a delimeter to specify queue is empty
```

Food for Brain

How is Pop_Front significantly different from Pop_Back when the deque has only one element?

4.8.5 Working: Front Operation

'Front' is the peeking operation at the front of the queue. It is the same operation as in case of single-ended queues with the same naming convention. Pseudocode 4.15 shows the 'Front' operation.

Pseudocode 4.15

```
If Queue is not empty
Then,
        Return value at Front
Else,
        Return 0 or a delimiter to specify
        queue is empty
```

4.8.6 Working: Rear Operation

This is similar to the 'Front' operation on the rear end. It is not present in single-ended queues, as it does not allow users to access the rear end. The algorithm is similar to the 'Front' operation. Pseudocode 4.16 shows the 'Rear' operation.

As 'Rear' and 'Front' are simple operations and similar to the ones used in single-ended queues, the same example can be referred from Section 4.6.1.

Pseudocode 4.16

```
If Queue is not empty
Then,
        Return value at Rear -1
Else,
        Return 0 or a delimiter to specify
        queue is empty
```

4.8.7 Implementation of a Deque

All the members of the class will remain the same as single-ended queues. Only the functionalities are increased. So, member functions will be 'Push_Front, Push_Back, Pop_Front, Pop_Back, Front and Back' accompanied by the utility functions, 'isEmpty, Size, and Print'. Most of the base cases will be same as single-ended queues, while some new base cases will be added for new accessing points. Due importance should be given to maintenance of the pointers. Python code 4.6 shows implementation of double-ended queues.

Python code 4.6

```
class deq:
        def __init__(self):
                  self.__q = []
                  self.__front = -1
                  self.__rear = -1
        def push_back(self,element):
                 if (self.isEmpty() == 1):
                            self.__front = 0
                            self.__rear = 0
                            self.__q.append(element)
                            self.__rear += 1
                 else:
                            self.__q.append(element)
                            self.__rear += 1
        def pop_back(self):
                 if (self.isEmpty() == 0):
                            temp = self.__q.pop(self.__rear - 1)
                            self.__rear -= 1
                            return temp
                 else:
                            return -1
        def push_front(self,element):
                 if (self.isEmpty() == 1):
                            self.__front = 0
                            self.__rear = 0
                            self.__q.append(element)
                            self.__rear += 1
                 else:
                            self.__q.insert(self.__front,element)
                            self.__rear += 1
        def pop_front(self):
                 if (self.isEmpty() == 0):
                            temp = self.__q.pop(self.__front)
                            self.__rear -= 1
                            return temp
                 else:
                            return -1
        def print_deq(self):
                 if (self.isEmpty() == 0):
                            print("front to rear:")
                            print(self.__q[self.__front:self.__rear])
                 else:
                            print("queue empty")
```

(contd)

(*contd*)

```
    def front(self):
        if (self.isEmpty() == 0):
            return(self.__q[self.__front])
        return -1
    def rear(self):
        if (self.isEmpty() == 0):
            return self.__q[self.__rear-1]
        return -1
    def size(self):
        if (self.isEmpty() == 0):
            return self.__rear - self.__front
        else:
            return 0
    def isEmpty(self):
        if(self.__front == self.__rear):
            return 1
        return 0
```

The implementation is just a way, but the maintenance of the pointers can be changed based on necessity. This code maintains 'Rear' at a position next to the last element. This is just to take care of the condition, 'isEmpty - (Front= =Rear)'. If there is only one element in the queue, then the 'Front' and 'Rear' may be in the same position, and hence, this method is followed. It is absolutely fine to change the condition of 'isEmpty' as 'if(size( )==0)' and maintain the 'Rear' pointer at the last element.

The naming conventions followed here can be also changed, such as 'Insert_Front, Insert_Back, Remove_Front, and Remove_Back'. The naming is just for readability.

As discussed in Section 4.7.6, deques can also be implemented using circular arrays. Again, it will be of fixed size. As it is straight forward and requires only small modifications from the code specified in Section 4.7.6, it is skipped in here. After going through the above codes, readers should also be able to implement deques using circular arrays. Thus, this section is left for self-exploration.

4.8.8 Complex Operations

Even though deques have more accessing points and functionalities, the basic algorithms of search and sort that were followed for single-ended queues apply here too. As said previously, the algorithms specified in this book are just basic algorithms to help the readers utilise the data structure more efficiently. Enhancement of an algorithm and minimising its cost are left for the users to experiment with. So, the same algorithm from Section 4.7.4 can be referred in here too. Alternatively, the same algorithm can also be run in the reverse order, that is, removing elements only from the back and adding the element only to the front. However, this will not make any constant difference to the running time of the algorithm.

4.8.9 Complexity Analysis

Similar to a single-ended queue, the basic operations of a deque are also of constant complexity, 'O(1)'. The 'Push_Front and Push_Back' operations are just adding an element to the front or back and updating the corresponding pointer. The 'Pop_Front and Pop_Back' operations are removing the element from the corresponding end and again updating the pointer. When the pointer is consistently being updated, all the operations become straight forward and simple. The process of updating the pointer is also not a big task, as it involves just incrementing or decrementing based on the work done. The process of 'Front' and 'Rear' functions is even simpler. It just reads the elements at the extremes. The supporting functions also work in a constant order, as count is consistently maintained. So, all the member functions, other than '`Print( )`', run at constant time. The '`Print()`' function is required to traverse across all the members, so it has a complexity of 'O(n)'. As the search and sort algorithms are retained from the single-ended queue, their complexities also remain the same.

Food for Brain

Try implementing deque data structure using queue ADT.

4.9 PRIORITY QUEUES

A priority queue is a normal queue with a priority for each element. Consider Figure 4.25 that shows a theatre with seats. The catch is that the first row alone has royal seats, while the other rows have normal seats. The royal seats are for special or VIP visitors. The normal seats, on the other hand, are for normal people. Here, all the people enter in a queue, but only the prioritised members get the front seats. The other people have to sit behind all the priority members. In the same way, a priority queue maintains priority for each element. It works as a queue with applied priority.

Figure 4.25 Priority seats in a theatre

Basically, in priority queues, the data does not follow the FIFO order. The order of data is by the order of their priority. So, the data gets into the queue, gets reordered based on priority, and then comes out. Generally, the order of priority will be from lower to higher, that is, element with priority value '0' will come first. This can be changed based on design.

4.9.1 Implementation of Priority Queues

The access modes of the priority queue are the same as normal queue. 'Enqueue' is used to send a data unit in, while 'Dequeue' is used to take the data unit out. The 'Front' pointer points to the front end of the queue. It is only the internal processing and maintenance that have changed in this case.

Implementation using Sorting of the Queue

The easiest way of implementation of priority queues is using the sorting process of the queue. Every data unit is no more just a single element. It is a compound data like a class object, which has the value along with its priority. After every enqueue, the queue is sorted based on the priority inside each data unit. Now, while dequeueing, the data comes out in the order of its priority. The sorting algorithm specified in Section 4.7.5 can be used in this case but with minor tweaks for the compound data.

Figure 4.26 is the visual representation of such a queue. It, initially, has an empty queue. Three data units are to be enqueued into the queue. They are, '2' with priority '3', '3' with priority '0', and '7' with priority '1'. Based on this implementation, the sort function is called after the new data is entered inside the 'Enqueue' function, which puts the data in priority order. This is shown in Figure 4.26. Here, every cell has two halves, the upper half is the value whereas the lower half is the priority.

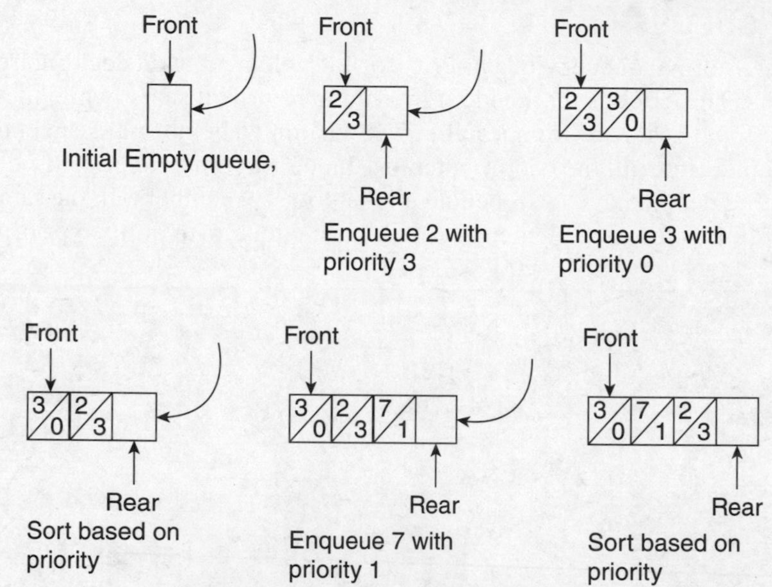

Figure 4.26 Visual representation of sorting-based priority queues and its working

It is to be noted that after every 'Enqueue' operation, the data is in required order. So, there is no change in the 'Dequeue' operation. In this implementation, the complexity of 'Enqueue' operation goes up to '$O(n^2)$', as it involves sorting too. All other operations retain the same complexity. Due to this complexity of the 'Enqueue' operation, this implementation of the data structure is not preferred.

Implementation using Multi-level Queues

Another way of implementing this data structure is using multi-level queues. Even though this method does not involve any sorting, the data comes out in the order of priority. It is done using internal processing and maintenance. Internally, here multiple queues are maintained and data in each queue has the same priority.

For example, in Figure 4.27, if three data units are entered, that is, '2' with priority '0', '3' with priority '1' and '7' with priority '0', then the data units '2' with priority '0' and '7' with priority '0' will be placed in a queue. The other unit, '3' with priority '1' will be placed in a different line. Here, multiple queues are maintained, one queue for one priority. In queue '0', all the data value whose priority is '0' will be stored. In queue '1', all the values whose priority is '1' will be stored. The working of these internal queues is same as the normal queue explained in the previous sections, with the same 'Enqueue, Dequeue, and Front' operations. So, a priority queue's enqueue will internally redirect to enqueue of any one queue based on the priority of the element entered. While dequeueing, all the elements of queue '0' will be taken out and then queue '1' will start dequeueing. Thus, the priority order is maintained. Similarly, any number of queues can be maintained based on the necessity of number of priorities.

The issue with this implementation is that the number of possible priorities must be known before starting with the implementation process. Only then, the number of queues inside can be fixed and implemented. Thus, it has a restriction over the priority value. If there is a new priority value coming in, which was not designed, the data structure fails. It will waste a lot of memory, if implemented with static arrays.

The best implementation of priority queues is not linear. It is implemented with a non-linear data structure called Heap discussed elaborately in Chapter 8. It is implemented in a non-linear fashion to be dynamic and limit space and time complexity. This implementation of multi-level queue-based priority queues is also used in applications where the number of priority is fixed. One important application of multi-level queues is processing instructions in operating systems. It maintains queues such as interrupt, system calls, user interaction, batch process, etc. from higher to lower priority instruction.

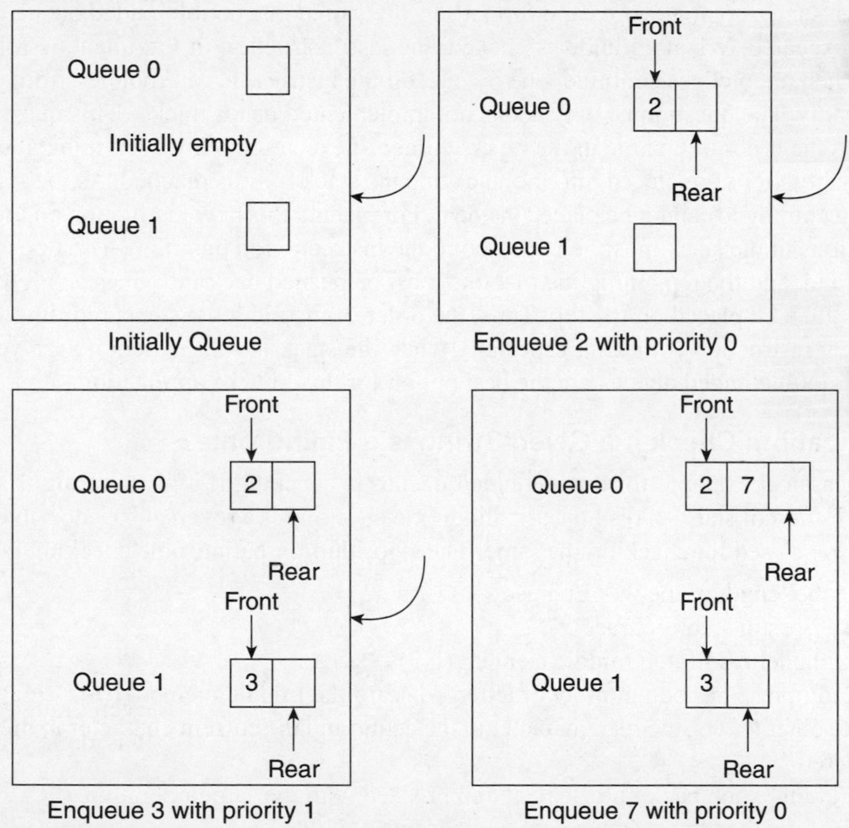

Figure 4.27 Multi-level, queue-based implementation of priority queues

Food for Brain

How to implement a bounded priority queue, a priority queue with a bound on the number of elements that can be stored?

4.10 APPLICATIONS OF QUEUES

The major application of queues is in handling jobs and processes in operating systems. When multiple jobs are initiated, the processor gets allocated only to one process at a time. So, all the processes are placed in a queue and get the processor one by one. However, this is not real time as all processes are not the same and cannot wait for every other operation. So, in reality, it is a multi-level queue (priority based). The queues are classified into batch processes, interactive processes, system processes, user processes, and so on. Then, comes the timing issue. A process cannot wait endlessly for another process to be completed. Just imagine how your personal computer would look like if it can handle only one job at a time. Then, it is no more a real-time system. So, what actually happens is that a small time frame is fixed and is evenly distributed across all the processes in the queue. But, how is it visualized? The first process gets the processor and executes for the time frame. Then, the execution stops and the process is moved out and added to the end of the same queue. In this way, the order of processes does not change and real-time parallelism is also achieved. This is just one algorithm for scheduling; similarly there are many other scheduling algorithms.

Another important application of queues is in processes that handle instructions like MS word. Here, all the instructions, such as typing words and formatting, are stored in a double-ended queue of a particular size and then executed. When an undo is clicked, the last instruction in the queue is rolled back and popped out. When undo clicks continue, one by one, all the instructions are popped from the back until the queue is empty. The question is, why is this not implemented using stacks? This question may arise in your mind as the order of undo is in the reverse order of execution. However, think about a situation where all the instructions are placed into the stack and the stack limit is reached. As the stack is full, the new instruction coming in cannot be placed inside it. For placing this new instruction on top of the stack, all the instructions in the stack must be popped out, the instruction in position 1 (first position of stack) must be discarded, and the remaining instructions must be pushed back into the stack. Finally, the new instruction can then be placed on the top. Thus, the order of instructions is ensured. Implementing this each time a new instruction comes in, especially when the stack is full, is definitely a very expensive option. Hence, double-ended queues are the best option for this kind of application.

4.10.1 Application: Check if a Given String is a Palindrome

A simple yet classical example for double-ended queues is checking if a given string is a palindrome. Isn't it an application of stacks? Yes it is, as palindrome checking is a reversal based problem. However, a deque can also be used for checking the same. The algorithm for palindrome checking is given below:

1. Calculate the length of the word/phrase
2. Traverse across the word/phrase
3. Pushback the letters till the middle element (n/2)
4. If the word/phrase has odd number of letters, discard the middle element ((n/2) + 1)
5. For all the other letters, the rear character in the deque and the current character in the string should be compared
6. If they are same, pop back one element and proceed with the same operation
7. If not the same, then the string is not a palindrome

Python code 4.7 shows the implementation of a Palindrome.

Python code 4.7

```
def palindrome(s):
    st = list(s)
    l = 0
```

(*contd*)

(*contd*)

```
    d = deq()
    for l in range (0,math.floor(len(st)/2)):
        d.push_back(st[l])
    print(st)
    l = l+1
    if((len(st) % 2) == 1):
        l=l+1
    while (l<len(st)):
        if((not d.isEmpty()) and d.rear() == st[l]):
            t = d.pop_back()
            l = l+1
        else:
            print(s+" is a not a palindrome")
            return False
    print(s+" is a palindrome")
    return True
```

Note This program requires Math library to be imported.

Some more real-life applications of single-ended queues are:

- Buffing elements and processing them in the order they come
- First-come-first-serve request service provider
- Breadth-first search algorithm
- A-Steal process scheduling for processors

Key Points to Remember

- Linear data structures are a type of data structure where the elements are stored one after the other in a linear sequence.
- Stacks are a non–primitive linear data structure. It is an ordered collection of data elements.
- Stacks have only one point of access for data, the 'Top' pointer. Stacks follow LIFO movement of data.
- Queues are non–primitive linear data structures that follow FIFO movement of data.
- Queues allow insertion in 'Rear' pointer and removal from a 'Front' pointer.
- There are three types of queues—single-ended queue (one-way motion), double-ended queue (two-way motion), and priority queue (multi-level queue).

Key Terms

Stack A linear data structure working on the 'last in first out' principle

Queue A linear data structure working on the 'first in first out' principle

Deque or Double-ended Queue A queue with two ends. Elements can enter and exit from either of the ends.

Push The operation of inserting a new element into the stack

Pop The operation of removing an element from the stack

Enqueue The operation of inserting a new element into the queue

Dequeue The operation of removing an element from the queue

EXERCISES

Multiple-choice Questions

1. The application of a stack data structure is:
   (a) Evaluation of Arithmetic expression
   (b) Function call
   (c) Both (a) & (b)
   (d) None of the above
2. In any stack, only the top element can be accessed.
   (a) True
   (b) False
   (c) None of the above
3. How many queues are needed to implement a stack?
   (a) 1
   (b) 2
   (c) 3
4. How many stacks are needed to implement a queue?
   (a) 1
   (b) 2
   (c) 3
5. Which of the following is an application of Queue?
   (a) Load Balancing
   (b) When data is transferred asynchronously
   (c) Both (a) & (b)
6. How many lists are needed to implement a stack?
   (a) 1
   (b) 2
   (c) 3
7. In a circular queue of size 10, the array index starts with '0', Front is '6', and Rear is '9'. In which index does the insertion of the next element happen?
   (a) 0 (b) 7
   (c) 10
8. What is the total worst case complexity of sorting a stack with one single-ended queue alone?
   (a) O(n) (b) $O(n^2)$
   (c) None of the above
9. What is the space complexity of multi-level, queue-based implementation of a priority queue with three possible priorities?
   (a) O(n) (b) $O(n^2)$
   (c) $O(n^3)$ (d) None of the above
10. What of the following is an example of a priority queue?
    (a) Ticket counter
    (b) System jobs waiting for processor
    (c) Customer waiting online for chat/call assistance
    (d) All of the above

Theoretical Review Questions

1. Which linear data structure can be implemented without pointers? How?
2. When arrays are continuous memory based, why are stacks/queues mandatory? Explain with scenarios.
3. What is LIFO? Explain it with a data structure that follows the same approach.
4. What is FIFO? Which data structure uses it? Elaborate.
5. What is a circular array based implementation of queues? Explain its significance with illustration.

Exploratory Application Exercises

1. Which is the best linear data structure that can be used for reversal of a string? Implement the same.
2. Using stacks evaluate a postfix expression.
3. Which linear data structure suits best for finding whether a given string is a palindrome or not? How to implement the same?
4. Which data structure can be used for forming the largest possible number with the digits in a given number? Explain the algorithm. E.g. – i/p: 25731, o/p: 75321
5. Implement a code if a given number is symmetric.
6. Write an algorithm for solving the 'Tower of Hanoi' problem.

7. Write a code to take an infix expression as a string and evaluate the same to get the result.
8. A given expression can have open and close parenthesis. A valid expression is when every open parenthesis has a close parenthesis with proper level of nesting. Identify if the expression is valid with respect to parenthesis using an appropriate data structure.
9. LRU is one of the techniques used in cache. It helps in identifying the least used content stored in cache. It also helps in swapping the least used content with another content which is in need for a space in the cache. Implement a LRU using an appropriate data structure. Let the content in the structure be characters and using it be depicted by 'read' operation.
10. Maintain a job queue, when every job arrives the queue is maintained in the sorted order such that the job with the highest priority moves first.

Picto Puzzles

Identify the logic and write code for each of the following.

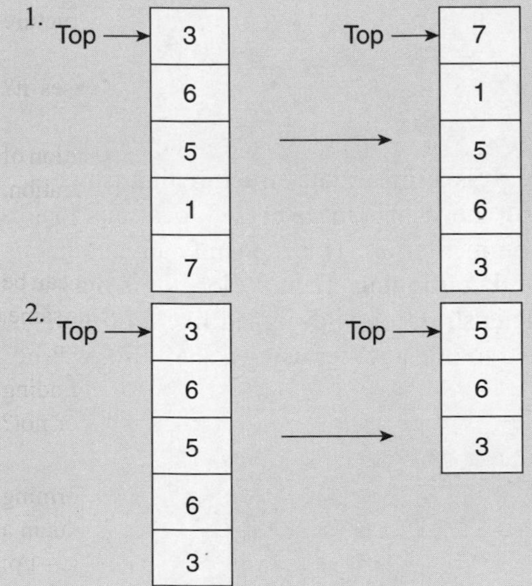

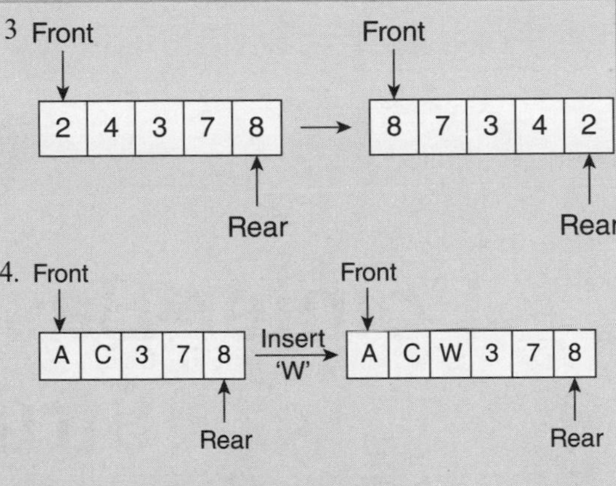

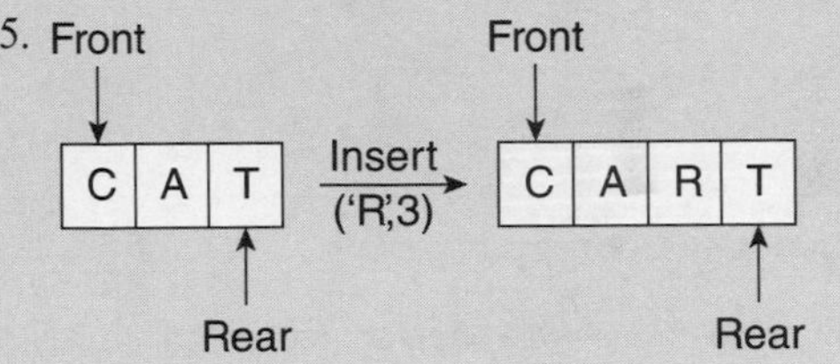

Mini Projects

1. How is a system stack implemented? Identify the hardware and software essentials and develop a small system stack that can be programmed over a controller.
2. Implement a stack using queue objects alone.
3. Implement a queue using stack objects alone.

Answers to Multiple-choice Questions

1. (c) 2. (a) 3. (a) 4. (b) 5. (c) 6. (a) 7. (a) 8. (b) 9. (a) 10. (a)

CHAPTER

5

Pointer-Based Linear Data Structures

LEARNING OBJECTIVES

After going through this chapter, readers will be able to understand:

- How is data stored in non-continuous memory chunks as a linear data structure?
- What are linked lists?
- How are linked lists different from other linear data structures?
- Different types of Linked Lists

5.1 INTRODUCTION TO LINKED LISTS

A linked list is a non-primitive and linear data structure. It is a linear data structure that is not stored in continuous memory locations. This feature of storing the values in dispersed locations makes it more efficient. This avoids internal problems such as fragmentation. This is mainly advantageous at times when a large amount of data has to be entered and continuous memory locations may not be available, raising some internal memory exceptions. This structure is designed like a normal train, as shown in Figure 5.1, where the coaches are connected to one another using a shaft. So, whenever

Figure 5.1 Train

necessary, a new coach can be added or removed. It is not mandatory to add or remove a coach only from the end, but it can be done at any point as all coaches are connected to its neighbours using removable shafts/links. For example, if a coach in the middle has some wiring issues, the train is stopped, that particular coach is removed and the rest is put in place. The starting point of the train is maintained using an engine, so if the engine is removed, it is no more a train but just coaches left behind. The data structure has all these features as explained in here for the train. The visualization of the data structure is shown in Figure 5.2.

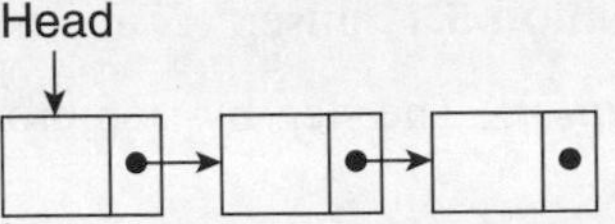

Figure 5.2 Visual representation of a linked list

A linked list is basically a collection of memory locations, connected to one another. Each location is termed as 'Node'. Every node has a value and a pointer to the next location. The pointer will point to the next node. If the pointer is lost or removed, then the next node cannot be reached as it is not stored in continuous memory locations. Here, each node is like coaches in a train. Each node is independent and connected to other nodes only through the 'Next' pointer. The 'Head' pointer points to the first node of the list. This 'Head' pointer is like the engine. So, if the 'Head' pointer is lost, then the list is also lost. Even if it is fully connected when the starting point is unknown, the list and the data are all lost. The only point of access to the user is the 'Head' pointer. To reach any other node, linear traversal across the nodes using 'Next' pointer is the only way. Unlike queues, linked lists do not have a 'Rear' pointer. As discussed about adding or removing a coach in the train, lists do not have a restriction over the point of addition or deletion. A node can be added or deleted at any position.

Some points to be noted about linked lists are:

1. Linked lists do not store elements in continuous memory locations.
2. Data is stored in memory location called 'Node', which has the value along with 'Next' pointer
3. Only the first node of the list can be accessed using the 'Head' pointer
4. Accessing the elements is possible only through linear traversal using the 'Head' pointer and 'Next' pointer of each node
5. Data can be inserted and deleted anywhere in a linked list.

There are three types of linked lists:

- Singly linked lists
- Doubly linked lists
- Circular linked lists

5.2 SINGLY LINKED LISTS

Singly linked lists (SLLs) are one-way lists. Here, the traversal along the list can only be in one direction. The train is a general example of linked lists. General linked lists have more features as compared to SLLs. For example, in case of a treasure hunt game, the player gets only one clue initially. Based on that clue, the next clue is searched. The process continues until the player reaches the end. However, at any point, the player does not move back to the previous clue/position. Same is the case with single linked lists. Every node is connected to the next node via the 'Next' pointer. Once the desired node is reached, there is no way to move back to the previous node, as its location is not known. In addition, the 'Next' pointer of the last node is 'null', stopping further movement. The visual representation of SLLs is same as normal linked lists.

5.2.1 Working—Insert Node Operation

'Insert Node' is the function for inserting a node into a list. Unlike, queues or stacks, here the position of insertion is not fixed. So, along with the element, the position must also be specified. Once the position is known, the movement is started from the 'Head' pointer and the particular node is reached where the new element is to be inserted. The 'Next' pointers of the nodes are altered such that the new node is inserted into the list (refer to Pseudocode 5.1).

Question 5.1 Insert '2' at position '4' of the linked list containing 3, 1, 4, 5.

Solution: The step-by-step process is shown in Figure 5.3.

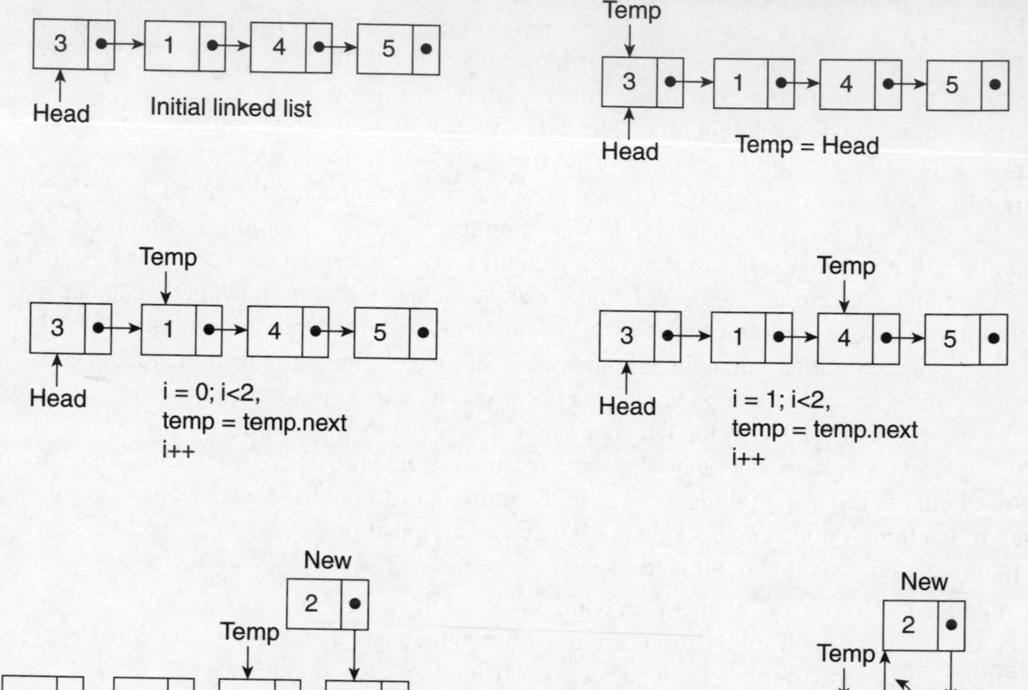

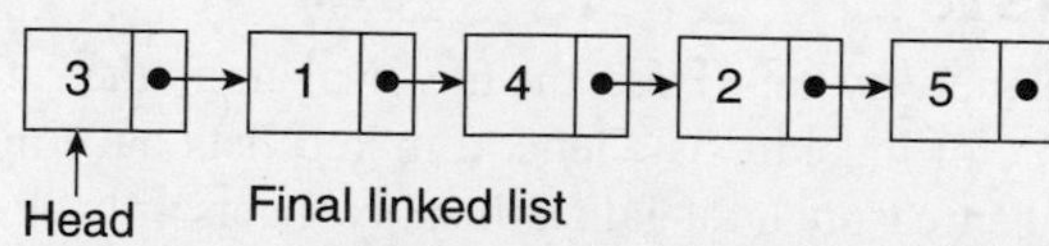

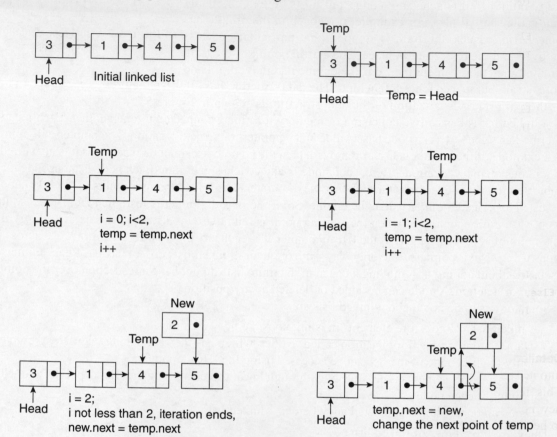

Figure 5.3 Step-by-step process of inserting '2' at position '4' of the linked list containing 3, 1, 4, 5

Pseudocode 5.1

```
Create a New node
New.value = element
If position < size of list
Then,
    If size of list = 0
```

(contd)

(*contd*)

```
    Then,
        Head -> New node
    Else If position = 0
    Then,
        New.next -> Head
        Head -> New
    Else If position < size
    Then,
        Temp = Head
        For i in range of 0 to position - 1
        /*position - 1 is used to reach the element after which the new node is to be inserted */
        Do,
            Temp -> Temp.next // traversal using next pointer
        New.next -> Temp.next
        Temp.next -> New
    Increment count
Else,
    Invalid insertion // position greater than size
```

Detailed Explanation for the Pseudocode First, the algorithm creates a new node and places the element into it. Then, it creates a temporary pointer and assigns the value of 'Head' pointer to this 'temp' pointer. This 'temp' pointer is used for traversal across the list. It traverses into the list to the node after which the new node is to be inserted by moving the 'temp' pointer to the consecutive nodes. The number of nodes to be crossed in this traversal is specified earlier as position. Then, the 'Next' pointer of the new node is assigned to the node that was being pointed by the 'Next' pointer of the node, reached after traversal. Finally, the 'Next' pointer of the node, reached after traversal, is pointed to the new node. Now, the old link of that node, reached after traversal, gets destroyed and the new link alone remains active. Thus, the list is ready with the element in the required location.

Can a newly inserted node be stored in a memory location that is lesser than the memory location of all the nodes already present in the list?

5.2.2 Working—Delete Node Operation

'Delete Node' is used to delete an element from the list. The 'Head' pointer is used to traverse to the position next to the node that is to be deleted. Then, the 'Next' pointer is changed to by-pass the node to be deleted and is pointed to the following node (refer to Pseudocode 5.2).

Question 5.2 Delete element at position '2' in a linked list containing 3, 1, 4, 2, 5.

Solution: The process is shown in Figure 5.4.

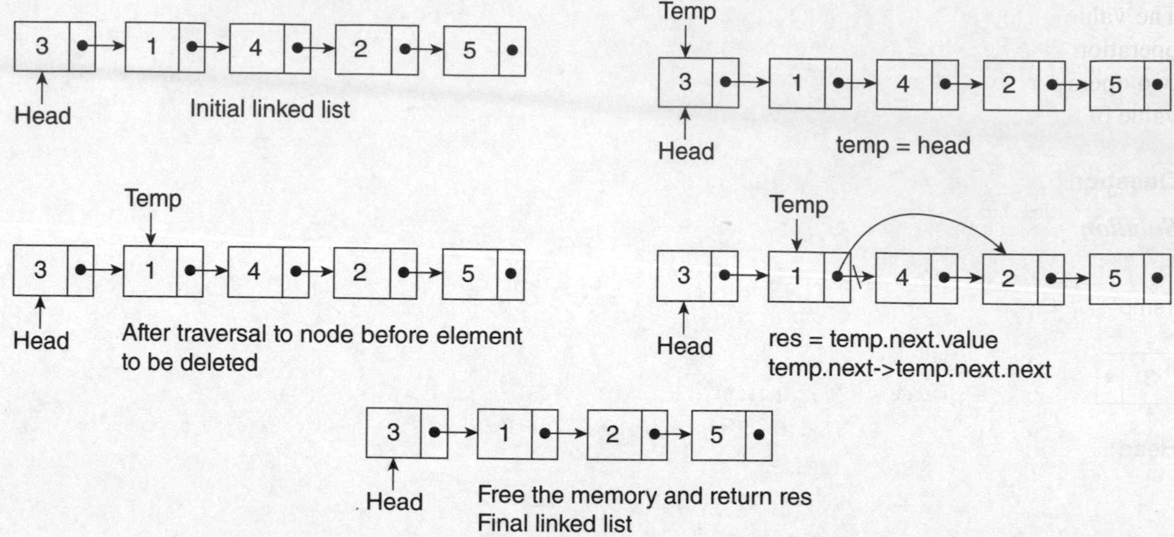

Figure 5.4 Step-by-step illustration of deleting element at position '2' in a linked list containing 3, 1, 4, 2, 5

Pseudocode 5.2

```
If list is not Empty and position < size
Then,
        temp = head
        for i in range of 0 to position - 1
        Do,
                temp -> temp.next
        res = temp.next.value
        temp.next -> temp.next.next
        Decrement count
        return res
Else,
        return 0 or a delimiter to specify List is empty
```

Detailed Explanation of the Pseudocode First, it checks if the list is not empty and if the position to be deleted is less than size. Failing either cannot be a valid operation, so it thrives as a base case. When the condition is satisfied, the deletion operation is performed, else the algorithm returns '-1'. First, a 'temp' pointer is created and assigned with the 'Head' pointer. This traverses across the list to reach the node whose next is to be deleted. The value of the node to be deleted is stored in a local variable for returning to the user. Then, the 'Next' pointer of the node, reached after traversal, is made to point to the node which was being pointed by the 'Next' pointer of the node to be deleted. Thus, the required node is bypassed and the link gets changed. Finally, the algorithm returns the value stored in the local variable.

5.2.3 Working—ValueAt Operation

'ValueAt' is the simplest of the operations of SLLs. It is just peeking into the list and checking the value stored at a particular location of the list. It is straight forward and simple. In this case, a 'temp' pointer is created and assigned the 'Head' position. The list is then traversed to reach the specified position.

The value of the node is read using the 'temp' pointer and then returned. The base cases of 'Delete' operation hold here too, as it is not possible to read an empty list or any location in it. Unlike the other two operations here, the list is traversed to directly reach the node itself and not its previous one as the value of the node is just read and not modified. Pseudocode 5.3 shows the ValueAt function.

Question 5.3 Find 'ValueAt' position '3' of a list containing 3, 1, 4, 2, 5.

Solution: The step-by-step solution is shown in Figure 5.5.

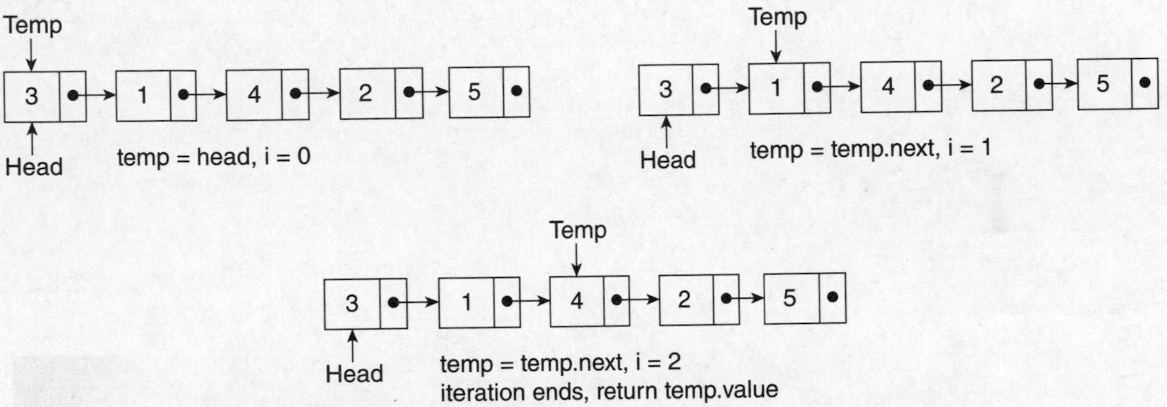

Figure 5.5 Illustration of 'ValueAt' position '3' of a list containing 3, 1, 4, 2, 5

Pseudocode 5.3

```
If list is not Empty and position < size
Then,
        temp = head
        for i in range of 0 to position
        Do,
                temp -> temp.next
        return temp.next.value
Else,
        return 0 or a delimiter to specify List is empty
```

Food for Brain

What if the 'Head' pointer itself is moved in case of the 'ValueAt' operation instead of creating a 'Temp' pointer and using it?

5.2.4 Implementation of Singly Linked Lists

Unlike other linear data structures, this is not stored in continuous memory locations. So, the only way of implementing a linked list is based on pointers. Python code 5.1 shows the implementation of linked lists.

Python code 5.1

```
class node:
        def __init__(self):
                self.value = None
                self.next = None
class SLL:
        def __init__(self):
                self.__head = node()
                self.__size = 0
        def insertAt(self,val,position): # position starting from 0
                t = node()
                t.value = val
                if (self.__size == 0 and position == 0):
                        self.__head = t
                        self.__size += 1
                elif (position == 0):
                        t.next = self.__head
                        self.__head = t
                        self.__size += 1
                elif (position<=self.__size):
                        temp = self.__head
                        for i in range (position - 1):
                                temp = temp.next
                        t.next = temp.next
                        temp.next = t
                        self.__size += 1
                else:
                        print("invalid insertion")
        def deleteAt(self,position):
                if (self.__size >0 and position<=self.__size):
                        temp = self.__head
                        for i in range(position - 1):
                                temp = temp.next
                        res = temp.next.value
                        temp.next = temp.next.next
                        self.__size -= 1
                        return res
                else:
                        return -1
        def print_list(self):
                if (self.__size > 0):
                        temp = self.__head
                        for i in range(self.__size):
                                print(temp.value," ")
                                temp = temp.next
                        print(" ")
                else:
                        print("list empty")
        def valueAt(self,position):
                if (self.__size > 0 and position<self.__size):
                        temp = self.__head
                        for i in range(position):
                                temp = temp.next
                        return temp.value
                else:
                        return -1
```

In the implementation, the position is referred from '0 to n-1', similar to index of an array. This may be changed based on necessity.

5.2.5 Complex Operations—Searching

Searching is straight forward, similar to the 'ValueAt' function. Initially, the base cases are checked. Then, a 'temp' pointer is assigned to the head node. The pointer traverses across the list until the element is found or the end is reached. Once the element is found, its position is returned, else '-1' is returned to indicate that the element is absent (refer to Pseudocode 5.4).

Question 5.4 Search '7' in the list containing 3, 1, 7, 4, 6.

Solution: The step-by-step process is shown in Figure 5.6.

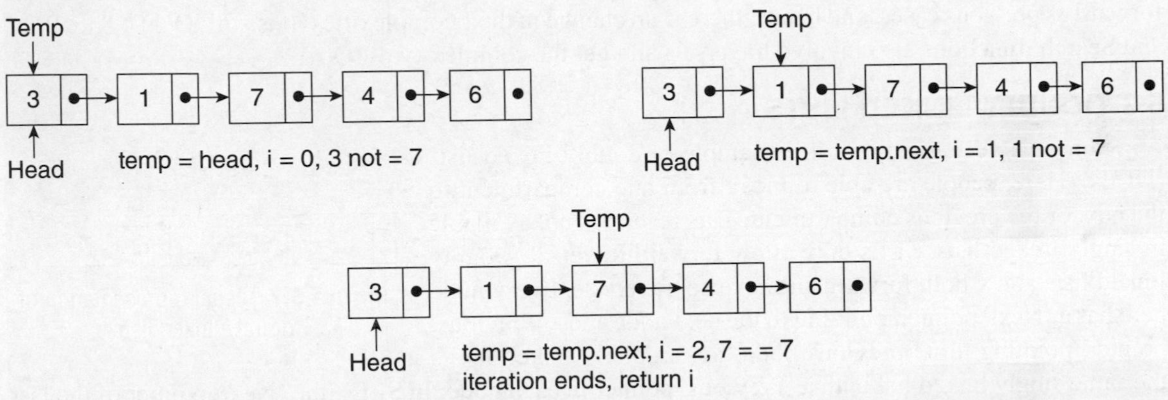

Figure 5.6 Step-by-step illustration of searching '7' in the list containing 3, 1, 7, 4, 6

It is also to be noted that the data structure has a function called `'DeleteNode( )'`. When a value is specified, this function deletes the corresponding node. Internally, the function calls the search function to find the position of the required node and then calls the above 'deleteAt' function with the value returned from the search function.

Pseudocode 5.4

```
If list is not Empty and position < size
Then,
        i = 0
        temp -> head
        While temp.next is not null //end is not reached
        Do,
                If temp.value = element
                Then,
                         Return i
                Else,
                         temp  -> temp.next
                         increment i
Else,
        Return -1
```

5.2.6 Complex Operations—Sorting

Sorting of linked lists is same as sorting of arrays, which is discussed in Chapter 12. Each node can be treated as an element and applied to all the algorithms. However, it is preferred to retain the nodes and just change the values inside the nodes. You can use any in-place sorting algorithm and change the values in between the nodes, retaining the structure. It minimises the risk of memory exceptions. Rather than swapping the nodes, along with their pointers, it is always better to swap the elements of the nodes alone.

5.2.7 Complexity Analysis

Unlike other linear data structures, here the complexity for all the operations is high. This is mainly because it allows inserting or deleting at any point. All the 'insertAt, deleteAt, and valueAt' operations have an internal traversal to the position required. In the worst case, the traversal will be until the end of the list. Thus, the complexity of all the three is 'O(n)'. The 'isEmpty' and 'Size' functions are straight forward as previous cases, and hence, there is no change in their complexities. It is still 'O(1)'. The 'Print and Search' functions also involve traversals and get the complexity of 'O(n)'.

5.3 DOUBLY LINKED LISTS

A 'Train' is a very good real-life example of doubly linked lists (DLLs). Here, people are able to move from one compartment to the next or the previous compartment. This feature is not available in singly linked lists. SLLs only allow forward traversal. Doubly linked lists allow both forward and reverse traversals. Every node here has a 'Next' pointer, pointing to the next node and a 'Previous' pointer, pointing to its previous node. So, a doubly linked list is the same singly linked list with a 'Previous' pointer in each node. In SLLs, the 'Next' pointer of the last node is 'null', similarly in DLLs, the 'Previous' pointer of the first node is 'null', marking the end points of traversal. Figure 5.7 shows the visual representation of DLLs.

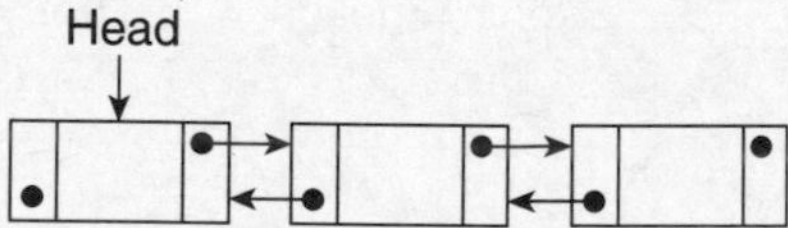

Figure 5.7 Visual representation of doubly linked lists

5.3.1 Working—Insert Node Operation

This is the same process of inserting a node at a specified position in a linked list. The base cases are the same. In a SLL, it is done by altering the 'Next' pointer of the node before the position where a node is supposed to be inserted. In a DLL, however, there is an additional 'Previous' pointer. The 'Previous' pointer of the node at the position where the new node is to be inserted must point to the new node. Only then, all the elements on the right of that position are shifted to right by '1'. In addition, the 'Previous' pointer of the new node must point to the node before the required position for continuity.

First, a 'temp' pointer is created that is assigned the value of the 'Head'. It traverses across the list to reach the position where the new node is to be inserted.

A new pointer 'temp1' is created and assigned with previous node of 'temp'. Now, we have three nodes into consideration. A new node, a node pointed by 'temp1', and a node pointed by 'temp'. The 'Next' pointer of the node pointed by 'temp1' is changed to point to the new node and the 'Next' pointer of the new node points to the node marked by 'temp'. This is done just like in case of a SLL.

Additional steps in a DLL include the 'Previous' pointer of the node marked by 'temp' to point to the new node and the 'Previous' pointer of the new node to point to the node marked by 'temp1'. This also follows the similar mechanism. If the node is to be inserted in the beginning of the list, then traversal is not mandatory. The 'Previous' pointer of the node currently pointed by 'Head' is made to point to the new node and the 'Next' pointer of the new node is pointed to the current 'Head'. Finally, the 'Head' pointer is assigned to the new node. Thus, the node is inserted successfully into the list (refer to Pseudocode 5.5).

Question 5.5 Insert '2' at position '4' of the linked list containing 3, 1, 4, 5.

Solution: The step-by-step process is shown in Figure 5.8.

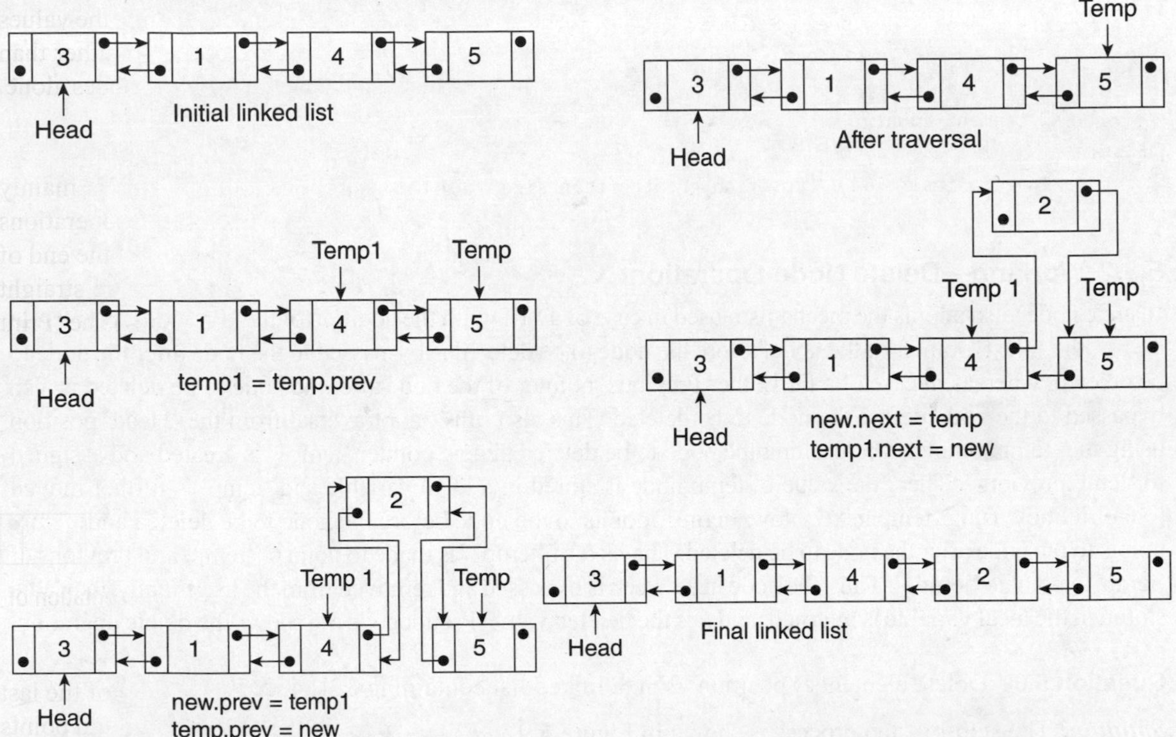

Figure 5.8 Step-by-step insertion of '2' at position '4' of the linked list containing 3, 1, 4, 5

Pseudocode 5.5

```
Create a New node
New.value = element
If position < size of list
Then,
        If size of list = 0
        Then,
                Head -> New node
        Else If position = 0
        Then,
                New.next -> Head
                Head.prev -> New
                Head -> New
        Else,
                Temp = Head
                For i in range of 0 to position
                Do,
                        Temp -> Temp.next // traversal using next pointer
```

(*contd*)

(*contd*)

```
                Temp1 = Temp.prev
                New.next -> Temp
                New.prev -> Temp1
                Temp1.next -> New
                Temp.prev -> New
        Increment count
Else,
        Invalid insertion // position greater than size
```

5.3.2 Working—Delete Node Operation

'Delete node' also adopts the mechanism used in case of a SLL with the addition of the 'Previous' pointer. In a SLL, the 'Next' pointer of the node before the node to be deleted is by-passed to the node after the node to be deleted, whereas in case of a DLL, the 'Previous' pointer of the node after the node to be deleted is also bypassed to the node before the node to be deleted. This also runs on a traversal from the 'Head' position using the 'temp' pointer. On reaching the node to be deleted, a new pointer 'temp1' is created and assigned to 'temp.previous'. Then, the value of temp node is stored in a local variable and 'temp' is further moved to the right by using 'temp.next'. Now, 'temp1' points to the node before the node to be deleted and 'temp' points to the node after the node to be deleted. The next of 'temp1' is made to point to 'temp' and previous of 'temp' to point to 'temp1'. Thus, the node in between is bypassed and removed from the list. Finally, the value stored in the local variable is returned, and it is the deleted value. Pseudocode 5.6 shows the delete operation.

Question 5.6 Delete element at position '2' in a linked list containing 3, 1, 4, 2, 5.

Solution: The step-by-step process is shown in Figure 5.9.

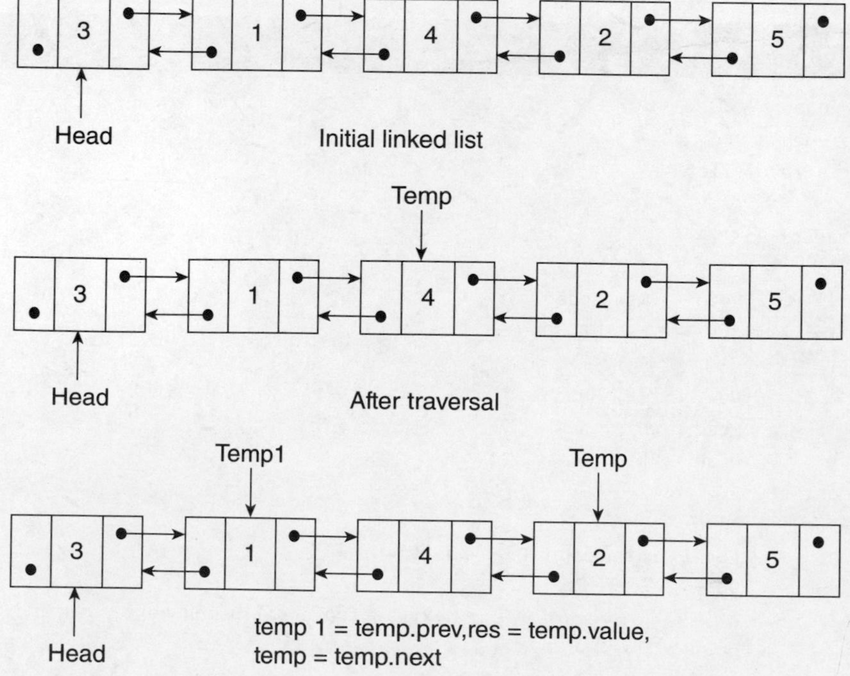

(*contd*)

(*contd*)

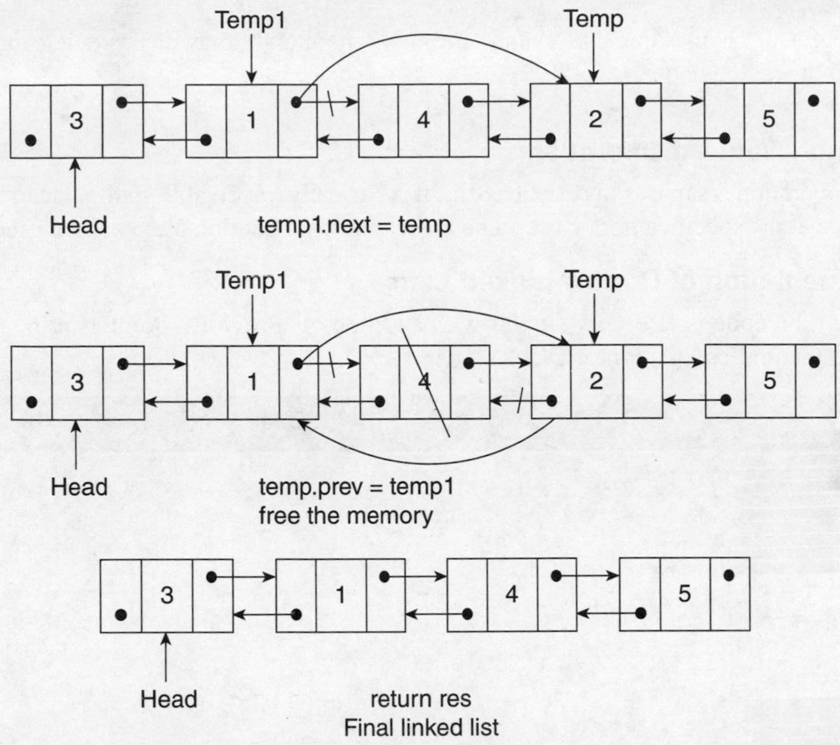

Figure 5.9 Deleting the element at position '2' in a linked list containing 3, 1, 4, 2, 5

Pseudocode 5.6

```
If list is not Empty and position < size
Then,
        temp = head
        for i in range of 0 to position
        Do,
                    temp -> temp.next
        temp1 = temp.previous
        res = temp.value
        temp = temp.next
        temp1.next -> temp
        temp.previous -> temp1
        Decrement count
        return res
Else,
        return 0 or a delimiter to specify List is empty
```

Food for Brain

Is it not enough to change the 'Next' and 'Previous' pointers alone in the delete process? Is it mandatory to delete the node as well?

5.3.3 Working—ValueAt Operation

The 'ValueAt' operation is same as in case of a SLL. It is basically traversal from the 'Head' to the position to read the value at the specified node. The same algorithm from Section 5.2.3 can be used here as well.

5.3.4 Implementation of Doubly Linked Lists

The implementation code is also very similar with addition of 'Previous' pointer in the nodes. Python code 5.2 shows the implementation of DLLs.

Python code 5.2

```
class node:
        def __init__(self):
                self.value = None
                self.next = None
                self.prev = None
class DLL:
        def __init__(self):
                self.__head = node()
                self.__size = 0
        def insertAt(self,val,position):
                t = node()
                t.value = val
                if (self.__size == 0 and position == 0):
                        self.__head = t
                        self.__size += 1
                elif (position == 0):
                        t.next = self.__head
                        self.__head.prev = t
                        self.__head = t
                        self.__size += 1
                elif (position<self.__size):
                        temp = self.__head
                        for i in range (position):
                                temp = temp.next
                        temp1 = temp.prev
                        t.prev = temp1
                        t.next = temp
                        temp1.next = t
                        temp.prev = t
                        self.__size += 1
                elif (position == self.__size):
                        temp = self.__head
                        for i in range (position - 1):
                                temp = temp.next
```

(*contd*)

(*contd*)

```
                        t.prev = temp
                        temp.next = t
                        self.__size += 1
                else:
                        print("invalid insertion")
        def deleteAt(self,position):
                if (self.__size >0 and 0<position<self.__size):
                        temp = self.__head
                        for i in range(position):
                                temp = temp.next
                        temp1 = temp.prev
                        res = temp.value
                        temp1.next = temp.next
                        temp.next.prev = temp1
                        self.__size -= 1
                        return res
                elif(self.__size >0 and position == self.__size):
                        temp = self.__head
                        for i in range(position):
                                temp = temp.next
                        temp1 = temp.prev
                        res = temp.value
                        temp1.next = None
                        self.__size -= 1
                        return res
                elif(self.__size>0 and position == 0):
                        temp = self.__head
                        res = temp.value
                        self.__head = temp.next
                        self.__size -= 1
                        return res
                else:
                        return -1
        def print_list(self):
                if (self.__size > 0):
                        temp = self.__head
                        for i in range(self.__size):
                                print(temp.value," ")
                                temp = temp.next
                        print(" ")
                else:
                        print("list empty")
        def valueAt(self,position):
                if (self.__size > 0 and position<self.__size):
                        temp = self.__head
                        for i in range(position):
                                temp = temp.next
                        return temp.value
                else:
                        return -1
```

The complex operations are also similar to that of SLLs. The addition of 'Previous' pointer does not make a significant difference in the algorithms. The searching is based on traversal and similar to 'ValueAt'. So, this algorithm is also same as the one used in case of SLLs. Refer to Sections 5.2.5 and 5.2.6 for complex operations on SLL.

5.3.5 Complexity Analysis

When there is no significant change in the operations or algorithm for DLL, the complexity will be same as that of SLLs. All the basic operations—insertAt, deleteAt, valueAt, print and search—all run to the complexity 'O(n)'. As usual, 'isEmpty' and 'size' alone run in 'O(1)' because of the count maintained. There is no difference in traversal, so there is no change in complexity of the operations.

5.4 CIRCULAR LINKED LISTS

Circular linked lists are normal linked lists with the last node pointing back to the first node. Consider the game of 'merry go round' played by children in Figure 5.10. Each child holds the hands of its neighbours in this game. So, it is difficult to figure out the start or the end. The same is the case with circular linked lists. When the last node points back to the first node, there cannot be an explicit 'Head' pointer pointing to the first node in the list. There cannot be a first node in the circle. So, a 'Current' pointer is used to point to one node in the circle at a time. The visual representation of circular linked lists is shown in Figure 5.11.

Figure 5.10 Children playing 'merry go round'

The 'Current' pointer is always assigned to the first node that was inserted into the list, just as a point of access. Even if the list has two elements, they will point to each other. The basic operations are:

1. Insert
2. Delete
3. ValueAt

These at are discussed below.

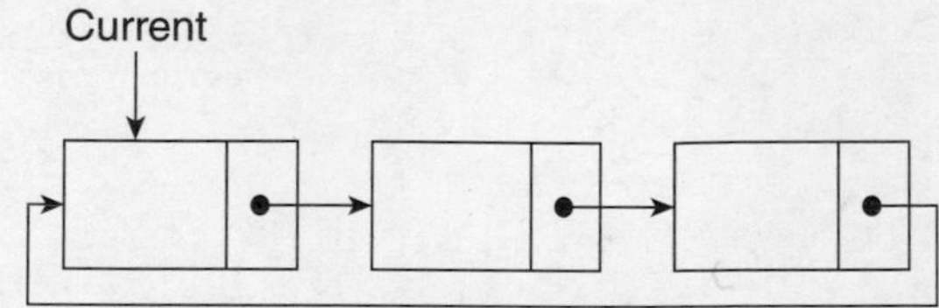

Figure 5.11 Visual representation of circular linked lists

5.4.1 Working—Insert Node Operation

The insert operation here is not much different from that discussed in case of SLLs. However, there is one important change. When the first element is inserted, it is made to point back to itself. Thus, it forms a circular list. So, then any normal insertion will retain the circular property of the list. Thus, a circular linked list is achieved.

Consider when an element is inserted at position '0'. In this case, a traversal is done from the current node to the last node, that is, node before the current node and pointing to it. After that, the same mechanism of changing the pointers takes place. Thus, a new traversal is added into the algorithm. In SLL, the best case running of algorithm is inserting in position '0', but here the best case is only when the list is empty. Pseudocode 5.7 shows the insert operation in a circular linked list.

Question 5.7 Insert 1, 2, 3 into an empty circular linked list.

Solution: The process is shown in Figure 5.12.

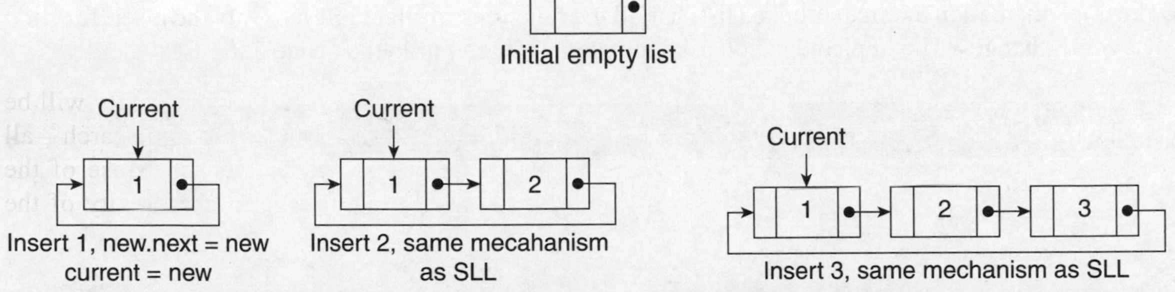

Figure 5.12 Illustration of inserting 1, 2, 3 into an empty circular linked list

Pseudocode 5.7

```
Create a New node
New.value = element
If position < size of list
Then,
        If size of list = 0
        Then,
                New.next -> New //self-pointing for circular property
                current-> New node
        Else If position = 0
        Then,
                Temp = current
                While Temp.next is not current
                /*Node before current is to be reached */
                Do,
                        Temp -> Temp.next // traversal using next pointer
                New.next -> current
                Temp.next -> New
                Current -> New
        Else If position < size
        Then,
                Temp = Head
                For i in range of 0 to position - 1
                /*position - 1 is used to reach the element after which the new node is to
                be inserted */
                Do,
                        Temp -> Temp.next // traversal using next pointer
                New.next -> Temp.next
                Temp.next -> New
        Increment count
Else,
        Invalid insertion // position greater than size
```

The operations, deletion and valueAt, are similar to the ones discussed in case of a SLL, so Sections 5.2.2 and 5.2.3 can referred to for more detail.

5.4.3 Implementation of Circular Linked Lists

The implementation of circular linked lists has all the functions similar to SLLs. Only the insert function has some changes. The implementation using pointers is shared in Python code 5.3.

Python code 5.3

```
class node:
        def __init__(self):
                self.value = None
                self.next = None
class CLL:
        def __init__(self):
                self.__current = node()
                self.__size = 0
        def insertAt(self,val,position): # position starting from 0
                t = node()
                t.value = val
                if (self.__size == 0 and position == 0):
                        self.__current = t
                        t.next = t
                        self.__size += 1
                elif (position == 0):
                        temp = self.__current
                        for i in range(self.__size):
                                temp = temp.next
                        t.next = self.__current
                        temp.next = t
                        self.__current = t
                        self.__size += 1
                elif (position<=self.__size):
                        temp = self.__current
                        for i in range (position - 1):
                                temp = temp.next
                        t.next = temp.next
                        temp.next = t
                        self.__size += 1
                else:
                        print("invalid insertion")
        def deleteAt(self,position):
                if (self.__size >0 and position<=self.__size):
                        temp = self.__current
                        for i in range(position - 1):
                                temp = temp.next
                        res = temp.next.value
                        temp.next = temp.next.next
```

(*contd*)

(*contd*)

```
                        self.__size -= 1
                        return res
            else:
                        return -1
    def print_list(self):
            if (self.__size > 0):
                        temp = self.__current
                        for i in range(self.__size):
                                    print(temp.value," ")
                                    temp = temp.next
                        print(" ")
            else:
                        print("list empty")
    def valueAt(self,position):
            if (self.__size > 0 and position<self.__size):
                        temp = self.__current
                        for i in range(position):
                                    temp = temp.next
                        return temp.value
            else:
                        return -1
```

In some sources, the 'Current' pointer in implementation will be referred to as 'Head'. It is not incorrect, but logically there cannot be a 'Head' in a circle. Hence, this naming convention is followed. Circular linked lists can also be implemented as a doubly linked form of circular linked lists. That is commonly known as circular doubly linked lists. It does not make any significant difference in implementation. In circular doubly linked lists, the first element's 'Next' and 'Previous' are made to point to the same node. In case of more number of elements, if a new element is to be inserted at position '0', then from the 'current' node, the 'previous' can be reached and insertion is easily done. The complex operations of search and sort are also similar to that of SLLs.

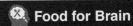

 **Food for Brain**

How many pointers will be there in an empty doubly circular linked list?

5.4.4 Complexity Analysis

When there is no significant change in algorithms, the complexity also sticks to that of SLLs. All the operations, 'insertAt, deleteAt, valueAt, print, and search', get the worst case complexity of 'O(n)'. The basic ones, 'isEmpty and size', as usual stick to 'O(1)'. This data structure is similar to a SLL, with an additional feature of roll over to front from back.

5.5 APPLICATIONS OF LINKED LISTS

Some of the applications of linked lists are given below:

Accessing Photos in a Computer Consider a photo stream in your personal computer. Open any one photo in the location using a photo viewer. From this photo, the user can move to any of the 'previous' or 'next' location. This can be implemented using a modified form of DLL. However, in actual applications, this is not used. In real time, all the photos in a location are stored in consecutive memory locations. So, moving back and forward is done by relative accessing.

Polynomial using ADT Another important application of linked lists is in representing and processing polynomial, where co-efficient of each literal is independent. The algorithm for the same is shared in here:

1. Traverse through the expression until the end
2. For every component, add a node in the list
3. If the expression has only one variable, then the node is actually a structure which contains the co-efficient and power of the variable
4. If the expression has multiple variables, then the node is actually a structure which contains the co-efficient and power along with the variable itself.
5. For manipulating two expressions, linked lists can be used. Say, for adding two expressions, the nodes of the linked lists can be added and the result can be saved into a new linked list. While adding, only the co-efficient inside the nodes should be added. Using the final linked list, a new expression can be formed which is the resultant expression.
6. While manipulation, a node can be added with a node which has the same variable and power

The implementation of polynomial using ADT is shared in Python code 5.4.

Python code 5.4

```
class exp:
        class exnode:
                def __init__(self,coeff,power):
                        self.coeff = coeff
                        self.power = power
                def print_exnode(self):
                        print(self.coeff,"x",self.power)
        def __init__(self,ex):
                self.n= SLL()
                e = ex.split(" ")
                for i in range (0,len(e)):
                        if (i ! = 0 and (not isOperand(e[i-1])) and e[i] == 'x' and i ! =
len(e) - 1 and (not isOperand(e[i + 1]))):
                                temp = self.exnode(e[i-1],e[i +1])
                                self.n.insertAt(temp,self.n.list_size())
                        elif((i == 0 or isOperand(e[i-1])) and e[i] == 'x' and i != len(e)
- 1 and (not isOperand(e[i + 1]))):
                                temp = self.exnode(1, e[i + 1])
                                self.n.insertAt(temp, self.n.list_size())
                        elif (i! = 0 and (not isOperand(e[i - 1])) and e[i] == 'x' and i
== len(e)-1):
                                temp = self.exnode(e[i - 1],1)
                                self.n.insertAt(temp,self.n.list_size())
                        elif((i == 0 or isOperand(e[i - 1])) and e[i] == 'x' and i ==
len(e)-1 ):
                                temp = self.exnode(1,1)
                                self.n.insertAt(temp,self.n.list_size())
                self.n.print_list()
                def isOperand(o):
                        op = ['+','-','*','/','^']
                        return True if o in op else False
```

The 'print_list' function of SLL should be modified. Instead of printing the value, it should call the 'print_exnode' as the value of the node in a SLL is now a new class object. It is suggested that the readers should try implementing the mathematical functions for this expression class.

Some Real-life Applications of Linked Lists

1. Web indexing, which means indexing pages to alphabets. So when searched, the journey will be from the first linked list to the linked list with the node that has the page. The traversal across these pointers will be same as the page name.
2. E-commerce websites where the categories are fixed but the number of elements are not fixed, it is implemented as a two-dimensional list. In the first list, each node is a category. Every category node is linked to a new list of products.
3. Implementing a music playlist with repeat mode
4. Instructions in software with undo and redo option. The instructions are stored in DLLs, so undo is previous shift and redo is next shift (An alternative over deques, but not as efficient as deques).

Thus, linked lists are organized. It is to be noted that the values are no more stored linearly. They are dispersed in the memory. It falls into linear category as the nodes are linked in a one-to-one basis, in a linear order. Changing the link strategy will lead to non-linear data structures.

Key Points to Remember

- Linked lists are non–primitive data structures. It is a linear collection of elements or nodes not stored in continuous memory locations.
- A linked list has no particular order of motion. It has no constraint on data insertion and removal.
- The different types of linked lists are as follows:
  - Singly linked list
  - Doubly linked list
  - Circular linked list
  - Circular doubly linked list
- A singly linked list has only one pointer or link to the next node present in the list.
- In a doubly linked list, each node contains two pointers called 'NEXT' and 'PREV' pointing to the next and previous node, respectively.
- In circular linked lists, the last node is connected to the first node, that is, the last node does not contain 'Null' but contains a pointer to the first node of the list.
- In a circular linked list with one element, the node should point to itself.

Key Terms

Linked lists A linear data structure designed to store elements in non-continuous memory locations using pointers from one memory location to the next location.

Singly linked lists/SLLs A linked list with pointer to traverse in forward direction. Every node will have a 'Next' pointer to move to the consecutive node, whereas there will not be any way to reach the previous node.

Doubly linked lists/DLL A linked list where every node has both 'Next' and 'Previous' pointers.

Circular linked lists A linked list where the last element points back to the first element to create a circular structure.

Head pointer The dedicated pointer that marks the first node/start point of the list.

Pointer-based linear data structures A data structure that uses pointers to associate a memory location to another memory location.

EXERCISES

Multiple-choice Questions

1. Which of the following about linked lists is true?
   (a) Insertion and deletion of elements is in constant runtime
   (b) Random access is not allowed in a linked list.
   (c) Linked lists can change sizes dynamically.
2. What is the worst case complexity of searching in a singly linked list of size 'n'?
   (a) n/2 (b) n
   (c) log 2n (d) log 2n-1
3. What is the output of the code?

```
def fun1(head)
    if(head==NULL):
        return
    fun1(head.next)
    print(head.data)
```

   (a) Print all the nodes in the list
   (b) Print all the nodes in reverse order
   (c) None of the above
4. Can nodes of a SLL be stored in continuous memory location?
   (a) True (b) False
5. The number of comparisons required to search a singly linked list of length 'N' in the worst case is:
   (a) N (b) N/2
   (c) Log N (d) $\text{Log}_2 \text{N}$
6. In linked list implementation of a queue, 'Front and Rear' pointers are tracked. Which of these pointers will change during an insertion into EMPTY queue?
   (a) Only 'Front' pointer
   (b) Only 'Rear' pointer
   (c) Both 'Front' and 'Rear' pointers
   (d) None of the above
7. Which data structure is used in case of breadth first search?
   (a) Stack
   (b) Queue
   (c) Linked Lists
8. What is the total complexity required for finding the first and last element in a circular doubly linked list with current pointer?
   (a) O(n) (b) O(1)
   (c) O(Log n)
9. In a SLL when a node is deleted and immediately another value is inserted at the same position, will the memory address of the new (inserted) node be same as the address of the old (deleted) node?
   (a) True (b) False
10. Can a linked list node contain objects of a class?
   (a) True (b) False

Theoretical Review Questions

1. Why pointer-based linear data structures are required? Is it mandatory in Python?
2. How is a SLL different from a DLL?
3. How to handle a SLL when Head has been deleted?
4. How to reconcile a broken linked list?
5. What is a circular linked list? Explain and elaborate with some real-time examples.

Exploratory Application Exercises

1. Try to implement a multi-dimensional list using a SLL?
2. What happens when a node in a linked list points to a node which is already in the linked list? How to find that node?
3. Which data structure is appropriate for searching and trimming a substring from a given string?
4. How to find the middle of a singular linked list using just pointers?
5. Delete a node in a sorted linked list.
6. Check if a given string is a palindrome using a doubly linked list.
7. Write an algorithm for A-Steal scheduling process.
8. A loop in a singular linked list is a node pointing to any node before it in the list. Identify the loop node in a given linked list.
9. Create and maintain a 'Rear' pointer for the SLL.
10. Given a DLL, create a new DLL such that it has unique elements only. If the input DLL has duplicate elements, the same should be removed else the input will be the output as well.

Picto Puzzles

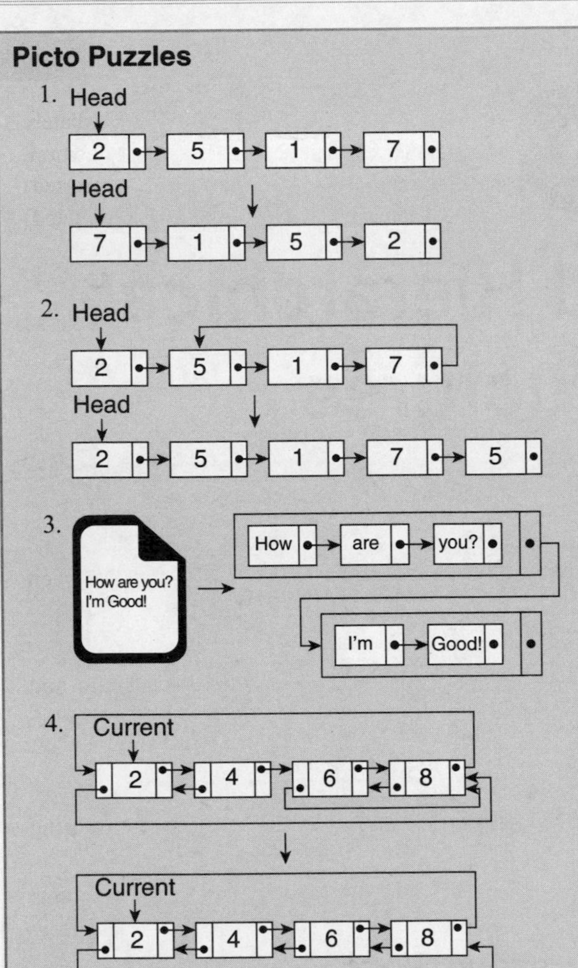

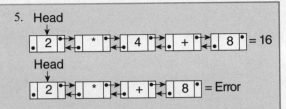

5. Head

2 * 4 + 8 = 16

Head

2 * + 8 = Error

Mini Projects

1. Design a structure to represent students in a classroom. Every student has a name, roll no, and address in the object. Every student can have any number of friends. In the list of students, every node contains the student object. Additionally, each node should be pointed to another list if friends. The friends will be replication of the student objects that are already present in the main students' list.
2. Implement a 'deque' using a DLL object alone. This will be a pointer-based implementation of queues.
3. Implement a stack using SLL object alone. This will be a pointer-based implementation of stacks.

Answers to Multiple-choice Questions

1. (c) 2. (b) 3. (b) 4. (a) 5. (a) 6. (b) 7. (b) 8. (b) 9. (b)
10. (a)

CHAPTER

6

Pointer-Based Hierarchical Data Structures

LEARNING OBJECTIVES

After going through this chapter, readers will be able to understand:

- What is a non-linear data structure?
- What is a tree?
- Types of trees
- How pointers are used to link a data to more than one data?
- How a data structure is classified as hierarchical data structure?

6.1 INTRODUCTION—NON-LINEAR DATA STRUCTURES

Non-linear data structures are the next type of data structures. Here, every data element may be connected to one or more elements, thus breaking the linear constraints. All non-linear data structures are implemented only using pointers. Using continuous memory to store data and establish a connection between multiple data elements is not directly possible. Thus, pointer-based implementation is the only go. A node has the data along with all the pointers, pointing to each of the connected node in the structure. A very important hierarchical data structure is trees. In this chapter, you will be taken through the basics of tree data structure.

6.2 TREES

The tree in Figure 6.1 is a typical tree. However, the tree structure is to be visualized exactly upside down. A tree is a data structure in which every node acts as a parent and the node can have 0, 1 or more children. A node contains the element/value and a set of pointers. The pointers are generally called a child pointer. It is to be noticed that every node will be present in a level and its children will be present in the next level.

(a)

(b)

Figure 6.1 (a) Typical tree (b) Tree data structure visualization

6.2.1 Definitions

A tree data structure has multiple components which are defined below. If all these components are understood, the data structure can be understood as a whole.

Node A node is same as in linked lists. It has the value/data and pointers to the next nodes.

Root Root is the top/first node of the tree. It doesn't have a parent. A tree can have only one root.

Parent A parent of a node is another node which points to this node. Any node other than the root will have a parent. Also, any node can have a maximum of one parent.

Child A node pointed by another node, the parent, is a child. A parent can have any number of children. The children will never have a pointer to the parent.

Levels Levels can be visualized as generations of trees. Root is considered as 'level 0', all the children of the root will go into 'level 1' whose children will proceed further. It is the levels which help the data structure to be treated as hierarchical. A notable fact is that no node will point to any node in previous levels in alignment to the hierarchical constraint.

Child Pointer The pointer in a node pointing to the children is the child pointer. Every child has an exclusive pointer.

Leaves The nodes at the last level of the tree are the leaves. It doesn't have children.

Sibling All the children of a particular parent are called siblings. All siblings will always be in the same level.

Ancestor All nodes above the current node, from which the current node is reachable, are ancestors. An ancestor cannot be reached from the current node as there is no pointer from a node to its parent. To check if a node is an ancestor of the current node, it is to be checked if the current node is reachable from the same.

Descendent All the nodes below the current node are the descendants. It is typically the children, children's children and so on. An alternative way of defining descendants is 'all the nodes in successive levels that are reachable from the current node'.

Subtree A sub-tree of a node is the tree rooted from the current node. The sub-tree consist all the descendants of the node and nothing else. Interestingly, a sub-tree can have another sub-tree. This is possible, as the sub-tree has some nodes, which in turn will have sub-trees.

Internal Node Any node that has children is an internal node. These are the nodes that lie in any level other than the lowermost level. That doesn't mean the root is an internal node, this is to be looked from the perception of children. The root has children, unless it is a single node tree, is an internal node.

Degree Degree of a node is the number of sub-trees from that node. If the node has three children, there will be three different sub-trees for this node. This will be directly equal to the number of children at the node.

Edge It is the connection between two nodes. In trees, it is always unidirectional due to the hierarchical nature. This is exactly the interpretation term for the child pointer.

Path A sequence of nodes and edges that start from a node and end at any of its descendants is a path. There can never be a path from a node to another node, which isn't a descendant of the former.

Node Height Height is the number of edges in the longest path between the node and a leaf. If the node itself is a leaf, then the height is zero.

Tree Height Height of the tree is the height of the node which has the largest height amongst all the nodes in tree. Typically, it is the height of the root as it is one level higher than all other nodes. If the height of the tree is zero, then the tree is a single node tree.

Depth Depth of a node is the number of edges from root to the current node. Depth of the root is always zero. Depth is not to be confused along with height. Height is node to leaf and depth is root to node.

Forest A forest is a collection of trees. This is a complex data structure finding application in complex algorithms like machine learning. By definition, a forest is a set of zero or more disjoint trees. So, a single tree is also technically a forest.

The major parts of a tree are marked in Figure 6.2.

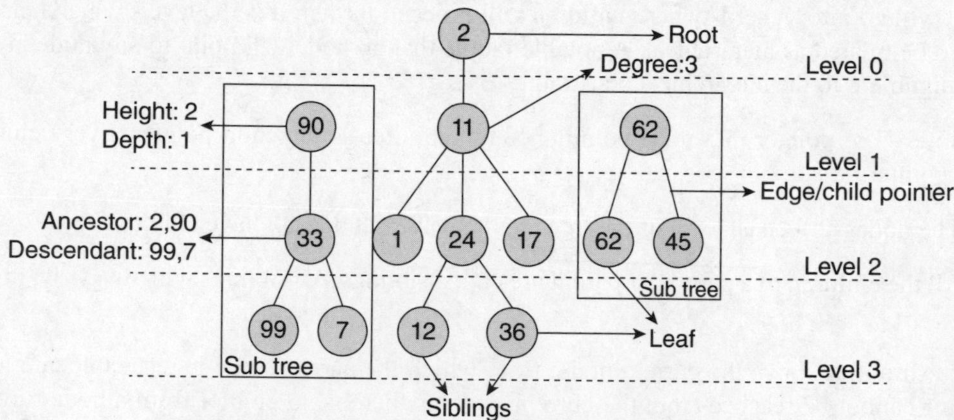

Figure 6.2 Visual representation of a tree data structure

6.3 BINARY TREES

A very common and useful variant of the tree data structure is the binary tree. All the definitions above will hold good for the binary tree as well. Albeit, there is an additional constraint on the above. Any node can have a maximum of two children. Typically, the children are called as left child and the right child. The tree depicted in Figure 6.2 is not a binary tree, however, Figure 6.3 shows a binary tree.

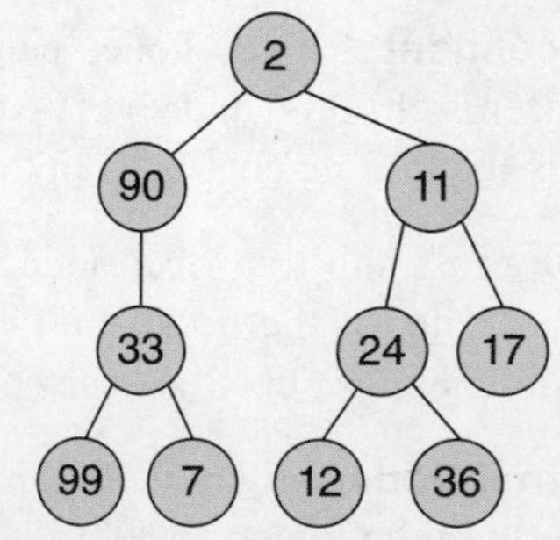

Figure 6.3 Binary tree representation

Can you think of a practical application where Binary trees can be used? Think about it!

6.3.1 Types of Binary Trees

A binary tree is further classified into multiple types. These are minor changes and constraints on the base binary tree. Undoubtedly, the constraint that a node can have a maximum of two children will apply to all the sub-forms. The different types of binary trees are discussed in detail in the following sections.

Full Binary Tree

A binary tree becomes a full binary tree when every node either has two children or zero children. Other than this there is no other constraint. It is straight forward and easily visualizable. The binary tree shown in Figure 6.4 is not a full binary tree. Figure 6.5 is an example for full binary tree.

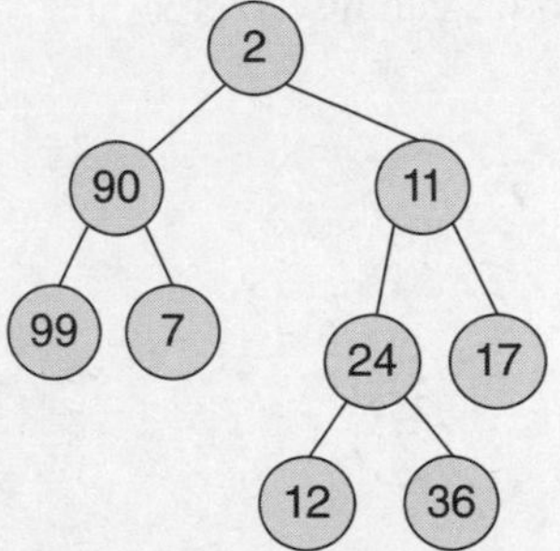

Figure 6.4 Full binary tree

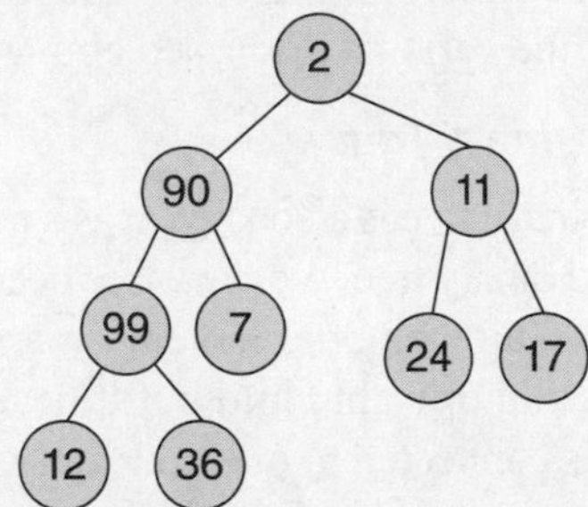

Figure 6.5 Complete binary tree

Complete Binary Tree

A complete binary tree also has the same constraint as the full binary tree. Every node should have two or no children. Above this is another constraint making it stricter. All levels other than the last level should be completely filled. While looking into the last level, the leaves in the left must be filled before the right. If it is the other way round, depicted in Figure 6.4, then the tree will be only a full binary tree but not a complete binary tree. A complete binary tree is shown in Figure 6.5.

Perfect Binary Tree

Perfect binary tree is the simplest variant of a binary tree. Just like the previous variants, all the nodes should have two or no children. The new constraint in here is all the levels of the tree must be fully filled. Figure 6.6 will be first perfect binary tree introduced to you.

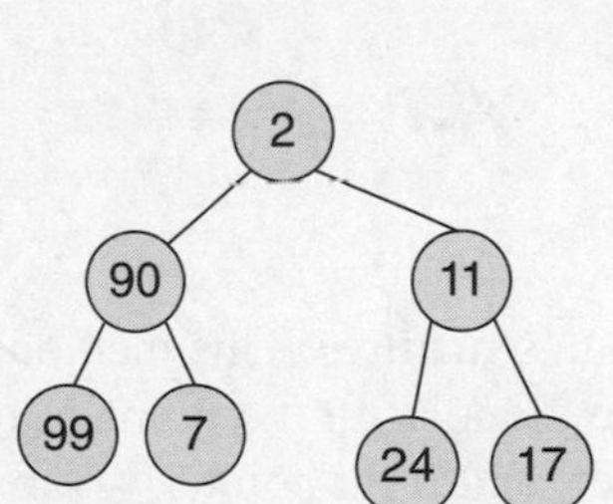

Figure 6.6 Perfect binary tree

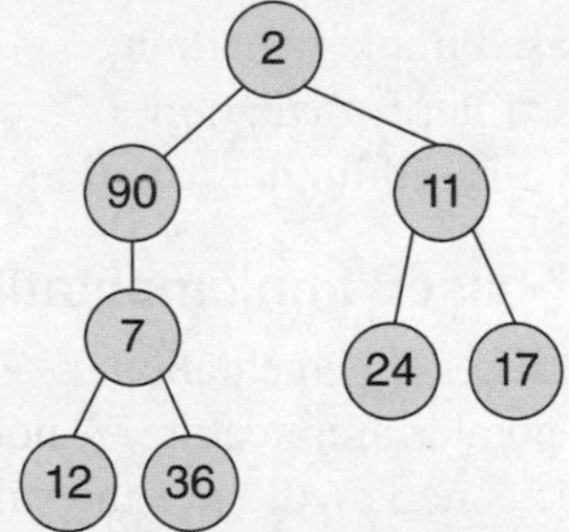

Figure 6.7 Balanced binary tree

Balanced Binary Tree

A binary tree becomes balanced if the heights of the root's left tree and root's right subtree have a maximum difference of one level. A perfect binary tree is always balanced as all the levels other than the last level is filled resulting in the difference of heights of left and right sub-tree of the root to be always zero or one. For computation, let us take the perfect binary tree which is balanced as well. The root is one element, and the children for the root are '2^1' which is '2'. The nodes in the next level will be '2^2' which will double at every node. Thus at any level the number of nodes will be '2^n'. So given 'k' nodes, half of the nodes will be at the lowermost level. From the remaining nodes, again half is taken and placed in the next level and this process of dividing by '2' for each level continues till just one node is reached for the root. For every level we divide by '2' and hence the number of levels will be 'O(log n)'. The height of a balanced binary tree with 'n' nodes is also 'O(log n)', as the perfect binary tree is the worst case balanced binary tree. The balanced property helps alarmingly in many applications and will be handled in detail in Chapter 7, AVL Trees. Figure 6.7 is a sample balanced binary tree and not to forget Figure 6.6 is also a balanced binary tree. An interesting fact to look at is that the nodes can have zero, one or two children unlike most of the variants discussed above.

Degenerate Binary Tree

A degenerate binary tree is also known as a pathological binary tree or a skewed binary tree. A binary tree becomes a degenerate binary tree when all the nodes have only one child. The child may be a left child or right child but it becomes a linked list as every node is connected to one node only. Figure 6.8 shows two different types of skewed trees. Thus the height of the tree becomes 'O(n)', making most of the process costly.

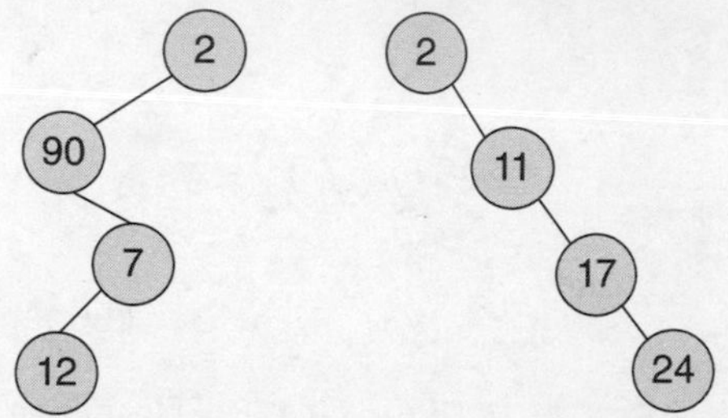

Figure 6.8 Skewed binary trees

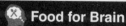

Create analogies like 'Perfect binary tree is always Balanced' by comparing the types of the binary trees.

6.4 IMPLEMENTATION OF BINARY TREES

Any tree is preferably implemented using the orthodox pointer based method. However, it can also be achieved in alternate methods. This section will discuss all possible ways of implementing binary tree. The methods discussed in here may not mandatorily be applicable for non-binary trees.

Few important implementation methods for binary trees are:

- Pointer-based Implementation
- Array-based Implementation
- Linked List-based Implementation

6.4.1 Pointer-based Implementation

This is the orthodox implementation of all non-linear based data structures. This method is completely relied on node-pointer architecture. A node contains the value along with the pointers to its children. For a binary tree, a node will have the values along with the left and right pointer. A sample tree and a pointer-based visual representation are shared in Figure 6.9. This is achieved by the Python class defined in Python code 6.1.

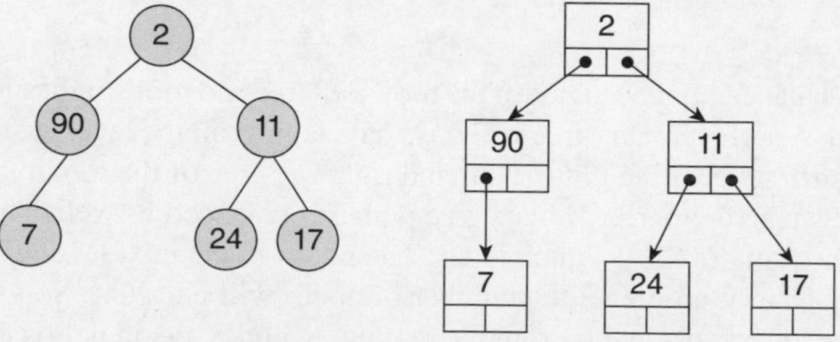

Figure 6.9 Pointer-based representation of a sample tree

Python code 6.1

```
class binary_tree:
    class Node:
        def __init__(self):
            self.node, self.left, self.right = None, None, None
        def __init__(self, node):
            self.node = node
            self.left, self.right = None, None

    def __init__(self):
        self.root = self.Node()

'''
The left and right variables inside Node class will be assigned with Node objects
itself making it act like pointers to next nodes in the tree
'''
```

From the definition perspective, the left and right in the node class are just placeholders. While inserting the nodes into the tree and connecting them, the left and right will hold other nodes. The functionality of Python helps in making them act similar to pointers in other programming languages. The tree is accessed by the object of the first node, which will be the root node.

6.4.2 Array-based Implementation

This is a logical way of implementing the binary tree. It is a maverick attempt of storing non-linear data structure's elements in a continuous memory. This is achieved by completely relying on the constraint that a node can have a maximum of two children. The implementation is done as:

- The root node is stored at first location of the array.
- The children of the root are stored in 1st and 2nd locations.
- Following down the levels, children of any node at location 'n' will be present in index '2n+1' and '2n+2'.

For this logic to work, an additional rule is applied to the above description. If a node doesn't have a left or right child, then the corresponding location is to be left empty. If it had been filled by the next element, then it will completely spoil the tree as nodes will then be mapped to different parents. Figure 6.10 will give a better understanding of the implementation.

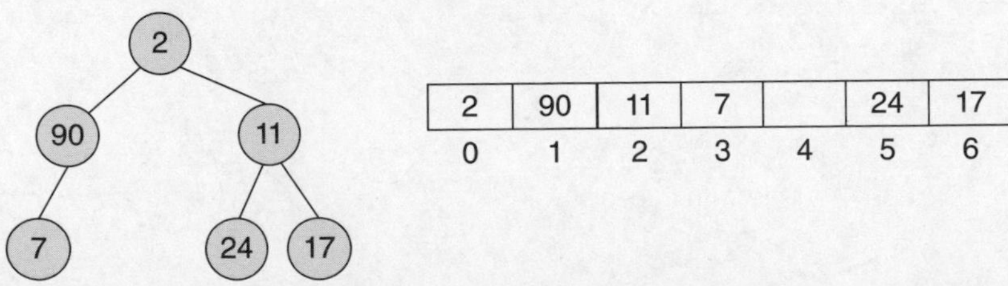

Figure 6.10 Array representation of a tree

Some interesting facts on this implementation are that for a tree with 'n' levels, the size of the array will be '$2^n - 1$'. All the nodes in the same level will be together in the array. The main issue with this implementation is while creating the tree. If there was an array of fixed size while creating the tree, then it is going to be an issue as it cannot accommodate newer nodes.

6.4.3 Linked List-based Implementation

The difficulties cited above while building the tree as the array is static, is overcome by using the linked list in the place of arrays. All the logic and rules are applicable in here as well. It is better over array-based implementations as linked lists are dynamic in nature. Figure 6.11 shows the linked list representation of the same tree shown in Figure 6.10.

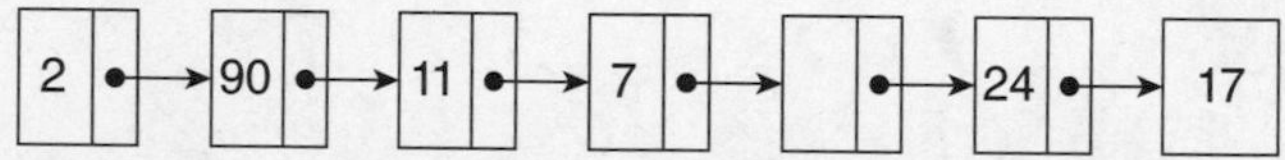

Figure 6.11 Linked List-based representation of the tree shown in Figure 6.7

 **Food for Brain**

Can you think of other ways of implementation of trees?

6.5 TRAVERSAL

Traversal means visiting or reading all the nodes in a tree without any duplication. This is simple in linear data structures. Starting from the first node, it is just moving in the forward direction, whereas, in hierarchical data structures, traversal is done using specific algorithms. At any node, there can be multiple paths moving forward. Moving down simultaneously is not possible. So, these algorithms come into the picture. In a nutshell, from a branching point, the movement is in one branch, once the end of the branch is reached, the origin is back-tracked and the next branch is taken. There are three popular traversal algorithms for trees:

- In-order Traversal
- Pre-order Traversal
- Post-order Traversal
- Level-ordered Traversal

6.5.1 In-order Traversal

This is the basic type of traversal. The traversal of any node is from left to right. The left child of the node is visited first and then the node itself and finally the right child. If the left child or right child had further branches, the entire subtree must be completed before proceeding further. In compliance with the above statement, the definition of in-order traversal is rephrased as, "the left-tree of the node is visited first followed by the node itself and finally the right sub-tree of the node is visited". Figures 6.12 and 6.13 show some sample trees and their in-order traversals.

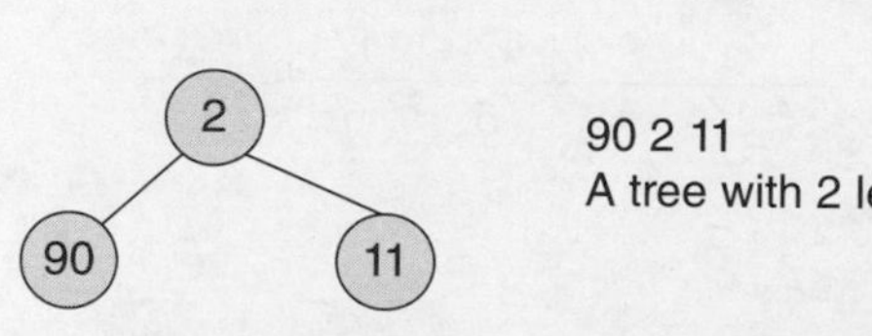

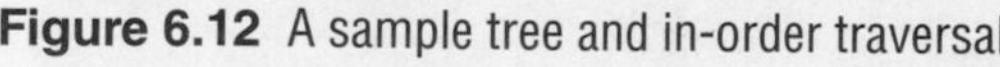
Figure 6.12 A sample tree and in-order traversal

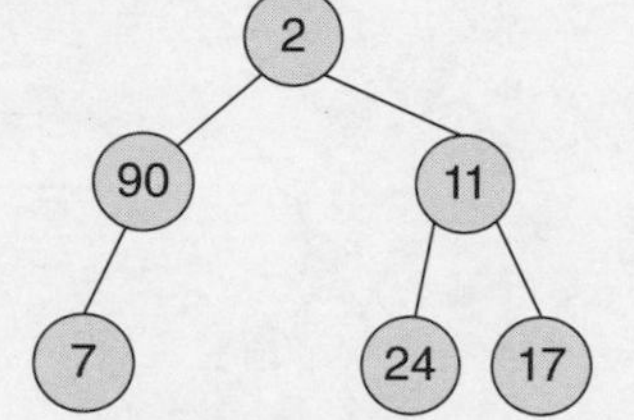

Figure 6.13 A sample tree and in-order traversal

This is achieved by recursion. A function starts from the root node and based on conditions calls itself with the left or right child as the argument (as shown in Python code 6.2).

Python code 6.2

```
def inorder(n):
    if n.left != None:
        inorder(n.left)
    print(n.value)
    if n.right != None:
        inorder(n.right)
```

6.5.2 Pre-order Traversal

This is similar to in-order traversal but the place where the root is visited is different. In pre-order traversal, the nodes' children are visited after the node itself. Putting it in clear terms, the node is visited first and then the left subtree is visited, and finally the right sub-tree is visited. A fact in this traversal is, for any tree the root will be visited first. Figures 6.14 and 6.15 share pre-order traversal of the same trees as discussed above (refer to Python code 6.3).

Python code 6.3

```
def preorder(n):
    print(n.value)
    if n.left != None:
        preorder(n.left)
    if n.right != None:
        preorder(n.right)
```

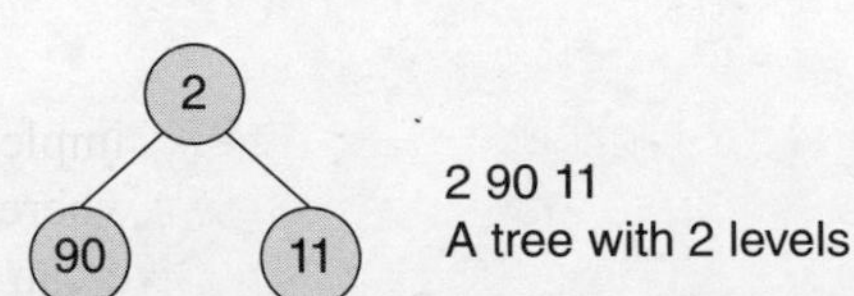

Figure 6.14 A sample tree with pre-order traversal

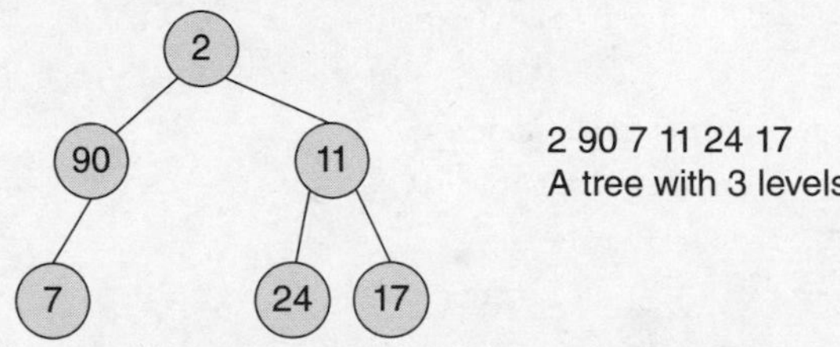

Figure 6.15 A sample tree with pre-order traversal

Python code 6.4

```
def postorder(n):
    if n.left != None:
        postorder(n.left)
    if n.right != None:
        postorder(n.right)
    print(n.value)
```

6.5.3 Post-order Traversal

In post-order traversal, the nodes' children are visited and then the node is visited. Putting it in clear terms, the left subtree is visited, then the right sub-tree is visited. Finally, the root is visited. A fact in this traversal is that for any tree, the root will be visited last. For the root to be visited, its left sub-tree and right sub-tree should have been visited. By then, the entire tree would have been traversed thus pushing the root to the last node to be visited. Figures 6.16 and 6.17 share post-order traversal of the same trees as discussed above (also refer to Python code 6.4).

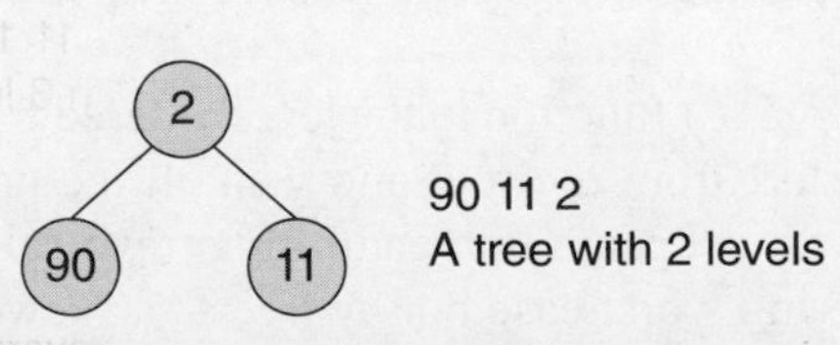

Figure 6.16 A sample tree with post-order traversal

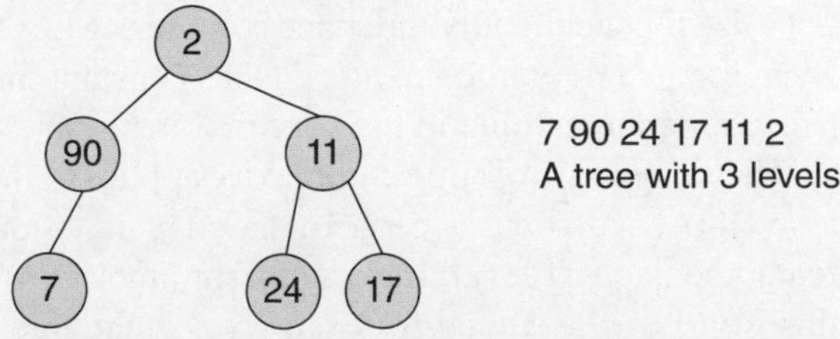

Figure 6.17 A sample tree with post-order traversal

6.5.4 Level-ordered Traversal

All the above three traversals are depth-first traversals, as they start from the root and reach a leaf. Then again move up to find other possible sub-trees and traverse to the other leaves one by one. This traversal is breadth-first traversal. Unlike the other traversal algorithms, this starts from the root and proceeds down level by level. First, the root are visited and then all the immediate children of the root are visited. Post-this, all the elements in 'level 2' are traversed and proceeds down till all the leaves are visited. Figure 6.18 shows a sample tree and its level-ordered traversal.

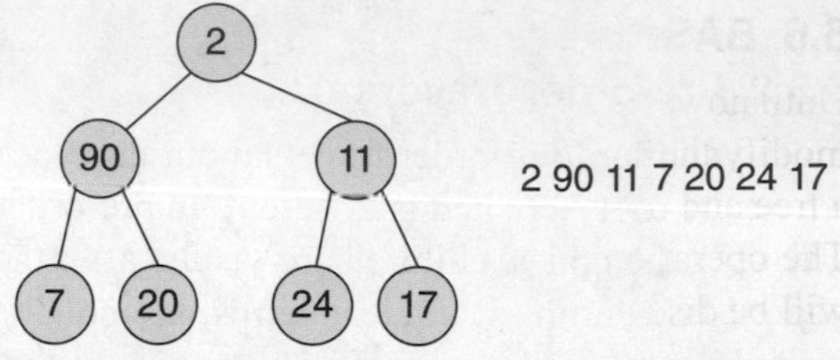

Figure 6.18 A sample tree with level-order traversal

Pseudocode 6.1

```
def  levelorder(tree)
    for i in tree.height
        printLevel(tree,i)

def printLevel(node, n)
    if tree is not null
        if n =1
            print(node-> value)
        else
            printLevel(node-> left, n-1)
            printLevel(node-> right, n-1)
```

In Pseudocode 6.1, the `printLevel()`, function starts from the root and moves to the nth level and print it. Every single element in the level is reached separately starting from the root. The last part of the `printLevel()` function has an iterator to recursively call the function for all the children of the current node.

Complexity Analysis of Traversal Algorithms

The general complexity of depth-first traversals for a binary tree is 'O(n)' as it has to visit all the nodes and complexity for reading every node is 'O(1)' summing up to 'O(n)' for 'n' nodes. Technically, the recursive algorithm can have a maximum of 'n' iterations arriving at the same complexity. As it is a recursive algorithm, it explicitly does not use any space. Thus, the space complexity is 'O(1)'. Far from that, it can be argued stating the system stack will be used for recursion and thus space complexity is 'O(n)'. Still, technically the space complexity is 'O(1)'. The time complexity has some exceptional cases. Even for an empty tree, traversal takes constant time 'O(1)', as the algorithm checks for the pointers and tries to point the value in the very first iteration.

The same logic of time complexity applies to the `printLevel()` function in the level ordered traversal as well. At worst case the `printLevel()` function has to start from the root and visit all the nodes to reach the deepest level, making its runtime 'O(n)'. However, the catch in breadth-first traversal is that this printLevel is called for each level in the tree. Considering worst case binary tree as a skewed tree with 'n' levels, the total complexity of level-ordered traversal makes up to 'O(n * n)' which is '$O(n^2)$'.

Euler tour of a tree visits all the nodes like drawing a border outside the tree. Explore Euler tour for a tree!

6.6 BASIC OPERATIONS

Until now, we have been seeing how to store a tree and traversing a stored tree. However, how to build or modify the tree hasn't been discussed. In here we discuss the basic operations like inserting a node into a tree and deleting a node from the same. These are applicable for not just binary trees, but for any tree. The operations specified in here can be dealt in multiple ways. Some common logic for the operations will be discussed in here.

6.6.1 Inserting a Node

A node can be inserted into a tree provided the parent node is available and it is known if that node will be the left or right child. There can be multiple cases. The parent node, for which the new node has to be added, may have a child or may not. Each case is considered separately and discussed in here.

Consider the parent doesn't have a right child and the new node has to be added as the right child for the node. This is straight forward and requires no additional effort. Consider the tree in Figure 6.19 and insert a value '7' as left child for node '11'.

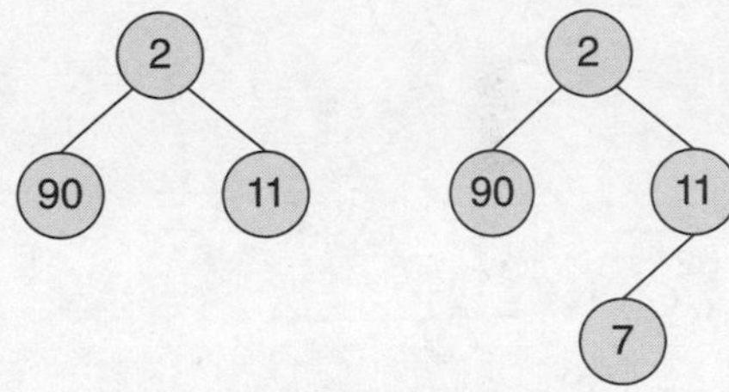

Figure 6.19 Inserting a node into a parent without child

Now, assume the same case, inserting '7' as left child for '11', but for the tree in Figure 6.20, where there is already a left child. Now, there is a conflict. Here, it can be treated in different ways. One commonplace method is adding the new node as the left child and moving the existing left child as the left child of the new node. This can be clearly understood from the figure.

Handling such a situation is purely based on the developer or conditions required. Say, instead of making '9' as left child of '7', it can also be made as right child of '7' which is not incorrect. It all depends on the conditions and requirements. If the tree was a complete binary tree, then the above method might break the property. Instead, the new node can be put in place of '9' and the node '9' can be moved to a new leaf in the last level. This method is just an attempt to hold the completeness of the tree. Again, the correctness of the solution purely depends on the scenario. Chapter 7 has a wide range of binary trees with constraints, where the insertion will be defined in a rigid way, in compliance with the constraints.

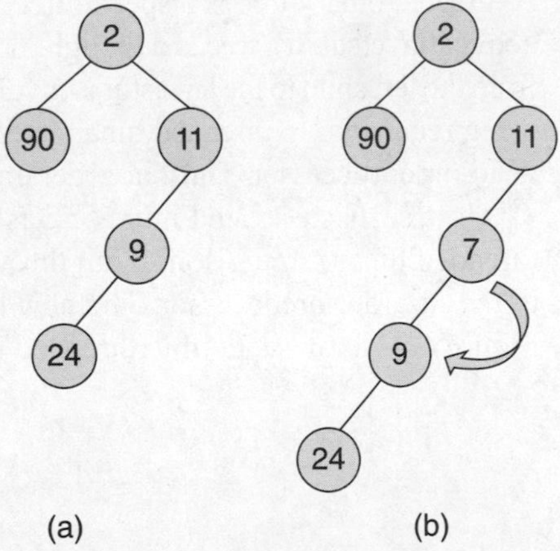

Figure 6.20 Inserting a node into a parent with child

6.6.2 Deleting a Node

A node can be deleted from a tree directly, without any additional requirement. The node to be deleted may or may not have children. Based on the same, the solution varies. If the node to be deleted is a leaf, then there is no thought to be put in there, it is straightaway deleted. If the node to be deleted has a left or right sub-tree, then the child is moved to the place of the current node which is represented in Figures 6.21 and 6.22.

The logic holds well when the node to be deleted has only one sub-tree. When the node has both the sub-trees, there is the pitfall of the logic. Which child will be moved to the place of its parent? What will happen to the other sub-tree? This can be handled in multiple ways. The sub-tree can be made as a sub-tree to any of the leaves. Else, if there is a descendent, to the node that moved to the parent's place, with only one child, the remaining sub-tree will be moved as a child to that node. Again, it all depends on the requirement. All these confusions will be solved when some more constraint is applied on the tree, which can be seen in the upcoming chapters.

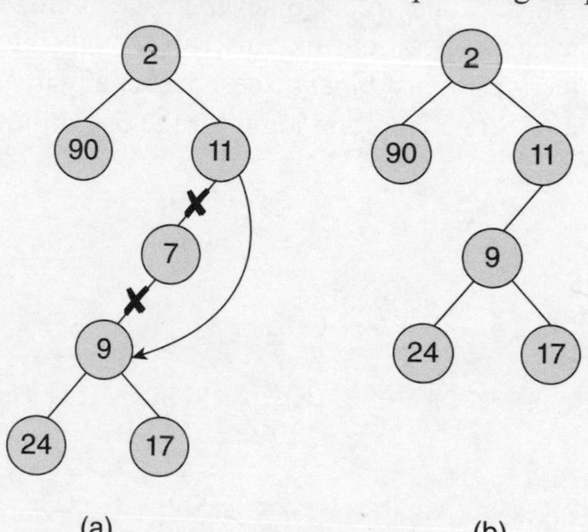

Figure 6.21 Deleting a node with one sub-tree

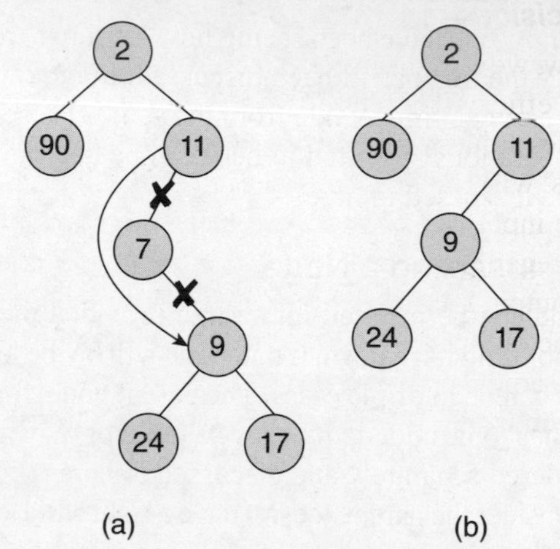

Figure 6.22 Deleting a node with one sub-tree from a little more complex tree using the same logic

6.7 THREADED BINARY TREES

A threated binary tree is a special tree. It is a typical binary tree with some additional pointers. As we saw above, traversal in a tree is a thought provoking process. Consider in-order traversal where we see a motion from the left child to the ancestor is involved. There is no pointer for that movement and the same was achieved using recursion. In threaded binary trees, all the nodes whose right child pointer is null is made to point to its in-order successor. Thus, in-order traversal is made easy. Figure 6.23 shows a single threaded binary tree.

The tree discussed in Figure 6.23 is a single threaded binary tree. Another variant of the same is double threaded binary tree. Along with the above threads, here when the left pointer is null it is made to point to the in-order predecessor. The new threads help in reverse in-order traversal and post-order traversal. Figure 6.24 shows a double threaded binary tree.

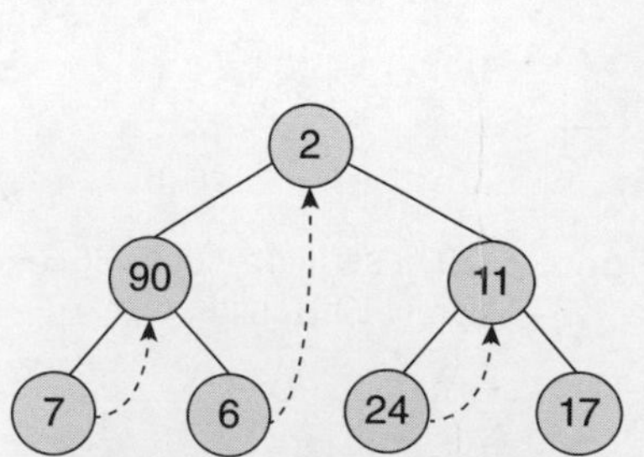

Figure 6.23 Threaded binary tree

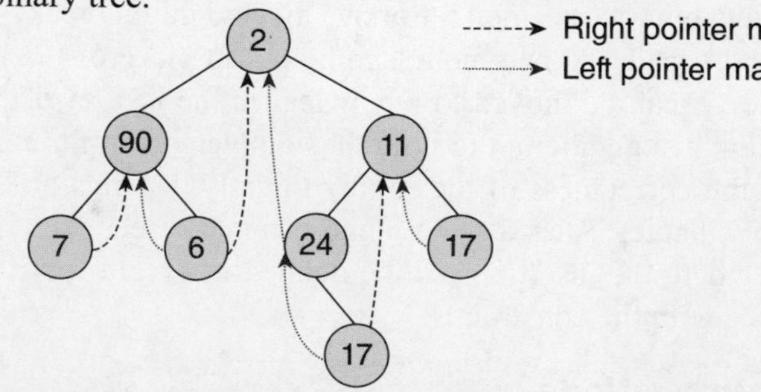

Figure 6.24 Double threaded binary tree

Can you find out one very frequently used application with threaded binary tree?

6.8 APPLICATIONS OF TREES

Binary trees can have numerous applications. The most important application of binary trees is storing and managing data (files as well). Other than storing files, trees can be used to represent any real world data that naturally has a hierarchy in it. Say, a family tree can be maintained easily using a tree data structure.

Decision Tree in Machine Learning

Now, we will discuss an interesting application of binary tree. In machine learning, there is an important and efficient model called decision tree. A decision tree is a tree that is built based on questions. At every node, a question is asked based on the features. The answer of the question will be a 'yes' or 'no'—'yes' will lead to a sub-tree and 'no' will lead to a sub-tree. In the next nodes, questioning will continue. The input has a set of features and an output variable for few records. The goal of building the tree is segregating the records based on output variable. As the tree is being built, in every level the mixture of output variables in the node will reduce. The process is stopped when a node has all records with same output variable and this becomes a leaf. Figure 6.25 has a sample data set and a decision tree for the same. What question to be asked at any node is decided by the algorithm used for building the tree, which is out of scope of this book.

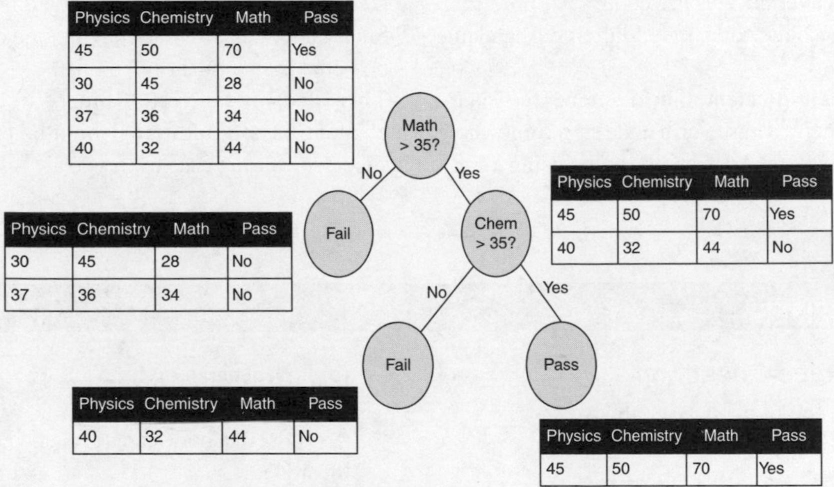

Figure 6.25 Sample data and a decision tree

KEY POINTS TO REMEMBER

- Data structures may not necessarily be linear.
- Non-linear data structures are implemented using pointers.
- 'Tree' is a hierarchical data structure, which can easily represent parent child relationship.
- A 'Binary' tree is a type of tree where a parent can have at most two child nodes.
- A 'Binary' tree can have further constraints improving efficiency in data handling.
- Traversal operation in trees is very important and involves different logics. The order of visiting differs in three ways, in-order, pre-order, and post-order traversal.
- Basic operations in a tree are insertion and deletion of a node and searching a node.

Key Terms

Hierarchical data structure A data structure that has the capability of representing a hierarchical representation among its elements. The relationship is a one-to-many relationship represented in different levels.

Tree A primary hierarchical data structure which has a root element at level 1 and has children/descendants in consecutive levels. There will not be a direct path from a descendant to root.

Binary tree A tree where any node can have a maximum of two child nodes only.

In-order traversal Traversal is an algorithm to logically visit all the nodes in the tree. In-order traversal first visits the left child and then the root and finally visits the right child of the node.

Pre-order traversal Here the node is visited first and then the children/descendants are visited.

Post-order traversal This is a contrast of pre-order. The node is visited after the children/descendants are visited.

Pointer based implementation of binary tree Binary tree is implemented based on a node structure, where every node is associated to another node using a child pointer.

Array based implementation of binary tree Simple representation of a tree in an array with a basic formula for associating an element at an index with another element as child.

Linked List based implementation of binary tree The same logic of representing binary trees in a linear fashion, but in a linked list.

Full binary tree A binary tree with all nodes having two or no children.

Complete binary tree A full binary tree with all levels other than the last level filled.

Perfect binary tree A full binary tree with all levels filled.

Balanced binary tree A binary tree where the absolute difference between the height of the left sub-tree and height of the right sub-tree is one or zero.

Degenerate binary tree/Skewed binary tree A binary tree with all nodes having one child only. It is no better than a linear linked list.

Threaded binary tree A binary tree where every element has an additional pointer to the in-order successor for the ease of traversal.

Exercises

Multiple-choice Questions

1. A node at top of the tree is called ________.
   (a) Sibling (b) Parent
   (c) Root (d) Leaf
2. A node without children is called ________.
   (a) Sibling (b) Parent
   (c) Root (d) Leaf
3. A node's parent can be reached directly from the node.
   (a) True (b) False
4. A threaded binary tree uses more space than the normal binary tree
   (a) True (b) False
5. What is a tree, in which all the nodes have only one child node, called?
   (a) Skewed tree
   (b) Linked list
   (c) Degenerate tree
   (d) All of the above
6. A sibling of a node can be reached directly from the node.
   (a) True (b) False
7. A perfect binary tree is always____________.
   (a) Degenerate (b) Balanced
   (c) Full (d) All of the above
8. Pick the odd one out.
   (a) In-order traversal
   (b) Level-order traversal
   (c) Pre-order traversal
   (d) Post-order traversal
9. _________ is the maximum number of levels in a perfect binary tree.
   (a) O(n) (b) $O(n^2)$
   (c) O(log n) (d) Cannot be computed

10. In a threaded binary tree, can there be a path to the sibling of a node?
(a) Yes (b) No

Theoretical Review Questions

1. Explain a data structure that represents a hierarchical relationship.
2. Graphically represent a tree data structure and mark all the parts of it and define the same briefly.
3. What are the different forms of trees? Explain with illustration.
4. Write a brief on threaded binary trees.
5. Why is tree traversal significant? What are the various traversal algorithms?

Exploratory Application Exercises

1. Given the in-order and post-order traversal, construct a binary tree? Write a Python code for the same.
In-order : 103 37 11 94 6 16 28 40 15 21
Post-order : 103 11 37 94 16 40 28 21 15 6
2. Given 'n' how many different binary trees can be formed with 'n' nodes provided all the nodes are same?
Example: If 'n' is 3, 5 different trees can be formed. The same is shared below.

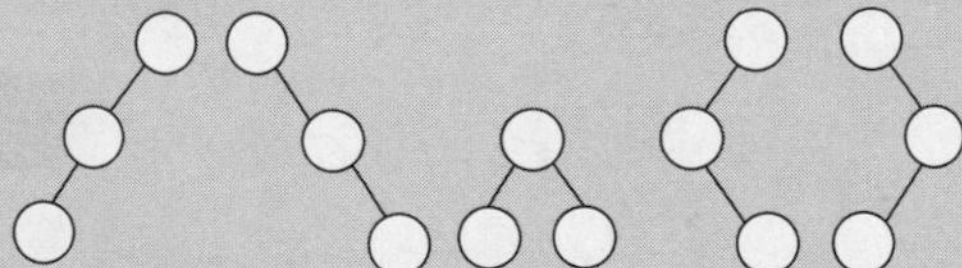

This is called Enumeration of binary trees. Write a Python code to compute the enumeration for any given 'n'.
3. Given a mathematical equation as string, write a code to construct a tree for easy evaluation of same.
Example : 'a+b*c' is represented as,

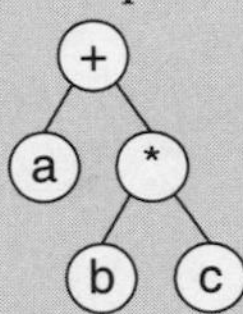

4. Write a code to evaluate a given expression tree and return the result.
5. A binary tree is a foldable tree if the right and left subtree of the root are mirror images structurally. Write a code to find if a given tree is foldable.

Foldable tree

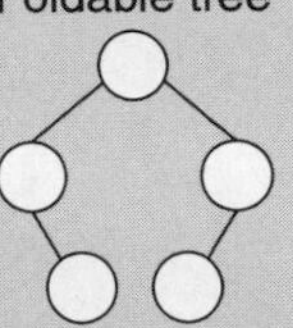

Non-foldable tree

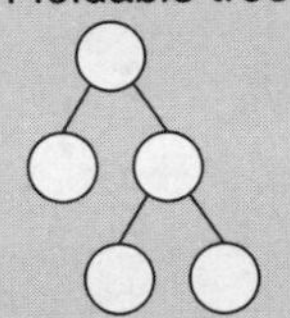

Foldable trees are also called symmetric binary trees.
6. Write a code to find all root-to-leaf paths in a tree.
7. Write a code to find the level-ordered traversal of a binary tree. Example,

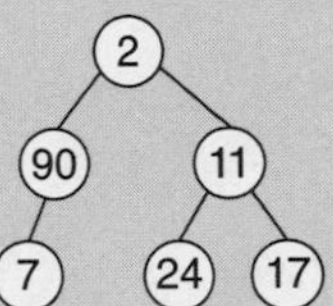

Level Order: 2 90 11 7 24 17
8. Given two nodes in a tree, write a code to find the lowest common ancestor of the node.
Example: In the tree given in above question, lowest common ancestor of nodes '7' and '24' is '2' and lowest common ancestor of '24' and '17' is '11'.
9. Given a tree, write a code to find the minimum of difference between a node and any of its descendants.
10. Write a code to find the top view of the tree.
Example: In top view, nodes in lower levels fall under the nodes in upper levels won't be visible.

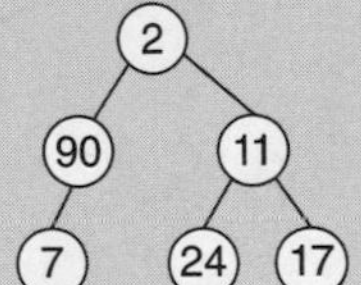

Top View: 7 90 2 11 17

Picto Puzzles

Identify logic for every question.

1.

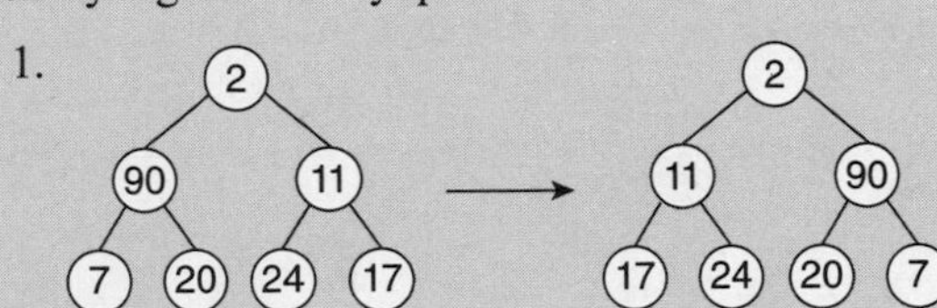

2.

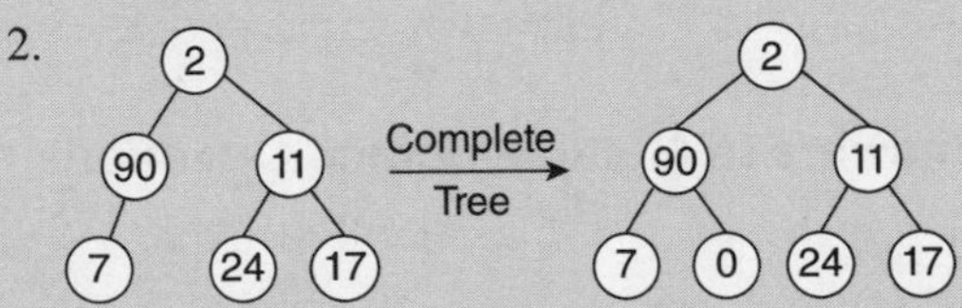

3.

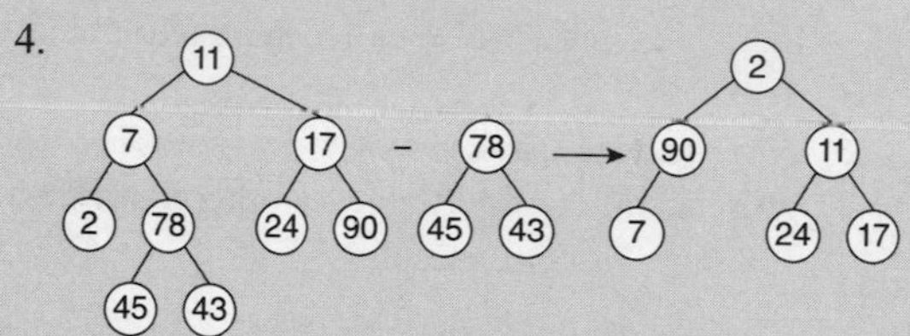

4.

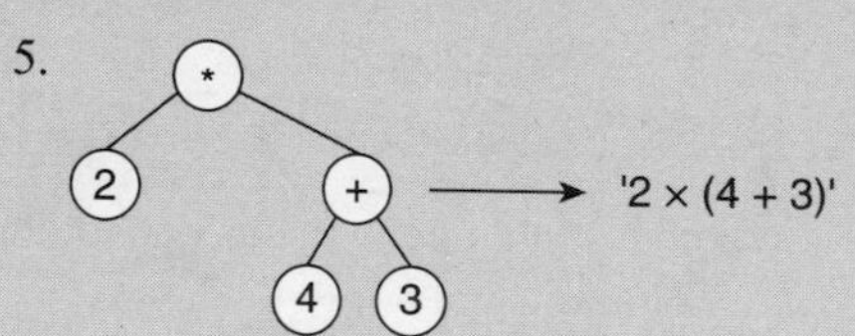

5.

*

2 +

4 3

'2 × (4 + 3)'

Mini Projects

1. Huffman encoding is an encryption technique. It is completely based on trees. Explore how Huffman encoding works and write Python code to execute encryption and decryption of a given text file. Also analyse the size of the encrypted file and decrypted file.
2. Create a tree to store numbers in a specific order. All the numbers to the left of a node should be lesser than or equal to the node and all the numbers in the right sub-tree should be greater than or equal to the node.
3. Create a tree to maintain a list of words efficiently. The root should point to all possible initial letters from the word list. Every alphabet's descendants will be all possible adjacent characters from the word list.

Answers to Multiple-choice Questions

1. (c) 2. (d) 3. (b) 4. (a) 5. (d) 6. (b) 7. (b) 8. (b) 9. (c)
10. (a)

Search Trees

LEARNING OBJECTIVES

After going through this chapter, readers will be able to understand:

- What is a search tree?
- Types of search trees and its advantages
- Search trees are not mandatorily binary.
- Self-modifying trees that change on adding or deleting elements
- Data handling can be made efficient using self-balancing trees.

7.1 INTRODUCTION

Trees are a generalized data structure which has the ability to represent hierarchical relationship. However, there is a gap in the logic of operation, such as when a node is deleted, it is unknown which child will take up the parent's place. These gaps can be potentially filled based on the additional constraints that will be applied to the generic tree data structure. These constraints are applied based on the application for which the tree is to be modified. This chapter deals with different binary tree structures along with their significance in the real world. Since each data structure has its own pros and cons, this chapter also deals with how the disadvantage of a particular data structure is overcome by its better version. The primary modification of binary trees is binary search trees, which applies an ordering constraint on the elements. The constraint helps in efficient searching of elements. The chapter will throw further light on this and similar data structures and their significance.

7.2 BINARY SEARCH TREES

A binary search tree (BST) is a meek binary tree unlike the complete or full binary tree, with a different constraint. In this case, a parent should always be greater than the left child and lesser than the right child. From the root's perspective, all the nodes in the left subtree will be lesser than the root and all the nodes in the right sub-tree will be greater than the root. Putting the constraint in actual words, the in-order traversal of the binary tree will be in ascending tree. A sample binary search tree is shown in Figure 7.1.

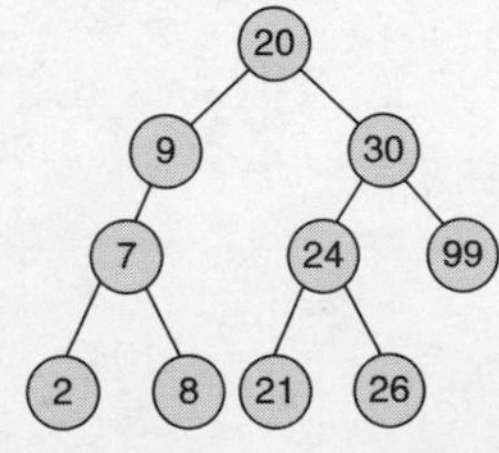

Figure 7.1 Binary search tree

All the search trees are built for storing and retrieving data efficiently. Given a chunk of data, a tree is built using the insert node operation. The basic operations are inserting a node, deleting a node, and searching for a given node.

For better understanding, first, we will deal with searching for a node in a binary search tree and then move into insertion and deletion operations.

Food for Brain

Provided the in-order traversal of the binary search tree will be in ascending order, how will the tree treat duplicate elements while building the tree?

7.2.1 Operation—Search Value

Given a value, the function finds if the value is present in the tree. The value of root is compared with the required element. If the element is smaller, the left sub-tree is to be checked. If the element is greater than the root, then the right sub-tree is to be checked. If the root is the required element, the same value is returned. The same is to be continued below. If a leaf is reached and the value in the node is not the required value, then '-1' is returned, implying the value does not exist (refer to Pseudocode 7.1).

Question 7.1 Search '5' in the binary search tree given in Figure 7.1.

Solution: Search begins with the root. Since '20' is greater than the required value, '5', the left sub-tree is considered. In next iteration, the node is '9'. Node '9' is greater than '5', henceforth, the left sub-tree is considered again. The next node is '7'. Node '7' is greater than '5' and the left sub-tree is taken to the next iteration. Now, the node is '2'. Node '2' is lesser than '5'. The right sub-tree of node '2' is checked and it is 'null'. Thus, the value is not present and returns '-1'. The node and sub-tree considered at each iteration are shared in Figure 7.2.

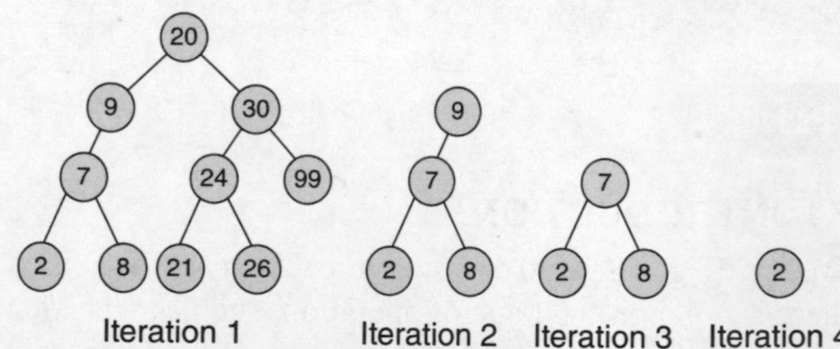

Figure 7.2 Searching a node in a BST

Pseudocode 7.1

```
def search(node, value)
    if node = value
    then,
        return node
    else if node > value
    then,
        if node.left is not null
        then,
            Search in left subtree
    else if node < value
    then,
        if node.right is not null
        then,
            Search in right sub-tree
    else,
        return -1
```

7.2.2 Operation—Insert a Node

In a typical binary search tree, insertion is always in as a leaf. Given a value, it is compared with each node and placed as a leaf at a suitable position. The algorithm is similar to search algorithm, where the leaf with a value closest to the new value is searched and then the new node is inserted as a child to that leaf, making the new node a leaf. The new value is compared with the root. If the root is greater than the value, the left sub-tree is considered, else the right sub-tree is considered. The process is continued until a leaf is reached. Now, the new node is added as a child to that leaf. The new node becomes the left child of the leaf, if the node's value is greater than the new value, else the new node gets added as the right child to that leaf (refer to Pseudocode 7.2). The function must be called with the root.

Question 7.2 Insert a value '25' in the BST shown in Figure 7.1.

Solution:

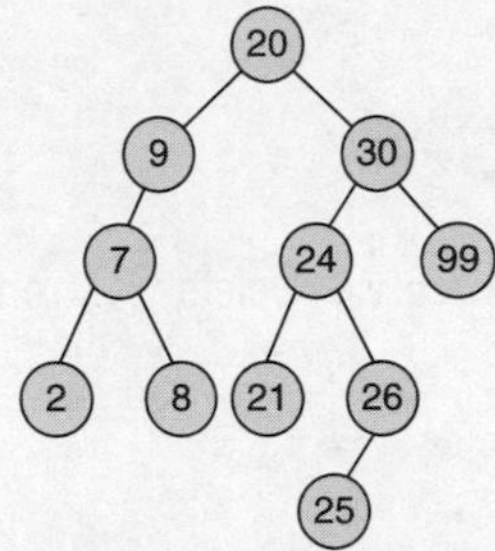

Figure 7.3 Inserting '25'

Question 7.3 Insert a value '20' in the BST shown in Figure 7.3.

Solution:

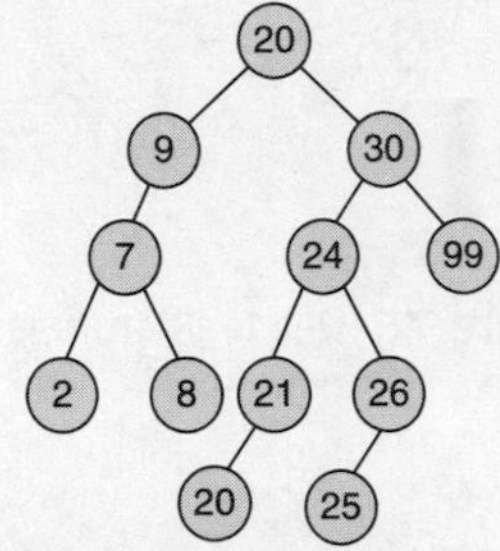

Figure 7.4 Inserting '20'

Pseudocode 7.2

```
def insert(node, value):
    if node is not null
    then,
        if node > value
        then,
            Insert value in the left sub-tree
        else if node < value
        then,
            Insert value in the right sub-tree
    else,
        insert value into node
    return node
```

Food for Brain

What will happen to a BST when the nodes are inserted in ascending or descending order?

7.2.3 Operation—Delete a Node

Compared to insertion, deletion is a complex operation. Deleting a node will collapse the constraint of a BST. Deletion may have more than one possible case.

Case 1 If the node is a leaf, it can be deleted straightaway without any additional work.

Case 2 If the node to be deleted has only one sub-tree, then the corresponding child is moved up to its parent's position.

Case 3 The above two cases are predictable and far from that is the third case. When the node to be deleted has both the sub-trees, then it is replaced with its in-order successor. This should pave way for a doubt - 'When the in-order successor comes as a replacement, what will happen to its place?' There will be a vacancy created in its space. This vacancy, in turn, is treated as a deleted node and the above procedure is repeated considering all the three cases.

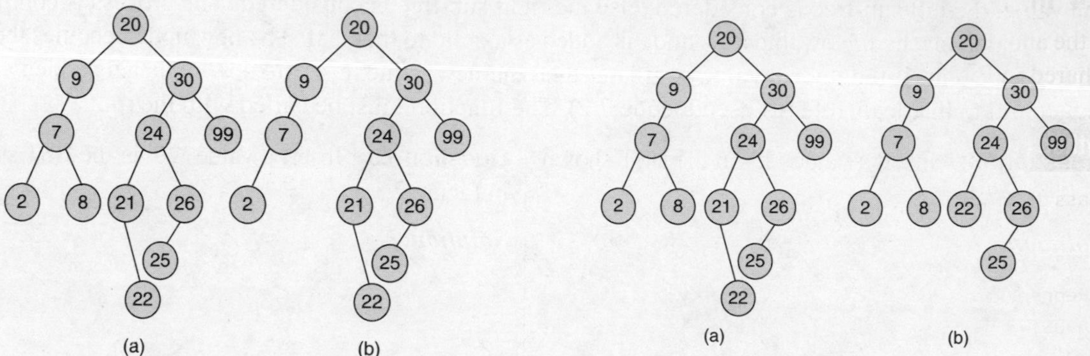

Figure 7.5 Delete '8' from left tree

Figure 7.6 Delete '21' from left tree

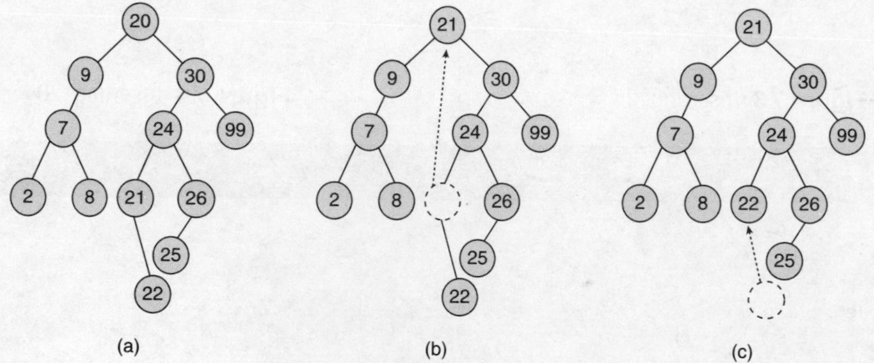

Figure 7.7 Delete '20' from left tree

Figures 7.5, 7.6, and 7.7 are examples for all the three cases, respectively. In Figure 7.7, '20' is replaced with its in-order successor '21' which creates a cavity as shown in Figure 7.7 (b). This new cavity is filled with the corresponding right child of the node as shown in Figure 7.7 (c). Pseudocode 7.3 explains the process.

Pseudocode 7.3

```
def delete(value):
    n=search(value)
    if n.left is null
    then,
        move the right child to parent position
    else if n.right is null
    then,
        move the left child to parent position
    else,
        move the in-order_successor(n) to 'n' position
    return n
```

Food for Brain

Develop a function to identify the minimum and maximum element from a BST.

7.2.4 Implementation of Binary Search Trees

All the above features are implemented as a class with a node class for representing each node. The same is shared in Python code 7.1.

Python code 7.1

```
class Node(object):

  """
  Represents a node in a Binary Search Tree (BST).
  A BST is a tree data structure where each node has at most two children.

  For a Binary Tree to be called BST:
    (i) The value of nodes on the left of root should be less than or equal to the value at
        root.
    (ii) The value of nodes on the right should be greater than the value at the root.

  Parameters
  ----------
     key : int
          The value of a node in the tree (Left or right of the root node)
   """

    def __init__(self,key):
        self.key = key
        self.left = None
        self.right = None

def insert(node, key):

    """
    Inserts node to the BST.

    Parameters
    ----------
      node: int or str
          The placeholder in the tree that holds a key
      key : int
          The value of a node in the tree (Left or right of the root node)
    """

    # If the tree is empty, return a single node (root), with value key
    if node is None:
        return Node(key)
    """
```

(*contd*)

(*contd*)

```
    If value of node is greater than the value to be inserted, then if left is empty, insert it
    to the left, else use recursion, to insert it.
    """
    if node.key is not None:
        if node.key > key:
            if node.left is None:
                node.left = Node(key)
            else:
                node.left = insert(node.left, key)
    """
    If value of node is less than the value to be inserted, then if right is empty, insert it
    to the right, else use recursion, to insert it
    """
        elif node.key < key:
            if node.right is None:
                node.right=Node(key)
            else:
                node.right = insert(node.right, key)
    else:
        node.key = key
    return node
def search(node, key, parent=None):

    """
    Searches for a node in the BST.

    Parameters
    ----------
      node: int or str
          The root of the tree
      key : int
          The value to be searched for
      parent : None
          The parent of a node. Default value of parent is None
    """

    # If key is found at root node, return root
    if node.key == key:
        return node, parent

    """
    If a node's value is greater than the value to be searched, or in other words, if the value
    to be searched for is less than a node's value, then go left. If left node is not empty,
    repeat the same process recursively, until a match is found.
    """
    elif node.key > key:
        if node.left is None:
            return None, None
        else:
            return search(node.left, key, parent = node.key)
```

(*contd*)

(*contd*)

```
    """
    If a node's value is less than the value to be searched, or in other words, if the value to
    be searched for is greater than a node's value, then go right. If right node is not empty,
    repeat the same process recursively, until a match is found.
    """
        elif node.key < key:
        if node.right is None:
            return None, None
        else:
            return search(node.right, key, parent = node.key)
    else:
        return node, parent

def minimum(node):
    """
    Returns the minimum of two children nodes.

    Parameters
    ----------
      node: int or str
          The root of the tree
    """
    while node.left is not None:
         node = node.left
    return node

def delete(node, key):

    """
    Deletes a node in the BST.
    To delete a node, you change the value in that node to None and remove its parent node link
    to this node (left or right).
    After the deletion, the tree should be a BST

    Parameters
    ----------
      node: int or str
          The root of the tree
      key : int
          The value to be deleted from the tree
    """

    # If node is empty, return empty node
    if node is None:
        return node
    if node.key > key:
        node.left = delete(node.left, key)
    elif node.key < key:
        node.right = delete(node.right, key)
    else:
```

(*contd*)

(*contd*)

```
        # If left node is empty, make its parent node none and return right node.
        if node.left is None:
            node = None
            return node.right

        # If left node is empty, make its parent node none and return right node.
        elif node.right is None:
            node = None
            return node.left

        # When deleting a node with 2 children, find the minimum from the two sub-trees and
        # return it as the left node.
        temp = minimum(node.right)
        node.key = temp.key

        #Delete value from right subtree
        node.right = delete(node.right, temp.key)
    return node
```

7.2.5 Complexity Analysis

Searching of a node in a binary tree has an average case of 'O(log n)', as at each step of recursion either only the left or right sub-tree is considered. However, consider a skewed BST where all the nodes are inserted in a descending order. Here, searching is literally a linear traversal on a linked list. Hence, the worst case complexity of searching is 'O(n)'. In case of the insertion operation, the complexity of finding the closest leaf makes up to 'O(n)' and creating the child is 'O(1)'. Putting it together, 'O(n) + O(1)' gives 'O(n)' complexity to insertion. The deletion process has its own complexity too. The first two cases in case of deletion are simple and have a complexity of 'O(1)'. The third case involves finding the in-order successor, copying it to the current position, and finally deleting the in-order successor. The process of finding the in-order successor has a complexity of 'O(n)' for a skewed BST. The deletion of the in-order successor is the catch here. It again has three cases and the process is repeated. However, the complexity of deleting the in-order successor is less than the process of finding it and is mostly constant, as it mostly falls into case 1 or case 2. Summing up the complexities, 'O(n) + O(1)', gives 'O(n)' in total for the deletion operation. None of the above operations use long memory spaces. Only some temporary buffer variable is used. Thus, they all have a auxiliary space complexity of 'O(1)'.

Food for Brain

How many recursive calls will it take to delete a root from a skewed binary tree with 'n' nodes? Which type of BST will have the worst case complexity while deleting the node?

7.3 AVL TREES

A binary search tree is a very good application of binary trees for efficient data handling. Despite dividing and storing data based on constraints, the complexity of all the operations still relies on 'n', that is, the number of elements stored. Which is the worst case complexities are all for skewed binary search trees.

To overcome this constraint, AVL trees were invented. It was invented by Adelson-Velskii and Landis and hence named with their initial letters. AVL trees are also called as self-balanced trees. The speciality of AVL trees is that the difference between the heights of the left and right sub-trees of any node is a maximum of '1'. Along with it, the previous constraint of BST also holds in here. This implies that the in-order traversal of an AVL tree will also be in ascending order. The act of balancing is done using the process of rotation. If the balance of the tree is lost while insertion or deletion or any node, then rotation is performed to gain the balance back. This will be discussed in detail in the corresponding sections.

7.3.1 Operation—Search Value

For searching, the same algorithm is used as discussed in case of a BST. Searching does not involve editing any node in the tree. So, the algorithm is still the same. Searching is done based on the original constraint of BST that the left child is less than the root and the right child is greater than the tree.

Rotation

Rotation is a sub-process. It takes place in both insertion and deletion operations. It is the act of balancing the height of a node in an AVL tree. Every time a node is modified in a tree, there is a possibility that the balance of the tree is lost. The change in balance may not mandatorily be in the point where the node was modified. The issue could arise in the ancestor of the node but not at the node which is not related to the modified node. First, the node which is not balanced is found. This is done by checking the height of sub-trees of every node and comparing them to see if the difference of their heights is greater than '1'. This comparison for checking imbalance in any node is done from the nodes in the lowermost level to the nodes in the higher levels. This order is vital because if a node is imbalanced, then all its ancestors are imbalanced as well. So, finding the lowest node which has the imbalance is the key part. Next, the path from the modified node to the lowest imbalanced node is considered. Assume 'x' is the lowest node which is imbalanced. Let 'y' be the child of 'x' on the imbalanced path from 'x' to a leaf and let 'z' be the grandchild of 'x' on the same path. Now, 'x', 'y', and 'z' can be arranged in four different ways as follows.

1. Right-Right case: 'y' is the right child of 'x' and 'z' is the right child of 'y'
2. Right-Left case: 'y' is the right child of 'x' and 'z' is the left child of 'y'
3. Left-Right case: 'y' is the left child of 'x' and 'z' is the right child of 'y'
4. Left-Left case: 'y' is the left child of 'x' and 'z' is the left child of 'y'

Each of the above case needs to be handled separately for balancing at the point 'x'.

Can there be a situation when an imbalanced node 'x' doesn't have a child 'y' or a grandchild 'z'?

Before getting into detail on how they are handled, we will discuss the two types of rotations. They are the left rotation and the right rotation. Rotation is based on a pivotal node. The pivotal node is the point of imbalance.

Left Rotation In left rotation, the pivot becomes the left child of its actual right child. However, what if there was already one left child to its actual right child. The existing left child becomes the right child of pivot after rotation. Left rotation for both the cases is depicted clearly in Figures 7.8 and 7.9.

The left tree is the initial tree and the right tree is the final tree after rotation in each figure, respectively.

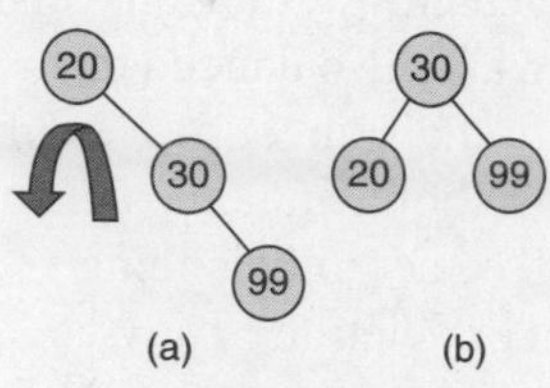

Figure 7.8 Left rotation at a node in which the right child doesn't have a left child

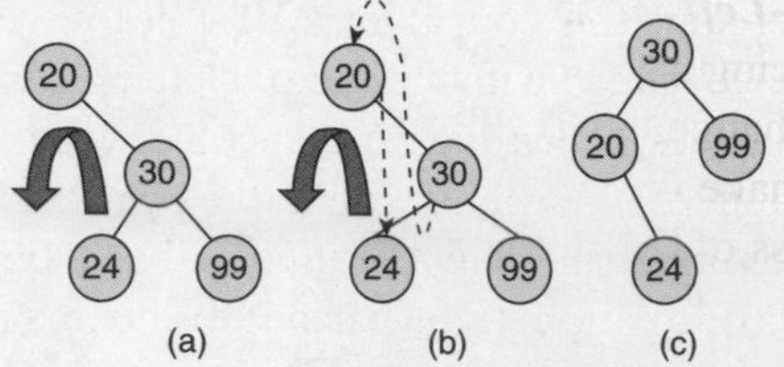

Figure 7.9 Left rotation at a node in which the right child has a left child

Right Rotation Given left rotation, right rotation becomes predictable. Here, the pivot becomes the right child of its actual left child. If the actual left child already had a right child for itself, then that right child becomes the left child for the pivot after rotation. Both the cases are depicted in Figures 7.10 and 7.11.

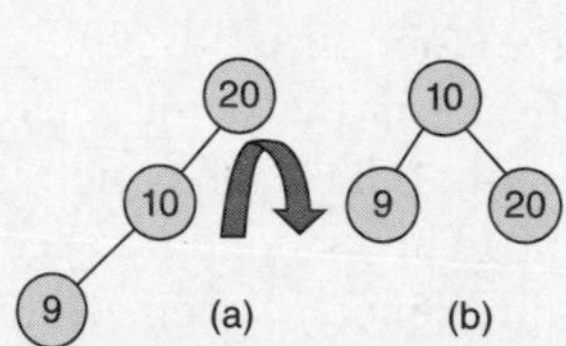

Figure 7.10 Right rotation at a node in which the left child doesn't have a right child

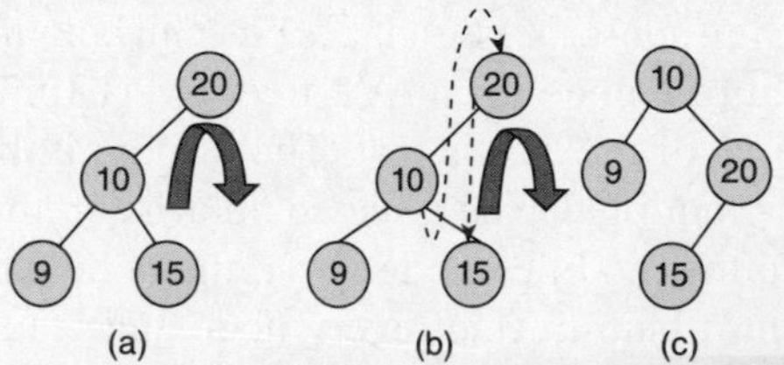

Figure 7.11 Right rotation at a node in which the left child has a right child

Food for Brain

What happens when the tree given below is left rotated with pivot 'x' and then right rotated with pivot 'y'?

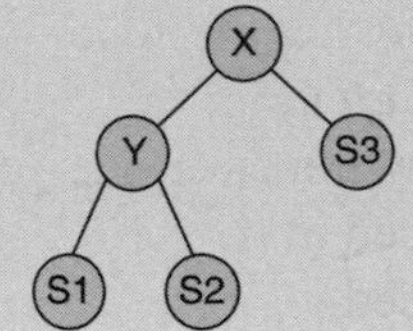

Now, the four cases of imbalance mentioned above will be discussed here.

Right-Right Case The right-right case is already discussed while explaining left rotation. A single left rotation balances the tree. Figure 7.12 has a tree which falls under the right-right case and shows how it is balanced.

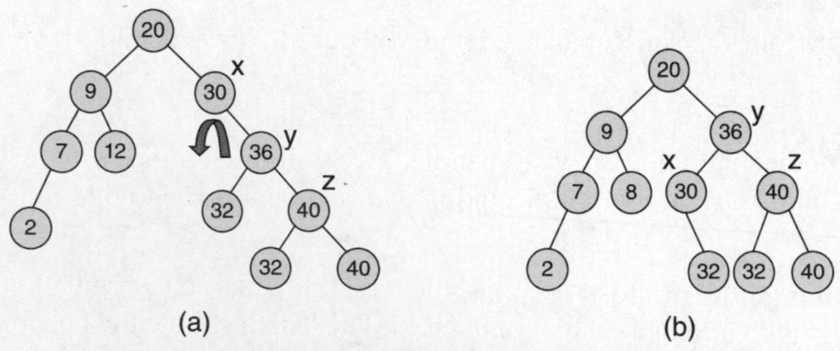

Figure 7.12 (a) A right-right unbalanced tree
(b) A balanced tree with left rotation at '30'

Right-Left Case Unlike the right-right case, the right-left case is a little complex. The process of balancing it results in two continuous rotations. First, a right rotation is performed with 'y' as pivot. This will change the tree from the right-left case to the right-right case. Now, a left rotation with 'x' as pivot will make the tree balanced. Figure 7.13 has a brief depiction of the right-left imbalanced tree and the process of balancing.

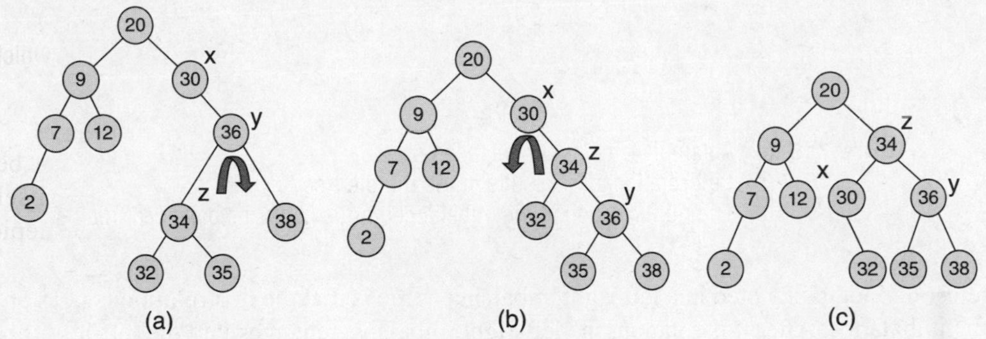

Figure 7.13 (a) A right-left imbalanced tree
(b) Result of first rotation
(c) A fully balanced tree after two rotations

Food for Brain

Why can't a right–left imbalanced tree be balanced by just one rotation?

Left-Left Case Just like the right-right case, the left-left case is also straight forward. This, in turn, was dealt while explaining the right rotation. A single right rotation at the imbalanced node makes the tree balanced in here. Figure 7.14 (a) shows a sample left-left imbalanced tree and Figure 7.14 (b) shows its balanced version.

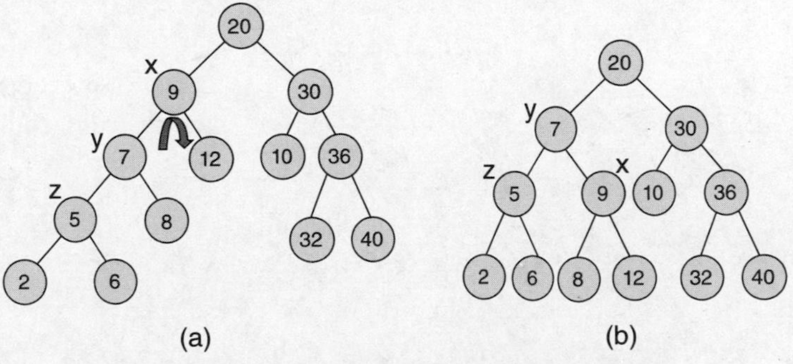

Figure 7.14 (a) A simple left-left imbalanced tree
(b) A balanced tree with the right rotation

Left-Right Case In line with the right-left case, here too, two rotations will balance the tree. First, a left rotation with 'y' as pivot is performed. This converts the left-right tree into the left-left tree. Finally, a right rotation pivoted at 'x' balances the tree. Figure 7.15 briefs up the balancing of a sample left-right tree.

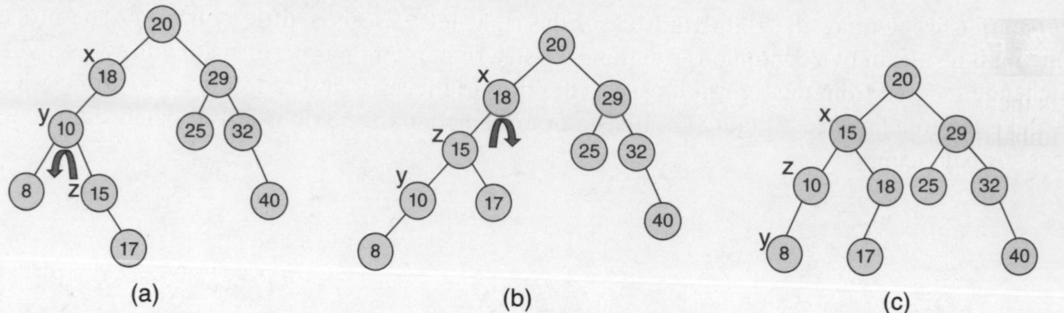

Figure 7.15 (a) A sample left-right imbalanced tree
(b) Left rotation at 'y' results in the middle tree
(c) The right rotation at the imbalanced node gives the balanced tree

An interesting fact to be noted in a left-right imbalanced tree is that the first rotation is not done at the point of the imbalance. After this rotation, the left-right imbalance changes into the left-left imbalance. A similar behaviour can be noticed in the right-left imbalanced tree as well. Pseudocode 7.5 shows the left and right rotation.

Pseudocode 7.5

```
def left_rotate(z):                  #        z                               y
    y = z.right                      #       / \                             / \
    T2 = y.left                      #     T1   y       Left Rotate(z)      z     x
    # Perform rotation               #         / \    --------------->    / \   / \
    y.left = z                       #       T2   x                      T1 T2 T3 T4
    z.right = T2                     #           / \
                                     #         T3    T4
    Update heights of z and y
    return y

def right_rotate(z):                 #        z                               y
    y = z.left                       #       / \                            /   \
    T3 = y.right                     #      y   T4      Right Rotate(z)    x     z
    # Perform rotation               #     / \        --------------->   / \   / \
    y.right = z                      #    x   T3                        T1  T2 T3  T4
    z.left = T3                      #   / \
                                     #  T1   T2
    Update heights of z and y
    return y

def update_height(node):
    if node is null
        then,
        return 0
    else
        return 1 + max (height(node.left) and height(node.right))
```

Is the tree shown below a right-left imbalanced tree or a right-right imbalanced tree?

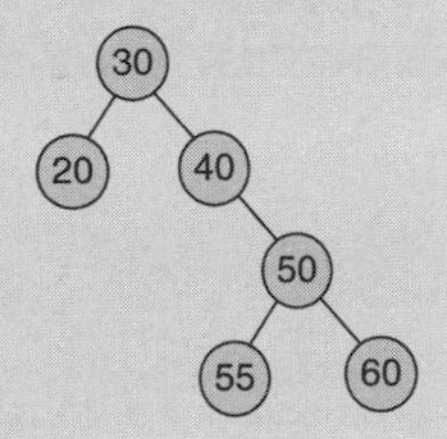

7.3.2 Operation—Insert a Node

In a BST, any node inserted is a leaf. In an AVL tree too, nodes are inserted as leaves. There is no change in the logic in which a node is to be inserted into the tree. After the new node is inserted, the balance of each node is checked from bottom until the root, as discussed earlier. This process ensures that the balance is checked only for the ancestors of the inserted node, as the other node's balance cannot be modified by the inserted node. In addition, this ensures that the lowest imbalanced node is found first. If there is an imbalance at a node, it is handled based on the four different cases discussed above. After the imbalance is fixed, there will be no more imbalances in the nodes in higher levels as the tree was already balanced before insertion. Thus, after insertion of every node, it is ensured that the balance of the tree is preserved. Figure 7.16 depicts a sample AVL tree and how insertion of a node modifies it. The pseudocode for insertion of a node in an AVL tree is shared below. One notable fact is insertion of a node may not mandatorily make the tree unbalanced. So, it is not mandatory for rotations to take place for every insertion operation. Pseudocode 7.6 shows Insertion of a node in a AVL tree.

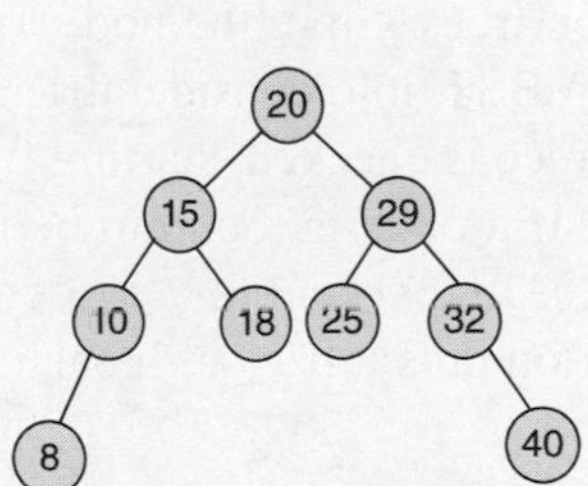

A sample tree in which a new value '9' is inserted

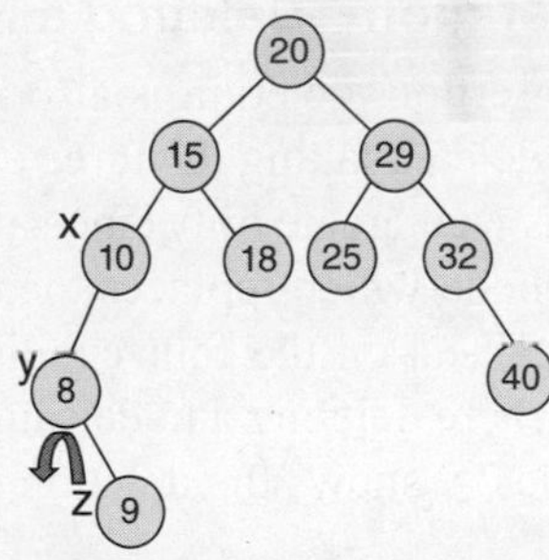

As a result of the insertion, there comes an imbalance which is of left-right case

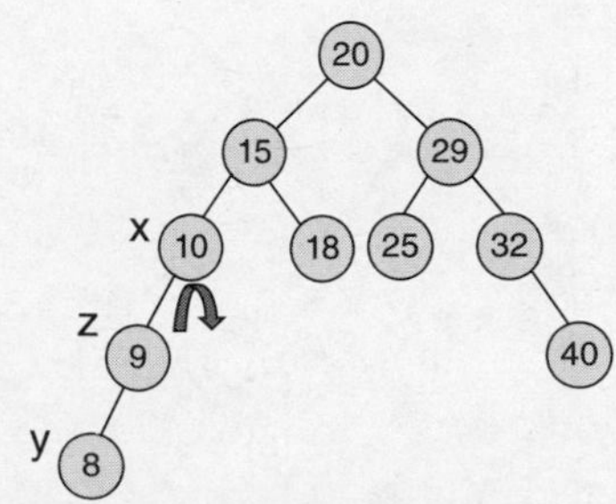

Imbalance is handled by left rotation at '8' followed by right rotation at '10'

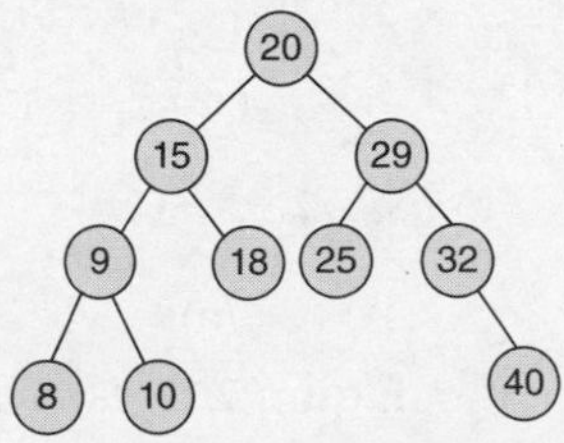

The final tree is a balanced AVL tree

Figure 7.16 Insertion process in an AVL tree

Pseudocode 7.6

```
def insert(node, value):
    Perform insert like BST
    Update_height(node)
    balance_factor = height(node.left)-height(node.right)
    if balance_factor > 1 and node.left > value
    then,
        return right_rotate(node)
    if balance_factor < -1 and node.right < value
    then,
        return left_rotate(node)
    if balance_factor > 1 and node.left < value
    then,
        node.left = left_rotate(node.left)
        return right_rotate(node)
    if balance_factor < -1 and node.right > value
    then,
        node.right = right_rotate(node.right)
        return left_rotate(node)
    return node
```

7.3.3 Operation—Deleting a Node

Just like insertion, deletion is also in line with the binary search trees. First, the node to be deleted is found and deleted taking the three cases of deletion, discussed in BST, into consideration. Deletion of a node can as well create imbalance at an ancestral node. The balance is checked, starting from the parent of the left node which replaces the deleted node, until the root. If a node is found to be imbalanced, it is handled based on the four conditions discussed in previous sections. Figure 7.17 depicts a sample AVL tree where deleting a node causes imbalance and then rotation puts it back as a balanced AVL tree. Pseudocode 7.7 shows the deletion process in an AVL tree.

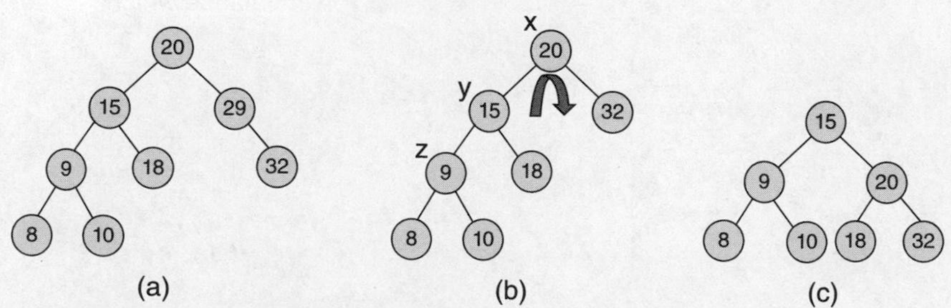

Figure 7.17 (a) A sample AVL tree where '29' is deleted
(b) Deletion results in a left-left imbalance
(c) A right rotation at '20' restores the balance of the AVL tree

Pseudocode 7.7

```
def delete(value):
    Perform standard BST delete
    #node - where the value was present and get the in-order successor
    balance_factor = height(node.right) - height(node.left)
    Based on balance_factor apply the same 4 cases of rotation as in insertion
    return root
```

7.3.4 Implementation of AVL Trees

The code for implementation of an AVL tree based on a node class is shared below (refer to Python code 7.2). The left rotation, right rotation, balance checking, and height calculation are all implemented as separate functions just to ensure reusability of the code.

Python code 7.2

```
class Node(object):
  """
  Represents a node in an AVL (Adelson-Velskii and Landis) Tree.
  An AVL tree is a BST. They are not perfectly balanced, but pairs of sub-trees differ in
  height by at most 1.

  For a BST to be an AVL tree,
    (i) The sub-trees of every node differ in height by at most one.
    (ii) Every sub-tree is an AVL tree.

  Parameters
  ----------
     key : int
          The value of a node in the tree (Left or right of the root node)
  """

  def __init__(self, key):
      self.key = key
      self.left = None
      self.right = None
      self.height = 1

class AVL(object):
  """
  Represents the AVL Tree class.

  Methods
  -------
     insert
          Inserting a value to the node

     left_rotate
          Rotate node to the left to balance the tree
```

(*contd*)

(*contd*)

```
    right_rotate
        Rotate node to the right to balance the tree

    delete
        Delete a node and rebalance the tree

    get_height
        Get the height of the tree

    update_height
        Update the height of the tree after rotation

    get_balance
        Get the balance factor

    minimum
        Get the minimum value between the trees
"""
def insert(self, node, key):
       # Step 1 - Perform normal BST
      if node is None:
          return Node(key)
      elif node.key > key:
          if node.left is None:
              node.left = Node(key)
          else:
              node.left = self.insert(node.left, key)
      elif node.key < key:
          if node.right is None:
              node.right = Node(key)
          else:
              node.right = self.insert(node.right, key)
      elif node.key is None:
          node.key = key

      # Step 2 - Update the height of parent
      if node.left is not None and node.right is not None:
          node.height = self.update_height(node)

      # Step 3 - Get the balance factor
          balance_factor = self.get_balance(node)

      # Step 4 - If node is unbalanced, try out the 4 cases
      # Case 1 - Left Left
          if balance_factor > 1 and node.left.key > key:
              return self.right_rotate(node)
```

(*contd*)

(*contd*)

```
    # Case 2 - Right Right
        if balance_factor < -1 and node.right.key < key:
            return self.left_rotate(node)

    # Case 3 - Left Right
        if balance_factor > 1 and node.left.key < key:
            node.left = self.left_rotate(node.left)
            return self.right_rotate(node)

    # Case 4 - Right Left
        if balance_factor < -1 and node.right.key > key:
            node.right = self.right_rotate(node.right)
            return self.left_rotate(node)
    return node
#T1, T2, T3, T4 subtrees of x, y, z

def left_rotate(self, z):          #          z                                          y
    y = z.right                    #         / \                                        /  \
    T2 = y.left                    #       T1    y          Left Rotate(z)             z     x
    # Perform rotation             #            / \       ----------------->          / \   / \
    y.left = z                     #          T2   x                                 T1  T2 T3  T4
    z.right = T2                   #              / \
                                   #            T3   T4

    # Update heights
    z.height = self.update_height(z)
    y.height = self.update_height(y)

    # Return new root
    return y

def right_rotate(self, z):     #          z                                         y
    y = z.left                 #         / \                                       /   \
    T3 = y.right               #        y    T4      Right Rotate(z)              x      z
                               #       / \         ----------------->            / \    / \
    # Perform rotation         #      x    T3                                  T1   T2 T3   T4
    y.right = z                #     / \
    z.left = T3                #   T1    T2

    # Update heights
    z.height = self.update_height(z)
    y.height = self.update_height(y)

    # Return new root
    return y

def delete(self, root, key):

    # Step 1 - Perform standard BST delete
```

(*contd*)

(*contd*)

```
        # If the tree has only one node, simply return it
        if root is None:
            return root

        elif root.key > key:
            root.left = self.delete(root.left, key)

        elif root.key < key:
            root.right = self.delete(root.right, key)

        else:
            if root.left is None:
                temp = root.right
                root = None
                return temp

            elif root.right is None:
                temp = root.left
                root = None
                return temp

            temp = self.minimum(root.right)
            root.key = temp.key
            root.right = self.delete(root.right,temp.key)

        # Step 2 - Update the height of the parent
        root.height = self.get_height(root)

        # Step 3 - Get the balance factor
        balance_factor = self.get_balance(root)

        # Step 4 - If node is unbalanced, then try out the 4 cases
        # Case 1 - Left Left
        if balance_factor  > 1 and self.get_balance(root.left) >= 0:
            return self.right_rotate(root)

        # Case 2 - Right Right
        if balance_factor  < -1 and self.get_balance(root.right) <= 0:
            return self.left_rotate(root)

        # Case 3 - Left Right
        if balance_factor  > 1 and self.get_balance(root.left) < 0:
            root.left = self.left_rotate(root.left)
            return self.right_rotate(root)

        # Case 4 - Right Left
        if balance_factor  < -1 and self.get_balance(root.right) > 0:
            root.right = self.right_rotate(root.right)
```

(*contd*)

(*contd*)

```
            return self.left_rotate(root)

        return root

    def get_height(self, root):
      #Get height of the Tree
        if root is not None:
            return 0
        return root.height

    def update_height(self, root):
      #Update height of the Tree after rotation
        if root is None:
            return 0
        else:
            return 1 + max(self.get_height(root.left), self.get_height(root.right))

    def get_balance(self, root):
      #Get the balance factor to check if it does not exceed 1
        if root is None:
            return 0
        else:
            return self.get_height(root.right) - self.get_height(root.left)

    def minimum(self, root):
      #Get the minimum value
        if root is None or root.left is None:
            return root
        return self.minimum(root.left)
```

7.3.5 Complexity Analysis

All the operations of the AVL tree discussed are just similar to that of the BST. However, the complexity of all these operations is far lesser than a BST. In a BST, all the operations were of complexity 'O(n)', whereas here, the complexity is 'O(log n)'. A search in an AVL tree is of complexity 'O(log n)', as the tree is always balanced. Complete traversal from first to last level takes a maximum time of only 'O(log n)'. The insertion and deletion processes have the complexity of 'O(log n)' as these are directly dependent on searching, just as explained in case of a BST. The rotation operations are all of constant time, 'O(1)', as they are straight forward. All the operations here are implemented in a recursive manner. The maximum number of recursions a function can take while searching is 'O(log n)', which is the maximum height of the tree.

7.4 RED—BLACK TREES*

An AVL tree has a good runtime for all the operations. It can efficiently manage data. However, one drawback in that method is that it involves lots of rotations. Nearly, every insertion or deletion triggers a rotation. Just to save some resources, red-black trees were devised. Red-Black trees are also self-balanced. It is not true that red-black trees do not involve rotations at all. It does involve rotations but only in some

* ▢ shows red nodes and ■ shows black nodes in Red-Black trees.

cases. Along with the constraints of BST and AVL trees, there are new additional constraints in here. All the constraints of the red-black trees are discussed below.

1. The parent node must be greater than the left child and lesser than the right child
2. A node can only either be in red or black colour
3. The root should always be a black node
4. A null node is considered black
5. A parent or child of a red node cannot be a red node
6. Every root-to-leaf path should have the same number of black nodes

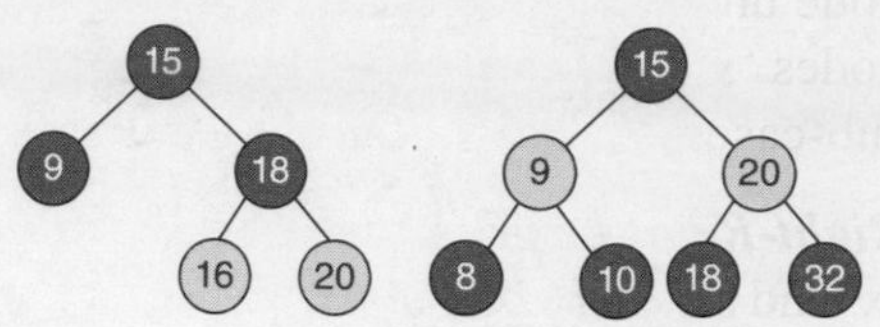

Figure 7.18 Sample Red-Black trees

How these properties are maintained when a node is inserted or deleted, where rotation is used, and how the process of rotation has been modified are all discussed in detail with the operations of a red-black tree. Figure 7.18 shows a sample red-black tree.

Searching, inserting, and deleting are the basic operations in red-black trees too. Searching is based on the same property of a BST. It has already been dealt in detail in BSTs and AVL trees. So, insertion and deletion are alone discussed in here.

7.4.1 Operation—Insertion

Given a node, it is inserted using the same logic involved in a BST. The node will always be inserted as a leaf. The colour of the inserted node will always be red. Now, the balance of the tree is restored involving re-colouration and rotation, whenever applicable. If the inserted node is the root, it is re-coloured to black. If the inserted node is not a root, then the parent must be black. If the parent is not black, then there is a clash in the property since a red node's parent or child cannot be red. This clash is handled based on two cases.

Before discussing the different possible cases for handling the inserted node, few properties are to be thrown light on. The inserted node is coloured red and is inserted only as a leaf. While inserting a node, if the parent to which the new node is to be added as a child is a leaf, it will be red in colour. This is because when a node is inserted, its ancestors' or uncle's colour is changed, but not the colour of the node. However, if the parent node already has a child and the new node is to be added as another child, then the parent node will be black. Since a parent or child of a red node cannot be red as per the properties of a red-black tree, the colour of the parent can be checked if red and then changed to black. This solution makes the tree hold good for this property. In odds, this remedy will clash with another property. The last property mentioned in the list states that the number of black nodes in every root of leaf path should be same. If there was a sibling to the parent node of the new node inserted and if the node was in red, then the previous remedy will make the tree lose this property. For this property to be held good, it is a good practice to change colours of all the siblings in one go. Keeping this in mind, the two cases of handling an inserted node while the parent is not black are discussed below.

Case 1 The colour of the uncle node is checked. Uncle node is a sibling of the parent of the inserted node. If there is an uncle node, its colour is checked. If the uncle node is red, then the parent and uncle are changed to black. The grandparent is then coloured red. This case does not involve any rotation. Now, the colour of the grandparent is red. The grandparent is considered and the balancing process is continued from there. The grandparent may result in recolouring of further ancestors or rotation (based on case 2) until the root. This process ensures that the tree holds good for all the colouring properties. While recursion if the root is coloured red, recursion cannot move further above. So, the root is again coloured black and recursion is stopped.

Case 2 The colour of the uncle node is checked and if it is already black, then rotations are performed. There may not be an imbalance in the tree currently. Even then, rotations take place. Let the current node under consideration be 'z'. Assume 'y' is the parent of 'z' and 'x' is the grandparent of 'z'. The nodes 'x', 'y', and 'z' can be arranged in four different ways, just as discussed in AVL trees. All these sub-cases and how these are handled are discussed in detail below.

Right-Right Case In case when 'y' is the right child of 'x' and 'z' is the right child of 'y'. Left rotate at 'x' and swap the colours of 'x' and 'y'. It can be seen that after rotation, 'x' and 'y' are on the same level. A sample tree which has a right-right case and how it is handled is depicted in Figure 7.19.

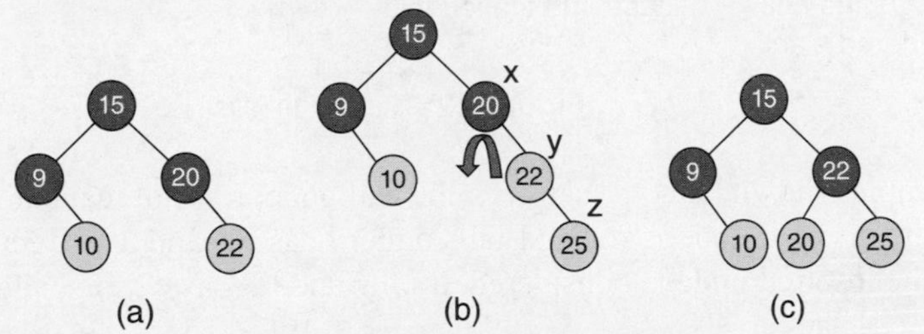

Figure 7.19 (a) A sample red-black tree, where '25' is inserted. Its uncle is black, so results in a right-right case.
(b) A left rotation at the grandparent of '22', which is '15'
(c) A swap of colours of '15' and '20' is done to handle the case

Note There is no uncle for the inserted node. So, the colour of uncle is considered black, as discussed in the property that a null node is black.

Right-Left Case Consider 'y' as the right child of 'x' and 'z' as the left child of 'y'. Right rotate pivoted at 'y' and then apply the right-right solution. If the right-right case is clear, this is straight forward. A sample process is shared in Figure 7.20.

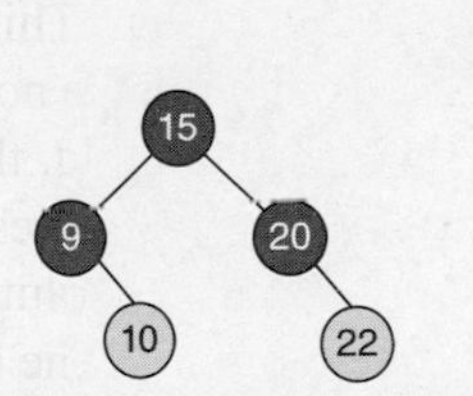

A sample tree where insertion of '21' results in right-left imbalance, as the uncle is null and black

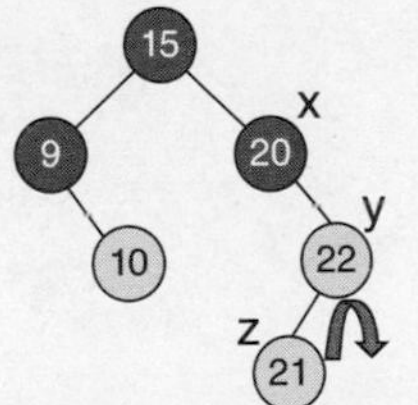

A left rotation at '22' changes it to right–right imbalance

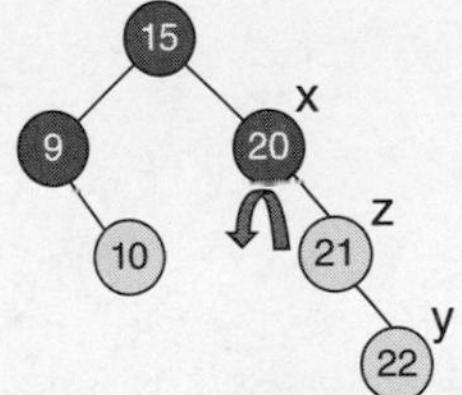

A left rotation at '20'

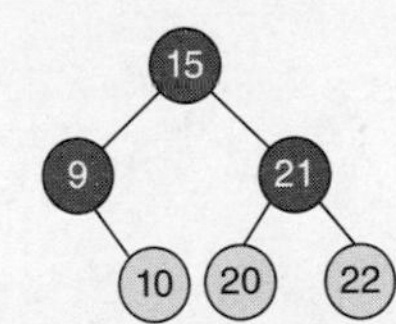

Swapping colours between '20' and '21' puts all the properties in place and gives the final red-black tree

Figure 7.20 Right-Left Case

Left-Left Case It is like the mirror image of the right-right case. A right rotation pivoted at 'x' and swapping the colours of 'y' and 'x' manage the balancing. A pictorial example is shared as a part of the next case, the left-right case, as it involves the left-left case while solving.

Left-Right Case It is the mirror image of the right-left case. First, a left rotation is done at 'y' which makes the left-right case into the left-left case. Then, the above solution of left-left is applied without any change. Figure 7.21 has a sample tree where insertion results in the left-right case. While handling the left-right case, the left-left solution is also shown.

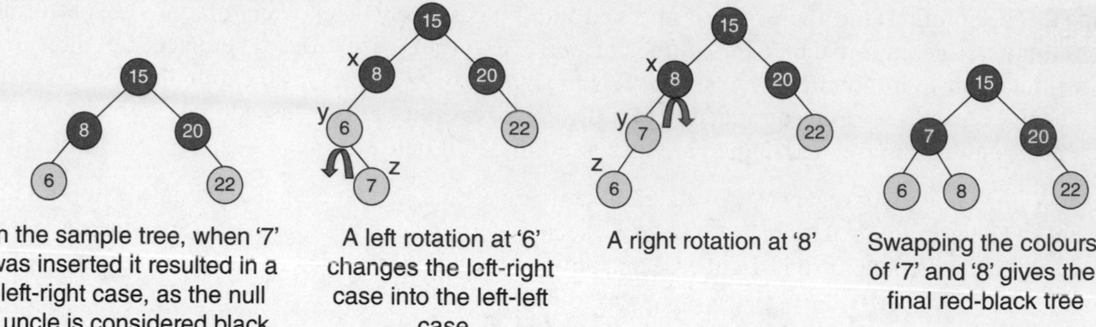

Figure 7.21 Left-Right case

In all the examples shown here, 'z' has been the leaf node. It is not mandatory in real time. There can be cases when the inserted node is red and falls under 'Case 1' and after rectifying the case, when the grandparent of the inserted node is considered, it falls under 'Case 2'. Pseudocode 7.9 shows insertion of a node into a red-black tree.

Question 7.4 Insert '17' into the red-black tree given in Figure 7.22.

Solution: Figure 7.23 shows the step-by-step process. In the given red-black tree, '17' is inserted, creating an imbalance that is handled as per 'Case 1'. Re-colouring the parent, uncle and grandparent and considering the grandparent for further balancing results in 'Case 2' imbalance at grandparent, node '18'. It has a right-left imbalance which is handled by a right rotation at '20' followed by a left rotation at '15' and finally by swapping the colours of '18' and '15.

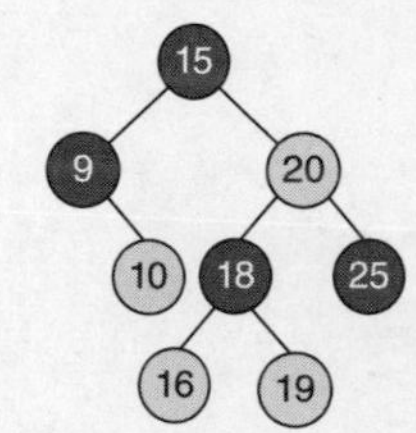

Figure 7.22 Red-Black tree

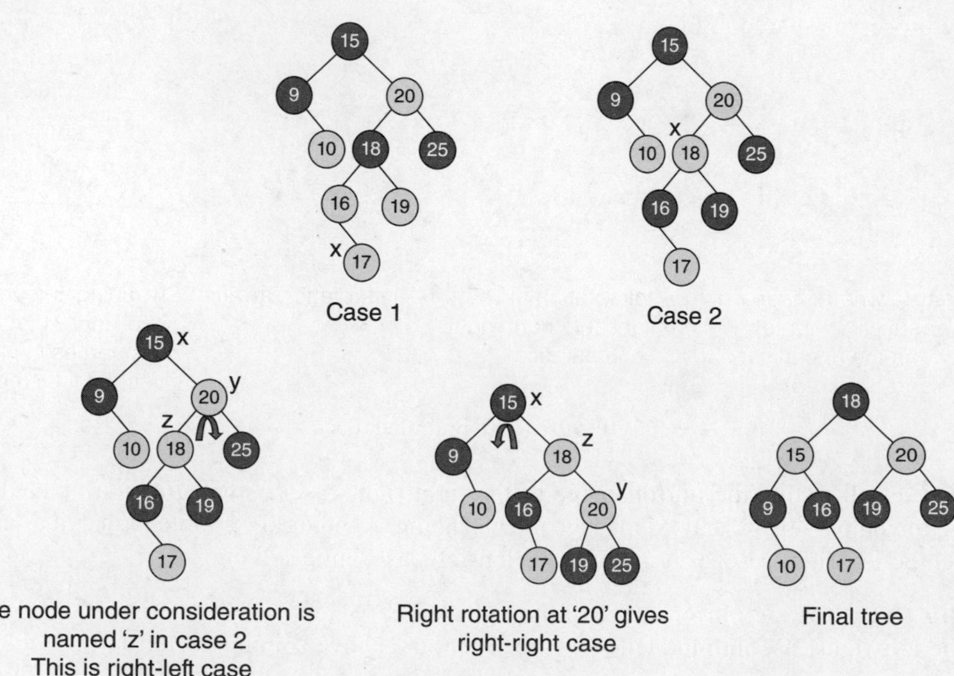

Figure 7.23 Step-by-step process to insert '17' into the Red-Black tree

(contd)

Pseudocode 7.9

```
def insert(value):
    Perform insert like BST
    value.color = RED
    z=value
    while z.parent.color = RED and z is not the root of the tree
    Do,
        if z.parent = z.parent.parent.left
        #node's parent is the left child of grandparent
        then,
            y = z.parent.parent.right
            if y.colour = RED    #uncle is RED
            then,
                z.parent.colour = BLACK
                y.colour = BLACK
                z.parent.parent.colour = RED
                z = z.parent.parent
            else,
                if z = z.parent.right
                then,
                    z = z.parent
                    rotate_left(z)
                z.parent.colour = BLACK
                z.parent.parent.colour = RED
                rotate_right(z.parent.parent)
        else,
        #node's parent is the right child of grandparent
            y = z.parent.parent.left
            if y.colour = RED
            then,
                z.parent.colour = BLACK
                y.colour = BLACK
                z.parent.parent.colour = RED
                z = z.parent.parent
            else,
                if z = z.parent.left
                then,
                    z = z.parent
                    rotate_right(z)
                z.parent.colour = BLACK
                z.parent.parent.colour = RED
                rotate_left(z.parent.parent)
    root.colour = BLACK
```

Food for Brain

When a node is deleted in a BST the actual node that is getting deleted, that is, the node of the final in-order successor that moves up, can have a maximum of how many children?

7.4.2 Operation—Delete a Node

Given a node, it is deleted using the same logic involved in a BST. When a node is deleted, if it is not a leaf, another node moves up. Then, the deletion of the replaced node takes place. This process continues until a leaf node or node without an in-order successor is deleted. From the balance or colour point of view, the last node that is moved up is important. The final node can be a leaf or can have one child, this is when the recursion in the BST delete process breaks, making it the base case. This implies that the final node deleted can never have two children. This deletion is handled under various different cases explained in detail below. Let the final node to be deleted be 'v' and the node considered for replacement be 'u'. The node 'u' can either be 'null' or the left child of 'v'.

Case 1

Consider that either 'u' or 'v' is a red node. It is to be kept in mind that both 'u' and 'v' cannot be red as they are parent and child. Even if 'v' is red and 'u' is null, as discussed earlier, colour of the null node is black. Now, 'v' is deleted and 'u' is moved up to the place of 'v' and then is marked black. So, the black height of the branch remains unchanged, irrespective of the colour of the node that is getting deleted. Figure 7.24 has a sample tree where the process of deletion of a node falls under the case explained above. In this figure, '9' is 'v' and '10' is the replaced 'u'.

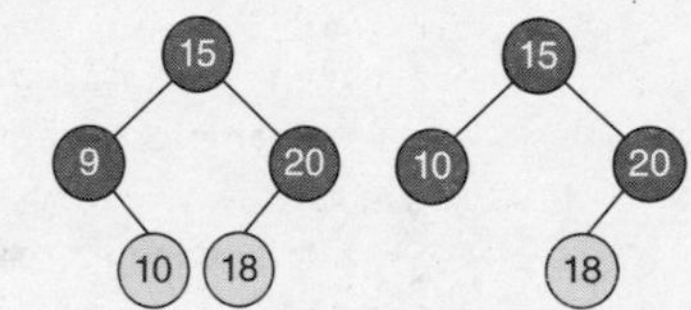

Figure 7.24 A sample tree where '9' is deleted

Case 2

When both 'u' and 'v' are black, then the real imbalance issue occurs. When one node is deleted, the total black height of the sub-tree loses the balance. This is handled in different ways based on the colour of the sibling and descendants of the deleted node. This has various possible sub-cases, say the sibling can be red or black and their children can also either be red or black. Each sub-case is to be treated in a unique way and explained in detail below. However, first, the deletion process is to be completed. The node 'v' is deleted and is replaced by 'u'. Finally, 'u' is coloured as double black. Double black is a temporary state which will be rectified using the below sub-cases. If 'v' was a leaf node, even then its children would have been 'null' and considered black. Thus, deletion of a black leaf node always falls under this category. Figure 7.25 shows a pictorial representation of a double black resulting in deletion of a node. The double black node need not always be 'null'. In this figure, it is 'null' because the children of the deleted node are 'null'.

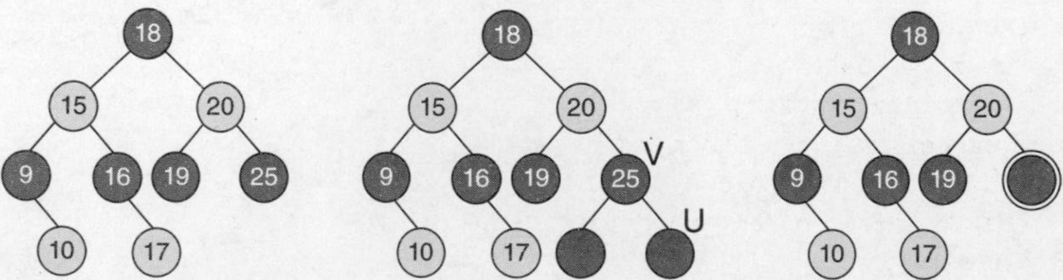

Figure 7.25 A sample tree where deletion of a black leaf '25' results in a double black node

If the sibling is black and has a red child/red children, then rotations are to be performed. The rotations are same as in AVL. The child of the sibling who is red is considered as 'z'. Let 'y' be the parent of 'z' and 'x' be the grandparent of 'z'. With 'x', 'y', and 'z' in place we have the four cases of rotation in here as well, same as in AVL trees. Based on the arrangement, rotation is done following the same logic defined in AVL rotations. Even though restructuring is same as in AVL, re-colouring is new in here. Each of these sub-categories is explained below.

Right-Right Case When the sibling 'y' is the right child of the parent 'x', which is also the parent of 'u', and the red child 'z' is the right child of the sibling 'y', it falls under right-right case. As explained in AVL trees, a left rotation at 'x' is done for restructuring. For recolouring, node 'z' is coloured black and then the double black 'u' is made single black. In general, a double black node finds a closeby red node and changes the (double black, red) nodes into (black, black) nodes. Figure 7.26 shows a sample tree where deletion creates a right-right case and explains the way it is handled.

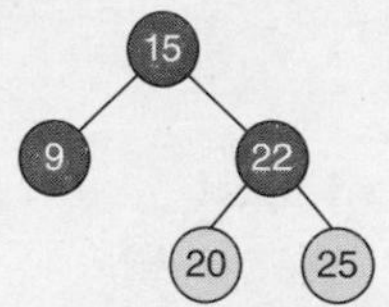

A sample tree where deletion of '9' creates a double black 'null'

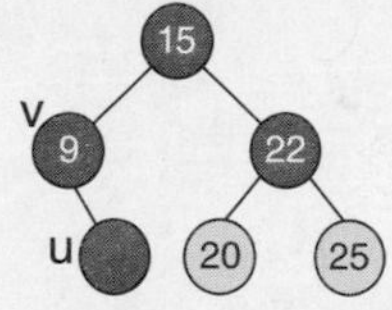

A sample tree where deletion of '9' creates a double black 'null'

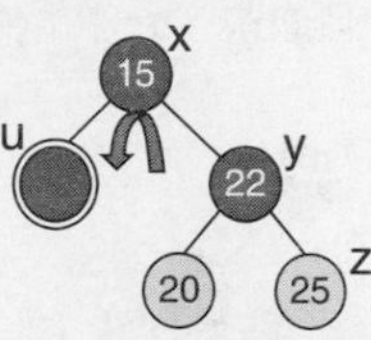

This is handled using the right-right case with a left rotation at '15'

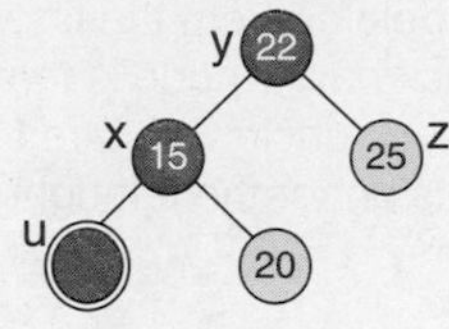

After rotation, 'u' and 'z' are in different sub-trees of 'x'

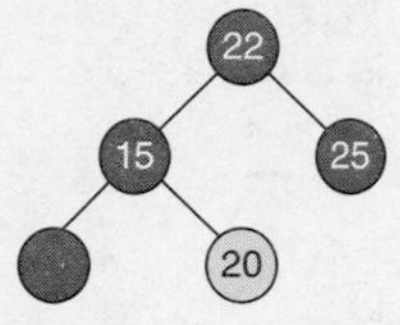

Finally, '25' is re-coloured black to compensate the double black

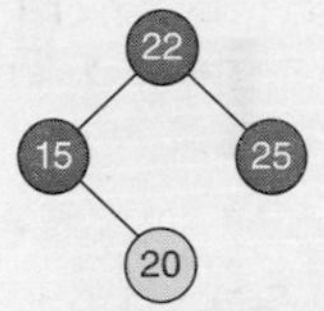

The final red-black tree is formed

Figure 7.26 Right-Right case

Right-Left Case When the sibling 'y' is the right child of 'x' and red node 'z' is the left child of 'y', it is called as the right-left case. Then, first a right rotation is performed at 'y'. This structurally converts the right-left case into the right-right case. After the right rotation at 'y', the colour of 'y' and 'z' is interchanged. This swapping of colour is done so that the black nodes are on the same level. After recolouring, 'x' and 'z' become black and 'y' becomes red. Now, a left rotation at 'x' is applied and then the colour of 'y' is changed to black. Finally, 'u' is `changed from double black to single black. Figure 7.27 shows the balancing of right-left imbalance in a red-black tree from deletion.

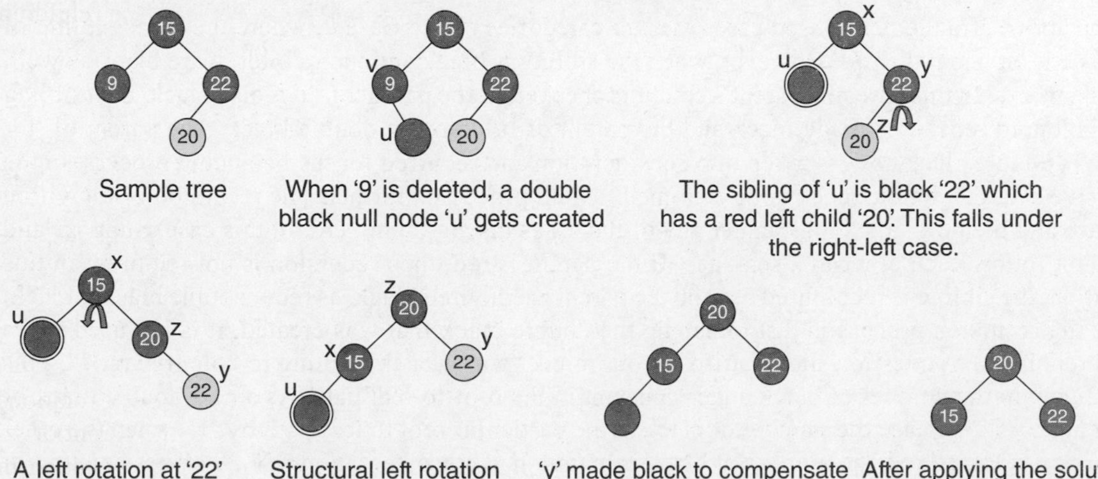

Sample tree

When '9' is deleted, a double black null node 'u' gets created

The sibling of 'u' is black '22' which has a red left child '20'. This falls under the right-left case.

A left rotation at '22' changes the tree into the right-right case

Structural left rotation for right-right case

'y' made black to compensate the double black

After applying the solution for right-right, the final tree is left with just black nodes

Figure 7.27 Right-Left case

Left-Left Case If the sibling 'y' is the left child of 'x' and 'z' is the left child of 'y', it is the left-left case. For balancing, a right rotation is done at 'x'. This is followed by colouring 'z' as black. In odds, if 'z' was the right child of 'y', it would have resulted in a left-right imbalance. Then, a left rotation at 'y' and swapping of colours between 'y' and 'z' would have been performed as an intermediate step. This changes the left-right imbalance into the left-left imbalance which is handled the same way as explained in the beginning of this paragraph. Figure 7.28 shows how the left-right imbalance is converted into the left-left imbalance and the way it is handled.

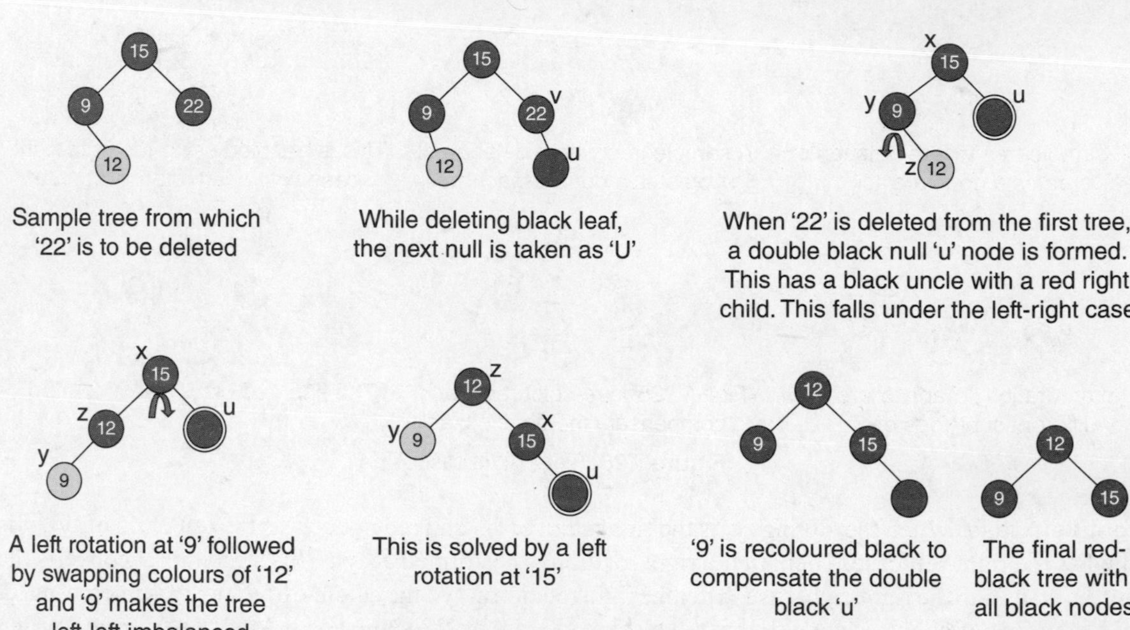

15
9
22
12
Sample tree from which '22' is to be deleted
15
9
22
V
12
u
While deleting black leaf, the next null is taken as 'U'
X
15
y
9
u
z
12
When '22' is deleted from the first tree, a double black null 'u' node is formed. This has a black uncle with a red right child. This falls under the left-right case.
X
15
Z
12
u
y
9
A left rotation at '9' followed by swapping colours of '12' and '9' makes the tree left-left imbalanced
12
Z
y
9
X
15
u
This is solved by a left rotation at '15'
12
9
15
'9' is recoloured black to compensate the double black 'u'
12
9
15
The final red-black tree with all black nodes

Figure 7.28 Left-Left case

Case 3

All the above arrangement-based cases are sub-categories of the Case 2, where the black sibling of 'u' has atleast one red child. However, when the sibling is black and their children are black as well, nothing works. In this case, the parent's colour is checked. If the parent of 'u' is also black, then sibling is re-coloured red, 'u' is made black and the parent of 'u' is made double black. The parent of 'u', which is double black now, is taken into consideration and recurred for the balancing process. In the recursive call, the double black node is termed 'u' and processed further. The recursion is not within the case and the new 'u' can fall under any of the cases discussed in here. In this case. Suppose and if cannot follow each other in a sentence. If the parent is red, then recursion is not required. In this condition, the sibling is recoloured red and the parent is coloured black, as red + double black = black. Since the recursion process is just to handle the double black that was created, it is not used when the parent is red. A question should arise in your mind, "why was the sibling re-coloured red?". This is to maintain the number of black nodes constant in the root-to-leaf path. As a new double black or black node will increase the number of black in the particular root to leaf path by '1', when the other child is re-coloured red, the number of black is maintained consistent. Figure 7.29 shows deletion of a node which has black siblings and children of siblings, but a red parent. While Figure 7.29 nullifies the double black and has no recursion involved, Figure 7.30 shows a tree where deletion falls under Case 3 and causes a recursion at the end.

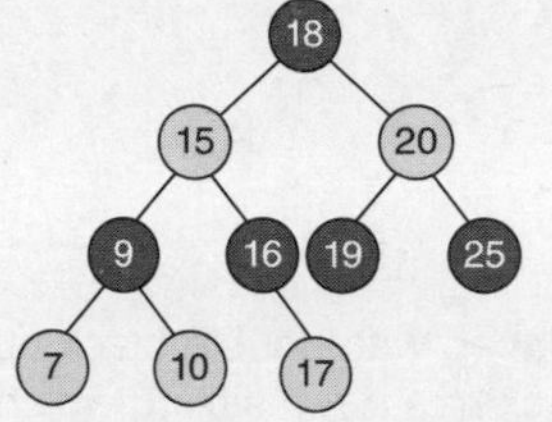

Sample tree with '19' as a black node

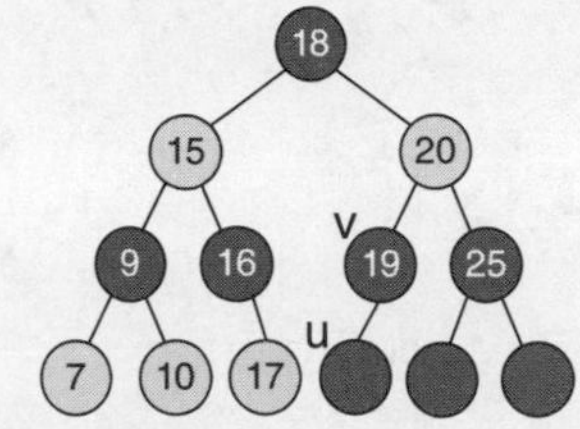

Sibling and children of sibling of '19' are black as well, as sibling has no children and null is black. Deletion of '19' creates a double black null node

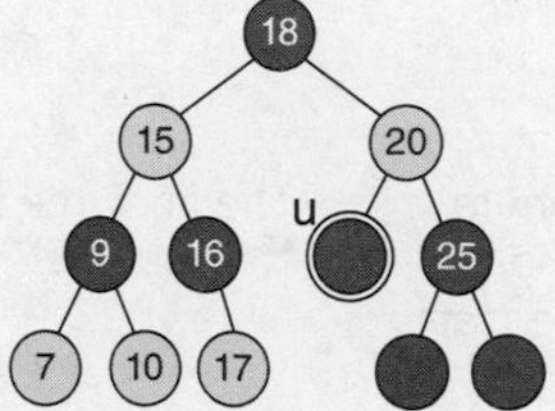

Parent of double black is red

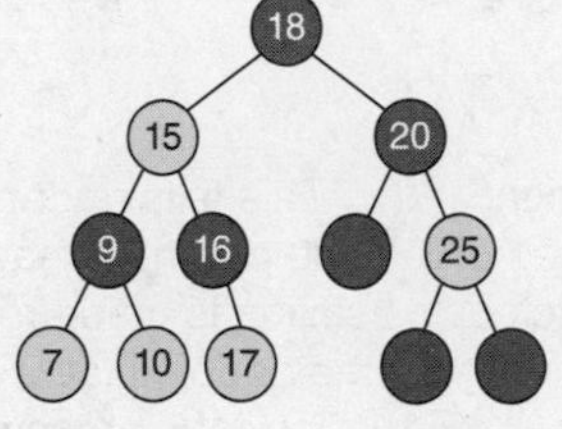

The parent is re-coloured black to convert double black into single black

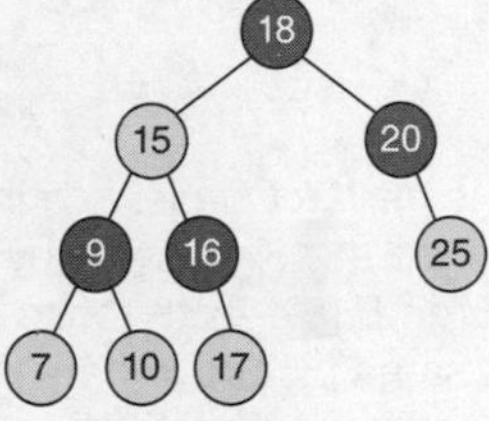

The final red-black tree

Figure 7.29 Nullification of double black with no recursion

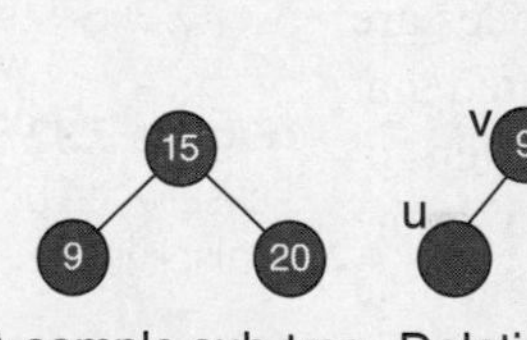

A sample sub-tree with a black node '9'

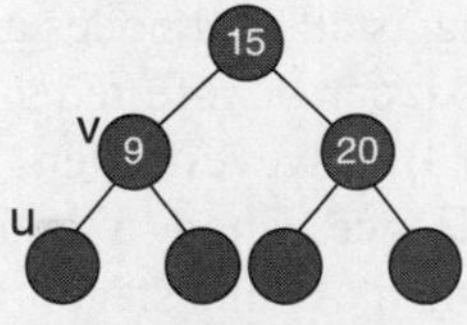

Deleting '9' creates a double black null as sibling and cousins of '9' are all black

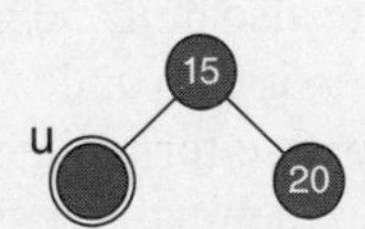

Parent of the double black is black as well

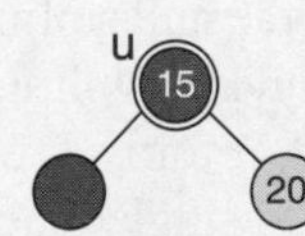

The parent is made double black

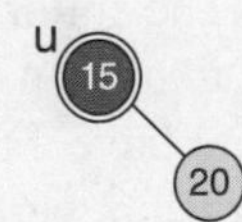

The 'u' node is recurred for further balancing

Figure 7.30 Deletion under case 3 causes recursion

Case 4

The sub-categories discussed above in Case 2 and Case 3 depends on the black sibling. If the sibling is red, then it is handled differently. This is considered as Case 4 in here. Here, the sibling of the double black node is red. This means the children of the red sibling are black, as children of red cannot be red. Next, the red sibling may be the right child of the parent or the left child. Thus, it forms two sub-categories in here as well. The '*Left Case*' is when the red child is left child of the parent. To balance in this instance, a left rotation is performed at the parent of 'u'. After this rotation, colour of the old parent and old sibling is swapped. This can also be stated as inverting the colours of the parent and grandparent of 'u' after rotation. Now, the new sibling is always black as the grandchildren before rotation were black. The tree can be handled by Case 3 or Case 4 as explained above. The right case is just the mirror image of the left case and the solution is also the mirror image as discussed in here. The '*Right Case*' means the red sibling is the right child of the parent of double black. Figure 7.31 depicts a deletion which leads to the left case in red sibling of a double black node and how it is handled.

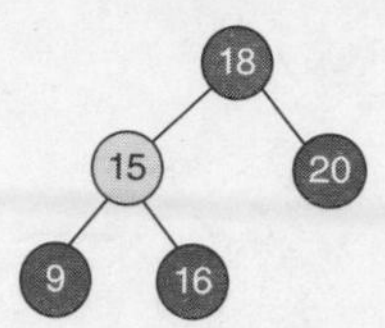

A sample tree from which '20' is to be deleted

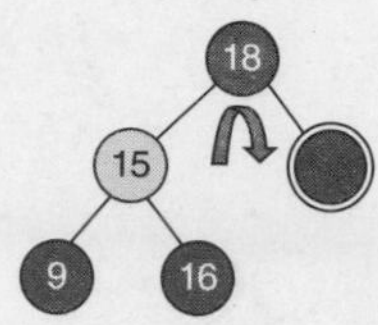

'20' is replaced with double black null. Double black has a red sibling which is the left child of the parent

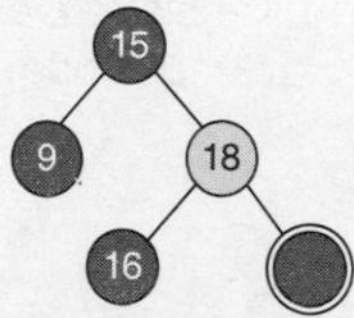

It is the '*Left Case*' and involves a right rotation at '18' followed by colour swap of '15' and '18'—both these steps depicted in same picture in here. Now, consider double black as 'u' and recurse

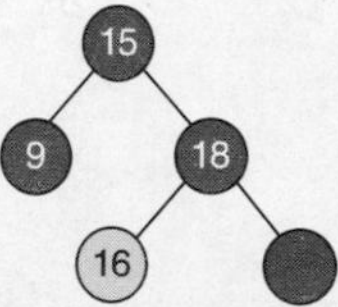

This falls under Case 3, where the parent is made black and the sibling is made red to compensate the double black. Thus, color of '18' and '16' are inverted and 'u' is made single black

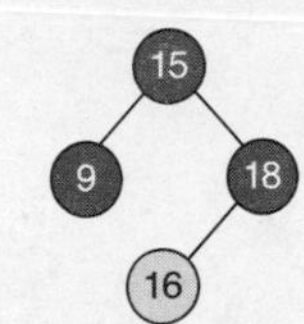

The final tree is formed

Figure 7.31 Deletion leads to the left case in red sibling of a double black node

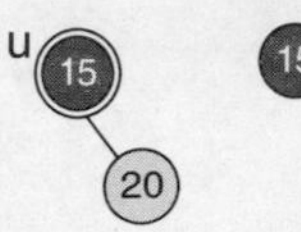

Figure 7.32 Base case when double black is the root

All the above cases work only if there is a parent of 'u'. This argument is based on the fact that only when there is a parent, there can be a sibling. Even if there is a parent but not a sibling, it means that 'u' has a black sibling as all null nodes are black. The children of the null siblings are also null and black. It can be inferred that when 'u' has a parent and no siblings, then it falls under Case 3. However, when 'u' does not have a parent, it forms the base case for recursion. Hence, when 'u' is the root, it is converted into single black and the final tree is formed. At this stage, the black height of the entire tree is reduced by '1'. Figure 7.32 shows a base case of the deletion recursion that resulted from example in Figure 7.30 where the double black node is a root. Pseudocode 7.10 shows deletion of a node from a red-black tree.

Food for Brain

What happens when a double black node is null with a black parent and null sibling? Which case does it fall into and how is it handled?

Pseudocode 7.10

```
def delete(self, z):
    Perform standard BST delete
    #X-replacement node
    while x is not the root and x.colour = BLACK,
    Do,
        if x=x.parent.left
        #X is the left child of the parent
```

(*contd*)

(*contd*)

```
    then,
        w = x.parent.right
        if w.colour = RED,
        then,
            w.colour = BLACK
            x.parent.colour = RED
            rotate_left(x.parent)
            w = x.parent.right

        if w.left.colour = BLACK and w.right.colour = BLACK
        #both children are black
        then,
            w.colour = RED
            x = x.parent

        else,
            if w.right.colour = BLACK
            then,
                w.left.colour = BLACK
                w.colour = RED
                rotate_right(w)
                w = x.parent.right

            w.colour = x.parent.colour
            x.parent.colour = BLACK
            w.right.colour = BLACK
            rotate_left(x.parent)
            x = root

    else if x = x.parent.right
    #X is the right child of the parent
    then,
        w = x.parent.left
        if w.colour = RED,
        then,
            w.colour = BLACK
            x.parent.colour = RED
            rotate_right(x.parent)
            w = x.parent.left
        if w.left.colour = BLACK and w.right.colour = BLACK
        #both children are black
        then,
            w.colour = RED
            x = x.parent

        else,
            if w.left.colour = BLACK
            then,
                w.right.colour = BLACK
                w.colour = RED
                rotate_left(w)
                w = x.parent.left

            w.colour = x.parent.colour
            x.parent.colour = BLACK
            w.left.colour = BLACK
            rotate_right(x.parent)
            x = self.root
x.colour = BLACK
```

Food for Brain

Should a red-black tree always be an AVL tree structurally?

7.4.3 Implementation of Red-Black Trees

The code for implementation of a red-black tree based on a node class is shared below (refer to Python code 7.3). The rotational operations are all implemented as separate functions just to ensure reusability of code, whereas re-colouring is done inline in the function as it is simple and case specific.

Python code 7.3

```
"""
A Red-Black Tree is a BST with an extra attribute for each node: its colour, which is either
RED or BLACK.
Each node has attributes 'colour', 'key', 'left', 'right' and 'p'. If a child or parent of a
node doesn't exist, the corresponding pointer attribute of the node contains the value NIL.
We shall regard NILs as being pointers to leaves (external nodes) of the BST and the normal
'key-bearing' nodes as being internal nodes of the tree.

It has the following properties:
  1) Every node in the tree is either Red or Black
  2) The root is Black
  3) Leaf (NIL) nodes are Black
  4) If a node is red, then both its children are black (implies that on any path from the root
to a leaf, red nodes must not be adjacent. However, any number of black nodes may appear in a
sequence.)
  5) Every simple path from a node to a descendant leaf contains the same number of black
nodes.
```

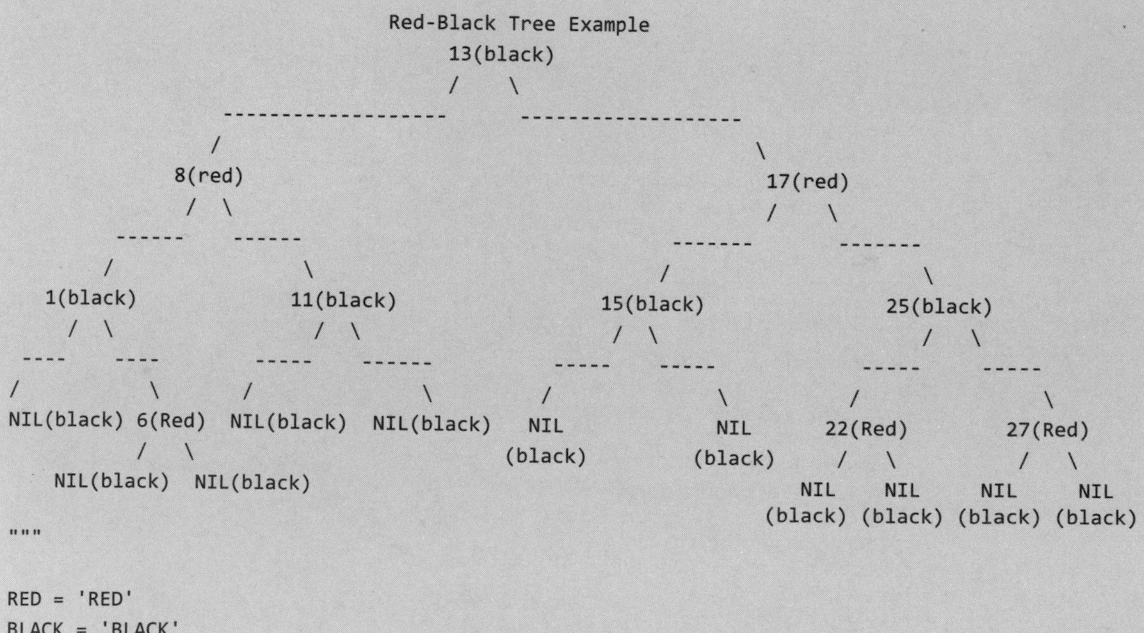

```
                              Red-Black Tree Example
                                   13(black)
                                    /    \
                   -----------------      -----------------
                  /                                        \
              8(red)                                     17(red)
               /  \                                       /    \
          ------   ------                          -------      -------
         /               \                        /                    \
    1(black)            11(black)             15(black)             25(black)
     /  \                 /  \                  /  \                  /  \
 ----    ----         -----   ------        -----   -----        -----    -----
/            \       /              \      /             \      /              \
NIL(black) 6(Red)  NIL(black)  NIL(black)  NIL          NIL      22(Red)        27(Red)
             /  \                       (black)       (black)    /   \          /    \
   NIL(black)  NIL(black)                                     NIL    NIL      NIL     NIL
                                                           (black) (black) (black) (black)
"""

RED = 'RED'
BLACK = 'BLACK'
```

(*contd*)

(*contd*)

```
class NilNode(object):

  """
  Represents the Nil class. Every leaf (NIL) node is BLACK
  """

    def __init__(self):
      #Initializer for the class
        self.colour = BLACK

#NIL Object
NIL = NilNode()

class Node(object):

  """
  Represents the node class for creating node placeholders.
  """

    def __init__(self, key, p=NIL, left=NIL, right=NIL, colour=RED):

    """
    Initializer for the class

    Parameters
    ----------
    key: int
      It is the value of a node in the tree

    p: int
      It is the parent of a node

    left: int
      It is the left node of a parent node

    right: int
      It is right node of a parent node

    colour: str
      It is the colour of a node

    """
        self.p = p
        self.left = left
        self.right = right
        self.colour = colour
        self.key = key
```

(*contd*)

(*contd*)

```
class RedBlackTree(object):
  """
  Represents the RedBlackTree class.

  Methods
  -------
    minimum
      It finds the node with the lowest value in a subtree rooted at given node

    rotate_left
      Rotate the tree to the left to balance it after insertion or deletion

    rotate_right
      Rotate the tree to the right to balance it after insertion or deletion

    insert
      Insert value to a node in the tree

    insertion_fixup
      Fix any violations happened due to insertion of a node

    balance
      Helper function to balance the tree after deletion of a node

    delete
      Deletes a node from the tree

    deletion_fixup
      Fix any violations that had occured due to deletion of a node
  """

    def __init__(self, root=NIL):
      #Initialize root of the tree as NIL object
        self.root = root
        #self.NIL = None
        #self.root.p = self.NIL

    def minimum(self, root):
      # Finds the node with the lowest value in a subtree rooted at given node (x)
        x = root
        if x and x != self.NIL:
            while x.left and x.left != self.NIL:
                x = x.left
            return x
        else:
            return None
```

(*contd*)

(*contd*)

```
def rotate_left(self, x):

  """
  Rotate the tree to the left to balance it after insertion or deletion
        y                                        x
      /   \      <- Left Rotate(x)             /   \
     x    T3     <=====================>      T1    y
    / \                Right Rotate(y)->            / \
  T1  T2                                          T2  T3

  T1, T2, T3 are sub-trees
  Note: in_order traversal of both trees will be T1 x T2 y T3

  Parameters
  ----------
  x: int
    Node to be rotated

  """

    y = x.right                          #set y
    x.right = y.left                     #turn y's left sub-tree into x's right sub-tree
    if y.left != self.NIL:
        y.left.p = x
    # else: y.left is NIL -- its p can be any value

    y.p = x.p                            #link x's parent to y

    if x.p == self.NIL:
        self.root = y
    elif x == x.p.left:                  # if x is the left child
        x.p.left = y
    else:                                # if x is the right child
        x.p.right = y

    y.left = x                           #put x on y's left
    x.p = y

def rotate_right(self, y):

  """
  Rotate the tree to the right to balance it after insertion or deletion
        y                                        x
      /   \      <- Left Rotate(x)             /   \
     x    T3     <=====================>      T1    y
    / \                Right Rotate(y)->            / \
  T1  T2                                          T2  T3

  T1, T2, T3 are sub-trees
```

(*contd*)

(*contd*)

```
        Parameters
        ----------
        y: int
          Node to be rotated

        """

         x = y.left                              #set x
         y.left = x.right                        #turn x's right sub-tree into y's left sub-tree
         if x.right != self.NIL:
             x.right.p = y
         # else: x.right is NIL -- its p can be any value

         x.p = y.p                               #link y's parent to x

         if y.p == self.NIL:
             self.root = x
         elif y == y.p.left:                     # if y is the left child
             y.p.left = x
         else:                                   # if y is the right child
             y.p.right = x

         x.right = y                             #put y on x's right
         y.p = x

    def insert(self, z):

        """
        Inserts node 'z' into binary tree and colours it RED.

        To remove any Red-Black tree property violations, Insertion_fixup is called to recolour
        nodes and perform rotations

        Parameters
        ----------
        z: int
          node z with some filled key
        """

        y = self.NIL                             # Set y as NIL object
        x = self.root                            # Start with root
        while x != self.NIL:
            y = x
            if z.key < x.key:
                x = x.left                       # Go left
            else:
                x = x.right                      # Go to right otherwise

        z.p = y                                  # y is parent of z
```

(*contd*)

(*contd*)

```
        if y == self.NIL:                       # If tree is empty
            self.root = z                       # z is root
        elif z.key < y.key:
            y.left = z
        else:
            y.right = z                         # z is right of y

        z.left = self.NIL
        z.right = self.NIL
        z.colour = RED                          # colour of z is RED
        self.insertion_fixup(z)

    def insertion_fixup(self, z):

        """
        Insertion_fixup is called to recolour nodes and perform rotations, to remove any Red-
        Black tree property violations

        Parameters
        ----------
        z: int
          node z with some filled key
        """

        z.colour = RED
        while z.p.colour == RED and z != self.root:   # While z's parent is RED
            if z.p == z.p.p.left:
                y = z.p.p.right                       # Set y to be z's uncle
                if y.colour == RED:                   # If uncle y is RED
    # Case 1: z's uncle y is RED

                    z.p.colour = BLACK                # Colour parent BLACK
                    y.colour = BLACK                  # Colour uncle BLACK
                    z.p.p.colour = RED                # Colour grandparent RED
                    z = z.p.p                         # Set z to grandparent

                else:
                    if z == z.p.right:                # If z is right of parent
    # Case 2: z's uncle y is BLACK and z is a right child

                        z = z.p                       # Set z to parent
                        self.rotate_left(z)           # Rotate z

    # Case 3: z's uncle y is BLACK and z is a left child
                    z.p.colour = BLACK                # Colour parent of z to BLACK
                    z.p.p.colour = RED                # Colour grandparent of z to RED
                    self.rotate_right(z.p.p)          # Rotate grandparent of z
```

(*contd*)

(*contd*)

```
        else:
            y = z.p.p.left                          # Set y to be z's uncle
            if y.colour == RED:                     # If uncle y is RED
 # Case 1: z's uncle y is RED

                z.p.colour = BLACK                  # Colour parent BLACK
                y.colour = BLACK                    # Colour uncle BLACK
                z.p.p.colour = RED                  # Colour grandparent RED
                z = z.p.p                           # Set z to grandparent
            else:
                if z == z.p.left:                   # If z is left of parent
 # Case 2: z's uncle y is BLACK and z is a left child
                    z = z.p                         # Set z to parent
                    self.rotate_right(z)            # Rotate z

 # Case 3: z's uncle y is BLACK and z is a right child
                z.p.colour = BLACK                  # Colour parent of z to BLACK
                z.p.p.colour = RED                  # Colour grandparent of z to RED
                self.rotate_left(z.p.p)             # Rotate grandparent of z

 # Case 0:  Root colour is BLACK
    self.root.colour = BLACK                        # Colour root to BLACK

 def balance(self, u, v):

 """
 Helper function to balance tree after deletion of a node

 Parameters
 ----------

 u: int
   node u with some filled key to be deleted
 v: int
   u's child node with some filled key

 To delete u, simply connect u's child v to u's parent
 """

    if u.p == self.NIL:                             # If u's parent is NIL
        self.root = v                               # then v is root
    elif u == u.p.left:                             # If u is left of its parent
        u.p.left = v                                # assign v to left of u's parent
    else:
        u.p.right = v                               # else assign v to right of u's parent
    v.p = u.p                                       # such that u's parent is now v's parent

 def delete(self, z):
```

(*contd*)

(*contd*)

```
    """
    Inserts node 'z' into binary tree and colours it RED.

    To remove any Red-Black tree property violations, Insertion_fixup is called to recolour
    nodes and perform rotations

    Parameters
    ----------
    z: int
      node z with some filled key, to be deleted
    """
        y = z                           # Assign z to node y
        y_original_colour = y.colour    # Original colour needs to be tracked to determine if
                                        # any fixes are required. If its RED, no fix required
        if z.left == self.NIL:          # Case 1: If z has only right child
            x = z.right
            self.balance(z, z.right)    # Put right child of z in z
        elif z.right == self.NIL:       # Case 2: If z only has left child
            x = z.left
            self.balance(z, z.left)     # Put left child of z in z
        else:                           # Case 3: Else if z has two children
            y = self.minimum(z.right)   # y is z's successor
            y_original_colour = y.colour
            x = y.right
            if y.p == z:                # If z is y's parent
                x.p = y                 # Make y as x's parent
            else:
                self.balance(y, y.right) # Put right child of y in y
                y.right = z.right       # Put right child of z in y's right
                y.right.p = y

            self.balance(z, y)
            y.left = z.left
            y.left.p = y
            y.colour = z.colour
        if y_original_colour == BLACK:
            self.deletion_fixup(x)

    def deletion_fixup(self, x):

    """
    Deletion_fixup is called to recolour nodes and perform rotations, to remove any Red-Black
    tree property violations

    Parameters
    ----------
    x: int
```

(*contd*)

(*contd*)

```
    node x with some filled key
"""
     while x != self.root and x.colour == BLACK:   # while x is BLACK and is not root
         if x==x.p.left:                           # if x is left child
             w = x.p.right                         # w is x's sibling
             if w.colour == RED:
# Case 1: x's sibling, w is RED

                 w.colour = BLACK                  # Colour w BLACK
                 x.p.colour = RED                  # Colour x's parent RED
                 self.rotate_left(x.p)             # Left rotate x's parent
                 w = x.p.right

             if w.left.colour == BLACK and w.right.colour == BLACK:
# Case 2: x's sibling, w is BLACK and both of w's children are BLACK

                 w.colour = RED
                 x = x.p

             else:
                 if w.right.colour == BLACK:
# Case 3: x's sibling, w is BLACK, w's left child is RED, and w's right child is BLACK
                     w.left.colour = BLACK
                     w.colour = RED
                     self.rotate_right(w)
                     w = x.p.right

                 w.colour = x.p.colour
# Case 4: x's sibling, w is BLACK and w's right child is RED

                 x.p.colour = BLACK
                 w.right.colour = BLACK
                 self.rotate_left(x.p)
                 x = self.root
         elif x == x.p.right:
             w = x.p.left
             if w.colour == RED:
# Case 1: x's sibling, w is RED

                 w.colour = BLACK
                 x.p.colour = RED
                 self.rotate_right(x.p)
                 w = x.p.left
             if w.left.colour == BLACK and w.right.colour == BLACK:
# Case 2: x's sibling, w is BLACK and both of w's children are BLACK
```

(*contd*)

(*contd*)

```
                w.colour = RED
                x = x.p

            else:
                if w.left.colour == BLACK:
# Case 3: x's sibling, w is BLACK, w's right child is RED, and w's left child is BLACK

                    w.right.colour = BLACK
                    w.colour = RED
                    self.rotate_left(w)
                    w = x.p.left

                w.colour = x.p.colour
# Case 4: x's sibling, w is BLACK and w's left child is RED

                x.p.colour = BLACK
                w.left.colour = BLACK
                self.rotate_right(x.p)
                x = self.root
    x.colour = BLACK
```

7.4.4 Complexity Analysis

In red-black trees, the worst-case complexity of searching is 'O(log n)' and so the complexity of insert and delete operations is also 'O(log n)', respectively. In AVL trees, there were continuous rotations to ensure that the tree is always balanced. A balanced tree has a height of 'O(log n)' which resulted in the same complexity for the searching, inserting, and deleting processes. In a red-black tree, there is no rotation for every insertion. Instead, it has some cases when to rotate and when not to rotate reducing the overheads. The step-by-step proof that the red-black trees are balanced is provided below.

- For a general binary tree, the minimum number of nodes in any root-to-leaf path is '2Log(n+1)', where 'n' is the number of nodes in the tree.
- Given the minimum number of nodes in a root to leaf path, the maximum number of black nodes in a root-to-leaf path is 'Log(n+1)'. This is same for all root-to-leaf paths as the number of black nodes is same in each sub-tree. In addition, all the nodes in the path will not be black and a red lies between two blacks. Thus, the maximum black nodes are half of the minimum number of nodes in a root-to-leaf path.
- Other than this, it is known that the maximum number of black nodes in a tree is 'n/2' (rounded off to previous integer).
- From the above two points, it can be inferred that height of a node cannot be more than '2Log(n+1)'.

7.5 SPLAY TREES

The primary purpose of search trees is to store data efficiently. As the name suggests, the primary purpose of a search tree is searching. In a BST, the search time is 'O(n)' for a skewed tree. In real time, if searching a value from a million data takes a million seconds, then it is considered to be inefficient. Thus, an AVL tree was introduced to maintain the tree balanced and bring down the search time to 'O(log n)'. It had the overheads in rotating the tree for every new entry. To reduce the rotations, red-black trees were brought into the picture. However, there was no betterment in the complexity of searching. If searching has been the primary operation, then why shouldn't there be a search tree dedicated for searching? Studies show that for any common application, 80 per cent of accesses are only on 20 per cent of data. Therefore, search-friendly splay trees were devised. In a splay tree, the most recently accessed element is moved to the root to reduce the search time. In the same example of one million data points, it will be sufficient that the top 'k' frequently accessed elements are placed in the main memory. As we know, these are the elements that will be accessed. If an element is not available in main memory, then it can be loaded from the disk. This reduces the processing time in real time as all BST, AVL, and red-black trees have the entire tree on main memory. In an attempt to bring the access time of recently-accessed item to 'O(1)', the worst case height of the tree gets compromised. The worst case height of the splay tree is 'O(n)' with an average height of 'O(log n)'. Despite this worst case height, splay trees are referred to as self-balancing trees. While inserting a node, it will be first checked if the same is already present in the tree. Only if it is not present, the element will be inserted. Thus, splay trees cannot have duplicate elements and this is ideal for file storage as there will not be any duplicates. How is this achieved and how the search operation is performed in such a structure is all discussed below.

Unlike the other search trees, searching is different in splay trees. Along with search, insertion and deletion are also dealt in detail in the following section. A peculiar fact about splay trees is that the search operation will also edit the tree. In search operation, the last accessed value is moved up to the root, hence editing the tree. In all the search trees which we have already discussed, the search operation does not edit the tree.

7.5.1 Operation—'Search a Value' or 'Splay a Value'

As explained above, search finds a value and moves it to the root. So, searching is started from the root. If the required value is in the root, then just the value is returned. This means the same node has been accessed two or more times in a line. Thus, the simplest search of the last accessed element is 'O(1)'. The node that is searched for can have a grandparent or just a parent or may be the root. So, when these cases are handled, it covers all positions of the node. Rotations are done to bring the concerned node to the root and then return the value. If the node is present deep in the tree, recursions help in rotation of the tree from that level until the root is reached. Rotations are the same as discussed in case of an AVL tree, just with a different name.

The simple case is when the required node is the direct child of the root. The child may be a left child or right child. If the required node is the left child of the root, a right rotation is done pivoted at the root and then the new root is returned. If the required node is the right child of the root, then a left rotation is done pivoted at the root and then the new root is returned. In splay, the left child case is termed as 'Zig' and the right child case is termed as 'Zag'.

As discussed above, search is a recursive process. At every recursion, there will be a primary node and the checks, and rotation will be done on its sub-tree. The node under consideration is the root of the sub-tree under consideration. In a given recursion, the node under consideration is the root for the part of the tree under consideration. If the root is the value that is being searched for, then the value is returned. If the required value is the left child of the root, it is the 'Zig' case. A right rotation is done at the root node. This brings the required node to the root position. Then, the new root is returned. On the other hand, when the required value is the right child of the root, it is the 'Zag' case. A left rotation at the root node moves the required node as the new root. Then, the new root value is returned. The 'Zig' and 'Zag' cases are straight forward and just handling the cases when the required node is the child of the root, that is the node under consideration in the current recursion. There can be cases when the required node is the grandchild of root of the sub-tree. There can be four different arrangements of the node classified as:

1. Zig-Zig
2. Zig-Zag
3. Zag-Zag
4. Zag-Zig

Zig-Zig

Zig-Zig is when the required node is the left child of its parent and its parent is the left child of the grandparent of the required node. This is just the 'left-left' case imbalance discussed in AVL trees. In splay trees, it cannot be considered as imbalance as it does not have the property of maintaining balanced trees. To handle this case, a right rotation is done at the grandparent followed by another right rotation at the parent of the required node. This ensures that the required node moves up to the root.

In recursion, from the grandparent node, the value of the left child is checked. When the left child is found to be greater than the required value, the function is recurred for the left child as new root, considering the left sub-tree of the grandparent. In the next recursive round, the above check fails as the left child is the required node. Then, the tree is rotated right and the recursion ends. The control then returns to the previous call, where one more rotation takes place. Thus, the final tree is rotated twice and the required node is brought to the root. This step might seem complicated but it is straight forward and can be easily understood using the example provided in Figure 7.33. The figure shows a sample splay tree where searching of a node results in the Zig-Zig case.

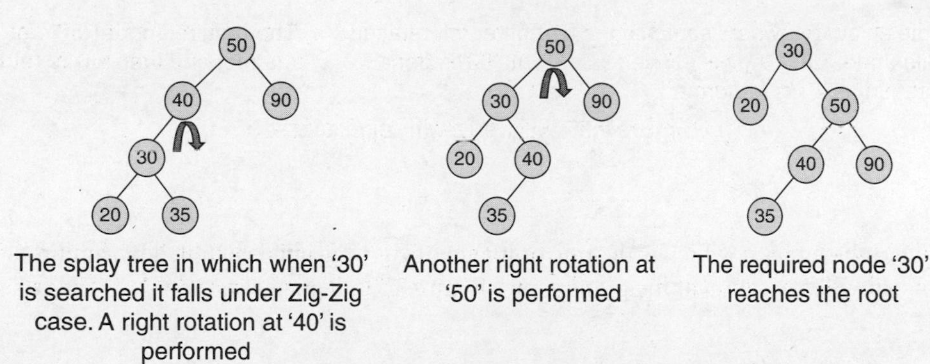
50
40
90
30
20
35
The splay tree in which when '30' is searched it falls under Zig-Zig case. A right rotation at '40' is performed
50
30
90
20
40
35
Another right rotation at '50' is performed
30
20
50
40
90
35
The required node '30' reaches the root

Figure 7.33 Splay tree with Zig-Zig case

Zig-Zag

Figure 7.34 shows a splay tree where searching a node falls under the Zig-Zag case. Zig-Zag is the case when the required node is the right child of the parent and the parent is the left child of the grandparent. This is the left-right case as discussed in case of AVL trees. In this case, a left rotation at the parent followed by a right rotation at the grandparent brings the required node to the root. Then, the value in the new root is returned.

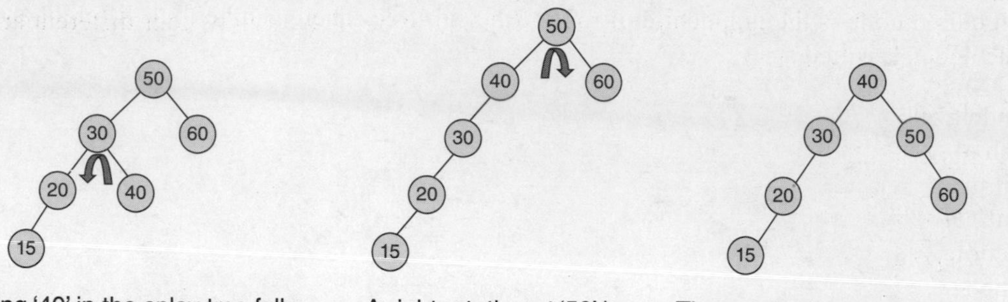

Searching '40' in the splay tree falls under the Zig-Zag case. A left rotation at '30', parent of '40', is performed

A right rotation at '50' is performed

The required node '40' reaches the root. Finally, '40' is returned

Figure 7.34 Splay tree with Zig-Zag case

Zag-Zag

Zag-Zag is the right-right case, which is the mirror image of Zig-Zig. It is handled by double left rotation just like double right rotation of Zig-Zig. Figure 7.35 shows a tree where searching a node falls under the Zag-Zag case.

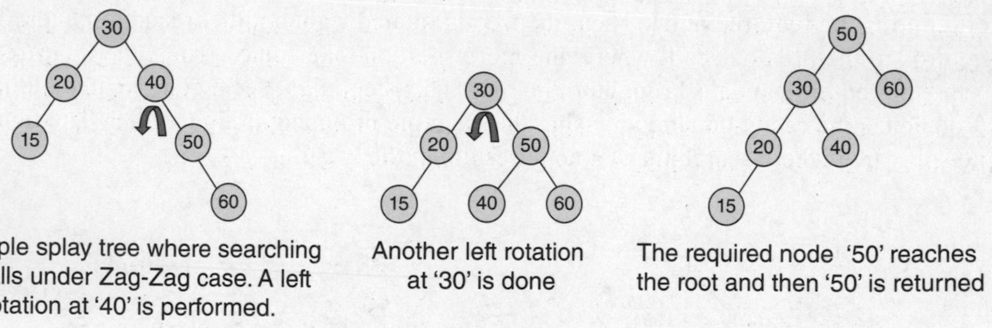

A sample splay tree where searching '50' falls under Zag-Zag case. A left rotation at '40' is performed.

Another left rotation at '30' is done

The required node '50' reaches the root and then '50' is returned

Figure 7.35 Splay tree with Zag-Zag case

Zag-Zig

Zag-Zig is the right-left case which is the mirror image of Zig-Zag and is handled by right rotation at the parent followed by left rotation at the grandparent. Figure 7.36 depicts a sample Zag-Zig case.

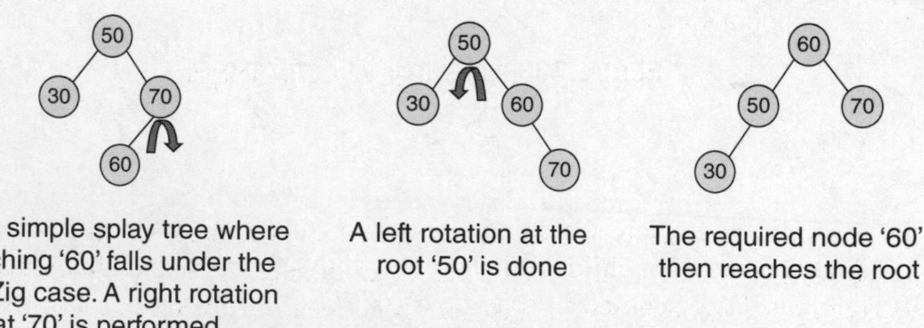

A very simple splay tree where searching '60' falls under the Zag-Zig case. A right rotation at '70' is performed.

A left rotation at the root '50' is done

The required node '60' then reaches the root

Figure 7.36 Splay tree with Zag-Zig case

In real time, when a node is searched for, it is not mandatorily in the first three levels of the tree. Instead, it may lie deep inside the tree. That is where recursion plays a major role. In every recursive call, the node, its parent, and grandparent are checked. If the node is lesser or greater than the grandchildren, then recursion comes into the picture. In that case, the required node is not within the reach of the current node. So, the recursive call is done with the grandchild. This process continues until the required node can be reached from the root of the recursion. Then, rotation starts from that point. Once all the rotation of the current recursion is done, the control returns back to the previous functions, that is, the point where it was recurred. There comes further rotations and this continues in the reverse order of recursion. Finally, when all the recursions are completed, the required node becomes the root. The basic logic for recursion is same as search in a BST. If the current node is lesser than the required value, then the right child is considered. If the node is greater, then the left child is considered. If the left or right child is the required node, then a right rotation is done to bring the left child to the root or a left rotation is done to bring the right child to the root. Post-rotation, the root is returned. Recursion does not come into the picture, if the left or right child is not the required element and if further sub-trees exist. If the required value is lesser than the left child, then it can be compared with the left child of the left child. Even then if the required value is lesser, then a recursive call is done with that particular grandchild as the root. This means recursive call happens skipping one level in the middle and once the recursive call is over, the control returns back to this same point. Remember that we are inside the left sub-tree case. So, after the control comes back, there will be a right rotation at the root. Similarly, there will be a left rotation inside the right sub-tree case. After this case is completed, there will be another rotation outside. It means when rotations have been completed inside the left child of the left child case, there will be a rotation inside the left child case. Thus, for two levels, two rotations come into the picture. The case left child and left child of left child discussed in detail above are Zig and Zig-Zig cases, respectively. Similarly, Zig-Zag, Zag-Zag, and Zag-Zig cases also involve two rotations based on different arrangements of the required value. Two important things to be taken from here are that recursive calls are present inside the grandchild checking part and corresponding rotations are done after the recursive call. The left child case will have a right rotation and the right child case will have a left rotation. This entire process of searching the node is also termed as Splaying.

Question 7.5 Search node '65' in the tree given in Figure 7.37.

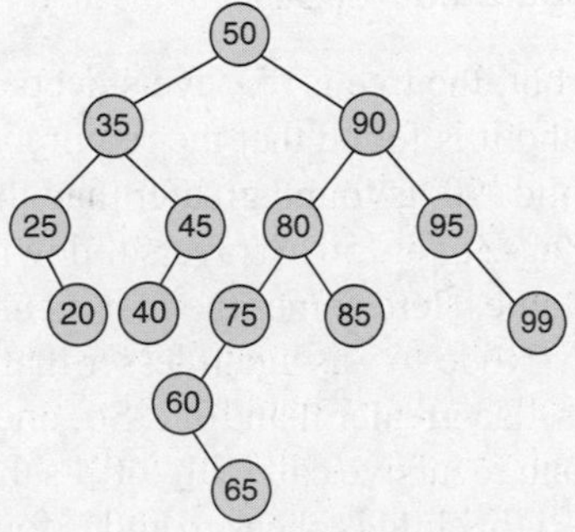

Figure 7.37 A sample tree where node '65' is searched

Solution: Figure 7.38 shows searching of a node deep inside the tree.

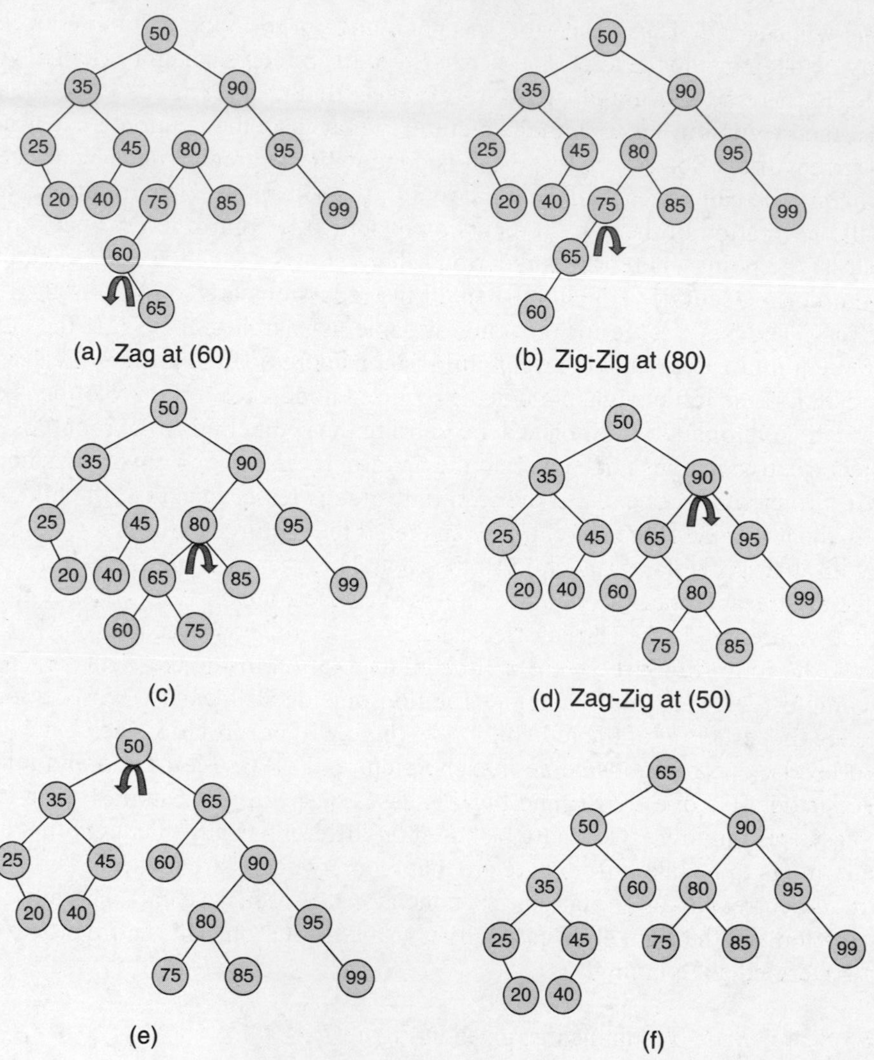

Figure 7.38 Solution to Question 7.5

In Figure 7.38, starting from the root, the tree is '5' levels deeper. So, it involves two recursive calls. From the root '50', the check starts and it is found that the required node is greater than the root. This is the right case, Zag. Then, the right child '90' is found greater than the required node. This is the left case, Zig. These two add up to form the Zag-Zig at '50'. Traversal down is not possible and the left child of '90' is also greater than the required value. Here comes the first recursive call with '80' as the new root for the next sub-tree under consideration. Node '65' is again lesser than '80' and gets into the left case, Zig. The left child of '80' is '75', which is also greater than '65'. So, one more left case is piled up and forms Zig-Zig at '80'. This invokes the second recursive call with '60' as the new root, as '65' is lesser than '75'. Now, '65' is greater than '60'. So, the right child is checked and is found to be '65', the required node. This adds a Zag at '60' and the recursion ends. In the innermost recursion, Zag at '60' is handled first with a left rotation at '60'. Then, the control returns to the previous call where the Zig-Zig at '80' is handled by two right rotations, one at '75' followed by another at '80'. Then, the control returns to the first function which initiated the first recursive call where the Zag-Zig at '50' is handled by a right rotation at '90' followed by a left rotation at '50'. This brings the required node '65' to the root and the same is returned. This is how the recursions in the pseudocode help in bringing values from deeper levels to the root.

All the above discussion ends with the base case that the required node is present inside the tree at any deeper level. What if the value is not present? This is the most interesting part of splaying. The logic of comparison and recursion will continue until a leaf node is reached. In the last recursion, the root called will be 'null' and the same will be returned to the previous call, as it cannot be rotated anyways. Then, rotations start getting triggered one by one in the reverse order. Eventually the last leaf node, which is closest to the required node, will move up to the root. Consider the same tree depicted in Figure 7.37.

If '66' was to be searched, the recursive process would have further proceeded down from '65'. Since '65' is lesser than the required value '66', a recursive call with the right child of '65' would have been performed. However, since the right child is 'null', the same would have been returned. After this stage, all the recursions behave in the same manner as described earlier. At the end, the same tree gets formed, moving '65' to the root as it was the last accessed node in the process of searching for '66'. After all, inside the recursions while rotating when a new node moves into the root position, it is never checked if it is the required node. Pseudocode 7.13 shows the search/splay operation.

Pseudocode 7.13

```
def splaying(node,value):
    if not node     #No rotation required
    then,
        return None
    if node = value
    then,
        return node
    if value < node
    then,
        if node.left is null
        then,
            return node
        if value < node.left
        then,
            node.left.left = splaying(node.left.left,value)
            node = right_rotate(node)
        else if value > node.left
        then,
            node.left.right = splaying(node.left.right,value)
            if node.left.right:
            then,
            node.left = left_rotate(node.left)
        if node.left is not null
        then,
            return right_rotate(node)
        return node
    else if value > node
    then,
        if node.right is null
        then,
            return node
        if value < node.right
        then,
            node.right.left = splaying(node.right.left,value)
            if node.right.left is not null
            then,
                node.right = right_rotate(node.right)
        else if value > node.right
        then,
```

(*contd*)

(*contd*)

```
        node.right.right = splaying(node.right.right,value)
        node = left_rotate(node)
    if node.right is not null
    then,
        return left_rotate(node)
    return node
```

7.5.2 Operation—Insert a Node

Inserting a node into a splay tree places it in the root. So when a node is to be inserted, it is first splayed. If the node is already present, then it becomes the root as it has already been splayed. Now, the new node is not inserted as it is already present in the tree. Thus, splay trees do not have duplicate elements. If the value is not present, then the node with the value closest to the value to be inserted becomes the new root, based on the splaying process discussed earlier. If the new node to be inserted is lesser than the current root after splaying, then the current root is made the right child of the new root. The right child of the old root is left unchanged, whereas the left child of the old root is made as the left child of the new root. So, the left child of the old root is made 'null'. Figure 7.39 shows insertion of a value into a splay tree which is lesser than the existing root. In case the new value is greater than the existing root, then the existing root is made the left child of the new node. The left child of the root is not changed but the right child of the old root is made the right child of the new node. The right child of the old root is made 'null'. Figure 7.40 shows insertion of a node greater than the root into a splay tree. There are just two cases of insertion into a splay tree. In splay trees, the node inserted last is also at the position of the root. Pseudocode 7.14 shows insertion a node into a splay tree.

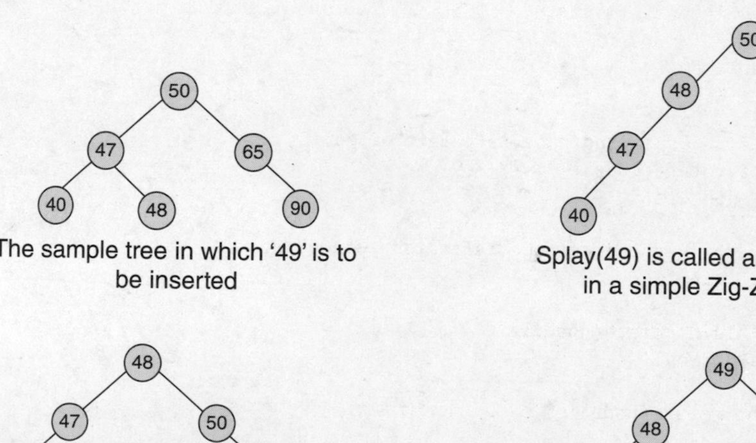

The sample tree in which '49' is to be inserted

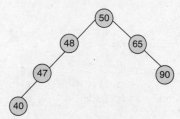

Splay(49) is called and that results in a simple Zig-Zag at '50'

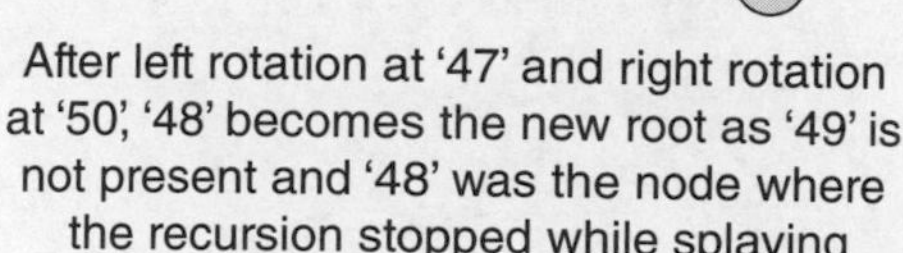

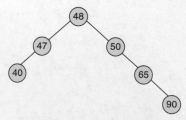

After left rotation at '47' and right rotation at '50', '48' becomes the new root as '49' is not present and '48' was the node where the recursion stopped while splaying

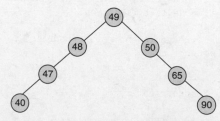

Node '49' is inserted into the tree as the root. Since '48' is lesser than '49', '48' and its left sub-tree are made the left sub-tree of '49'. The right sub-tree of '48' is made as the right sub-tree of '49' and the right of '48' is left blank. This is the final splay tree after insertion of '49' which is in the root position.

Figure 7.39 Insertion of a value into a splay tree which is lesser than the existing root

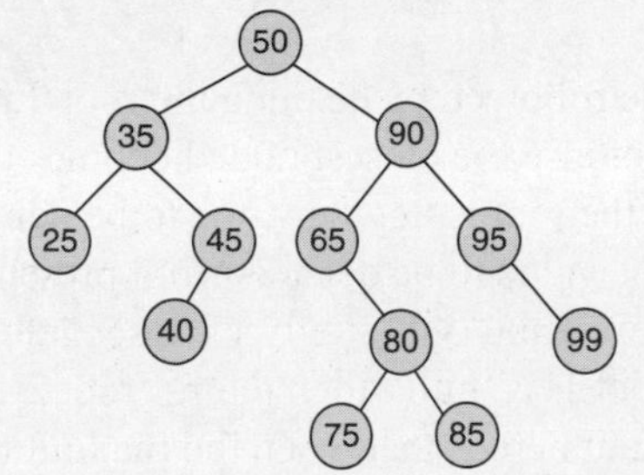

A sample tree where '60' is to be inserted

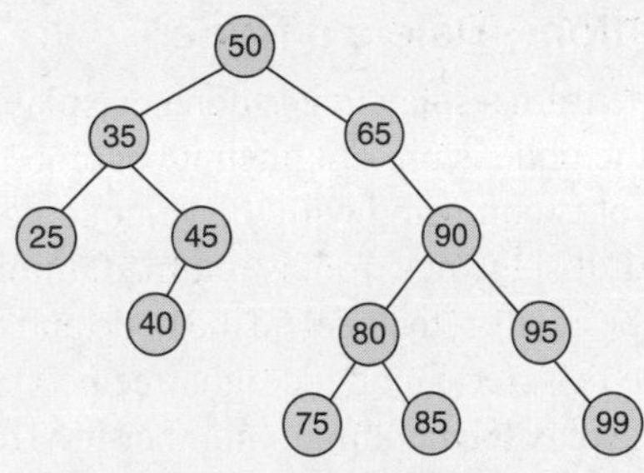

When splay(60) is called, the closest node '65' is reached and it results in Zag-Zig case at '50'

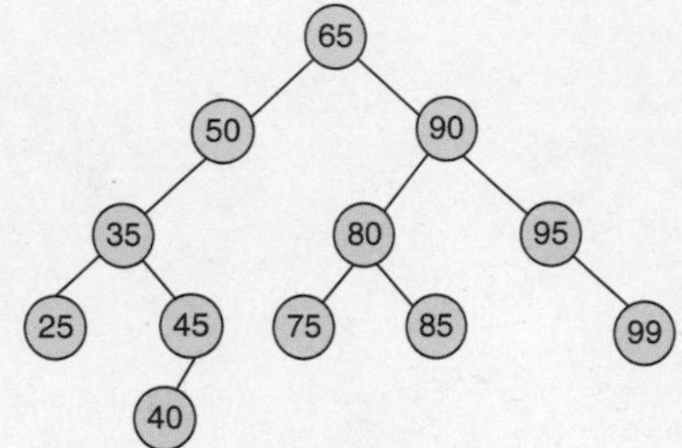

After splaying, '65' becomes the new root

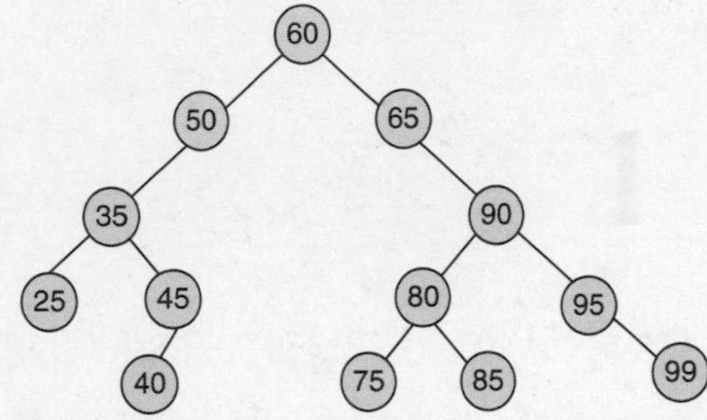

When '60' is inserted, '65' and its right child form the right sub-tree whereas the left sub-tree of '65' becomes the left sub-tree of '60'

Figure 7.40 Insertion of a node greater than the root into a splay tree

Pseudocode 7.14

```
def insert(value):
    if root is null
    then,
        root = value
        return
    root = splaying(root,value)
    if root = value #after splay operation
    then,           #element already present, no insertion
        return
    else if root > value
    then,
        node = Node(value)
        node.right = root
        node.left = root.left
        root.left = null
        root = node
    else,
        node = Node(value)
        node.left = root
        node.right = root.right
        root.right = null
        root = node
```

7.5.3 Operation—Delete a Node

Deleting a node from a splay tree is done by splaying the node followed by deleting the root. First, the node is splayed. If the node is present, then it becomes the new root else the closest node becomes the root. The value of the root is compared with the value to be deleted. If the root is not the value to be deleted, then no node is deleted. Just the new root is returned, implying that the value to be deleted is not present. If the root is the value to be deleted, then delete the node and consider the left and right sub-trees as separate splay trees. Let the left tree be 'Tree 1' and the right tree be 'Tree 2'. If 'root 1' is 'null', then return 'root 2'. When 'root 1' is not 'null', splay the maximum number in 'Tree 1'. A fact in here is that when the maximum element is splayed in 'Tree 1', the right child of the root becomes 'null' as all other elements in 'Tree 1' are now lesser than the root. 'Tree 2' can then be made as the right sub-tree of the 'root 1'. This forms the final splay tree after deletion of the specified node. Figure 7.41 shows deletion of a node in a tree. Pseudocode 7.15 shows the deletion process.

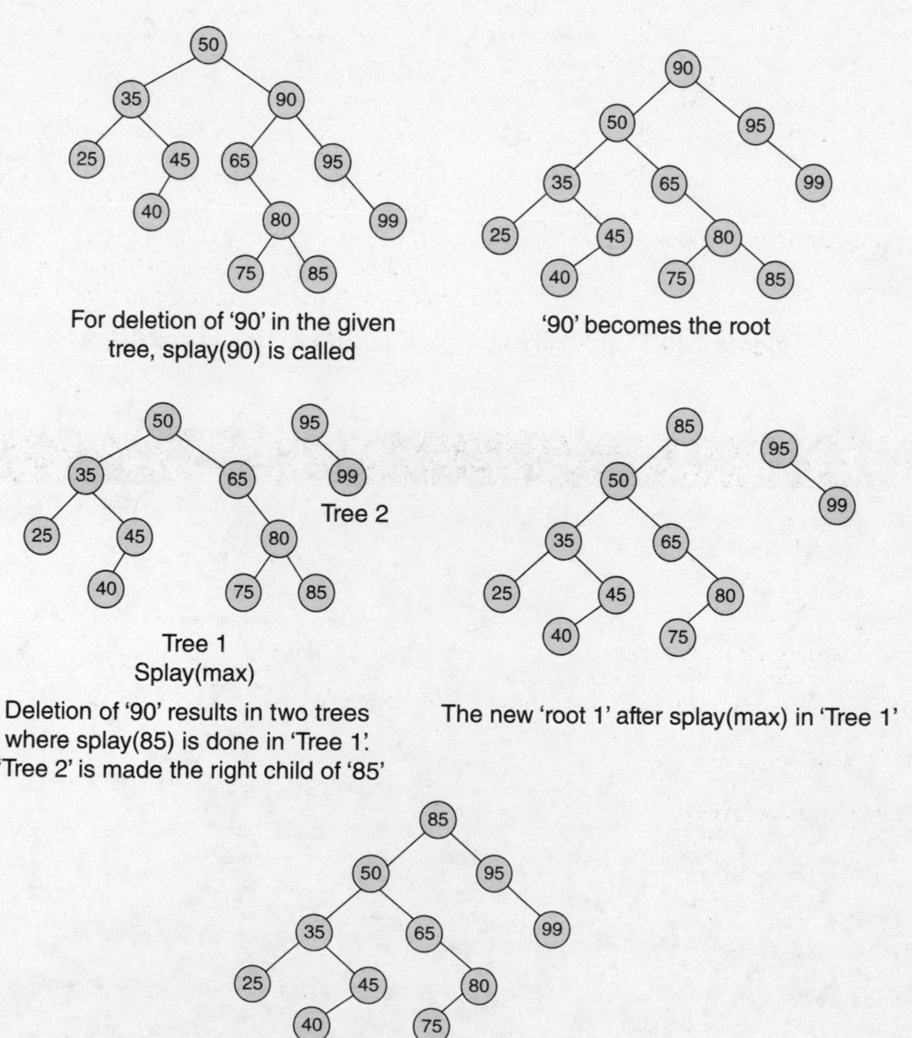

For deletion of '90' in the given tree, splay(90) is called
'90' becomes the root
Tree 2
Tree 1
Splay(max)
Deletion of '90' results in two trees where splay(85) is done in 'Tree 1'. 'Tree 2' is made the right child of '85'
The new 'root 1' after splay(max) in 'Tree 1'
The final tree

Figure 7.41 Deletion of a node in a Splay tree

Pseudocode 7.15

```
def delete(value):
    if root is null
    then,
        print("empty tree")
        return
    root = splaying(root,value)
    if root != value                          #after splay operation
    then,                                     #element not there in tree
        return
    else,                                     #element found and moved to root, delete root
        if root.left = None
        then,
            root = root.right
        righttree = root.right
        root = splaying(root.left,value) #next smallest element is moved to the root
        root.right = righttree
```

7.5.4 Implementation of Splay Trees

Both the insertion and deletion operations involve splay operation. Splay involves both the left and right rotations. Just as previous search trees, all the functionalities are implemented using modules here as well. Python code 7.4 shows for implementation of splay trees.

Python code 7.4

```
"""
 A Splay Tree is a self-adjusting BST, where every operation on element will rearrange the tree
such that the element is brought to the root of the tree by appropriate rotations.

 All operations in a Splay Tree are invloved with a common operation called Splaying, followed
by the standard BST insertion/search/deletion.

 By splaying, most frequently used elements are brought closer to the root of the tree.

 To splay any element, we use the following rotation operations (combinations of zig-zag):
 1. Zig
 2. Zag
 3. Zig-Zig
 4. Zag-Zag
 5. Zig-Zag
 6. Zag-Zig

 Zig involves insertion/access to the left
 Zag involves insertion/access to the right

Splaying a node, to move it to the root involves a double rotation, rather than a single rotation.

 The splaying operations are shown below:

 x - node to be splayed, y - parent, g - grandparent T1, T2, T3, T4 - sub-trees
```

(*contd*)

(*contd*)

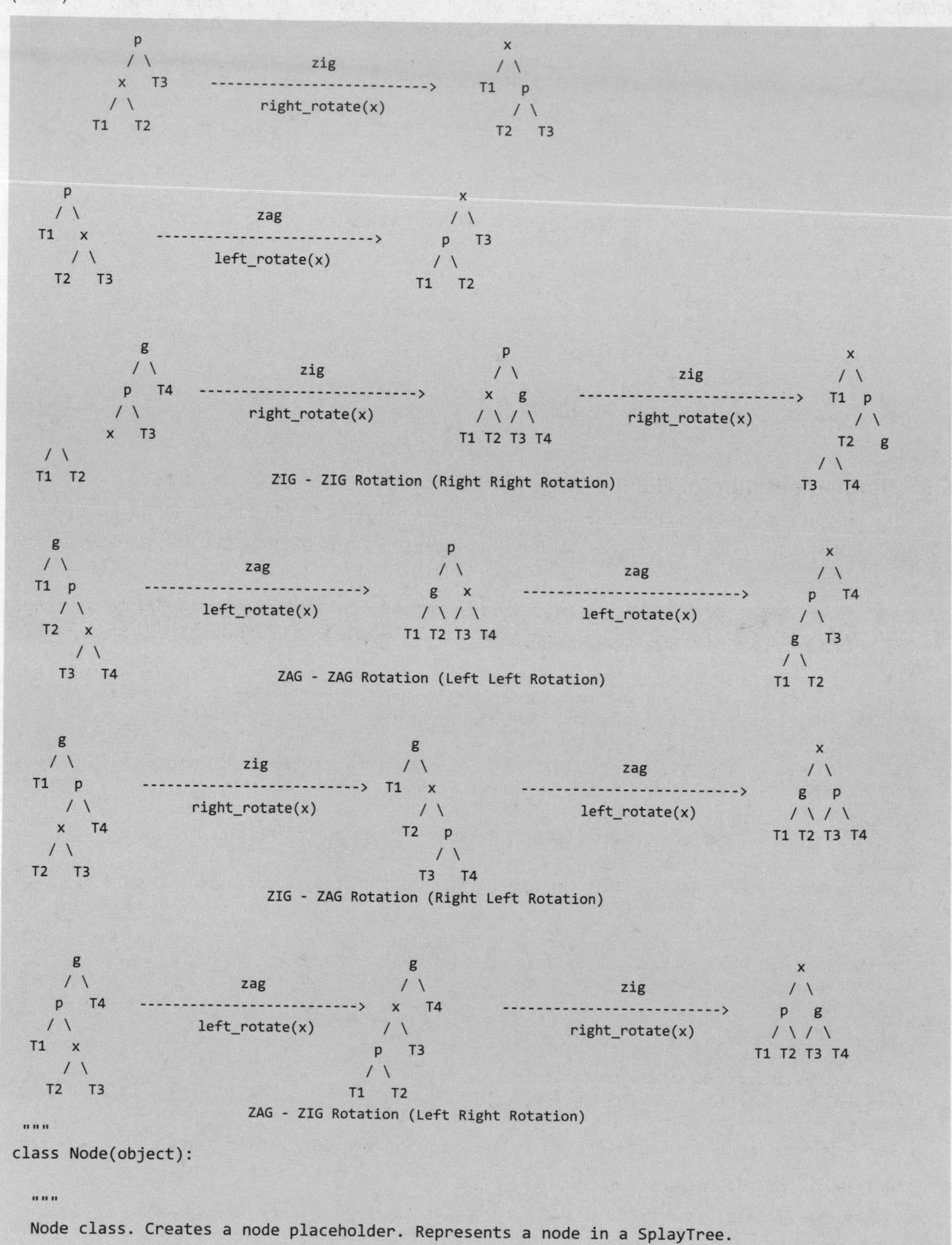

```
              p                                      x
             / \             zig                    / \
            x   T3   ------------------------->   T1   p
           / \            right_rotate(x)              / \
          T1  T2                                      T2   T3

       p                                      x
      / \            zag                     / \
     T1  x   ------------------------->     p   T3
        / \        left_rotate(x)          / \
       T2  T3                             T1  T2

              g                                 p                                    x
             / \          zig                  / \              zig                 / \
            p   T4  ------------------------->  x   g  ------------------------->  T1   p
           / \        right_rotate(x)         / \ / \     right_rotate(x)              / \
          x   T3                             T1 T2 T3 T4                              T2   g
     / \                                                                                  / \
    T1  T2             ZIG - ZIG Rotation (Right Right Rotation)                        T3   T4

      g                                   p                                      x
     / \           zag                   / \             zag                    / \
    T1  p   ------------------------->  g   x   ------------------------->     p   T4
       / \       left_rotate(x)        / \ / \      left_rotate(x)            / \
      T2   x                          T1 T2 T3 T4                            g   T3
          / \                                                               / \
        T3   T4          ZAG - ZAG Rotation (Left Left Rotation)           T1  T2

      g                                  g                                       x
     / \           zig                  / \              zag                    / \
    T1  p   ------------------------->  T1  x    ------------------------->    g   p
       / \       right_rotate(x)           / \        left_rotate(x)          / \ / \
      x   T4                              T2  p                              T1 T2 T3 T4
     / \                                      / \
    T2  T3                                   T3  T4
                          ZIG - ZAG Rotation (Right Left Rotation)

       g                                 g                                        x
      / \          zag                  / \              zig                     / \
     p   T4  ------------------------->  x   T4   ------------------------->    p   g
    / \         left_rotate(x)          / \          right_rotate(x)           / \ / \
   T1  x                               p   T3                                 T1 T2 T3 T4
      / \                             / \
     T2  T3                          T1  T2
                       ZAG - ZIG Rotation (Left Right Rotation)
"""
class Node(object):

  """
  Node class. Creates a node placeholder. Represents a node in a SplayTree.
```

(*contd*)

(*contd*)

```
  """

  def __init__(self,key):

    """
    Initializer for the Node class

    Parameters
    ----------
    key : int
         The value of a node in the tree
    """
        self.key = key
        self.left = None
        self.right = None

class SplayTree(object):
  """
  Represents the SplayTree class.

  Methods
  -------

  insert
    Inserts a node with key to the SplayTree

  search
    Searches for a key among nodes in a SplayTree

  delete
    Deletes a node from the SplayTree

  splaying
    Perform splaying operations on a key bearing node

  left_rotate
    Rotate the SplayTree to the left, at a specified node

  right_rotate
    Rotate the SplayTree to the right, at a specifed node
  """
    def __init__(self):
        self.root = None                          # Initially, the root is empty
    def insert(self,key):

      """
      Inserts a node with key to the SplayTree by standard BST insertion and set it as root

      Parameters
```

(*contd*)

(*contd*)

```
    ----------
    key: int
        key of a node
    """

      #node = self.root
      if not self.root:
          self.root = Node(key)                  # If its not root, make the new node as root
          return

      self.root = self.splaying(self.root,key)   # Perform splaying operations, to make the
                                                 # new node as root

      # Standard BST Insertion

      if self.root.key == key:                   # If key is already there in the tree, do
                                                 # nothing
          return
      elif self.root.key > key:
          node = Node(key)
          node.right = self.root
          node.left = self.root.left
          self.root.left = None
          self.root = node

      else:
          node = Node(key)
          node.left = self.root
          node.right = self.root.right
          self.root.right = None
          self.root = node

def search(self,key):

    """
    Search for a key among nodes in the SplayTree.
    Splay the tree at that node and set it as root
    If the key is not found, set the last splayed node as root

    Parameters
    ----------
    key: int
       key of a node
    """

      self.root = self.splaying(self.root,key)
      if self.root.key == key:
          return self.root.key
      return None
```

(*contd*)

(*contd*)

```
    def delete(self,key):

      """
      Search for a key among nodes in the SplayTree.
      If found, splay the tree at parent of the node and set it as root

      Parameters
      ----------
      key: int
         key of a node
      """
        if not self.root:                          # Tree is empty
            print("empty tree")
            return
        self.root = self.splaying(self.root,key)
        if self.root.key != key:                    # Key not in tree
            return

        else:
            if self.root.left == None:
                self.root = self.root.right

                righttree = self.root.right
                self.root = self.splaying(self.root.left,key)
                self.root.right = righttree

    def splaying(self,node,key):

    """
    Perform splaying operations on a key bearing node
    1. Zig (Right Rotation)
    2. Zag (Left Rotation)
    3. Zig-Zig (Right Right Rotation)
    4. Zag-Zag (Left Left Rotation)
    5. Zig-Zag (Right Left Rotation)
    6. Zag-Zig (Left Right Rotation)

    Parameters
    ----------
    node: node object
        key bearing node

    key: int
        key of a node
    """
        if not node:
            return None
        if key == node.key:
            return node
        if key < node.key:
            if node.left == None:
                return node
```

(*contd*)

(*contd*)

```
            if key < node.left.key:
                node.left.left = self.splaying(node.left.left,key)      # Case: Zig-Zig
                node = self.right_rotate(node)                          # Case: Zag

            elif key > node.left.key:
                node.left.right = self.splaying(node.left.right,key)    # Case Zig-Zag
                if node.left.right:
                    node.left = self.left_rotate(node.left)             # Case Zig

            if node.left:
                return self.right_rotate(node)                          # Case: Zag

            return node
        elif key > node.key:
            if node.right == None:
                return node

            if key < node.right.key:
                node.right.left = self.splaying(node.right.left,key)    # Case: Zag-Zig
                if node.right.left:
                    node.right = self.right_rotate(node.right)          # Case: Zag

            elif key > node.right.key:
                node.right.right = self.splaying(node.right.right,key)  # Case: Zag-Zag
                node = self.left_rotate(node)                           # Case: Zig

            if node.right:
                return self.left_rotate(node)                           # Case: Zig

            return node

def left_rotate(self,node):

        """
        Rotate the SplayTree to the left, at a specified node

        Parameters
        ----------
        node: node object
            key bearing node
        """

#        p (node)                                 x
#       / \                   zag                / \
#    T1    x (child)    --------------->      p    T3
#         / \            left_rotate(p)      / \
#       T2   T3                            T1    T2
```

(*contd*)

(contd)

```
        if not node:                # If node doesn't exist do nothing
            return None
        child = node.right          # assign node's right to child
        if not child:               # if child doesn't exist return node
            return node
        node.right = child.left     # Assign child's left to node's right  (child.left)
        child.left = node           # Finally assign child's left to node
        return child

    def right_rotate(self,node):

       """
       Rotate the SplayTree to the left, at a specified node

       Parameters
       ----------
       node: node object
           key bearing node
       """
#      (node) p                                  x
#          / \             zig                  / \
#    (child) x   T3      --------------->    T1   p
#          / \          right_rotate(p)          / \
#        T1   T2                               T2   T3
#              (child.right)

        if not node:                # If node doesn't exist do nothing
            return None
        child = node.left           # assign node's left to child
        if not child:               # if child doesn't exist return node
            return node
        node.left = child.right     # Assign right of child to node's left
        child.right = node          # Finally assign child's left to node
        return child
def postorder(node):
    if node is not None:
        lst.append(node.key)
        postorder(node.left)
        postorder(node.right)
        print(node.key,en d=" ")
```

7.5.5 Complexity Analysis

The core operation for all functionalities is splaying. It has the worst case complexity of 'O(n)' as the worst case height of a splay tree is 'O(n)'. The average case complexity of splay is 'O(log n)'. Complexities of insertion and deletion processes are also 'O(n)', respectively, as they directly rely on the splay operation. An interesting fact in splay trees is that even though the worst case height is 'O(n)', the trees are called self-balancing as rotations while inserting the new node balance the height while building the tree. The key point with splay tree is, as already said it is not build on the entire lot of elements. With 'm' elements a limited 'n' is determined based on the problem and the data set and then the tree is built on that. Then the true impact on search time is felt, especially when 'm' is very large when compared to 'n'.

Food for Brain

Is the splay tree balanced if the nodes are inserted in ascending order without any other operation before insertion of all nodes?

7.6 B-TREES

This is the most important form of search trees. It is widely used in real-time applications. Here, the entire data is present in secondary memory and need not be loaded completely into main memory for accessing or processing specific nodes. This is also known as 'm-n' trees. A format of this tree is a (2-4) tree which is handled in detail in this chapter. Unlike other search trees, here the node can have more than two children. So, B-trees are also known as multiway search trees. The number of keys in the node depends on the order of the tree. The (2-4) trees or (2-3-4) trees are B-trees of 'order 4'. The number of possible children of a node is the number of keys in the node plus 1. The properties of B-trees are shared below.

1. All the leaf nodes are at the same level
2. All nodes other than the root must have '[m/2]-1' keys, where 'm' is the order of the tree
3. All nodes other than the root can have a maximum of 'm-1' keys
4. All non-leaf nodes other than the root must have at least [m/2] children
5. If the root is not a leaf, it must have at least two children
6. A node with 'n-1' keys can have a maximum of 'n' children
7. All the keys within a node will be in ascending order

If the order is '6', then it is either a (3-6) tree or a (3-4-5-6) tree. The children are arranged in a specific order. The first child, that is the left-most child, and the subtree are lesser than the first key. The second child and the second subtree, in turn, are greater than the first key and lesser than the second key. Similarly, the third subtree is greater than the second key and lesser than the third key. The final subtree, that is the rightmost child's subtree, is greater than the third key in the node. An example of a (2-4) tree is shown in Figure 7.42.

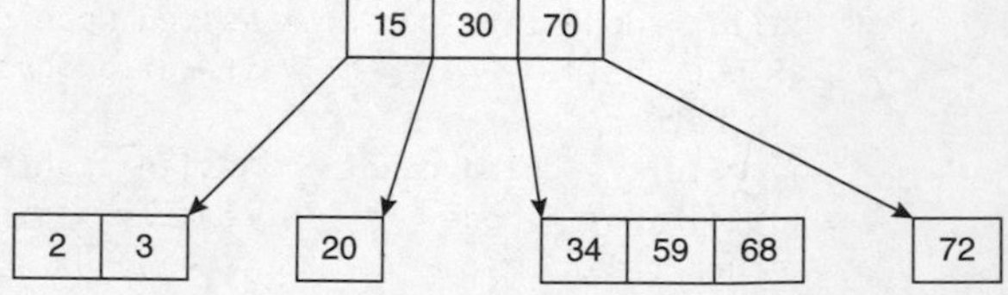

Figure 7.42 A sample (2, 4) tree

In a (2, 4) tree based on the above property, the nodes can have 1, 2, or 3 keys at max. Such trees are called multiway trees as there are more than two subtrees for each node. Traversal or searching is just based on the facts that the keys inside the node are in ascending order and the range of the subtree distribution is explained above. As the tree has a different structure, traversal algorithms also change for B-trees. All the operations are explained in the sections below.

7.6.1 In-order Traversal

As known already, in-order traversal of a search tree is in ascending order but how it is achieved has a different logic. The base logic is still the same. The sub-tree to the left of a key is visited before visiting the key. The recursion starts with the root. Consider the current node, that is, if the first child is not 'null' then a recursive call performs the in-order traversal of the first sub-tree. Following this, the first element is printed or visited. If the second child exists, a recursive call for the second sub-tree is done and then the second key is visited. After this, there could be a third child. When the third child exists, recursive call for in-order traversal of the third sub-tree is done. Finally, if there is a third child, it is visited, followed by a recursive call for the fourth and final sub-tree, if it exists. The in-order traversal of the example tree shared in Figure 7.42 is 2, 3, 15, 20, 30, 34, 59, 68, 70, 72.

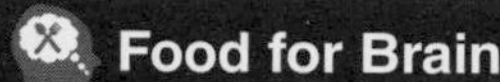

How to perform pre-order and post-order traversal of a B-tree?

7.6.2 Operation—Search a Node

Given a value, it is searched starting with the root. Searching is also handled using recursive calls. In the current node, if the required value is lesser than the first case, the first sub-tree is searched. If the first key is the required value, then just the key is returned. If the required value is greater than the first key, then it is compared with the second key. When the required value is between the first and second keys, the second sub-tree is searched using a recursive call. If the value searched for is equal to the second key, then the second key is returned. When any of the above cases is not satisfied, the search value is compared with the third key. When the value is lesser than the third key, the third sub-tree is searched. On the contrary, if the third key is the required value, the same is returned. The final case is when the required value is greater than the third key, which means the fourth child is searched in this case. In all the above cases, there might be a possibility that the corresponding child or key does not exist. In the recursion cases, if the corresponding child is not present, then the required child is not present in the tree and '-1' is returned. The logic explained above is for a 4-node which has three keys. Similarly, a node can be a 3-node or a 2-node. In a 3-node when the value is greater than the second key as the third key is not present, the case calls the same sub-tree as above. In a 2-node, the logic is just same as search in a BST. Thus, searching is handled based on the number of keys in the node. Pseudocode 7.16 explains the searching process.

Pseudocode 7.16

```
#called from the root node of the B-Tree
def search(val):
    i = 0
    while (i < len(current_node) and value[i] < val)
    Do,
        increment i     #to reach the value inside the node
    if i < len(current_node) and value[i] = val
    then,                #value found in current node
        return node and index
    #when value not found in the node
    if current_node is a leaf
    then,                #value not present in the tree
        return
    else,                #check for value in the corresponding subtree
        return children[i].search(k) #Multiple recursive calls
```

7.6.3 Operation—Insert a Node

For inserting a key, it is first searched in the tree. If the key is already present, then it is not inserted. Hence, B-trees do not have duplicate elements. When the key is not present, the search operation just ends at a leaf node. It may be a 2-node, 3-node, or 4-node. Inside the node, the new key is inserted and placed in an appropriate position such that all the keys are still in an ascending order. This may sound simple, but has a pitfall. When the node is already a 4-node, it has '3' keys within it, which is the maximum capacity of a node in a (2, 4) tree. Now when the new key is added, the size of the node violates the properties of the B-tree. This condition of a node is overflow. This is handled by split. Split is done by moving the 3rd key above its parent and the node is split into two different nodes. The first two keys become a node, that is, 'node 1', and the 4th key is made as another node, that is, 'node 2'. The 3rd key that was moved above the parent is placed in the position to hold the ascending order. The new 'node 1' is made the child to the left of the key moved up and the new 'node 2' is made the right child of the key moved up. Now, there is a possibility that the parent where the key has been moved violates the property in the similar way. The parent might already be a 4-node, then moving a key up will violate the property. This, in turn, will break the parent into two and move the key further above. This is done using recursion until a node where the key inserted does not exceed the maximum limit is reached. If the root is reached in recursion and even then the size violation occurs, the 3rd key from the root is moved one level up and made as the new root. As said here, if a new root is created, then the height of the entire tree is increased by '1'. Figure 7.43 depicts insertion of '35' into a sample (2, 4) tree given in Figure 7.42. Pseudocode 7.17 shows insertion into a B-tree.

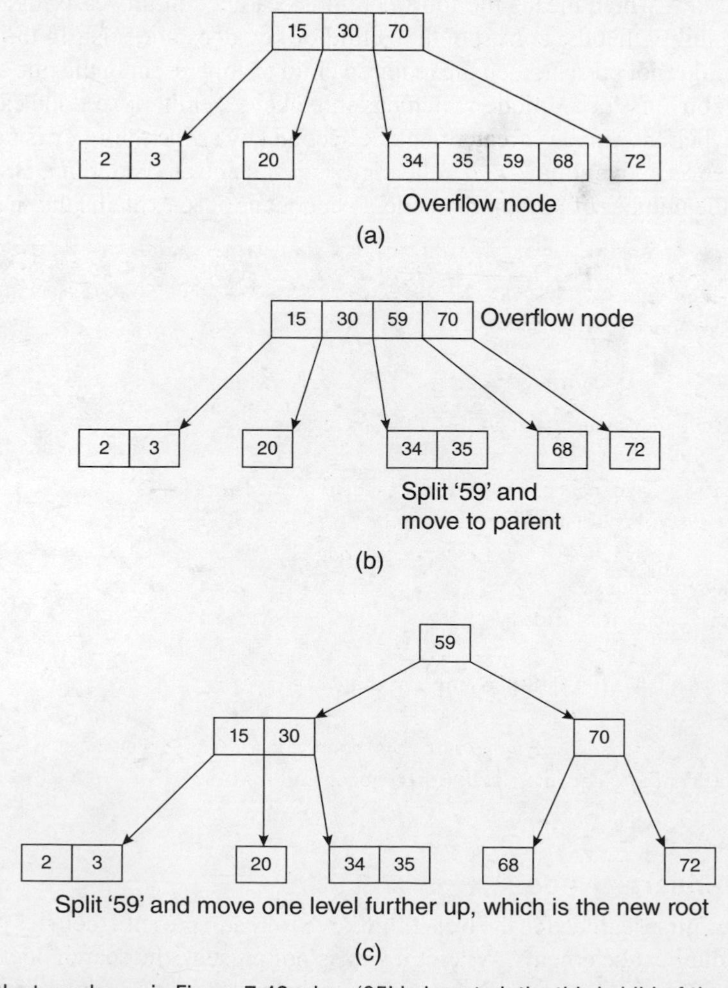

Figure 7.43 (a) In the tree shown in Figure 7.42 when '35' is inserted, the third child of the root becomes the overflow node.
(b) This results in moving '59' to the root, which in turn, becomes the overflow node
(c) Finally, '59' is moved further up and becomes the new root

Pseudocode 7.17

```
def insert(val):
    r = root
    if len(r) = 2 * order of tree - 1 #if node is full
    then,
        s = new node
        s.children.append(r)  # make root as child of new node so that inserting the new node
                              # in root
        s.split_child(0, r)
        s.insert_nonfull(val) # insert into the new node
        root = s
    else,                     # node is not full direclty insert into it
        r.insert_nonfull(val)
#Split_child functionality of the node
#Order of a node in a 2-4 tree is 4 (which marks the max length of values in it)
def split_child(i, y):
    z = new Node
    if y is a leaf
    then,
        make z a leaf node
    z.value = y.value[order_of_y:]
    if y is not a leaf
    then,
        z.children = y.children[order_of_y:]
    children.insert(i + 1, z)
    value.insert(i, y.value[order_of_y - 1])

    y.value = y.value[0:order_of_y-1] #y gets the remaining part of value & children
    y.children = y.children[0:order_of_y]
#insert function of the node, which is not full
def insert_nonfull(val):
    if current node is a leaf
    then,
        i = 0
        for i in range(len(current node))
            if val < value[i]
            then,
                value.insert(i, val)
                return self
        value.append(val)
    else,
        i = 0
        # identifying the correct subtree to insert, as a value should be to the left of all
        # greater values
        while (i < len(value))
        Do,
            if val < value[i]
            then,
                break
            i += 1
        c = children[i]
        if (len(c) = 2 * order of tree - 1)
            split_child(i, c)
            if k > value[i]
                c = children[i + 1]
        c.insert_nonfull(k)
```

7.6.4 Operation—Delete a Node

Just like insertion, deletion also starts with searching the key in the tree. If the key is not present, then just return '-1', implying that the key is not available. When the key is found, it is deleted out of the node and replaced with the in-order successor. Deletion can also break the property. If the node is a 2-node, it will have only one key. When the key is deleted, the node may be an internal or external node. If the node is external, then deleting the key leads to deleting the entire node and finally reducing the height of the sub-tree which violates the property that all leaves must be on the same level. If the node is an internal node, then it may have one or two children whose parent no more exist. This is called underflow. Underflow is the case when the number of keys in the node is lesser than the lower limit explained in the properties. The node which has underflow is handled based on two cases.

Case 1

It occurs when the underflow node has a 2-node sibling adjacent to it. In this case, the underflow node and the adjacent 2-node sibling are merged. The key in the parent, whose left and right children are merged, is moved down to the merged node. After merging, two different children of the parent become a single child. The new merged node now has '2' keys. The children of the nodes before merging are positioned according to the definitions provided above. This merging process is called fusion.

Case 2

It occurs when the adjacent sibling of the underflow node is a 2-node or a 3-node. In this scenario, a child of the adjacent sibling is moved into the underflow node. The child moved will be the first child or the last child of the adjacent sibling. If the adjacent sibling is on the left, then the last child of the adjacent sibling is moved to the underflow node. In odds, if the adjacent sibling is on the right side, then it is the first child that is moved to the underflow node. Then, the corresponding key in the adjacent node is moved up to the parent. Finally the key in the parent, whose left and right children are the underflow node and its adjacent node, respectively, is moved into the underflow node. Figure 7.44 depicts deletion of a key from a 3-node. Figure 7.45 depicts deletion of a key in a 2-node in 'Case 1' and Figure 7.46 depicts deletion of a key in a 2-node in 'Case 2'. Pseudocode 7.18 shows the deletion process.

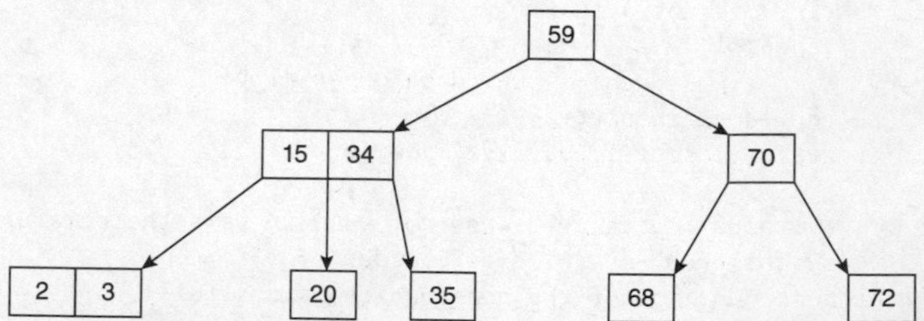

Figure 7.44 From the final tree in Figure 7.41 when '30' is deleted, its in-order successor '34' comes as a replacement

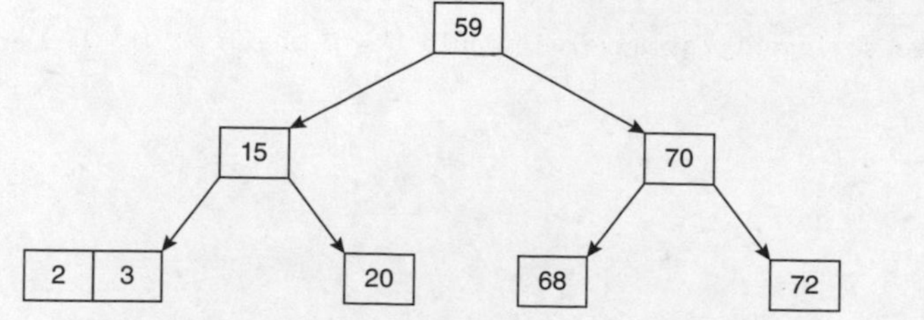

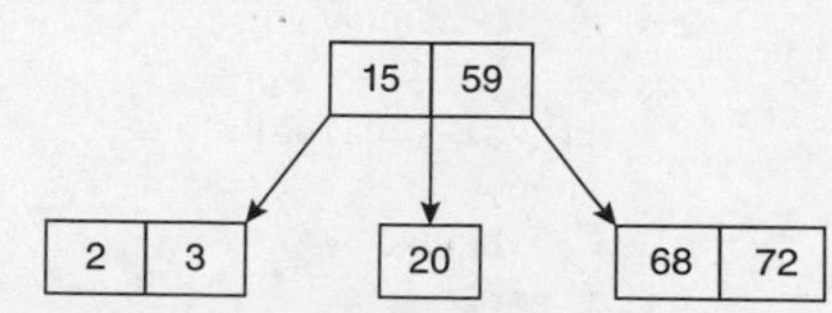

The nodes are merged and the key parent moves down. The children are re-arranged based on the new keys. The new node with '15' and '59' is the fusion node.

Figure 7.45 Deletion of a key in a 2-node in `Case 1'

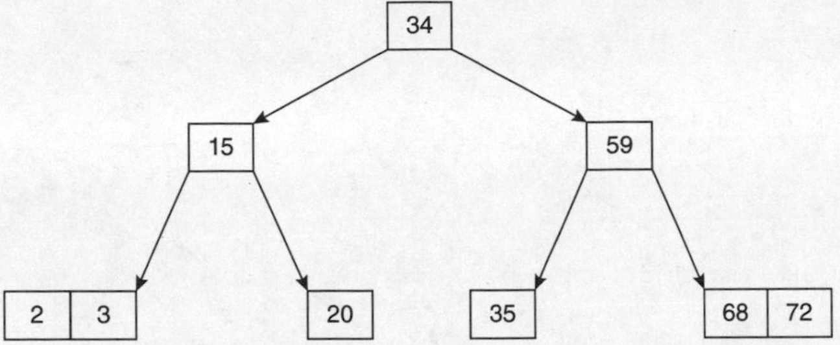

From the tree in Figure 7.44, '70' is deleted. It is a 2-node deletion whose adjacent sibling is a 3-node. Thus, '34' moves from the sibling to the parent and '59' moves from the parent down to the 2-node where '70' is deleted. The children are re-arranged based on the new keys in the node

Figure 7.46 Deletion of a key in a '2-node' in 'Case 2'

Pseudocode 7.18

```
def delete(val):
    flag=False
    i=0
    for x in value
    Do,
        i+=1
        if val = x
        then,
            flag=True
            if current node is a leaf
            then,
                value.remove(val)
            else,
                if i > 0 and len(children[i]) > order of node - 1
                then,
                    value[i] = children[i].value.pop()
                else if len(children[i + 1]) > order of node - 1:
                then,
                    value[i] = children[i + 1].value.pop()
                else,
                    Append value.pop() and children[i + 1].value into children[i].value
                    delete children[i + 1]
                    children[i].delete(val)
    if flag is False
    then,
        i = 0
        #identifying the correct subtree
        While (i < len(value))
        Do,
            if val < value[i]
            then,
                break
            i += 1
```

(*contd*)

(*contd*)

```
        c = children[i]
        if len(c) > order of node - 1
        then,
            c.delete(val)
        else,
            if i > 0 and len(children[i - 1]) > order of node - 1
            then,
                flag = True
                insert value[i - 1] into c.value
                value[i - 1] = children[i - 1].value.pop()
            else if len(value[]) > i and len(children[i + 1]) > order of node - 1
            then,
                flag = True
                append value[i] into c.value[]
                value[i] = children[i + 1].value.pop()
            if flag is True
            then,
                c.delete(val)
            else,
                if i > 0
                then,
                    append children[i - 1].value and value[i-1] from current node into the
                    beginning of c.value
                    remove value[i-1]
                    delete children[i - 1]
                else,
                    append value[i] and children[i + 1].value into c.value
                    remove value[i]
                    delete children[i + 1]
                c.delete(val)
```

7.6.5 Implementation of B-Trees

An implementation of (2, 4) trees is shared in Python code 7.5. Only in-order traversal is added in here in the code and the pre-order and post-order traversals are left for the reader to define based on the use case required.

Python code 7.5

```
class BTree(object):

    """

    Represents the BTree class. B-Trees are Balanced Search Trees (BST).
    They are similar to Red-Black trees except that, B-Tree nodes have many children, from a
    few to thousands.
    This is an implementation of a simple BTree with t = 2, which is called a 2-4 or 2-3-4
    B-Tree.

    Here are the rules of 2-3-4 trees:
    1. Each node stores 1, 2, or 3 key values
    2. Each node has 2, 3, or 4 child pointers
    3. All pointers to empty subtrees are the same distance from the root.
```

(*contd*)

(*contd*)

```
    Methods
    -------
    insert
        Inserts a node with key(k) to a tree

    delete
        Deletes a node from the tree

    search
        Searches for a node in the tree

    """

    def __init__ (self, t = 2):

        """
        Initializer for the class

        t = 2 implies that the tree is a 2-3-4 B-Tree
        """

        self.t    = t
        self.root = BTree.Node(t)
        self.root.is_leaf = True

    def insert(self, k):

        """
        Inserts a node with key k to the tree

        Parameters
        ----------
        k: int
            key with some value
        """

        r = self.root
        if len(r) == 2 * self.t - 1:
            s = BTree.Node(self.t)
            s.children.append(r)
            s.split_child(0, r)
            s.insert_nonfull(k)
            self.root = s
        else:
            r.insert_nonfull(k)

    def delete(self, k):

        """
        Deletes a node with key k from the tree, if it exists
```

(*contd*)

(*contd*)

```
        Parameters
        ----------
        k: int
            key with some value
        """

        r = self.root
        if r.search(k) is None:
            return
        r.delete(k)
        if len(r) == 0:
            self.root = r.children[0]

    def search(self, k):
        """
        Searches for a node

        Parameters
        ----------
        k: int
            key with some value
        """

        return self.root.search(k)

class Node(object):

    """
    Represents the Node class

    Methods
    -------
    search
        Searches for a key in nodes of a BTree

    split_child
        Splits a full node

    locate_subtree
        Locates a subtree, rooted at an internal node

    insert_nonfull
        Recursive procedure that inserts key into a node

    delete
        Recursive procedure which deletes a key from the B-tree rooted at a node
    """

    def __init__(self, t):
```

(*contd*)

(*contd*)

```
        """
        Initializer for the class

        Each node in the tree will have these attribute information.

        Parameters
        ----------
        t: int
            degree of the node. Since its a 2-3-4 tree, t is 2
        """

        self.t        = t
        self.keys     = []          # Number of keys in a node, in ascending order
        self.children = []          # Number of children of a node
        self.is_leaf  = False

    def __len__(self):
        return len(self.keys)

    def search(self, k):

        """
        Just like BST search, but instead of making a two-way branching decision, we make a
        multiway branching decision, according to the number of the node's children.

        Parameters
        ----------
        k: int
            key to be searched
        """

        i = 0
        while (i < len(self) and self.keys[i] < k):
            i += 1

        if i < len(self) and self.keys[i] == k:
            return (self, i)

        if self.is_leaf:
            return
        else:
            return self.children[i].search(k)

    def split_child(self, i, y):

        """
        Splits a full node having 2t-1 keys around its median key into two nodes having t-1
        keys each.
```

(*contd*)

(*contd*)

```
        Parameters
        ----------
        i: int
            int value
        y: dict
            dictionary
        """

        t = self.t
        z = BTree.Node(t)

        z.is_leaf = y.is_leaf
        z.keys    = y.keys[t:]
        if not y.is_leaf:
            z.children = y.children[t:]

        self.children.insert(i + 1, z)
        self.keys.insert(i, y.keys[t - 1])

        y.keys     = y.keys[0:t-1]
        y.children = y.children[0:t]

    def locate_subtree(self, k):

        """
        Locates the subtree rooted at an internal node, for inserting key into a leaf node
        """

        i = 0
        while (i < len(self)):
            if k < self.keys[i]:
                return i
            i += 1
        return i

    def insert_nonfull(self, k):

        """
        Recursive procedure that inserts key to a node, which is assumed to be nonfull
        when this procedure is called. 'insert' operation followed by the operation
        'insert_nonfull', ensures that this assumption is true.
        """
        # Case when node is a leaf node
        if self.is_leaf:
            i = 0
            for i in range(len(self)):
                if k < self.keys[i]:
                    self.keys.insert(i, k)
```

(*contd*)

(*contd*)

```
                return self
            self.keys.append(k)

        else:
            i = self.locate_subtree(k)
            c = self.children[i]
            if (len(c) == 2 * self.t - 1):
    # checks whether recursion needed for a full child
                self.split_child(i, c)
    # split full child into two nonfull children
                if k > self.keys[i]:
    # to find, in which of the two children, should the key be inserted
                    c = self.children[i + 1]
    # ensures recursion happens only in subtree and not full tree
            c.insert_nonfull(k)
    # recurse to insert k at appropriate subtree

def delete(self, k):

    """
    Deletes key from a subtree rooted at a node
    """

    t = self.t
    flag = False

    for i, x in enumerate(self.keys):
        if k == x:
            flag = True                         # k found
            if self.is_leaf:
    #Base Case: key k exists in leaf node

                self.keys.remove(k)         # remove k from the list of keys
            else:
    #Case 1: key k exists in an internal node
                if i > 0 and len(self.children[i]) > t - 1:
    #Case 1a: If a child precedes k in a node having t keys, then find predecessor k' of
    #k in subtree rooted at that node, replace k by k' and remove k'
                    self.keys[i] = self.children[i].keys.pop()
                elif len(self.children[i + 1]) > t - 1:
    #Case 1b: If node has fewer than t keys, symmetrically examine the child that
    #follows k in node. If that child has atleast t keys, then find successor k' of k in
    #subtree rooted at that child. Delete k' and replace k by k' in node
                    self.keys[i] = self.children[i + 1].keys.pop(0)
                else:
    #Case 1c: If both node and its child have only t-1 keys, merge k and all of child
    #into node so that the initial internal node loses both k and its pointer to this
    #child node and now node contains 2t-1 keys. Then free the child and recursively
    #delete k from node
```

(*contd*)

(*contd*)

```
                        self.children[i].keys += [ self.keys.pop(0) ] + self.children[i +
                        1].keys
                        del(self.children[i + 1])
                        self.children[i].delete(k)

        if not flag:
        #Case 2: Find subtree rooted at c which has key k, if k is in tree at all
            i = self.locate_subtree(k)
            c = self.children[i]
            if len(c) > t - 1:
                c.delete(k)
            else:
        #Case 2a: c has t-1 keys but siblings has atleast t keys
                if i > 0 and len(self.children[i - 1]) > t - 1:
                    flag = True
                    c.keys.insert(0, self.keys[i - 1])
                    self.keys[i - 1] = self.children[i - 1].keys.pop()
                elif len(self) > i and len(self.children[i + 1]) > t - 1:
                    flag = True
                    c.keys.append(self.keys[i])
                    self.keys[i] = self.children[i + 1].keys.pop(0)

                if flag:
                    c.delete(k)
                else:
        #Case 2b: The left and right brothers only had t-1
                    if i > 0:
                        l = self.children[i - 1]
                        c.keys = l.keys + [ self.keys.pop(i - 1) ] + c.keys
                        del(self.children[i - 1])
                    else:
                        r = self.children[i + 1]
                        c.keys += [ self.keys.pop(i) ] + r.keys
                        del(self.children[i + 1])
                    c.delete(k)

# 2-4 BTree creation - client code
tree = BTree(4)
```

7.6.6 Complexity Analysis

The worst case height of the tree is 'O(log n)' when all the nodes are 2-nodes. Then, the worst case search time is also 'O(log n)', as it will visit all the nodes in any one root-to-leaf path and all leaves in (2, 4) trees are on the same level. Just like other search trees, in B-trees too, insertion and deletion depend on searching and with the same complexity as searching. So, all the operations in B-trees are of 'O(log n)' worst case complexity.

Food for Brain

Delete '59' from the given tree.

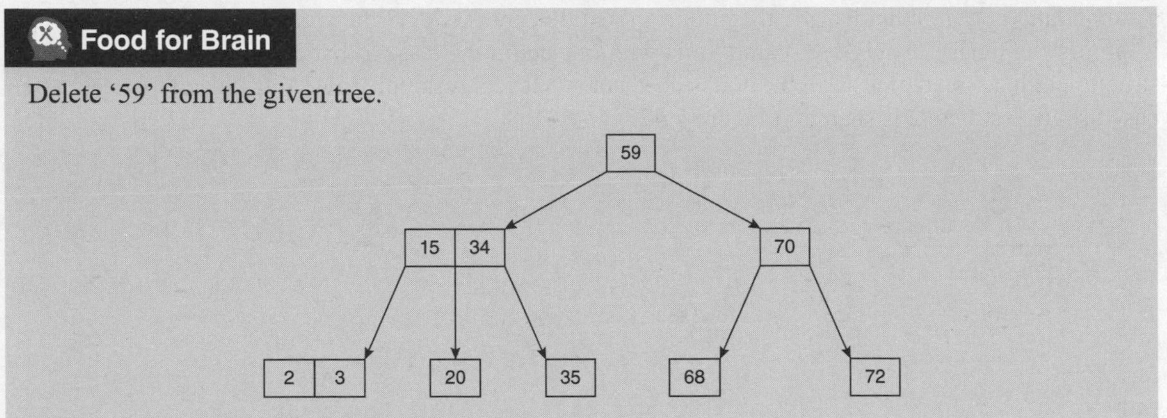

7.7 APPLICATIONS OF SEARCH TREES

There are many real-time applications for search trees. One very interesting application is the working of network and routers, which have become a part of our day-to-day life. Within a network, when a system tries to communicate to another system, data is sent as packets. The packet starts from the source system and moves to the router, to which it is connected to. From there, it starts moving across routers until it finds the router to which the destination is connected to. Then the packet moves into that subnetwork and crosses all the systems until it reaches the destination. Every router or system is connected to multiple systems. It is the IP of any connected system that helps the router to identify the correct neighbour to jump to. The jumping process is formally known as hop. This process of finding the route and hoping will be dealt in detail in the networking course. After the packet identifies the neighbour to hop to, the next job is to identify the port to which that particular neighbour is connected. This is where routing table comes into the picture. A routing table has the list of IPs of the neighbours and the port they are connected to. From the table, the system/router searches for the neighbour that they want to hop to. The process of selection involves considering all the available neighbours and selecting the best one closest to the destination. This routing table can be stored as self-balancing binary search trees or AVL trees.

Process: First, a normal binary tree is created from the list of ports where the key in the node is the IP address of the system connected to the port. The tree is created based on the logic discussed in Chapter 6, that is, regarding storing binary trees in a one-dimensional array. Once the tree is created, an algorithm is run to traverse through the nodes and perform the following check. Is there a node with a supernet of the current node in the left sub-tree. A supernet is an IP for which the current IP is a subnet. A subnet is an internal network or a node inside the network. For example, if 56.32.20.12 is a subnet of 56.32.0.0, it means 56.32.20.12 is a system inside the network 56.32.0.0. Simply, it can be understood that if the initial parts of the IP are common, then the larger IP will be a subnet of the smaller IP, provided that the uncommon components are '0' in the smaller IP. It is also to be remembered that the subnet IP will have '0' as the last component in the IP. After the binary tree is built, it is re-arranged such that an IP that is the left child of the current IP is smaller and the IP to the right of the current IP is bigger. The smaller and bigger is based on comparison of each of the four components in the IP. This ensures that all the supernets of the node are ancestors to the node. The tree is also partially balanced without rotating the subnets in the structure. So, when a packet wants to enter into the network from a node, if the destination IP is lesser than the current IP, then the left child is chosen and proceeds forward in the left sub-tree. However, if the destination IP is greater than the current IP, the right child is chosen and the process continues. If the current node is a subnet and not an individual IP, then the right child is checked and the closest node is selected. This is simply the binary search tree search logic with one additional case to handle subnets. Thus, the data structure reduces read time as all the nodes need not be visited. A sample routing table and the search tree based routing structure is shared in Figure 7.47.

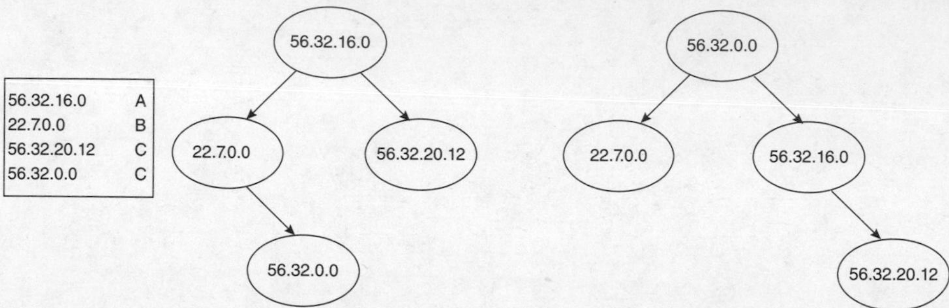
56.32.16.0 A
22.7.0.0 B
56.32.20.12 C
56.32.0.0 C
56.32.16.0
22.7.0.0
56.32.20.12
56.32.0.0
56.32.0.0
22.7.0.0
56.32.16.0
56.32.20.12
A sample routing table followed by the initial binary tree
After re-arranging, supernet is the ancestor of subnets and the BST rule is depicted in the final tree. Here, 56.32.16.0 is a subnet in the network 56.32.0.0 and 56.32.20.12 is a subnet (system) inside the network 56.32.0.0

Figure 7.47 A sample routing table and the search tree based routing structure

Points to Remember

- A binary search tree is a binary tree with a constraint on storing the elements. The left child should be lesser than the parent and the right child should be greater than the parent.
- A binary search tree makes searching easier with an average case 'O(logn)'.
- The worst case height of the BST is 'O(n)', when the elements are inserted in a sorted order and when the search time also hits 'O(n)'.
- Inserting a value always adds a new leaf to the tree with the value.
- Deleting a node from the BST replaces the node with its in-order successor.
- In-order traversal of a BST is in ascending order.
- A BST can be built using its pre-order and post-order traversals.
- Height of the BST is to be maintained 'O(log n)' to ensure efficient searching, which is achieved by self-balancing search trees, that is, the AVL tree.
- When the absolute difference between the left and right subtrees' height is greater than '1', then the node is considered to be unbalanced.
- An unbalanced node is balanced using rotations.
- Left rotation is rotating a right skewed sub-tree towards left/anti-clockwise such that the middle elements become the new root and the sub-tree becomes balanced.
- Right rotation is rotating a left skewed sub-tree towards right/clock-wise such that the middle element becomes the new root and the sub-tree becomes balanced.
- There are four different cases in handling unbalance-right-right, right-left, left-right, and left-left based on the imbalance factor.
- Some rotations in AVL trees can be skipped and still the trees can be maintained with optimized height.
- Red-Black trees aim at avoiding unwanted rotations.
- In Red-Black trees, every node should be either red or black.
- The root in Red-Black trees should always be a black and a 'null' node is considered as black.
- A parent or child of a red node cannot be a red node.

- Every root-to-leaf path should have the same number of black nodes.
- While deleting, if the number of black nodes in the root-to-leaf path loses balance, then the last black is made double black, which is a temporary state in the process of rotation.
- A Splay tree is for efficient memory management.
- A Splay tree has the BST constraints, but maintains the recently accessed elements in the main memory.
- Every time an element is searched/splayed, it is moved to the root.
- If the element sought after is not present, then the closest element is moved to the root.
- A B-Tree is a search tree where a node can have more than two children.
- A BST is a B-Tree of order 2.
- The constraint based on which the elements are stored is 'value[i]<children[i+1].value[ ] <value[i+1]'.

KEY TERMS

Binary Search Trees A binary tree with a constraint on storing the elements. The left child must always be lesser than the root and the right child should always be greater than the root.

AVL trees/Self-balancing binary search trees When the height of the right sub-tree and left sub-tree is not balanced, it involves rotations to balance the sub-trees.

Red-Black tree A self-balancing search tree with a constraint on colouring of the nodes to reduce the number of unwanted rotations from AVL trees

Splay tree An unorthodox tree which has the ability to maintain only the recently accessed elements in the main memory. It moves the recently accessed element to the top of the tree, making the lastly accessed element as root.

B-tree/M-N tree A BST which can have more elements and more children. The constraint based on which the elements are stored is 'value[i]<children[i+1].value[]<value[i+1]'.

2-4 tree A B-tree of order 4. Each node can have '4' values with three children.

Left rotation Rotating a right skewed sub-tree towards left/anti-clockwise such that the middle element becomes the new root and sub-tree becomes balanced.

Right rotation Rotating a left skewed sub-tree towards right/clock-wise such that the middle element becomes the new root and sub-tree becomes balanced.

Left-Right, Left-Left, Right-Left, Right-Right Four different cases of rotations in balancing AVL trees

Zig-Zig, Zig-Zag, Zag-Zig, Zag-Zag Four different cases of rotations in balancing splay trees

EXERCISES

Multiple-choice Questions

1. A balanced binary search tree is:
   (a) BST (b) AVL tree
   (c) B-Tree (d) None of the above
2. All the nodes in a Red-Black tree can be black.
   (a) True (b) False
3. A Red-Black tree is always balanced in height.
   (a) True (b) False
4. What is the complexity of rotation operation?
   (a) O(n) (b) O(log n)
   (c) O(2) (d) None of the above
5. How many child/children can be there for a 3-node in a (2, 4) tree?
   (a) 2 (b) 3
   (c) 4 (d) All of the above
6. Can a B-Tree be rotated?
   (a) Yes
   (b) No
7. An AVL tree is also a:
   (a) BST (b) Red-Black tree
   (c) B-Tree (d) All of the above

8. A (2, 4) tree is also a:
   (a) B-tree of order 3
   (b) (3, 6) tree
   (c) B-Tree
   (d) All of the above
9. What is a B-tree of 'order 3' called?
   (a) (2,3) Tree (b) (2, 4) tree
   (c) (1,3) Tree (d) None of the above
10. An average case height of a splay tree is:
   (a) O(n) (b) O(log n)
   (c) O(m), where 'm' is the number of operations taken place from the point of creation of the tree like insertion, search, and deletion.
   (d) O(n/2)

Theoretical Review Questions

1. What is a binary search tree and how is it efficient in searching of elements?
2. What is the disadvantage of a BST and how is it overcome?
3. Write a note on Red-Black trees and how is it different from AVL trees?
4. Design a tree to reduce search time of an element, especially when the number of elements are huge.
5. Write a note on the structure of trees with multiple elements in the same node. How are the children arranged in the next level?

Exploratory Application Exercises

1. Develop a function to compute the height of a BST.
2. Modify the BST to efficiently handle a large number of duplicate elements. Every element must have a counter to denote the number of instances to restrict the height of the tree.
3. Design a BST to store decimal values.
4. Given the pre-order and post-order traversals, build the BST.
5. Write a code to balance a given BST.
6. Create a dictionary of words for efficient search of words. Note that once the dictionary is created, no new words will be added to it.
7. Given a binary tree, check if it is height balanced like a Red-Black tree.
8. Build a data compressor using Splay trees.
9. Write a code to store and represent a (2, 4) tree in a one-dimensional array.
10. Write a note on modification of AVL trees. What could happen if the balancing condition is relaxed to a height difference of '2' instead of '1' among the sub-trees? What could be the pros and cons of this modification. Give supportive computations for the claim.

Picto Puzzles

1.

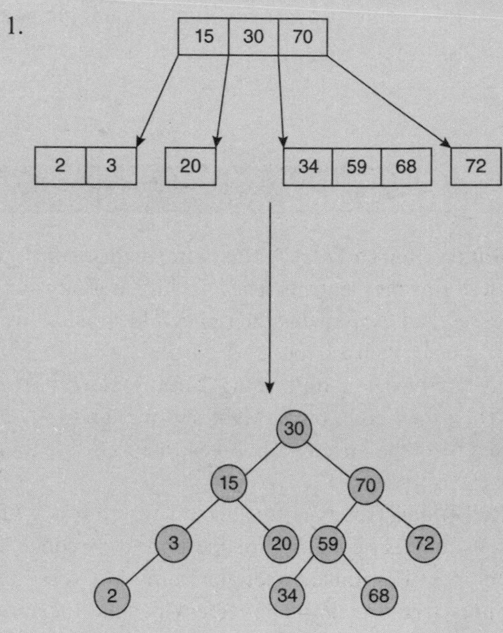

2.

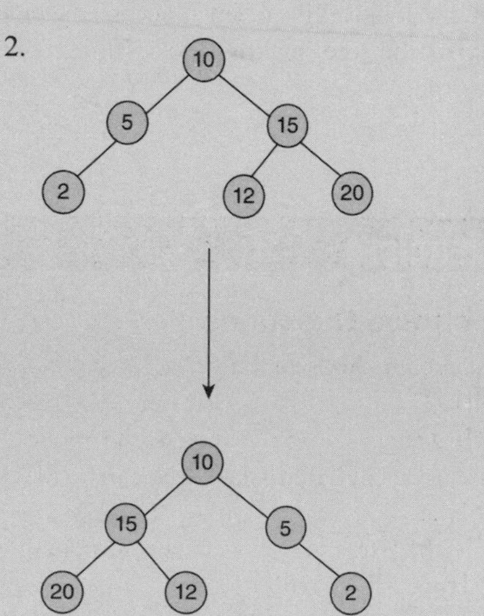

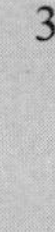

3.

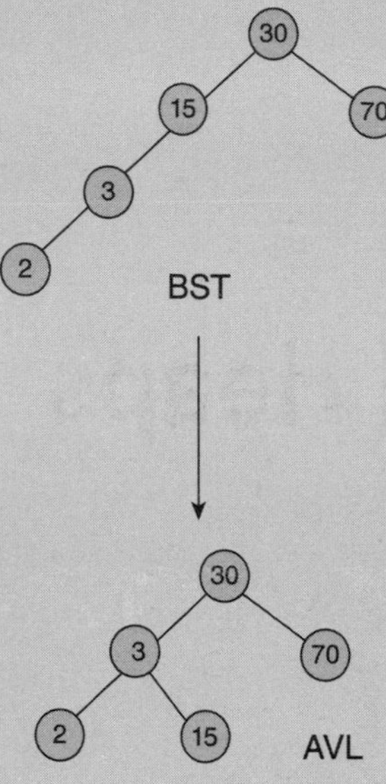

4.

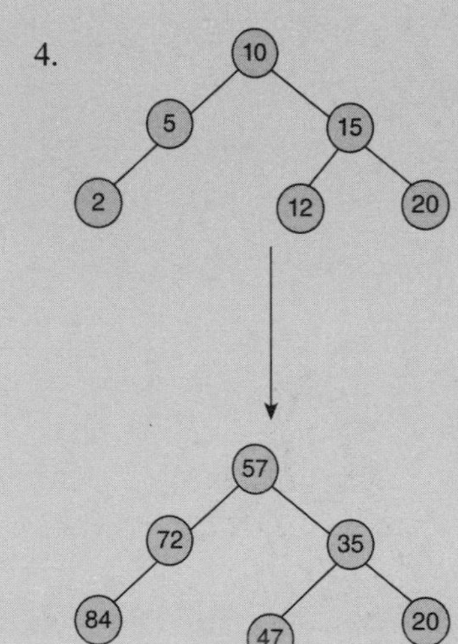

5.

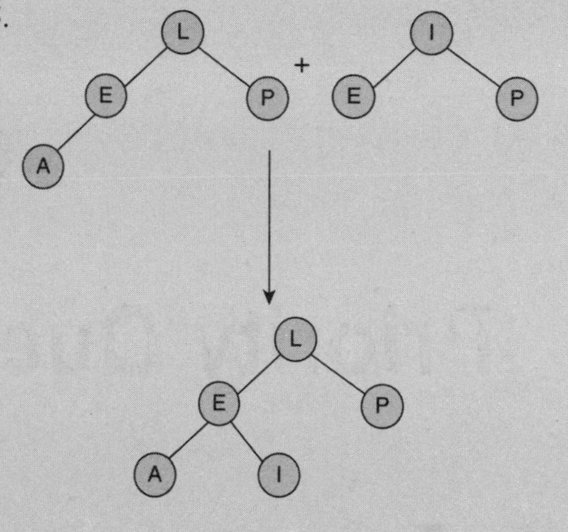

L E P A I

Mini Projects

1. Explore the structure, Left Leap Red-Black trees.
2. Explore the structure, Tango trees.
3. Design a tree to efficiently store and search strings in it. Search or insert should be at max 'O(l)', where 'l' is the length of the string.

Answers to Multiple-choice Questions

1. (b) 2. (a) 3. (a) 4. (c) 5. (d) 6. (a) 7. (a) 8. (c) 9. (a)
10. (b)

CHAPTER

Priority Queues and Heaps

LEARNING OBJECTIVES

After going through this chapter, readers will be able to understand:

- Different types of hierarchical data structures and their use
- What is a heap?
- What are the various modifications of heaps?
- How to implement priority queues using heaps?

8.1 INTRODUCTION—HEAP

A heap is a complete tree-based data structure with some different properties. Just like search trees, heaps are variants of hierarchical tree structures. For example, in case of a heap of stones, when sand is poured over this heap, it sneaks in and moves down the stones. This is because of the smaller size of the sand granules as compared to the stones. Figure 8.1 shows a heap of rocks, stones, and sand. Heaps are inspired by such structures. The heap is a tree structure with an additional property of weight of nodes. The weight of a parent should be greater or lesser than all its children. This chapter throws light on different types of heaps, their working, and implementation.

Figure 8.1 A heap of sand, stone, and rock

8.2 BINARY HEAPS

A binary heap is a version of heap which is a variant of a complete binary tree. Here, the parent node can either be smaller or larger than both its children. When the parent is greater than its children, it is called as max heap. If the parent is lesser than the children, it forms a min heap. The property holds good for all the nodes in the heap. Thus, for a max heap, the largest element in the lot will always be the root. Similarly, in a min heap, the minimum element will be the root. Figure 8.2 shows a sample min heap.

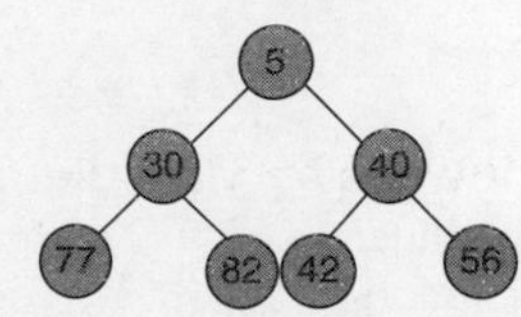

Figure 8.2 Sample min heap

While it is important to learn how to build a binary heap, it is also important to learn how to maintain the heap. The basic operations in a heap are insertion and deletion. Unlike search trees, there is no search or lookup operation in a heap.

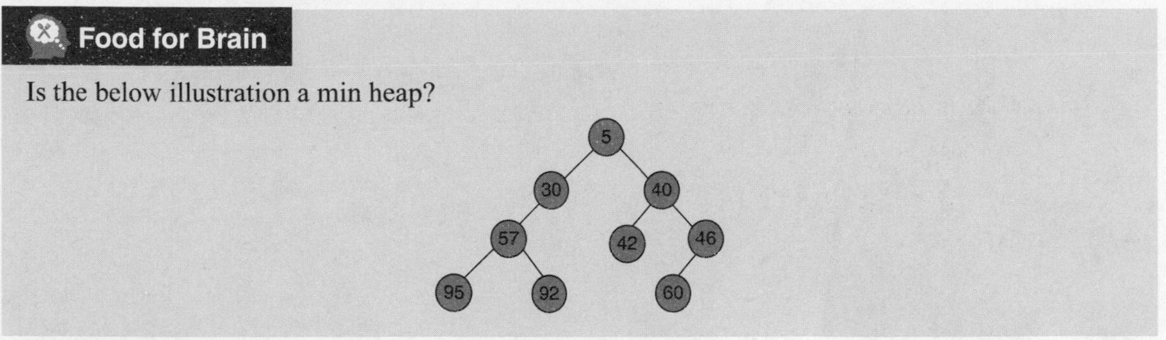

8.2.1 Operation—Insertion

Insertion of an element is always in the last level. As already mentioned, heaps are a variant of complete trees. So, binary heap insertion follows the rules of insertion of a complete binary tree. Once the new node is placed in the heap, the heap property is checked. For a max heap, the new node must be lesser than its parent, whereas in min heap, the new node must be greater than its parent. If the new node is compliant with the corresponding heap's property, then no further action is required. If the heap property is violated, then the heap is to be modified to regain the property. This process involves a new operation called 'Heapify'. Heapifying means swapping a parent and child to make them inline with the heap property. In case in a min heap the new node inserted is smaller than its parent, the heapify operation gets initiated. First the parent and the child will be swapped and then the new parent will be compared with its parent for the same property. Thus, heapify is a recursive process which will run until the root or the parent-child pair that meets the property is reached. Pseudocode 8.1 shows the insertion process.

Question 8.1 Insert '45' into the max heap shown in Figure 8.3.

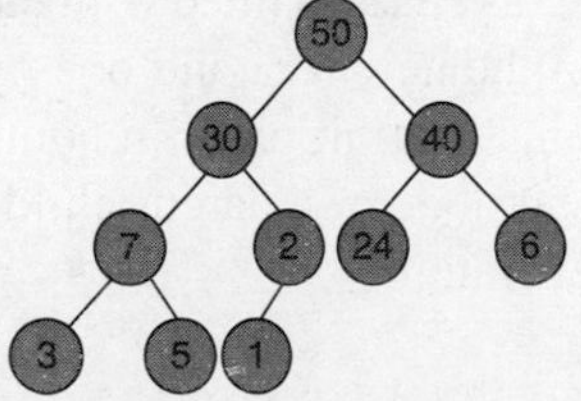

Figure 8.3 Initial max heap

Solution: The process is shown in Figure 8.4.

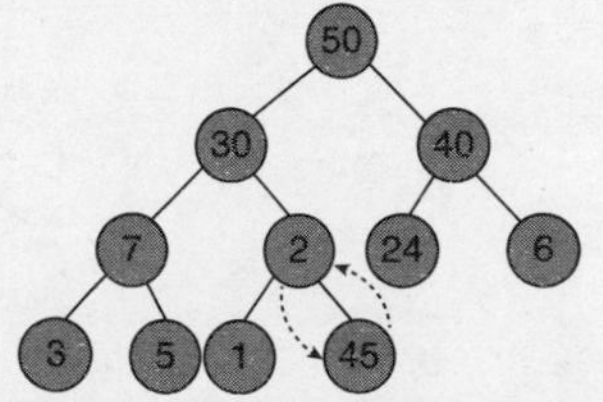

Inserting '45' in the last leaf. Property violation Heapify to swap '45' and '2'.

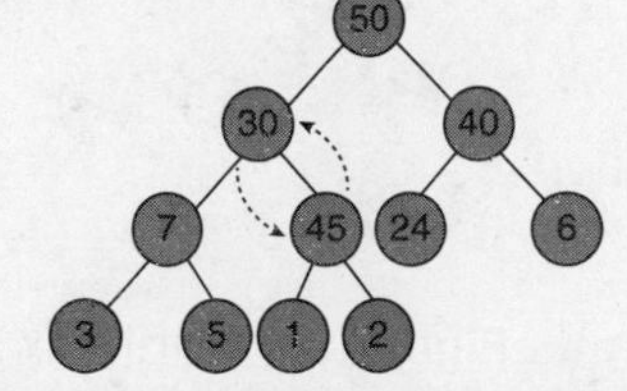

Property violation. Heapify to swap '45' and '30'

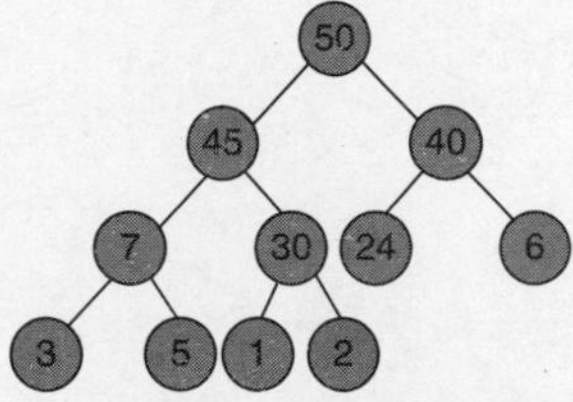

Final max heap

Figure 8.4 Illustration of insertion of an element into a max heap

Pseudocode 8.1

```
#using array/list based implementation as heaps are based on complete binary trees
heapify(L, node)
    root = node
    left, right = 2 * node + 1, 2 * node + 2
    for i in range of left to right
        if i < size of(L) and L[i] > L[root]
        then,
            root = i
    if root is not node
    then,
        swap L[root] and L[node]
        node = root
        heapify(L, root)
insert(L, value)
    append value into L
    Heapify(L, value)
```

8.2.2 Operation—Deletion

While insertion is always done at a leaf node, deletion also has a constraint. In a heap, any given element cannot be deleted as it may distort the heap and crumble it. Deletion happens only at the root. The deleted root creates a vacant space in the heap. This space is filled with the last leaf in the heap. This replacement may violate the heap property between the new root and one of its children. Thus, again, the heapify operation is triggered to put the elements back in place in compliance with the heap property. In this case, heapify will stop on reaching a leaf node or a parent-child pair which satisfies the heap property. Pseudocode 8.2 explains the deletion operation.

Question 8.2 Delete '50' from the Figure 8.5.

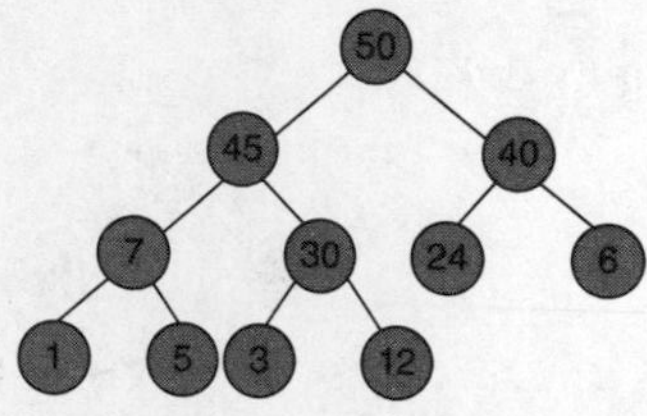

Figure 8.5 Initial max heap

Solution: The process is shown in Figure 8.6.

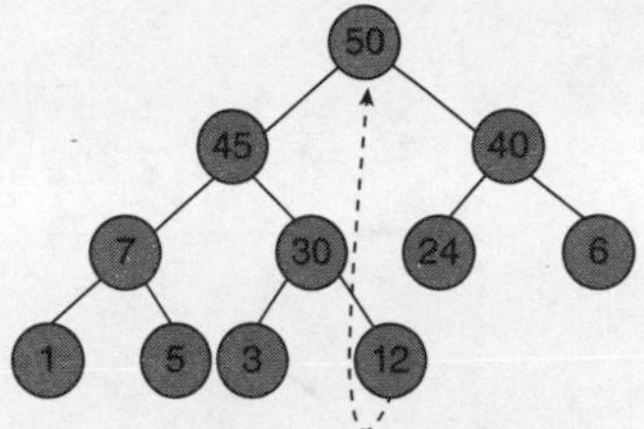

Initial max heap. Delete root '50' and replace with last leaf '12'.

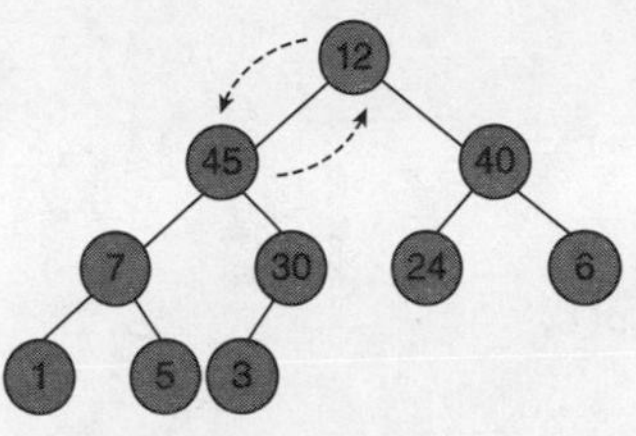

Property violation at the new root. Swap '12' and '45'.

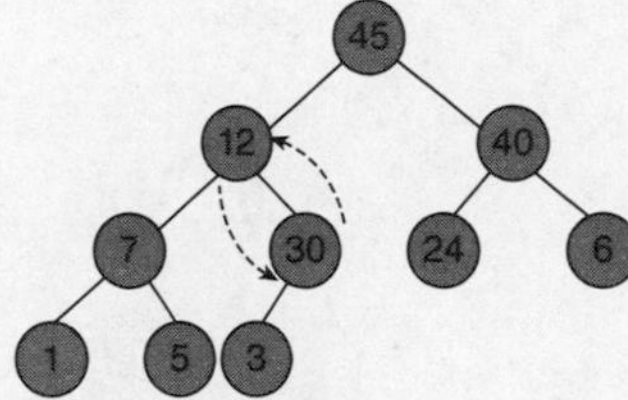

Swap '30' and '12' due to property violation

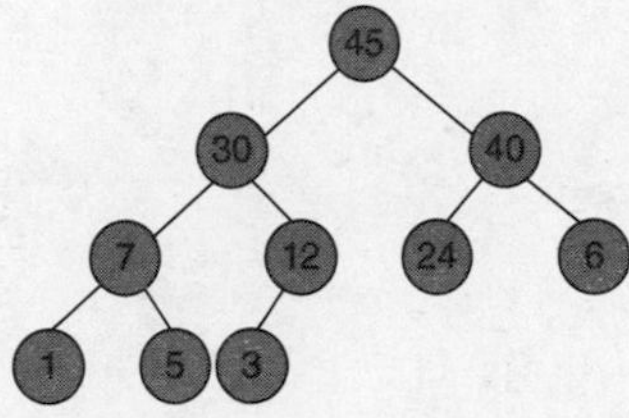

Final max heap post-deletion

Figure 8.6 Step-by-step illustration of deletion operation on a max heap

Pseudocode 8.2

```
def delete(L):
    Swap first and last element
    L.pop(last element)
    heapify(L, 0)
```

8.2.3 Implementation of Max Heap

The implementation of max heap is shared below with the same operations of insert and delete. Min heap is left for the users to explore which can be built in the similar way just by changing the comparison conditions. As binary heaps are completely binary-based, array-based or list-based is the most preferred implementation of heaps (refer to Python code 8.1).

Python code 8.1

```
def max_heap(L):
    n = len(L)
    parent = (n-1)//2   #Last Parent
    for node in range(parent, -1, -1):
        heapify(L, node)
    print("Constructing Max Heap - Parent > both left and right child")
    return L
def heapify(L, node):
    n = len(L)
    root = node
    left, right = 2 * node + 1, 2 * node + 2
    for i in [left,right]:
        if i < n and L[i] > L[root]:
            root = i
    if root is not node:
         L[root], L[node] = L[node], L[root]
         node = root
         heapify(L, root)
```

(contd)

(*contd*)

```
def insert(L, val):
    n = len(L)
    L.append(val)
    rebalance_up(L, n)
    return L
def rebalance_up(L, node):
    parent = (node - 1)//2
    if L[parent] < L[node]:
        L[parent], L[node] = L[node], L[parent]
    if parent <= 0:
        return
    else:
        rebalance_up(L, parent)
def delete(L):
    n = len(L) - 1
    L[0], L[n] = L[n], L[0]
    L.pop(n)
    heapify(L, 0)
    print(L)
```

8.2.4 Complexity Analysis

Both the insertion and deletion are single-step operations. However, the maintanence of the heap post-insertion or post-deletion impacts the complexity of the operations. A single swap in the heapify operations is 'O(1)', as it is just concerned with two nodes. The maximum possible number of swaps will be same as the height of the tree. This is because, in insertion, heapify starts from a leaf and can swap nodes maximum until the root. Similarly, in deletion, swapping starts from the root and can continue until leaf, as no more elements exist to be swapped. In either cases, the worst case number of swaps is 'height-1'. Thus, the complexity of heapify is equal to the height of the tree. It is already known that height of a complete binary tree is 'O(log n)'. Thus, complexity of heapify operation is 'O(log n)'. Considering complexity of the heapify operation, the complexity of both insertion and deletion operations is 'O(log n)'.

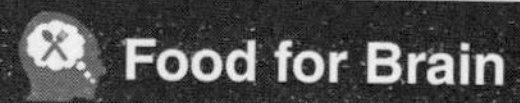

How to maintain the heap with a duplicate element? How to modify the heap property?

8.3 LEFTIST HEAPS

A leftist heap is a version of min heap. The min heap property of maintaining the parent lesser than the children is followed in here. Unlike binary heaps, leftist heaps are not in the form of complete binary trees. Instead, there is another constraint along with the min heap property. Before we proceed with leftist heaps, an important fact to be kept in mind is that in case of leftist heaps, a leaf is a null node and not the node in the last level, unlike regular trees.

The next new definiton in here is the `'Dist()'` function. For any node 'n', `'Dist(n)'` is a distance function defined as `'i + Dist(right(n))'`. So, this distance function is a recursive function that will calculate the number of nodes on the path to the rightmost leaf. A property based on this distance function is that `'Dist(right(n))'` should be less than or equal to `'Dist(left(n))'`. Here, the `'right(n)'` and `'left(n)'` correspond to the right and left children of node 'n'. When the tree is build in compliance with this distance property, the shortest root-to-leaf path is from the root to the rightmost leaf of the heap.

For better understanding of this distance computation, different structured leftist heaps and the computation of the distance of nodes is explained below. First, let us start with a single node heap. The single node will be the root and no more children. So the distance of the node will be '0', as it has a right 'null' child. Now, consider the leftist heap in Figure 8.7. It just has two nodes—a root and a left child of the root.

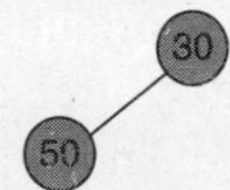

Figure 8.7 A sample leftist heap for distance computation

Here, the node '50' does not have a right child or a 'null' right child. Hence, the distance of node '50' is '0'. Similarly, node '30' also does not have a right child and has a distance '0'. What if node '30' also had a right child as shown in Figure 8.8.

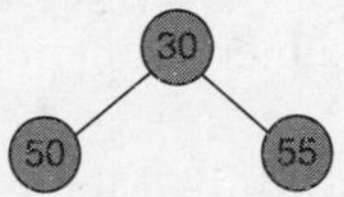

Figure 8.8 Example of leftist heap

In this case, the distance of node '50' and node '55' is '0' as there is no right child. The node '30' has a right child '55', so when `'Dist(30)'` is called, it returns `'1 + Dist(55)'`. As discussed previously, `'Dist(55)'` is '0' as there is no more right child. Thus, `'Dist(30)'` sums up to '1'.

Food for Brain

Compute the distance of each node in the leftist heap given below.

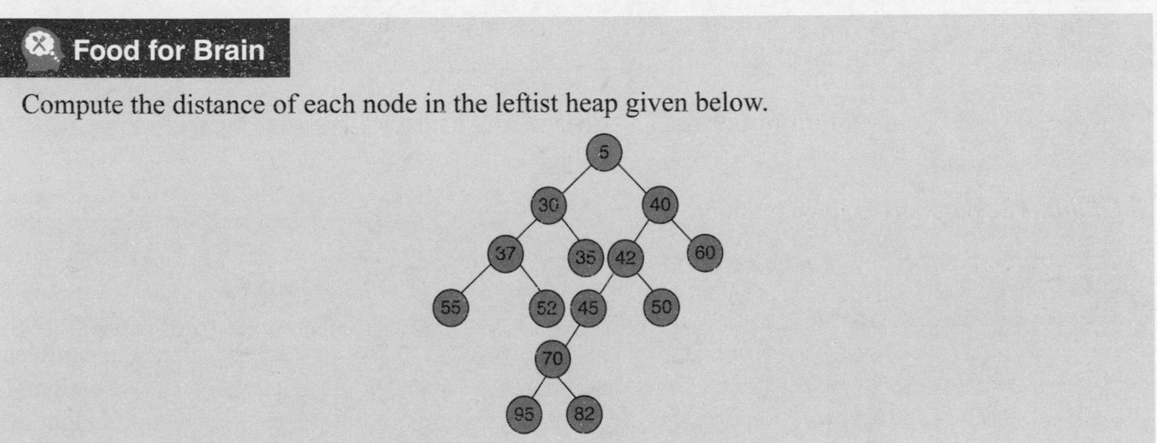

Given the root to the rightmost leaf path is the smallest, if there are 'x' nodes in that path then the tree will have at least '2^x-1' nodes. This makes the rightmost leaf path of 'O(log n)'.

Along with the basic heap operations, leftist heaps have another important operation of merging two heaps. The three basic operations of leftist heaps—merging, insertion, and deletion— are discussed in the sections below.

8.3.1 Operation—Merging

Given two leftist heaps, this is the process of combining them into a new leftist heap. Merging is a long and recursive process. It begins with the roots of two heaps. For merging, a stack is mandatory. In the first level, when the two roots are compared, the smaller element is pushed into the stack. The node pushed into the stack and its left subtree can be skipped for now from the corresponding heaps. The right child of the same node is taken into consideration and compared with the other node, which was greater in the previous comparison. This process of comparison and pushing into the stack continues until a node without a right child/with a right leaf child is pushed into the stack. When a node with the right child 'null' is pushed into the stack, the next node to be taken into consideration is 'null'. This is the final comparison when an element is being compared with 'null'. Now, this element along with its left subtree is made the right child of the current top of the stack. After this, the next element is popped out of the stack and the element and its left subtree are again made as the right child of the new top of the stack. This process continues until the end of the stack is reached to get the merged heaps. An important fact to be kept in mind is that when a node is pushed into the stack, the node along with the left subtree can be skipped temporarily and while popping from the stack and making it the right child, the node along with its left subtree is made as the right child of the corresponding parent. In addition, while adding the element as the right child, there is a possiblity that the leftlist heap's distance property, Dist(right) <= Dist(left), gets violated. In any insertion if the property gets violated, then the left and right child are immediately swapped to regain the leftist structure. Pseudocode 8.3 shows the merge operation.

Question 8.6 Merge leftist 'heap 1' and leftist 'heap 2' given in Figure 8.9.

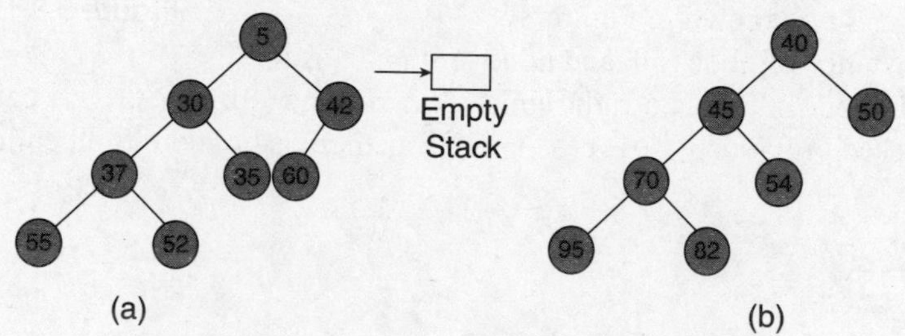

Figure 8.9 (a)Leftist 'heap 1', (b) Leftist 'heap 2'

Solution: The process is shown in Figure 8.10.

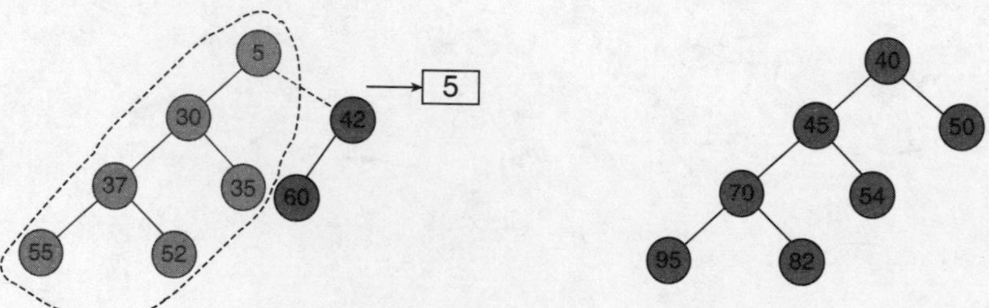

Compare '5' and '40' . Since '5' is smaller, push '5' into the stack and skip '5' and its left subtree (showed with a layer to hide). Then consider '42', the right child of '5' for next comparison.

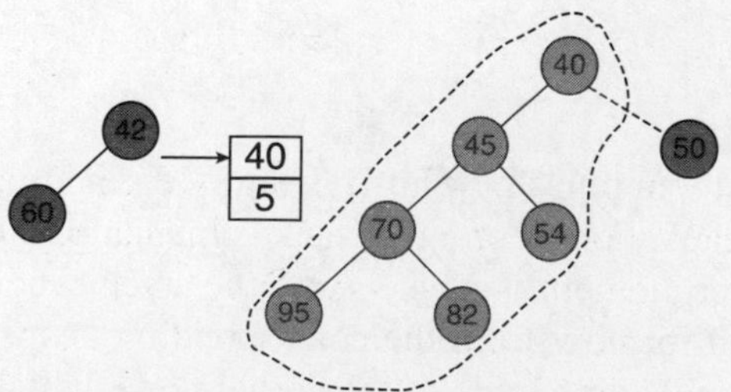

Compare (42,40). Push '40' into stack and skip the node with its left subtree

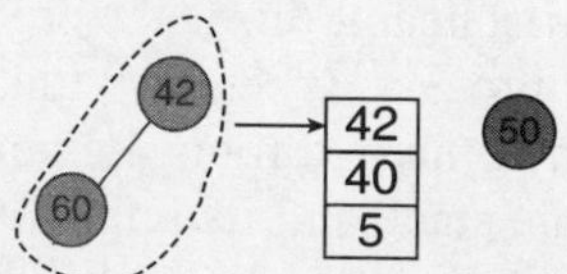

Compare (50,42). Push '42' into stack and skip '42' and the left subtree

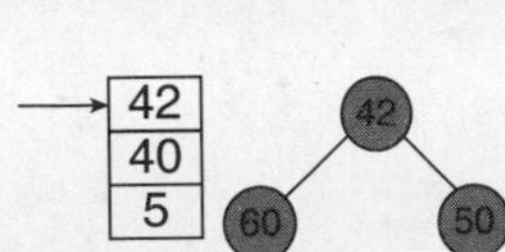

One heap has reached 'null', as all nodes have been skipped now. So, compare(50, null). Make '50' the right child of current top of stack '42'.

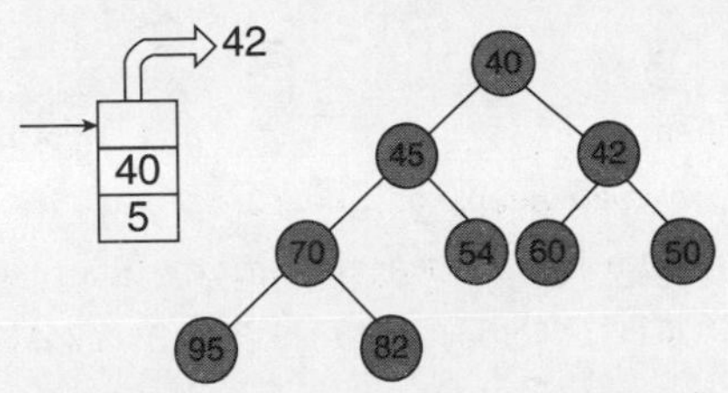

Pop '42' and make the subtree rooted at '42' as the right subtree of current top of stack '40'.

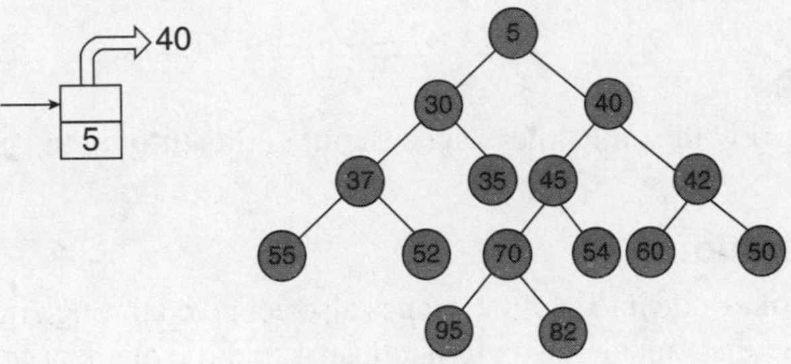

Pop '40' and make the subtree rooted at '40' as right child of the current top of stack '5'.

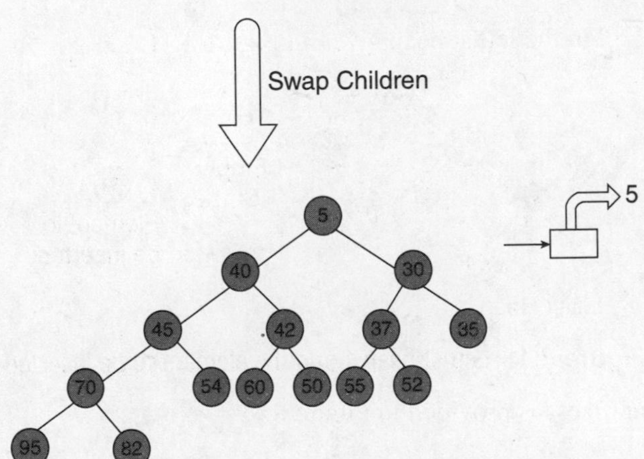

Here, the distance of right child of '5' is greater than left child of '5', which violates the leftist heap's property. Thus, the left and right subtrees are swapped. Finally, '5' is popped out and the stack is empty. This is the final merged leftist heap.

Figure 8.10 Detailed, step-by-step illustration of merging two leftist heaps

Merging is the most important operation in leftist heaps. Other two basic operations of insertion and deletion are directly implemented based on this operation.

Pseudocode 8.3

```
merge(Heap1, Heap2):
    if Heap2 is null then return Heap1
    if Heap1 is null then return Heap2
    if Heap1.root < Heap2.root
```

(contd)

(*contd*)

```
then,
    swap Heap1 and Heap2
Heap1.right = Merge(Heap1.right, Heap2)
if dist(Heap1.right) > dist(Heap2.left)
then,
    swap Heap1.right and Heap2.left
```

Food for Brain

Can the stack be replaced with some other data structure efficiently in the merge process?

8.3.2 Operation—Insertion

As already said, insertion of a node into a leftist heap is also achieved through merging. The heap in which the element is to be inserted is considered as leftist heap 1 and the element to be inserted is considered as leftist heap 2 as a heap of size '1'. Now, these two are merged based on the same logic as explained in Section 8.3.1. Pseudocode 8.4 shows the insertion process.

Question 8.8 Insert '20' in the leftist heap given in Figure 8.11.

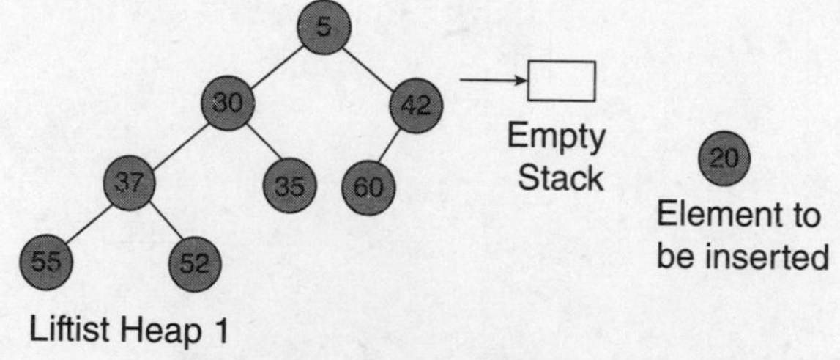
5
30
42
37
35
60
55
52
Liftist Heap 1
Empty
Stack
20
Element to
be inserted

Figure 8.11 Leftist heap 1 and the element to be inserted

Solution: The complete process is provided in Figure 8.12.

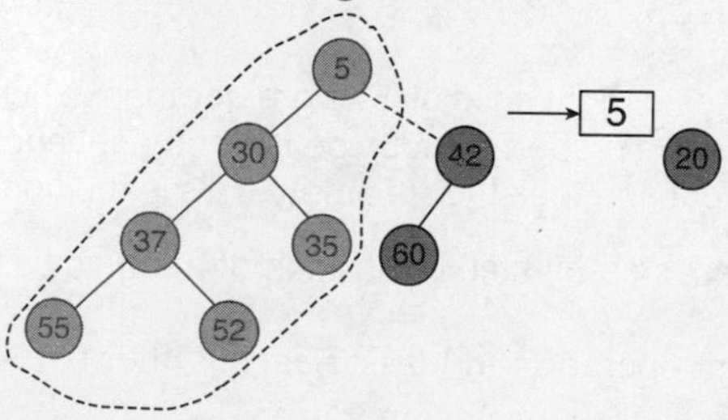
5
30
42
37
35
60
55
52
5
20
Compare (5,20). Since '5' is smaller, push '5' into stack and skip the left sub tree.

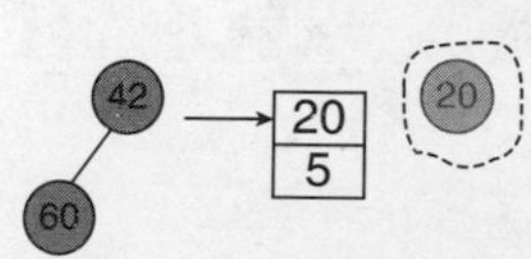
42
60
20
5
20
Compare (42,20). As '20' is
smaller, push '20' into the stack.

20
5
20
42
60
Swap Children
20
42
60
Compare(42,null). Make '42' the right child of top of stack – 20.
Now, Dist(right) > Dist(left) at '20', so swap the children
and make '42' and the subtree as left child of '20'.

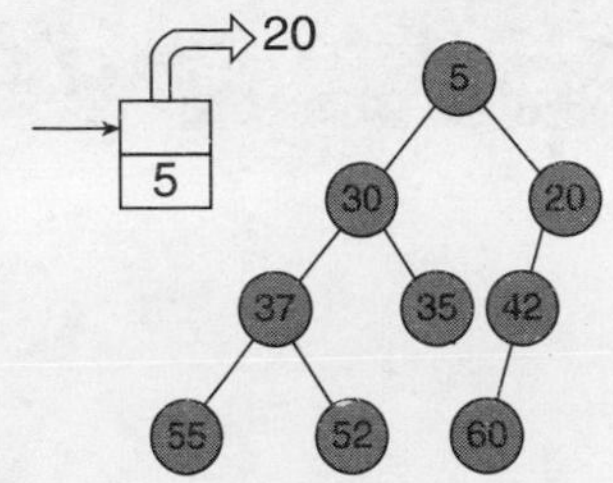

Pop '20' and make the subtree the right child of new top of stack, '5'

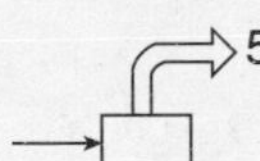

Pop '5' and the stack is empty. The heap in the previous step is the final heap.

Figure 8.12 Detailed illustration of insertion of an element into a leftist heap

Pseudocode 8.4

```
insert(Heap, value)
    value.left = Null
    value.right = Null
    Merge(Heap, value)
```

8.3.3 Operation—Deletion

Just like binary heap, deletion removes the root from the leftist heap. This removes the minimum element and returns the same. The removal of root forms two leftist heaps—one rooted at the left child of the minimum element and another rooted at the right child of the minimum element. Now, these two heaps are merged just as explained in Section 8.3.1. Pseudocode 8.5 shows the deletion process.

Question 8.9 Delete '1' from the sample leftist heap shown in Figure 8.13.

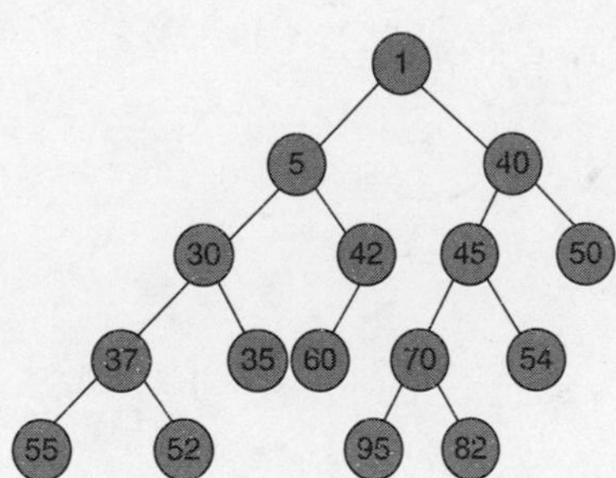

Figure 8.13 Sample leftist heap to delete

Solution: The complete process is explained in Figure 8.14.

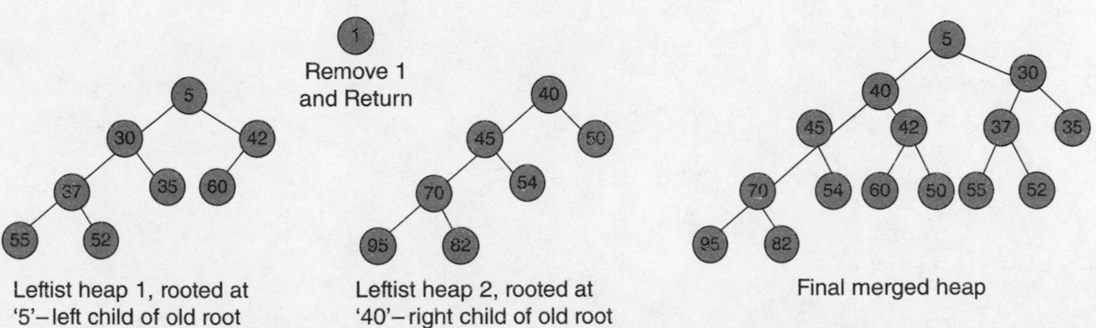

Figure 8.14 Brief illustration of deletion process from a sample leftist heap

Pseudocode 8.5

```
delete(node):
    p = parent(node)
    if node = p.left
    then,
        p.left = merge(p.left.left,p.left.right)
    else,
        p.right = merge(p.right.left,p.right.right)
parent(root,value):
    if root.left == value or root.right == value
    then,
        return root
    else,
        parent(root.right,value)
        parent(root.left,value)
```

8.3.4 Implementation of Leftist Heaps

The implementation of a leftist heap is shared below. First the merge fuction is implemented and then based on modular programming, insertion and deletion operations are implemented (refer to Python code 8.2).

Python code 8.2

```
class node(object):
    def __init__(self, data, rank = 1, dist = 1, left = None, right = None):
        self.data = data
        self.rank = rank
        self.dist = dist
        if left is None or right is None:
            if left is not None:
                self.left = left
            else:
                self.left = right
            self.right = None
        else:
            if left.dist < right.dist:
                left, right = right, left
            self.left = left
            self.right = right
            self.dist += self.right.dist
class leftHeap(object):
    def __init__(self, root = None):
        self.root = root
    def merge(root, t):
        if root is None:
            return t
        if t is None:
            return root
        if root < t:
            root, t = t, root
```

(*contd*)

(*contd*)

```
        root.right = leftHeap.merge(root.right, t)
        if root.left is None or root.right is None:
            root.rank = 1
            if root.left is None:
                root.left, root.right = root.right, None
        else:
            if root.left.rank < root.right.rank:
                root.left, root.right = root.right, root.left
            root.rank = root.right.rank + 1
        return root
    def insert(self, dummy_node):
        if not isinstance(dummy_node, node):
            dummy_node = node(dummy_node)
        if self.root is None:
            self.root = dummy_node
            return
        if self.root == dummy_node:
            self.root.dist += 1
            return
        parent = self.findParent(self.root, dummy_node, None)
        if parent is None:
            self.root=leftHeap.merge(self.root, dummy_node)
        else :
            if parent.left == dummy_node:
                parent.left.dist += 1
            else:parent.right.dist += 1
    def remove(self, dummy_node):
        if not isinstance(dummy_node, node):
            dummy_node = node(dummy_node)
        if self.root == dummy_node:
            self.root = leftHeap.merge(self.root.left, self.root.right)
        else:
            parent = self.findParent(self.root, dummy_node, None)
            if parent is not None:
                if parent.left == dummy_node:
                    parent.left = leftHeap.merge(parent.left.left, parent.left.right)
                else:
                    parent.right = leftHeap.merge(parent.right.left, parent.right.right)
    def findParent(self, root, dummy_node, parent):
        if not isinstance(dummy_node,node):
            dummy_node = node(dummy_node)
        if root is None or root < dummy_node:
            return None
        if root == dummy_node:
            return parent
        l = self.findParent(root.left, dummy_node, root)
        if l is not None:
            return l
        else:
            self.findParent(root.right, dummy_node, root)
```

> **Note** A shortcoming in leftist heaps is that it cannot be represented as an array without any class. In a binary heap, an array-based representation is achievable as the structure is a complete binary tree structure and can be represented in an array.

8.3.5 Complexity Analysis

The complexity of merge function determines the complexity of the other two operations. As already known, merge is a recursive function. So, the complexity of merge is determined based on the number of recursive calls. The maximum number of recursive calls is the sum of the heights of rightmost leaves of the two heaps to be merged, as the condition for breaking the recursive call is reaching the rightmost leaf. If the first heap has 'n' nodes and the second heap has 'm' nodes, then the corresponding heights of rightmost leaves will be 'O(log n)' and 'O(log m)'. So, the worst case complexity of merge operation is 'O(log n)+O(log m)', that is, the sum of heights from both the heaps. It eventually is 'O(log n)' if $n > m$, else it is 'O(log m)'. Thus, the complexity of insertion or deletion is 'O(log n)'.This proves that both the leftist heaps and binary heaps have the complexity of 'O(log n)' for insertion and deletion operations, but merging two binary heaps cannot be achieved in 'O(log n)'. This is where leftist heaps outperform binary heaps.

8.4 PRIORITY QUEUES USING HEAPS

A priority queue is a queue where every element is inserted and taken out based on their priority. Based on the priority, the elements are re-arranged within the queue and the one with the highest priority always gets in front of the queue. Implementing this using linear data structures is very difficult as the queue is supposed to be sorted for every new element coming in or going out. This raises the complexity of insertion/deletion operation to '$O(n^2)$', which is the standard complexity of sorting an array. When the same is implemented using heaps, the functionality can be achieved with a complexity of 'O(log n)' itself. For every new element inserted, the heap ensures that the element with the highest priority moves to become the root. Similarly, on deleting an element, the next highest priority moves up to the root. At any moment the order of the numbers inside the structure does not matter, as priority queues concentrate only on the number that is at the front or the element that will exit the queue next. Thus, heaps are used in implementing priority queues with a limited space complexity of 'O(n)'. Usually, in computerscience concepts, priority is represented using an integer and the highest priority is for the least number. Thus, priority queues are implemented as min heaps. At any point, the element with the highest priority could be in the root. This is very helpful in operating system concepts where the process is scheduled based on priority.

Adaptable Priority Queues

A modification of a priority queue is an 'Adaptable Priority Queue'. In a normal priority queue, elements are inserted and deleted based on their priority. This is a straightforward process in case of a min heap. In an adaptable priority queue, the priority of the elements can be modified even after placing the element in the queue. Along with the normal priority queue functions, in this case, the structure will have additional methods to modify the elements. Before proceeding into the implementation of this structure, it is important to understand the significance of such a structure. Assume there is a sale happening online. Within the day you can find some goods getting their price changed based on demand and stock. So, how is this done? At every point of time, the items have a priority (critical value) based on which the price is modified at certain intervals. This priority varies based on demand, such as the number of items ordered and stock available. Thus, at any moment, the priority of any item can increase or decrease. Such a scenario demands modifiable priorities. Another scenario is a typical computer operating system. There can be many jobs waiting in the queue. If a job is waiting for a long time, then it is about to be starving.

Thus, jobs waiting for a long time must be put on high priority to avoid starvation. This again demands a dymanic change of priority in queue entries. So, how is this implemented?

Adaptable priority queues can also be implemented in a linear fashion using a doubly linked list, but each entry of the list will point to an entry (object) that has the <key,value> pair. The 'key' is the priority value and 'value' is the element itself. The list is maintained in ascending order of the priority of elements. So, when an element is to be inserted, it traverses all the nodes with lesser priorities and inserts the element in the right slot. However, deletion of the element is straight forward. Removing the head and making the next element as head is the `'remove()'` operation. As already discussed, an adaptable priorty queue has two more operations—replaceKey(element, key) and replaceValue(element,value), where 'element' is an object. These two functions take the element object and directly change the key/value correspondingly. For this function to work, a supporting function is required that returns the element given the 'key' – getElement(key). An illustration of a doubly linked list based adjustable priority queue is shown in Figure 8.15.

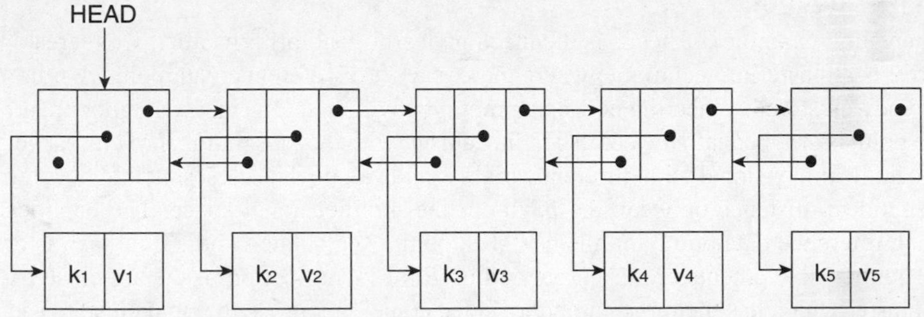

Figure 8.15 Doubly linked-list based adjustable priority queue

In this implementation, when an entry is to be searched, the structure demands linear search, that is, one by one the elements are checked for the required key. So, this increases the cost of the data structure. Thus, adjustable priority queues are also maintained as a heap. Every node of the heap has similar <key,value> pairs as an entry. When a 'key' of an entry is modified, the heapify operation is immediately triggered to bring the heap back to form. Thus, the implementation is very similar to normal priority queues along with an adjustable option.

What will be the complexity of maintaining a min heap based adjustable priority queue?

8.5 APPLICATIONS OF HEAPS

As already explained, heaps are a data structure used majorly for implementing priority queues. Other than priority queues, heaps can also help in sorting a set of numbers with less complexity, which is explained in Chapter 12. In fact, heaps are a special, non-linear data structure designed from trees for efficiently handling sorting operations. Various applications of heaps are discussed below.

Operating Systems

In operating systems like Linux Kernel, multiple jobs wait for processor/memory. There is a priority set for each job that is in the queue. The priority varies depending on the length of the job, resources required, user/system job, and so on. It is based on these priorities that a job gets its resources and gets executed. For example, a print job has a lesser priority when compared to a memory optimization job. Such a scheduling is called as priority scheduling. When any new job is created, it is placed in the priority queue/adjustable priority queue, which places the job based on its priority. At any moment, the next job to be executed will be of the highest priority. This queue is completely maintained using min heaps in operating systems. This is a very brief explanation and so the readers are suggested to explore different scheduling alogrithms to understand this further.

Crucial Algorithms

Heaps also find their place in crucial algorithms, where the lowest or the highest number should be identified efficiently. Some examples of such crucial algorithms are graph algorithms like Prim's algorithm (as discussed in Chapter 11) and Djikstra's algorithm (see Chapter 11). These have a good scope of heaps. Other algorithms like finding the kth smallest/largest element can also be efficiently achieved using heaps. Finding the Kth element is like finding the 4th largest element in a given set.

K-Nearest Neighbours

Another interesting example for heaps is the machine learning algorithm called K-Nearest Neighbours (KNN). KNN is a clustering technique, where there is a set of reference data points within the model, which is already clustered. When the new data point is provided, its K-closest neighbours are identified and the data point is grouped into the corresponding cluster with the most number of closest neighbours. A data point is multi-dimensional with different variables and values. The closest neighbours are computed using the euclidean distance between the points in the n-dimensional space. The euclidean distance between each reference data point and the new data point is calculated and a min heap is created with the same. The first 'k' elements are taken out and used for identification of the apt cluster for the data point. The cluster which has the most number of selected neighbours is the final cluster. There can also be class values given to the cluster that use this algorithm for prediction of events/values. Based on the 'k' value, this algorithm requires continuous sorting of the values which is a time consuming task. The min heap in that can support any 'k' value without much effort and hence best suits the purpose. A use case for this will clearly explain the process.

Consider a program that has recorded the atmospheric temperature and the temperature of the water you took bath (hot water) with for one month. In the next month, this program will take in the atmospheric temperature and predict the temperature of water, that will suit you, to take bath. This is achieved by finding the distance between the new atmospheric temperature values and the recorded atmospheric temperatures. Let us assume a 'k' of '3'. The KNN finds '3' days from the last month where the atmospheric temperature was closest to the current temperature, takes the temperature of water that you took bath with, and predicts today's apt water temperature as the average of the water temperature from those '3' days. With '5' reference data points, this step-by-step process is illustrated in Figure 8.15.

Atmospheric Temperature (in °C)	Water Temperature (in °C)
29	25
25	30
26	29
24	31
32	23

Sample reference points

Atmospheric Temperature (in °C)	Water Temperature (in °C)	Distance from 23 °C
29	25	6
25	30	2
26	29	3
24	31	1
32	23	7

Eucledian distance of 23°C from each reference point's atmospheric temperature

(contd)

(*contd*)

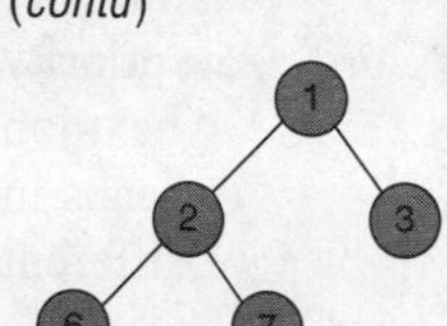

Min heap build with the calculated distances

Atmospheric Temperature (in °C)	Water Temperature (in °C)	Distance from 23 °C
29	25	6
25	30	2
26	29	3
24	31	1
32	23	7

With K = 3, the '3' closest points are identified from the heap. The predicted temperature of water will be Average (30,29,31) which is '30'.

Figure 8.15 Step-by-step for predicting the temperature of water

Points to Remember

- Heaps are hierarchical data structures designed specifically for sorting.
- A min heap has the parent lesser than or equal to its children, whereas in max heap, the parent is greater than or equal to its children.
- Binary heap is a complete tree-based data structure, so list based implementation is always preferred.
- Heapify is a process of swapping a parent and child, when the heap property is violated.
- Heaps are concerned only about the root. In min heap, the smallest element will be placed as the root, whereas in max heap, the largest element is placed as the root. The order of other elements in the heap does not matter much, provided they meet the heap property.
- The complexity of insert/delete operation in heaps is 'O(log n)'.
- A leftist heap is not a complete tree-based heap.
- A leaf is a null node in leftist heaps.
- The distance of a node is the number of nodes in the path to the rightmost leaf.
- At any node, Dist(right) <= Dist(left). So, the shortest root-to-leaf path is the path to the rightmost leaf.
- Two leftist heaps can be merged easily.
- Priority queues are implemented using binary heaps.
- A heap can be used to sort elements and the method is called as heap sort.

Key Terms

Heap A tree-based data structure which has a constraint on the parent-child relationship alone

Binary heap A complete binary tree based heap

Min heap A heap where the minimum most element is maintained in the root

Max heap A heap where the maximum most element is maintained in the root

Leftist heap A min heap where the height of right sub-tree from the root is greater than the height of the left sub-tree

Priority queue A queue where the position of elements is changed based on priority of elements implemented using heaps

Adjustable priority queue A priority queue where the priority of an element can be changed after placing inside the queue

EXERCISES

Multiple-choice Questions

1. Heap is a _______ based structure.
   (a) Binary Tree (b) BST
   (c) Complete Binary Tree
   (d) List
2. _______ is a swap operation of parent and child in a heap when the property is violated.
   (a) Raise (b) Push
   (c) Heapify (d) Skew
3. _______ is the time complexity of maintaining the heap when an element is inserted/deleted.
   (a) O(1og n) (b) O(1)
   (c) O(n) (d) $O(n^2)$
4. Binary Heaps are always symmetric.
   (a) True (b) False
5. _______ is the time complexity of maintaining the leftist heap when an element is inserted/deleted.
   (a) O(1og n) (b) O(1)
   (c) O(n) (d) $O(n^2)$
6. In a leftist heap, when the Dist(right) > Dist(left), the left and right subtrees are _______.
   (a) Swapped (b) Rotated
   (c) Interchanged (d) Trimmed
7. A binary tree is always a leftist heap.
   (a) True (b) False
8. A leftist heap also follows _________ property.
   (a) Binary Heap (b) Min Heap
   (c) Max Heap
9. Is this a leftist heap?

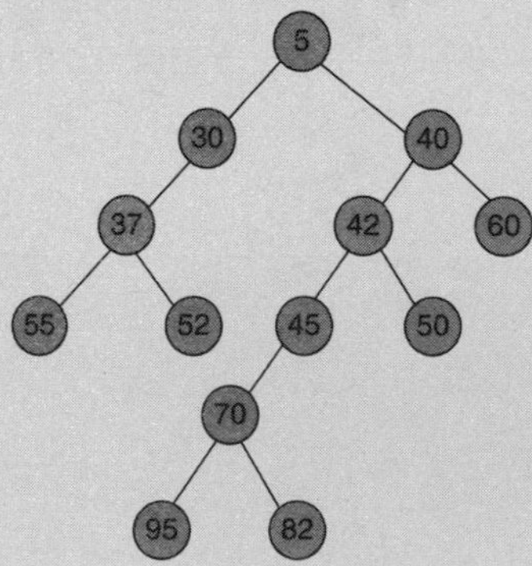

   (a) True (b) False
10. Every subtree in a leftist heap will be a __________.
   (a) Min Heap (b) Max Heap
   (c) Binary Heap (d) Leftist Heap

Theoretical Review Questions

1. What are heaps? How are these implemented?
2. Explain binary heaps along with the importance of heapify operation?
3. How is a heap maintained at O(log n) complexity for insertion/deletion?
4. Explain leftist heaps and how these are better over binary heaps?
5. Explain merge friendly heaps and their merge operation with illustration?

Exploratory Application Exercises

1. From a given set of elements, find the kth smallest element.
2. From a list of 'N' elements, find the three largest products of any two numbers from the list.
3. Implement a double bit priority queue where the first bit is priority 1 and the second bit is priority 2. The order of priority will be based on bit 1. When bit 1 is equal, bit 2 is used for next level priority.
4. Write a program to sort a k-sorted array. A k-sorted array is almost sorted with just k-element misplaced.
5. Develop a module to check if a binary tree is a binary heap.
6. Sort a given array using heap property.
7. Implement a k-array heap. When k=2, it is a binary heap. Other properties of the heap remain the same.
8. Write a procedure to fetch the minimum element from a max heap.
9. Create a function to find all the elements lesser than a given 'X' in a max heap.
10. Write a procedure to fetch the median element from a heap.

Picto Puzzles

Identify logic for every question and develop a code for the same.

1.

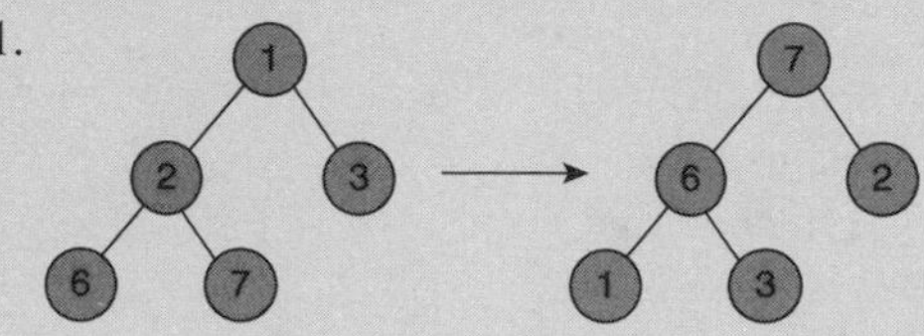

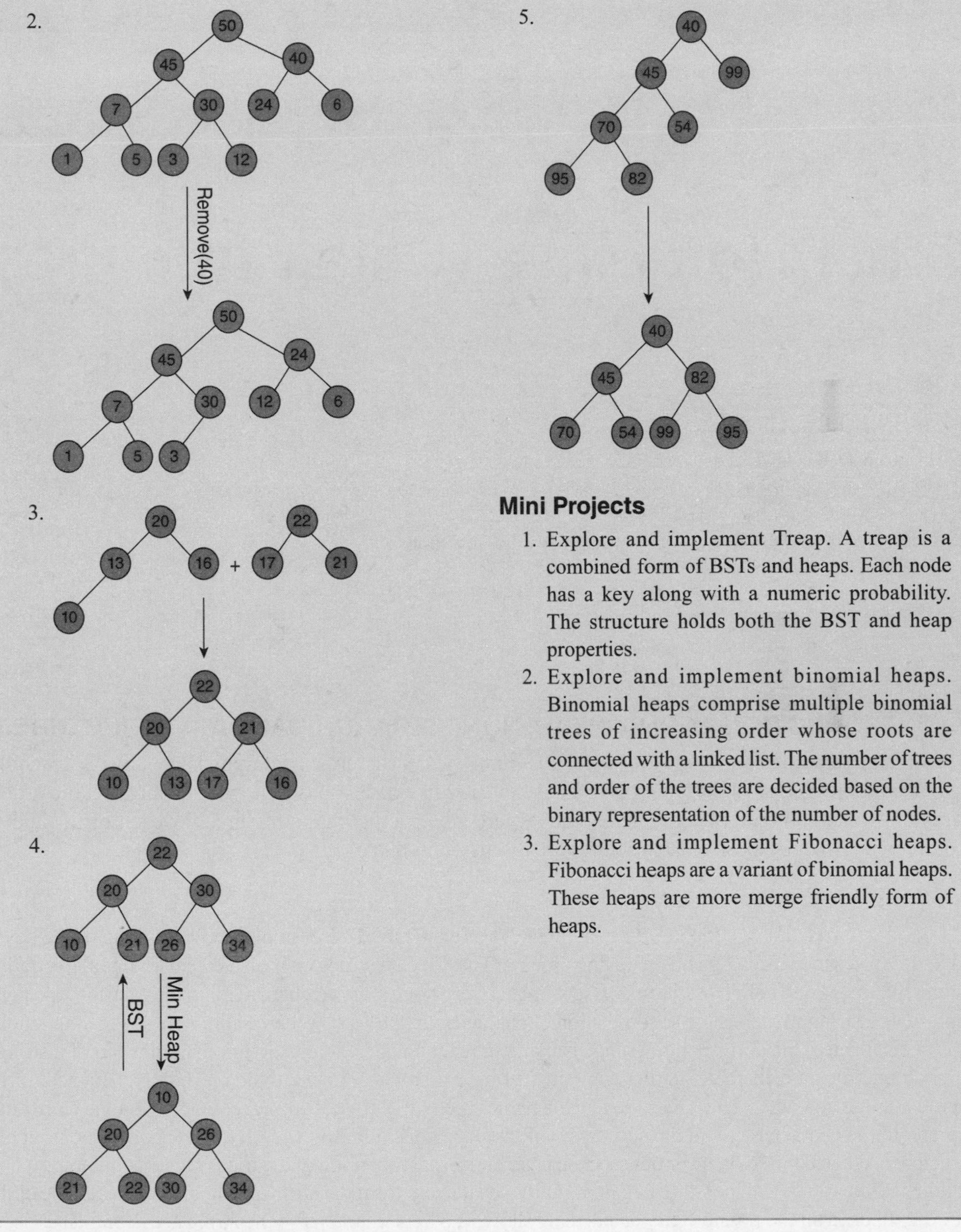

Mini Projects

1. Explore and implement Treap. A treap is a combined form of BSTs and heaps. Each node has a key along with a numeric probability. The structure holds both the BST and heap properties.
2. Explore and implement binomial heaps. Binomial heaps comprise multiple binomial trees of increasing order whose roots are connected with a linked list. The number of trees and order of the trees are decided based on the binary representation of the number of nodes.
3. Explore and implement Fibonacci heaps. Fibonacci heaps are a variant of binomial heaps. These heaps are more merge friendly form of heaps.

Answers to Multiple-choice Questions

1. (a) 2. (c) 3. (a) 4.(a) 5. (a) 6. (a) 7. (b) 8. (b) 9. (b) 10. (d)

CHAPTER

9

Other Non-Linear Data Structures

LEARNING OBJECTIVES

After going through this chapter, readers will be able to understand:

- Learn about some more non-linear data structures other than tree and heap
- Know how tabled data is maintained in data structures
- Gain knowledge about sets and map structures and how these are useful
- Understand if hierarchy always plays a role in the non-linear data structures

9.1 INTRODUCTION—NON-LINEAR, NON-HIERARCHICAL DATA STRUCTURES

Other than trees and heaps, there are some more non-linear structures. Hierarchy is not always available in the data. There can also be tabled data and set/cluster like data. Above all, without any specific order, data points can be connected to one another. There are specific data structures for each of the above requirement. Most of those data structures are discussed in this chapter.

9.2 TRIE

A trie is a tree-based data structure for handling keys or elements. There is no specific ordering of the keys, but it optimises the searching and retrieving process. The trie data structure is also called as digital tree/radix tree/prefix tree. Trie is often used for storing strings. Every node stores a character and the root-to-node path represents a string, which is the accumulation of characters in the path. When a complete string in the input data set is formed, the corresponding node is marked. All the nodes, which do not mark the end of a string, form an intermediate character in the string. In a string, for any character, all the preceding characters form a prefix to that character. This gives the tree the name 'prefix tree'. All the predecessors of a node constitute a prefix to the character and all the successors of the node constitute to the suffix of the node. The trie data structure is created based on the input set of strings. The initial root node of the trie is always null/empty. The children of the root are all possible beginning/initial characters from the string set. In the next level, the child of every node is all the possible characters that follow its parent character in the string set. A branch ends, if a string in the input set has been represented, and there is no superstring comprising the same. The structure can be better understood by interpreting the example trie shared in Figure 9.1 based on a set of strings.

In the tree shown in Figure 9.1, the root is empty as already defined. The children of the root are 'I', 'M', 'C', and 'L' because these are the unique set of initial characters of the strings in the given set. The strings beginning with 'I' are 'I', 'Is', 'India', and 'Indians'. The unique set of second characters from this list are ‘s’ and ‘n’. So ‘I’ has two children, ‘n’ and ‘s’. This proceeds further and ‘n’ has only one child. The word ‘India’ is represented. To mark this word, ‘a’ is marked in the figure with an underline. However, there is another word ‘Indians’ in the list. ‘India’ is a prefix in the word ‘Indians’, so even if ‘a’ marks the end of a word, it has children and grows down to represent further words. Thus, ‘a’ has a child ‘n’ and grandchild ‘s’. The character ‘s’ marks the string ‘Indians’ and the same is shown with an underline in Figure 9.1. Thus, strings are represented in a hierarchical fashion based on adjacent characters and all prefix substrings of a word are represented as a predecessor of the last node of the superstring, just like ‘India’ in ‘Indians’. Any node in the middle cannot be read without reading all the predecessors of the node. If a new word ‘try’ was in the input set, it would have not been represented in the existing branches. Even though the branch for ‘country’ has a ‘try’ in it, it cannot be used to represent the same as the string should start from the root’s children and not somewhere in the middle. Instead, the word ‘count’ can be represented by the same branch by marking ‘t’ as end of a word since ‘count’ is a complete prefix of ‘country’.

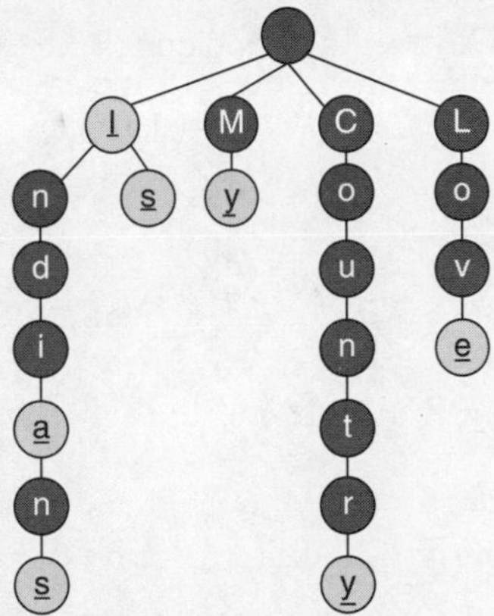

Figure 9.1 Sample trie created from the word set {‘India’, ‘Is’, ‘My’, ‘Country’, ‘I’, ‘Love’, ‘Indians’}

As explained, trie is built on string keys. There are only two operations on the trie structure—insertion of a key and searching a key in the trie. These two operations are explained in the sections below.

9.2.1 Insertion of a Key

Insertion of a new string into a trie can fall under two cases. The first case is the simplest case in which the key is already present in the trie. This is possible if the string to be inserted is a substring of another string that is already present in the trie. So, the last character node is marked and the string is inserted. The counter case is when the string is not a part of the trie. Now, this is the actual insertion or updating process of the trie. Starting from the root, the first character of the string is searched in the root’s children. If the child is found, the corresponding branch is taken and continued further, else the node and all the successive characters are inserted as descendants. When the required child is found, the next character in the string is searched for the children of that node. When the required node is not found, the same is inserted along with the consecutive characters as children of that particular node. If the required node is found, the branch is taken and the same process is repeated. This ensures that the prefix of the new string to be inserted is identified and used properly in the trie. Figure 9.2 illustrates the steps of insertion of a string into a trie.

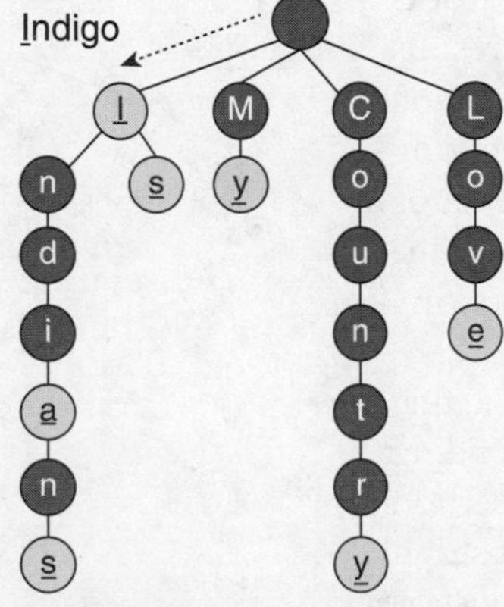

The first character ‘I’ is considered (indicated with underline in the string). Root’s child ‘I’ is found.

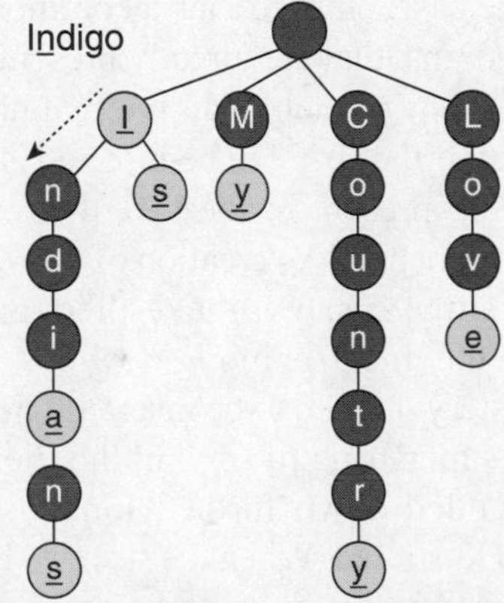

The next character ‘n’ is considered. From the children of ‘I’, ‘n’ is found and branch is taken.

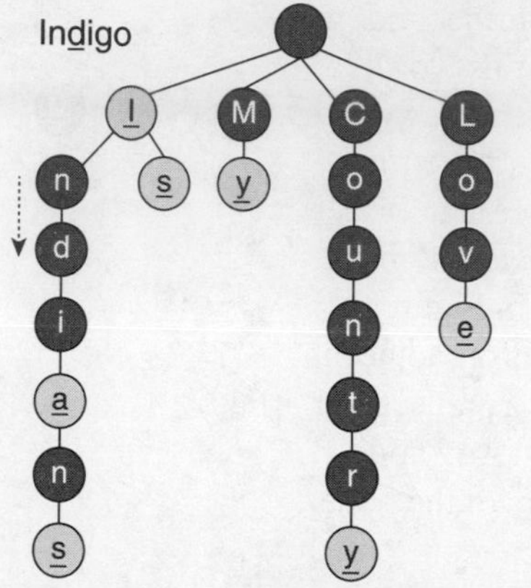

The next character 'd' is found to be child of 'n'

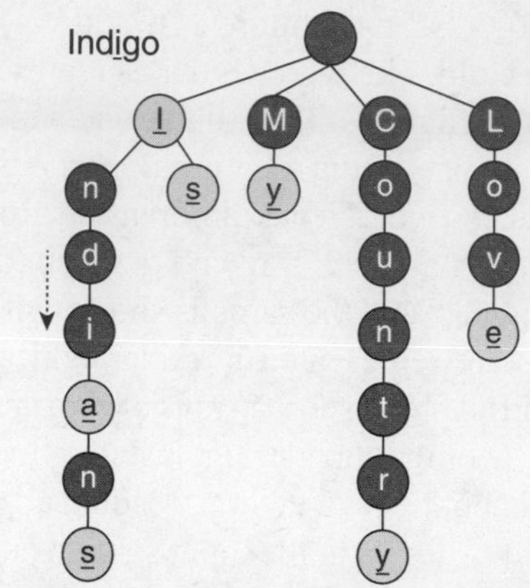

The next character 'i' is found as child of 'd'

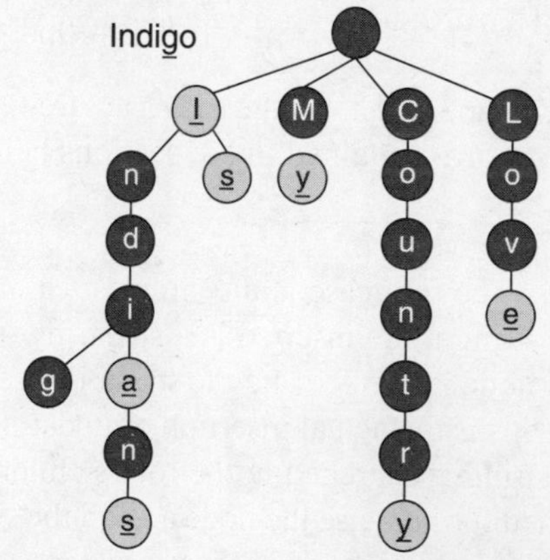

The next character is 'g'. But, 'i' doesn't have a child 'g'. So a new child 'g' is added to the 'i' node.

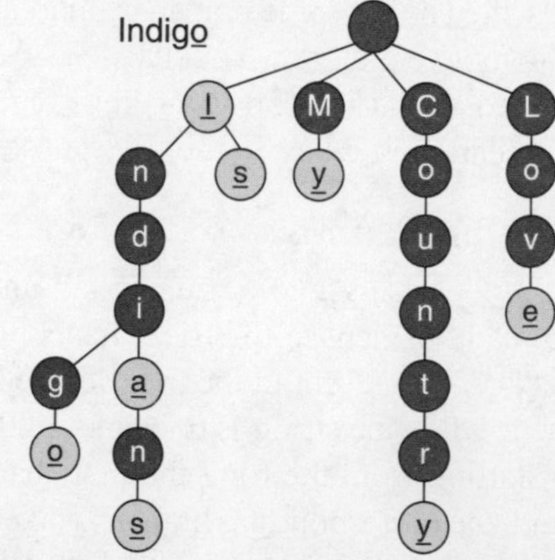

'g' is a new node and doesn't have any child. 'o' is inserted as child of 'g' and marked as end of the new string.

Figure 9.2 Step-by-step illustration of insertion of string 'Indigo' into a sample trie shared in Figure 9.6

In the above case, 'Indigo' has a common prefix with the words 'India' and 'Indians' that are already present in the trie. This results in creation of a new branch in an internal node where the common prefix gets over. If the string to be inserted is a complete superstring of another string present in the trie, then it can be interpreted as extension of a branch unlike creation of a new branch as shown in the above case. Figure 9.3 shows the result of insertion of a superstring of a word into the final trie in Figure 9.2.

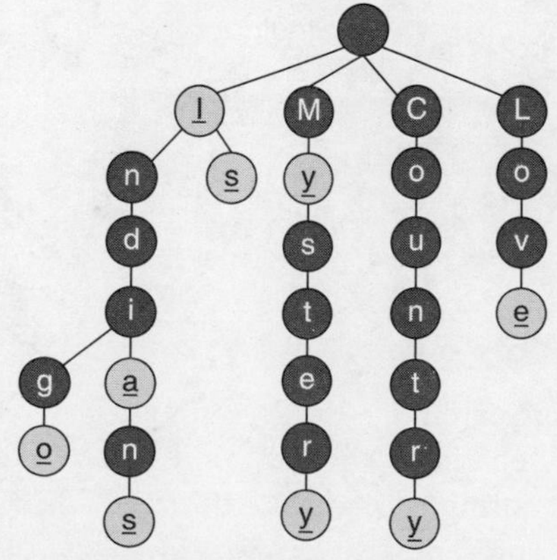

Figure 9.3 Insertion of 'Mystery' into the final trie in Figure 9.2

When 'Mystery' is tried to be inserted into the trie, it is found that 'mystery' is a superstring of 'my' in the trie. So, the corresponding branch is extended down further. Finally, the simplest insertion operations are illustrated. When the string to be inserted is a substring of an existing string in the trie, the search process begins just as illustrated in Figure 9.2. All the required nodes are present in the trie so no new child is inserted at any point. When the final node is found, the same is marked and the process is completed. An example for this case is shown in Figure 9.4. The counter case is when no prefix of the new string is present in the trie. Here, the entire string is inserted as a new branch from the root as shown in Figure 9.5. As said previously, inspite of different cases of handling, insertion is a single process of checking for required nodes one by one. Hence, it is an iterative process for proceeding down the levels. Pseudocode 9.1 explains the insertion process.

Question 9.1 Insert 'count' and 'hot' into the trie shown in Figure 9.3.

Solution: Insertion of 'count' is shown in Figure 9.4 and insertion of 'Hot' is shown in Figure 9.5.

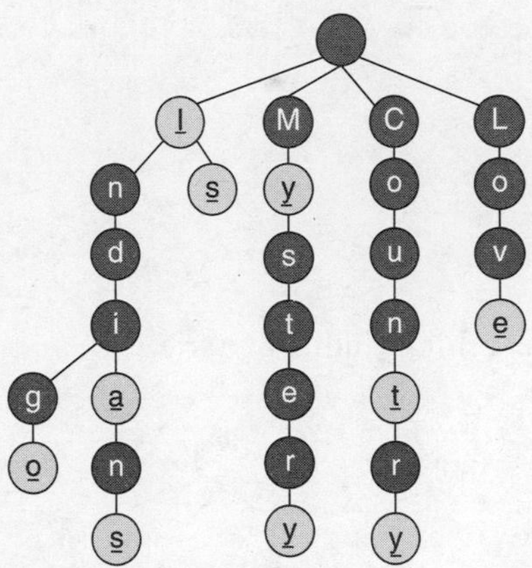

Figure 9.4 Insertion of 'Count' into trie in Figure 9.3

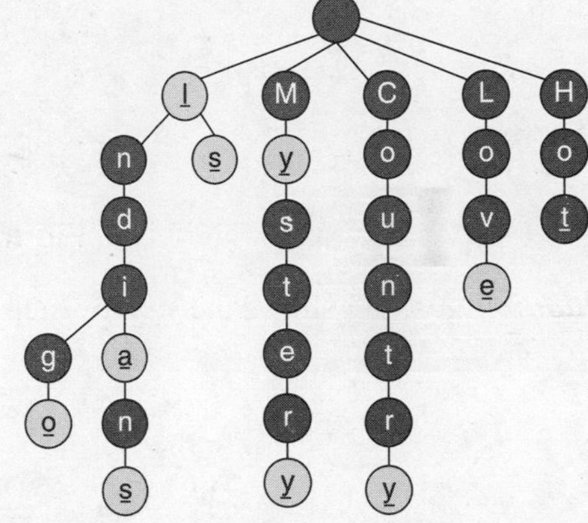

Figure 9.5 Insertion of 'Hot' into trie in Figure 9.3

Pseudocode 9.1

```
def insert(word):
    current_node = root
        if char is not in node.children
        then,
            add char as a child for the current node
        current_node = current_node.children[char]
    Mark current_node as end of a string
```

Food for Brain

What will be the depth of the trie with just English words?

9.2.2 Searching a Key

Searching a string in trie is just similar to insertion. Starting from the roots' children, one by one, the characters in the string are compared with the node and moved down continuously. When the end of the string is reached, the node should already be marked as end of string. Only then it means that the string is present in the trie. If the required character is not available among the children of a node or the node that corresponds to the last character of the string is not marked as end of string, then the string is not present in the trie and '-1' is returned to indicate the same. Pseudocode 9.2 shows the search process.

Question 9.2: Search 'India' in the trie shown in Figure 9.6.

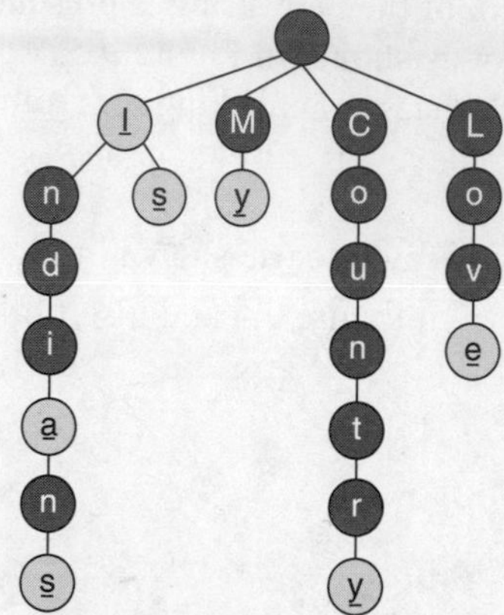

Figure 9.6 A sample Trie

Solution: Figure 9.7 shows the step-by-step illustration of searching 'India' in a trie.

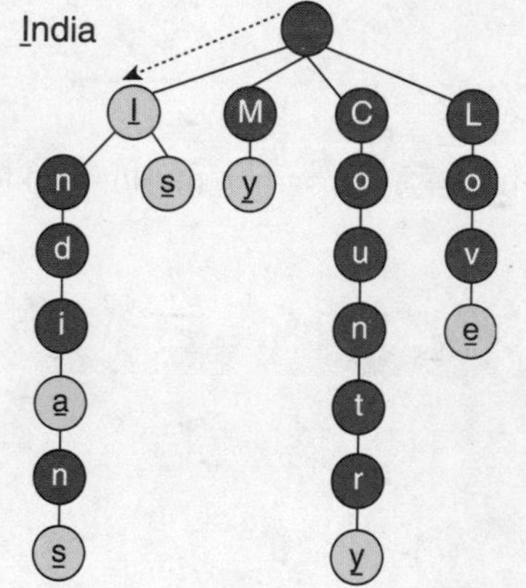

First character 'I' is found as the child of root

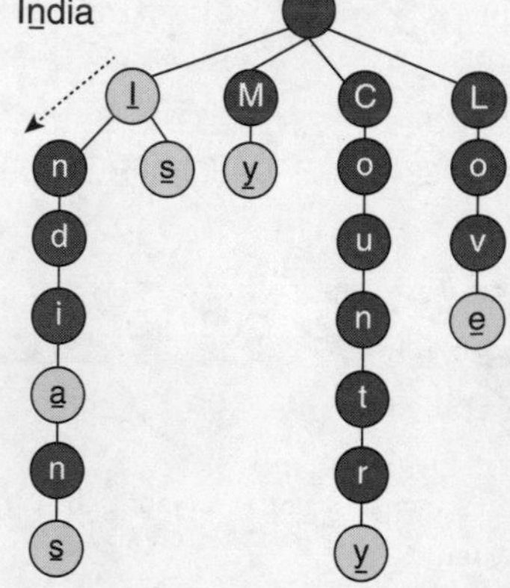

Next character 'n' is also child of 'I'

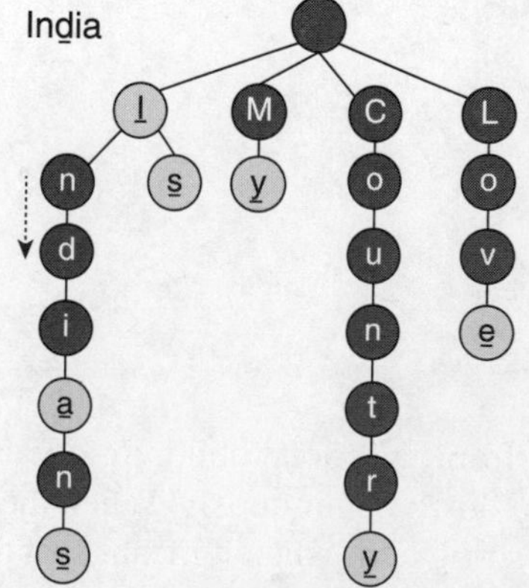

The next character is 'd', a child of 'n'

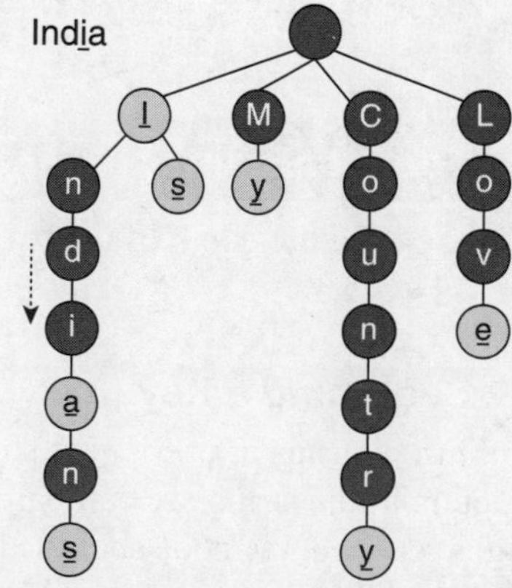

The next character 'i' is child of 'd' in trie

(contd)

(contd)

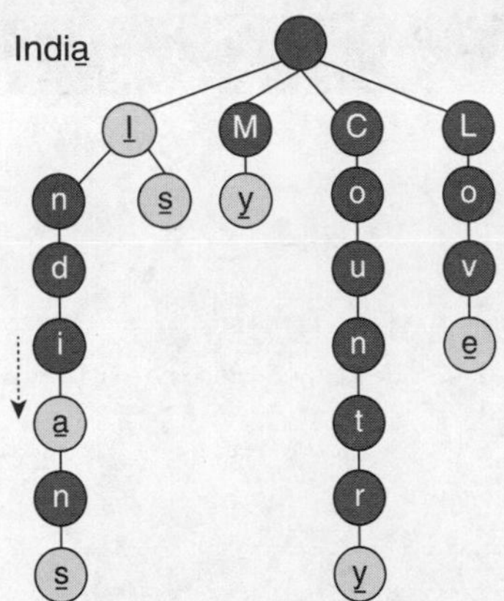

Moving down from 'i', the final character 'a' is reached. The node also marks end of a string.

Figure 9.7 Detailed illustration of searching 'India' in a trie

In the above illustration when 'India' is searched, starting from the root, the process moves down in search of the consecutive characters and reaches the last character 'a' which is marked as end of string. Thus, it returns a positive response to indicate the presence of the string. If 'Indian' was searched instead of 'India' in the same trie, the process would have moved down further cross 'a' and reached 'n'. Now, the end of string would have been reached, but the node is not marked as end of string. So, even if the string is present in the trie it is not used in the input set for building the trie. Thus, '-1' is returned to indicate absence of the string. While moving down in search of consecutive characters, the required node is not present at any point, that too, indicates the absence of the required string and '-1' is retuned in here as well.

Pseudocode 9.2

```
def search(prefix,node,word):
    prefix += node
    if prefix = word
    then,
        if current_node is end of string
        then,
            return word
        else,
            return -1
    else,
        next_char = word[len(prefix)+1]
        for i in range(node.children)
            if node.children[c] = next_char
            then,
                return search(prefix,node.children[c],word)
        return -1
```

9.2.3 Implementation

Trie is a search optimising data structure which has only two operations–Insertion and Searching. By default, trie does not support deletion. The implementation is shown in Python code 9.1.

Python code 9.1

```
class Trie(object):

    """
    List implementation of Trie

    A trie is a data structure that is designed for re'TRIE'val.

    Represents the Trie class
    """

    def __init__(self, char):

        """
        Initializer for the Trie class

        Parameters
        ----------
        char: str
            The character of a word node in a Trie

        children: list
            List of words in the Trie

        is_end: bool
            End of a word
        """

        self.char = char
        self.children = []
        self.is_end = False             # is this the end of the word?


def insert(root, word):

    """
    Function to insert words in the Trie.

    Parameters
    ----------
    root: object
        Object of the Trie class

    word: str
        Word to be inserted
    """
```

(contd)

(contd)

```
    node = root
    for char in word:
        found = False
        for child in node.children:    # check if character is present in current node's
                                       # children
            if child.char == char:     # if character is found, point node to the child that
                                       # contains it
                node = child
                found = True
                break
        if not found:                  # word not found, so add a new chlid
            new_node = Trie(char)
            node.children.append(new_node)
            node = new_node            # and then point node to the new child
    node.is_end = True                 # word added. Mark it as end

def search(root, word):

    """
    Function to search for a word in the Trie and return True or False

    Parameters
    ----------
    root: object
        Object of the Trie class

    word: str
        Word/prefix to be searched
    """

    node = root
    if not root.children:              # if root has no children (empty), return False
        return False
    for char in word:
        char_not_found = True
        for child in node.children:    # search all children of current node
            if child.char == char:     # if search character is found in child
                char_not_found = False
                node = child           # make child containing the character as node and break
                break
        if char_not_found:             # if character not found, return False
            return False
    return True                        # to check for prefix only, uncomment this line and
                                       # comment the next three lines
```

(contd)

(*contd*)

```
    if node.is_end:                      # if character found, and is a complete word, return True
        return True
    else: return False
root = Trie('*')
insert(root, "india")
insert(root, 'is')
insert(root, 'my')
insert(root, 'country')
insert(root, 'love')
insert(root, "indians")
insert(root, 'indigo')

print(search(root, 'india'))
print(search(root, 'indian'))
print(search(root, 'is'))
```

9.2.4 Complexity Analysis

Both the operations of trie are based on iterative movement down the tree. So, the complexity of the operations directly depends on depth of the trie. Depth is decided by length of strings inserted into the trie. If the length of the longest string is 'M', then the depth of the tree is 'O(M)'. Insertion will reach the deepest point for the worst case, so both the operations are 'O(M)'. While searching a string of length 'N', the complexity is based on the smallest of 'M' and 'N'. If 'N' is smaller, search stops on reaching 'N' and it does not proceed till the deepmost point, so the complexity is 'O(N)'. If 'M' is smaller, then the end of trie is reached before reaching the end of the required string, so the complexity becomes 'O(M)'. While a string that is present in the trie is searched, the worst case length is 'M' which will be the deepest branch constituting its complexity to 'O(M)'. Thus, the worst case search complexity is referred to as 'O(M)'. Even when 'N<M', the complexity of 'O(M)' accommodates 'O(N)' within the limits. So as a standard reference, the complexity of search operation is 'O(M)'. If the similar structure is implemented using search trees, the depth of the tree is 'M log(N)' for 'N' strings. In this case, both insertion and searching are accommodated in linear time, making it a search efficient structure.

9.2.5 Applications of Trie

As already discussed, trie is a search-oriented data structure. It is widely used for search applications where search on a large chunk of data is frequently performed. A potential application of trie is in search engines. Frequent search operation takes place in the ocean of web links. A trie of all the possible search terms is created. The search terms are keywords provided in the domain itself by the website publisher. At every node which marks the end of a character, the links of the websites of the corresponding keywords are stored. All keywords are mostly of same length and there is no skewing when compared to the volume. This creates a very wide and medium height trie. The root will have 26 children for characters and some for numbers and symbols as well. However, as moving down, the width is not exponential. The child 'A' can have all the children just like the root, but according to English grammar rules, 'q' should always be followed by 'u', so the node 'q' only has one character child 'u' along with number and symbol children. Thus, the width of the tree is designed based on the keywords from the language. In English the longest word is 'pneumonoultramicroscopicsilicovolcanoconiosis', which is the name of a disease. So, the depth of the trie also cannot cross this point for characters. Thus, web trie has a constant length and a growing width, making search time constant compared to the growing volume.

9.3 DICTIONARY

Real-time data does not have just hierarchical relationships, but it also exhibits tabular relationship. Every data point has a set of features associated with each other. Here, the features are represented as columns and every data point is a record. Tabular data plays a very important role in data analytics and real-time learning. A basic data structure to support tabular data is dictionary. At a low level, dictionary can be visualized as a set of <key,value> pairs associated as a structure. A very simple dictionary is:

D = {1: 'a' , 3: 'b' , 2: 'c' }

This is the definition of a dictionary in Python, which is a primitive type. In the above dictionary, the set of keys are '1', '3', and '2'. Each key has values 'a', 'b', and 'c' correspondingly. There is no constraint on the number of <key:value> pairs or the order of keys in a standard dictionary.

Every key should have a value and there cannot be any key without value. The keys should only be immutable/constants. Inside the dictionary, the values can be accessed only through their keys. So, if the keys were modified after placing them in, there is a possibility to miss the values. In addition, duplicate keys are not allowed as the values clash, so modifying keys after placing might make them duplicates. Thus, keys are designed to be immutable in dictionaries. While keys had these many constraints, values do not have any constraint. It can be of any type and any value, mutable or immutable. Thus, with immutable keys and mutable or immutable values, a dictionary is created. The basic operations in dictionary are Inserting a <key:value> pair, modifying a value of a key, deleting a key, which also deletes its value, and finally merging two dictionaries.

9.3.1 Inserting a Key and its Value

Inserting a key is done just like lists. Instead of using subscripts as numbers, keys are used to update the dictionary. The term, Dictionary[key]= 'value', inserts the value with the key into the dictionary. This operation is more than insertion as it is also used for updating/modifying the dictionary. In the operation, if the key is already present in the dictionary, then it is updated with the new value. The code for insertion is shared in Snippet 9.1.

Snippet 9.1

```
"""
The following are different ways of creating a dictionary in Python
"""

# Empty dictionary can either be created using empty brackets or by calling Python's dict()
# function

d1 = {}

d1 = dict()

# Values can be added into the dictionary in any of the following ways
d1['a'] = 1
d1['b'] = 1
d1['c'] = 1

d2 = {'a':1, 'b':1, 'c':1}
d3 = dict(a = 1, b = 1, c = 1)
```

(contd)

(*contd*)

```
d4 = dict([('a', 1), ('b', 1), ('c', 1)])

x = ['a', 'b', 'c']
d5 = dict.fromkeys(x,1) # for creating keys with a default value, from elements of a list

print(d1,d2,d3,d4,d5, sep='\n')
```

The above snippet also shows how to insert elements into an empty dictionary. The final dictionary in 'd5' will be { 'a': 1 , 'b': 1 , 'c': 1 }. The same operator for updating is shared in Snippet 9.2.

Snippet 9.2

```
d6 = {'a':2, 'e': 2} # d6 is a dictionary

d6['a'] = 1          # value of key 'a' is updated
d6['b'] = 1          # new key:value pair is inserted
d6['c'] = 1          # new key:value pair is inserted

print(d6)            # {'a': 1, 'e': 2, 'b': 1, 'c': 1}
```

In the above snippet, the initial dictionary is { 'a': 2 , 'e': 2 }. While dict['a'] is assigned, it updates the dictionary. The old value is overwritten by the new value. Thus, after all the updates, the final dictionary will be { 'a': 1 , 'e': 2 , 'b' : 1 , 'c':1}.

9.3.2 Deleting a Key along with Value

Deleting a key is achieved using the 'del' operator. While deleting a key, its value also gets erased out of the dictionary. As already said, dictionary is a dynamic data structure and the order of elements within the data structure does not matter. So, deleting a <key:value> pair does not create any vacant space in the middle of the dictionary. Snippet 9.3 shows deletion of a key.

Snippet 9.3

```
d7 = {'a': 1, 'e': 2, 'b': 1, 'c': 1}

del(d7['b'])                  # d7 will be {'a': 1, 'e': 2, 'c': 1}

#del(d7['x'])                 # throws KeyError, because key 'x' does not exist in d7

if 'x' in d7:                # will not throw KeyError
    del(d7['x'])

d7.pop('e')                   # Python's pop() can be used to delete a key. It returns the
                              # value of the key removed
```

(*contd*)

(contd)

```
d7.pop('z','No such key exists') # pop() function can take an additional default parameter that
                                 # is returned when value doesn't exist
d8 = {'a': [1, 3, 4, 9, 2]}
d8['a'].remove(9)                # removes only a specific value for a key containing multiples
                                 # values
```

A key can have multiple values it the form of a list/ 'del' operator will completely delete the key and the list of values as well. This is where `'remove( )'` function of Python lists can be helpful in deleting a selected value alone.

9.3.3 Merging Dictionaries

Merging dictionaries can be seen as concatenation of two lists. When two dictionaries have a distinct set of keys, merging them creates a pool of keys which is the union of keys from both the dictionaries. This does not modify any <key:value> pair from both the dictionaries. This merge operation is achieved through update function. The update function gets called by the source dictionary and takes another dictionary as argument. The code for merging dictionaries using the update function is shared in Snippet 9.4.

Snippet 9.4

```
d9 = {'a':2, 'e': 2}
d10 = {'a':1, 'b': 1, 'c': 1}
d10.update(d9)              # Python's update() function can also be used to update values of
                            # a key from one dictionary to another

print(d10)                  # {'a': 2, 'b': 1, 'c': 1, 'e': 2}

# when the source dictionary has a key, which is also present in dictionary to be merged, the
# key just gets the value from the source.

d11 = {'a': 1, 'e': 2}
d11.update(a = 5, b = 3)
print(d11)                  #{'a': 5, 'e': 2, 'b': 3}
```

Update function not only merges the dictionary with a given dictionary, but also can modify/append any given key and its value.

9.3.4 Handling Tabular Data

Since dictionaries map values to the keys and store them, these are also referred to as 'Maps' in some other programming languages. As already said, the values need not be mutable. Even lists can be stored as values. Now, dictionaries get the actual tabular form. Every key plays the role of a field header. The value is a list of entries of the field. So, every value list is a column. The representation of a sample table as a dictionary is shown in Figure 9.8.

Roll Number	Name	Gpa
13201	Abhishek	9.52
13202	Akash	8.65
13203	Akshaya	7.63
13204	Anjana	6.24
13205	Aswin	8.98

```
Student = {'Roll Number':[13201,13202,13203,103204,13205],
           'Name': ['Abhishek','Akash','Akshaya','Anjana',
           'Aswin'],
           'GPA':[9.52,8.65,7.63,6.24,8.98]}
```

Figure 9.8 A simple table and dictionary representation of the same table

This table-to-dictionary and dictionary-to-table conversion is possible only when all values in the list are of same length. If the length of the value list is not same, it cannot be interpreted as a proper table. Another difficulty in using dictionary for tabular data is that records cannot be directly fetched from the structure. A record is an entry in the table which will have one entry for each field. The first record from the table in Figure 9.8 is <13201, 'Abhishek', 9.52>. In dictionary, a record has one element from each field list, accessing which is difficult. Even if it can be accessed, they do not get collated and returned as a single entity. Instead, a record is fetched as individual entries from each value list. To fetch n[th] record out of a dictionary as a single list, the function shown in Snippet 9.5 can be used.

Snippet 9.5

```
Students = {'Roll Number' : [13201, 13202, 13203, 13204, 13205],
            'Name' : ['Abhishek', 'Akash', 'Akshaya' ,'Anjana', 'Aswin'],
            'GPA' : [9.52, 8.65, 7.63, 6.24, 8.98]}

# Fetching a record from a dictionary by index position
n = 1       # for the above dictionary this will fetch the values for Akash, because Python
            # indexing starts from zero
s = []
for student in Students:
    s.append(Students[student][n])
print(s)

# the above code can be simplified as follows
[Students[student][n] for student in Students]

# the following code can be used to fetch a record from a dictionary by value
t = []
for student in Students:
    for stu in Students.values():
        if 'Akshaya' in stu:
            t.append(Students[student][stu.index('Akshaya')])
print(t)
```

All the values in the list need not be of the same type. The list might contain a mix of types, which is again a violation of a regular table property, where every field is of one single type. This gives dictionary the ability of handling nested or complex data types as well. Given these abilities of mixed value types and varied length values, dictionaries can handle hash tables, HTML/XML data, and much more column oriented data. HTML/XML are tag-based languages where the tags are stored as keys and attributes for the tags can be represented in the value. These attributes are of different types and lengths, making dictionaries the best for the purpose.

How can two tables be merged using Python Dictionaries?

9.3.5 Implementation

Implementation of dictionaries can be visualised as a class comprising two lists. One list will have all keys and other lists will have the values of the keys in the corresponding position. When a <key:value> pair is inserted into the dictionary, if the key is placed in 3rd location of the key lists, then the value will also be placed in the 3rd location of the value lists. At any point, the length of the lists will be consistent. When the first lists, that is the key lists, will be one dimensional, the second lists/value lists can go two dimensional as values can be in the form of lists for tabular data. As dictionaries are primitive in Python, their implementation is not discussed much and any development code for the same is not shared. This description would have given the basic idea about how dictionaries are implemented in Python or in other languages. It is left for the users to explore.

As a supportive proof for the above description, Python also has the ability to build a dictionary from two lists. Two lists of same length can be taken and a dictionary can be created out of them. Either of the lists can be key lists and the other can be values, provided the key lists have all constants/immutable data. This is achieved by applying 'zip' over the lists and then applying 'dict' function over the zipped lists. Snippet 9.6 shows the code for creating a dictionary out of two lists.

Snippet 9.6

```
letters = ['a', 'b', 'c', 'd']
numbers = [1, 2, 3, 4]

d12 = dict(zip(numbers,letters)) # merging two lists of same length into a dictionary
```

The zip function combines the lists into tuples as (key, value). This can be used by the dict constructor to convert them and build a final dictionary as {1: 'a', 2: 'b', 3: 'c', 4: 'd'}.

9.3.6 Complexity

The time complexity of insertion is 'O(1)', as it just appends the pair into the dictionary. While searching for a key, worst case can be traversal through all elements making the search complexity as 'O(n)'. The space complexity of dictionary will be 'O(n)' for 'n' keys and 'n' values.

9.3.7 Applications of Dictionary

Most of the applications of dictionaries have already been shared above. It finds opportunity in storing and representing tabular data. It can represent tabular data and tag based data like HTML/XML. In tag-based data, the tag name will become the key and the content of the tags will be values. Other than these applications, dictionary also finds its applications in implementation of other data structures/algorithms. Implementation of graph data structure using adjacency list can be easily implemented using dictionaries. The same has been discussed and elaborated in Chapter 11. In addition, counting sort for strings explained in Chapter 12 can be easily achieved through dictionaries. The Trie data structure elaborated in Section 9.2 as well can be implemented easily using dictionaries. The implementation of Trie using dictionary is shown in Python code 9.2.

Python code 9.2

```
from collections import defaultdict
class Trie(object):

    """
    Dictionary implementation of Trie
    """

    def __init__(self):
```

(contd)

(*contd*)

```
        self.children = defaultdict(Trie)  # defaultdict() creates an entry in the dictionary
                                           # if key does not exist. dict() will throw an error
                                           # if key not found.
        self.is_end = False                # variable to store the end of string


def insert(root, word):

    node = root
    for char in word:
        node = node.children[char]         # insert character to dictionary
    node.is_end = True                     # word added. Mark it as end


def search(root, word):
    node = root
    for char in word:
        if char not in node.children:
            return False                   # if character not found, return False
        node = node.children[char]
   #return True                            # to check for prefix only, uncomment this line and
                                           # comment the next line

    return node.is_end                     # if character found, and is a complete word, return
                                           # True


root = Trie()
insert(root, "india")
insert(root, 'is')
insert(root, 'my')
insert(root, 'country')
insert(root, 'love')
insert(root, "indians")
insert(root, 'indigo')

print(search(root, 'india'))
print(search(root, 'indian'))
print(search(root, 'is'))
```

9.4 HASH TABLES

A hash table is a table oriented data structure that can be used for just organising the data. Hash tables convert a list-based data into table-based structure for efficiently handling the same. It works on a mechanism called hashing. It is a mechanism of grouping the data based on a key value. It is a function that groups data of random size into a fixed size. It has two parts, a hash function and a hash table. A hash table has all the given input reordered and mapped to specific keys. The hash function generates the 'key' for every data. It can be designed in such a way that all the data items get specific keys. Figure 9.9 shows a small hash table.

Working

The aim of hash function is to fully order the data. However, in some cases it may not be possible, so it partially orders the data. It visualizes ordering as much as possible. A hash table is visualized as a linear array. Every element is an entity stored value pair at an index which is same as the key. When the element is a value, its key is computed using the hash functions. For building a hash table, first the hash function is to be devised. For simpler implementation, it may be modulo function. If there are ten numbers, then 'mod 10' is used. If the length of the expected final table is eight, then 'mod 8' is used. In general small-scale applications/problems, 'mod n' hash function is mostly used. A hash table with 12, 23, 34, 45, 56 is shared in Figure 9.10 for reference. For a hash table of length 'five', let hash function be 'a[i]%5'.

Figure 9.9 Hash table of some common things

0	1	2	3	4
45	56	12	23	34

Figure 9.10 Sample hash table

Problem of Collision

There is a problem in the hash building procedure. According to the procedure, the element is to be placed in the index where the index is same as key. The key is generated using the hash function. Consider a scenario where more than one input element gets the same key. This situation is called collision. Collision can be handled in two different ways discussed in the following sections.

- Linear Probing
- Chaining the Elements

9.4.1 Linear Probing

This is based on the fact that there are only 'N' elements for a hash table of length 'N', so every element must have a location for sure in the output. While insertion, the hash function generates a key and then the table at key is checked. If the position is empty, then the element is placed in it. If the position is already occupied, then it linearly searches for the next empty slot and places the element in there. So, it achieves partial ordering. While searching for the element, the key is found. The position is checked in the hash table. If the element does not match, then a linear search is done starting from that point until the element is found. Just because any element can be placed at any index, this method is referred to as open addressing. Pseudocodes 9.3 and 9.4 are for insertion and searching, respectively.

Pseudocode 9.3

```
key = hash_function(element)
d = data_item(key,element)
hash_index=key
while hash_index is not empty
do,
    increment hash_index
    hash_index %= size to wrap within limits
hash_array[hash_index]=d
```

Pseudocode 9.4

```
hash_index = hash_function(element)
while hash_array[hash_index] is not empty
do,
    if hash_array[hash_index]== element
    then,
        return hash_index
    else,
        increment hash_index
        hash_index %= size to wrap within limits
return -1 as no match found
```

A sample hash table with elements '12, 23, 34, 45, 55' of size '5' is shown in Figure 9.11 to illustrate linear probing. Since the hash table is of size '5', the hash function will be 'a[i]%5'.

0	1	2	3	4
45	55	12	23	34

Figure 9.11 Sample hashing to illustrate Linear Probing

A drawback in the solution is that the misplaced elements further cause misplacement of appropriate elements. Say, we have '5, 10, 11, 12, 13', then '5' is placed in index '0' as usual. Then comes collision for '10', which is placed at index '1'. Following this, '11' is placed in index '1', but the previous linear probing causes this to collide. Similarly, the following '12' and '13' also collide. So, solving one collision causes three new collisions. This increases the searching cost.

9.4.2 Chaining the Elements

This is an idea to use additional space. It creates a linked list of elements at any key when there is collision. When the linked list is created, the head of the list is stored in the base array of the hash table. Now, hash table starts growing in two dimensions—one in the base array and another in the list for colliding elements. Thus, it gets the table structure, key as columns and value as records. So, the implementation has some free slots using additional memory. So when there is a collision for an index, next element is appended into the list. A sample hash table with five elements '12, 23, 34, 45, 55' is shared in Figure 9.12. For a hash table of 'size=5', hash (mod) function is 'a[i]%5'.

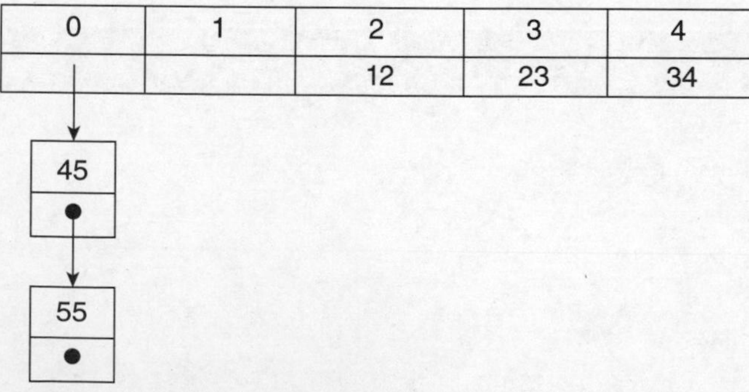

Figure 9.12 Illustration of chaining in hash tables

A drawback in here is it wastes some space and implementation is difficult. Consider this scenario when the whole array is skewed. An example of creating a hash table with elements '5, 10, 15, 20, 25' is shared in Figure 9.13. Here, the whole array is empty and all the elements are added in one list itself, wasting more space and making the data no better when compared to the original form.

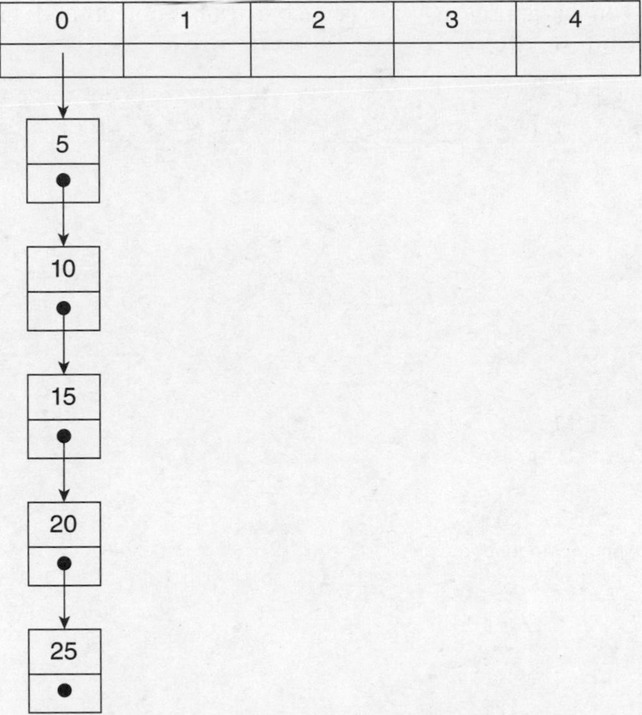

Figure 9.13 Illustration of a skewed list in chaining

Despite the above drawbacks, chaining is the preferred hashing implementation. The reason is in linear probing—the length of the hash table is same as the length of input list. For efficiently handling large amount of elements in a limited width, chaining-based table structure is the best. The above drawback of skewed list for one key alone can be overcome by efficiently designing the hash functions. While mod functions perform for normal applications like the examples shared in here, for real-time data, a complex hash function will be designed and even at times it may be polynomial of higher degrees.

How can strings be hashed?

Other than these two algorithms, collision can be handled in many ways. In open addressing, the algorithm which we discussed was linear probing. In linear probing, when the requested location is engaged, the next location is checked, which is the required + 1. Here, '1' is a constant and a linear function. Even this '1' can be replaced by '2' and still remain a linear probing design. When a quadratic function is used in place of a linear function to find the next available slot faster, the algorithm is referred to as quadratic probing.

Another out-of-the-box thinking is double hashing or rehashing. Here, for balancing the load of nodes, the hashed value is hashed again using level two hash function. This further randomizes the values and balances the load. These algorithms are left for the users to explore.

9.4.3 Implementation

The linear probing mode of hashing is implemented here. A separate class is used to store the value along with the key. Initially, the hash table of required size is created and filled with dummy items with key '-1'. So if a position is found to have key '-1', it is treated as empty. The implementation shown in Python code 9.3 is based on this approach. The hash_table just has objects and can be simply overwritten with a new object at any time easily.

Python code 9.3

```
class DataItem:
    def __init__(self,k,v):
        self.key = k
        self.value = v

class hash_table:
    def __init__(self,a):
        self.size = len(a)
        self.hash_array = []
        dummy = DataItem(-1,0)

        for i in range(self.size):
            self.hash_array.append(dummy)
        for i in range(self.size):
            self.insert(a[ i ])

    def hash_function(self,element):
        return element % self.size


    def search(self,element):
        hash_index = self.hash_function(element)
        temp = hash_index
            while(self.hash_array [hash_index].key != -1):
                if(self.hash_array [hash_index].value==element):
                    return hash_index
                hash_index += 1
                hash_index %= self.size
            if (temp == hash_index):
                return -1

    def insert(self,element):
            k = self.hash_function(element)
            item = DataItem(k,element)
            hash_index = k
            while(self.hash_array[hash_index].key != -1):
                hash_index+=1
                hash_index %= self.size
            self.hash_array[hash_index] = item
```

(*contd*)

(*contd*)

```
def get_data(self,i):
        if (i != -1):
            print("key: ",self.hash_array[ i ].key)
            print("value: ",self.hash_array[ i ].value)
        else:
            print("value not existing")
```

Python has a built-in `hash()` function that converts any given value into a integer. In Python 3.3 for any value, the `hash()` function will give a different value in every new run. The value is so unpredictable making it fit for encryption and digital transfer. A program creating the hash and sending it over online and a counter program to convert the hashed value back into the original value will be a very good secured transfer. Python also has a hashlib library, which has various functions. However, the utility of the function is different. It has different functions built based on different encoding techniques as core hash function. These can be used for encoding values into specified format like 'sha256' and 'md5'.

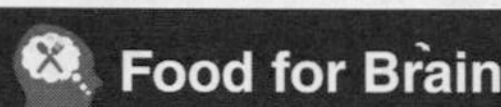

How to implement hash tables using Python Dictionaries?

9.4.4 Complexity

The complexity of creating the hash table is 'O(n) * complexity of hash function'. So, the total complexity is determined by the hash function. Here, the hash function is just a simple function which is of complexity 'O(1)'. So, the total building complexity is 'O(n)'. The searching complexity best case is 'O(1)', where the element will be stored in the expected position, while the worst case search is 'O(n)'. This is possible when linear probing has moved the element by 'n' digits or chaining has formed a skewed list. Hashing is still preferred for organising large volumes of data. This is because, with the right choice and design of hash function, collision can be avoided for any set of data. Thus, the worst case search can be brought down to 'O(1)'. Hence, searching at constant time 'O(1)' is possible using hash tables.

9.4.5 Applications of Hash Tables

As already discussed, hash tables are specialized data structures handling 'store and search' efficiently. So, the primary application of hash tables is in searching. Other than searching-based applications, another potential application of hash tables is data handling algorithms like machine learning. When the data is continuous and the range is very long, hashing can be used to limit the range and use the data more efficiently. In case of categorical data when the number of categories are too wide, hashing can be done to bucket closer categories and significantly reduce the processing time. Continuous string values can be one-hot encoded into vectors. One-hot encoding is a technique for vectorizing the string values. In a vector, every entry is mapped to a possible word in the reference data set and the value is made 1/0 based on the words' occurrence in the current data point. Now, this vector will be very long, say a length of 2000 for encoding URLs. These vectors can be hashed for efficiently reducing the diversity/length and then use them. In addition to reducing the diversity, this reduces the complexity of processing data in the algorithms. With large iterative process like machine learning, this definitely impacts the complexity of the final result to a great extent. A set of five sample URLs and the vectorization is shared in Figure 9.14 just to add clarity to the understanding. Other than this, hashing plays a very important role in encryption and compression techniques. Based on standard encoding of digital transfer, value of any type can be hashed using the hashing function which will result in standard encoding bits. Since hashing can reduce the space used, it can be used as a compression technique as well.

URL	**<global, india, oup, com, academic, education, contact>**
global.oup.com	<1,0,1,1,0,0,0>
india.oup.com	<0,1,1,1,0,0,0>
global.oup.com/academic/	<1,0,1,1,1,0,0>
global.oup.com/education/	<1,0,1,1,0,1,0>
India.oup.com/contract	<0,1,1,1,0,0,1>

Figure 9.14 Sample one-hot encoding of URLS

9.5 SETS

Set is a data structure which has elements associated with each other, but without any relationship among them. This can be directly related to set theory in mathematics. By definition, 'Set' is an unordered collection of data. Sets are also primitive in Python and many other programming languages. All the mathematical properties of set hold well in the data structure. So, no duplicate elements can be placed in a set. The declaration of a set in Python is shared in Snippet 9.7.

Snippet 9.7

```
S = {'a','e','i','o','u'} #Simple Declaration

S = set(['a','e','i','o','u']) #Constructor Based Method
```

As shown in the snippet, declaration of a set is similar to that of a dictionary, but the elements for a dictionary were a 'key' and a 'value' pair. In Set, the elements alone are enclosed in curly braces. As already said, sets cannot have duplicate values. So, at the time of declaration if duplicate elements are specified, then those are removed while storing. Irrespective of the elements specified, a set only has unique elements.

As defined, set data structure is a mathematical set representation. Thus, most of the mathematical operations over a set are defined in Python as discussed in the sections below.

9.5.1 Operation—Insertion of an Element

Insertion of elements after definition of a set is achieved using `'add()'` function. It allows insertion of a new element into the set. The type of the element does not matter. Just like dictionary, there is no constraint of data type in set. Any element can be added using this function. If the element is already present, then the element is just skipped without modifying the set. The syntax of the function can be referred in Snippet 9.7 that is shared after explaining all the functions.

9.5.2 Operation—Removal of Elements

For removing elements out of a set, `'remove()'` function has been defined in Python. It can be called using the set object. It takes in one argument, which is the element to be removed out of the set. However, a drawback of this method is that if the element is not available in the set, the `'remove()'` function will give an error. To overcome this, Python set has another function, `'discard()'`. This function will remove the element if it is present in the set, else skip the operation without giving any exception. Finally, Python also has a function to refresh the set. A function `'clear()'` has been defined to delete all the elements out of the set, making it empty. This function has its own utilities in certain applications.

9.5.3 Binary Set Operations

Two primary set operations in mathematics are union and intersection. Union of sets is creating a new set with the combined elements from the two sets. This can be achieved using the `'union()'` function that updates the set. The syntax of calling the function is `'set1.union(set2)'`. The union of set1 and set2 is returned. Intersection operation is implemented as `'intersection()'` function. It takes in a set as an argument and creates an intersection set based on the elements of the argument set and the calling set. Intersection of { 'u', 'e', 'a', 'o', 'i' } and { 'a', 'b', 'c', 'd', 'e' } is { 'a', 'e' }, which are the common elements from both. Some more binary operations available in Python are `'isdisjoint()'`, `'issubset()'`, and `'issuperset()'`. The syntax for all these functions is the same. Two sets are said to be disjoint if they do not have any elements in common. The function `'isdisjoint()'` checks if both the sets, set1 and set2, are disjoint and return a Boolean value. Set1 is a subset of set2 if all the elements in set1 are present in set2. The function `'issubset()'` checks the same and returns the Boolean result. When set1 is a subset of set2, then set2 can be referred to as superset of set1. If set1 has all the elements of set2, then set1 is a superset of set2. The same is checked in `'issuperset()'` functions. Let set1 be { 'u', 'e', 'a', 'o', 'i' } and set2 be { 'a', 'e' }. Here, set1 is a superset of set2 and set2 is a subset of set1. Superset can be identified by merely comparing the sets using greater than operator '>'. Set1 > set2 or set1 >= set2 gives the same result as `'set1.issuperset(set2)'`. Similarly, subset check can be done using the lesser than operator as set1 <= set2.

9.5.4 Other Utility Functions

Other than the primary functions discussed in the above sections, there are some more utility functions defined for sets in Python. There is a function to arbitrarily remove and return an element out of the list. This is the `'pop()'` function which does not take any argument. Another binary operation on set is difference of two sets. The difference operation can be seen as subtraction of a set from another. When the function is called as `'set1.difference(set2)'`, all the elements from set1 which are not present in set2 are returned as a new set. This function can also be called using minus '-' operator. Let set1 be {'u', 'e', 'a', 'o', 'i'} and set2 be {'a', 'e'}. So, result of set1- set2 / set1.difference(set2) will be a new set {'u', 'o', 'i'}. There is also a function `'difference_update()'`, which also computes the same difference. In `'difference()'` function, the difference is created as a new set and returned but in `'difference_update()'`, the result is updated into the set1. Till now, there has been many utility functions discussed in all the above sections. There is one final and important function called `'copy()'`. The usual assignment operator '=' can also be used to assign a set to another set in Python 3. In previous versions of Python, the assignment operator just creates an empty set, hence these functions were defined explicitly. So assigning a set into a new set, say for backup purpose, is achieved through `'backup_set = set.copy()'`. Snippet 9.8 explains all the functions.

Snippet 9.8

```
S = {'a','e','i','o','u'}
S.add('x')
S1 = {'a','b','c','d'}
S.remove('a')
S.discard('z')
S.clear()
S2 = {'a','b'}
S1 = S1.union(S2)
print(S1.intersection(S2))
print(S1.issuperset(S2))
```

(*contd*)

(*contd*)

```
print(S1 >= S2) #for superset check
print(S2.issubset(S1))
print(S2 <= S1) #for subset check
print(S1.isdisjoin(S2))
print(S1.pop())
print(S1.difference(S2))
print(S1-S2)
S1.difference_update(S2)
S_bkp=S1
print(S_bkp)
S_bkp = S1.copy()
print(S1)
print(S_bkp)
```

9.5.5 Implementation

As defined, the operations for updating a set are insertion and deletion. There is no search function as sets are not meant for the same. So, it is important to maintain the complexity of insertion and deletion as minimum as possible. This is achieved with the help of hash tables. Thus, sets are internally built over hash tables. The constraints of hash tables apply in here as well. Thus, sets cannot have mutable elements like list. All the set elements can be constants only to maintain a consistent hash table. The readers can feel free to try implementing set as a class over the hash table with all the above defined functions.

9.5.6 Complexity Analysis

Since sets are implemented over hash tables, the complexity of insertion/removal is 'O(1)'. The complexity of binary operations will be 'O(n)', where 'n' is size of the larger set. This is because these functions handle the set as a whole.

9.5.7 Applications of Set

General sets are used in algorithms where disjoint sets are to be maintained and processed. In graph data structure, sets can be used to maintain the connected components. In minimum spanning tree algorithms for graph, sets are used to maintain the tree. In both the above instances, sets suit best only because the vertices are of major concern and the edges do not bother much in either case. Another example of sets is in clustering algorithms, where the data points are to be maintained in separate clusters. This is achieved by maintaining each cluster as a set. Similarly, in algorithms which handle data in independent chunks, sets play an important role.

9.5.8 Variants of Set Data Structure

The basic set discussed above is referred to as general set, which is always preferred for disjoint sets of data. These sets are used to maintain data in chunks, say cluster. A data point in a cluster cannot be present in another cluster, thus making the set disjoint. Thus, the general sets are referred to as disjoint sets.

Another version of sets is frozen sets. Frozen sets are same as general sets, but here the sets are immutable. Once the frozen set is created, no element can be inserted or deleted. The same application of cluster can show the importance of this data structure. In clustering, the data points are taken and the final number of required clusters is fixed. For 'k' clusters, the first 'k' elements are randomly placed into the clusters. After that, each element is placed into the cluster which has the closest data point. The closest data point is identified using the Euclidean distance. The closest data point is the one with minimum

Euclidean distance. Once all the elements are distributed into 'k' clusters, first iteration is complete. As already said, these clusters are implemented as sets. Then, the second iteration begins. The average value of elements inside each cluster is computed and placed as the centres of the clusters. In this iteration, again the Euclidean distance of each data point with the centres is computed and the data points are re-arranged within the clusters based on the new distance. This process continues until the convergence is reached. By convergence, it means that the contents of clusters do not change in iterations. That point is considered as final results and each cluster has the corresponding elements. This is just a brief explanation of K-means algorithm. The readers are encouraged to explore the algorithm further for better understanding. Just to ensure the final result to remain unchanged during any computation, the clusters can be frozen using frozen sets. Thus, the significance of frozen sets comes into the picture.

Weight
15 gms
20 gms
21 gms
25 gms
30 gms
12 gms
10 gms

Figure 9.15 Sample data for clustering

For the ease of understanding the process of clustering, we will start with a sample of weights as use case for building a 3-means model. The sample data is shown in Figure 9.15. Three data points are randomly selected and the process is initiated.

For building three clusters, first select three random elements. Let the numbers be '20, 21, and 25'. You can feel free to try with different numbers. The final cluster will still be the same as it is an iterative process moving towards convergence. In the first iteration, the elements '15, 20, 12, and 10' are all closer to '20' and will be placed in cluster 1, whereas cluster 2 will just have '21'. The final cluster will have '25' and '30'. This is shown in Figure 9.16. After this iteration, the new means of the clusters will be '14.25, 21, and 27.5' correspondingly. Now, in second iteration, there will be changes in the elements within the clusters. Values '15, 12, and 10' will remain in cluster 1 whereas '20' will move from cluster 1 to cluster 2, as distance of '20' from '14.25 is 5.75' while distance from '21' is just '1'. Other than this, there will not be any change in the elements. Now, the new means will be '12.33, 20.5, and 27.5'. With these means, the next iteration begins. However, there is no change in the elements in this iteration. Hence, the clusters are fixed and the output is given. All the three iterations are depicted in the Figure 9.16.

Weight \ Mean	20	21	25
15 gms	15		
20 gms	20		
21 gms		21	
25 gms			25
30 gms			30
12 gms	12		
10 gms	10		

Weight \ Mean	14.25	21	27.5
15 gms	15		
20 gms		20	
21 gms		21	
25 gms			25
30 gms			30
12 gms	12		
10 gms	10		
New Means:	14.25,	21,	27.5

Weight \ Mean	12.33	20.5	27.5
15 gms	15		
20 gms		20	
21 gms		21	
25 gms			25
30 gms			30
12 gms	12		
10 gms	10		
New Means:	12.33,	20.5,	27.5

Figure 9.16 Step-by-step clusters formed from the initial set. The tables are in order, iteration 1, iteration 2, and iteration 3.

The final clusters are {15, 12, 10}, {20, 21}, and {25, 30}. If the initial data set is a general set with elements {15, 12, 10, 20, 21, 25, 30}, the final three sets are frozen sets to maintain the cluster consistent. The declaration of the frozen set is shared in Snippet 9.9.

Snippet 9.9

```
frozen_set = frozenset(['a','e','i']) #Straight Declaration

set = {'a','b','c'}
frozen_set = frozenset(set) #Declaration from General Set
```

9.6 COUNTER/MULTISETS

A counter is a sub-class of dictionary. It is also referred to as multiset/bag. In a nutshell, a counter is a set with duplicate elements. The counter contains the elements with the number of instances of each element. It can be built over a list or a dictionary. The list or dictionary is to be created and passed to the constructor to create the counter. For building a counter from a dictionary, the keys are the elements and the value is the count of instances. In addition, the constructor can be called with keyword arguments to create the counter. The arguments are the values to be stored in the counter. Each value must be initialised to the corresponding value. This set of values is separated with a comma and passed to the constructor. Apart from all these methods, the constructor can also be called with a string argument. It splits the string into characters and creates the counter. Even if the string has space or any other special character, the same is also considered as a key and value for them is generated as well. So when a character repeats, its value is incremented. If the string is 'I Love India', then the counter will be, {'I': 2, ' ': 2, 'L': 1, 'o': 1, 'v': 1, 'e': 1, 'n': 1, 'd': 1, 'i': 1, 'a': 1}. From this example, it can also be noted that these keys are case sensitive and the constructor does not change any case or format in the input string. All these three methods of defining counters can be viewed in the Snippet 9.10.

Snippet 9.10

```
from collections import Counter
c = ['a','b','c','d','e','a','e','i','o','u']
coun = Counter(c) #Define from List

c1 = {'a':1, 'b':2, 'c':3, 'd':4, 'e':1, 'f':0, 'g':-1}
coun = Counter(c1) #Define from Dictionary

coun = Counter(a=1, b=2, c=3, d=4, e=1, f=0) #Define using Keyword Arguments

coun = Counter('I Love India') #Define from String
```

Food for Brain

Can a counter be implemented over sets instead of dictionaries?

As said above, counters can be defined using a list of elements or a dictionary of <element : count> pair. The counter has the element and count stored in it. When the list has repeated elements, the counter will have it only once by increasing the corresponding values. Once the counter is initialised, there can be multiple operations in counter like accessing the elements and some modification operations.

9.6.1 Accessing

Both the elements and their counts can be fetched from the counter. Given an element, its count can be accessed right away. This access is just like accessing values in dictionaries, as the values in counter are the count of the instances of a particular element. The element is used as a subscript for fetching the count.

Other than printing the counter or accessing the counts of the elements, counters have another ability of accessing elements. The `'counter.elements()'` functions fetch all the elements from the bag but the order of the elements cannot be assured. Other than these methods, counter also has a function called `'most_common()'`. It takes in an argument 'k' and returns the top 'k' elements along with their counts from the counter. The elements come out in the descending order of number of instances. The `most_common(1)` is the element with maximum count. All these accessing methods can be referred in Snippet 9.11.

Snippet 9.11

```
print(coun)
print(list(coun.elements()))
print(coun['a'])
for letter,count in coun.most_common(2):
    print(letter,count)
```

9.6.2 Binary Operations on Counters

The first modification operation is the update operation. By update, it is meant that new elements are added to the counter. This is done using the `'update()'` function.This function can take in arguments in all formats that are supported by the `'Counter()'` constructer. It takes in new elements and updates their counts into the counter. If the element is already present in the counter, its value will be incremented. If the element is not a member, then it will be inserted as new. This operation can be achieved using the '+' operator. So, `'Counter(['a','b','c']) + Counter(['a','b'])'` will be {'a': 2, 'b': 2, 'c': 1}. It is to be noted that both the function and the operator update the result into the calling counter, which is the first operand. The syntax and usage of both can be referred below in Snippet 9.12.

Snippet 9.12

```
coun.update(['a','b','c'])
coun.update({'a':2, 'b':1, 'c':1})
coun.update(a=2, b=1, c=1)
coun.update('ace')
coun + Counter(['a', 'b', 'c'])
```

In the above code, all the lines update the 'coun' counter with new elements. Explicit assignment like, `coun = coun .update('ab')`, may or may not be used. The next operation is subtraction. Subtraction is removing the elements of a specified counter from another counter. So, if a counter has {'a': 2, 'b': 2, 'c': 1}, then subtracting {'a': 1, 'c': 1} from it will result in {'a': 1, 'b': 2}. Two things to be given thought about in here are, what happens if a key in subtract has a value greater than the value of the key in the counter. Another question is what happens when a key that is not present is subtracted? In either cases, the key will get a negative value which is absolutely fine in counters. Just like `'update()'`, `'subtract()'` function also can take in arguments of all types and subtract them from the calling counter. This operation can also be achieved by '-' operator. Subtract operation also updates the result into the calling counter as shown in Snippet 9.13.

Snippet 9.13

```
coun.subtract(['a', 'c'])
coun.subtract({'a':2, 'c':3})
coun.subtract('ace')
coun.subtract(a=1, c=1)
coun - Counter(['a', 'c'])
```

Other than the addition and subtraction operations, counter also supports intersection and union operations. Intersection operation is the process of identifying the common elements in the given counters. If one counter is {'a': 2, 'b': 3, 'd': 3} and another counter is {'a': 2, 'b': 1, 'c': 1}, then the intersection will be {'a': 2, 'b': 1}. This basically means if the first counter had 3 b's and second counter had only 1 b, then the common element is only 1 b. Thus, while identifying the intersection, keys that are present in both the counters are only taken. The value for the key will be the minimum of the values among the counters. Union, on the other hand, is the merging of the keys. It gets all the keys from both the counters. When a key is present in both counters, the maximum of the values is taken as the final union value. If one counter is {'a': 2, 'b': 3, 'd': 3} and another counter is {'a': 2, 'b': 1, 'c': 1}, then the union will be {'a': 2, 'b': 3, 'd': 3, 'c': 1}. This means when a set has 3 b's and another has 1 b, then there union will be 3 b's and not 4 b's. This is because 1 b is like a subset of the 3 b's. Thus, the values will be the maximum from either set. So, intersection gets the minimum of the value and union gets the maximum of the value. Intersection is achieved using '&' operator and union is achieved through '|' operator. Unlike update and subtract, these operations do not update the result directly into the counter. The result is retuned as a new counter instead. Hence, the assignment is mandatory for storing the result, if required later. The usage of these operators is shown in Snippet 9.14.

Snippet 9.14

```
print(c1&c2)
coun = c1|c2
#c1 and c2 are two different counters
```

As already said, counters are a subclass of dictionary data structure. Hence, no further insight is required on the implementation and complexity fronts, as they can be referred from Sections 9.3.5 and 9.3.6. The applications of counters are similar to sets like clustering where duplicate elements play a mandatory role. Other than all these types of non-linear data structures, there is one more data structure. The elements in the data structure can be related/associated to any other element. There is no pattern or condition for relationship. To capture such a random behaviour, we have the more powerful Graph data structures. It does not have any restrictions in terms of elements or its connections. It just has the ability to maintain the elements and connections. To visualize the power of graphs, more algorithms are applied over the data structure to extract the value/result out of them. The data structure and its essential algorithms are handled extensively in Chapter 11.

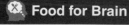

Food for Brain

Will multi-dimensional arrays handle tabular data more efficiently than Dictionary? Explore data frames in Python and R!

Points to Remember

- Other than hierarchical relationship, non-linear data can have various relationships.
- Trie is a hierarchical data structure but with a different condition, unlike search trees.
- Trie is used for storing strings. Every consecutive character is represented in consecutive levels in the structure.
- All the characters in the prefix of a word will be present as ancestors of the remaining characters of the word in the tree.
- The children of a node are the set of all possible next characters from various words.
- The width and height of a trie is bound to an upper limit, hence these are search efficient for online search engines.
- Dictionary is a data structure to store key value pairs indexed using keys.
- It can also handle tabular data.
- The order of keys does not matter in dictionary.
- A hash table is used for efficiently storing data, whereas a hash function is used to find the key for a value.
- With efficient hash function, the complexity for read or write will be 'O(1)'.
- It is used to reduce the granularity and range of the input data for efficient handling.
- A Set is an unordered collection of unique keys. It just represents mathematical sets, which can be used in algorithms like clustering.
- Sets can be mutable or immutable, but the values in the sets are always immutable.
- Counters are sets with duplicate elements, also referred to as bag/multiset.
- For every element, counter maintains a key value pair where the element is the key and the number of instances of the elements is stored as values.

Key Terms

Trie/Prefix tree/Digital tree/Radix tree A hierarchical, tree like data structure which can store strings for efficient searching. Each node is a character and the prefix of the character is the accumulation of ancestors of the character. End of string is marked specially in a variable.

Dictionary/Map A collection of <Key:value> pairs, where the order of the elements doesn't matter. It can represent tabular data. 'Key' is immutable and 'value' is mutable.

Hash function A function which gets an index for a given value. It can be linear or quadratic polynomial and even multi-layered functions at times.

Hash table A table designed to efficiently store and retrieve data, where load & store can happen in 'O(1)'. For storing a value, the index is found using the hash function. The index is the key for which the value is placed inside a dictionary like structure.

Probing This is the open addressing way of handling collision in hash table. When an index already has an element, the current element is placed at the next available space. Probing is based on a fact, when the number of elements and width of the hash table are equal.

Chaining In hash table, while collision occurs at a key, the new value is appended along the existing value making it a list of values. Used generally in application as it can reduce the granularity/width of real-time data.

Sets Unordered distinct collection of values on which all mathematical set properties and functions are applicable.

Counter/Multiset/Bag A set with duplicate elements. It maintains the distinct elements as 'key' and count of occurrence of each element as 'value' stored as a dictionary.

EXERCISES

Multiple-choice Questions

1. Trie is a _______ data structure.
   (a) Hierarchical
   (b) Tabular
   (c) Collection based
   (d) None of the above
2. Trie is also called _______ .
   (a) Radix tree
   (b) Deep tree
   (c) String Search Tree
   (d) None of the above
3. End of a string in a trie is marked by _______ .
   (a) Leaf
   (b) Specially marked node
   (c) Even node
   (d) Any node which has the last character of a string
4. Dictionary is a _______ based data structure.
   (a) Table
   (b) Map
   (c) <Key:Value> pairs
   (d) All the options
5. _______ is a way of handling collision in a hash table.
   (a) Linear probing (b) Chaining
   (c) Open addressing (d) All the options
6. _______ is a collection of unordered elements.
   (a) Bag (b) Multiset
   (c) Hash Tables (d) Set
7. Sets are implemented over _______.
   (a) Bag (b) Multiset
   (c) Hash Tables (d) Tree
8. _______ is the complexity of insertion of an element in a set.
   (a) O(n)
   (b) O(1)
   (c) O(log n)
   (d) Depends on the way of implementation – O(1) / O(n)
9. Counters are implemented over ________ .
   (a) Hash tables (b) Set
   (c) Dictionary (d) Tree
10. A Counter can have negative values.
    (a) True (b) False

Theoretical Review Questions

1. What is Trie? How is it different from search trees?
2. What is an unordered collection of elements? How is it useful in applying mathematical properties on data?
3. Explain multiset and how it is different from frozen set?
4. How is collision handled in a hash table?
5. Elaborate dictionaries with the help of an example.

Exploratory Application Exercises

1. Write a function to find all the prefixes of a given word from a trie.
2. Implement a trie to handle binary numbers. What will be the width of the tree at a level n?
3. Write a function that takes in a line and checks if the same can be formed from the trie.
4. Create a function to count the number of words present in a trie.
5. Develop a function to take in two tables in dictionary format and perform inner join operation over them based on a specified column.
6. Write a code to efficiently sort a list of number with duplicates using a Counter.
7. Design a function to create subset of prefixes, given the set of string.
8. Create a dictionary of English words. It should have ability to insert new words and search for words.
9. Design a hash table with double hashing to avoid collision.
10. Develop a hash table for storing strings.

Picto Puzzles

Identify logic for every question and develop a code for the same.

1. {In, Inter, Enter, Into, Great, Eat, Seat}

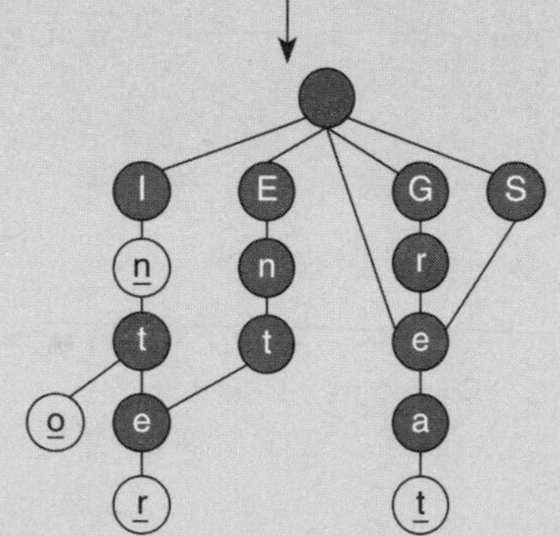

2. {0: [22,4,35], 1: [17,65,34], 2: [98,71,20]}

   ↓

   {0: [22,17,98], 1: [4,65,71], 2: [35,34,20]}
3. {Date: ['12-06-2018', '12-06-2018', '12-09-2018','12-09-2018'],
   Time: [14:0:0, 12:0:0, 8:0:0, 9:0:0],
   Temperature: [32, 32, 26, 28]}

   ↓ Group by (Date, Temparature)

   {Date: ['12-06-2018,'12-09-2018','12-09-2018']},
   Temperature: [32, 26, 28]}
4. {5: 6, 2: 1, 4: 0, 3: 2} ⟶ 38
5. {'TN 38 AP 1214', 'TN 38 SG 5218', 'TN 66 D 5578', 'KA 05 LP 5545', 'KA 01 DA 0001',}

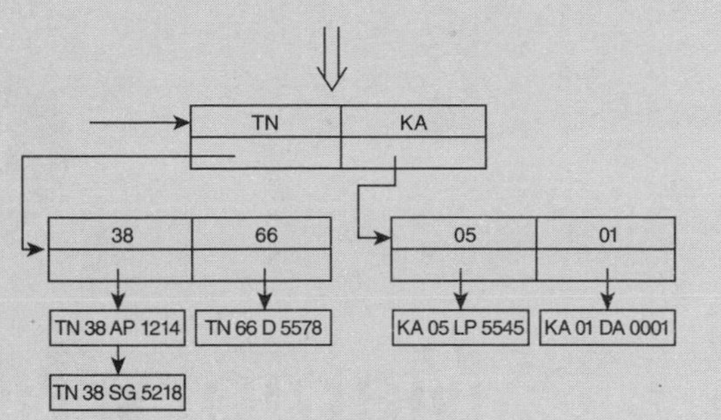

Mini Projects

1. Use a hash map to optimise the trie memory handling.
2. Design and develop cryptographic algorithm using hash functions for secure message transfer.
3. Implement K-means clustering algorithm on a sample data, stored in a dictionary, using sets.

Answers to Multiple-choice Questions

1. (a) 2. (a) 3. (b) 4.(c) 5. (d) 6. (d) 7. (c) 8. (b) 9. (c) 10. (a)

CHAPTER

10

Memory Management

LEARNING OBJECTIVES

After going through this chapter, readers will be able to understand:

- The importance of data structures in memory management
- The data structures involved in handling memory and data items in computer systems
- How pointers to data block in memory reduce processing time?
- What is a B+ tree?

10.1 INTRODUCTION—MEMORY MANAGEMENT

The core aim of the book states that data structures play a very important role in efficiently using memory space for handling data. A computer system stores data in memory and the memory units are treated as memory blocks arranged linearly. Each memory block has an index for accessing it. Since the blocks are linear, the indices are also linear and sorted. For accessing a data item, its block is first identified and then the same is accessed. This can be directly associated to arrays/lists. For storing an element at a position, its index is used in the subscript. The location, A[3]= '7', stores '7' at index '3' of the list. This is the fourth block in the array. Internally, this block will have another address which is associated to the name. Not only lists, every variable will have a block address. Every time a variable is accessed, internally, its memory address is identified and accessed for modification.

Other than the traditional memory based computer systems, a typical scenario exists in relational databases as well. Every record in a table is uniquely identified using a primary key. For reading or modifying the record, its key is used to access the record. The records are arranged in a linear fashion one after another in data blocks/pages. The records are stored based on a sorted order of the primary keys. These explanations in here are just a briefing of operating systems/database concepts of indexing memory locations. The users are strongly encouraged to read the process of indexing memory blocks and accessing memory in computer systems.

While accessing is simple using the index, allocation of memory blocks is something tricky and involves some algorithms towards it. Memory management is the process of controlling and handling memory spaces in a computer system. In an operating system (OS), memory management has more to do with allocation of memory to variables and functions based on users' demand. The initial memory is considered as a large block and chunks of memory are divided and allocated to jobs. In hardware, memory is made of flip flops/quantum magnetic particles which can store a certain number of binary digits, which decide the size of the memory unit. It is important to understand that in hardware a memory block means a basic memory unit which stores value. In OS, a memory block means a collection of memory units that are virtually concatenated and treated as a single empty space. The length of an OS block is same as the sum of the length of the hardware blocks within that. How memory is allocated and how data structures can be used for allocating or accessing memory is discussed in this chapter.

10.2 DATA STRUCTURES IN MEMORY MANAGEMENT

There are different memory allocation algorithms handled by different operating systems. Some operating systems treat memory spaces as separate blocks of non-uniform size. Every time a new request is received, a block of memory is allocated to it so that the block has the required space. The allocation of memory block can be done in three different ways, using three different algorithms—the first fit, best fit, and worst fit.

In first fit, a list of memory blocks is traversed and the first block that has size greater than or equal to the required space is allocated to the job. A dynamic linear data structure can be used to maintain the list of available memory blocks. Hence, a linked list/queue best suits the purpose. The algorithm just involves traversal and comparison until the condition is met.

In best fit, a list of memory blocks is traversed and the block whose value is greater than and closest to the required space is allocated to the job. In this algorithm, all the memory blocks are to be checked. However, in first fit, the first block greater is allocated and the process is stopped. As the process is similar, the same data structure is used in here. Linked lists are the most widely used data structures for both first-fit and best-fit algorithms.

In worst fit, the job gets the largest available block, if it is greater than the required space. For every job, identification of the largest available block involves searching. This is achieved by using max heaps. At any point, the largest block is at the root and can be easily removed. While best fit and first fit use a linear data structure, worst fit demands a hierarchical data structure (Heap) for identifying the maximum element in the lot. This is how data structures are employed in memory allocation algorithms.

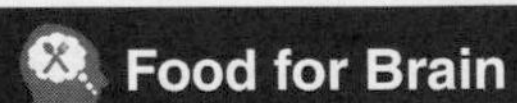

How to implement best-fit algorithm with heap?

When a block is allocated to a job, if there is some free (extra) space in the block, it goes wasted. A block can be allocated to only one job. Thus, the additional space is claimed wasted. Say, in best fit a job requires 8 MB space and a block of 10 MB has been allocated to it, then 2 MB of the block goes wasted and cannot be used until it is released by the job. Hence, in case of the worst-fit algorithm, more space gets wasted. This wasted space problem is termed as internal fragmentation. Consider there are 10 blocks of memory in the system and each has a small space wasted in it. Let the wasted space be 10 MB, when a new job which requires 8 MB comes in, it cannot be allocated any block as the free spaces are not continuous. This problem of wasting space and holding jobs is defined as internal fragmentation. To overcome this issue, memory allocation was re-designed with a different algorithm, known as dynamic memory allocation.

In dynamic algorithm, the entire memory is treated as a pool/hole which is a virtual concatenation of all hardware memory blocks. When a new job request is placed, the space is allocated as a small hole to the job. The remaining space is still maintained as a single new hole. Thus, no additional space is wasted. In this case, a hardware block can be assigned to multiple jobs. So, how is it achieved? Every position/digit stored in a memory space has its index, as explained in Section 10.1. The operating system internally maps every position to the job, to which it has been allocated. Thus, hardware memory blocks can be partially assigned to a job. To achieve this, a table/map data structure is really useful. The job ID is associated with every index of the memory block allocated to it as the entries of the map/table.

While all the above discussion is about memory allocation, there is also memory management on operating systems. As discussed in Section 10.1, each block is indexed and each variable/table record is mapped to an index for referral and access. For every access, linear search cannot be used as the number of indices can be huge in a real-time computer system. So, taking advantage that the indices are in sorted order, a search tree can be built for efficient access. Still the search tree cannot be binary, as the depth will be very high with large number of indices. Hence, non-binary search trees like B-Trees can be used for the application. B-trees store the key along with the value in memory. 'Key' in here is the index and value is the value present at that location. In a real-time system, this is not possible to maintain as the main memory will not be that large to accommodate all the content. To overcome this shortcoming, B-trees were modified to have key and a pointer to the main memory block in place of the value. This reduces the size of the B-tree, but still the number of elements that can be packed in a node can be optimized. Thus, to aid in maintaining an optimized indexing tree, B+ trees were designed. B+ trees have been discussed in detail in Section 10.3.

Other than these data structures, stacks also play a very important role in computers. Each processor has a system stack. This is related to program execution. When a program is executed, it usually happens line by line. At a point if there is a function call in the program, then the control of execution is shifted to the function, implement and then returned back to the line where it was called. This is achieved using a stack. In case of a function call, all the context variables are stored in the Process Control Block (PCB) and placed on top of the stack. When a function gets completed, the top of the stack is popped out and control is returned to that program line. The usage of stack for this application can be well understood by considering the scenario of nested functions, that is, function1 calling function2, which in turn, calls function3. Control shifts from function1 to function2 and from function2 to function3. When function3 completes execution, the control returns back to the remaining part of function2. Post-completion of function2, the control moves to function1. After completing function1, the stack gets empty and the job is considered completed. Thus, the retuning path is the exact reverse of the order of function calls. When reversal is the expected property, stacks are the best data structure to use. Thus, system stack plays an important role in maintaining the execution control in a processor. In a system, the maximum possible function calls depend on the size of the system stack. When the stack capacity is reached and a new function call is encountered, the stack overflow exception is thrown. This means the stack cannot store any more function context and thus the function call fails and the job is terminated to clear the stack. This is how various data structures impact memory management in computer systems.

10.3 B+ TREES

B+ trees are the modified version of B-trees. A B+ tree is also a search tree with each node having multiple keys. For a node with 'k' trees, there can be 'k+1' children implemented using children pointer. Some notable differences between B-tree and B+ tree are that only the indices are stored in the tree and the corresponding values are still present in the secondary memory. The leaf nodes have <key, value> pairs where key is the index and value is the pointer to that index in secondary memory. So, on reaching the node of a particular index, the value can be easily accessed. Only the leaf nodes have these pointers to the memory location. Thus, to achieve this, all the indices should be present in the leaf nodes. This requires another modification in the tree structure. At every level, the keys from the previous nodes are also accommodated in the corresponding children. This might seem like repetition of keys and waste of space, but this is very small when compared to B-tree's architecture of storing the values in the main memory itself. Other than these two modifications, all the leaves of B+ trees are connected to a single list.

10.3.1 Working

From the above discussion, a B+ tree can be visualized as the linked list of blocks of indexes in the last level of a B-tree. A B+ tree follows all the properties of a B-tree which was discussed in Chapter 7. Above those properties are the two modifications—every parent key is a part of the child key as well and leaves alone have values, pointers in here, whereas other nodes have only keys. A sample B-tree's and B+ trees' modification is shown in Figure 10.1.

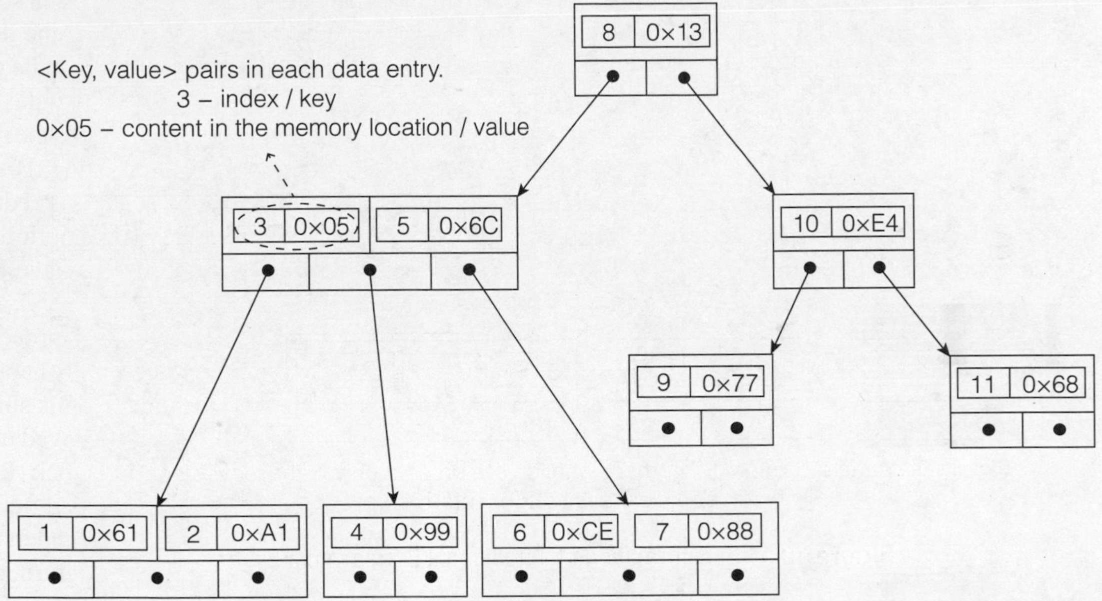

Typical B-tree with index and values in main memory

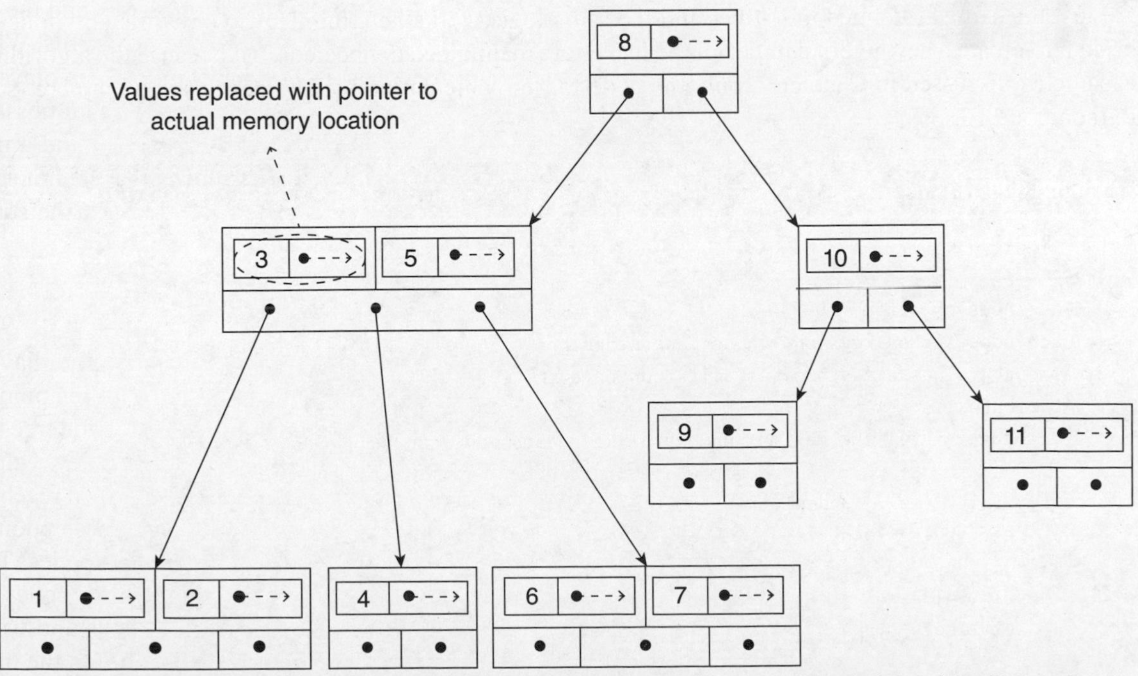

The data values replaced with pointers to actual memory location to reduce weight of the B-tree

(*contd*)

(contd)

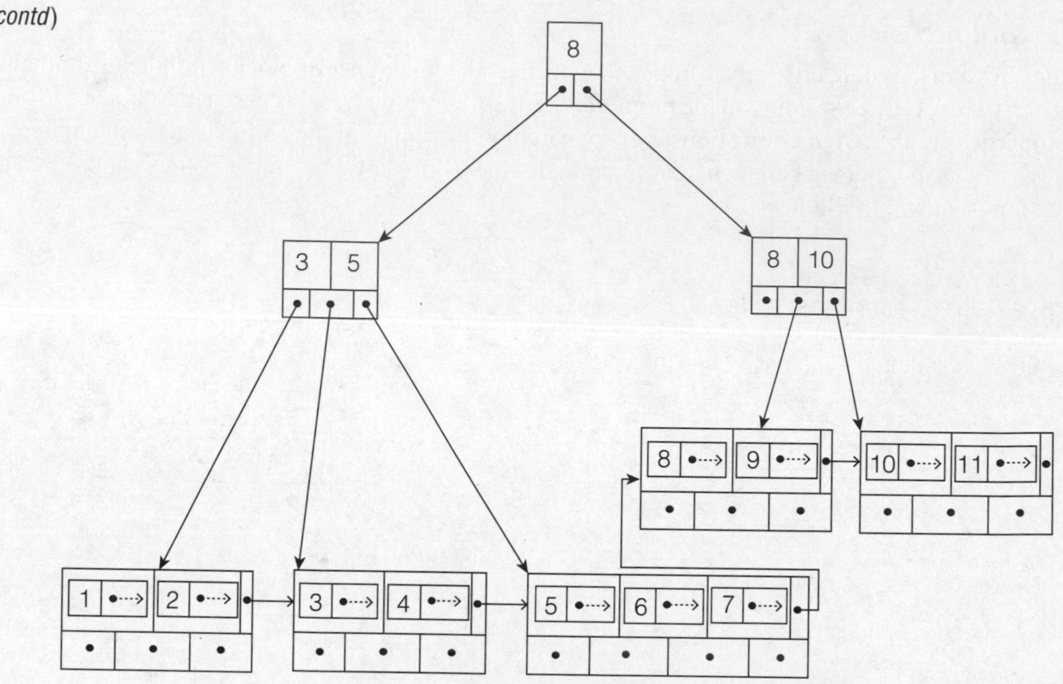

B+ tree where pointers to memory location are present only in the leaves and all leaves are connected

Figure 10.1 Transformation of a traditional B-Tree into a B+ Tree

The primary operations in a B+ tree are insertion and searching of an index. Both the operations are just the same as defined in B-trees and the same logic works here too. However, while any node is broken to create a new internal node, all the leaves are maintained connected. Just because the algorithm is same as discussed in Chapter 7, only the code for implementation of B+ trees is shared in here (see Python code 10.1).

Python code 10.1

```
class Node(object):
    '''
    Base node object.
    Each node stores keys and values. Keys are not unique to each value, and
    as such values are stored as a list under each key.
    Attributes:
        order (int): The maximum number of keys each node can hold.
    '''
    def __init__(self, order):
        self.order = order
        self.keys = []
        self.values = []
        self.leaf = True
```

(contd)

(*contd*)

```
    def add(self, key, value):
        '''
        Adds a key-value pair to the node.
        '''
        if not self.keys:
            self.keys.append(key)
            self.values.append([value])
        return None
        for i, item in enumerate(self.keys):
        if key == item:
            self.values[i].append(value)
                break
            elif key < item:
                self.keys = self.keys[:i] + [key] + self.keys[i:]
                self.values = self.values[:i] + [[value]] + self.values[i:]
                break
            elif i + 1 == len(self.keys):
            self.keys.append(key)
            self.values.append([value])
            break
    def split(self):
        '''
        Splits the node into two and stores them as child nodes.
        '''
        left = Node(self.order)
        right = Node(self.order)
        mid = self.order / 2
        left.keys = self.keys[:mid]
        left.values = self.values[:mid]
        right.keys = self.keys[mid:]
        right.values = self.values[mid:]
        self.keys = [right.keys[0]]
        self.values = [left, right]
        self.leaf = False
    def is_full(self):
    '''
        Returns True if the node is full.
        '''
        return len(self.keys) == self.order
    def show(self, counter=0):
        '''
        Prints the keys at each level.
        '''
        print counter, str(self.keys)
        if not self.leaf:
            for item in self.values:
                item.show(counter + 1)
```

(*contd*)

(*contd*)

```
class BPlusTree(object):
    '''
    B+ tree object, consisting of nodes.
    Nodes will automatically be split into two once it is full. When a split
    occurs, a key will 'float' upwards and be inserted into the parent node to
    act as a pivot.
    Attributes:
        order (int): The maximum number of keys each node can hold.
    '''
    def __init__(self, order=8):
        self.root = Node(order)
    def _find(self, node, key):
    '''
        For a given node and key, returns the index where the key should be
        inserted and the list of values at that index.
        '''
        for i, item in enumerate(node.keys):
            if key < item:
            return node.values[i], i
        return node.values[i + 1], i + 1
    def _merge(self, parent, child, index):
        '''
        For a parent and child node, extract a pivot from the child to be
        inserted into the keys of the parent. Insert the values from the child
        into the values of the parent.
        '''
        parent.values.pop(index)
        pivot = child.keys[0]
        for i, item in enumerate(parent.keys):
            if pivot < item:
                parent.keys = parent.keys[:i] + [pivot] + parent.keys[i:]
                parent.values = parent.values[:i] + child.values + parent.values[i:]
                break
            elif i + 1 == len(parent.keys):
                parent.keys += [pivot]
                parent.values += child.values
                break
    def insert(self, key, value):
        '''
        Inserts a key-value pair after traversing to a leaf node. If the leaf
        node is full, split the leaf node into two.
        '''
        parent = None
        child = self.root
        while not child.leaf:
            parent = child
            child, index = self._find(child, key)
```

(*contd*)

(*contd*)

```
        child.add(key, value)
        if child.is_full():
            child.split()
            if parent and not parent.is_full():
                self._merge(parent, child, index)
    def retrieve(self, key):
        '''
        Returns a value for a given key, and None if the key does not exist.
        '''
        child = self.root
        while not child.leaf:
            child, index = self._find(child, key)
        for i, item in enumerate(child.keys):
            if key == item:
            return child.values[i]
        return None
    def show(self):
        '''
        Prints the keys at each level.
        '''
        self.root.show()
```

Food for Brain

What will be the complexity of searching and inserting a value into the B+ Tree?

10.4 MEMORY HIERARCHY AND CACHING

There are different hardware memories available for any computer system. These are arranged on a hierarchy based on their cost and handling speed. Memories which are costly are present in smaller amount. The hierarchy of memory devices is shown in Figure 10.2.

Registers are the basic memory blocks in the system made with flip flops. It is pure storage hardware and does not have much processing power. The OS uses system registers to store some critical values. It is very expensive and present in a very small amount in any computer. Thus, hardly, any data structures are employed in here.

Before looking at cache, let us discuss RAM. Random Access Memory (RAM) is the main memory where all the processing takes place. RAM again is made up of flip flops. This is present in some GBs, say 8GB to 32GB. When jobs require RAM, chunks of data are moved from secondary memory to main memory. While moving this data, accommodating large data in a limited space is the problem. This is where the fit/memory allocation algorithms come into the picture. In addition, while executing functions, there might be function calls to be handled. RAM also has in-memory spatial indexing trees to support faster implementation and access. So, linked lists, heaps, stacks, and trees are some data structures that support RAM.

Hard Disk Drive (HDD) is the secondary and permanent memory of the system. All permanent memory devices are built over quantum magnetic particles that can store data without power supply. It is very huge and comparatively cheap. HDDs of size 750GB to 1TB are present in commodity systems itself. With

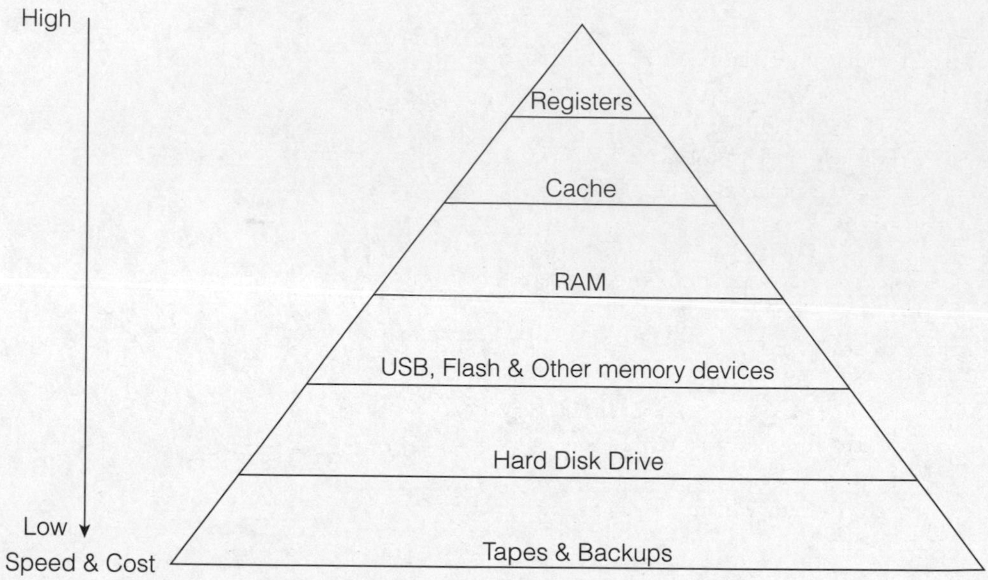

Figure 10.2 Hierarchy of memory devices

such huge space, indexing becomes mandatory for easily accessing the data. If this indexing is done using B-Trees, the tree along with all the values are to be stored in main memory (RAM) which is not possible. Thus, B+ Trees are designed for this purpose. Indexing trees play a major role in permanent storage devices.

USB and other Flash devices are tertiary, mobile, and permanent storage devices. Their position above HDDs in hierarchy is only because of the accessing speed and high cost. On the notion of making these devices easily portable, a huge size constraint is placed, resulting in high accessing speed and high cost for mobility. The memory capacity of a USB device is similar to RAM, but it is made with quantum magnetic particles. So, indexing tree is present for aid in access within the device drivers.

Tapes/Backups are magnetic devices used for a permanent backup. These are very cheap and huge. This also has spatial indexing trees in their driver for aiding in access.

When a job begins, the associated data is required in the RAM. While the data is requested for the first time by a job, it is highly unlikely to be present in the RAM as it is a limited space and filled with data of current jobs. When this request is sent to the secondary memory, a copy of the corresponding data is moved from secondary memory to main memory. If the data is very huge, it erases data of all other jobs that are currently getting executed in the main memory. Hence, data in disk is split as small chunks and only the required chunk is transferred to the main memory. This process is referred to as blocking in caching techniques. These chunks/blocks are referred to as pages in the secondary memory. This process still erases some data which is dormant in the RAM, as multiple independent jobs run simultaneously. Consider the scenario when a page of data replaces a dormant chunk from RAM. In the next step, the erased page is again required by another job. This request loads the page back into memory, replacing something else. This 'miss' and request process might continue. Thus, the load time might increase and affect the runtime of the jobs. This scenario is mainly because RAM and disk are in opposite extremes of the range. So, an intermediate cache is introduced. Cache is designed for faster access and is thus more expensive than RAM. The cache is a small intermediary memory space. When RAM requires a page, it is checked in the cache. If the data is present, it is a hit and loaded into RAM. Since searching and loading time for cache is lesser than HDD, the total running time also gets controlled to a greater extent. In addition, the cache is in order of twice or thrice the size of main memory, thus accommodating more data that can be handled by multiple jobs that are running in main memory. When the required data is missing in cache, it is a 'miss'. In this case, the same data is loaded from secondary memory, a copy of it is placed in cache, and then it is sent to the RAM for processing. This load time is same as the load time of normal disk to RAM. So, lesser number of cache 'miss' will optimise the running time of jobs. When a new page is to be loaded into the cache and the cache is full, then again replacement is the only option. The new page of data will replace an old page of data. This replacement is optimized using algorithms. Some traditional algorithms are LIFO, FIFO, LRU, and LFU.

LIFO is Last In First Out, where the page that came in last will be replaced first. FIFO is 'First In First Out', where the page that came in first/oldest gets replaced first. Both LIFO and FIFO are not optimal enough, whereas LRU and LFU are optimized algorithms. LRU means the 'Least Recently Used' cache. In LRU, the page that was not requested in the recent past is overwritten by the new page. The detail of the last accessed time stamp for every page is maintained and based on this order the oldest or last recently accessed can be identified and replaced with the new page. LFU is the 'Least Frequently Used' cache, where the number of times a data page is accessed is maintained instead of the access time. Based on this frequency, the page which has been accessed least number of times is replaced. LRU is the best amongst the traditional algorithms.

While we have defined what happens in LRU and LFU, how is this achieved is still a big question. In a computer system, cache is always a separate hardware placed close to the processor. This is a special hardware which is very fast in accessing the block. This hardware is organized only by the OS. For LRU, the cache controlling software uses a linked list/queue and a hash table. The elements are stored in the linked list and the address of the data pages is stored in the hash tables. The key is the page number and the value is the address. Whenever a page is requested, it is checked in the hash table and the address is fetched. Using this address the page can be directly accessed, read, and loaded to the RAM. At the same time, the linked list node with the page is taken out and placed in the front end and the new address is updated in the hash table as well. In case of a 'miss', the page is loaded from disk and placed on the front end and a new entry is done in the hash table. Every time a page is moved/added front, all other nodes move towards the rear end. The page which is not at all accessed reaches the rear end. If the list is already full, the new load deletes an element at the rear end. The deleted element is the least recently used element.

While the LRU requires a linked list or a linked list based queue to aid in moving the data nodes based on the access, LFU demands to maintain the nodes in order of number of accesses. So, each data item is stored as a <key, value> pair in a vector. The key is the page content and the value is the counter which represents the number of times the page was accessed. These vectors are stored in a linear list, but with a constraint. The list-based implementation of min heap is chosen for storing these vectors, where the heap is maintained based on the counter variable. So, at any instance, the least frequently used element is at the root which is 'index 1' of the list. Along with the list-based heap, the hash map stores the address of each page, just like LRU. Whenever a page is accessed, its counter is incremented and heapify operation is called. In case of a cache 'miss' condition when the list is full, the element at 'index 1', that is the least frequently used element, is removed and the new element is added to 'index 1' of the list with 'counter 1'. The same changes are reflected in the hash table as well. When there is a tie on the frequency, LRU is used to identify the page to be replaced.

Even though LRU and LFU are optimized, further scope of optimization still exists. So, modified algorithms like P-LRU (Pseudo-LRU) were introduced. Other than the change in algorithms, latest systems have multi-level cache, that is, multiple caches are linearly configured between RAM and disk. When a page is requested by RAM, it is checked in L1 cache. If it is a 'miss' in L1 cache, then L2 cache is checked. This proceeds to L3 as well, if the system has a L3 cache. Some systems are configured with L1 and L2 cache, whereas some have L3 cache. When there are multi-level caches, all of them are configured with the same replacement algorithm. The sole reason for using multi-level cache is reduction in the load time from disk to cache, as this creates more space to store more pages. However, size of the cache is not increased as it will raise the access time, instead multiple individual caches are added to keep the access time in control.

All the concepts explained in here are operating system related basics and the role of data structures played in it. We strongly encourage the readers to explore the operating system basics of memory management and explore how cache associates pages from cache to RAM. All the algorithms explained in here are basic and traditional algorithms, to serve as a proof of concept for applying data structures in various operating systems requirements. Modern day sophisticated operating systems need not necessarily have the same algorithms / data structures to achieve the same.

Food for Brain

Can different levels of cache have different replacement algorithms? Will there be a change in access time observed explicitly?

POINTS TO REMEMBER

- Data structures play an important role in operating system algorithms for memory allocation and management.
- Memory allocation is the process of allocating RAM space for a data from disk.
- RAM space may be treated as individual blocks and assigned to different disk pages.
- Worst fit is where a page gets the largest available block.
- In first fit, the page gets the first block that can accommodate the page.
- Best fit allocates the page to the closest block which can accommodate the page.
- Fit algorithms waste some space in the blocks as only one job can get a block.
- The waste space is internal fragmentation, which is overcome by pooled allocation based memory, where job gets only the required space from the pool memory.
- While execution of an instruction, if there is a function call, the current context is saved in a stack and the control moves to the next function.
- The returning order from a function is the reverse of the function calls.
- Data in the disk/flash is huge. To aid in access, indices are maintained in a search tree which points the index to the space directly.
- The indexing tree is B+ Tree.
- Cache acts as an intermediary storage space for RAM and disk to reduce the overall load time from disk to RAM.
- Cache can accommodate twice or thrice the capacity of RAM.
- When a new page is moved into cache that is full, an existing page is to be deleted.
- Various replacement algorithms are in place to achieve this like LRU and LFU.
- There can be multi-level caches to further reduce the 'miss' rate and all the caches have the same replacement algorithm.

KEY TERMS

B+ Tree A binary tree which stores secondary memory address and helps in indexing for memory management.
Data structures in OS Apt choice of data structures for deployment in operating system algorithms like First-fit, Best-fit, Worst-fit, indexing, function handling, LRU cache, LFU cache and some more.

EXERCISES

Multiple-choice Questions

1. Data structures are a part of _______ for memory allocation.
   (a) Hardware Memory
   (b) Operating System
   (c) Device Driver
   (d) None of the above
2. _______ data structure is used in memory allocation.
   (a) Linked Lists (b) Queue
   (c) Heap (d) All of the above
3. _______ data structure is used memory in management.
   (a) Tree (b) Linked List
   (c) Heap (d) All of the above
4. A B-Tree can be used for memory allocation.
   (a) True (b) False
5. A B+ Tree can be used for memory allocation.
   (a) True (b) False
6. Complexity for search in a B+ Tree is _______.
   (a) O(n) (b) O(log n)
   (c) O(1) (d) None of the above
7. Height of a B+ Tree is in order of _______.
   (a) O(n) (b) O(log n)
   (c) O(1) (d) None of the above
8. _______ data structure is used in cache for LRU.
   (a) Hash Table (b) Linked Lists
   (c) Queue (d) None of the above
9. _______ data structure cannot be used in operating system for memory management.
   (a) Set (b) Table
   (c) Stack (d) None of the above
10. Can different levels of cache have different algorithms?
    (a) True (b) False

Theoretical Review Questions

1. How data structures play an important role in memory allocation?
2. What is indexing? Why is it important? How is it achieved?
3. Elucidate the difference between a B-Tree and a B+ Tree.
4. Explain various cache replacement algorithms and how data structures are used in it.
5. Explain the hierarchy of memory units in an operating system and data structures used in each level.

Exploratory Application Exercises

1. Write a function to extract all the indexes and address values from a B+Tree.
2. Write a function that takes in a list of available holes and implements best-fit algorithm for a new request.
3. Write a function that takes in a list of available holes and implements first-fit algorithm for a new request.
4. Write a function that takes in a list of available holes and a request to identify the worst fit.
5. Implement a variable table that stores all different variables and their corresponding memory address in main memory. When a job is executed in the instruction if a variable is accessed, immediately, this table has to be accessed to fetch the address of the variable. Write a function to handle this process on the developed table as well.
6. Define a class called Process Control Block (PCB) to store all the context variable of a function and create a stack which can store these PCB objects. Using this stack, mimic the function call handling system stack.
7. Mimic the LIFO and FIFO cache algorithms. Which data structures can be used for the same?
8. Implement LRU cache using a hash table and a doubly linked list.
9. Implement LRU cache using a hash table and a doubly ended queue.
10. Implement LFU cache using a min heap and a hash table.

Picto Puzzles

Identify logic for every question and develop a code for the same.

1.

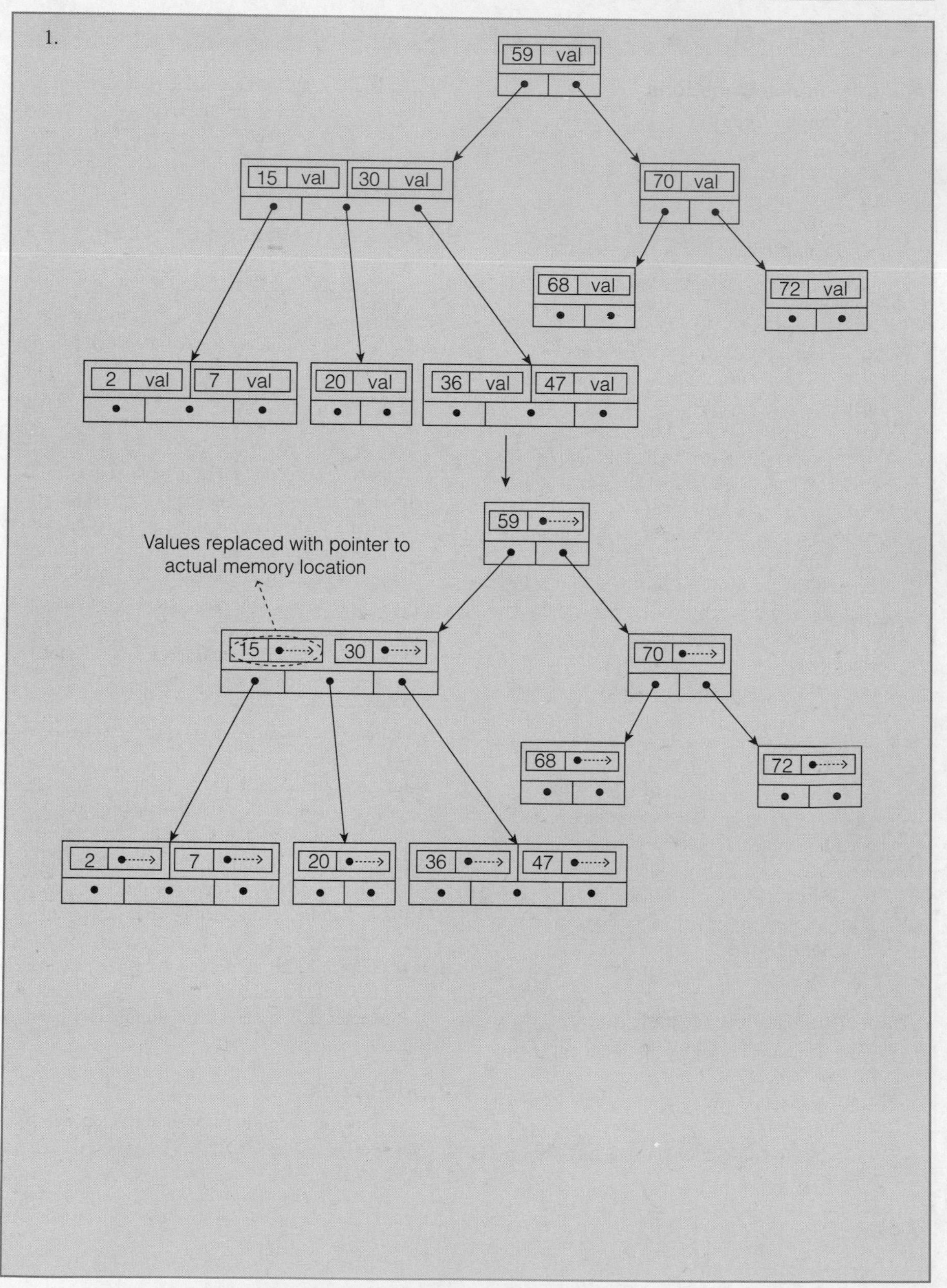
59 val
15 val
30 val
70 val
68 val
72 val
2 val
7 val
20 val
36 val
47 val
59
Values replaced with pointer to actual memory location
15
30
70
68
72
2
7
20
36
47

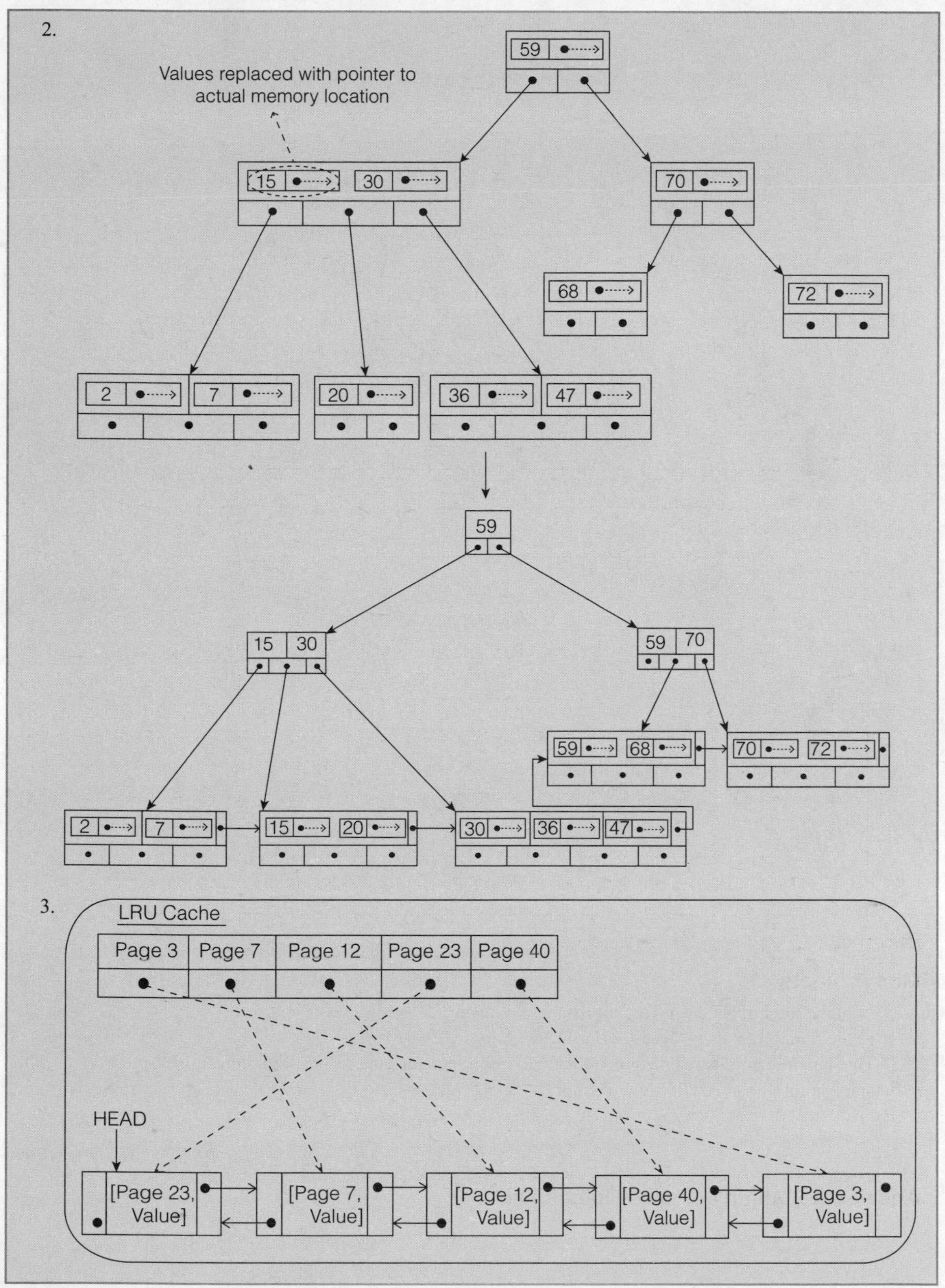
2.
Values replaced with pointer to actual memory location
59
15
30
70
68
72
2
7
20
36
47
59
15 30
59 70
59
68
70
72
2
7
15
20
30
36
47
3.
LRU Cache
Page 3
Page 7
Page 12
Page 23
Page 40
HEAD
[Page 23, Value]
[Page 7, Value]
[Page 12, Value]
[Page 40, Value]
[Page 3, Value]

4.

5.

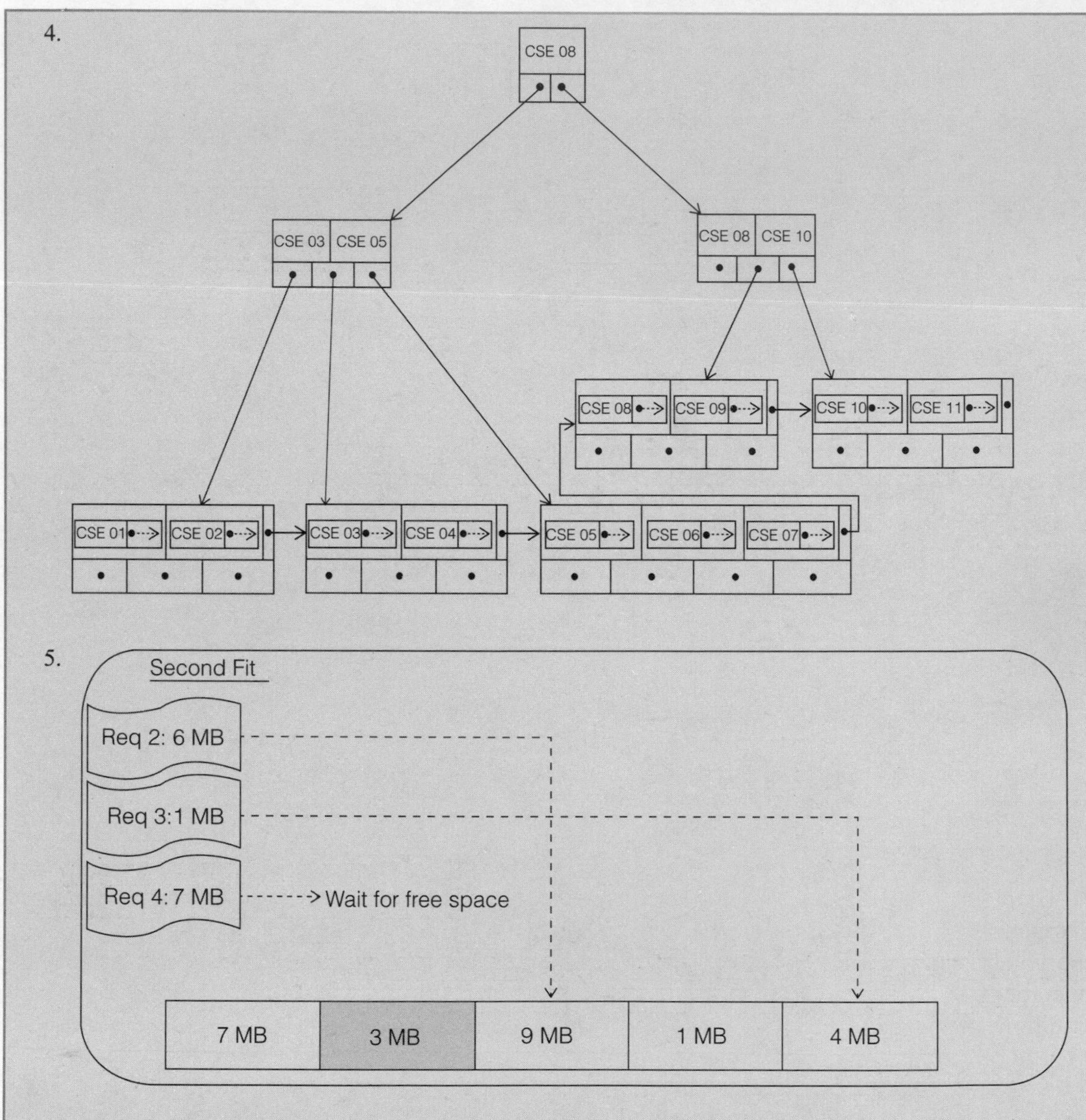

Mini Projects

1. Explore and implement T-Tree for database indexing.
2. Explore and implement Tree-LRU using a binary tree.
3. The dynamic hole-based memory allocation is implemented over a heap. Explore and mimic how a heap helps in dividing and allocating memory.

Answers to Multiple-choice Questions

1. (b) 2. (d) 3. (a) 4. (b) 5. (b) 6. (d) 7. (d) 8. (b) 9. (a)
10. (b)

CHAPTER

Graphs

LEARNING OBJECTIVES

After going through this chapter, readers will be able to understand:

- What is a non-hierarchical, non-linear data structure?
- What are the uses of graphs over trees?
- A graph contains a tree within it. How to bring it out?
- Real-life problems based on graphs and popular algorithms to solve them
- Disconnected data structures

11.1 INTRODUCTION

A 'Graph' is a non-linear data structure where a component may be connected to/pointing to multiple components. Unlike trees, graphs are not hierarchical. Any node can be connected to any node overcoming the levelled architecture of trees. This chapter will explore the data structure, its components, and operations. This chapter will also take you through some real-life applications of the structures and traditional algorithms for solving those real-time problems.

11.2 COMPONENTS OF A GRAPH

Some important components of graphs are:

- Node/vertex—where the value is stored
- Edge—the connection that runs from one node to another. The pointer is represented using an edge. In a directed edge the pointer runs along the arrow, whereas in un-directed edge both the nodes point to each other. An edge running from node 'A to B', pointed at 'B', is read as 'A to B'. If the pointed arrow is missing, then the edge may be read as 'A to B' or 'B to A'.
- Path—a combination of vertices and connecting edges, starting from a vertex and ending at another
- Cycle—a path which starts and ends at the same vertex
- Degree—the number of edges incident for a vertex

A sample graph with some components marked is shared in Figure 11.1.

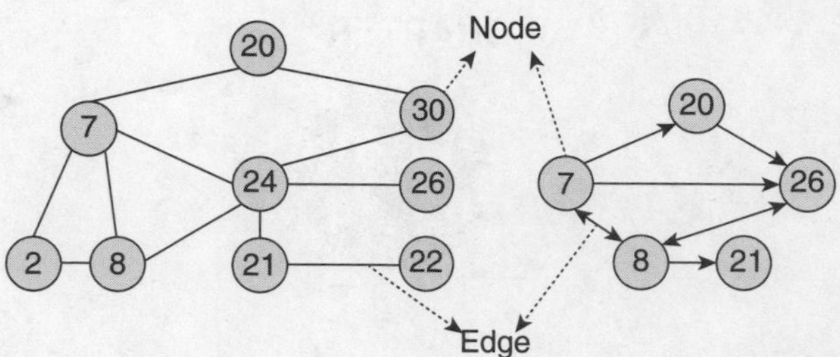

Figure 11.1 Sample directed and undirected graphs with marked nodes and edges

11.3 GRAPH REPRESENTATION

This section mainly deals with various possible ways of storing and representing graph data structure. There are three notable representations:

- Array-based/Linked List-based representation
- Matrix-based representation
- Pointer-based representation

11.3.1 Linked List-based Representation

Linked list-based representation is not a one-dimensional representation but a two-dimensional representation. This is also known as adjacency list representation. There is a base list which has all the nodes. When a new node is added, it is appended towards the end of the list. Every node has an additional pointer along with the pointer in the linked list definition. This additional pointer points to a new list which has all the nodes that the current node is connected to. When a new node is added to the graph, it is appended towards the end of the main linked list and when a new connection is added then the destination node is added to the secondary list pointed by the source node. In an undirected graph, when a new connection is added, there are no source and destination nodes present. Thus, the first node is added to the secondary list pointed by the second node and vice-versa. The same is applicable for bi-directed edges in directed graphs. The representations of the graphs shared in Figure 11.1 are shared below in Figure 11.2.

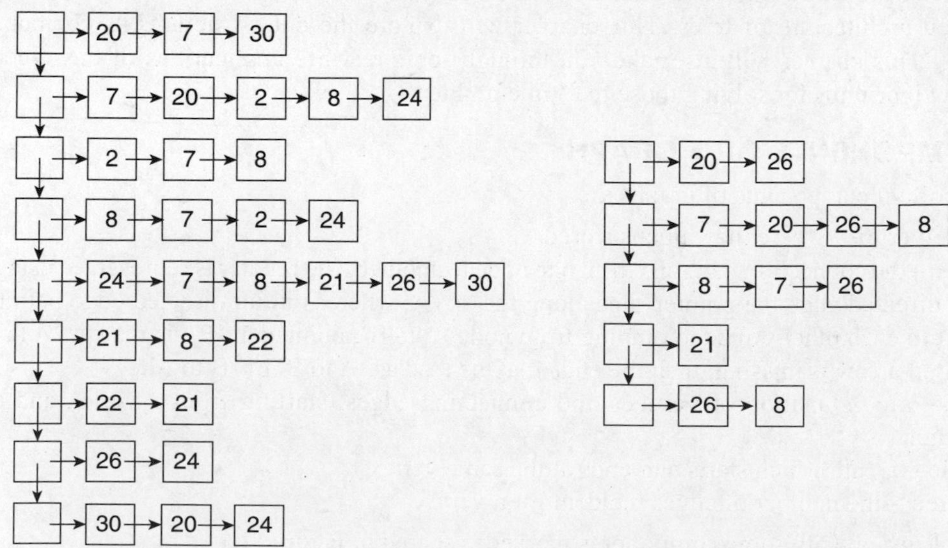

Figure 11.2 Linked List-based representation of the graphs shared in Figure 11.1

11.3.2 Matrix-based Representation

In matrix-based representation, a matrix is built to represent the graph. There are two different matrix-based representations.

- Adjacency matrix
- Incidence matrix

Adjacency Matrix-based Representation

It is a square matrix, where the list of nodes is along the row and column headers. If there is an edge running from NodeA to NodeB, then the entry [A][B] in the matrix will be '1', else '0'. The diagonal elements of the graph will mostly be zero as nodes generally do not have an edge pointing to itself. In an undirected graph, the adjacency matrix will be symmetric as an edge from NodeA to NodeB will have an entry '1' at both [A][B] and [B][A]. The adjacency matrix of sample graphs displayed in Figure 11.1 has been shared below in Figure 11.3.

	20	7	2	8	24	21	22	26	30
20	0	1	0	0	0	0	0	0	1
7	1	0	1	1	1	0	0	0	0
2	0	1	0	1	0	0	0	0	0
8	0	1	1	0	1	0	0	0	0
24	0	1	0	1	0	1	0	1	1
21	0	0	0	0	1	0	1	0	0
22	0	0	0	0	0	1	0	0	0
26	0	0	0	0	1	0	0	0	0
30	1	0	0	0	1	0	0	0	0

	20	7	8	21	26
20	0	0	0	0	1
7	1	0	1	0	1
8	0	1	0	1	0
21	0	0	0	0	0
26	0	0	1	0	0

Figure 11.3 Adjacency matrix representation of graphs shared in Figure 11.1

Incidence Matrix-based Representation

Unlike adjacency matrix, incidence matrix is neither a square matrix nor a symmetric matrix. It has nodes along row headers and edges along column headers. For an undirected graph, the entry is '1' if the corresponding vertex meets the edge, else the entry is '0'. In a directed graph, the edge is pointed towards one of the two nodes which also should be represented in the matrix. So the entry is '1' at the node which is pointed by the edge and the entry is '-1' for the vertex from which the edge moves out. If the edge is bi-directed, then both the entries in the particular column are '1'. An interesting fact in this representation is that every column has two non-zero entries at max for any type of graph as the edges are along the column headers and an edge can connect a maximum of two nodes. Figure 11.4 shows a sample graph and incidence matrix.

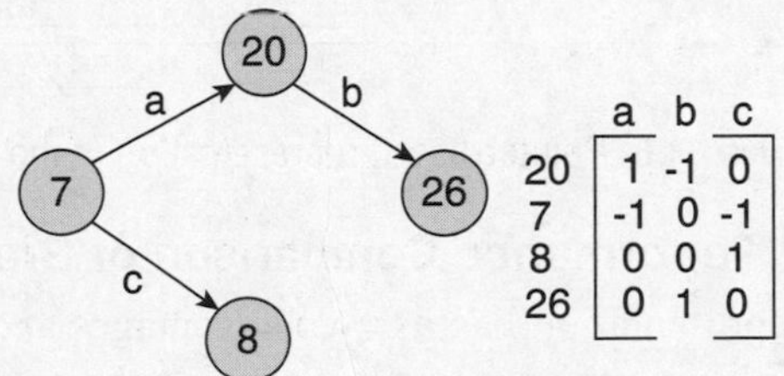

	a	b	c
20	1	-1	0
7	-1	0	-1
8	0	0	1
26	0	1	0

Figure 11.4 A sample directed graph and incidence matrix

11.3.3 Pointer-based Representation

Pointer-based representation is similar to the data structures discussed earlier. Every node maintains a list of pointers which point to all the nodes they are connected to. Every node has a linked list along with the value. Every time an edge is added into the structure, a node is added to the linked list which has a pointer to the corresponding node. This definition of a data structure inside another data structure makes it a little complicated. The definition of the structure depends on the problem for which the structure is used. Figure 8.5 shows the pointer-based representation of graphs shared in Figure 11.1. The pointer-based representation is hardly used in real-life problems due to its complexity to access nodes. There should be a starting pointer maintained separately to access the graph, just like a root in the tree. Any node of the graph cannot be accessed directly without crossing all the nodes in the path from the starting node. Thus, the representation increases the cost of access in graphs so it is avoided while solving real-life problems.

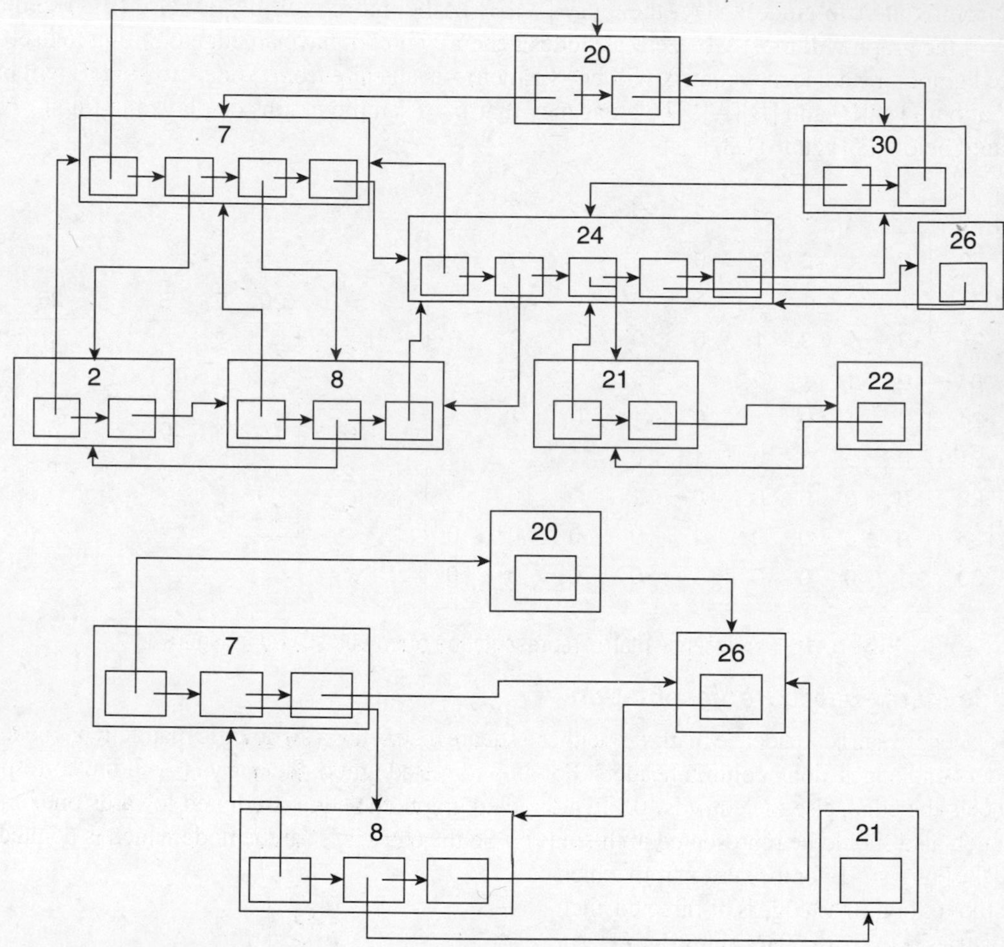

Figure 11.5 Pointer-based representation of the graphs corresponding to the graphs shared in Figure 11.1

11.3.4 Performance Comparison of Graph Representation

Each representation has its own advantages and disadvantages. The use of multiple representations is for simplifying the process by reducing the number of steps. For example, checking if there is a direct edge from node 'a' to 'b' is simple and just a single read using matrix-based representation. It can be found by reading matrix[a][b]. However, in adjacency list-based representation the same operation is more complicated. First, the main list is to be traversed to node entry 'a' and then the sub-list is to be traversed to see if there is a 'b' entry available. Only then it can be decided if there is a direct path from 'a' to 'b'. The same operation is highly complicated and time consuming in a pointer-based representation.

Due to these shortcomings, pointer-based representation is generally not preferred. But why is such an implementation even available? Think about an online game, where every level has one level along with some bonus level opened once the current level is completed. Now think of a maze where you can take multiple possible routes only after reaching the current node. Such a mandatory pre-requisite condition can be achieved only through this representation. A node cannot be reached directly if its in-degree (number of inward edges) is greater than '0'. This abstraction-based data model demands pointer-based implementation. Even though matrix-based implementation is for light-weight applications where any node and any edge can be directly accessed, for problems related to associativity among nodes rather than associativity in the whole data set matrix-based representation is preferred. Thus, the auxiliary space complexity of all the representations is constant. The time complexity for basic operations like addition/deletion of an edge or a vertex is still constant at 'O(1)' in matrix-based representation. The performance varies in operations like finding the path and so on. For those complex applications, the algorithms should select the representation based on the frequently done operation and its complexity. The various traversal algorithms and their complexity for each representation is shared in Section 11.5.

 **Food for Brain**

Think of an application that prefers adjacency list-based representation of graphs!

11.4 TYPES OF GRAPHS

Two types of graphs have already been discussed—directed and undirected. A directed graph has all the edges directed/pointed towards one or two nodes. An undirected graph has edges which do not point to any of the node. Some basic types of graphs are shared here:

- Directed Graph
- Undirected Graph
- Weighted Graph
- Complete Graph
- Disconnected Graph
- Acyclic Graph
- Planar Graph
- Isomorphic graph

In a directed graph when an edge runs from node A to node B pointed to node B, then node A is connected to node B, but the vice-versa is not true. In a weighted graph, all the edges will have a weight associated with it. A complete graph is when every node is connected, either directly or indirectly, to every other node. A cycle in a graph is a path across some nodes and edges such that a node can be reached starting from itself. A graph without any such cycle is called an acyclic graph. Unlike all other types, disconnected graphs may have two or more unconnected parts within a single graph.

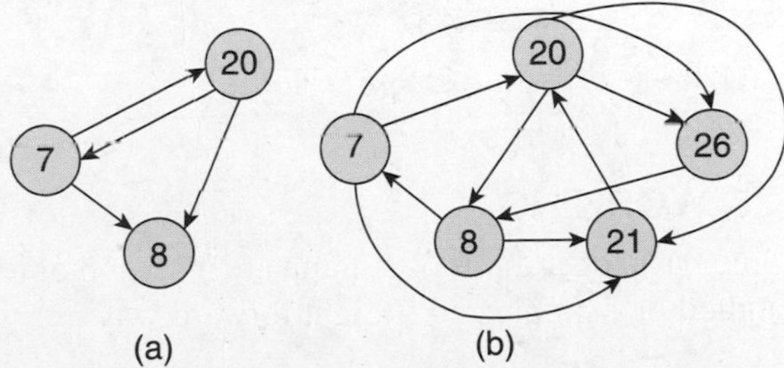

Figure 11.5 (a) Planar graph (b) Non-planar graph

Any of the above graphs can be a planar graph. A planar graph is a graph where all the edges can be represented in a two-dimensional plane without intersection of any of the edges. Figure 11.5 shows a sample planar and a non-planar graph and Figure 11.6 shows the rearrangement of edges to make the graph planar.

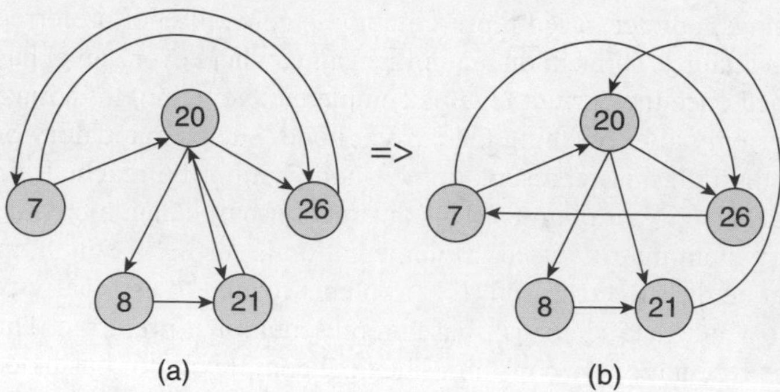

Figure 11.6 Rearranging the edges makes a non-planar graph into a planar graph.

Unlike the other types of graphs, isomorphic graphs are not a single graph. Isomorphic graphs are like equivalent graphs. Two graphs are isomorphic if the first graph can result in second graph by just displacing the vertices. The number of vertices and edges should be the same in both the graphs. If the first graph is planar, then second one should be planar as well. Isomorphic graphs are identified by mapping each vertex and edge from 'graph 1' to the corresponding vertex and edge in 'graph 2'. Figure 11.7 shows a set of isomorphic graphs with their corresponding vertices and edges marked.

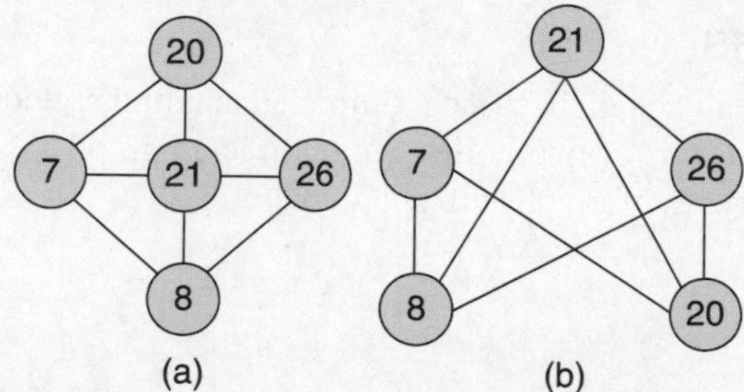

Figure 11.7 (a) Isomorphic graph 1
(b) When the vertices in 'graph 1' are displaced, 'graph 2' is formed.

What is a directed acyclic graph?

11.5 WORKING

Some basic operations of a graph are insertion of a node or edge and deletion of a node or edge. This is handled in a simple and straight forward way.

11.5.1 Insertion of a Node

In pointer-based implementation when a new node is added, it is a node object with the value and the empty pointer list. The pointer list is empty as there are no edges in the newly added node. In the adjacency matrix-based representation, a new row and a new column are added with the header as the new node. All the entries in the added row and column will be '0' as the node inserted is new and doesn't have an edge connecting it to other nodes in the graphs. In the incidence matrix, a new row alone is added with all '0s'. In an adjacency list representation, a new node is added in the main linked list which points to an empty list.

11.5.2 Insertion of an Edge

Inserting an edge in pointer-based implementation is straight forward. A pointer is added in the list inside the node which points to the corresponding node. In the matrix-based implementation, the corresponding entries alone are added. In the adjacency list representation, the destination node is added into the list pointed by the source node.

11.5.3 Deletion of an Edge

Deleting an edge in pointer-based implementation is removing the pointer from the source node's pointer list. In the matrix-based implementation, the corresponding entries are just made '0'. In the adjacency list implementation, the destination node in the source nodes' adjacent list is deleted removing the connection in turn.

11.5.4 Deletion of a Node

In pointer-based implementation, before deleting a node all the pointers in the list inside the node are first deleted and then all the pointers that point to the node to be deleted are removed. Finally, the node gets disconnected from the remaining graph. Then, the node is deleted. In adjacency matrix, the corresponding row and column can be straightaway deleted. In an incidence matrix, the corresponding row is traversed in search of non-zero. When there is a non-zero entry, the columns are removed out of the matrix. Finally, the row of the vertex is removed out of the matrix. In adjacency list, the vertex to be deleted is removed from the lists pointed by every node. Finally, the node in the main linked list, corresponding to the vertex to be deleted, is deleted. This ensures that the deleted vertex is not present anywhere in the structure post-deletion.

11.6 TRAVERSAL

Traversal in graphs is also noteworthy. Traversing doesn't mean visiting all the nodes in graph in any order or along a random path. Traversing involves visiting the nodes through proper edges. As nodes can be connected in any order and in any degree, visiting all the nodes needs special logics. Traversing a graph visits all the nodes, but all the edges need not be visited mandatorily. In an adjacency list representation, visiting all the nodes in the primary linked list is not traversal. Traversal is visiting the vertices by tracing path/connection between them. There are two main traversal algorithms, depth first search and breadth first search, which will be discussed in detail in following topics.

11.6.1 Depth First Search

Depth First Search (DFS) is also known as depth first traversal. The key idea behind the algorithm is traversing all the vertices until a vertex which doesn't have any outward edge is reached. This is the deepest vertex in this path. Once the deepest vertex is reached, travel back until another vertex above this with an alternative edge, that is the edge that was not taken earlier, is reached. Then, proceed forward from that vertex in the alternative edge. This process continues until all the nodes are visited. The logic is important in backtracking the vertices already visited and finding if any of them has an alternative edge. It is to be kept in mind that backtracking should exactly be in reverse of the order in which they were traversed so that no new edges are visited while backtracking. As stated here, the order should be reverse so a stack is used to store the nodes as and when they are visited.

Algorithm for DFS in a Pointer-based Implementation

1. DFS should start with a vertex that must be given by the user.
2. If the vertex is not visited, then it is marked visited and printed.

(a) From the list of pointers, the vertex pointed by the first pointer is checked if it is already marked or visited. If the first vertex is not visited, then the vertex is visited.
(b) If the vertex gets already visited, then the list of pointers is traversed checking for the next unvisited vertex and visits the same.

3. Visiting a vertex is done by passing the vertex to the recursive call-DFS. Before this recursive call, the current vertex is pushed into a stack, which is a useful step while backtracking.
4. If the vertices do not have any pointers forward or all the pointers are pointing to vertices that are already marked visited, then pop one value out of the stack and call DFS(popped value).
5. The process continues until the stack is empty. If the stack is empty, it implies that all the nodes have been visited.

This algorithm works fine only for a connected graph. If the graph is unconnected, then the logic to visit all the nodes simply fails. Instead, it visits all the nodes that are in the same component in which the initial node, provided by the user, was present.

Implement DFS for an unconnected graph implemented using pointers?

The above problem can be overcome by using adjacency list-based implementation of an unconnected graph. The DFS of the tree in the list-based implementation is comparatively easier. For each vertex, if it is not visited then mark it as visited, print it and call DFS of vertex for the vertices in the list pointed by the vertex. This is implemented using a list iterator inside the recursive function.

Implementation of DFS for Incidence Matrix

Once the user specifies a vertex,

1. If the vertex is not visited, then it is marked visited and printed.
2. The row corresponding to the vertex specified by the user is traversed to find an edge that runs out from the vertex. This is denoted by the entry '-1' in the directed graph.
3. Once the entry is found, the corresponding column is traversed from the beginning to find the entry '1'.
4. The vertex corresponding to that row is checked if it is already visited.
   (a) If it is not visited, then the current vertex is pushed into the stack and recursive call for the destination vertex is done.
   (b) If the vertex was already visited, then control returns to the same row where it was searching for '-1' and proceeds further searching for next '-1' and the same continues.
5. If the row doesn't have any '-1' or if all the destination vertices of '-1' have been visited, then the stack is popped out and DFS(popped vertex) is done.
6. This continues until the stack becomes empty.

The problem with this logic is every time a vertex is connected to an already visited vertex, it involves a nested traversal which uses more steps. This can be avoided by storing the visited edge along with the visited vertex in the stack. This is implemented as follows:

1. Given a vertex, if it is not visited then it is marked visited and printed.
2. The row corresponding to the vertex specified by the user is traversed to find an edge that runs out from the vertex. This is denoted by the entry '-1' in the directed graph.
3. Once the entry is found, the node and edge are made into a tuple and pushed into a stack.
4. Now, the column corresponding to the edge is traversed from the beginning through the last row to find '1'.

5. When the entry '1' is found, the corresponding vertex is taken and the recursive call for DFS is made.
6. If the row corresponding to the vertex doesn't have any '-1', then a tuple is popped out of the stack and DFS for the vertex in the tuple is called.
7. In this call, the row will be traversed not from the first edge, but from the edge that was specified in the tuple.
8. The same process continues until the stack is empty. Once the stack is empty, it means all the vertices in the connected component have been visited.

These algorithms also have the same issue of missing out vertices if the graphs have unconnected components. Provided the above algorithms, DFS for adjacency matrix can be easily implemented and is left for the readers to explore. Figure 11.8 shows a directed graph and its DFS.

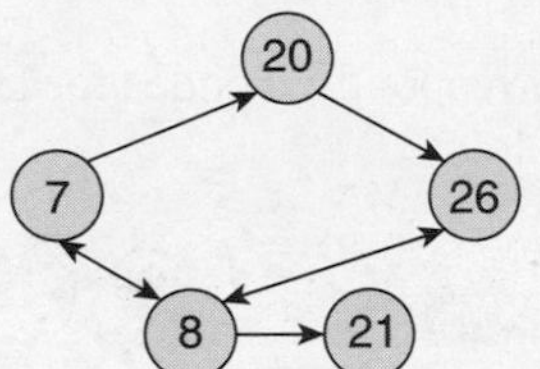

DFS(20): 20 26 8 21 7 or 20 26 8 7 21
Depends on the order in which the edges were inserted.
DFS(7): 7 20 26 8 21 or
7 8 21 26 20 or
7 8 26 20 21
Depends on the order in which the edges were inserted.

Figure 11.8 A sample tree and DFS of the tree starting from different nodes

In Figure 11.8, it is specified that the order in which the vertices will be printed is dependent on the type of implementation used and the order in which the edges are inserted. While performing DFS manually from the visual representation of the graph, when the order of insertion of edges is not known, any of the specified order is correct as the end goal of DFS is to visit all the vertices using some logic.

11.6.2 Breadth First Search

The key idea behind the Breadth First Search (BFS) algorithm is traversing the vertices in the same level simultaneously. In DFS, the forward motion is only along one edge whereas in BFS all the edges from the current vertex are taken forward. All the children of a node are visited simultaneously. As the motion is along the width of the structure, it is called as breadth first traversal. When DFS uses a stack for reversing the order while backtracking, BFS uses a queue to retain the order of the children while traversing.

BFS Algorithm for Pointer-based Implementation

1. Given a vertex, it is marked visited and appended into the queue
2. While the queue is not empty,
   2.1 Pop a value out of the queue and print the same
   2.2 For every connected/adjacent vertex, if it not visited then append it into the queue

This ensures that the children of a vertex are printed continuously. All the vertices in the same level, that are non-siblings, are also printed continuously. The same logic will work for BFS in adjacency list-based implementation and adjacency matrix-based representation. In the adjacency matrix, the list of adjacent vertices is not readily available. So, it is found using the same logic as in DFS. The row corresponding to the vertex is traversed for '-1', the outward edge. Then, the column corresponding to the entry '-1' is searched for '1', the destination vertex. The vertex of the row corresponding to the entry '1' in the column is an adjacent vertex. Similarly, all adjacent vertices can be found and then applied in the algorithm as explained above. In a similar way, BFS for incidence matrix is designed which is left for the users to explore. Figure 11.9 shares BFS of the same tree presented in Figure 11.5. Just like DFS when the visual representation of graph is given without any information on the order in which the edges or nodes were inserted, there can be more than one BFS order starting from a given node.

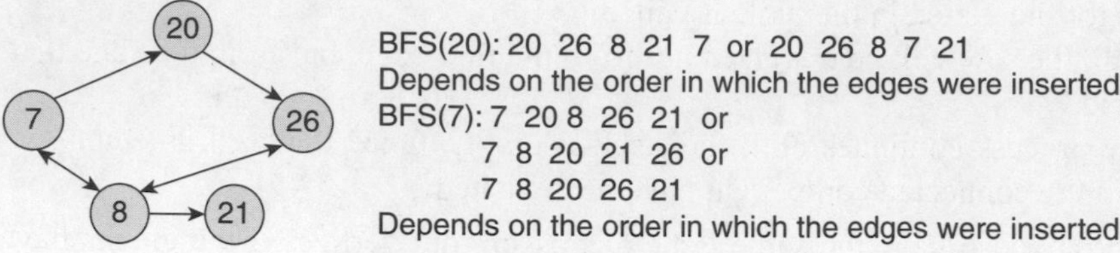
20
7
26
8
21
BFS(20): 20 26 8 21 7 or 20 26 8 7 21
Depends on the order in which the edges were inserted.
BFS(7): 7 20 8 26 21 or
7 8 20 21 26 or
7 8 20 26 21
Depends on the order in which the edges were inserted.

Figure 11.9 BFS of sample graph

Implementation

Pseudocode 11.1 shows the implementation of BFS and DFS. The corresponding codes for DFS and BFS are shared along with the graph's implementation code in Section 11.7.

Pseudocode 11.1

```
def dfs(v):
    push v into stack
    while stack is not Empty:
    Do,
        C = stack.pop()
        if C not in visited:
        then,
            mark C as visited
            for w in C.next:
            Do,
                push w into stack
def bfs(v):
    add v into queue
    while queue is not Empty:
    Do,
        C = q.dequeue()
        if C not in visited:
        then,
            mark C as visited
            for w in C.next:
            Do,
            add w into queue
```

Complexity Analysis of Traversal Algorithms

In adjacency list-and pointer-based implementations, complexity of DFS and BFS is '$O(V + E)$', where 'V' is the number of vertices and 'E' is the number of edges. In DFS, all the vertices and edges are visited at the worst case. So, it sums up to this complexity. The complexity of the same in matrix-based implementation is '$O(V^2)$'. This is when the graph is a complete graph, so for every vertex the row has all entries as '1'. This, in turn, results in complete traversal of all the columns summing up to 'V^2'. Thus like deletion, traversal operations also have different complexities for different implementations. Henceforth, while choosing a method to implement, it is important to take the frequent and primary operations into consideration and then choose the implementation method based on optimal overall complexity of all operations.

11.7 IMPLEMENTATION OF GRAPHS

The implementation codes for graph data structure using adjacency list, adjacency matrix and incidence matrix are shared in the sections below. Implementation codes for DFS and BFS are given for adjacency list-based implementations alone and the implementation of the same for the other representations is left for exploration by the readers as they are comparatively simple and straight forward.

11.7.1 Adjacency List-based Representation

The ADT has the main list of node objects. Each node object has a list of node objects which are connected with a direct edge. Python code 11.1 shows the implementation.

Python code 11.1

```
class Node:
    def __init__(self,val):
        self.value = val
        self.next=[]

#Implementation of unweighted directed graph
class Graph:
    def __init__(self,vertices=""):
        self.list = []
        if vertices != "":
            for v in vertices:
                V = Node(v)
                self.list.append(V)

    #Function to add edge
    def add_edge(self,a,b):
        a_flg = 0
        b_flg = 0
        for v in self.list:
            if v.value == a:
                a_flg=1
            if v.value == b:
                b_flg=1
        #When the vertices itself are not present, add the vertex first
        if a_flg == 0:
            self.add_vertex(a)
        if b_flg == 0:
            self.add_vertex(b)
        #Add the edge by appending the destination as the neighbour in the source nodes 'Next'
        #list
        for i in self.list:
            if i.value == a:
                if b not in i.next:
```

(contd)

(*contd*)

```
                i.next.append(b)
                return

    #Function to add vertex
    def add_vertex(self,a):
        for v in self.list:
            if v.value == a:
                print("vertex is already present")
                return
        V = Node(a)
        self.list.append(V)

    #Function to remove vertex, done by just removing the destination
    #from the source's 'Next' list
    def remove_edge(self,a,b):
        a_flg = 0
        b_flg = 0
        for v in self.list:
            if v.value == a:
                a_flg=1
            if v.value == b:
                b_flg=1
        if a_flg==0 or b_flg==0:
            print("vertices not present")
            return
        elif a_flg==1:
            for i in self.list:
                if i.value == a:
                    if b in i.next:
                        i.next.remove(b)

    #Function to remove vertex, by deleting it from the 'Next' lists of all nodes and finally
    #the object itself
    def remove_vertex(self,a):
        ind=-1
        for j in range(0,len(self.list)):
            if self.list[j].value==a:
                ind=j
        if ind>-1:
            del self.list[ind]
        for i in self.list:
            if a in i.next:
                i.next.remove(a)

    def print_vertices(self):
        tmp =[]
        for i in self.list:
```

(*contd*)

(*contd*)

```
            tmp.append(i.value)
        print(tmp)

    #Function to print the graph in the adjacency list format
    def print_graph(self):
        for i in self.list:
            print(i.value," -> ", i.next)
```

Instead of master list in graph class, a dictionary object can be used. This avoids unnecessary loops within some modules, optimizing the performance further. The new implementation code is shared below (refer to Python code 11.2). The code also has the DFS and BFS implementations for adjacency, list-based graphs.

Python code 11.2

```
#Stack and Queue for DFS and BFS
from stack import *
from queue import *

#Here the self.list is a dictionary object instead of a list for the ease of access
class Graph:
    def __init__(self,vertices=""):
        self.list = {}
        if vertices != "":
            for v in vertices:
                self.list[v] = []

    def add_edge(self,a,b):
        if a not in self.list.keys():
            self.list[a]=[b]
        else:
            self.list[a].append(b)
        if b not in self.list.keys():
            self.list[b]=[]
        return

    def add_vertex(self,a):
        if self.list.has_keys(a):
            print("vertex is already present")
            return
        self.list[a] = []

    def remove_edge(self,a,b):
        if not(a in self.list and b in self.list):
            print("vertices not present")
```

(*contd*)

(*contd*)

```
            return
        elif a in self.list:
            if b in self.list[a]:
                self.list[a].remove(b)

    def remove_vertex(self,a):
        if a in self.list:
            t = self.list.pop(a)
        for i in self.list.values():
            if a in i:
                i.remove(a)

    def print_vertices(self):
        print(list(self.list.keys()))

    def print_graph(self):
        for i in self.list.keys():
            print(i," -> ", self.list[i])

    #The function for Depth First Search traversal
    def dfs(self,v):
        visited =[] #A separate list to maintain the nodes already visited by the algorithm
        s = stack()
        s.push(v)
        while not(s.isEmpty()):
            C = s.pop()
            if C not in visited:
                visited.append(C)
                for w in self.list[C]:
                    s.push(w)
        print(visited)

    #The function for Breadth First Search traversal
    def bfs(self,v):
        visited=[] #A separate list to maintain the nodes already visited by the algorithm
        q = queue()
        q.enqueue(v)
        while q.isEmpty()==0:
            c=q.dequeue()
            if c not in visited:
                visited.append(c)
                for w in self.list[c]:
                    q.enqueue(w)
        print(visited)
```

11.7.2 Adjacency Matrix-based Representation

The adjacency matrix-based implementation of graphs is shown in Python code 11.3.

Python code 11.3

```
class Graph:
    #Adjacency matrix representation for unweighted undirected graph
    #The matrix will always be symmetric as the direction of edge is neutral
    #Matrix is implemented using a nested list in Python
    #The matrix will always be a square matrix as both rows and columns signifies the vertices
    #only
    def __init__(self,vertices=""):
        self.list = []
        self.adj_matrix = []
        if not (vertices == ""):
            for v in vertices:
                self.add_vertex(v)
    def add_edge(self,a,b):
        if a not in self.list:
            self.add_vertex(a)
        if b not in self.list:
            self.add_vertex(b)
        a_ind = self.list.index(a)
        b_ind = self.list.index(b)
        self.adj_matrix[a_ind][b_ind]=1
        self.adj_matrix[b_ind][a_ind]=1
        #Undirected graph, so edge is denoted by a connectivity 1 from 'a' to 'b' and 'b' to
        #'a' as well
        #For a weighted graph, the edge weight is added instead of '1' and for undirected
        #graph, negative number is used for the entry 'b' to 'a'
        return

    def add_vertex(self,a):
        if a in self.list:
            print("vertex is already present")
            return
        #For every vertex, a row and column is to be added into the matrix
        self.adj_matrix.append([0]*len(self.list))
        self.list.append(a)
        for row in self.adj_matrix:
            row.append(0)

    def remove_edge(self,a,b):
        if not(a in self.list and b in self.list):
            print("vertices not present")
            return
        else:
            a_ind = self.list.index(a)
            b_ind = self.list.index(b)
            self.adj_matrix[a_ind][b_ind]=0
            self.adj_matrix[b_ind][a_ind]=0
            #By making the entry 0, the edge from 'a' to 'b' is removed
```

(contd)

(*contd*)

```
    def remove_vertex(self,a):
        if not(a in self.list):
            print("no such vertex")
            return
        else:
            a_ind = self.list.index(a)
            #The row of the vertex in the matrix is deleted
            self.adj_matrix.pop(a_ind)
            #For every other vertex, the entry corresponding to the vertex to be deleted is to
            #be removed as deleting a vertex will delete all the edges leading there. This can
            #be simply intepreted as deletion of the corresponding column from the matrix.
            for row in self.adj_matrix:
                row.pop(a_ind)
            self.list.pop(a_ind)

    def print_vertices(self):
        print(self.list)
    def print_graph(self):
        print("matrix:")
        print("\t","\t".join(str(i) for i in self.list))
        for i in range(len(self.list)):
            print(self.list[i],"\t","\t".join(str(j) for j in self.adj_matrix[i]))
```

11.7.3 Incidence Matrix-based Representation

The incidence matrix-based implementation of graphs is shown in Python code 11.4. The incidence matrix is not a square matrix, unlike the adjacency matrix. The rows in here signify the vertices and the columns signify the edges.

Python code 11.4

```
class Graph:
    #Incidence matrix representation for unweighted directed graph
    def __init__(self,ver=""):
        self.vertices = []
        self.edges = [] # A separate list to maintain edges
        self.incid_matrix = []
        if ver != "":
            for v in ver:
                self.add_vertex(v)

    def add_edge(self,e,a,b):
        if a not in self.vertices:
            self.add_vertex(a)
        if b not in self.vertices:
            self.add_vertex(b)
```

(*contd*)

(*contd*)

```
        if e in self.edges:
            print("edge already present")
            return
        self.edges.append(e)
        a_ind = self.vertices.index(a)
        b_ind = self.vertices.index(b)
        #Adding a new edge is adding a new column, done by adding an element at the end of
        #every row
        for row in self.incid_matrix:
            row.append(0)
        self.incid_matrix[a_ind][len(self.edges)-1]=-1 #-1 for outward edge
        self.incid_matrix[b_ind][len(self.edges)-1]=1  #1 for inward edge
        return

    def add_vertex(self,a):
        if a in self.vertices:
            print("vertex is already present")
            return
        self.incid_matrix.append([0]*len(self.edges))
        self.vertices.append(a)

    def remove_edge(self,e):
        if not(e in self.edges):
            print("edge not present")
            return
        else:
            e_ind = self.edges.index(e)
            #Removal of the edge is done by deleting the column from the matrix
            #In nested list, the corresponding element from each row is deleted
            for row in self.incid_matrix:
                row.pop(e_ind)
            self.edges.pop(e_ind)

    def remove_vertex(self,a):
        if not(a in self.vertices):
            print("no such vertex")
            return
        else:
            #Deleting the vertex is deleting the row and also the edges encountering the
            #vertices
            a_ind = self.vertices.index(a)
            incidents =[]
            for e in range(len(self.edges)):
                if self.incid_matrix[a_ind][e]!=0:
                    incidents.append(self.edges[e])
            for e in incidents:
                self.remove_edge(e)
            print("deleted edges incident with vertex", a)
```

(*contd*)

(*contd*)

```
            self.incid_matrix.pop(a_ind)
            self.vertices.pop(a_ind)

    def print_vertices(self):
        print(self.vertices)

    def print_graph(self):
        print("matrix:")
        print("\t","\t".join(str(i) for i in self.edges))
        for i in range(len(self.vertices)):
            print(self.vertices[i],"\t","\t".join(str(j) for j in self.incid_matrix[i]))
```

11.8 COMPLEXITY ANALYSIS OF GRAPHS

The complexity of insertion and deletion of an edge is 'O(1)', as it is independent of any other operation or part of the graph. Insertion of a vertex is also 'O(1)', as it doesn't trigger any additional process. Deletion of a vertex can be 'O(E)', where 'E' is the total number of edges in the graph. The worst case is all the edges in the graph are connected to the node, so the iteration in the pointer will run across 'E' elements. The complexities given in here are generic and are subjected to change in some implementations based on the representation. For example, adding a vertex in adjacency list representation is 'O(1)', whereas the same in adjacency matrix is 'O(V)' as adding a vertex needs addition of a row and column. Adding a column is achieved by adding an element to every row. On the other hand, for deletion the complexity is 'O(E)' in all the list and matrix based representations, as in worst case a vertex might encounter all the edges. However, it need not mandatorily be the same for other implementations like pointer-based representation. The specific complexity computations for each representation and for different types of graphs like weighted/unweighted and directed/undirected graphs are left for the readers to explore. Based on the problem and the most frequently used operations, the representation of graph should be chosen. This optimizes the solution to a great extent.

11.9 TOPOLOGICAL SORTING

Topological sorting is ordering of vertices based on a criterion. In a way, topological sorting is similar to traversal, where a new order for visiting the vertices is defined. This is based on one simple condition, if there is an edge running from 'i' to 'j', then 'i' must be ordered/visited before 'j'. Topological sorting is possible only in an acyclic graph, that is, if the graph has a cycle then the above condition will fail for at least one vertex as there will be a pointer back from the last node to the starting node. In an undirected graph, every edge may be considered two ways but such a condition doesn't make any sense. So, topological sorting is done only on directed acyclic graphs. A stack is used for this traversal. The algorithm is explained in detail below.

Algorithm for Topological Sorting

1. Create a list of in-degree of each vertex, where in-degree is the number of edges pointing to the corresponding vertex.
2. Initiate a counter to '0'.
3. If a vertex has in-degree '0', push it into the stack.
4. When the stack is not empty, pop the top element.
5. Add the element into the topological sorted list with the counter. Then, increment the counter by '1'.

6. For every vertex adjacent to this vertex, decrement the in-degree by '1'.
7. If any of the adjacent vertex's new in-degree becomes '0', push it into the stack.

If the final sorted list doesn't contain all the vertices, then it means the graph contains a cycle as the in-degree of those vertices never came down to '0'. Unlike DFS and BFS, this doesn't skip unconnected parts of a graph, as the criterion is just based on in-degree. Figure 11.11 shows the step-by-step illustration of topological sorting of a graph with intermediate stack values. The implementation code for topological sorting is shared in Section 11.9.1.

Question 11.1 Perform topological sorting of the graph provided in Figure 11.10.

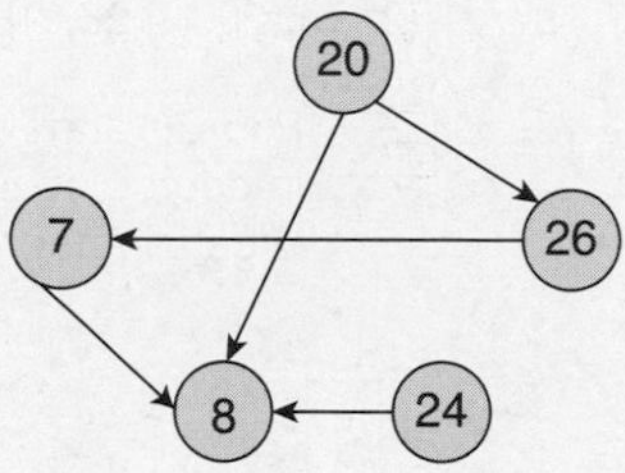

Figure 11.10 Sample graph

Solution: Figure 11.11 shows the step-by-step process.

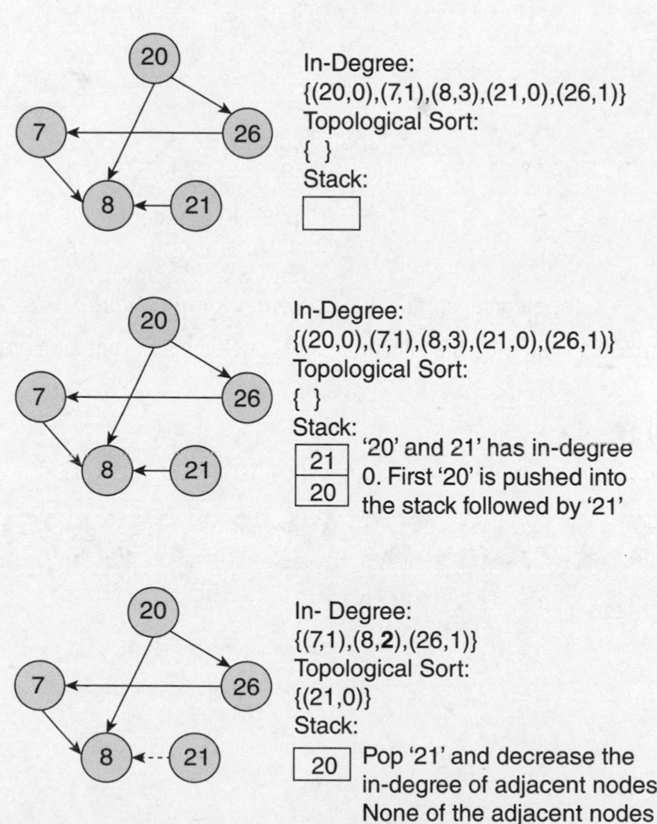

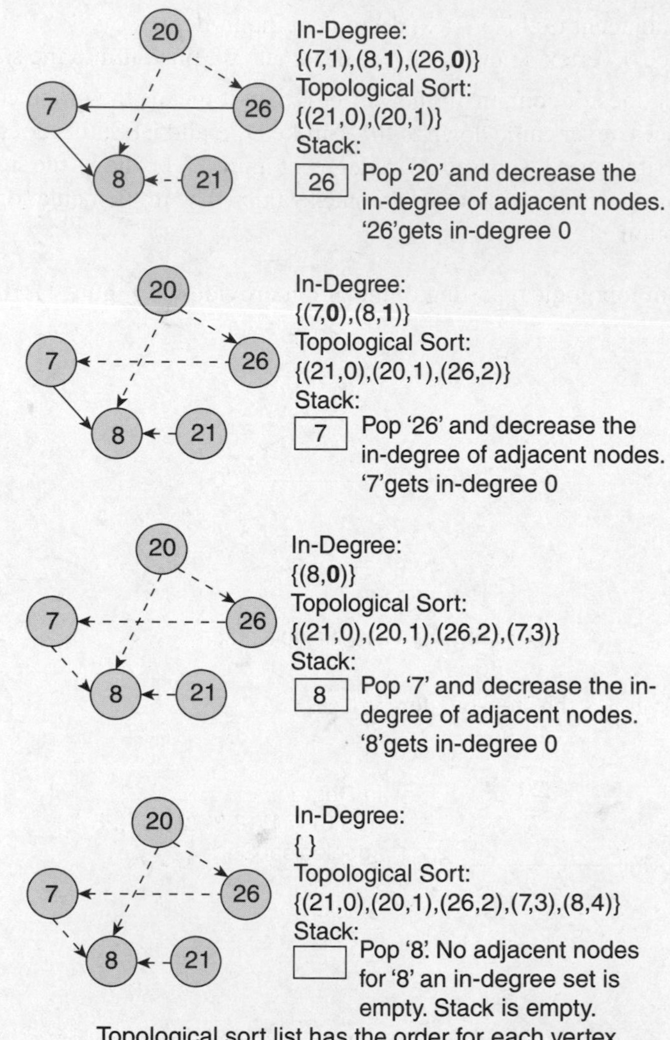
20
7
26
8
21
In-Degree:
{(7,1),(8,1),(26,0)}
Topological Sort:
{(21,0),(20,1)}
Stack:
26
Pop '20' and decrease the in-degree of adjacent nodes. '26'gets in-degree 0
In-Degree:
{(7,0),(8,1)}
Topological Sort:
{(21,0),(20,1),(26,2)}
Stack:
7
Pop '26' and decrease the in-degree of adjacent nodes. '7'gets in-degree 0
In-Degree:
{(8,0)}
Topological Sort:
{(21,0),(20,1),(26,2),(7,3)}
Stack:
8
Pop '7' and decrease the in-degree of adjacent nodes. '8'gets in-degree 0
In-Degree:
{ }
Topological Sort:
{(21,0),(20,1),(26,2),(7,3),(8,4)}
Stack:
Pop '8'. No adjacent nodes for '8' an in-degree set is empty. Stack is empty.
Topological sort list has the order for each vertex.

Figure 11.11 Step-by-Step illustration of Topological Sorting of a graph

11.9.1 Implementation

The implementation of topological sorting based on adjacency list representation is shown in Python code 11.5.

Python code 11.5

```
#Topological sort for Adjacency List based representation
def topological_sort(self):
    top_sort=[]
    in_degree = {u:0 for u in self.list.keys()}
    C=0
    #Compute the in-degree for each vertex
    for u in self.list.keys():
        for v in self.list[u]:
```

(*contd*)

(*contd*)

```
        in_degree[v]+=1
s=stack()
#push nodes with in-degree 0 into the stack
for v in in_degree.keys():
    if in_degree[v]==0:
        s.push(v)
#pop elements one-by-one and decrement adjacent vertices' in-degree
while s.isEmpty()==0:
    cur=s.pop()
    top_sort.append((cur,C))
    C+=1
    for w in self.list[cur]:
        in_degree[w]-=1
        if in_degree[w]==0:
            s.push(w)
print(top_sort)
```

11.9.2 Complexity Analysis

From the complexity point of view, topological sorting is very similar to DFS algorithm. The complexity of topological sorting is 'O(V+E)', where 'E' is the number of edges. Here, the number of edges is impacting the complexity because for every edge the in-degree of multiple vertices is edited.

Perform topological sorting of the below graph.

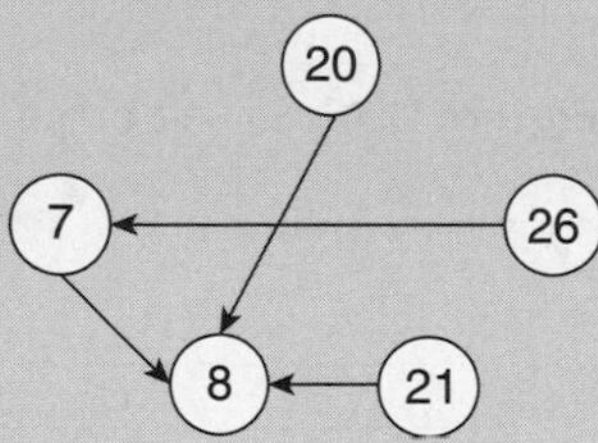

11.10 SPANNING TREES

As discussed in sections above, graphs are multiple relationship models breaking rules of hierarchy. However, in every graph, there is an embedded tree. This is identified by all the nodes and some essential edges alone. A spanning tree is an attempt to represent a tree from a graph. The core aim is to remove redundant edges and bring hierarchical policies into a graph. Creation of a spanning tree from a graph is selecting all the nodes and some edges, which in turn, converts the graph into a tree such that all the connected components in the graph remain connected even after removing the unwanted edges. A spanning tree might be helpful in multiple applications, especially hierarchy-oriented problems. A minimum spanning tree (MST) is a spanning tree with the minimum most weight in the graph. Thus, it also implies that a graph can have multiple trees in it. Minimum spanning trees are associated only with weighted graphs, but in unweighted graphs spanning trees cannot be compared with one another for their cost. MSTs are applicable only with undirected graphs. The same concept in directed graphs is a more complex process, referred to as optimum branching, and has a set of different algorithms. There are two traditional and useful minimum spanning tree creation algorithms:

- Kruskal's algorithm
- Prim's algorithm

11.10.1 Kruskal's Algorithm

Kruskal's algorithm for solving the minimum spanning tree problem is a Greedy algorithm. As discussed above, the end goal of Kruskal's algorithm is to create a tree out of the graph by selecting the edges such that their total weight is minimum. Initially, the tree is empty. First, all the edges are taken as a list and are sorted in ascending order of weights. Now, the list is traversed considering each edge in the order. If adding an edge into the spanning tree doesn't create a cycle, then add the edge along with the corresponding vertices into the tree. This check ensures that the tree doesn't get a cycle within it just because that edge is smaller than some other edge in the graph. In addition, it ensures that the tree is one single component and is not disconnected. A fact inferenced here is that 'A MST has V-1 edges', where 'V' is the number of vertices. Figure 11.13 shows a sample graph and step-by-step building of the MST using Kruskal's algorithm.The pseudocode for Kruskal's method is shown below too (refer to Pseudocode 11.2).

Question 11.2 Create the minimum spanning tree of the given graph using Kruskal's algorithm.

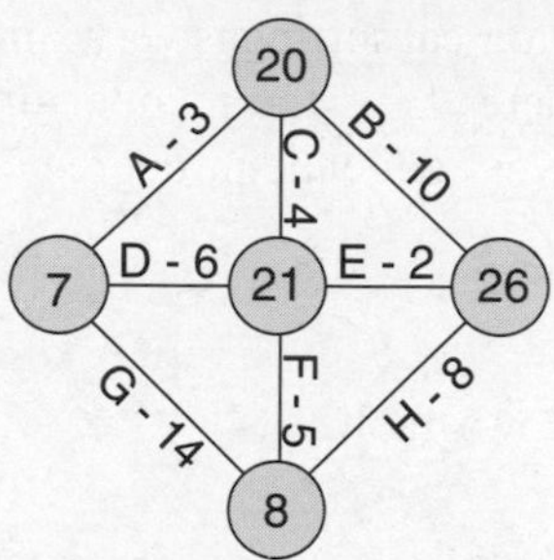

Figure 11.12 Sample graph

Solution: The step-by-step process is shown in Figure 11.13.

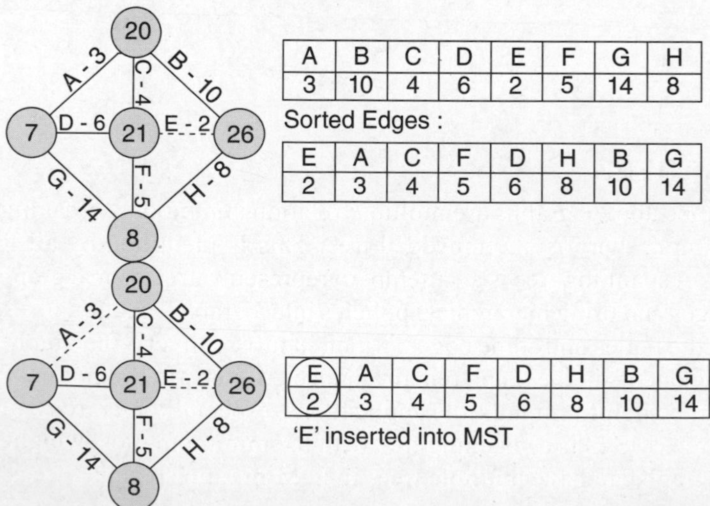

A	B	C	D	E	F	G	H
3	10	4	6	2	5	14	8

Sorted Edges :

E	A	C	F	D	H	B	G
2	3	4	5	6	8	10	14

E	A	C	F	D	H	B	G
2	3	4	5	6	8	10	14

'E' inserted into MST

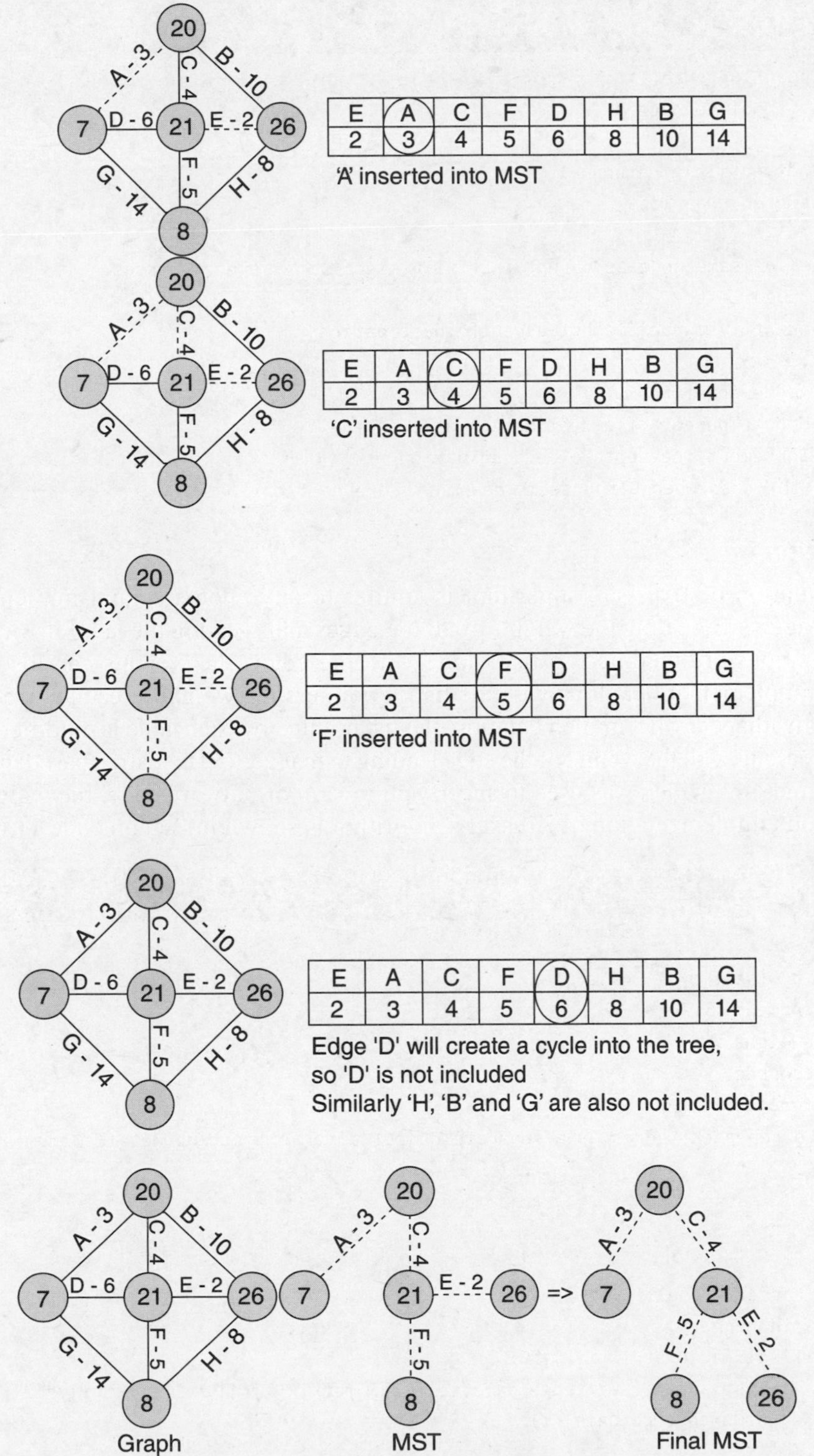

Figure 11.13 Step-by-step illustration of Kruskal's algorithm. The vertices are considered in sorted order, and added into the MST if the edge is not creating a cycle in the MST

Pseudocode 11.2

```
def minimum_spanning_tree():
    if graph is not connected
    then,
        MST not possible return -1
    edges = sorted edge list
    parent = {}
    #Initiate the same node as parent initially signifying seperate trees
    for e in edge list:
        if parent[e.source] is not parent[e.destination]
        then,
            Add e into the MST
            Update parent of e.destination as e.source
            Increment the depth of e.destination
    #This is the case when e.source is deeper than e.destination
```

Implementation

The implementation of Kruskal's algorithm is similar to any another graph implementation. The difference in logic is collecting the weights of all the edges and creating the list. For weighted graphs, the implementations are modified so that along with the edges the weights can also be stored. In pointer-based implementation, along with the list of pointers the weight of each corresponding edge can be stored. In adjacency list implementation, the list pointed by each node is modified to contain the adjacent vertex along with the weight of the edge leading to that vertex. In matrix-based implementation, instead of '1' and '-1', which was used to specify an inward or outward edge, the weight of the edge is used. The code implementation of Kruskal's algorithm is shown in Python code 11.6.

Python code 11.6

```
class edge:
    def __init__(self,n="",w=1,s="",d=""):
        self.name=n
        self.weight=w
        self.source=s
        self.destination=d
#Edge class to represent edges as a separate object after extracting details from a graph

def edges(self):
    list=[]
    name='a'
    for i in range(len(self.list)):
        for j in range(i):
            if self.adj_matrix[i][j]>0:
                list.append(self.edge(name,self.adj_matrix[i][j],self.list[i],self.list[j]))
                name=chr(ord(name)+1)
    return list
#To be changed for each implementation of graph
```

(contd)

(*contd*)

```
#This is specific to adjacency matrix implementation
#Default representation doesn't have edge names, so added in here

#Minimum Spanning tree, which extracts edges from a graph and then works on it
def minimum_spanning_tree(self):
    if(self.isConnected()) == False:
        print("Disconnected graph.. So there cannot be a Minimum Spanning Tree")
        return
    parent={} #Store the parent of every node in the tree
    level={} #Level of each node in the tree from the root

    #Each vertex is made into a tree, later based on edge weights the trees shall be merged
    def segment(v):
        parent[v]=v
        level[v]=0  #Initiate each node as a seperate tree so everything is a root
    #Segment each vertex and add it into the tree
    #Each element's parent is assigned as the same element

    #Module to efficiently find the root of a segmented tree
    def root(v):
        if parent[v]!=v:
            parent[v]=root(parent[v])
        return parent[v]
    #Recursive function to find the root of a node by moving up the ancestors

    #Merging two trees by attaching the smaller tree as leaf of deeper tree
    def union(v1,v2):
        root1=root(v1)
        root2=root(v2)
        if root1 != root2:
            #Find the deeper node and then add the leaf into the deeper tree
            if level[root1] > level[root2]:
                parent[root2] = root1
            else:
                parent[root1] = root2
            if level[root1] == level[root2]:
                level[root2] += 1
    #When two elements are merged into a the tree the level of the later is incremented

    for v in self.list:
        segment(v)
        mst={}
        #Create a list of edges
        edge_list = self.edges()
        #Sort the edges
        for i in range(len(edge_list)):
            for j in range(len(edge_list)):
```

(*contd*)

(*contd*)

```
            if edge_list[i].weight<edge_list[j].weight:
                edge_list[i],edge_list[j]=edge_list[j],edge_list[i]

for i in edge_list:
    if root(i.source)!=root(i.destination):
        union(i.source,i.destination)
        mst[i.name]=i
#This is a greedy algorithm, so when the edge is sorted the loop runs
#over the list.
#At every point, the next optimal edge is taken and inserted into the tree.
#If the source/destination belongs to a new segment
print("Minimum Spanning Tree edges: ")
for i in mst.values():
    print("weight ",i.weight," connecting ",i.source," and ",i.destination)
```

Complexity Analysis

The time complexity of Kruskal's algorithm is directly dependent on the time for sorting. Thus, the given code (Python code 11.6) is of complexity '$O(E^2)$'. The best possible time for sorting is 'O(n)', which is 'O(E)' in here. However, the implementation will use lots of additional memory. More reliable sorting algorithms with comparatively lesser time are of complexity 'O(E log E)', where 'E' is the number of edges. Such algorithms are handled in upcoming chapters. Once the edges are sorted, it is just a linear traversal with comparison which makes to 'O(E)' only. Thus, total time complexity is 'O(E log E) + O(E)', which is just 'O(E log E)'. This is also equal to 'O(E log V)'. This is possible since the maximum number of edges is 'V^2' in a complete graph. While applying log, '$\log E = \log V^2$' can be reduced to '2 log V' and '2' can be removed from complexity as it is just a constant multiplied to a variable. Thus, it derives to 'O(E log V)'.

11.10.2 Prim's Algorithm

Prim's algorithm is also a Greedy algorithm, but a little complicated when compared to Kruskal's algorithm. In Prim's algorithm, there is a MST set maintained along with the tree. Initially, both are empty and weight of vertices is maintained in a separate set. All the vertex weights are set to positive infinity. The weight of vertices connected by the minimum most edge is set to '0'. It is an iterative algorithm.

Steps for Prim's algorithm

1. Find the minimum-most vertex weight from the set. Add the vertex into the MST and fix its weight.
2. Update the adjacent vertices' weight. The new weight will be minimum of current weight and weight of the edge that is connecting it from the last added vertex.
3. Once the weights of some vertices are updated again, the minimum most is found and added to the MST along with the edge. The same are removed from the list.
4. Steps 2 and 3 continue until all the vertices are added into the MST.

Figure 11.15 depicts step-by-step building of a MST from a graph using Prim's algorithm. Pseudocode is also shown below (refer to Pseudocode 11.3).

Question 11.3 Create the minimum spanning tree of the given graph using Prim's algorithm.

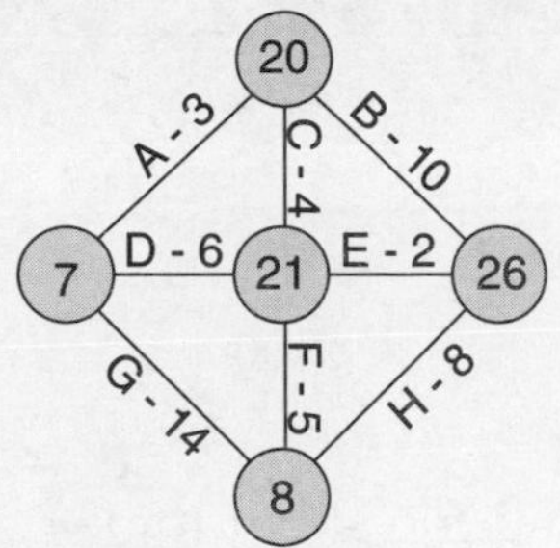

Figure 11.14 Sample graph

Solution: Figure 11.15 explains the complete process.

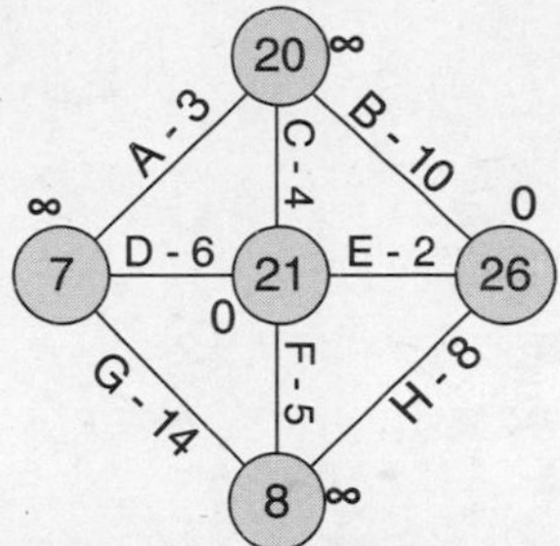

Minimum most edge 'E' with weight 2.
So '21' and '26' alone gets 0 and all others get infinity as weights.
'21' and '26' added into MST with edge 'E'.

New min weight for '20' is 4 from the edge 'C' from '21' to '20'
New min weight for '7' is 6 from the edge 'D' from '21' to '7'
New min weight for '8' is 5 from the edge 'F' from '21' to '8'

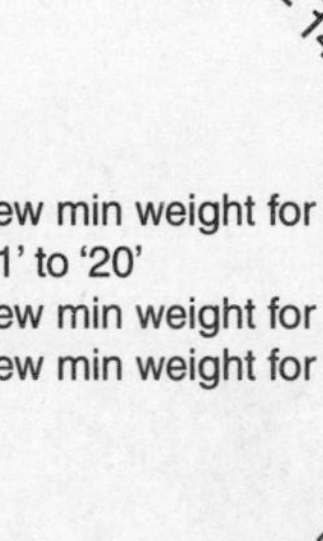

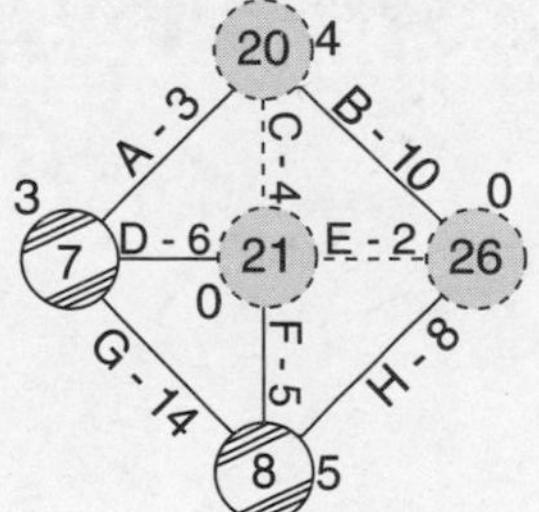

'20' with weight 4 is next min, added into MST with edge 'C'
New min weight for '7' is 3 from the edge 'A'
Weight of '21', '26' and '20' cannot be updated anymore.

'7' with weight 3 is next min, added into MST with edge 'A'
No Update in adjacent node as 'G' from '7' to '8' gives it a weight of '14' which is more than the current weight '5'.

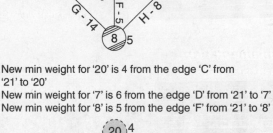

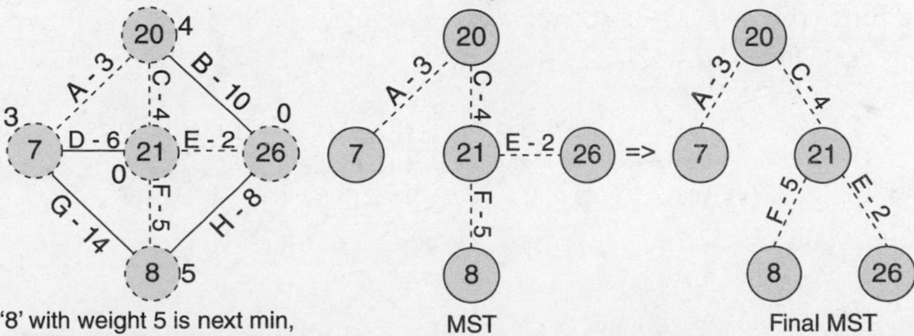

Figure 11.15 Illustration of Prim's MST algorithm. The MST is same as in Figure 11.12.

Pseudocode 11.3

```
def minimum_spanning_tree():
    if graph is not connected
    then,
        MST not possible return -1
    mst_node=[]
        #Find the minimum most edge to start with
    min_edge_weight=min_edge.weight
    min_src,min_dst=min_edge.source,min_edge.destination
    node_cost[min_src]=0
    node_cost[min_dst]=0
    A loop to consider each vertex:
        min_node = next minimum node in each iteration
        min_node_weight=min_node.weight
        mst_node.append(min_node)
        for every neighbour in the min_node.next:
            if node_cost[neighbour]>self.adj_matrix[min_node][neighbour]
            then,
                node_cost[neighbour]=adj_matrix[min_node][neighbour]
```

Implementation

The basic implementation is based on an adjacency matrix which has weight of the corresponding edges in the entry. Python code 11.7 shows the implementation of Prim's algorithm.

Python code 11.7

```
def minimum_spanning_tree(self):
    if(self.isConnected()) == False:
        print("Disconnected graph.. So there cannot be a Minimum Spanning Tree")
        return
    parent={}
    mst_node=[]
    min_edge_weight=math.inf
    min_src,min_dst=0,0
    node_cost={}
    for v in self.list:
        node_cost[v]=math.inf
    #Find the minimum most edge to start with
    for i in range(len(self.list)):
        for j in range(i):
            if self.adj_matrix[i][j] > 0 and self.adj_matrix[i][j]<min_edge_weight:
                min_edge_weight=self.adj_matrix[i][j]
                min_src,min_dst=self.list[i],self.list[j]
    node_cost[min_src]=0
    node_cost[min_dst]=0
    parent[min_src]='NA'
    parent[min_dst]=min_src
    #Loop to add all other nodes into the MST
```

(*contd*)

(*contd*)

```
    for i in range(len(self.list)):
        min_node_weight=math.inf
        min_node = math.inf
        #Next minimum node to fix cost
        for (node,weight) in node_cost.items():
            if weight < min_node_weight and node not in mst_node:
                min_node_weight=weight
                min_node = node
        #Next minimum node added into MST
        mst_node.append(min_node)
        min_index = self.list.index(min_node)
        #Update neighbours based on the current node
        for j in range(len(self.list)):
            #For every neighbour which is not yet added into the
            #tree, cost update if path is lesser
            if self.adj_matrix[min_index][j] > 0 and self.list[j] not in mst_node and node_
cost[self.list[j]]>self.adj_matrix[min_index][j]:
                node_cost[self.list[j]]=self.adj_matrix[min_index][j]
                parent[self.list[j]]=min_node    #Parent of the neighbour is the current node
                                                 #in the tree
    print("Minimum Spanning Tree edges: ")
    for i in mst_node:
        if parent[i] != 'NA':
            print("weight ",self.adj_matrix[self.list.index(parent[i])][self.list.index(i)],"
connecting ",parent[i]," and ",i)
```

Complexity Analysis

The complexity of the algorithm depends on cost of identifying the next smallest node. Thus, the complexity of Prim's algorithm is '$O(V^2)$'. For adjacency list-based representation, the Prim's algorithm can be implemented in 'O(ELogV)', using a min Heap of nodes aiding in faster fetching of next minimum nodes in every iteration.

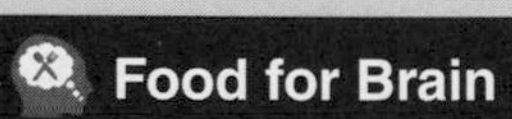

Implement Prim's algorithm for adjacency list-based representation using Heap. How to modify keys after inserting into the heap?

11.11 SHORTEST DISTANCE

Another problem of practical importance from graphs is finding the shortest distance between any two nodes. The shortest distance is in terms of sum of weights of the edges on the path. For an unweighted graph, shortest distance is calculated based on the number of hops from source to destination. Real-time significance is high for shortest path in a weighted graph. So, different algorithms for finding the shortest distance from a weighted graph have been devised. Few traditional algorithms are:

- Dijkstra's algorithm
- Floyd-Warshall algorithm

11.11.1 Dijkstra's Algorithm

Dijkstra's algorithm is very similar to Prim's algorithm. A set to store the cost of vertices is created which is initiated as '0' for the source node and 'infinity' for all other nodes. Other than this, there is a set to store the shortest path alone. The algorithm runs around the source and destination vertices. Starting from the source node,

1. Take the vertex with minimum weight and add it into shortest path set
2. For every neighbor of this vertex, update the weight as the minimum of current weight and sum(weight of this vertex ,weight of the edge that is connecting this vertex).

The above steps are repeated until the destination node is added into the shortest path set. Once the destination node is reached, it might be a tree. Branches whose leaves are not the destination can be completely removed. Thus, the final path is ensured to be linear. The step 2 in this algorithm, where in every iteration the weight of a node is reduced if there is a better edge leading into it is referred to as '*Relaxation of Edges*'. The algorithm is very similar to Prim's algorithm. There is only one difference that Prim's algorithm is a Greedy algorithm where the update of weight is just based on the weight of the edge running into it. In odds to it, in Dijkstra's algorithm the weight of the vertex is based on the sum of weights of all the edges in the path from the source vertex to the current node. So, it is not a Greedy algorithm. Figure 11.17 depicts building the shortest path from a vertex to another using Dijkstra's algorithm. Refer to Pseudocode 11.4 too.

Question 11.4 Identify the shortest path from 'node 26' to 'node 7' in the given graph using Djikstra's algorithm.

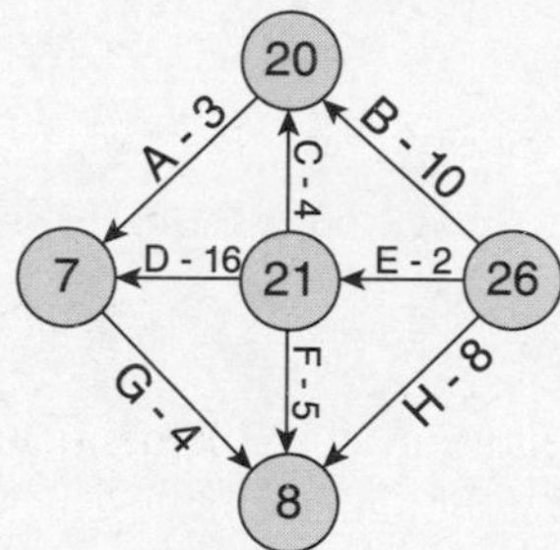

Figure 11.16 Sample graph

Solution: Figure 11.17 shows the complete process.

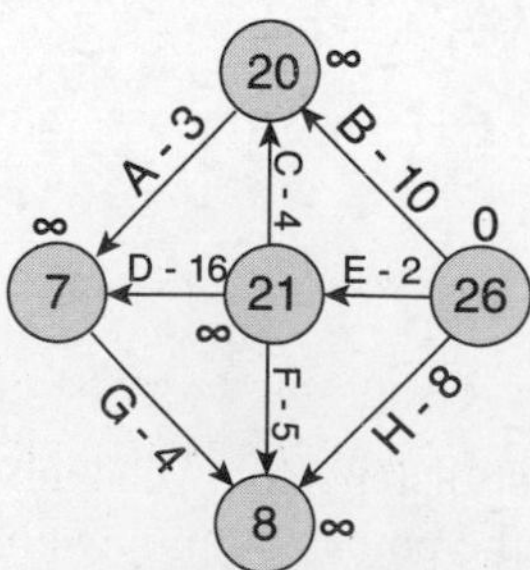

Shortest Path from '26' to '7'
Cost of source '26', is 0

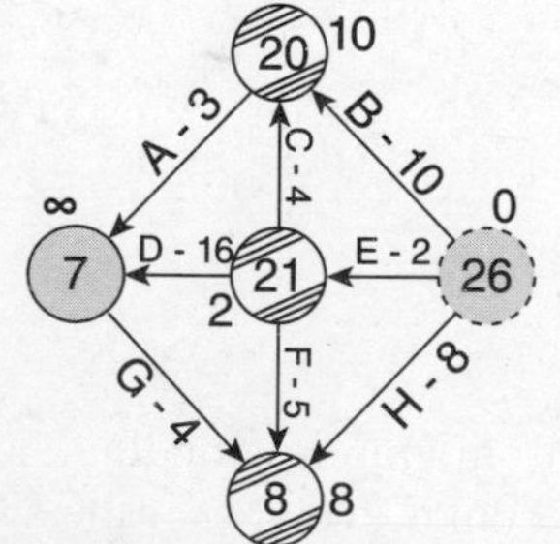

Cost of '20' becomes 10 from edge 'B'
Cost of '21' becomes 2 from edge 'E'
Cost of '8' becomes 8 from edge 'H'

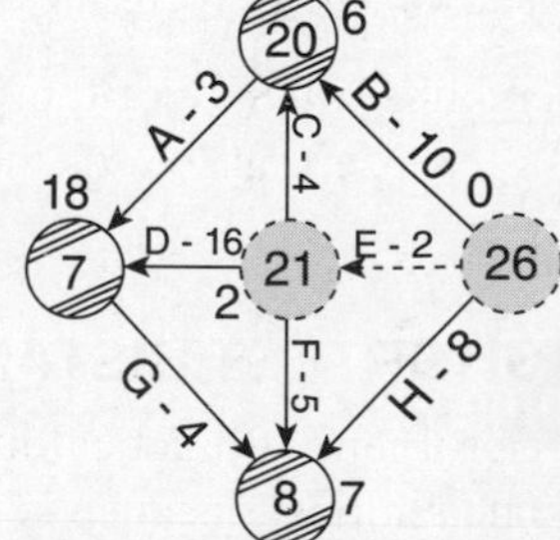

Cost of '21' is next min, added to the path
Cost of '20'becomes 2+4 from edge 'C'
Cost of '7' becomes 2+16 from edge 'D'
Cost of '8' becomes 2+5 from edge 'H'

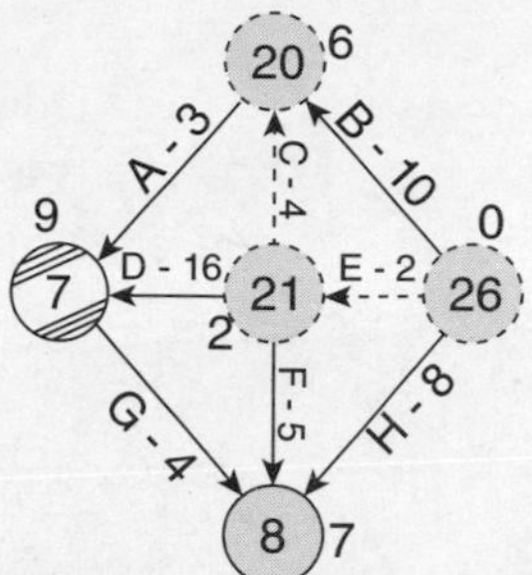

Cost of '20' is next min, added into path
Cost of '7' becomes 6+3 from edge 'A'

Cost of '7' is next min, added into path
Destination Reached

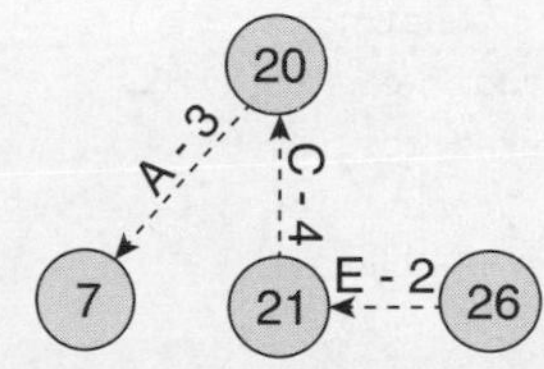

Min Cost path from '26' to '7', with total cost of 9 (final cost of destination)

Figure 11.17 Finding shortest path from '26' to '7' using Dijkstra's algorithm

Pseudocode 11.4

```
def mininmum_distance(source,destination):
    path={V: for V in vertices}
    fixed_cost={inf: for V in vertices}
    node_weights={inf: for V in vertices}
    fixed_cost[source]=0
    node_weights[source]=0
    current_min=source
    while current_min != destination:
        for every neighbour of current_min:
            if node_weights[neighbour]>node_weights[current_min]+edge cost to neighbour
            then,
                node_weights[neighbour]=node_weights[current_min]+edge cost to neighbour
                path[neighbour]=path[current_min]+neighbour
        current_min=next minimum node from node_weights
    #The path[destination] will have the shortest distance path from source
    #fixed_cost[destination] will have the cost of the shortest path from source
```

Note Another interesting point with this algorithm is that from a node shortest path to all other nodes can be computed. All these paths can be added into a tree, with the root as the source and this creates the minimum spanning tree of the graph. Thus, it can be used as an alternative to create the minimum spanning tree of graphs.

Implementation

Python code 11.8 shows the implementation of Dijkstra's using dictionaries for adjacency lists representation of graph.

Python code 11.8

```
#Djikstra's algorithm for minimum distance in Adjacency list representation
def minimum_distance(self,s,d):
    path={}
    node_weights={}
    fixed_cost={}
    for v in self.list.keys():
```

(contd)

(*contd*)

```
        fixed_cost[v]=math.inf
        node_weights[v]=math.inf
        path[v]=str(v)
    node_weights[s]=0
    fixed_cost[s]=0
    current_min=s
    fail_flag=0
    counter=0
    #Loop to reach the destination from source
    while current_min != d:
        #Update weights of neighbours if cost of edge is lesser
        for neigh in self.list[current_min]:
            if node_weights[neigh[0]]>(node_weights[current_min]+neigh[1]):
                path[neigh[0]]=path[current_min]+','+str(neigh[0])
                node_weights[neigh[0]]=(node_weights[current_min]+neigh[1])
        #Add current mininum into the fixed list and make it inf in the current list to help find
        #next min easily
        if node_weights[current_min]< math.inf:
            fixed_cost[current_min]=node_weights[current_min]
            node_weights[current_min]=math.inf
        val_list = list(node_weights.values())
        #Finding the next minimum after changing the previous minimum's weight to infinity
        current_min=list(node_weights.keys())[val_list.index(min(val_list))]
        counter+=1
        #If all the nodes has been explored and destination has not been reached, set fail flag
        if(counter==len(self.list)):
            fail_flag=1
            break
    #After loop completes, based on fail flag the path is printed
    if fail_flag:
        print("no path from ",s," to ",d)
    else:
        #Add the final node into the fixed cost
        fixed_cost[current_min]=node_weights[current_min]
        print("minimum distance path from ",s," to ",d," is ",path[d]," with cost ",fixed_cost[d])
```

Complexity Analysis

The complexity of Python code 11.8 is '$O(V^2)$', where the worst case is when every node is directly connected to every other node. This means the inner loop runs for 'V' iterations for every iteration of the outer loop. Similar to the previous algorithms, while using heaps the complexity of the algorithm becomes 'O(ElogV)'. The normal heaps do not have the property to modify the key of the elements and this is the reason why heaps cannot be used to represent the node costs. A complex format of heaps known as Fibonacci heaps will help bringing down the cost of searching of next minimum to 'LogV', making the total complexity to 'O(ElogV)'.

11.11.2 Floyd-Warshall Algorithm

Floyd-Warshall algorithm is a dynamic programming-based algorithm. It is based on an adjacency matrix-based representation, with some modifications. In the matrix, if there is an edge from node 'u' to 'v', then the entry at position 'g[u][v]' carries the weight of the corresponding edge. If there is no direct edge, then the position has infinity. All the diagonals are maintained '0', as self-pointing edges should never be added into the shortest path. Once the matrix is ready, the algorithm runs as:

1. Consider every node as 'k' and try modifying at all entries in the graph 'g[i][j]'.
2. Update 'g[i][j]' to 'g[i][k]+g[k][j]', where 'g[i][j]' is greater than 'g[i][k]+g[k][j]'. This means that the weight of the path from 'i' to 'j' is dynamically changed based on intermediate nodes.

Once all the nodes have been considered and the entire matrix has been updated, every 'g[i][j]' will have the minimum possible value for the path from 'i' to 'j'. A drawback of Floyd-Warshall algorithm is that it will just give the weight of the shortest path but not the actual path for the nodes. An advantage of the algorithm is that the final matrix has the shortest path cost for all pairs. Thus, multiple iterations for finding shortest path cost for multiple pairs can be skipped, reducing cost in problem solving. Figure 11.19 shows computation of shortest path matrix using Floyd-Warshall algorithm for a sample graph.

Question 11.5 Identify the shortest path from 'node 26' to 'node 7' in the given graph using Floyd Warshall algorithm.

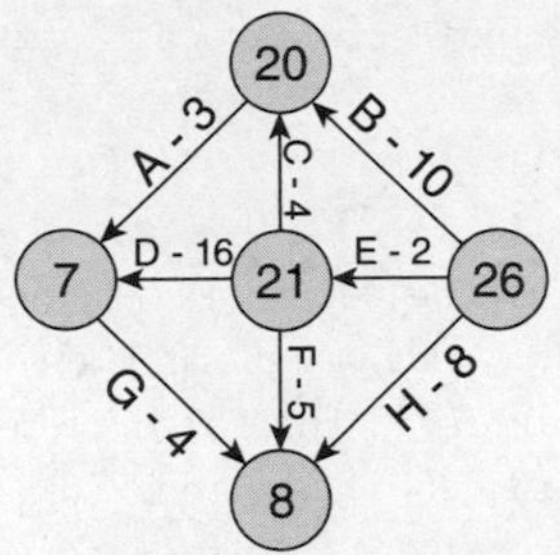

Figure 11.18 Sample graph

Solution: Figure 11.18 shows the step-by-step process.

	20	7	8	21	26
20	0	3	INF	INF	INF
7	INF	0	4	INF	INF
8	INF	INF	0	INF	INF
21	4	16	5	0	INF
26	10	INF	8	2	0

Initial Matrix

	20	7	8	21	26
20	0	3	INF	INF	INF
7	INF	0	4	INF	INF
8	INF	INF	0	INF	INF
21	4	**7**	5	0	INF
26	10	**13**	8	2	0

Consider '20' as 'k' and update Every other entry. New less cost path from '26' to '7' and '21 to '7'.

	20	**7**	8	21	26
20	0	3	7	INF	INF
7	INF	0	4	INF	INF
8	INF	INF	0	INF	INF
21	4	7	5	0	INF
26	10	13	8	2	0

Consider '7' as 'k' and update. New less cost path from '20' to '8'.

	20	7	8	21	26
20	0	3	7	INF	INF
7	INF	0	4	INF	INF
8	INF	INF	0	INF	INF
21	4	7	5	0	INF
26	10	13	8	2	0

Consider '8' as 'k' and update. No new less cost path as there is no outword edge from '8'.

	20	7	8	21	26
20	0	3	7	INF	INF
7	INF	0	4	INF	INF
8	INF	INF	0	INF	INF
21	4	7	5	0	INF
26	**6**	**9**	**7**	2	0

Consider '21' as 'k' and update. New less cost path from '26' to '20' and '26' to '7' and '26' to '8'.

	20	7	8	21	26
20	0	3	7	INF	INF
7	INF	0	4	INF	INF
8	INF	INF	0	INF	INF
21	4	7	5	0	INF
26	6	9	7	2	0

Consider '26' as 'k' and update. No new less cost path as there is no inward edge into '26'. Final Shortest path matrix, min cost of '26' to '7' is 9.

Figure 11.19 Illustration of Floyd-Warshall algorithm for a sample graph

Implementation

The implementation of Floyd-Warshall algorithm is shown in Python code 11.9.

Python code 11.9

```
def minimum_distance(self,s,d):
    #Weight matrix for each node weight in a weighted directed graph
    node_weights=[[0 for i in range(len(self.list))]for j in range(len(self.list))]
    #Read edge weights when there is an edge, else assign infinity
    for i in range(len(self.list)):
        for j in range(len(self.list)):
            if self.adj_matrix[i][j]>0 or i==j:
                node_weights[i][j]=self.adj_matrix[i][j]
            else:
                node_weights[i][j]=math.inf
    #For every node 'k' check for an indirect less cost path
    for k in range(len(self.list)):
        for i in range(len(self.list)):
            for j in range(len(self.list)):
                if node_weights[i][k]+node_weights[k][j]<node_weights[i][j]:
                    node_weights[i][j]=node_weights[i][k]+node_weights[k][j]
    #Only cost of shortest path available in this algorithm
    if node_weights[self.list.index(s)][self.list.index(d)] < math.inf:
        print("Shortest path from ",s," to ",d," is of cost ",node_weights[self.list.index(s)]
[self.list.index(d)])
    else:
        print("No path from ",s," to ",d)
```

Complexity Analysis

This is one algorithm which has a very high running time. The algorithm has three leveled nested loops. Thus, the complexity of the algorithm is 'O(v^3)'. Such algorithms are generally referred to as dynamic programming algorithms, where the intermediate results are based on results from previous steps and mostly the computation cost is in order of cubes.

Design the number of hops based shortest distance algorithm for unweighted graphs.

11.12 GRAPH CONNECTIVITY

A graph can be connected or unconnected. In an unconnected graph, there may be more than one component. Identifying the unconnected graph's component is important as algorithms like DFS, BFS, and other MST-like algorithms should be applied separately for each component. Algorithm for identifying connected components in a graph is discussed in this topic. The best way to find if a graph is connected is by performing DFS or BFS. If the traversal gives all the vertices in the graph then it is connected, else the graph has unconnected components. This has already been discussed while explaining DFS and BFS. In directed graphs, connected graphs are classified as strongly connected graph and weakly connected graph. A strongly connected graph is one in which there is a path between any two pairs of vertices.

Graphs which don't have the same are classified as weakly connected graphs. Figure 11.20 shows types of graphs based on connectivity.

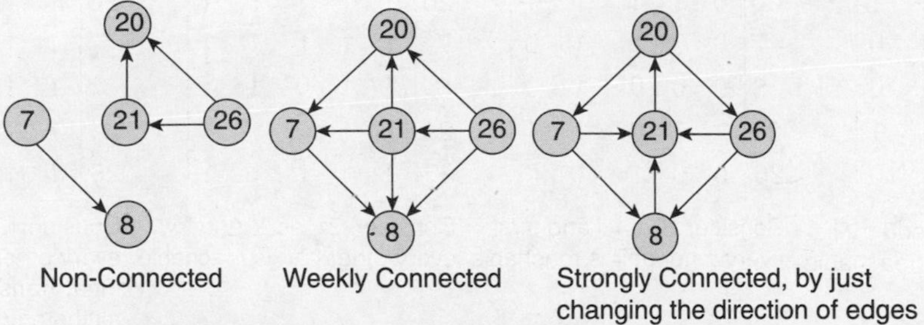

Figure 11.20 Types of graphs based on connectivity

An algorithm to find if a given graph is strongly connected is to create the transitive closure of the graph. Transitive closure of a graph is finding if every node is reachable from every other node. It is similar to Floyd-Warshall's dynamic programming based algorithm. A matrix similar to adjacency matrix is created. If there is a straight edge from node 'i' to 'j', then 'g[i][j]' is '1'. The following logic is applied over the adjacency matrix representation.

1. Consider each vertex separately as 'k'.
2. For every pair of vertices in the graph 'i' and 'j', if there is an edge from 'i' to 'k' and 'k' to 'j', then 'i' and 'j' are considered connected and the entry g[i][j] is made '1'.

The implementation of the same algorithm is shared in Python code 11.10. After this algorithm, if all the entries of the matrix are '1', then the graph is strongly connected. Figure 11.22 traces this algorithm for a sample graph.

Question 11.6 Find transitive closure of the graph provided in Figure 11.21.

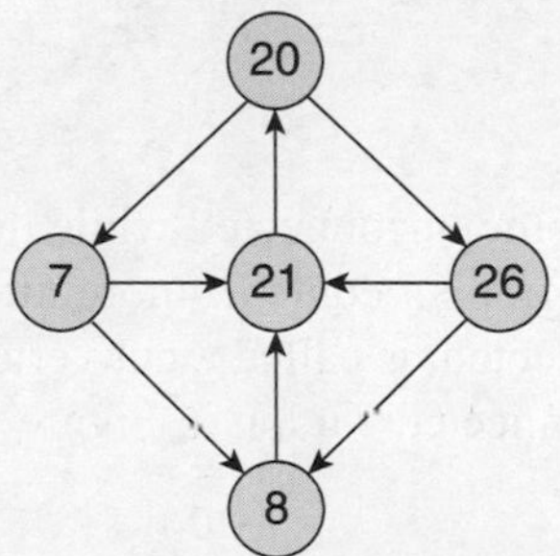

Figure 11.21 Sample graph

Solution: The process is shown in Figure 11.22.

	20	7	8	21	26
20	0	1	0	0	1
7	0	0	1	1	0
8	0	0	0	1	0
21	1	0	0	0	0
26	0	0	1	1	0

Initial Matrix

	20	7	8	21	26
20	0	1	0	0	1
7	0	0	1	1	0
8	0	0	0	1	0
21	1	**1**	0	0	**1**
26	0	0	1	1	0

Consider '20' as 'k' and try if every other pair is reachable

(contd)

(*contd*)

	20	7	8	21	26
20	0	1	1	1	1
7	0	0	1	1	0
8	0	0	0	1	0
21	1	1	0	1	1
26	0	0	1	1	0

Consider '7' as 'k' and try if every other pair is reachable

	20	7	8	21	26
20	0	1	1	1	1
7	0	0	1	1	0
8	0	0	0	1	0
21	1	1	0	1	1
26	0	0	1	1	0

Consider '8' as 'k' and try if every other pair is reachable

	20	7	8	21	26
20	1	1	1	1	1
7	1	1	1	1	1
8	1	1	0	1	1
21	1	1	0	1	1
26	1	1	1	1	1

Consider '21' as 'k' and try if every other pair is reachable

	20	7	8	21	26
20	1	1	1	1	1
7	1	1	1	1	1
8	1	1	1	1	1
21	1	1	1	1	1
26	1	1	1	1	1

Consider '26' as 'k' and try if every other pair is reachable. Final Transitive closure where all the entries are 1

Figure 11.22 Creation of transitive closure matrix of a sample graph

Implementation

The transistive closure implementation for graph connectivity is shown in Python code 11.10.

Python code 11.10

```
#This is the transitive closure algorithm for unweighted undirected graph
def isConnected(self):
    transitive_closure = self.adj_matrix
    #For every node k check if there an indirect path from i to j via k
    for k in range(len(self.list)):
        for i in range(len(self.list)):
            for j in range(len(self.list)):
                transitive_closure[i][j]=transitive_closure[i][j] or (transitive_closure[i][k]
and transitive_closure[k][j])
    if min(min(transitive_closure))==0:
        return False
    return True
```

A connected graph may also become unconnected while deleting a vertex or a node. Hence, while processing, especially deleting the graph's content, more attention should be paid. A vertex, which when deleted makes a graph unconnected, is called a cut vertex. Similarly, cut edge is an edge, which when removed, makes a graph unconnected. Graph in Figure 11.23 shows a cut vertex and cut edge.

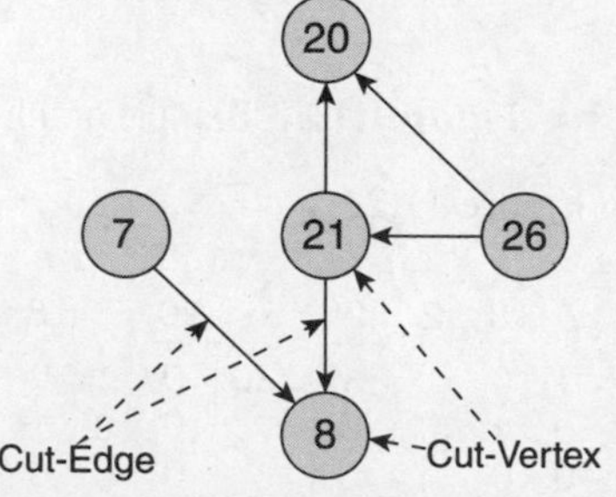

Figure 11.23 A connected graph with marked cut-edge and cut-vertex

Food for Brain

How to traverse a non-connected graph?

11.13 APPLICATIONS OF GRAPHS

A real-time application of graphs is the World Wide Web. In today's world, the Internet has become the part and parcel of life. The World Wide Web is an information space where every document or resource is identified using a unique address known as Uniform Resource Locator (URL). These URLs are formed as hyperlinks and used to move from one page to another. The whole of web space is represented by a graph called webgraph. A webgraph consists of web pages as nodes connected by directed links. Every page can be linked to various different pages in the web using hyperlinks. Every linked page is connected by a directed edge from the source page to the destination page. Every 'page X' linked to 'page Y' has a directed edge running from 'page X to page Y'. The famous PageRank algorithm is an algorithm that is applied on this graph. When a user is present at a webpage, there can be multiple pages linked to it. There is a probability for each of the connected pages to be visited. This is the damping factor and based on this damping factor, all the pages are ranked. There are many algorithms other than PageRank running in the web for various different purposes like web crawling algorithms and phishing detection algorithms. All those are not handled in here as it would deviate from the scope of the book. Figure 11.24 shows an illustrative subgraph of the webgraph concerning to the Oxford University Press website.

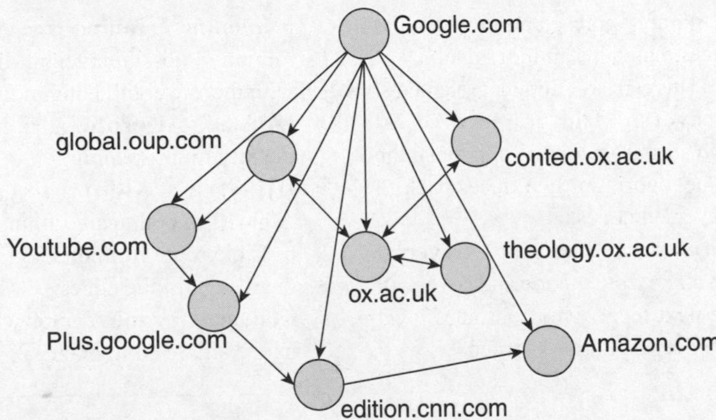

Figure 11.24 Subgraph of webgraph. Websites connected to Oxford University Press from Google

POINTS TO REMEMBER

- Graphs are non-hierarchical, non-linear structures.
- Graphs can be implemented using linked lists, pointers and matrices.
- Traversal of a graph can be depth wise or breadth wise, termed as depth first search and breadth first search correspondingly.
- DFS or BFS may not visit all the vertices if the graph is not connected.
- Graphs can be directed, undirected, unconnected, planar, cyclic and acyclic.
- Topological sorting of nodes in a directed acyclic graph is ordering them based on dependencies such that all the nodes pointing to the current node are listed before listing the current node.
- In weighted graph, there can be more than one path from one node to another. Shortest path is the path with minimum weight found using algorithms like Djikstra's or Floyd-Warshall.
- A graph may have a tree or trees within it. A spanning tree is a tree formed with all the vertices in the graph connected with some edges from the graph such that there is a hierarchical structure in place.

- A minimum spanning tree is a spanning tree of minimum weight. It can be found using algorithms like Prim's or Kruskal's.
- If there is a path from a vertex to every other vertex, then the graph is a strongly connected graph, else it is a weakly connected or unconnected graph.
- Some connected graphs can be made disconnected by removing an edge or a vertex. The same is termed as cut edge or cut vertex.

KEY TERMS

- **Graphs** Non-hierarchical, non-linear data structure which can represent one to many relationship
- **Adjacency matrix** A graph representation where the vertices are represented as rows and columns as well, for every edge 'i to j', 'graph[i][j]' will have the weight of the edge.
- **Adjacency list** A graph representation where the base list of vertices maintains an individual list of adjacent vertices. This can have duplicate elements.
- **Depth first traversal** The graph traversal algorithms which start from a node and reach the deepest point. The algorithm then traces back to cover any un-traversed nodes.
- **Breadth first traversal** The graph traversal algorithm which starts from a node and covers all the nodes in the next level. This continues level by level until the deepest node is visited.
- **Topological sorting** An algorithm to solve problems on pre-requisites. It orders nodes based on its in-degree.
- **Spanning tree** A tree representation of a graph which has all the nodes and removes redundant edges.
- **Minimum spanning tree** A spanning tree with minimum possible weight. It tries to avoid edges with more weight using indirect edges.
- **Kruskal's Algorithm, Prim's Algorithm** To find the minimum spanning tree
- **Djikstra's Algorithm, Floyd–Warshall Algorithm** Graph algorithms used to find shortest possible route from one node to another based on the weight of the edges
- **Connected graph** A graph where all the nodes are in one single component.

EXERCISES

Multiple-choice Questions

1. Graphs can be implemented using _______.
   (a) Arrays / list (b) Pointers
   (c) Linked List (d) Matrices
   (e) Either of the above
2. What is the complexity of DFS?
   (a) O(V) (b) O(E)
   (c) O(V+E) (d) O(V.E)
3. Shortest path between two vertices in an unweighted graph is calculated based on __________.
   (a) Number of Hops made in the path
   (b) Number of nodes crossed in the path
   (c) Number of edges taken in the path
   (d) Either of the above
4. In topological sorting, can there be two vertices at same index?
   (a) Yes (b) No
5. What is the minimum most weight possible for a path in an unweighted graph?
   (a) 0 (b) 1
   (c) 2 (d) None of the above
6. Floyd-Warshall algorithm can be applied to graphs implemented using adjacency list.
   (a) True (b) False
7. There can be more than one shortest path for a vertex pair in a graph.

(a) True (b) False

8. Every pair's shortest path should be a part of the minimum spanning tree.
   (a) True (b) False
9. All the edges from a cut vertex are cut edges in a connected graph.
   (a) True (b) False
10. The transitive closure of a complete graph is a ________.
    (a) Unit Matrix
    (b) Diagonal Matrix
    (c) Symmetric Matrix
    (d) None of the above

Theoretical Review Questions

1. How are Graphs implemented? Write a brief review on different implementation of a graph using illustrative examples.
2. What are the common graph traversal algorithms? What are its disadvantages? Give an illustrative example of each algorithm.
3. How is Kruskal's algorithm different from Djikstra's algorithm?
4. Explain Floyd-Warshall algorithm and how is it different from transitive closure.
5. What is topological sorting? Explain the algorithm with illustrations.

Exploratory Application Exercises

1. Given an adjacency matrix-based weighted directed graph, convert it into an adjacency list-based implementation.
2. Modify DFS algorithm to visit all the vertices in the graph irrespective of its connectedness.
3. Write Djikstra's algorithm for unweighted graphs.
4. Produce a code to identify cycles in a graph.
5. Given a graph, identify if it is strongly connected or weakly connected using a function.
6. Write a function to identify all the cut vertices and cut edges in a given adjacency matrix based graph.
7. Write a program to check if two graphs are isomorphic.
8. Given a list of cities and the distance between them, develop a function to find the shortest route from a city to every other city.
9. Given two directed graphs, write a program to find if the graphs are mirror images of each other.
10. In a crowd of 'n' people, there is a celebrity. A celebrity is a person known by everybody else but he doesn't know anybody. Design this problem in a graph and identify the celebrity using just the above information.

Picto Puzzles

Identify logic for every question and develop a code for the same.

1.

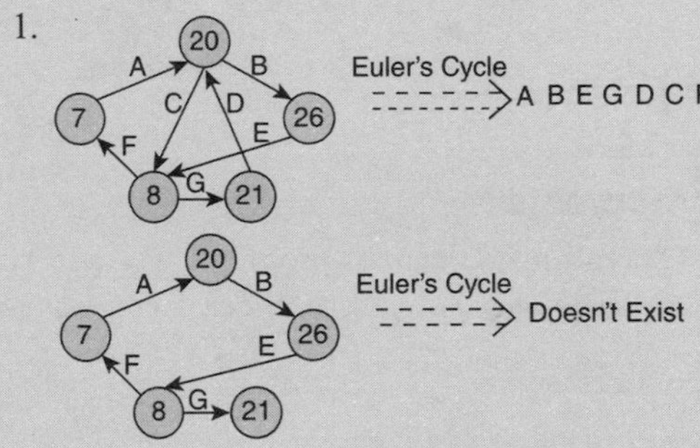

2.

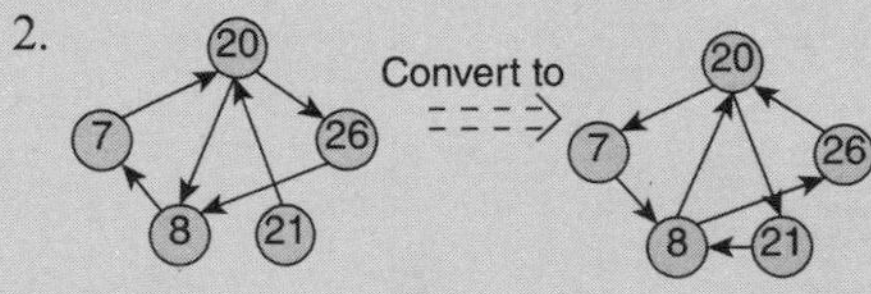

3. Does the path 'ACDEDBFG' exist in the graph?

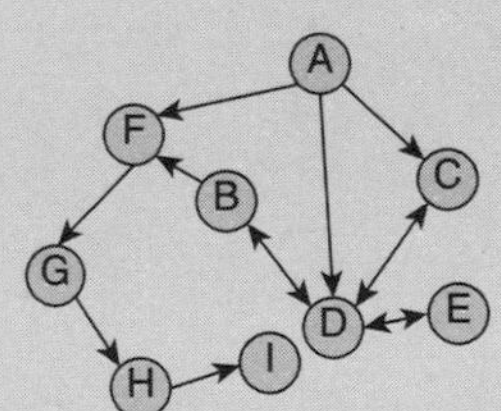

4. Propionic acid ($C_3H_6O_2$) is represented using graphs as shown. Identify if it has acid (shown in image) as a part of the molecule.

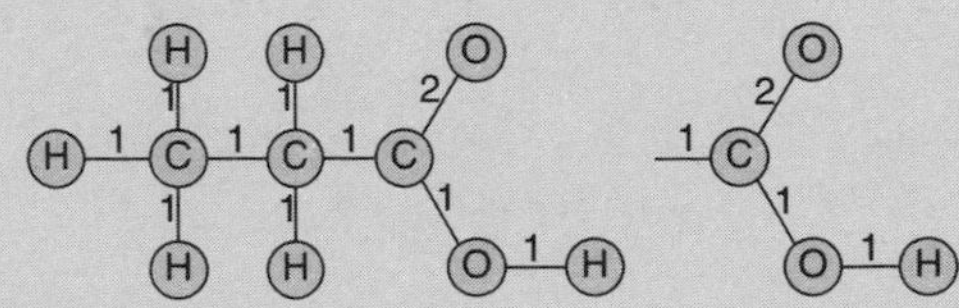

5. Five River Islands are connected by '7' bridges. Starting from any city, find a path that visits every city and returns to starting city crossing every bridge just once.

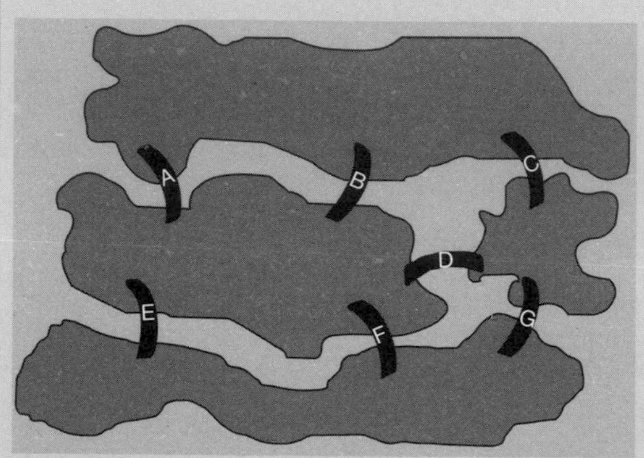

Mini Projects

1. Travelling Salesman problem: Given a set of cities and the paths between them, write a program to identify if the salesman can travel all the cities and return back to his home town visiting every city just once.
2. Graph colouring is a problem when every vertex can have any colour, but no two adjacent vertices are of the same colour. Write a function to identify the minimum number of colours required for performing this graph colouring.
3. Write a program to represent a network. It should have functions to identify topology, find the shortest path for the packets to travel from one node to another, and add or delete routers within the network. Keep in mind that adding routers will create subnetworks inside the network.

Answers to Multiple-choice Questions

1. (e) 2. (c) 3. (d) 4. (a) 5. (d) 6. (b) 7. (b) 8. (a) 9. (b)
10. (a)

CHAPTER

12

Sorting

LEARNING OBJECTIVES

After going through this chapter, readers will be able to understand:

- What is sorting?
- Why is sorting important?
- What are the various possible ways of sorting?
- What is 'Divide and Conquer' strategy?
- How to code for all the sorting techniques using Python?

12.1 INTRODUCTION TO SORTING

Sorting is a set of algorithms that help arrange the data in a specific order. This is more significant in organizing data. When arranging the elements is the key intent, what is that order? When we talk about order, the first thing that strikes our mind is ascending order and descending order. In ascending order, the elements are arranged from smallest to largest. However, in descending order, the elements are arranged from largest to smallest. This can be completely relevant to numbers and even to alphabets, but what about objects? Assume you want to sort a set of toys which has balls and Rubik's cubes. Now we can decide on any feature of the objects based on which we want to sort them. For example, these can be sorted based on their area or even volume. Deciding the criteria based on which the elements should be sorted is purely based on the solution design/logic. This chapter will introduce different sorting algorithms that can be applied over any data by just modifying the criteria as required.

12.2 IMPORTANCE OF SORTING ALGORITHMS

When a large amount of data is to be handled, it must be organized in an intelligent way for ease and efficiency. Sorting is a technique for organizing data. Consider a collection of details of one million students. If a student's details are to be fetched, then all the records have to be traversed to identify the required information. However, what is the worst case complexity of this read operation? It is 'O(n)', that is, from a million records fetch will cost a million operations. If the records are organized using sorting techniques, this cost gets reduced drastically. So, how is it possible? How to sort the numbers and what is its impact on searching? All these questions will be clarified in this Chapter and the next.

12.3 EXCHANGE SORT

Exchange sort is a basic and naive sorting technique that just compares a pair of data and swaps it on necessity. The common form of exchange sort, which is considered as a naïve algorithm, is the bubble sort.

12.3.1 Bubble Sort

Bubble sort is the simplest of all sorting algorithms. The fact that bubbles rise when water or any other liquid is poured into a vessel helps in understanding this concept. All these bubbles will reach the surface of the liquid, but there will be a pattern in it. It is the biggest bubble that reaches the surface first. For the larger bubble to reach the surface, it has to swap itself with all other smaller bubbles on the way to the top. This sort has been sculpted with the same mechanism. Here, the numbers are compared with every following number and are then swapped with the smaller ones. After 'n' iterations, last 'n' numbers will be in a sorted order. Figure 12.1 represents how bubbles start to swap once they are created.

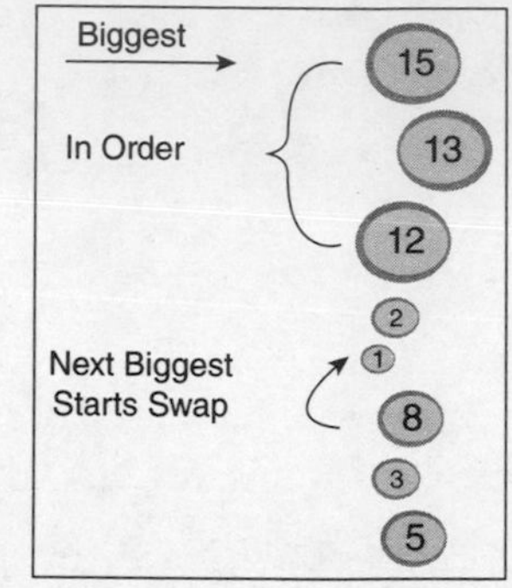

Figure 12.1 Bubbles in water

Working

Initially, the first two numbers are compared. If the second one is smaller, they will be swapped else will be left unchanged. Then, the second and third numbers will be considered. This continues until the largest number reaches the end. Now, the first iteration is over. After this, the next iteration begins. The same process is repeated for the next iteration as well. Now, the last two numbers get in order. After 'n' such iterations, the sorted list is achieved.

At the end of second iteration, it is to be noted that the last number will never be smaller than the new number that has moved to the penultimate position in the iteration. This means, the number taken to the last position in iteration '1' is fixed and will never change in lateral iterations. This inference can be accepted as in iteration '1' it is the biggest number that reaches the end. Similarly, in the second iteration, the next biggest number reaches the penultimate position and cannot reach the final position. So, in every 'ith' iteration, the last 'i' elements are in order. So, the last 'i' comparisons go useless and the same may be skipped while implementation. Pseudocode 12.1 shows the basic algorithm.

Question 12.1 Sort the numbers 10, 13, 2, 7, 5 using Bubble Sort.

Solution: The step-by-step process is shown in Figure 12.2.

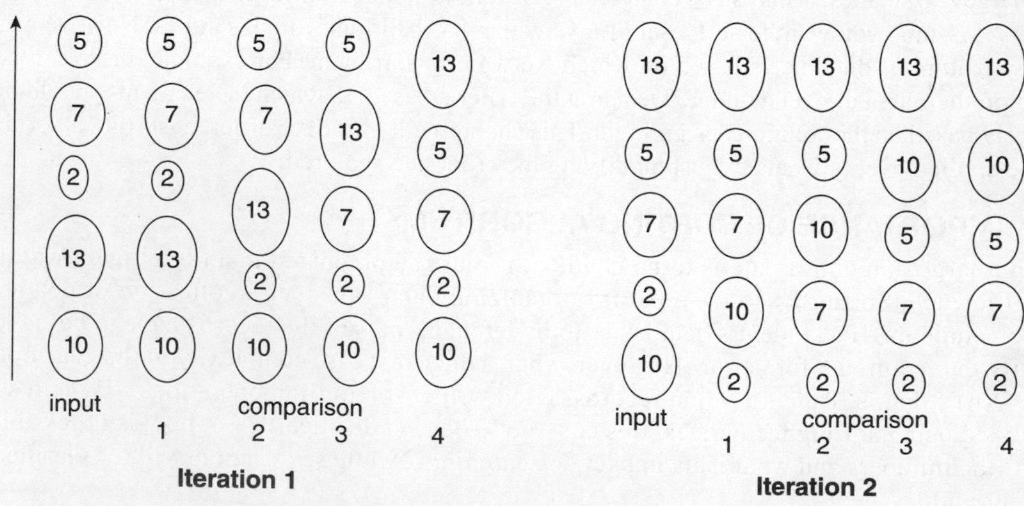

(*contd*)

(*contd*)

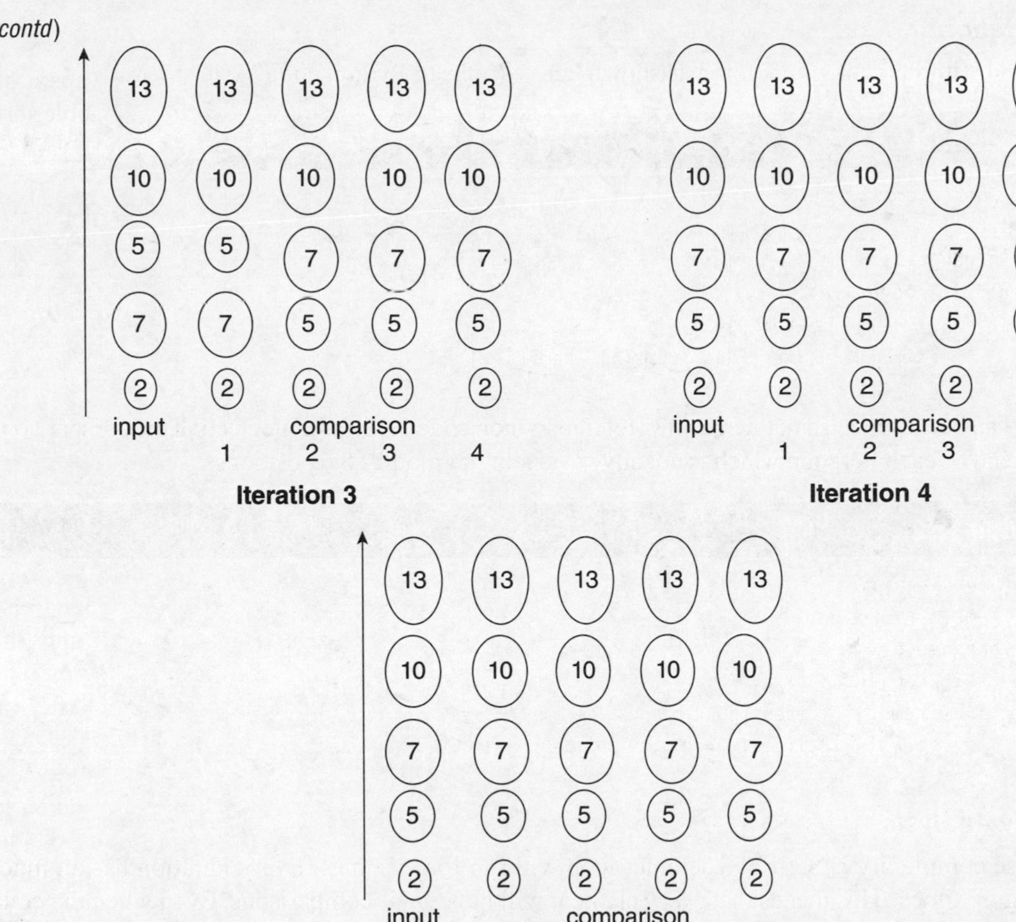

Figure 12.2 Bubble sort iterations

Pseudocode 12.1

```
n=length(list)
for i in 1 to n-1
Do,
    for j in 1 to n-1
    Do,
        if list[ j ] < list[ j-1 ]
        then,
            swap list[ j ] and list[ j-1 ]
```

Note

- The number of iterations is equal to the number of elements present.
- The number of comparisons in every iteration is equal to number of elements – 1.
- The last 'i' comparison results of the 'i[th]' iteration are identical, so can be neglected in implementation.
- For arranging in ascending order, the comparison condition must be changed accordingly.

Implementation

This sort can be implemented in Python as shown below (refer to Python code 12.1).

Python code 12.1

```
def Bubble_Sort(items):
    n=len(items)
    for i in range(1,n):
        for j in range(1,n):
            if (items[j] < items[j-1]):
                items[j-1],items[j]= items[j],items[j-1]
```

The code can be optimized as shown below (refer to Python code 12.2), after neglecting the comparisons towards the end of each iteration which is not anyways going to modify the positions.

Python code 12.2

```
def Bubble_Sort(items):
    n=len(items)
    for i in range(n-1):
        for j in range(1,n-i):
            if (items[j] < items[j-1]):
                items[j-1],items[j]= items[j],items[j-1]
```

Complexity Analysis

Its worst case complexity is '$O(n^2)$'. The outer loop will run for 'n' times. Every iteration has an inner loop running 'n' times. This means that every element will have 'n-1' comparisons. Even when the code gets optimized, the total comparisons will be 'n(n+1)', summing up to 'n^2'. The best case complexity is 'O(n)' when the numbers are already sorted. This is because the inner loop will never execute anything when numbers are in order. Even the average case sticks to '$O(n^2)$'. There is no additional space used by the program, so the auxiliary space complexity is 'O(1)'.

12.4 SELECTION SORT

Selection sort is an intelligent sorting algorithm wherein, the minimum or the maximum element is selected from the list and swapped with another misplaced element. There are two types of selection sorts—straight selection and heap sort. Straight selection directly swaps the element with the element that is wrongly placed in its position. Heap sort has a special pattern of working which is based on binary heap. Selection sort is an in-place sort. The first one elaborated here is the straight selection sort.

12.4.1 Straight Selection Sort

This is an appreciable and smart sorting algorithm. In this case, the smallest number is selected and swapped with the element in that place.

This can be explained better with an example. Consider the scenario of a doctor's clinic, where even though the patients are given tokens they are sitting in some random order. When the doctor arrives, person with token number '1' will immediately move to seat '1'. Now, the person at that place moves to the place where the person '1' was sitting. Seeing this patient, person '2' does the same. The same continues and finally all the people are seen sitting in order. At any point the first 'n' members will be swapped and the others will be patient to avoid chaos. Figure 12.2 shows a sample scenario of people sitting in a row.

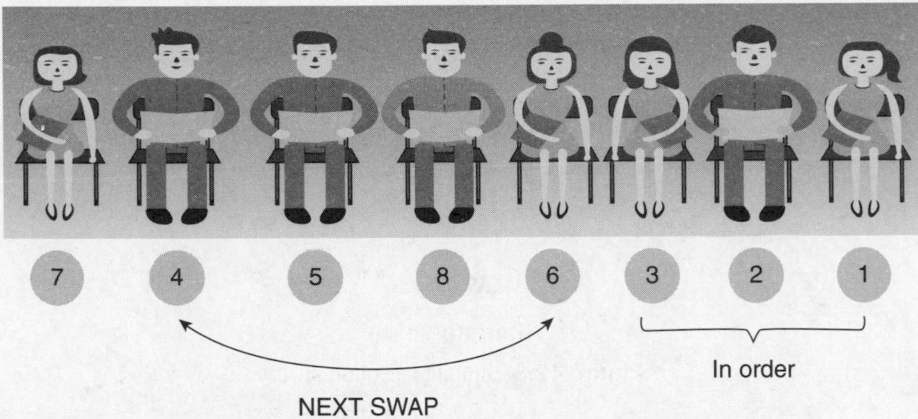

Figure 12.2 Scenario of people sitting in a queue

Working

The above mechanism must be slightly generalized, as while sorting numbers it is not necessary that the numbers are continuous. Hence, in first iteration, the smallest number is selected and swapped with the element at first position. Then, the next smallest number is selected and swapped with the number at position '2'. This continues for 'n-1' iterations, so all the numbers get in order. There will be at max 'n-1' swaps. In addition, in 'i^{th}' iteration, the first 'i' numbers will be in order. So, should not be considered while finding the next minimum number for the iteration. The basic algorithm is shown in Pseudocode 12.2.

Question 12.2 Sort the numbers 5, 7, 2, 13, 10 using Selection Sort.

Solution: The step-by-step process is shown in Figure 12.3.

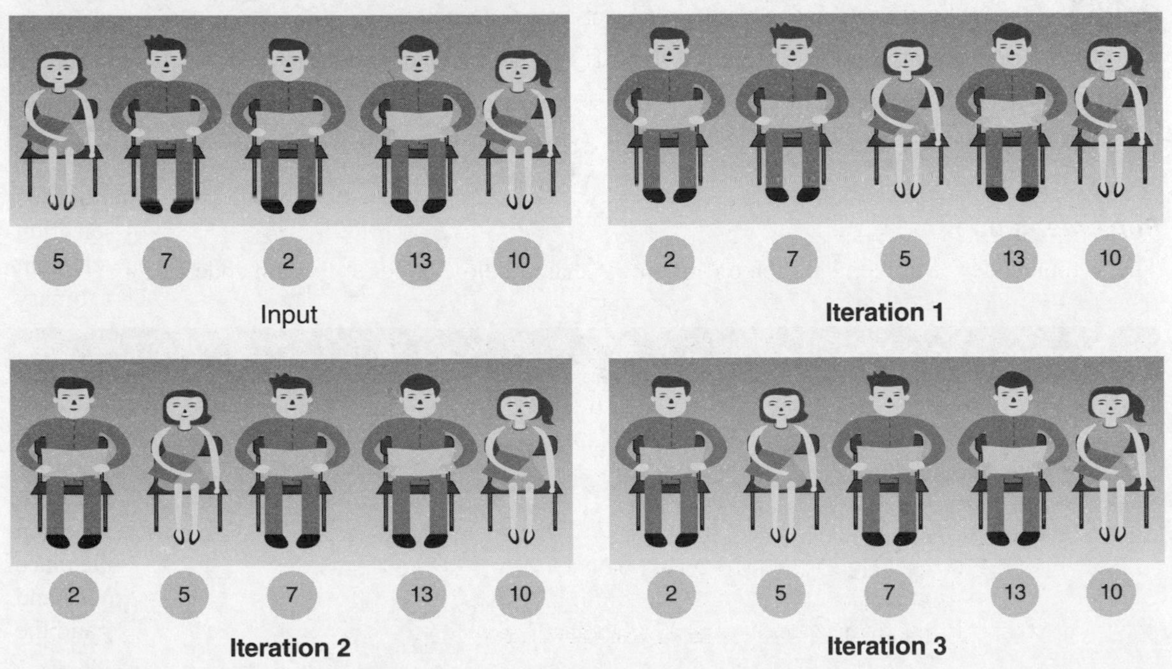

(*contd*)

(*contd*)

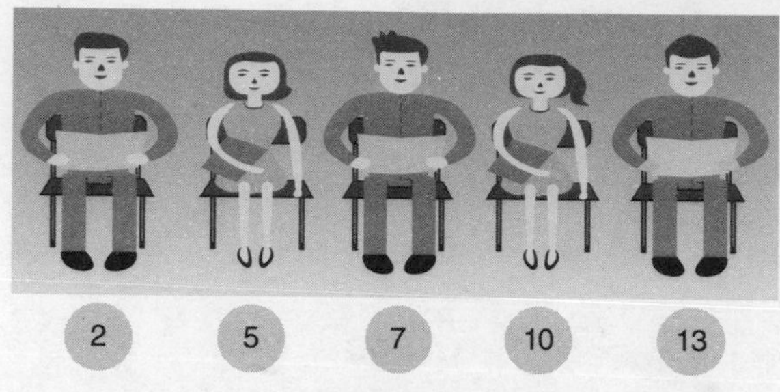

Iteration 4

Figure 12.3 Straight selection sort

Pseudocode 12.2

```
n=length(list)
for i in 0 to n-1
Do,
    min index = i
    for j in i to n-1
    Do,
        if list[ j ] < list[ min index ]
        then,
            min index = j
    swap list[ i ] list[ min index ]
```

Note

- The number of iterations is equal to the number of elements present - 1.
- The number of comparisons in every iteration is equal to the number of elements – 1.
- The first 'i' elements will be in order in 'i^th' iteration, so should not be considered while finding the next smallest number.
- For arranging in descending order, the comparison condition must be changed accordingly.

Implementation

The Python code for implementation of this sort is shared below (refer to Python code 12.3).

Python code 12.3

```
def Selection_Sort(items):
    n=len(items)
    for i in range(n):
        min_index = i
        for j in range(i,n):
            if (items[j] < items[min_index]):
                min_index = j
        items[i],items[min_index] = items[min_index],items[i]
```

Complexity Analysis

Its worst case complexity is 'O(n^2)', that is 'n' iterations with 'n-1' comparisons in each iteration. Here, both the best case and average case complexities also stick to 'O(n^2)'. Even when the list is sorted, there will be 'n' comparisons in the inner loop and hence the best case complexity. Considering the additional space that is used, it has only one variable for storing the minimum index in every iteration. So, it makes up to 'O(1)' auxiliary space complexity.

 **Food for Brain**

How is selection sort significant over bubble sort?

12.4.2 Heap Sort

Heap sort is based on the data structure 'HEAP' that has been discussed in Chapter 8. The elements are passed in a list and then heapified to sort the list. A heap is a situation when smaller objects dropped over larger objects move down, allowing the larger objects to stay above. Figure 12.4 shows a heap of sand, stone, and rock. In a pile of stones, if sand is poured, then the sand granules tend to slip through the gaps in the stones and move down. This makes the sand move down and stones to stay up. This can be completely related to a heap structure where the elements with lesser weight move down.

Figure 12.4 A heap of sand, stone, and rock

Working

This list-based implementation makes the data structure act as a sorting algorithm. The representation makes a[0] to be the root and a[i] to be the parent of a[2i] and a[2i+1]. This representation is applicable only when a node has two children and all nodes other than the last node are filled (heap property). Given a list to sort it (ascending order), the first step is to max heapify all the elements except the leaf nodes. Then, the last node is swapped with the first node and the first element is heapified neglecting the last node. With this, the penultimate node is swapped with the first node and again the first element is heapified neglecting the last two nodes. Then, the third node from the last is swapped with the first element, last three nodes are skipped, and the first node is heapified. This continues until the first node is reached and the list gets sorted. The heapify operation over a node checks if the node is larger than both its children. If not, then it will be swapped with the larger of the two children. The element the node is swapped with (left or right child) gets heapified again. Thus, it is a recursive process. It stops when the property is met or a leaf is reached. The basic algorithm is shown in Pseudocode 12.3.

Question 12.3 Sort the numbers 5, 7, 2, 13, 10 using Heap Sort.

Solution: The step-by-step process is shown in Figure 12.5.

5	7	2	13	10
0	1	2	3	4

Tree: 5 (0); 7 (1), 2 (2); 13 (3), 10 (4)

Input

5	13	2	7	10
0	1	2	3	4

Tree: 5 (0); 13 (1), 2 (2); 7 (3), 10 (4)

heapify(1)

(*contd*)

(*contd*)

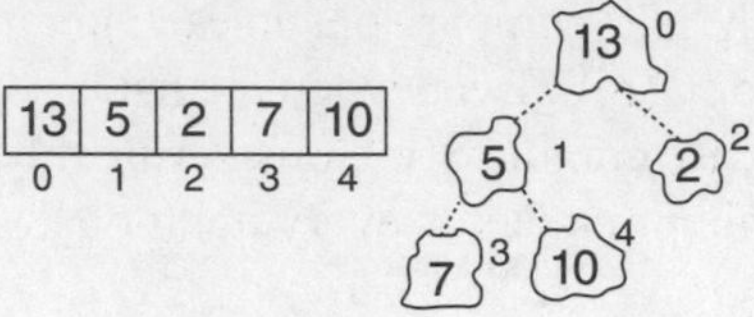

heapify(0) induces heapify(1)

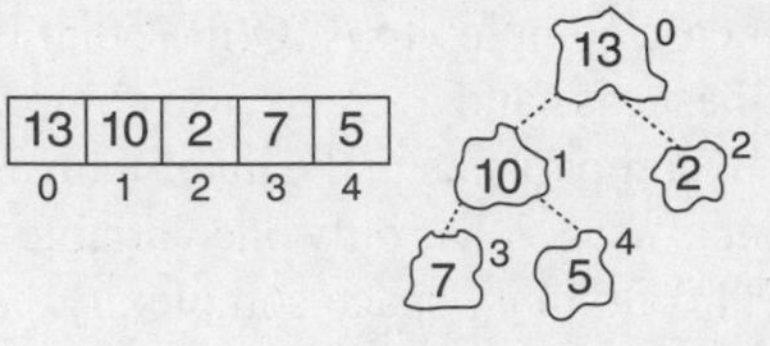

heapify(1)

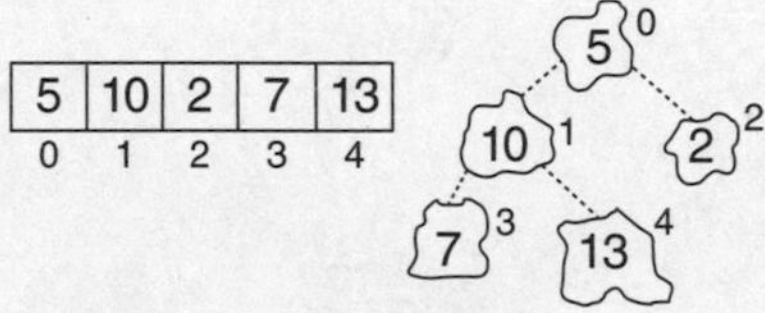

swap list[4] and list[0]
This moves the biggest element to last position.

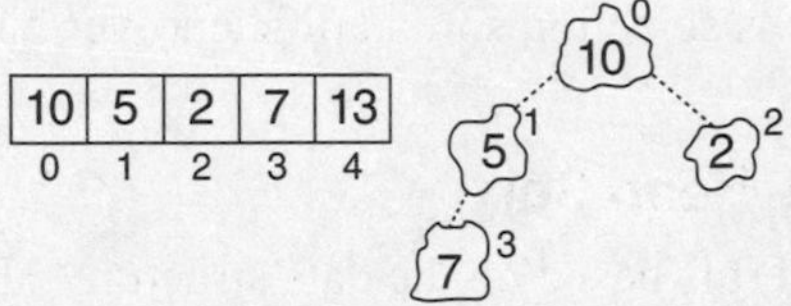

heapify(0) neglecting 13 induces heapify(1)

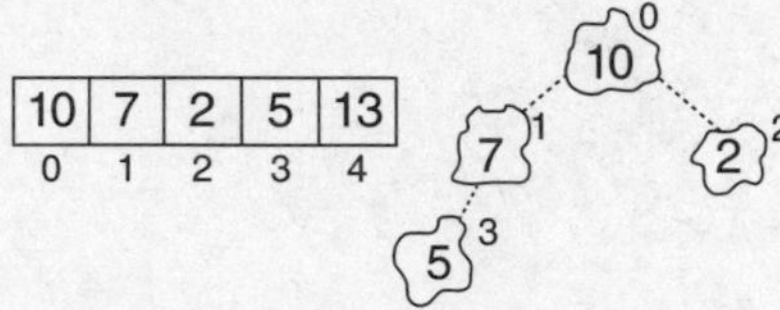

heapify(1) neglecting 13

swap list[3] and list[0]
This moves the second biggest number to penultimate position.

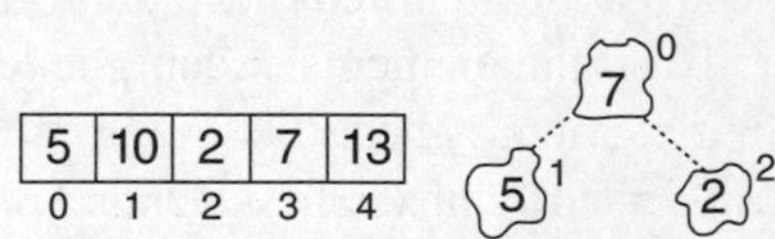

heapify(0) neglecting 10, 13

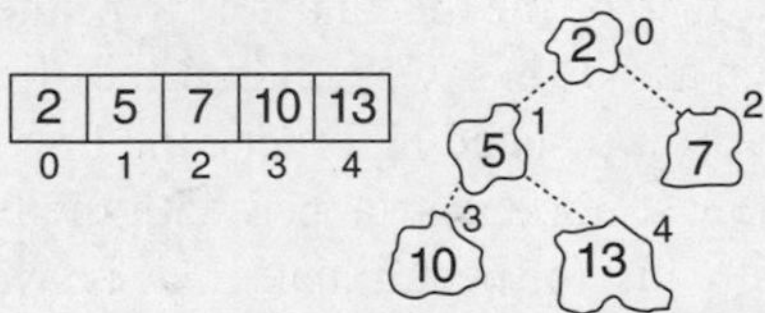

swap list[2] and list[0]

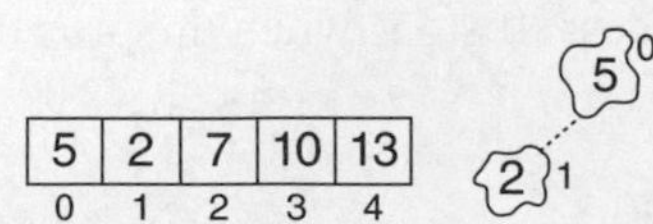

heapify(0) neglecting 7, 10, 13

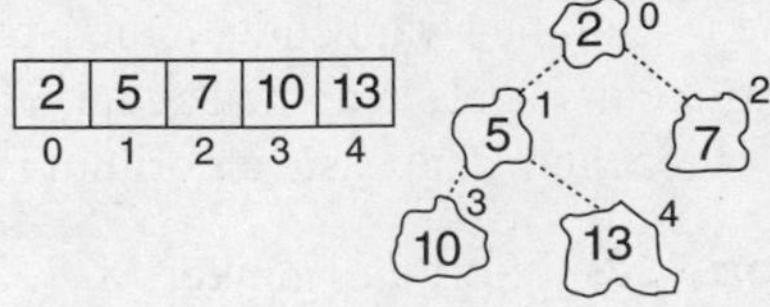

swap list[0] and list[1] – output

Figure 12.5 Illustration of heap sort

Pseudocode 12.3

```
n=length(list)
for i in n/2-1 to 0
Do,
    heapify(list,n,i)
for i in n-1 to 0
Do,
    swap 'i'th element with the first element
    if i!=1
    then,
        Heapify(list,i,0)

Heapify(list,n,i):
    max=i
    left,right=2*i+1,2*i+2
    if list[left]>list[max]
    then,
        max=left
    if list[right]>list[max]
    then,
        max=right
    if max has been updated
    then,
        swap list[i] and list[max]
    recursive call for max index
```

Implementation

As the heap is a complete binary tree, it has [n/2 + 1] leaves and [n/2 – 1] inner nodes. All these nodes are heapified, one followed by other. Then, swapping from the last node begins using a simple loop from 'n-1' to '1' (refer to Python code 12.4).

Python code 12.4

```
def Heap_Sort(items):

    #The heapify function used internally
    def Heapify(items, heap_size, idx):

        max_index = idx
        # Recall that in a max-heap, largest element is in the root index
        left_child = (2 * idx) + 1
        right_child = (2 * idx) + 2

        # If the left child of the root is a valid index, and the element is greater than the
        # current largest element, then update the largest element
```

(*contd*)

(*contd*)

```
        if left_child < heap_size and items[left_child] > items[max_index]:
            max_index = left_child

        # Do the same for the right child of the root
        if right_child < heap_size and items[right_child] > items[max_index]:
            max_index = right_child

        # If the largest element is no longer the root element, swap them
        if max_index != idx:
            items[idx], items[max_index] = items[max_index], items[idx]
            # Heapify the new root element to ensure it's the largest
            Heapify(items, heap_size, max_index)

    n = len(items)

    # Create a Max Heap from the list
    # The 2nd argument of range means we stop at the element before -1 i.e. the first element of
    # the list.
    # The 3rd argument of range means we iterate backwards, reducing the count of i by 1
    for i in range(n // 2, -1, -1):
        Heapify(items, n, i)

    # Move the root of the max heap to the end of
    for i in range(n - 1, 0, -1):
        items[i], items[0] = items[0], items[i]
        Heapify(items, i, 0)
```

Complexity Analysis

Its worst case complexity is 'O(n log n)'. This is because it has a tree structure. The height of a binary tree is 'log n'. So, for any operation, there will be at most 'log n' swaps. In total, for 'n' elements, it gives 'n log n'. Even the average case complexities will be 'O(n log n)'. However, the best case complexity is 'O(n)'. When the elements are already sorted, there is no action in heapify operation, thus bringing down the complexity to 'O(n)'. The auxiliary space complexity of heap sort is also 'O(1)' as it uses a temp just for swapping.

 **Food for Brain**

Can a heap be built with elements of different types? How to fix the criteria for maintaining it?

12.5 INSERTION SORT

Selection sort is more efficient for smaller lists as it uses in-place swaps. The main advantage of selection sort is that it does not use an auxiliary space. Selection sort performs well only when the list is completely random. When the list is semi-sorted or mostly sorted, then selection sort will have many unwanted swaps. Thus a new type of sorting algorithm, insertion sort, was designed to be more efficient when the elements in a list are in a nearly sorted order. Insertion sort is a type of sort in which the appropriate element will be inserted in its position rather than swapping. However, here, the following elements must be moved which is tedious in cases when the input is huge. It has two main types – simple insertion sort and shell sort. Simple insertion just finds the minimum or maximum number in every iteration and inserts it in appropriate index. Shell sort is a special form of insertion sort, which tries to reduce the number of shifts. Simple insertion is an in-place sort, where the sorting process happens within the same original list of elements itself.

12.5.1 Simple Insertion Sort

This sort is modelled after playing cards. When a player holds a set of cards, they wish to have it in sorted order (Note: Recollect the way cards are played). The way of sorting is selecting the minimal card and inserting it into the first position. Then, picking the second minimum card and inserting it in position 2. This continues until the entire lot is sorted. As the sort is modelled after the same mechanism, it is named as insertion sort. As the name suggests, it inserts the number at the appropriate index. Figure 12.6 shows an example of insertion in a playing card.

Figure 12.6 Insertion in playing cards

Working

In the first iteration, the minimum element is found. Then, it is to be inserted at index '0'. Insertion is done by moving all the elements until the index of the selected minimum is moved to the right by '1' and then the minimum is placed at index '0'. Then, in the next iteration, the minimum element is selected excluding the element at index '0'. Now, all the elements from index '1' to the index of the element selected are moved to the right by '1'. Then, the number is placed at index '1'. This continues until the entire list is sorted. The basic algorithm is shown in Pseudocode 12.4.

Question 12.4 Sort the numbers 10, 4, 8, 5, 7 using Insertion Sort.

Solution: The step-by-step process is shown in Figure 12.7.

Input

Iteration 1
Smallest element '4' moves to 1st position

Iteration 2
'5' moves to 2nd position

Iteration 3
'7' moves to 3rd position

Iteration 4
'8' moves to 4th position

Figure 12.7 Illustration of insertion sort

Pseudocode 12.4

```
n=length(list)
for i in 0 to n
Do,
    min index=i
    for j in i to n
    Do,
        if list[min index]> list[j]
        then,
            min index = j
    insert list[ min index ] into 'i'th position of list
```

Implementation

In a list for every 'i^th^' iteration, the first 'i' elements will be skipped and the minimum of the remaining elements is selected. The element and its index are kept in a temporary variable. All the elements from 'i' to the index selected is moved right by '1'. Then, the selected element is placed in index 'i' and the next iteration proceeds. The implementation is shown in Python code 12.5.

Python code 12.5

```
def Insertion_Sort(items):
    n=len(items)
    for i in range(n):
        m_ind=i
        for j in range(i,n):
            if(items[m_ind] > items[j]):
                m_ind = j
        Insert_element(items, i, m_ind)
def Insert_element (items,starti,endi):
    min = items[endi]
    i=endi
    while(i>starti):
        items[i] = items[i-1]
        i-=1
    items[starti] = min
```

Complexity Analysis

The total order is '$O(n^2)$' as there are 'n - 1' outer iterations with 'i' inner iterations. Summing up to '(n-1)n' giving n^2 as order, that is, 'n-1' comparisons and 'i' swaps in each iterations. However, when the list is sorted, there will not be any shifts in the inner list. So, the best case complexity is 'O(n)', but the average case complexity still remains '$O(n^2)$'. Even here, the auxiliary space complexity is 'O(1)', as it uses only some temporary variables.

 **Food for Brain**

What will be the maximum number of iterations and swaps in insertion sort?

12.5.2 Shell Sort

Shell sort is a clever sorting algorithm based on insertion sort. It follows an intelligent pattern to reduce the number of shifts in the insertion algorithm, which was an overhead for longer lists. The algorithm sub-divides the list and sorts it. The sub-division size is continuously increased and finally the full list is considered as a single division and normal insertion sort is performed.

Working

The division concept is based on 'gaps'. The logical sub-divisions are based on this gap. If the gap is '4', sub-division '1' will be { a[0], a[3], a[6],... }. The number of elements in the sub-division will be increasing and finally the entire list will be considered as a whole when the gap becomes '1'. In the subdivision, insertion sort is done to make them in order. If an element is in wrong place, it will be inserted in the appropriate position. Finally, when the whole list is considered, insertion sort is done. Finding the appropriate gap is the most important factor. There are many sequences of gap that can be followed. One primary factor in selecting the gap sequence is that it should end with '1'. If the last gap is not '1', then the whole list will not be considered, and thereby the list will not be sorted. A suggested way is assuming the initial gap is length/2. The gap is continuously divided by '2' until it becomes '1'. After 'gap' sorting, the list is said to be 'gap-sorted'. Say, the gap is '4', then the list is '4-sorted'. The elements at {a[0], a[3], a[6],....} will be in order. Similarly, elements at {a[1], a[4], a[7]....} will be sorted. Thus, when the gap becomes '1', the list becomes '1-sorted', which means 'fully sorted'. The basic algorithm is shown in Pseudocode 12.5.

Question 12.5 Sort the numbers 10, 4, 8, 5, 7 using Shell Sort.

Solution: The step-by-step process is shown in Figure 12.8.

Input

Sub-division by interval 2

Insertion sort in sub-division 1

Insertion sort in sub-division 1

(*contd*)

(*contd*)

Insertion sort in sub-division 2

Sub-division by interval 1 (2-sorted)

Insertion sort in 2-sorted list

Insertion sort in 2-sorted list

Figure 12.8 Step-by-step illustration of shell sort

Pseudocode 12.5

```
n=length(list)
for gap in n/2 to 0
Do,
    for i in 0 to gap
    Do,
        for elements in gap intervals, if it is less than previous number
        Do,
            swap the numbers
    gap = gap/2
```

Implementation

This is implemented with three nested loops in place (as shown in Python code 12.6). The outer loop is to determine the gap value. The middle loop runs from the gap to the end indices. The inner loop starts from the index of the middle loop and moves to elements before it at intervals of 'gap'. So, for any gap value, the inner loop runs in reverse order. The elements are moved forward by 'gap' intervals and the appropriate number is inserted. Say the gap is '4', then a number (a[0]) will be moved to an index which is '4th' from it, that is (a[3]), leaving the elements in the middle unchanged. Thus, it visualizes shifting in 'gap' sub-division.

Python code 12.6

```
def Shell_Sort(items):
    gap = len(items) // 2                          # Initialize the Gap
    while gap > 0:
        for start_position in range(gap):          # Loop over the sublist

            # Using the gap, insertion sort the items at respective indices
```

(*contd*)

(*contd*)

```
        for i in range(start_position + gap, len(items), gap):
            current = items[i]                  # Store the element at index position in
                                                # current
            pos = i                             # Store the index position in pos
            while pos >= gap and items[pos - gap] > items[pos]:
                items[pos] = items[pos - gap]   # Move the item
                pos = pos - gap
                items[pos] = current
    gap = gap // 2
```

Complexity Analysis

The worst case complexity of total working is 'O(n $\log^2$ n)'. Log^2 results due to continuous divisions. As the computation is on overlapping sub-lists, it gives (log n * log n). The complexity also depends on the 'gap'. The above complexity holds only for the best gap. If the 'gap' is worst, it is as good as normal insertion sort. So, worst case complexity for worst gap is 'O(n^2)'. Depending on the 'gap', the average case complexity differs. Still, the best case complexity is constantly 'O(n log n)', irrespective of the 'gap'. The auxiliary space complexity in here is 'O(1)'. It is to be noted that for all the above algorithms, the auxiliary space is 'O(1)' as it sorts the lists in their actual space itself.

When will shell sort work best over insertion sort and when will it work just like insertion sort?

12.6 DIVIDE AND CONQUER

'Divide and conquer' is a strategy where the given data is divided into sub parts, sorted, and merged together. It is preferred because of its ability to independently sort the sub divisions, making full use of the available hardware. These algorithms are mostly tweaked to form solutions of problems other than sorting. The two main divide and conquer algorithms are merge sort and quick sort.

12.6.1 Merge Sort

Merge sort is a basic divide and conquer sorting algorithm. It divides the given set into sub-divisions. The divisions continue until the sub-division has only one element. Then, the divisions are merged one by one in sorted order. As the elements are merged in sorted order, it is named as merge sort. It is also to be noted that the computation while merging and diving is straight forward. Figure 12.9 shows a sketch of merge sort.

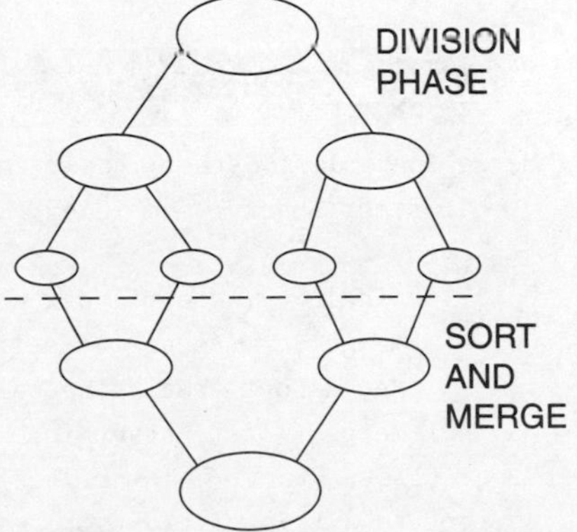

Figure 12.9 Merge sort sketch

Working

The entire working is divided into two phases. The first phase is the dividing phase, in which the elements are divided into subsets. Every subset will be half the length of its parent. This procedure continues until each sub-set has only one element. Then, the conquer phase starts. In this phase, every two elements will be merged into a new subset in sorted order. Subsequently, pairs of the new subsets formed will be merged in sorted order again. This continues until it forms one full, sorted set. The merging process is performed using the following guidelines:

1. The first elements of both sub divisions are compared. The minimum of the two is selected and placed at first position of the newly created sub division.
2. Then, the second element of the sub division from which the first element was taken and the first element of the other sub division is considered. The same procedure continues till either of the sub division ends.
3. The remaining elements of the other sub division are then added in order.

The basic algorithm is shown in Pseudocode 12.6.

Question 12.6 Sort the numbers 5, 7, 2, 13, 10 using Merge Sort.

Solution: The step-by-step process is shown in Figure 12.10.

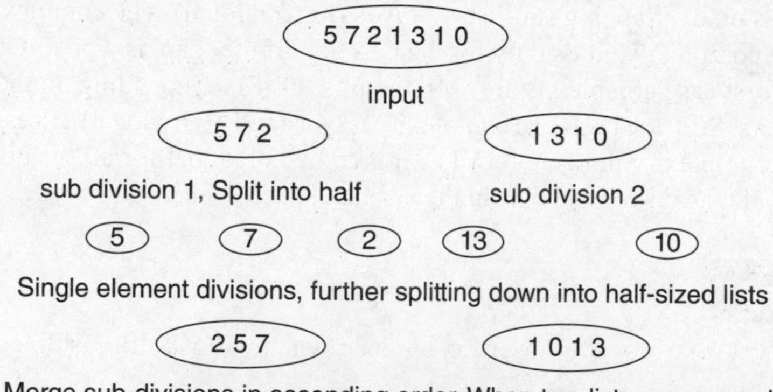

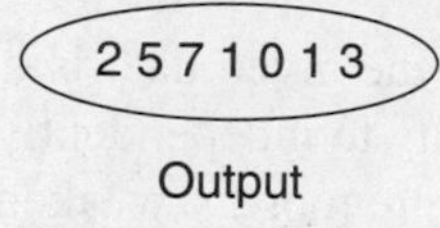

Figure 12.10 Merge sort

Pseudocode 12.6

```
Merge_Sort (list, start_index, end_index)
    if start_index < end_index
    then,
        middle = ( start_index + end_index ) / 2
        Merge_Sort recursive call start_index to middle
        Merge_Sort  recursive call middle to end_index
        Merge ( list, start_index, end_index, middle )
Merge (list, start, end, middle )
    create a temp list of size end - start
    i = start
    k = 0
    j = middle + 1
    while i <= middle and j <= end
```

(contd)

(*contd*)

```
Do,
    if list[ i ] < list[ j ]
    then,
        place list[ i ] at temp[ k ]
        increment k and i
    else,
        place list[ j ] at temp[ k ]
        increment k and j
while i<= middle
Do,
    place list[ i ] at temp[ k ]
    increment k and i
while j <= end
Do,
    place list[ j ] at temp[ k ]
    increment k and j
for i in start to k + start
Do,
    Update the input list using temp as list[ i ]=temp[i - start]
```

Implementation

Division is not physically done but logically achieved by passing the entire list with a start and end index. The division phase is achieved using recursion. The list is passed as an argument to the function along with its size. In every recursive call, the size of the list to be passed alone is divided into smaller subparts varying the start and end index arguments. Inside the function the merge phase will be called after the recursive call of the two sub divisions, thus it will be merged after division in the reverse order. Merging is done with three separate loops. The motto is grouping the lists passed into a single list. The arguments will be the list itself, and the start, end and middle index. So, logically the two lists will be the 'start to middle' and 'middle to end'. A new empty list is generated to store the merged result and later the original list is updated. The elements at first index and middle index +1 are considered as first elements of the two logical lists. The same procedure continues with two pointers at different positions of the same list. The minimum element selected at each comparison is inserted into the new created list. The comparison stops when the first pointer reaches the middle or the second pointer reaches the end. If the first pointer reaches the middle, then the remaining elements between the second pointer and end are added in order into the new list. However, if the second pointer reaches the end, all the elements between the first pointer and middle index are added in order into the list. Finally, the list is copied into the original list, from starting index to ending index as shown in Python code 12.7.

Python code 12.7

```
def Merge_Sort(items):

    def Merge(items, start_index, middle, end_index):
        temp = [0] * (end_index - start_index + 1)
        #Temporary list to stored to merged sorted list
```

(*contd*)

(*contd*)

```
        i = start_index
        j = middle+1
        k = 0
        while i <= middle and j <= end_index :
            if items[i] <= items[j]:
                temp[k] = items[i]
                i += 1
            else:
                temp[k] = items[j]
                j += 1
            k += 1
        while i <= middle:
            temp[k] = items[i]
            i += 1
            k += 1
        while j <= end_index:
            temp[k] = items[j]
            j += 1
            k += 1
        for i in range (0,len(temp)):
            items[i+start_index]=temp[i]
            #Updating the original list's specific interval with the sorted list

    #Utility function used inside mergesort
    def _Merge_Sort(items,start_index,end_index):
        if start_index < end_index:
            middle = int((end_index+start_index)/2)
            #Divide phase
            _Merge_Sort(items, start_index, middle)
            _Merge_Sort(items, middle+1, end_index)
            #Conquer phase after those recursions complete
            Merge(items, start_index, middle, end_index)

    _Merge_Sort(items,0,len(items)-1)
```

The recursive implementation of this algorithm is shared in Python code 12.8. In this approach, the list is not logically divided by sending the sub-division indexes. Instead, the list is physically divided into two in the merge call.

Python code 12.8

```
def Merge_Sort(items):
    def Merge(left, right):
        result = []
        while left and right:                                  # If both lists aren't empty
```

(*contd*)

(*contd*)

```
            result.append((left if left[0] <= right[0] else right).pop(0))
        return result + left + right
    if len(items) <= 1:
        return items
    mid = len(items) // 2    # Splitting the list at the mid point
    # Recursive merge to sort and merge sublists split at mid point
    return Merge(Merge_Sort(items[:mid]), Merge_Sort(items[mid:]))
```

Complexity Analysis

The total complexity of this sort is 'O(n log n)'. With every recursion, the partition is divided by '2', so there are 'log n' divisions and every element goes through at most 'n' comparisons. All the three cases stick to the same complexity. The auxiliary space used in here is 'O(n log n)'. In every call of the merge function, a temporary list of size 'end – start + 1' is created. Mathematically, it creates a list of size 'n' in the outermost recursion of merge. Then, two lists of size 'n/2' in second recursion, four lists of size 'n/4' in the next corresponding recursion, and so on. So, at the end of sort, a total of 'n' spaces are used additionally in merging in every recursion. Since there are a total of 'log n' recursions, the auxiliary space complexity is 'O(n log n)'. This can be reduced using an efficient algorithm. A temporary list must be passed to the 'merge' in the call itself and will be used in every inner merge. So, the temporary list created in every call can be skipped and this list can be used instead. Thus, auxiliary space can be brought down to 'O(n)'. That algorithm is left for the readers to explore.

12.6.2 Quick Sort

Quick sort is another divide and conquer algorithm used to sort elements. It divides the set into sub-divisions continuously until each sub-division has only one element, but this division is not straight. It is based on a pivot that is selected from the current sub-division. Later, all the sub-divisions are merged in pairs. Figure 12.11 shows a sketch of quick sort.

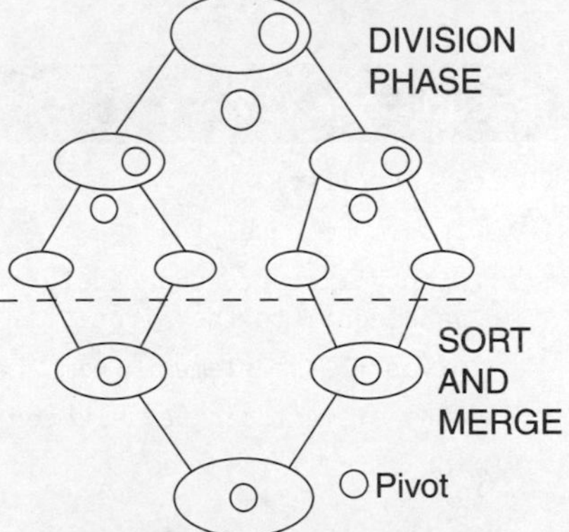

Figure 12.11 Quick sort – A diagrammatic representation

Working

The algorithm is based on portioning the given list. The pivot can be selected from the list itself. There are multiple ways of selecting the pivot. It can be the last, middle, or first number. Even the pivot can be taken as average of all the elements of the given list, but it needs additional overhead. All the elements lesser than the pivot will be placed in a list, whereas all the elements greater than the pivot will be placed in a different list. The pivots will be kept in a third list. All the three lists (partitions) are quick sorted separately and then concatenated. The concatenation will be in order of partition with elements less than the pivot, with all the pivots, and with elements greater than the pivot. The partitioning stops when each partition has only one element. The basic algorithm is shown in Pseudocode 12.7.

Question 12.7 Sort the numbers 5, 7, 2, 13, and 10 using Quick Sort.

Solution: The step-by-step illustration is shown in Figure 12.12.

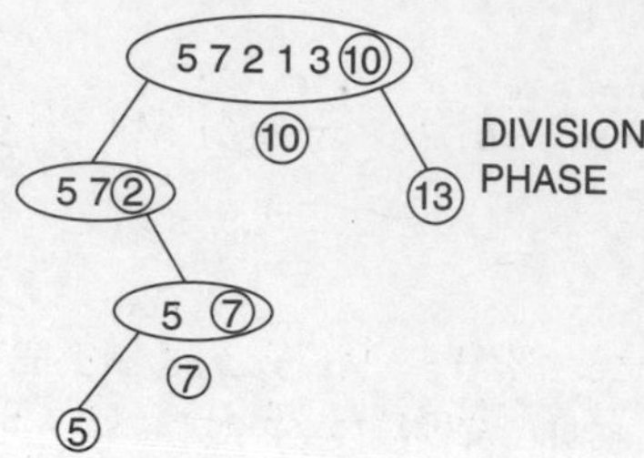

At every node, the median element is taken as pivot. In the first lot, '10' is the median and taken as pivot. Based on the median, all the elements less than the pivot are placed in one group and all the elements greater than the pivot are placed in the second group. This continues down and finally each element is in a separate list.

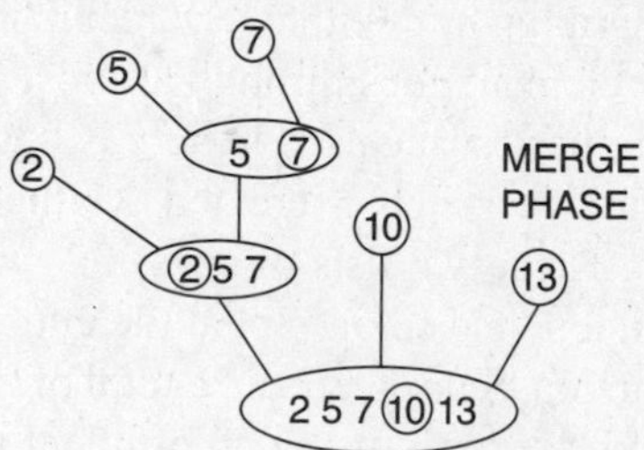

While merging, it starts with all the individual elements. At each step, the elements are arranged in the required order. So in first step of merging it is only two elements, the pivot and the single element which are placed in ascending order while merging. Now, this is merged along with the pivot and other sub-set in the same order. This continues down till all the elements are merged into one list.

Figure 12.12 An illustration of quick sort through an example

Pseudocode 12.7

```
Quick_Sort(list)
    less,more,equal=[ ]
    #Empty lists to separately store the elements less than the pivot, greater than the pivot
    #and equal to the pivot.
    pivot = last element from the list
    #Any element can be selected as pivot
    for X in list
    Do,
        if x <= pivot
        then,
            add x into less[ ]
        else if x > pivot
        then,
            add x into more[ ]
        else,
            add x into equal[ ]
    return concat(Quick_Sort(less),Quick_Sort(more))
```

Implementation

The implementation uses additional space which is waste. So, the portioning is based on two popular schemes. These schemes do not waste the extra space. Hence, they are referred to as in-place quick sort.

Lomuto Scheme First is the very popular Lomuto partition scheme. It chooses the last element as pivot for any partition. The partition is traversed from the start to end. Every time an element less than the pivot is identified, it gets swapped with the elements at the beginning. The index of the last element inserted is kept track of, so when next small element is to be swapped it comes into the next index. Once all the elements smaller than the pivot are placed in the beginning, the pivot gets swapped with the first element that is greater than the pivot. Thus, the elements smaller than the pivot get placed in the beginning. Then, the pivot is present in the middle which is followed by elements greater than it. Thus in every partition the numbers are distributed in the order - lesser elements < pivot < greater elements. Down the line when the partitioning is complete the elements can be directly merged in order of lesser elements, pivot followed by greater elements without any re-arranging. All the sorting happens while placing the pivots, in the divide phase making the conquer phase straight forward. The implementation is presented in Python code 12.9.

Python code 12.9

```
def Quick_Sort(items):

    #Lomuto Scheme of partition
    def Partition (items,start_index,end_index):
        pivot = items[ end_index ]                  #Last element is fixed as pivot
        small_index = (start_index - 1)
        #The index to mark smaller elements for swapping towards the beginning and for finally
        #placing the pivot
        for j in range(start_index,end_index):
            if (items[ j ] <= pivot):               #When the element is less than pivot
                small_index += 1                    #Increment the index to next position and then
                                                    #swap the lesser number
                items[ j ], items[ small_index ] = items[ small_index ], items[ j ]
        #After all the smaller numbers are placed in the beginning, the small_index+1 will be
        #pointing to the first element that is greater than the pivot.
        #Swap with pivot to bring pivot in the middle
        items[ end_index ], items[ small_index + 1 ]=items[ small_index + 1 ], items[ end_index ]
        return ( small_index + 1 )

    #Internal utility function
    def _Quick_Sort(items,start_index,end_index):
        if (start_index < end_index):
            pivot_index = Partition(items, start_index, end_index)
            #Divide phase
            _Quick_Sort(items, start_index, pivot_index - 1)
            _Quick_Sort(items, pivot_index + 1, end_index)
            #After the two recursions complete and come back it is merged and that is the
            #conquer phase
            #This is in-place quick sort as the process happens inside the original list

    items=_Quick_Sort(items,0,len(items)-1)
```

Question 12.8 Sort the numbers 5, 7, 2, 13, 10 using Quick Sort's Lomuto scheme.

Solution: The step-by-step process is shown in Figure 12.13.

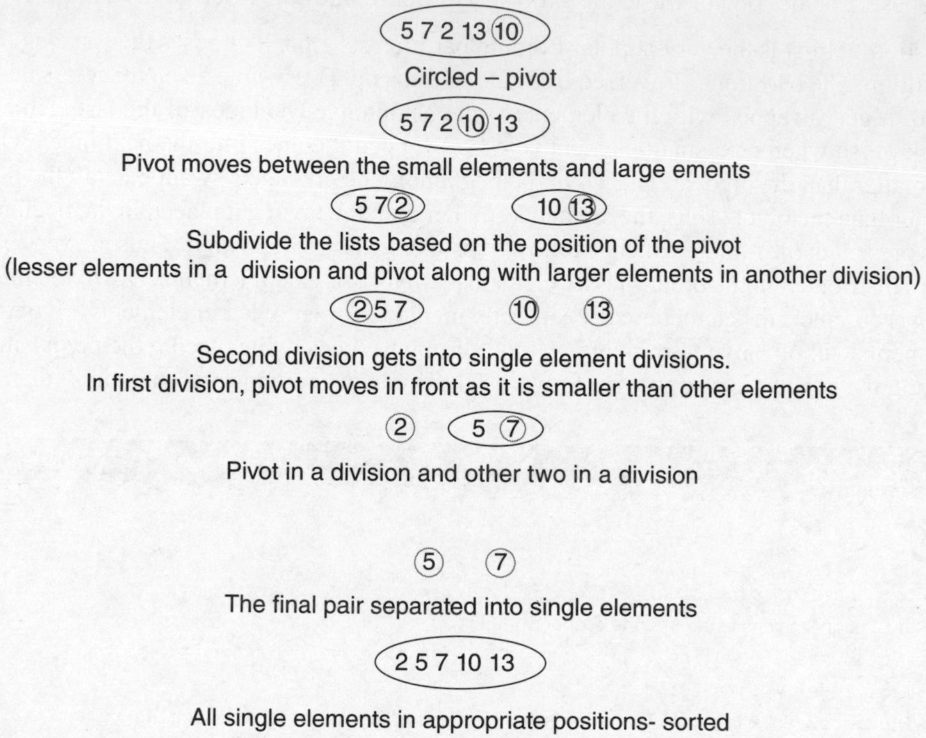

5 7 2 13 (10)

Circled – pivot

5 7 2 (10) 13

Pivot moves between the small elements and large ements

5 7 (2)   10 (13)

Subdivide the lists based on the position of the pivot
(lesser elements in a division and pivot along with larger elements in another division)

(2) 5 7   (10)   (13)

Second division gets into single element divisions.
In first division, pivot moves in front as it is smaller than other elements

(2)   5 (7)

Pivot in a division and other two in a division

(5)   (7)

The final pair separated into single elements

2 5 7 10 13

All single elements in appropriate positions- sorted

Figure 12.13 Lomuto partition

Hoare Partition Scheme Another scheme is Hoare partition scheme. Initially, two pointers will be placed at the two extremes of the list. Both will move towards each other until the inversion pair is identified. An inversion pair is one element less than the pivot and another element greater than the pivot. Here, the pivot is preferably the first element. The algorithm stops when the two pointers meet. The point where they meet acts as the partition index (middle index). It is more efficient than the Lomuto scheme. Implementation is presented in Python code 12.10.

Python code 12.10

```
def Quick_Sort(items):

    #Hoare Scheme of partition
    def Partition(items, start, end):
        pivot = items[start]          #First element is made the pivot
        i = start-1
        j = end+1
        #Loop to swap all the mismatch pairs
        while True:
            i += 1
```

(contd)

(*contd*)

```
        while items[i] < pivot:
            i += 1       #Incremenet 'i' till an element greater than pivot is found
        j -= 1
        while items[j] > pivot:
            j -= 1       #Decrement 'j' till an element lesser than pivot is found
        if i >= j:
            return j
        # element at i > greater than pivot > element at j - so swap them
        items[i], items[j] = items[j], items[i]

#Internal utility function
def _Quick_Sort(items,start_index,end_index):
    if (start_index < end_index):
        pivot_index = Partition(items, start_index, end_index)
        #Divide phase
        _Quick_Sort(items, start_index, pivot_index)
        _Quick_Sort(items, pivot_index + 1, end_index)
        #After the two recursions complete and come back it is merged and that is the
        #conquer phase
        #This is in-place quick sort as the process happens inside the original list

items=_Quick_Sort(items, 0, len(items)-1)
```

Question 12.9 Sort the numbers 5, 7, 2, 13, and 10 using Quick Sort's Hoare scheme.

Solution: The step-by-step process is shown in Figure 12.14.

Start with the first element. With this, the left and right element is fixed such that one is lesser than the considered element. Light - left and Dark - Right

2 7 5 13 10

Swap left and right and move left and right by 1 index
(here, left remains unchanged as it is not moved)

2 7 5 13 10

Subdivisions – '0' to right, left to end.

5 7 13 10

Swap the left and right of the subdivision
(Left and right cross here)

5 7 13 10

Subdivisions are called
(Left and right overlapped in subdivision, no swap possible)

(*contd*)

(*contd*)

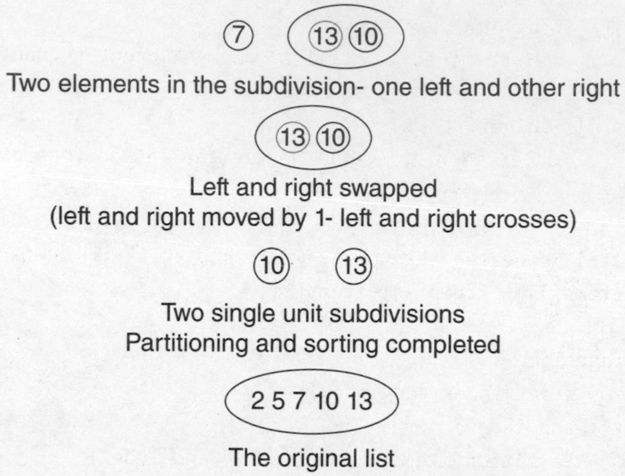

Two elements in the subdivision- one left and other right

Left and right swapped
(left and right moved by 1- left and right crosses)

Two single unit subdivisions
Partitioning and sorting completed

2 5 7 10 13

The original list

Figure 12.14 Hoare scheme

Both the above schemes sort the elements within the same list without extracting the partitions. This logically division and merging is called as 'In-place Quick Sort' as the elements are sorted in the native list itself. When auxiliary space can be used, the program can be made much simpler using Python's utilities. The below implementation (Python code 12.11) shows physically extracting the partitions and creating the sorted list in new space. The code is simpler, but has its own drawbacks of using more auxiliary space.

Python code 12.11

```
def QuickSort(items):
    if len(items) <= 1: return items
    start, pivot, end = Partition(items)
    return Quick_Sort(start) + [pivot] + Quick_Sort(end)
def Partition(items):
    pivot, items = items[0], items[1:]
    start = [x for x in items if x <= pivot]
    end = [x for x in items if x > pivot]
    return start, pivot, end
```

Complexity Analysis

The worst case complexity is when the given list is already sorted. The complexity will be 'O(n^2)'. The best case complexity will be 'O(n log n)'. This is because the list is continuously divided into two and there can be atmost 'n' comparisons for an element. Hence, the average case complexity also goes by 'O(n log n)'. So when the given list is sorted, merge sort must be preferred over quick sort. One thing to be noted in here is unlike merge sort, no additional space is used in here. The auxiliary space complexity in both schemes of quick sort is 'O(1)'. The auxiliary space complexity computation of the physically partitioning quick sort code (Python code 12.11) is left for the users to explore.

Can divide and conquer algorithm be used for problems other than sorting?

12.7 DISTRIBUTED SORT

In this technique, the input is divided and distributed across different structures based on some criteria and all the structures are sorted separately. This also induces parallel processing. There are three main distributed sorts—Bucket sort, Counting sort, and Radix sort.

12.7.1 Bucket Sort

It is the direct distribution sorting algorithm. The mechanism has fixed number of buckets, each with a fixed range. The elements falling under the range will be dropped into the particular bucket and sorted. Hence, it is named as bucket sort. This is also called as bin sort. Figure 12.15 shows the scenario of bucket sort.

Figure 12.15 A scenario of sorting elements using buckets

Working

The entire process is based on buckets. The number of buckets is initially fixed. It may also be determined based on the input for better efficiency. Once the number of buckets is fixed, the range for each bucket is assigned. The elements are distributed across the buckets based on the range in which they fall into. Then, all the elements inside every bucket are sorted using any other simple sort like bubble, selection, or insertion. Finally, the contents of all the buckets are appended into a single list which is the required output.

Question 12.10 Sort the numbers 5, 7, 2, 13, and 10 using Bucket Sort.

Solution: The step-by-step process is shown in Figure 12.16.

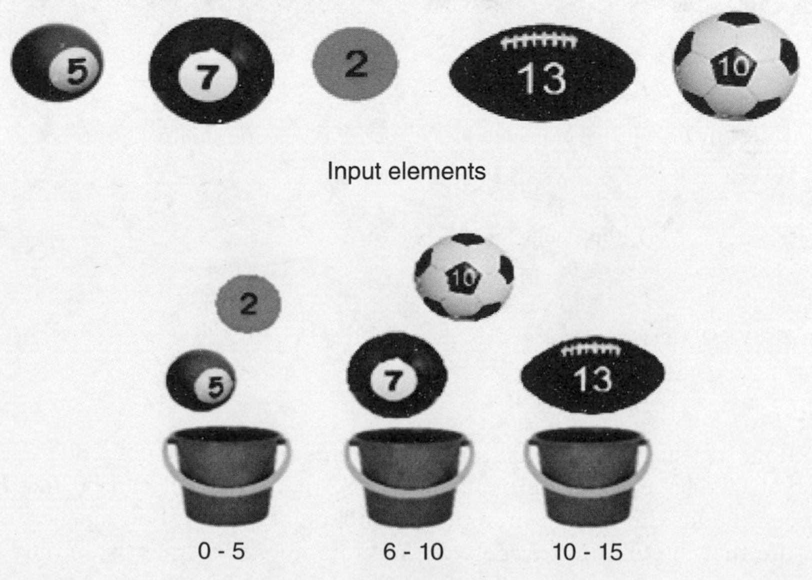

(*contd*)

(*contd*)

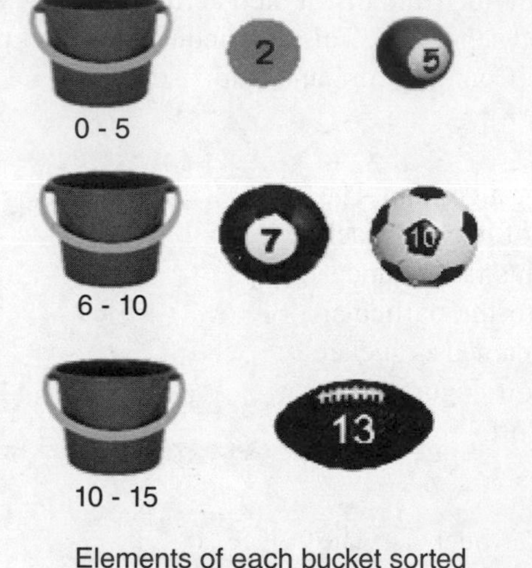

Elements of each bucket sorted

Sorted contents concatenated

Figure 12.16 Bucket sorting

The implementation of the above solution is presented in Pseudocode 12.8.

Pseudocode 12.8

```
create 'n' buckets
max = maximum of the list
min = minimum of the list
range = ceil of max-min/n
for i in list
Do,
    bucket_index = (i - min) mod range
    place i into bucket[ bucket_index ]
sort all the buckets
place every element from every bucket into the output list in order
```

Implementation

For implementation, 'n' buckets are fixed for 'n' elements (refer to Python code 12.12). So, in best case, every bucket will have only one element. Range of the bucket can be fixed by finding the difference between the maximum and minimum numbers, and then dividing the difference by 'n'. We also make sure that the first bucket gets the minimum most element so empty buckets can be skipped and resources can be controlled. The buckets are visualized as a single dimensional list. So, for sorting each bucket, the corresponding list is sorted. Here, the lists are sorted using a built-in sorting function in Python. Finally, a nested loop is used to concatenate the contents of all the buckets.

Implementation of example question 12.10 where the bucket range is fixed based on the input range is shown in Figure 12.17.

Only the distribution changes, the remaining processes are followed without any change and the final result is achieved. This change is done to reduce the overhead of sorting the contents of each bucket.

Figure 12.17 Bucket sorting with dynamic bucket range

Python code 12.12

```
def Bucket_Sort(items):
    n=len(items)
    buckets = [[] for x in range(n)]
    #'n' buckets for 'n' elements
    maxi,mini = max(items),min(items)
    #built in function for maximum & minimum in a list
    rg = (maxi-mini)/n + 1
    #range of buckets based on extremes from the list
    for i in range (n):
        b_ind = (items[ i ] - mini)//rg
        #bucket index based on size
        buckets [ int(b_ind) ].append( items[ i ] )
    for i in range(n):
        buckets [ i ].sort()
        #Built-in function to sort a list
    sorted_list=[]
    for i in buckets:
        for j in i:
            sorted_list.append(j)
    return sorted_list
```

Complexity Analysis

This is the most interesting segment of bucket sort. It has a worst case complexity of 'O(n)'. It is mainly because the only big process is distribution. Inside the buckets, the number of elements is negligibly small. So, its sorting complexity goes unnoticed. The issue here is that it uses a large additional space. It has an auxiliary space complexity of 'O(n)'. The best and average cases also stick to 'O(n)'. In the best case, no sorting is required for any bucket. This is possible only when every bucket has only one element. The worst case is subjected to change, based on the number and range of the buckets. If the range of buckets is fixed directly without finding the difference between the maximum and minimum elements, say every bucket will have a range of '10', then there is a possibility that all the elements fall under the same bucket. Then, the complexity worsens to 'O(n^2)'.

Looking into the generalized complexities, it is 'O(n + k)', where 'n' is the number of elements and 'k' is the number of buckets, each sorted in 'O(1)'. In this implementation, it is 'n' elements and 'n' buckets, thus summing to '2n', which is 'O(n)'. When the number of buckets is decreased, the complexity of sorting the buckets increases. So, the complexity is then determined by the buckets. This results in 'O(n^2)' as explained previously. When the auxiliary space used is taken into consideration, there are 'k' buckets created and the list elements are distributed equally in the same. So, an auxiliary space of 'O(n)' is used.

Variants of Bucket Sort

The same bucket sort can be implemented in a different way. The number of buckets can be made very large, say the number of buckets is the largest number in the list. Every bucket gets an index from 0 to the maximum number and is initialized with a count '0'. Then, for any element the count of bucket with the same index is incremented. Finally, a loop traverses through all the buckets. For every bucket, if the count is greater than '0', the corresponding index is duplicated based on the count of the bucket and inserted into the original list. Some more variants of bucket sort are shared below.

Generic Bucket Sort The sort implemented here is the generic bucket sort. In normal bucket sort, the range of the bucket is not fixed based on the input and is easy to implement, but has problems in complexity. However, to stick to the complexity of 'O(n)', the range is fixed by dividing the total range of the input with its length. Hence, the variation is termed as generic bucket sort.

Proxmap Sort It divides the list of keys into sub lists. These sub lists are formed using the 'map & key' function, which preserves a partial ordering. The sub lists are sorted using insertion sort. Finally, when all the sub lists are sorted, the whole list gets sorted. The main difference in proxmap is with using a map key function to approximately place the element in a sub list.

Postman's Sort It is based on the hierarchical structure of the elements. This structure is described by the set of attributes. This is used by letter sorting machines in post office. In post office, it first sorts domestic and international packages. Then, sorting happens with the following attributes in order: state, territory, destinations office and source office, etc. This is very similar to radix sort. The comparisons are not among the keys, but it is on some 'c' attributes for 'n' elements. So, complexity is 'O(cn)'.

Shuffle Sort It is a special variant of bucket sort. It removes the first 1/8 elements and sorts it recursively. This is placed into a list. Every element of this list acts as an individual bucket and these elements inserted act as referral element of each bucket. The remaining 7/8 elements are distributed into these buckets. An element is inserted into the bucket which has the closest referral element. Then, these buckets are sorted and all bucket contents are concatenated. The factor of 1/8 is an idea to stick to the complexity of 'O(n)'.

Can distributed sort behave like divide and conquer? How is that possible?

12.7.2 Counting Sort

This is a form of distribution algorithm and is not based on comparing numbers with each other. Consider a scenario where a bag with black and red balls is to be sorted. It is known that all black balls are uniform in size and same is the case with all red balls too. So, in here, it is not preferable to compare all the elements with each other. It will be enough if one black and one red ball is compared and the smallest is found among them. For example, if red is smaller, then all red balls should be placed first, followed by all black balls. This sort works with the same mechanism. As the name suggests, it is a sorting algorithm based on counting techniques. Given the input elements, it counts the number of occurrences of each element and sorts them based on the count. As in this case, the number of black balls and red balls is counted initially. After finding the smallest ball, all the balls are put first, followed by all larger balls. Here to make sure no ball is left, the count is mandatory. It has a map like structure to keep note of the count of all the elements within the given input range. This list is preferred when the elements have a lot of duplicates. The scenario is explained in Figure 12.18.

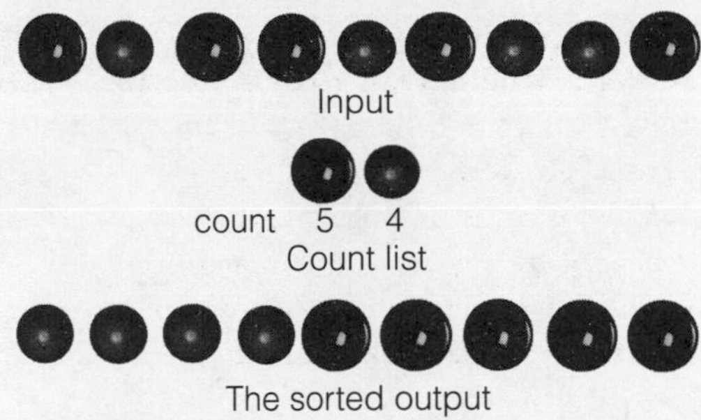

Figure 12.18 Counting sort scenario
are black balls and are red balls

Working

First, a list which can maintain all the elements in the given range is created. The count of occurrence each element in the input list is updated into this list. This is called a count list, which looks like a map structure. If an element does not exist in the given input, its count will be '0'. Then, the count list is modified. Every entry is made the sum of all its preceding entries. A new output list is created. Every element in the input list is placed in the output list at index which is its count value. Then, the value of its count is decremented. Again, the value is placed at the new index which is the new count. The count is decremented again. This continues until the count becomes '0' or the output list already has an element at the same index. There will be no overwriting. Finally, when all the elements of the input have been placed, the output list becomes sorted.

Question 12.11 Sort the numbers 5, 7, 5, 2, 5, 7, 10, 13, 13, and 10 using Counting Sort.

Solution: The step-by-step process is shown in Figure 12.19.

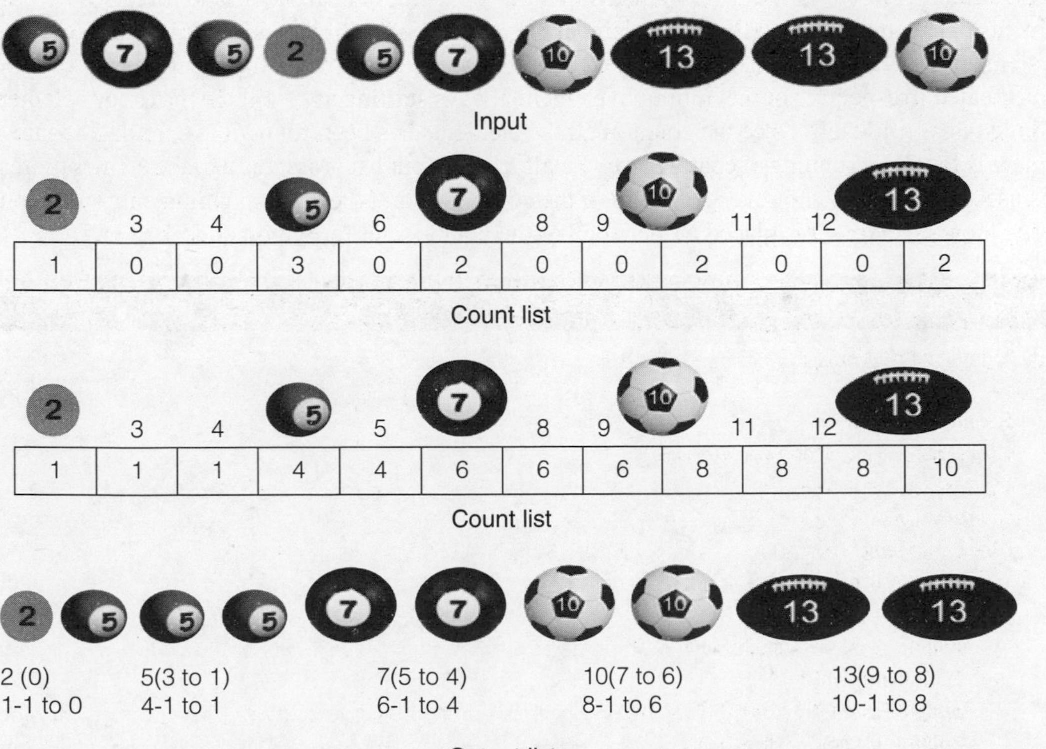

Figure 12.19 An example for Counting sort scenario

Pseudocode 12.9

```
Create output of size n
min = minimum of input list
max = maximum of input list
range = difference of max and min
create a count list of size equal to range
initialize the count_list to 0
for i in 0 to n
Do,
    increment count[ list[ i ] ]
for i in 1 to range
Do,
    find cumulative sum of count[ i ]
for i in 0 to n
Do,
    place list[ i ] at output[ count of list[ i ] ]
    decrement count of list[ i ]
Copy the output list into original list
```

Implementation

Initially, the count list of size equal to the given range is created. If the minimum element is '2' and the maximum element is '7', then the list is of size '6 (7 – 2 + 1)'. Now, a loop traverses across all the elements of the input list and for every element the corresponding index is incremented. Here, the index for element 'i' is 'a[i + min element]' as the count list is created based on the input elements. If the count list is created irrespective of the minimum element always starting at '1' till the maximum element, then the index is 'a[i]' itself. Once the count of all the elements has been found, the cumulative sum of each element is found by running a separate loop. Finally, the output list is created and the elements are placed. This uses nested loops. For every element, if the count != 0 and the corresponding entry at output list is empty, then the element is placed at the index of the count (refer to Python code 12.13).

Python code 12.13

```
def Count_Sort(items):
    n= len(items)
    output = [0] * (n)
    maxi, mini=max(items),min(items)
    rg = maxi-mini + 1
    count = [0] * (rg)
    for i in range(n):
        count[ items[ i ] - mini ] += 1
    for i in range(1,rg):
        count[ i ] += count[ i-1 ]
    for i in range(n):
        output[ count[ items[ i ]- mini ] - 1 ] = items[ i ]
        count[ items[ i ] - mini ] -= 1
    for i in range(n):
        items[ i ] = output[ i ]
```

Complexity Analysis

It uses many individual loops, which are all of complexity 'O(n)'. Only one loop is a nested loop where in inner loops run the count number of times of the outer loop. In the worst case, all the elements are the same, so the inner loop runs for 'n' times, but in that case the outer loop has only one element. So, the complexity cannot cross 'O(n)'. Above all, there is one loop which runs across the count loop. So, the complexity depends on that too. Say the range is 'k', the complexity then is 'O(n + k)'. In best case, when there are 'n' distinct continuous elements, the complexity becomes 'O(n + n)', which is 'O(n)'. With respect to the space, here, a new list of size 'k' is used for maintaining the count. So, auxiliary space is 'O(k)'.

 **Food for Brain**

Implement counting sort using the Counter data structure from Python Collections.

12.7.3 Radix Sort

Radix sort is a distribution based sort and the only sort that does not involve any direct comparison of the element. It clubs the digits as keys and sorts the element based on the key, retaining their input order. From the given list, if an element's key is lesser than any of the keys of the preceding elements, then they are swapped else the order of input is preserved. Consider a scenario of sorting students based on their marks. The mark has three components: annual exam marks, half yearly exam marks, and quarterly exam marks. The weightage of annual exam is the maximum and the weightage of quarterly exam is the minimum. Say, a guy scores '5' marks lesser than another guy in quarterly exam but scores '2' marks more than the other guy in half yearly. So, finally based on weightage, it is concluded that 'guy 1' has more marks than 'guy 2' irrespective of the difference in the marks. This is the mechanism of radix sort. So, for sorting numbers, digits are considered from least significant bit to most significant bit (LSB to MSB) and sorted following the same procedure. Figure 12.20 shows sorting of students based on marks with '3' components.

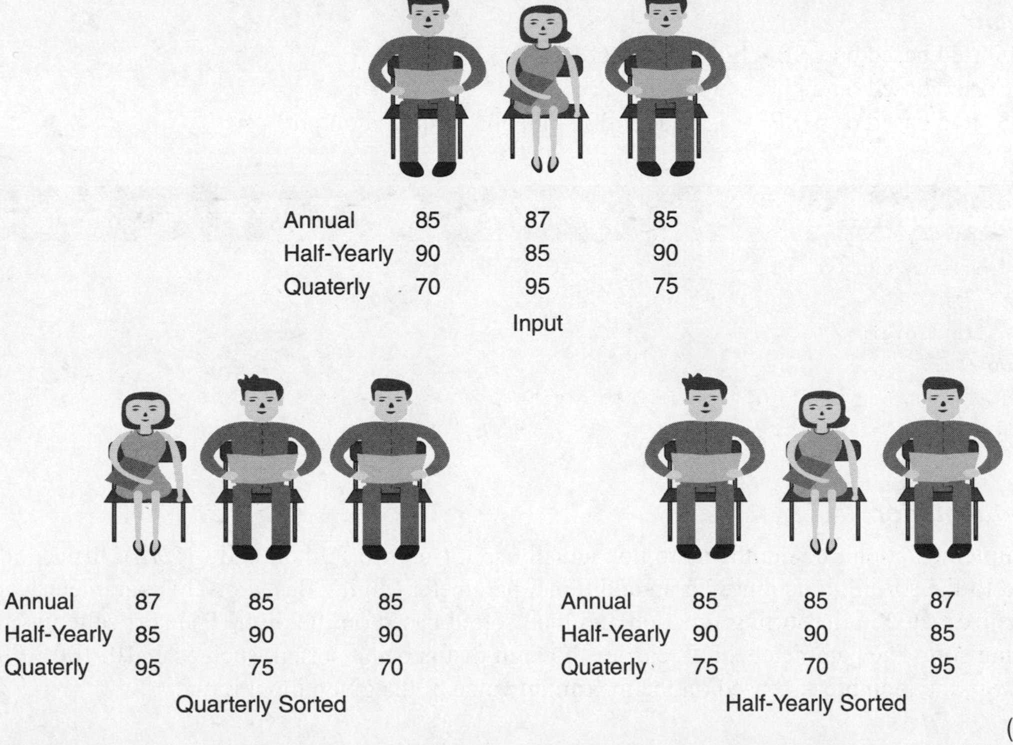

(contd)

(contd)

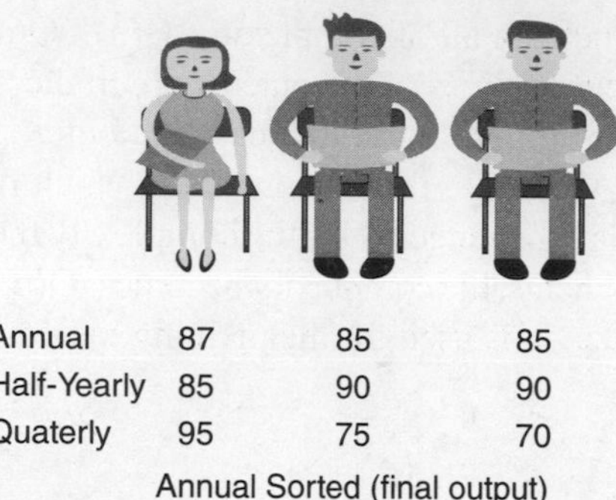

Figure 12.20 Sorting students with Radix sort

Working

Given a list, the elements are first separated into digits. Based on the digits, the list is sorted continuously from LSB to MSB. This sorting is done with any stable sort algorithm such as counting sort. A stable sort is a sort which changes the position of the misplaced elements alone and retains the input order for other elements. If 'A' follows 'B' and 'A' is less than 'B', then 'A' and 'B' will be displaced, else they will maintain the same position as in the input. Finally, when the list has been sorted based on all the digits, the resultant list will be sorted. For one digit element, the digit is LSB and not MSB. While comparing the third digit of numbers, if there is a two digit number then the third digit is considered as '0' and continued. Similarly, all missing digits are considered as '0'. The basic algorithm is shown in Pseudocode 12.10.

Question 12.12 Sort the numbers 503, 37, 12, 9, and 68 using Radix sort.

Solution:

- Sorted based on LSB - 12, 503, 37, 68, 9
- Sorted based on digit 2 – 503, _9, 12, 37, 68
- Sorted based on MSB – _09, _12, _37, _68, 503 (required output)

Pseudocode 12.10

```
max = maximum of list
digit = 1
    while m/digit > 0
    Do,
        Count Sort list with respect to digit
        digit *= 10
```

Implementation

For implementation, the numbers are not actually split (refer to Python code 12.14). Instead, they are passed to the sorting function with an additional parameter 'digit'. Based on this parameter value, the digit is extracted in the sorting function and then sorted based on the digit. The sort called is mostly a counting sort. The parameter 'digit' carries the digit that is being sorted, such as 1, 10, 100, 1000,..and so on. So, the loop breaks based on the maximum value of the given input range.

Python code 12.14

```
def Count_Sort(items,digit):
    n= len(items)
    output = [0] * (n)
    count = [0] * 10 #Number of possible digits is 10 only
    for i in range(n):
        count[ int(items[ i ] / digit) % 10] += 1
    for i in range(1,10):
        count[ i ] += count[ i-1 ]
    for i in range(n-1,-1,-1):
    #Run in reverse order to retain order sorted from previous digit
        output[count[ int(items[i]/digit)%10 ] - 1] = items[i]
        count[ int(items[i]/digit)%10 ]-= 1
    for i in range(n):
        items[ i ] = output[ i ]
def Radix_Sort(items):
#Radix sort for positive numbers only, negative requires different logic
    maxi = max(items)
    i=1
    while (int(maxi/i) > 0):
        Count_Sort(items,i)
        i *= 10
```

Complexity Analysis

The complexity calculation of radix sort is tedious. It is 'O(d * (n+b))', where 'b' is the base representation of the numbers, '10' for decimals base, and 'n' for the number of input elements. The additional variable 'd' is 'O($\log_b$ (k))', where 'k' is the largest possible value. Thus, the overall complexity is 'O($\log_b$ (k) * (n+b))'. This is the case when all the elements are relatively maximum elements. This is very large as compared to normal comparison based sorting. So, as an attempt to limit 'k', apply constraint 'k = n^c' where 'c' is a constant. Now, the complexity comes a way down to 'O(n $\log_b$ n)'. In the next criteria, 'b' is made equal to 'n'. This brings down the sort to 'O(n)'. If the maximum possible length of the number or word is 'w', the complexity is 'O(wn)'. The auxiliary space complexity is same as counting sort 'O(k)'.

Implement radix sort using linked lists. Make each digit as a separate node of a linked list. Will that reduce the sorting cost?

12.8 COMPARISON OF SORTS

Comparison of all the sorting algorithms discussed in this chapter is given in Table 12.1. The best complexity possible in sorting is 'O(n)'. This is because without looking at the elements, it cannot be sorted. So, complexity of a sorting or related algorithm can never go lesser than 'O(n)'. The next better complexity is 'O(n log n)'. This is tolerable complexity and mostly preferred. The worst is 'O(n^2)', which is a form of naïve algorithm. The 'O(n)' running algorithm always uses 'O(n)' or more additional space. So, when the system runs out of space or it is a busy system, then 'O(n log n)' is the better choice.

Comparing the usage of all sorts of resources such as space and time and keeping in mind the intelligence and ability at weird and skewed cases, in-place Quick Sort is found to be the best sorting algorithm (either of the schemes specified in the chapter). Radix sort has a special case. It is preferred over the most efficient quick sort, when the given input is a wide range and most of the elements have '$\log_2 n$' digits. These comparisons are subjected only to number sorting. When the problem requires some tweaking in the algorithm for different scenario (not sorting), then it may change.

Table 12.1 Comparison of Sorting Algorithms

Sort	Best Case Complexity	Worst Case Complexity	Auxiliary Space Complexity	Strategy
Bubble Sort	O(n) – Numbers sorted	$O(n^2)$	O(1)	Exchange
Selection Sort	$O(n^2)$	$O(n^2)$	O(1)	Selection
Heap Sort	O(n) – Numbers sorted	$O(n^2)$	O(1)	Selection
Insertion Sort	O(n) – Numbers sorted	$O(n^2)$	O(1)	Insertion
Shell Sort	O(n log n) – Numbers sorted	$O(n^2)$ – worst gap O(n log n) – best gap	O(1)	Insertion
Merge Sort	O(n log n)	O(n log n)	O(n) – new space	Divide & Conquer
Quick Sort	O(n log n)	O(n log n)	O(1)	Divide & Conquer
Bucket Sort	O(n + k)	$O(n^2)$	O(n)	Distributed
Counting Sort	O(n)	O(n + k)	O(k)	Distributed
Radix Sort	O(w . n)	O(w . n)	O(k)	Distributed

POINTS TO REMEMBER

- Sorting is ordering of data in any specific order.
- The naive algorithm is Bubble Sort which continuously swaps pairs of data with '$O(n^2)$'.
- Selection is a form of sort which selects the minimum element in every iteration and swaps with the element at its position.
- Straight Selection Sort is the simplest form of selection sort, where in every iteration the appropriate element is placed at its position and swapped with the wrong element in there. It has a complexity '$O(n^2)$'.
- Straight Selection Sort does a maximum of 'O(n)' comparisons.
- Heap Sort is based on heapify operation with complexity 'O(n log n)'.
- Insertion Sort is inserting the element at its correct position with complexity '$O(n^2)$'.
- Insertion Sort has an overhead of shifting. This is minimized by shell sort, which performs insertion at intervals with complexity '$O(n \log^2 n)$'.
- Divide and Conquer is a strategy of diving input and computing.
- Merge Sort is direct divide and merge (conquer) with complexity 'O(n log n)'.
- Quick Sort is a very intelligent sort that works in the list itself based on a pivot with complexity 'O(n log n)'.
- Distributed Sorting is an intelligent way of distributing the data across structures and sorting it simultaneously. However, they always use additional space.
- Bucket Sort is distributing element across buckets with fixed range, and sorting the buckets individually, with total complexity 'O(n)'.
- Counting Sort is a map like structure maintaining the count of elements. It is preferred when there are many duplicate elements. It has a complexity 'O(n)'.
- Radix Sort is the only sort not based on comparison of elements. It does not compare the elements with each other. It sorts the data based on sub keys. It has a complexity 'O(n)' after constraints.
- The space complexity of all sorting algorithms is O(n), the n elements to be sorted. However, auxiliary space complexity varies from one algorithm to another.

EXERCISES

Multiple-choice Questions

1. What is the best sorting algorithm?
   (a) Quick Sort
   (b) Radix Sort
   (c) Both 'a' and 'b'
2. Choose the best sort from the following?
   (a) Merge sort
   (b) Quick Sort
   (c) Bucket Sort
3. What will be the total number of steps in insertion sort of 'n' elements?
   (a) n^2 (b) $2n^2$
   (c) $n^2 + 2n$
4. What is the worst case time complexity for Radix sort?
   (a) $O(\log_{10}(k) * (n+b))$
   (b) $O(n \log_{10} n)$
   (c) $O(n)$
5. Which algorithm deals best when the given list is already sorted?
   (a) Selection sort
   (b) Insertion sort
   (c) Bucket sort
6. Can Shell sort be tweaked to perform as simple Insertion sort?
   (a) Yes (b) No
7. What is the sort where the data is divided and given to separate structures and sorted simultaneously?
   (a) Divide and Conquer
   (b) Distributed sorting
   (c) Insertion sorting
8. What sort must be used to sort the individual buckets in Bucket sort?
   (a) Insertion sort
   (b) Recursive bucket sort, until each bucket gets only one element
   (c) Any sort of the users choice
9. What sort must be used to sort the elements based on key in Radix sort?
   (a) Insertion sort
   (b) Counting sort
   (c) Any sort of the users choice
10. When the given list is sorted, Shell sort is a better choice over Quick sort.
    (a) True (b) False

Theoretical Review Questions

1. Compare and contrast recursion and iteration based bubble sort.
2. Explain heap sort and the data structure used in it. What is its advantage over selection sort?
3. Explain simple insertion sort and shell sort. Think about a scenario where shell sort can work worse than insertion sort.
4. What is divide and conquer strategy and how it is used for sorting efficiently?
5. How is distribution sort efficient over other sorting techniques? Think of a scenario when bucket sort complexity is same as or worse than other.

Exploratory Application Exercises

1. Implement the recursive bubble sort.
2. Implement the recursive selection sort.
3. Implement iterative quick sort.
4. A table has marks that the students have scored in various subjects. Find the schema of the table below.

Roll No	Name	Maths mark	Science Mark	Language Mark

   Sort this table by the marks. Sorting should be in the order of Maths, Science, and Language, that is, when two students have the same marks in Maths, then science marks are considered for ordering them.
5. Write a program to read a binary string and sort it to form the largest possible number. For example, 1001 should be re-arranged to 1100 to get the largest value.
6. Get a list of Amazon pay gift voucher numbers and sort them. NOTE: Amazon pay gift vouchers are alpha numeric and have '4' components. So, sort it segment by segment with more priority for alphabets over numbers.
7. Given a list of elements, first identify the largest element and place it in the last position. Then, consider the remaining list, that is, the list of size 'n-1'. Again, move the largest element and continue the iteration until sub-list of size '1' is reached. This sorting technique is called pancake sort and may be treated as a variant of selection sort. Implement pancake sort and compare it with other selection sorting techniques.

8. The bubble sort can be modified by splitting it into two phases. In first phase, all the elements in the odd index are sorted and then in second phase the elements from even index are sorted. Both the phases take place in every iteration and the iteration stops while list is sorted. This is called as odd-even sort or brick sort. Implement this and compare it with bubble sort.
9. Implement 3-way quick sort where the list is split into '3' instead of '2' at every step.
10. In Gome Sort the elements are considered in pairs and sorted continuously. Once the end is reached, pairs from the beginning are considered again and the next iteration begins. The iteration stops when the lists remains unchanged for two consecutive iterations. Implement Gome sort, and discuss its pros and cons.

Picto Puzzles

1. 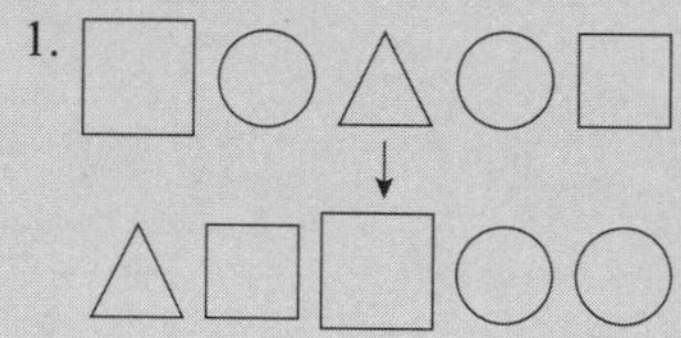

2.

3. DATA STRUCTURES ⟶ ACDERSTU
4. CROSS-SUBSIDIZE ⟶ SIBCDEORUZ
5. (5*2).(4+3).(8-2) ⟶ (4+3).(8-2).(5*2)

Mini Projects

1. Create a dictionary of words which maintains words in sorted order as and when they are inserted.
2. Using divide and conquer algorithm efficiently to pair up piles of nuts and bolts. For every bolt in the pile, identify the corresponding nut.
3. Create and maintain a queue that maintains the sorted order of jobs / processes based on priority in real time. The class should have functionality to modify the priority of job and re-arrange efficiently based on the updated priority.

Answers to Multiple-choice Questions

1. (b) 2. (c) 3. (a) 4. (a) 5. (b) 6. (a) 7. (b) 8. (c) 9. (c) 10. (a)

CHAPTER

13

Searching

LEARNING OBJECTIVES

After going through this chapter, readers will be able to understand:

- How to search for a required element from a pile of elements?
- How to efficiently search data using its sorted property?
- How can hashing be used for organization of data?
- How to code for all the searching techniques using Python?

13.1 INTRODUCTION—WHAT IS SEARCHING?

Searching is a very important process in data handling. It is simply the process of finding information from a group of data. In an attempt to find the required information if the complete data needs to be traversed, then it may not be the most optimized solution as the cost spent in this process would be very high. So, this chapter will introduce various searching techniques and their pre-requisites. Why is searching that important? In this data centric era, the world's most valuable resource is data. However if you have all the data and you cannot read it, then what is the value of that data? The value of data is visualized only after reading the information. This is where the searching operation comes into picture for reading the required data. When multiple read operations are to be performed, search cost directly impacts the solution's performance. Thus, searching is of great significance in designing/organizing data.

13.2 LINEAR SEARCH

The most naive form of searching is linear searching. When we want to find a student's answer script from a pile of scripts, we will just look at the first script and check if it is the required one or move to the next script. In this manner, the whole set of scripts will be checked until the required note is reached. This mechanism is termed as linear search. The name implies that all the data will be searched, one followed by next, in a specified order without any jumps or skips. Searching is not done randomly, as we can lose track of data already checked. Figure 13.1 shows a scenario of searching an answer script from the bundle.

13.2.1 Working

It is a very simple search. It does not change anything in the given input. It just traverses across all the elements in the given order and checks for the required element. It checks if the first element is the required element, else skips it and continues with the second element. This continues until the required element is found or the end is reached. This is a simple and straight forward method of searching. Pseudocode 13.1 represents the basic algorithm.

Figure 13.1 Linear search with answer sheet bundle

Question 13.1 Search '10' in 5, 7, 2, 13, 10.

Solution: The step-by-step process is shown in Figure 13.2.

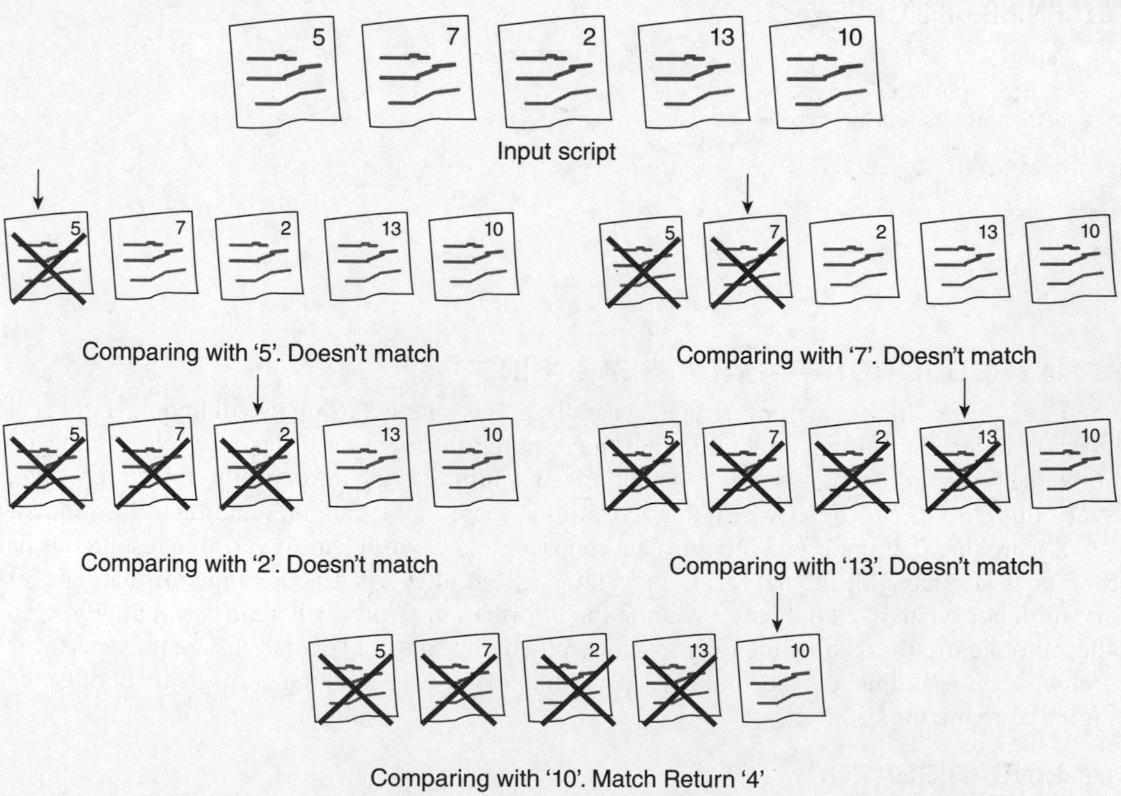

5 7 2 13 10

Input script

Comparing with '5'. Doesn't match

Comparing with '7'. Doesn't match

Comparing with '2'. Doesn't match

Comparing with '13'. Doesn't match

Comparing with '10'. Match Return '4'

Figure 13.2 Linear search for '10' in 5, 7, 2, 13, 10

Pseudocode 13.1

```
for i in 0 to n
    if a[ i ] is the required element
        return i
    return -1 as element is not present
```

13.2.2 Implementation

It just requires one loop for traversing through all the elements which has been represented in Python code 13.1.

Python code 13.1

```
def linear_Search(a,element):
    for i in range(len(a)):
        if(a[ i ] == element):
            return i
    return -1
```

13.3.3 Complexity Analysis

The complexity just sticks to 'O(n)' as it is just one simple loop across all the elements. Here, average case and worst case bind strictly to 'O(n)'. The best case is just determined based on the given input. It may even be 'O(1)', when the required element is the first element itself.

13.3 BINARY SEARCH

The process of searching is always easy when the given elements are structurally ordered or sorted. So, the searching job also can be made easy using lesser time. If there are more things to be found from a large set of data, it is wiser to sort the data and then search intelligently. Binary search is a search which uses the property of the given data. Let us consider the same example of answer scripts. First, it is mandatory that the scripts are arranged based on the roll numbers of the students. When there is a need of an answer script of roll number '60', it is wiser to start checking from the second half of the pile. First, the pile must be divided into two based on the number of students and this roll number '60' must be searched only in the second half, as the first half cannot have roll number '60'. This is ensured only because the scripts are sorted. Now, in the second pile, it need not be fully checked. Divide it further into two halves. Then based on the strength of the class, roll number '60' could be in either of the halves. The same process continues until roll '60' is reached. This is an intelligent search only because at every iteration it skips 'n/2' of the considered elements irrelevant, thus reducing resources. Figure 13.3 shows a scenario of searching roll number '60' from a class of '65'.

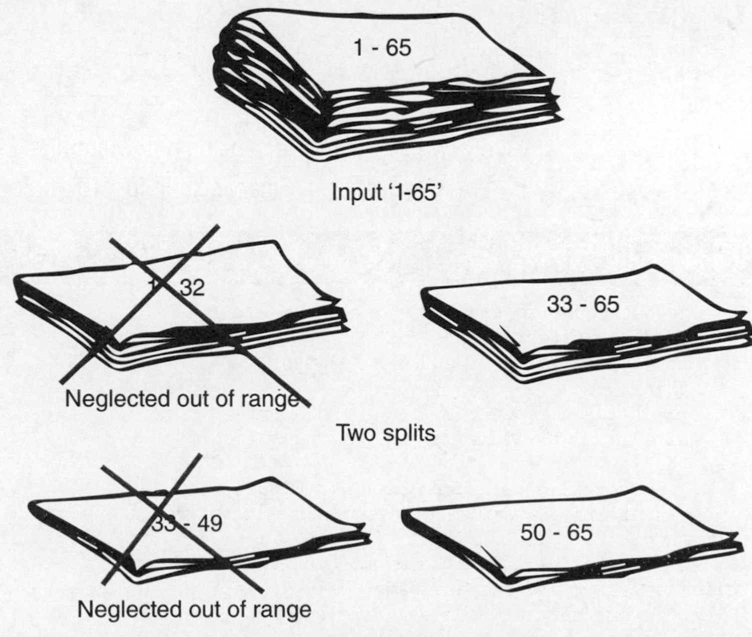

Figure 13.3 Binary search

13.3.1 Working

This works even if the input is not continuous, but it should always be in sorted order. It works based on the key that the middle element of a sorted list is always the median, based on which the divisions take place. The given element is checked with the middle element. If it matches, then the index of middle element is returned. If the required element is less than the middle element, then it is searched in first half of the list. If the required element is greater than the middle element, it is searched in second half of the list. Based on the middle value, the required half is fixed. Now, inside the selected half, the local median is selected and compared with the required element. Then again based on the value, the selected half is further divided into two halves. This continues, then the final half is left with only one element. This element is then compared with the required element. If they match, the index is returned, else the element is marked as missing. Pseudocode 13.2 shows the basic algorithm.

Question 13.2 Search '10' in 2, 5, 7, 10, 13 using Binary Search.

Solution: The step-by-step process is shown in Figure 13.4.

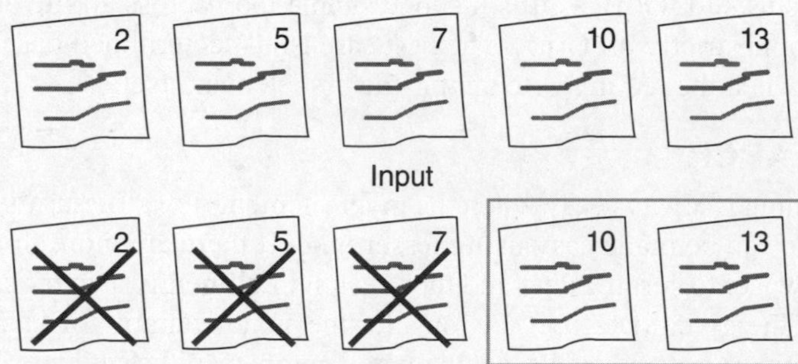

Split into half. So, two sub lists are created (0-2), (3-4). As 10>7, choose second half.

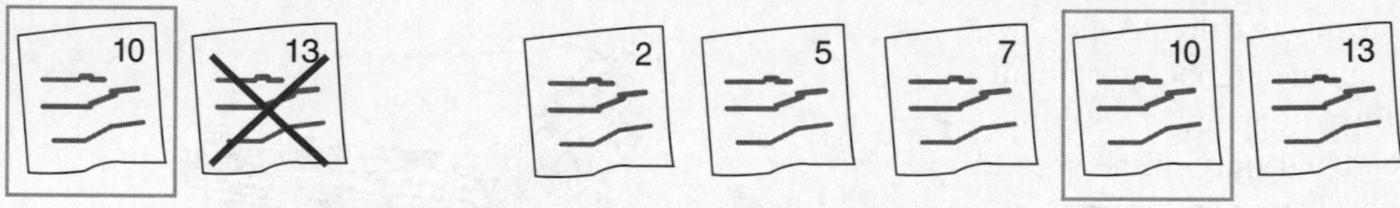

Only two elements. Each being a new sub-list.10= =10. Return 3

Figure 13.4 Binary search for '10' in 2, 5, 7, 10, 13

Pseudocode 13.2

```
if end not equal to start
    middle = (start + end) / 2
    if  middle value is equal to element
    then,
        return middle
    else if middle value is greater than element
    then,
        recursive call from start to middle
    else if middle value is lesser than element
    then,
        recursive call from middle to end
else the start and end are same, only one element in the subdivision
    if start element is equal to element
    then,
        return start
    else,
        return -1
```

13.3.2 Implementation

While implementing the sort, the original list should not be deformed. So, this is implemented using recursive calls with start and end index of the sub division (refer to Python code 13.2). So, in every call to find the middle element, the difference between end and start is found and divided by two.

Note An important part is the start index should be added to half of the difference. Consider the scenario when the middle of '3' to '9' is '6'. The difference is '6' and half of it is '3'. It means the middle element is '3' digits to right of the starting index, which is '6'. So, this is implemented by adding the start_index to half of the difference.

Python code 13.2

```
def binary_Search(a,start_index,end_index,element):
    if ( end_index!= start_index):
        middle = (start_index + end_index)/2
        if( a [ middle ] == element):
            return middle
        elif ( a [ middle ] > element):
            return binary_Search(a, start_index, middle, element)
        elif ( a [ middle ] < element):
            return binary_Search(a, middle + 1, end_index, element)
    else:
        if (0 <= start_index < len(a) and a[ start_index ] == element):
            return start_index
        else:
            return -1
```

The same binary search algorithm can also be accomplished by iteration instead of recursion. The Python code 13.3 is an iterative version of the search. Algorithmically, there is no change in the steps, but it uses iteration in place of recursion.

Python code 13.3

```
def binary_Search(a,start_index,end_index,element):
    while ( end_index!= start_index):
        middle = (start_index + end_index) /2
        if( a [ middle ] == element):
            return middle
        elif ( a [ middle ] > element):
            end_index = middle
        elif ( a [ middle ] < element):
            start_index =  middle + 1
    if (0 <= start_index < len(a) and a[ start_index ] == element):
        return start_index
    else:
        return -1
```

13.3.3 Complexity Analysis

The complexity just sticks to 'O(log n)', as at any call it neglects one half of the given input and focuses on the required half alone. Here, the worst case and average case complexities stick to 'O(log n)' as it fully divides the given input until the end. Again here, the best case is simply dependent on the scenario.

Think about an n-nary search, where at every iteration the list is divided into 'n' sub-lists.

13.4 TREE-BASED SEARCH

When a large volume of input is given and lot of data is to be sought, then it is advisable to sort the information first and then search one by one. In addition, for faster retrieval of such a vast data, tree data structure can be used. The binary tree and its variants described in Chapter 7 can be used in such a situation. A binary search tree is to be built using the given data. This reduces the search cost and improves the efficiency. The same binary search tree can also be used for sorting the given data. The binary search tree (BST) is built with the given data and finding the in-order traversal gives the sorted order of the data.

13.5 HASHING

A hash table is a data structure that can efficiently store and organize data, explained in Chapter 9. Hashing is the process of storing the data in a tabular format within hash tables. Hashing has two stages, the application of hash function on the data and storing the data as value to the key, generated by the hash function. As already explained in Chapter 9, in hash tables with an efficiently designed hash function the cost of read can be bound to 'O(1)'. Thus for a search intensive application, where from a lot of data frequent search operations is to be triggered, it is wise to build a hash table on the data and perform all the search operation on 'O(1)'. Instead of sorting the data and then performing binary search on the same, this can definitely be an alternative as cost of building the hash table is lesser than sorting that huge data. The search cost after sort as well is higher than search cost (read cost) on a hash table, provided the hash function is efficiently designed. Another advantage of hash over sort and search option is when the data points are complex objects, sort can be performed only on one value from the object. However, in hashing, the entire object can be directly hashed. Instead of extracting a feature from the object and sorting on the same, hashing can be preferred on such scenarios to expedite the process.

Implement the chaining-based hash table, where in each node, the chain is always maintained in a sorted order.

13.6 CASE STUDIES OF SEARCHING TECHNIQUES

In this section, let us discuss some real-time examples on searching.

1. Consider the *fit* algorithms in operating systems. There are first-fit, best-fit, and worst-fit algorithms in memory management. The algorithms and the process has already been completely discussed in Chapter 10. Searching plays a very crucial role in the best-fit and first-fit algorithms, in the processing of finding the suitable memory block from the available blocks.

2. Let us consider a simple scenario of shopping. At the time of billing, the bar code is scanned and the entries get populated into the bill. The staff just confirms the quantity and the bill is instantly ready. So, how does this work? When the stocks are received, all the details are entered into the database along with the bar code. The bar code is the primary key of that table, as it is unique for every product. At the time of billing, when the bar code is scanned the software hits the table with this primary key. Then, a search happens on the records and the corresponding record is fetched and returned. The details are then auto-populated into the billing software, making the process fast and easy. So, searching is closely associated in our routine life. There can even be a B+-tree indexing the records to expedite this search process further.
3. Take example of a biometric punching machine. Whenever a person's details and finger prints are registered for the first time, it is placed in cloud space with the primary key as the finger print object. So every time the machine is punched, the finger print is scanned and an object is created. Then, the details of that corresponding object are searched from the already registered details. How the object is created and what details it has is left for the readers to explore. This is the exact scenario where hashing can be preferred over sort and search, as objects can be easily hashed and search cost is also maintained to 'O(1)'.

Points to Remember

- The space complexity for searching is always 'O(n)' for storing the elements. So, auxiliary space complexity is 'O(1)'.
- Searching is the process of fetching data. Linear search is the naïve searching with time complexity 'O(n)'.
- Binary search uses the sorted property of the data with time complexity 'O(log n)'.
- Data organized in a Binary Search Tree can be searched easily.
- Hash tables can be built to organize the data. Building of hash table takes 'O(n)' time, whereas read cost is limited to 'O(1)'.

Key Terms

Binary search At every moment, the list is split into two halves and the required element is searched for one half directly. This requires the list to be sorted, so that the required element can be compared with the median and the irrelevant half can be neglected straight forward.

Dictionary based hash tables Dictionary is an unordered collection of key value pairs. How the key is decided for a value is again decided based on the solution. Deploying a hash function to build a dictionary where a key can have a list of values will give a perfect implementation of hashing, as the 'key' in a dictionary is directly accessible without searching in 'O(1)' time.

Hashing Hashing is an efficient organizing algorithm in which the elements are segregated based on a hash function. The larger set is split apart into smaller sets, now searching/organizing the smaller sets is simpler and efficient.

Linear search The naive searching algorithm, where the elements are stored in a linear fashion and one by one the required element is checked for.

Search in an ordered list Using the sorted property of the list / collection to efficiently search for an element. It helps in reducing the number of comparisons and ideally the search time.

Searching The algorithm used for efficiently checking if a required element is present in a lot.

Tree search How tree-based searching structures can be used to organize data and search efficiently.

EXERCISES

Multiple-choice Questions

1. Which searching algorithm uses the sorted property of the given file?
   (a) Linear search (b) Binary search
   (c) Binary search tree
2. Which of the following is correct recurrence for worst case of Binary Search, where 'T(n)' is total number of accesses made for 'n' elements?
   (a) T(n)=2T(n/2)+O(1) and T(1)=T(0)=O(1)
   (b) T(n)=T(n-1)+O(1) and T(1)=T(0)=O(1)
   (c) T(n)=T(n/2)+O(1) and T(1)=T(0)=O(1)
   (d) T(n)=T(n-2)+O(1) and T(1)=T(0)=O(1)
3. Is Binary Search a 'Divide and Conquer' algorithm?
   (a) Ture (b) False
4. Does hashing always give proper ordering of the data?
   (a) Yes (b) No
5. What can be worst case of building a hash table?
   (a) O(n) (b) O(n log n)
   (c) Exponential
6. Is hashing a sorting or searching technique?
   (a) Sorting (b) Searching
   (c) Both
7. When more data is to be searched from a large amount of data, is sorting the preferred technique?
   (a) Yes (b) No
8. What is k-sorting in heap sort?
   (a) Using a heap array of size 'k'
   (b) Using a heap array of size 'n' but stopping after 'k' iterations
   (c) Either of the above based on implementation
9. Find the error in the following code.

```
import math
def BinarySearch (Y,x):
    i=0
    j=len(Y)-1
    k=math.floor((i+j)/2)
    while(Y[k]!=x and i<j):
        if(Y[k]<x):
            i=k
        else:
            j=k
        k=math.floor((i+j)/2)
    if (Y[k] == x):
        print("x is in the array " )
    else:
        print("x is not in the array ")
```

   (a) The floor function doesn't divide the interval equally as expected for binary search. So, the program gets into never ending loop at times.
   (b) No error
10. Can the k-sorting in heap sort be implemented as a 'Divide and Conquer' strategy?
   (a) Yes (b) No

Theoretical Review Questions

1. What is binary search and what is its prerequisite?
2. Explain hashing and how is it achieved?
3. What is linear search? Explain its disadvantage.
4. How binary search tree can be used for searching? How is it different from binary search?
5. Explain the significance of sorting and searching in data organization. Compare and contrast this method with hashing and reading method.

Exploratory Application Exercises

1. Think about implementing a search which skips blocks of equal size while searching in a linear order on a sorted list. How to implement it?
2. When a list has sorted elements which are uniformly distributed, can the property be used for increasing the efficiency of linear search?
3. Given two linked lists, check if one list is a sublist of another.
4. Try implementing a ternary search over a sorted list. At any point, divide the interval into three and choose an interval to search further based on the value. Compare its performance with binary search.
5. Search for a given number in a sorted list using Fibonacci numbers. This is a variation of binary search where Fibonacci numbers are used to fix the range of the list to be searched for.
6. Given a list of Fibonacci numbers, search for a given number efficiently.
7. Develop a 'find and replace' program for whole word matches in a paragraph.
8. Write a module to read a mathematical equation and a dictionary of <variable:value> pairs.. The program must substitute the values in the equation and evaluate the final result.
9. Given a binary string, search for a given pattern and indicate it.

10. From an inventory of items, identify the best item to buy. The best item with price closest to the required value. If multiple items had the same value, quantity is considered to see which adds more value.

Picto Puzzles

1.

2.

3.

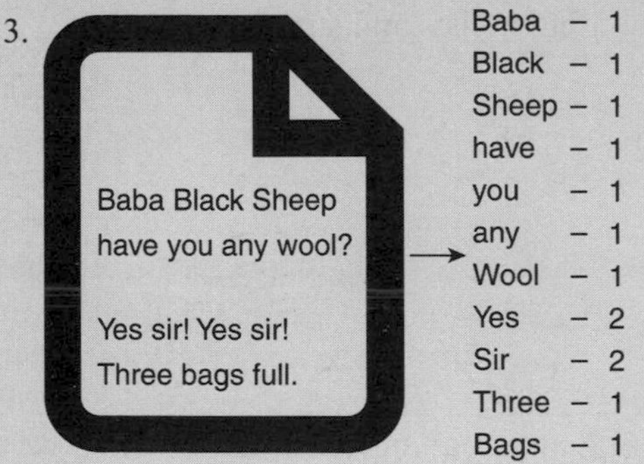

4. Structure ⟶ 0

   Data ⟶ 2

   Labal ⟶ 1

5.

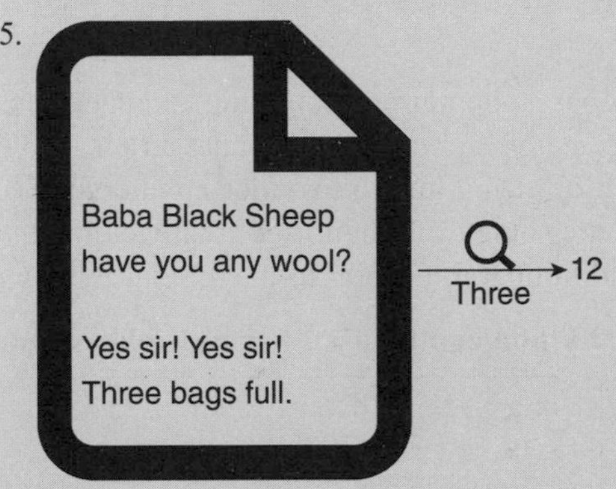

Mini Projects

1. Write a function to find the name and address of a person from a telephone directory.
2. In an operating system, when a process requires a hole in the main memory to start execution, best fit algorithm identifies the closest hole and uses it. Develop the best fit algorithm that takes in a list of holes and finds the best fit for a given demand.
3. Write an encryption and decryption algorithm which maintains the map for each alphabet in an external file. Given a text, the encryption module will replace the characters with its security keys and decryption converts it to the original text by replacing the security keys to actual characters. Say, for example, character 'E' has security key as 'L', then all the 'E' in the given text will be replaced by 'L' while encryption and all 'L' will be converted to 'E' while decryption.

Answers to Multiple-choice Questions

1. (b) 2. (c) 3. (b) 4. (b) 5. (a) 6. (c) 7. (a) 8. (c) 9. (a) 10. (b)

APPENDIX

Python is a popular programming language because it is highly readable and expressive. It is often joked as *'Executable Pseudocode'*. It has a rich set of standard libraries. You can check all the default libraries at the following link: https://docs.python.org/3/library/index.html
Here are some of Python tricks that we thought would simplify your life.
For additional info, refer to the official Python documentation at https://docs.python.org/3/

1. Python can be used for multiple assignments

```
>>> x, y = 5, 6
>>> x, y
(5, 6)
```

```
>>> x, y = 5, 6
>>> x, y = (5, 6)
>>> (x, y) = (5, 6)
>>> (x, y)  = 5, 6
```

All of these mean

```
>>> x, y, z = 5, 6, 7
```

Internally, this creates a tuple of the values, loops over the values and then assigns them to x, y, z.

Not only for tuples but multiple assignments can be used on lists and strings as well.

```
>>> x,  y =  [5, 6]
>>> X
5
>>> x, y = 'hi'
>>> X
'h'
>> y
'i'
```

Multiple assignments will work on any number of variables and objects.

```
>>> numbers = 5, 6, 7
>>> x, y, z = numbers
>>> x, y, z
(5, 6, 7)
```

Swapping variables is easy

```
>>> x, y = 5, 6
>>> x, y
(5, 6)
>>> x, y = y, x
>>> x, y
(6, 5)
```

Multiple assignments can be used to unpack dictionaries into key-value pairs.

```
>>> fruit_dictionary = {'Name':  "Apple", 'Origin': "Kashmir"}
>>> for k, v in fruit dictionary.items():
        print(f'{k} {v}')
Name Apple
Origin Kashmir
```

Note f before the quotation mark inside print statement indicates that it is a formatted string literal.

Multiple assignments can be used to make the code more readable.

```
>>> dob = '20-07-1998'
>>> day,month,year = dob.split('-')
>>> day
'20'
>>> month
'07'
>>> year
'1998'
>>>
```

Note Instead of using `date = dob.split('-')` and the using `date[0]`, `date[1]`, `date[2]` to access day, month and year, we could use multiple assignments to make it more readable. Note the use of `split()` function in the above code.

* can be used as a multiple assignment operator in Python.

```
>>> X = [5, 6, 7, 8, 9]
>>> first, *rest = x
>>> first
5
>>> rest
[6, 7, 8,  9]

>>> first, *middle last = x
>>> first
5
>>> middle
[6, 7, 8]
>>> last
9
```

2. Enumerate function

The enumerate function adds a counter to an iterable (string/list/tuple/dictionary) and returns an iterable object. The enumerate function also allows us to specify the start of the counter.

```
>>> Metros = ['Chennai', 'Mumbai', 'Kolkata', 'Delhi']
>>> for counter, values in enumerate(Metros):
    print(counter, values)

0 Chennai
1 Mumbai
2 Kolkata
3 Delhi
>>> for counter, values in enumerate(Metros, 1):
    print(counter, values)

1 Chennai
2 Mumbai
3 Kollkata
4 Delhi
```

3. zip() and zip_longest() function

The zip() function returns an iterator of tuples based on the iterable object. It is mainly used for combining data of two iterable elements together, i.e., looping over multiple lists at the same time.

```
>>> Products = ['Carrot', 'Apple', 'Banana']
>>> Colours = ['Orange', 'Red', 'yellow']
>>> Prices = [45, 100]
>>> for prod, col, price in zip(Products, Colours, Prices):
    print(f'{prod} {col} Rs. {price}')

Carrot Orange Rs. 45
Apple Red Rs. 100

>>> import itertools
>>> for prod, col, price in itertools.zip_longest(Products, Colours, Prices):
    print(f'{prod}  {col} Rs.  {price}')
Carrot Orange Rs. 45
Apple Red Rs. 100
Banana Yellow Rs. None
```

Note If the lists are not of equal length, then zip() function terminates at the length of the shortest list. To continue iteration, we could use the zip_longest() function found in the itertools Python library. It produces a None value when the shorter iterator is exhausted.

Zip function can also be used to retrieve the lists that have been merged by a previous zip function. For this we have to use a * operator before the zipped list.

```
>>> Products = ['Carrot', 'Apple', 'Banana']
>>> Colours = ['Orange', 'Red', 'Yellow']
>>> ZippectList = list (zip (Products, Colours))
>>> ZippedList
[('Carrot', 'Orange'), ('Apple', 'Red'), ('Banana', 'Yellow')]
>>> P, c = zip(*zippedList)
>>> P
('Carrot', 'Apple', 'Banana')
>>> list (P)
['Carrot', 'Apple', 'Banana']
>>> list(C)
['Orange', 'Red', 'Yellow']
```

Note Original lists can be retrieved completely only if they were of the same length.

Creating a dictionary out of two lists is easy using the dict() and zip() functions.

```
>>> keys = ['x', 'y', 'z']
>>> values = ['5', '6', '7']
>>> dict(zip (keys, values))
{'x': '5', 'y': '6', 'z': '7')
```

4. The use of _ and operator

We can use _ as names for variables we don't care about. They're called throwaway variables.

```
>>> x, _, z = 5, 6, 7
>>> x, *, z = 5, 6, 7, 8, 9
>>> X
5
>>> z
9
```

_ can be used to separate numbers and digits (binary, octal, hexadecimal parts).

```
>>> lakh = 1_0 0_0 0 0
>>> million = 1_000_000
>>> lakh
100000
>>> million
1000000
>>> binary = Ob_1010
>>> octal = Oo_70
>>> hex = Ox_162_e
>>> binary                    # bin(5) = Ob1O1
5
>>> octal                     # oct(56) = 0o70
56
>>> hex                       # hex(567) = 0x162e
5678
```

_ can also be used to store the last expression in the Python interpreter.

```
>>> 5 + 6

11

>>> _

11

>>>
```

5. Reversing strings and lists

Reversing stings or lists is very easy in Python. To reverse a string, you could use [::-1] or use the reversed() function. The reversed function returns a list object containing the characters in the string. They can be joined together to create the reversed string using the join() function.

To reverse a list you could simply call the reverse() function from the standard python library. To remove duplicates in a list, simply use the set function. The set function returns a set (notice the paranthesis below) which can be converted to a list using the list() function.

```
>>> x = 'hello'
>>> x[::-1]
'olleh'
>>> list (reversed (x))
['o', '1', '1', 'e', 'h']

>>> "".join(reversed (x))
'olleh'

>>> x=[1, 2, 3, 4, 1, 5, 1, 2]

>>> x.reverse()
>>> x
[2, 1, 5, 1, 4, 3, 2, 1]

>>> set(x)
{1, 2, 3, 4, 5}
```

To calculate how many times an element had occurred in a list, count method can be used.

```
>>> x = 'hello'
>>> x.count ('1')
2
```

6. List/Dictionary comprehension

List/Dictionary comprehension is a faster and handy way to create a list or dictionary in Python. It helps us write easy to read for loops in a single line reducing the number of lines of code.

```
>>> numbers = list(range(10))            # numbers = [0, 1, 2, 3, 4, 5, 6, 7, 8, 9]
>>> even = []                            # empty list
>>> odd = []                             # empty list
>>> for number in numbers:
        if number%2 == 0:
            even.append(number)

#List comprehension of the above for and if loops
>>> even = [number for number in numbers if number%2 == 0]
>>> odd = [number for number in numbers if number not in even]

>>> fruits = ['Apple', "Orange", "Mango"]
>>> 1 = {}                               # empty dictionary
for fruit in fruits:
    f[fruit] = len(fruit)

#Dictionary comprehension of the above for loop
>>> {fruit:len(fruit) for fruit in fruits}
```

7. Useful libraries

Collections is a very useful library. The Collections module provides additional data structured to store collections of data (list, dict, set, tuple, etc).

```
>>> from collections import OrderedDict, Counter
>>> x = [5, 6, 7, 8, 5, 6, 4, 3, 5, 7, 8, 9, 5, 2, 1, 6]
>>> Counter (x)
Counter({5: 4, 6: 3, 7: 2, 8: 2, 4: 1, 3: 1, 9: 1, 2: 1, 1: 1})
>>> Counter(x) .most_common(3)
[(5, 4), (6, 3), (7, 2)]
>>> max(set(x), key = x.count))

# Without importing any library, the most frequent value in the list can be
# obtained by the following
>>> max(set(x), key = x.count)
5

# Checking for anagrams i.e., words with the same characters
>>> Counter('listen') == Counter('silent')
True

# OrderedDict remembers the order in which values were inserted into a dictionary
>>> d = OrderedDict()
>>> d['a']=1
>>> d['b']=2
>>> d['c']=3
>>> d
OrderedDict([('a', 1), ('b', 2), ('c', 3)])
```

```
# Ordered Dictionary of most common letters
>>> l=['x', 'y', 'x', 'z', 'y', 'y' 'y', 'z', 'x' 'y', 'x', 'y' 'z']
>>> cnt = Counter(l)
>>> d = OrderedDict(cnt.most_common())
>>> d
OrderedDict([('y', 6), ('x', 4), ('z', 3)])
```

Deque is another list like container with fast appends and pops on either ends. Unlike list append and pop operations that have a O(n) time complexity, deque does it with O(1) complexity.

```
>>> from collections import deque
>>> x = deque([5, 6, 7])
>>> x.append(8)
deque([5, 6, 7, 8])
>>> x.appendleft(4)
deque([4, 5, 6, 7, 8])
>>> x.pop()
deque ([4, 5, 6, 7])
>>> x.popleft()
deque ([5, 6, 7])
>>> x.clear()
deque([])
```

The queue can also be rotated from specific positions.

```
>>> import collections
>>> Q = collections.deque ([6, 5, 2, 1, 3, 4])
>>> Q
deque([6, 5, 2, 1, 3, 4])
>>> Q.rotate(3)
>>> Q
deque([1, 3, 4, 6, 5, 2])
>>> Q.rotate(-3)
>>> Q
deque([6, 5, 2, 1, 3, 4])
```

namedtuple is another important container in the collections module. They can be very handy when you have to name each position in a tuple. Instead of using integer indexes for accessing members, you can access them with their names. This allows for more readable code.

```
>>> Weather = ('Chennai', 'India', 28)
>>> print(Weather[2])
28

#namedtuples converts the above tuples into convinent containers
>>> from collections import namedtuple

>>> Climate = namedtuple('Weather', 'City Country Temperature')
>>> Ch = Climate(City='Chennai', Country='India', Temperature=28)
>>> Ln = Climate(City='London', Country='UK', Temperature=12)
```

```
>>> Climate
<class '__main__.Weather'>
>>> Ch
Weather(City='Chennai', Country='India', Temperature=28)
>>> Ln
Weather(City='London', Country='UK', Temperature=12)

#Accessing tuple by their field names
>>> Ch.City
'Chennai'
>>> Ln.Country
'UK'

#Accessing tuple by their index number
>>> Ln[2]
'India'

#Converting namedtuple into an OrderedDict
>>> Ch._asdict()
OrderedDict([('City', 'Chennai'), ('Country', 'India'), ('Temperature', 28)])
```

defaultdict in collections module works similar to a dictionary, except that, it does not throw a KeyError when you try to acess a non-existent key. Instead defaultdict initializes the new key with a function called default_factory that takes no arguments and provides the default value for a nonexistent key.

```
>>> from collections import defaultdict
>>> fruits = [('apple', 5), ('orange', 3), ('pineapple', 6), ('apple', 2)]
>>> d = defaultdict(list)
>>> for key, value in fruits:
    d[key].append(value)

>>> d
defaultdict(<class 'list'>, {'apple': [5, 2], 'orange': [3], 'pineapple': [6]})

>>> d['apple']
[5, 2]
>>> d['banana']
[]
>>> d
defaultdict (<class 'list'>, {'apple': [5, 2], 'orange': [3], 'pineapple': [6], 'banana': []})
```

In the above code, the key banana does not exist. However, KeyError is not raised and the key is added into the dictionary with a value [], which is an empty list.

Notice in the below code, how defaultdict can be combined with Python's lambda function.

```
>>> from collections import defaultdict
>>> f = defaultdict(lambda : None)
>>> f['carrots'] = 10
>>> f['raddishes'] = 5
>>> f
defaultdict(<function <lambda> at 0x000002F3D65E7158>, {'carrots': 10, 'raddishes': 5})
>>> f['cabbages']
>>> f
defaultdict(<function <lambda> at 0x000002F3D65E7158>, {'carrots': 10, 'raddishes': 5,
'cabbages': None})
```

Itertools sliding window

The Python itertools library has functions for producing different kinds of iterators. Finding combinations, permutations are some of them. Itertools can work on two or more lists as well. Look at the zip_longest() function explained in section (3) above.

```
>>> from itertools import combinations
>>> c = ["x", "y", "z"]
>>> for i in combinations(c, 2):
        print(i)

('x', 'y')
('x', 'z')
('y', 'z')

>>> from itertools import permutations
>>> c = ["x", "y", "z"]
>>> for i in permutations(c, 2):
        print(i)

('x', 'y')
('x', 'z')
('y', 'x')
('y', 'z')
('z', 'x')
('z', 'y'
```

Sliding windows can be created using zip and iterators.

```
>>> from itertools import islice
>>> def n_grams (a, n):
    z = (islice(a, i, None) for i in range(n))
    return zip(*z)

>>> x =  [5, 6, 7, 8, 9, 10]
>>> n_grams (x, 3)
<zip object at 0x0000021B8E019588>
>>> list(n_grams(x, 3))
[(5, 6, 7), (6, 7, 8), (7, 8, 9), (8, 9, 10)]
>>> list(n_grams(x, 4))
[(5, 6, 7, 8), (6, 7, 8, 9), (7, 8, 9, 10)]
```

Heapq

Heaps and queues can be easily implemented in Python using the heapq/Queue module.

```
>>> import heapq
>>> x = [5, 6, 7, 8, 9, 10, 2, 4, 6, 3,]
>>> heapq.nsmallest(3, x)
[2, 3, 4]
>>> heapq.nlargest(4, x)
[10, 9, 8, 7]
```

```
>>> y = [8, 1, 2, 7, 9, 3]
>>> y[0]                # y is a list. Hence y[0]  is the first element in the list
8
>>> heapq.heapify(y)    # list y is converted into a heap
>>> y[0]                # y[0] is the smallest element, since y is a heap
1
>>> heapq.heappush(y, 6)
>>> y
[1, 7, 2, 8, 9, 3, 6]
>>> heapq.heappop(y)    # Pops the smallest element from the heap
1
>>> y
[2, 7, 3, 8, 9, 6]
>>> heapq.heappushpop(y, 10) #Pushes item into the heap while removing the smallest
element
2
>>> y
[3, 7, 6, 3, 9, 10]
>>> heapq.heapreplace(y, 5)  # Pops the smallest element and replaces it with the given
item
3
>>> y
[5, 7, 6, 3, 9, 10]
```

Queue

A simple Python list can act as a queue and stack. However, they are slower in performance when working on large number of elements because a simple insert or delete operation at the beginning requires shifting of elements by one which requires O(n) time.

The Queue module supports multithreading and helps implement queue data structures, like First In First Out (FIFO) queues, Priority Queues, etc.

```
>>> from queue import Queue
>>> q = queue()  #Queue Object

# Adding values in the Queue object
# This is a FIFO Queue
>>> q.put('A')
>>> q.put('B')
>>> q.put('C')
>>> q.put('D')
»> q.put('E')

# retrieving the values from Queue
>>> if not q.empty():
      for i in range(q.qsize()):
          print(q.get())
A
B
C
D
E
# Size of Queue object after retrieving
>>> q.qsize{)
0
```

LIFO Queue

```
from queue import LifoQueue as LQ

q = LQ()

for i in range(5):
    q.put(i)

while not q.empty():      #Same as for i in range(q.qsize()):
    print(q.get{})

4
3
2
1
0
```

Priority Queues

In priority queues, the objects are returned in order of priority. Least priority item is returned first. Priority Queues in Queue module are time synchronized and allow locking and concurrency during multithreading.

```
>>> import queue
>>> q = queue.PriorityQueue()

>>> q.put((l, 'A'))
>>> q.put((3, 'B')]
>>> q.put((2, 'C'))

>>> for i in range(q.qsize()):
        print(q.get())

(1, 'A')
(2, 'C')
(3, 'B')
```

Index

Bibliography

1. Huskey, Harry, The state of the art in electronic digital computing in Britain and the United States, 1947.
2. Dijkstra, E.W. Recursive Programming. Numer. Math. 2, 312–318, 1960.
3. Newell, Allen; Shaw, F. C. "Programming the Logic Theory Machine". Proceedings of the Western Joint Computer Conference: 230–240, 1957.
4. Hazewinkel, Michiel, ed. "Binary tree", Encyclopedia of Mathematics, Springer Science+Business Media B.V. / Kluwer Academic Publishers, ISBN 978-1-55608-010-4, 1994
5. Parlante, Nick. "Binary Trees". CS Education Library. Stanford University, 2001.
6. Heger, Dominique A., "A Disquisition on The Performance Behavior of Binary Search Tree Data Structures" (PDF), European Journal for the Informatics Professional, 5 (5): 67–75, 2004.
7. Adelson-Velsky, Georgy; Landis, Evgenii, "An algorithm for the organization of information". Proceedings of the USSR Academy of Sciences, 146: 263–266.
8. Leonidas J. Guibas and Robert Sedgewick, "A Dichromatic Framework for Balanced Trees". Proceedings of the 19th Annual Symposium on Foundations of Computer Science. pp. 8–21, 1978.
9. Bayer, R.; McCreight, E., "Organization and maintenance of large ordered indices" (PDF). Proceedings of the 1970 ACM SIGFIDET (Now SIGMOD) Workshop on Data Description, Access and Control - SIGFIDET '70. Boeing Scientific Research Libraries. p. 107, July 1970.
10. Williams, J. W. J, "Algorithm 232 - Heapsort", Communications of the ACM, 7 (6): 347–348, 1964.
11. Management and Processing of Complex Data Structures: Third Workshop on Information Systems and Artificial Intelligence, Hamburg, Germany, Proceedings, ed. Kai v. Luck, Heinz Marburger, p. 76, 1994.
12. Eckert Jr., John Presper and Mauchly, John W.; Electronic Numerical Integrator and Computer, United States Patent Office, US Patent 3,120,606, filed 1947-06-26, issued 1964-02 04; invalidated 1973-10-19 after court ruling on Honeywell v. Sperry Rand.
13. Dijkstra, E. W. "A note on two problems in connexion with graphs" (PDF). Numerische Mathematik. 1: 269–271, 1959.
14. Prim, R. C., "Shortest connection networks And some generalizations", Bell System Technical Journal, 36 (6): 1389–1401, November 1957.
15. Kruskal, J. B. "On the shortest spanning subtree of a graph and the traveling salesman problem". Proceedings of the American Mathematical Society. 7 (1): 48–50, 1956.
16. Biggs, N.; Lloyd, E.; Wilson, R. (1986), Graph Theory, 1736-1936, Oxford University Press.
17. Donald Knuth. The Art of Computer Programming, Volume 1: Fundamental Algorithms, Third Edition. Addison-Wesley, 1997. ISBN 0-201-89683-4.
18. Thomas H. Cormen, Charles E. Leiserson, Ronald L. Rivest, and Clifford Stein. Introduction to Algorithms, Second Edition. MIT Press and McGraw-Hill, 2001. ISBN 0-262-03293-7.

19. Goodrich M T, Tamassia R and Michael H. Goldwasser, "Data Structures and Algorithms in Python++", Wiley publication, 2013.
20. Tremblay J P and Sorenson P G, "An Introduction to Data Structures with Applications", Second Edition, Tata, McGraw-Hill, 2002.
21. https://www.geeksforgeeks.org/data-structures/ (last accessed on July 7, 2020)
22. http://web.stanford.edu/class/cs166/ (last accessed on July 7, 2020)

About the Authors

Shriram K. Vasudevan is Principal at K. Ramakrishnan College of Technology, Samayapuram, Trichy, Tamil Nadu. Previously, he was Assistant Professor in the Department of Computer Science and Engineering at Amrita Vishwa Vidyapeetham, Coimbatore, Tamil Nadu. Author/co-author of 40 books in various fields, he is an M Tech, MBA, and PhD with over 12 years of industrial and academic experience. He received his Master's degree and Doctorate in the field of Embedded Systems. Dr Shriram has published 115 international papers and has worked with major multinational companies like Wipro and Aricent Technologies.

The team led by Dr Shriram won the HackHarvard Global Hackathon @ Harvard University in 2019. He has been awarded by Sabre Technologies, Stop the bleed, Hack Harvard (Harvard University), Accenture Digital (India), NEC (Nippon Electric Company, Japan), Thought Factory (Axis Bank Innovation Lab), Rakuten (Japan), Titan, Future Group, Institution of Engineers of India (IEI), Ministry of Food Processing Industries (MoFPI – Govt. of India), Intel, Microsoft, Wipro, Infosys, IBM India, SOS Ventures (USA), VIT University, Amrita University, Computer Society of India, TBI – TIDE, ICTACT, Times of India, Nehru Group of institutions, Texas Instruments, IBC Cambridge, Cisco, CII (Confederation of Indian Industries), Indian Air Force, DPSRU Innovation & Incubation Foundation, ELGi Equipments (Coimbatore), etc. for his technical expertise. Dr Shriram is listed in many famous biographical databases.

Abhishek S. Nagarajan is working as a Data Scientist in [24]7.ai. Being a multi-faceted engineering graduate, he is a programmer, research enthusiast, author, teacher and motivational speaker. His primary responsibility at work is building machine learning models for predicting customer intents in a web journey. He has published nearly 10 research articles in various globally reputed journals.

Mr Abhishek has also co-authored 7 books on core computer science areas such as programming and IoT. Mr Abhishek has built some gadgets for day-to-day usage and his out-of-the-box thinking and innovative ideas have resulted in many open-ended projects.

Karthick Nanmaran is Assistant Professor, Department of CSE, SRM Institute of Science and Technology, Chennai.

Related Titles

Python Programming using Problem Solving Approach, First Edition (9780199480173)

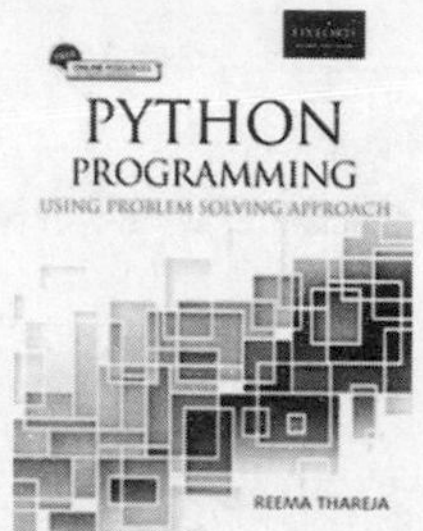

Reema Thareja, Assistant Professor, Department of Computer Science, Shyama Prasad Mukherji College for Women, University of Delhi.

Python Programming is designed as a textbook to fulfil the requirements of the first-level course in Python programming.

Features

- Numerous programming examples along with their outputs; and notes and programming tips to highlight the important concepts and help readers avoid common programming errors.
- Strong chapter-end pedagogy.
- 7 Annexures and 5 appendices covering types of operating systems, differences between Python 2.x and 3.x, installing Python, debugging and testing, iterators, generators, getters, setters, Turtle graphics, plotting graphs, multi-threading, GUI and Web Programming provided to supplement the text.
- Case studies on creating calculator, calendar, hash files, compressing strings and files, tower of Hanoi, image processing, shuffling a deck of cards, and mail merge demonstrate the application of various concepts.

Advanced Data Structures, First Edition (9780199487172)

Reema Thareja, Assistant Professor, Department of Computer Science, Shyama Prasad Mukherji College for Women, University of Delhi

S. Rama Sree, Professor, Department of Computer Science and Engineering, Aditya Engineering College, Andhra Pradesh

Advanced Data Structures aims to introduce the complex and advanced concepts of data structures and illustrate their use in problem solving. It provides a comprehensive introduction to the design and analysis of advanced algorithms and data structures.

Features

- Provides comprehensive coverage for k-way merge sort, hashing techniques, heaps, AVL trees, red-black trees, B-trees, B+ trees, Patricia, digital search trees, multi-way tries, and graphs.
- Includes algorithms along with examples for each operation on the various data structures.
- Provides numerous solved examples and programs using C++.
- Includes plenty of chapter-end exercises and two solved model question papers.

Data Structures using C, Second Edition (9780198099307)

Reema Thareja, Assistant Professor, Department of Computer Science, Shyama Prasad Mukherji College for Women, University of Delhi.

This second edition of Data Structures Using C provides a comprehensive coverage of the concepts of data structures and their implementation using C language.

Suitable for: A textbook for undergraduate engineering students of computer science as well as postgraduate students of computer applications.

Features

- Sections on omega and theta notations, multi-linked lists, forests, 2-3 trees, binary heap implementation of priority queues, interpolation search, jump search, tree sort, bucket hashing, cylinder surface indexing
- Programs on header linked lists, parentheses checking, evaluation of prefix expressions, priority queues, multiple queues, tree sort, file handling , address calculation sort
- Appendices on dynamic memory allocation, garbage collection, backtracking, Johnson's problem
- Integrates theoretical aspects of data structures with practical implementation of algorithms using tested C programs
- Provides analysis of all major algorithms in terms of their running times and provides numerous end-chapter exercises

Big Data Analytics, First Edition (9780199497225)

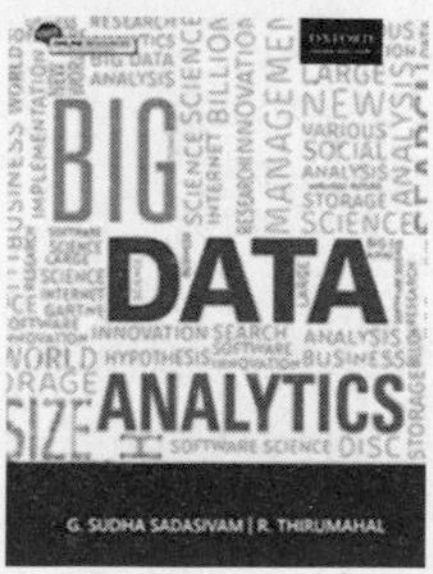

G. Sudha Sadasivam, Professor and Head of the Department of Computer Science and Engineering, PSG College of Technology, Tamil Nadu

R. Thirumahal, Assistant Professor (Selection Grade) in the Department of Computer Science and Engineering, PSG College of Technology, Tamil Nadu

The book has been written to cover the basics of analytics before moving to big data and its analytics. It seeks to translate the theory behind big data into principles and practices for a data analyst.

Features

- Illustrative discussion on big data frameworks and infrastructure
- Algorithms for data analytics on big data frameworks and tools
- Solved numerical examples and practice exercises and codes for various case studies on Hadoop, R, Spark, MongoDB, Storm, and Neo4j
- Interview questions highlighted as boxed items in each chapter
- Point-wise summary and chapter-end exercises

Other Related Titles

Programming in C, Pradip Dey and Manas Ghosh [9780199491476]
Cloud Computing, Shailendra Singh [9780199477388]
Cyber Forensics, Dejey & S. Murugan [9780199489442]
Mobile Computing, Raj Kamal [9780199455416]